REPLICATIONS

REPLICATIONS

Archaeology
Art History
Psychoanalysis

Whitney Davis

With the Editorial Assistance of Richard W. Quinn

The Pennsylvania State University Press
University Park, Pennsylvania

Library of Congress Cataloging-in-Publication Data

Davis, Whitney.
Replications : archaeology, art history, psychoanalysis / Whitney Davis ; with the editorial assistance of Richard W. Quinn.

p. cm.
Includes bibliographical references and index.
ISBN 0-271-01523-3 (cloth: alk. paper)
ISBN 0-271-01524-1 (paper: alk. paper)
1. Art—Themes, motives. 2. Art and society. 3. Psychoanalysis and art. I. Quinn, Richard W. II. Title.
N7560.D32 1996
701—dc20 95-397
CIP

Printed in the United States of America
Published by The Pennsylvania State University Press,
University Park, PA 16802-1003

It is the policy of The Pennsylvania State University Press to use acid-free paper for the first printing of all clothbound books. Publications on uncoated stock satisfy the minimum requirements of American National Standard for Information Sciences—Permanence of Paper for Printed Library Materials, ANSI Z39.48-1992.

Contents

List of Illustrations vii

Preface xiii

Acknowledgments xv

Introduction: Replication in Archaeology, Art History, and Psychoanalysis 1

REPLICATION IN ARCHAEOLOGY

1 Finding Symbols in History 35

2 The Origins of Image Making 46

3 Replication and Depiction in Paleolithic Art 66

4 The Deconstruction of Intentionality in Archaeology 95

REPLICATION IN ART HISTORY

5 Beginning the History of Art 131

6 Style and History in Art History 171

7 Narrativity and the Narmer Palette 199

8 Opticality and Rhetoricity in Paul de Man's "Historical Materialism" 232

REPLICATION IN PSYCHOANALYSIS

9 Winckelmann Divided 257

10 Pleasure and Its Contents: Bersani and Dutoit's Assyrian Reliefs 266

11 Sigmund Freud's Drawing of the Dream of the Wolves 286

12 HomoVision: A Reading of Freud's "Fetishism" 318

Index 347

List of Illustrations

Fig. 1.1. Polydigital tracing in the cave of Gargas, French Pyrenees, about 20,000 B.C. (?). Photo courtesy Claude Barrière.

Fig. 1.2. "Panel of the Great Bulls," cave of Gargas. Reprinted from Claude Barrière, *L'art pariétal de la grotte de Gargas* (Oxford, 1976), by permission.

Fig. 2.1. Varieties of representation.

Fig. 2.2. Aurignacian images on limestone blocks from rock shelters near Les Eyzies, Dordogne, France, about 32,000–26,000 B.C. *a.* Blocks 11–12, Abri Blanchard (painted legs and underbelly of a herbivore). *b.* Block 1, Abri du Renne, Belcayre (incised outline of a stag or ibex). Reprinted from Brigitte Delluc and Gilles Delluc, "Les manifestations graphiques aurignaciennes sur support rocheux des environs des Eyzies (Dordogne)," *Gallia Préhistoire* 21 (1978), by permission.

Fig. 2.3. Incised bison, cave of La Grèze, Marquay, Dordogne, France, about 20,000 B.C.

Fig. 2.4. Modes of representation dependent on vision.

Fig. 2.5. Types of marking.

Fig. 2.6. Drawings by chimpanzees. *a–d.* Typical clusterings and strokes. *e.* "Advanced" control over mark making. *f.* Image of a face by a human infant, about thirty months old. After Desmond Morris, *The Biology of Art: A Study of the Picture-Making Behavior of the Great Apes and Its Relationship to Human Art* (New York, 1962).

Fig. 2.7. Nonfigurative, "self-sufficient" marks of the Mousterian (Neanderthal) period. *a.* Incised bone from La Ferrassie, France. *b.* Engraved bone from Bacho Kiro, Bulgaria. After Alexander Marshack, "Some Implications of the Paleolithic Symbolic Evidence for the Origin of Language," *Current Anthropology* 17 (1976).

Fig. 3.1. Aurignacian images on limestone blocks, from rock shelters near Les Eyzies, Dordogne, France (about 32,000–26,000 B.C.). *a.* Block 1, Abri Cellier (animal horns?). *b.* Block 5, Abri Cellier (horns and head of an animal). *c.* Block 2, Abri Cellier (head of a horse?). *d.* Block 1, Abri Blanchard (horns and head of an ibex?). *e.* Block 5, Abri Blanchard (forepart of animal head?). After Delluc and Delluc, "Les manifestations graphiques."

Fig. 3.2. Block 16, La Ferrassie (incised legs and underbelly of a herbivore). Photo and drawing courtesy Gilles Delluc and Brigitte Delluc.

Fig. 3.3. Block 10, Abri Blanchard (incised "signs," including parallel scratches, hollows, and punctuations, and "female genitals"). Photo and drawing courtesy Gilles Delluc and Brigitte Delluc.

Fig. 3.4. The sorting of features of marks. *a.* The Constitutive Criterion (CC): Some particular features of the visual display must be determinable as signifying. *b.* The Criterion of Specific Resemblance (CSR): Some particular resemblances between features of the visual display and "reality" denote what they resemble. *c.* The joint sorting of CC and CSR: CC and CSR each classify different features of the visual display but conjointly establish the image.

Fig. 3.5. Canonical form of the chain of replications necessary and sufficient for depiction. M = mark; R = features resembling object initially perceived in seeing-as; ~R = features not resembling object initially perceived in seeing-as; T = object perceiving in seeing-as ("thing"); ‖ = judgment of perceptual identity.

Fig. 3.6. Polydigital tracing in the cave of Gargas, French Pyrenees, about 20,000 B.C. (?). Photo courtesy Claude Barrière.

Fig. 3.7. Polydigital tracing in the cave of Gargas, French Pyrenees, about 20,000 B.C. (?) (head and horns of an animal?). Photo courtesy Claude Barrière.

Fig. 3.8. Monodigital tracings depicting aspects of bison, in "Les Crevasses," Room 3, cave of Gargas. *a.* Double S curve (head). *b.* Double S curve (horns, dorsal line, and tail). *c.* Two double S curves (dorsal and frontal outlines). *d.* Two fitted double S curves and strokes (outline; modern damage to the head). *e.* Three superimposed double S curves and strokes (outline). *f.* Abbreviated and double S curves and strokes (outline). *g.* Abbreviated and double S curves and circular stroke (dorsal line, head, and eye). After Barrière, *L'art pariétal de Gargas*.

Fig. 3.9. Incised outline of a horse with surrounding linear incisions, "Chambre du Camarin," cave of Gargas. Reprinted from Barrière, *L'art pariétal de Gargas,* by permission.

Fig. 3.10. Incised panel with bovids, horses, and mammoth (not shown), in "Le Baldaquin," cave of Gargas. (Drawing shows left two-thirds of panel.) Reprinted from Barrière, *L'art pariétal de Gargas,* fig. 30, by permission.

Fig. 3.11. "Panel of the Mammoths" (top of figure), cave of Gargas, incised palimpsest with several bison, a mammoth, serpentine form, and other marks, above "La pierre noire" (bottom of figure), incised palimpsest with two bison, two ibexes, two horses, and mammoth. Both panels have many additional markings. (Drawing shows right and larger portion of panels, separated from each other by a flow of calcite.) Reprinted from Barrière, *L'art pariétal de Gargas,* fig. 52, by permission.

Fig. 4.1. Oldowan bifacially flaked pebbles ("pebble-tool culture"), Olduvai Gorge (Tanzania), Bed 1, early Middle Pleistocene. After L.S.B. Leakey, *Olduvai Gorge* (London, 1951).

Fig. 4.2. Simplified schema of a reduction sequence, from raw material ("blank") (1) toward "finished" tool (5), an "idea" possibly motivating "reduction" *(a–c)* also incorporating "changes of mind" *(d).*

Fig. 4.3. Reconstruction of the excavated area of Neolithic houses and shrine at Çatal Hüyük VII, Anatolia. Reprinted from James Mellaart, *The Archaeology of Ancient Turkey* (London, 1978), by permission.

Fig. 4.4. Plan of Neolithic houses with hypothetical circulation and communication routes at Lepenski Vir. Reprinted from D. Srejovic, *Europe's First Monumental Sculpture: New Discoveries at Lepenski Vir* (New York, 1982), fig. 12.

Fig. 5.1. Painting of horses (left horse is 3' 8" long) and engraving of bison (4' 5" long), entrance to the Axial Gallery, cave of Lascaux, about 15,000 B.C.

Fig. 5.2. Camille Pissarro, *Mardi-Gras on the Boulevard Montmartre, Paris,* 1897. Collection of the Harvard University Art Museums, by permission.

Fig. 5.3. Richard Estes, *Paris Street Scene,* 1972; gift of Sydney and Frances Lewis. Photo courtesy and copyright © 1994 Virginia Museum of Fine Arts, Richmond.

Fig. 5.4. Eric Fischl, *The Power of Rock and Roll,* 1984. Photo by permission Mary Boone Gallery, New York.

Fig. 5.5. Jan Vermeer, *Young Lady Standing at a Virginal,* about 1670. Collection of the National Gallery, London, by permission.

Fig. 5.6. Eric Fischl, *The Sheer Weight of History,* 1982. Photo by permission Mary Boone Gallery, New York.

Fig. 5.7. Sleeping hermaphrodite (the "Borghese Hermaphrodite"), now in the Louvre, Paris, about 150–100 B.C. Photo the author.

Fig. 5.8. Detail of wooden tomb relief of vizier Hesire, from Tomb of Hesire, Sakkara, Third Dynasty (about 2700 B.C.). Photo the author.

Fig. 5.9. Henri Breuil's line copy of wall paintings and engravings ("Panel of the Hut"), cave of La Mouthe, Dordogne, France, about 15,000 B.C. Reprinted from Henri Breuil, *Four Hundred Centuries of Cave Art* (Montignac, 1954).

Fig. 5.10. Henri Breuil's line copy of bison, cave of Font-de-Gaume, about 15,000 B.C. Reprinted from Breuil, *Four Hundred Centuries of Cave Art.*

Fig. 5.11. Henri Breuil's line copy of mammoths and other animals, cave of Les Combarelles, about 15,000 B.C. Reprinted from Breuil, *Four Hundred Centuries of Cave Art.*

Fig. 5.12. Cartailhac's palimpsest.

Fig. 5.13. Emile Bayard, *The Precursors of Raphael and Michelangelo, or The Birth of the Arts of Drawing and Sculpture in the Reindeer Age,* 1870, lithograph to illustrate Louis Figuier, *L'homme primitif* (Paris, 1870).

Fig. 5.14. "Figurine" from Berekhat Ram, Golan Heights, Acheulean period, about 230,000 B.C. Drawing courtesy Naama Goren-Inbar.

Fig. 5.15. Henry de Lumley's reconstruction of an "ovoid hut" at Terra Amata (Nice), Acheulean period, about 220,000 B.C. Drawing by Eric Mose. Reprinted from Henry de Lumley, "A Paleolithic Camp at Nice," *Scientific American* 220, no. 5 (1969), by permission.

Fig. 5.16. Emile Bayard, *Interior of a Hut of the Reindeer Age,* 1870, lithograph to illustrate Figuier, *L'homme primitif.*

Fig. 5.17. Marked bones from Bilzingsleben, Germany, Acheulean period, about 300,000 B.C. After Dietrich Mania and Ursula Mania, "Deliberate Engravings on Bone Artefacts of Homo Erectus," *Rock Art Research* 5 (1988).

Fig. 7.1. The Oxford Palette (left: obverse; right: reverse), late predynastic period (Nagada IIc/d), about 3200 B.C. Courtesy the Visitors of the Ashmolean Museum, Oxford University.

Fig. 7.2. The Hunter's Palette, late predynastic period (Nagada IId?), about 3200 B.C. Courtesy the Trustees of the British Museum.

Fig. 7.3. The Battlefield Palette (top: obverse; bottom: reverse), early First Dynasty (?) (Nagada IId/III?), about 3000 B.C. Collection of the British Museum (large fragment) and Ashmolean Museum (small fragment); photo courtesy the British Museum. Courtesy the Trustees of the British Museum.

Fig. 7.4. The Narmer Palette (left: obverse; right: reverse), early First Dynasty (Nagada IIIa/b or Horizon A/B), about 3000 B.C. Photo the author.

Fig. 7.5. Story structure of the Narmer Palette.

Fig. 7.6. Episodes of the story of the Narmer Palette.

Fig. 7.7. Reading the text of the Narmer Palette.

Fig. 11.1. Serge Pankejeff (the Wolf Man), drawing of his dream of the wolves, present whereabouts unknown. Reprinted from Sigmund Freud, "Aus der Geschichte einer infantilen Neurose," *Gesammelte Schriften*, vol. 8 (Vienna, 1924).

Fig. 11.2. Serge Pankejeff (the Wolf Man), untitled painting of his dream of the wolves, about 1950–60, from the collection of Muriel Gardiner. Photo courtesy Library of Congress.

Fig. 11.3. Caspar David Friedrich, *Oak Tree in the Snow*, 1829. Collection of the National Gallery, Berlin, by permission.

Fig. 11.4. Sigmund Freud, "Schematic pictures of the psychic apparatus." Reprinted from Sigmund Freud, *Die Traumdeutung* (Vienna, 1900), figs. 1–3.

Fig. 11.5. Sigmund Freud, schema of the structure of Emma's hysterical repression. Reprinted from Sigmund Freud, "Project for a Scientific Psychology" [1895], in *Standard Edition*, 1:354, courtesy Sigmund Freud Copyrights, The Institute of Psycho-Analysis, and The Hogarth Press.

Fig. 11.6. Sigmund Freud, schematic picture of sexuality *(Sexualschema)*. Reprinted from Sigmund Freud, manuscript titled "Melancholia," dated 7 January 1895, in *Standard Edition*, 1:202, courtesy Sigmund Freud Copyrights, The Institute of Psycho-Analysis, and The Hogarth Press.

Fig. 11.7. Sigmund Freud, "The Architecture of Hysteria." In the original, the dotted lines, arrows, and numerals are in red ink, as well as the word "Work" and the line preceding it. Reprinted from Sigmund Freud, manuscript titled "The Architecture of Hysteria," dated 25 May 1897, in *The Complete Letters of Sigmund Freud to Wilhelm Fliess, 1887–1904*, ed. and trans. Jeffrey M. Masson (Cambridge, Mass., 1985), 247, by permission Harvard University Press.

Fig. 11.8. Schema for sensory, motor, and conduction aphasias. Reprinted from Sigmund Freud, *Zur Auffassung der Aphasien* (Vienna, 1891).

Fig. 11.9. Psychological schema for the word concept. Reprinted from Freud, *Aphasien*.

Fig. 11.10. Sigmund Freud, drawing of the nerve processes of the spinal ganglia of *Petromyzon*, present whereabouts unknown. Reprinted from *Sitzungsberichte der kaiserlichen Akademie der Wissenschaften, Math.-Naturwissensch. Kl.* 78 (1878).

Fig. 11.11. Schema for the binding of nerve fibers and bodies in the medulla oblongata. Reprinted from *Neurologisches Centralblatt* 5 (1886).

Fig. 11.12. *a.* Schema for the passage of quantity in the psychic system. *b.* Schema for the passage of quality in the psychic system. Reprinted from Sigmund Freud, "Project for a Scientific Psychology" [1895], in *Standard Edition*, 1:314, 324, courtesy Sigmund Freud Copyrights, The Institute of Psycho-Analysis, and The Hogarth Press.

Fig. 11.13. Schema for the structure of the forgetting of the name of Signorelli. Reprinted from *Standard Edition*, 2:294, courtesy Sigmund Freud Copyrights, The Institute for Psycho-Analysis, and The Hogarth Press.

Fig. 11.14. "The probable effect of the action of natural selection through divergence of character and extinction, on the descendants of a common ancestor." Reprinted from Charles Darwin, *The Origin of Species* (London, 1876).

Fig. 11.15. "The lineage of mankind." Reprinted from Ernst Haeckel, *Anthropogenie* (Berlin, 1874).

Fig. 11.16. Schema for the psychogenesis of mankind. Reprinted from George John Romanes, *Mental Evolution in Man* (London, 1888).

Fig. 11.17. Family tree of the Freud family, after 1902, present whereabouts unknown. Reprinted from Marianne Krüll, *Freud and His Father* (New York, 1986).

Fig. 11.18. Family portrait of Freud and his brother and sisters, about 1875. Photo the author.

Fig. 11.19. Illustration from Freud's heirloom picture book. Reprinted from Friedrich von Tschudi, *Das Thierleben der Alpenwelt* (1865).

Fig. 12.1. The constitution of fetishism according to Freud's "Fetishism" (1927).

Preface

The chapters of this book were written over the past ten years for archaeologists, for art historians, and for students of psychoanalysis and culture (or of what has often been called "subjectivity"). These groups of readers have different approaches to what can often be exactly the same materials—images and artifacts produced in the past, surviving in one form or another into the present. But despite the fact that archaeologists, art historians, and psychoanalysts rarely have any professional exchange, I believe they often have common concerns.

A number of readers have encouraged me to collect some of my essays in a single book, partly because several chapters have not been published in their entirety before. Even those that have been fully published have appeared in scattered, specialized places, making it difficult for readers to get an overview of the work and especially of its underlying coherence. I hope that archaeologists will be interested in reading the studies in psychoanalytic topics, that art historians will be interested in reading the more archaeological essays, and so on. In this way, I hope that the arguments I make within each of these disciplines, though they are meant to stand on their own, will be seen to have a broader rationale. Although much of my work is "interdisciplinary," it does not follow the pattern of established interdisciplinary inquiries. It is not the same thing, for example, as "cultural studies" or the "history of consciousness." Some of its chief intellectual points of reference—the social anthropology of "cultural" conventions; the philosophy of language, notation, and "art"; and, more recently, literary theory—have not been projects to which I have contributed directly. Instead, I have drawn on them for some of the terms of what, for me, is a separate matter—namely, the archaeology, or history, of the ways in which an artifact or image "replicates" previous or other artifacts or images.

I have tried to include a range of essays in order to represent the overall shape of this problem. Despite the technical nature of some chapters, I have chosen them because they do make general, or generalizable, points. Since the chapters were first written, I have changed my mind about particular arguments, often in response to criticism, and in some areas a considerable literature has built up, but I have not systematically revised them for this book. I have corrected printing errors, eliminated unnecessary passages or overlaps in content, and standardized the format and apparatus. Apart from restoring the unpublished full text of several essays, the main difference between these chapters and the original versions is the addition of a number of cross-references and explanations designed to highlight links between them. Some of the chapters review formulations to be found in other chapters, but I hope that such modest repetition will be helpful rather than distracting—especially for those readers who do not intend to read all of the chapters in sequence. I have not tried to resolve deeper conflicts between the chapters, though I continue to believe that many of my arguments can be coordinated. Instead, in addition to cross-referencing the chapters, I have written a new Introduction for this volume. It outlines some of the interests animating all the essays and briefly discusses relations between them.

I want to acknowledge the support with which many of these chapters were written. From 1983 to 1986, the Society of Fellows at Harvard University offered an ideal environment for reading and research. Several chapters were written (although not published) at the time, and I was able to do the background work for several others. In 1986–87, the Department of History of Art at the University of California at Berkeley invited me to serve as its J. Paul Getty Fellow in the History of Art and the Humanities. During that year I completed a full-length treatment of the theory of depiction, style, and culture; although unpublished, it is cited in several chapters under the title *Seeing Through Culture: The Possibility of the History of Art* and underlies many ideas presented in this book (Chapters 3 and 6, in particular, draw from it). From 1987 to 1996, Northwestern University—through its Department of Art History, Program of African Studies, Program in Comparative Literary Studies, Center for the Humanities, College of Arts and Sciences, and Office of Research and Sponsored Programs—supported my work with travel grants, research funds, and a Humanities Research Award (in 1989–90). I owe a special word of thanks to the librarians and curators in the Interlibrary Loan Department and the Special Collections Department at Northwestern University Library; they know all too well how much they have helped me in the past few years. In 1992–93, a John Simon Guggenheim Memorial Foundation Fellowship and an Andrew W. Mellon Visiting Scholarship at the Stanford Humanities Center enabled me to begin preparing this book. It has been completed with the help of a publication subvention from the Office of Research and Sponsored Programs of Northwestern and funds from the Arthur Andersen Teaching and Research Professorship in the College of Arts and Sciences at Northwestern, an appointment I held in 1994 and 1995.

Many readers over many years have helped me develop or revise my work, especially by responding, often in detail, to drafts or to the published texts of these essays: I think especially of Svetlana Alpers, Michael Baxandall, Leo Bersani, Tim Clark, Meg Conkey, Iain Davidson, Peter Fenves, Joel Fineman, Nelson Goodman, Oleg Grabar, Wolfgang Kemp, André Leroi-Gourhan, Alex Marshack, Patrick Maynard, Bill Noble, Michael Podro, Alex Potts, David Rabinowitch, Dan Sperber, Peter Ucko, Irene Winter, Richard Wollheim, Alison Wylie, and Henri Zerner. David Carrier, Margaret W. Conkey, and Philip Winsor enthusiastically supported this project and made many helpful suggestions about its shape. I especially wish to thank Richard W. Quinn for his careful and creative editorial work. His judgment has helped craft a more cohesive, and I hope a more useful, volume. Where necessary, copyright holders have kindly granted permission to reprint the essays. Details can be found in the Acknowledgments. Sources and acknowledgments for illustrations are noted in the List of Illustrations.

Acknowledgments

Chapter 1. "Finding Symbols in History" was originally published in *Material Culture and Symbolic Expression*, ed. Ian Hodder (London: Unwin Hyman, 1989), and a different version (reprinted here) in *Representations in Archaeology*, ed. Jean-Claude Gardin and Christopher Peebles (Bloomington, Ind.: Indiana University Press, 1992). Reprinted by permission of the editors and Indiana University Press.

Chapter 2. "The Origins of Image Making" was originally published in *Current Anthropology* 19 (1986), with twelve invited comments by other writers and a "Reply" by the author (not reprinted here). Copyright 1986 by The Wenner-Gren Foundation for Anthropological Research, all rights reserved. Reprinted by permission of the University of Chicago Press.

Chapter 3. A longer version of "Replication and Depiction in Paleolithic Art" was originally published in *Representations* 19 (1987). Reprinted by permission of The Regents of the University of California.

Chapter 4. A shorter version of "The Deconstruction of Intentionality in Archaeology" was published in *Antiquity* 66 (1992). This version has not been previously published.

Chapter 5. A shorter version of "Beginning the History of Art" was published in *Philosophy and the Histories of the Arts*, ed. Donald W. Crawford, a special issue of the *Journal of Aesthetics and Art Criticism* 51 (1993). This version has not been previously published.

Chapter 6. "Style and History in Art History" was originally published in *The Uses of Style in Archaeology*, ed. Margaret W. Conkey and Christine Hastorf (Cambridge: Cambridge University Press, 1989). Reprinted by permission of the editors and Cambridge University Press.

Chapter 7. A shorter version of "Narrativity and the Narmer Palette" was originally published in *Narrative and Event in Ancient Art*, ed. Peter J. Holliday (New York: Cambridge University Press, 1993). Reprinted by permission of the editor and Cambridge University Press.

Chapter 8. A shorter version of "Opticality and Rhetoricity in Paul de Man's 'Historical Materialism'" was published (in German) in *Texte zur Kunst* 4, no. 14 (1994). This version has not been previously published.

Chapter 9. "Winckelmann Divided" was originally published in *Artistic Exchange: Proceedings of the Twenty-Eighth International Congress of the History of Art, Berlin, 1992*, ed. Thomas W. Gaehtgens (Berlin: Comité Internationale pour l'Histoire de l'Art, 1993).

Chapter 10. A shorter version of "Pleasure and Its Contents: Bersani and Dutoit's Assyrian Reliefs" was published in *Art History* 11 (1988). This version has not been previously published.

Chapter 11. "Sigmund Freud's Drawing of the Dream of the Wolves" was originally published in *Oxford Art Journal* 15 (1992). Reprinted by permission of the Editorial Group and Oxford University Press.

Chapter 12. A longer version of "HomoVision: A Reading of Freud's 'Fetishism'" was originally published in *Genders* 15 (1992). Reprinted by permission of the editor and the University of Texas Press.

Introduction

Replication in Archaeology, Art History, and Psychoanalysis

The following twelve chapters present elements of what has been, for me, a continuous and coherent project crossing the disciplines of archaeology, art history, and psychoanalysis. In this book, I interpret artifacts both as *replications* of one another and of prior artifacts or images, models, stories, or fantasies in a sequence—or what I often call a chain—of replications.

"Replication" and "Culture"

By "replication," I mean the sequential production of similar material morphologies—made or imagined material forms that are always "artifacts" and often images—that are substitutable for one another in specific social contexts of use. Qualifications and refinements of this concept are presented in many chapters. Strictly speaking, for example, there are no perfect substitutables—no artifactual or semantic synonyms. Moreover, substitutability among artifacts is an emergent, not a given, property of a tradition of production. It must be organized in a particular way—for example, in an irreversible direction in which a later artifact is partly substitutable for an earlier, but never an earlier for a later. Substitutability varies with changing ways of using artifacts or reasons for doing so. Equally important, the production of substitutable morphology, "replication," is always accompanied by the production (sometimes deliberate) of *non*substitutable morphology. Similarity itself, the condition of any judgment of substitutability or nonsubstitutability, is entirely relative to a particular perceptual standard or to a conventional metric.

The concept of replication presents these and many other difficulties. As several of the chapters show, for example, sometimes replication involves the actual manufacture of later artifacts tied causally, in one way or another, to earlier ones—the sense most likely to be highlighted by archaeologists and art historians. But sometimes replication involves the imaginary projection or the recollected image of such artifacts—a sense that theorists of consciousness or psychoanalysts might be more likely to emphasize.

At the most general level, I suggest that through examining the relations of replication we come to understand the history, and sometimes the "prehistory," of images and artifacts. The most important point is simply that an image or an artifact cannot be understood on its own, divorced either from the replicatory chains to which it belongs historically or from the replicatory assemblages in which we discover, perceive, and interpret it. Although this proposition is surely a truism, its implications have not, I believe, been as thoroughly explored as they deserve. Thus I set myself firmly against the view that images or artifacts—especially those artifacts we call "works of art"—are characterized by wholeness, completeness, autonomy, or self-sufficiency, or, in my terms, by nonreplicatoriness. At best, nonreplicatoriness could only be an imaginary, ideal condition of some artifacts (or perhaps a particular ideology of replication partly coordinating certain historical replicatory sequences). It follows that I set myself against the view that the object of study in art history, the discipline that has principally guided my thinking, is something called "*the* object" (or "*the* art object"). There is no such thing. More exactly, if there is such a thing, it should interest physicists and not art historians.

Archaeologists have been more interested than art historians in an artifact or an image as an object qua physical thing. Compared with contemporary art history, contemporary archaeology does, indeed, involve a strong dose of "physics": archaeologists consider the physical parameters which constrain the replication of objects and with which replication interacts, such as the durability of materials or their behavior in chemical environments. In addition, precisely because the object—artifact or image—can only be discovered in a material environment (a continuum of objects such as an archaeological "site"), archaeology insists that the proper focus of analysis is the environment and the "assemblages" within it, rather than the individual "object" detached from it.

At the other end of the continuum of analytic possibilities I explore in this book, psychoanalysts have been more interested than art historians in an artifact or an image as an object qua "not-thing": psychoanalysts (and other theorists of consciousness, like some of the philosophers and literary critics considered in Chapters 4, 8, and 9) investigate a representation (even a "fantasy" or other "internal, psychic object") whose physical realization has little or no interest apart from the ways in which it has been continually imagined and remembered by an individual consciousness. Some of the most complex internal objects investigated by psychoanalysts—such as the "fetish-images" I discuss in Chapter 12—need not have any physical realization whatsoever (although they might be partly replicated in the actual "fetish effigy," the material object employed in a fetishist's erotic practice). Often enough we cannot readily infer the florid properties of the internal, or psychic, object from its rather ordinary, paltry, or reduced material realization. In light of this, it is not surprising that many psychoanalysts look cautiously on art history's interest in studying "the object." In psychoanalysis, to recall Freud's formula, the finding of an object is always a *refinding* of it.[1] In a movement within psychoanalysis that has particular importance for me, psychoanalysis insists that "object relations" should be our focus: we should explore the replicatory connections and disjunctions between internal, psychic objects and external, material ones. Again, however, the object exists in an environment or assemblage—an intra- and intersubjective psychic environment or assemblage—from which it cannot be detached.

In order to explicate an image or an artifact, archaeology and psychoanalysis pursue very different replicatory histories. In archaeology, an object is never outside the *physical* assemblage in which it is found. In psychoanalysis, an object is never outside the *psychic* assemblage in which it is found. Obviously, physical assemblages are not psychic ones, and vice versa; the problem of passing from "matter" to "meaning," or vice versa, is one of the chief themes of this book. But in their different ways both archaeology and psychoanalysis are more dedicated than art history to the idea that the historical reality of images and artifacts is a replicatory reality. Art history has been beholden to the peculiar doctrine that some objects—namely, objects of art—must escape or rise above history (see esp. Chapters 5 and 9). Thus it has often resisted the so-called reduction that archaeology or psychoanalysis would enforce; for many art historians, to inquire too closely either into the "physics" or into the "psychics" of an art object is supposedly to compromise its self-sufficiency and to stray off the narrow replicatory paths in which this self-sufficiency is thought to have been historically organized. But in fact without the physics and the psychics there is nothing left. One way of putting my concern in this book is simply to say that, suitably interconnected, a physical and psychic account of artifacts or images should be exhaustive. It follows that there is no reason why a healthy art history cannot accommodate the replicatory histories proposed within archaeology and psychoanalysis. By the same token, a healthy archaeology should be able to embrace the replicatory histories suggested within art history and psychoanalysis, and a healthy psychoanalysis the replicatory histories suggested within archaeology and art history.

Every replication, each individual artifact or image, must be seen as the intersection of many different chains of replications (for case studies, see esp. Chapters 7 and 11). Some of these chains are situated materially in human persons (such as the intrapsychic "fetishism" considered in Chapter 12), some of them emerge intersubjectively in a person's

1. Sigmund Freud, *Three Essays on the Theory of Sexuality* [1905], vol. 7 of *The Standard Edition of the Complete Psychological Works of Sigmund Freud,* 24 vols., ed. and trans. James Strachey et al. (London, 1953–74), 222.

social relations with others (relations that often depend materially on the manufacture and exchange of images and artifacts) (see Chapter 11), and some of them coordinate the practices of large social groups (see Chapter 6). Some chains can be partly reconstructed analytically, but most of them are beyond all of our forensic powers. Furthermore, every replication potentially inaugurates other chains of replication—no one of which it determines. Admittedly it is difficult to develop a precise and flexible analysis of this structured dynamic of variability in the human production of artifacts.

For me, the "meaning" of an image or an artifact for the human beings who make and use it lies in the fact of its actual or possible replication. More exactly, the meaning of any image or artifact is constructed cumulatively and recursively—a pro- and retrospective "activation"—in and through the structure and history of its replication (see esp. Chapters 3, 7, 8, and 12). On these grounds, replicated images and artifacts can be treated as fossilized evidence of cognition and, in narrower cases, of human consciousness. This is not a small matter when we are studying human "prehistory" itself—that is, the possibility of a time *before* human history or consciousness.

I do not believe that human cognition or consciousness preexists and thus causally determines replication itself. Instead, to describe certain structures or dynamics in replication is, in itself, to describe cognition and consciousness. Thus, in addition to focusing on replication rather than objects, I set myself against the view that the appropriate context for interpreting replications historically is what is often called the cultural context. It is not so much that the "cultural" context of replication does not exist; it does. But the past and ongoing history of replicatory practices occurs within a social network that is in itself partly coordinated in the very elaboration of replications. As that phrasing suggests, to invoke the "cultural" context of and for replication to *explain* a replicatory history is, in the strict terms I want to uphold, a tautology: by "culture" we simply mean socially coordinated replicatory histories.

It follows that for any fundamental issues of historical interpretation it will not do to assume the consequent—to assume "culture." "Cultural" historians suppose that the social group they are studying already possesses a culture—a system the historian can take for granted in explicating replicatory histories supposedly proceeding from it. But apart from avoiding the historical question itself (whence this "culture," if not in the system of replicatory histories?), this assumption imposes far too much regularity on social life.

In several chapters, I dramatize these questions by exploring the case of "prehistoric" culture. In the case of some remote histories, at any rate, it would be unreliable to make the cultural-historical assumption—to assume the preexistence of "culture," the social coordination of replicatory histories, as the historical context of replication. It is logically possible that at some point the social coordination of replicatory histories did not exist (it is an open question whether apes, for example, who make tools, even through imitative induction, make tools in a *style*). But to some extent my interest in remote prehistory is metaphorical. I am interested in the "prehistoricity" of *all* social life—in its capacity to generate a coordination of replicatory histories that we can then, retrospectively, label as a "culture" and that we should not, anachronistically, assume in order to explain those histories in the first place. For me, the social history of replication is logically prior to the culturological explanation of replications. In this I would like to invert the usual direction of assumption and explanation in many of the anthropological and historical disciplines that study artifact production.

Needless to say, however, in many cases it may be analytically convenient to appeal to the supposed preexistence of replicatory traditions, or "culture," to account for a specific set of links in the chain of replications. To explain why a certain image or artifact has taken the form it has, it is often useful, for example, to invoke a preexisting artistic "style" (a way of making things) or social "ideology" (a way of thinking things). We like to say, for example, that a painter learned a style from a predecessor or that a sculptor adopted an ideology current in a social group. Most archaeological, art historical, and psychoanalytic histories are written on the basis of one or more of these simplifying assumptions.

But in fact it is very difficult to show that an apparently "later" replication in a chain of replications actually is an instance of replicating just that, rather than some other, perhaps unidentifiable, chain; it is very difficult to show that a "culture"—or "cultural" glue—is actually there.[2] The problem is familiar to analytic philosophers and literary critics in the form of puzzles about "meaning"; it is powerfully stated, for example, in the question attributed to Ludwig Wittgenstein, analyzed by Saul Kripke, with which I begin Chapter 1, and underlies what I take (in Chapter 8) to be Paul de Man's effort to conceive a material *history* of "meaning." In different forms, it occasionally crops up in forensic debates within archaeology and art history (see Chapters 4 and 6). Despite its centrality in much of the best theoretical work carried out in the historical and humanistic disciplines in the twentieth century, it deserves greater attention at the heart of cultural and historical analyses, which tend to be overly, and sometimes quite mistakenly, cultur*ological* and historic*ist*—fundamentally nineteenth-century inquiries. The methodological difficulties in identifying the coherence of replication (and thus what Gilles Deleuze and Felix Guattari call the "plane of consistency" and the "lines of flight" of human thought)[3] are certainly tremendous. The theoretical problem is fatal. There simply is no good reason to suppose that replication works like a cookie cutter, turning out the latest specimens according to preexisting specifications. Thus concepts like style and ideology must be handled very cautiously if they are to be useful instruments of historical analysis. In considering the replication of a style or an ideology, we must give priority to the similarity, not the identity, of replications (whether physical or psychic objects); to their substitutability, not their interchangeability; and to variations introduced by continuous use: in the very fact of its supposed repetition, a thought that has been thought again cannot be exactly the same thought. When this injunction is disregarded, it will appear that abstract Styles, Ideas, or Cultures (or, in more recent writing, abstract Subjectivities, Ideologies, or Rhetorics) march across the historical stage rather than the thoughts and actions of people making and using representations.

2. This problem derives from the way in which the concept of "culture" emerged in the eighteenth, nineteenth, and early twentieth centuries. A fine account of this development can be found in Christopher Herbert, *Culture and Anomie: Ethnographic Imagination in the Nineteenth Century* (Chicago, 1991).

3. Gilles Deleuze and Felix Guattari, *A Thousand Plateaus*, trans. Brian Massumi (Minneapolis, 1987), e.g., 5–7.

REPLICATION IN ARCHAEOLOGY

In Chapter 1, "Finding Symbols in History," I briefly introduce some of the questions followed up in other chapters. A "cultural" event in remote prehistory—markings made on the walls of the cave of Gargas in the French Pyrenees about 25,000 B.C.—dramatizes problems of historical interpretation that confront the archaeology and anthropology of all later symbol making as well. Although prehistorians protest the strategy, we can use "prehistoric" evidence to identify analytic issues in the study of "historical" periods. Chief among these must be the assumption that historians are not obliged to account for the origins of the conventions they take for granted in explaining culture—as if conventions are not constructed in historical processes. My example is not meant to suggest that prehistoric societies were outside history. I simply propose that in this case we can imagine a mark maker making what seem to us to be images—they are mostly depictions of bison and other large mammals—*without* art historical context, that is, without taking account of, making reference to, or otherwise replicating earlier images, or even replicating the mere possibility of image making itself. At the limit, I suggest, we can imagine that the mark maker had no preexisting knowledge of images and how they might be made.

The historical situation at Gargas supports such an imaginary scenario (at least, there is no compelling evidence that rules it out). But ultimately it is immaterial whether the "Robinson Crusoe" scenario I identify at Gargas actually existed there. I argue that *at some theoretical point* in human evolution, mark makers produced depictions without any prior knowledge of them: the cave at Gargas is a limited, and no doubt partial, representation of this purely logical possibility. This inaugural production goes on regularly at all times, and in Chapter 5, I devote attention to the forensic problems of actually identifying this hypothetical moment, or period, or event.

In Chapter 1, I am interested chiefly in handling what appear to be two insurmountable problems that arise if we grant that the logical possibility is intelligible: depictions had to have been made at least once without any replicatory relationship to other depictions. How did this "first" depiction get made? And how do we know that the marks in the caves of Gargas, which appear *to us* to be depictions, were *in fact* depictions for the mark makers? These two questions, I believe, are systematically related, and in this chapter I sketch the outline of a theoretical answer and also some empirical proposals and predictions. (Chapters 2 and 3 develop this fairly formal analysis at greater length.) I conclude in this chapter that the determining replicatory event in the "origin" of depiction is inaccessible to archaeological observation, although not to psychological inference. This result does not necessarily block archaeology. Instead, I see it as a call for archaeology to develop a body of theory that will guide our psychological inferences from the archaeological evidence. Throughout the first section of the book (Chapters 1–4), I really say nothing one way or another about the structure or content of that psychological inference as such. Instead, I merely assert that archaeology should focus on the forensic evidence for an inferred psychological event, what I call seeing-as (following Wittgenstein), which accounts for certain material properties of the morphological evidence, such as its distribution in an assemblage, its frequency, its chronology, and so forth. In the third section of the book

(Chapters 9–12), it becomes obvious that what seems to be a simple, unitary perceptual and cognitive event—the seeing-as that makes a mark remark—must itself be a replication with a complex psychological history. Psychoanalysis is not the only means of describing this history, but it does offer a rich vocabulary and intriguing group of methodological and theoretical proposals for doing so.

Chapter 2, "The Origins of Image Making," is a first attempt at showing how depictions might be generated from a basis of nondepictive markings, whether we suppose, as I do in this and the next chapter, that these antedate the depictive marks or were made at the same time, in the same "act," as the depictive marks (as Chapter 4 recognizes). I strive for minimum assumptions and maximum generality in my account. Replication—the remaking of a mark in order to preserve or to vary certain morphological and psychological properties—is an integral, in fact the essential, property of depiction. Depiction, I propose, is potentially emergent in any sequence of marks organized replicatorily. It follows that the morphology of a replicatory history can—although it might not—be evidence for the presence of depiction. (This is a way of solving the problem, bedeviling the study of early and nonhuman marking behaviors and of many other situations of marking as well, that what looks depictive "to us" might not have been depictive "to them," and what was depictive "to them" might not be depictive "to us.") There are notable logical flaws in this presentation. Far and away the most important was pointed out in 1986, shortly after the chapter was originally written, by the philosopher Patrick Maynard. He noted that I wrongly expected depiction to materialize in a replicatory sequence that actually secured only the preservation of resemblances between marks and of resemblances between marks and things. No amount of resemblance, in itself, suffices for depiction. But I believe the basic approach employed in Chapter 2 is correct. Depiction rides on replication, which generates a pattern of resemblances of mark to mark, and mark to things, as well as a pattern of *non*resemblances.

In Chapter 3, "Replication and Depiction in Paleolithic Art," I adjust the formal account to accommodate Maynard's criticism. The analysis becomes substantially more complex. We need, I suggest, to identify what I call a canonical chain of replications—the chain that is necessary and sufficient for the emergence of depiction in a replicatory sequence of marks. Armed with the appropriate formal analysis of this "canonical chain," I explore some of its archaeological implications. We can predict, for example, that in a history of specifically *depictive* replications certain mark-to-thing resemblances should be preserved and certain mark-to-mark resemblances should be abandoned. Without knowing, in advance, if prehistoric mark makers were making marks that depicted something, we can, by examining the morphology, frequency, distribution, and chronology of marking, determine that their production did, in fact, generate depiction. At the end of Chapter 3, I note that the formal analysis also shows why depiction is so closely entwined, at both material and logical levels, with nondepictive mark making (or "not-depiction"). This concern becomes increasingly important in later chapters (especially Chapters 4, 8, and 10). There I explore various "deconstructive," "de Manian," and psychoanalytic ideas about the relations between material morphology and the "meaning" threading through but never identical with it.

Some of the arguments mounted in Chapters 2 and 3 are unnecessary or misguided; the formal analysis could probably be streamlined. After Chapter 2 was published, a number of other writers took up the issue, both as a theoretical problem and in relation to the historical interpretation of prehistoric art. None of them, I believe, seriously undermined my account, although the debate was taken into areas Chapters 2 and 3 did not go. Several alternative scenarios for the "origins of image making" were proposed, but I found all of them more unsatisfactory than my own. The most elaborate, a scenario conceived by the archaeologist Iain Davidson and the psychologist William Noble, purports to do the same work as my own, but it fails, as I point out in Chapter 5, to explicate reference, or referring, continuing to assume it to be an essential human capacity or activity.

Some of the aims that animate Chapters 1–3 have been carried into later chapters. Most important, I hope to secure a nontautologous view of the evolution of human symbol making or "culture" broadly conceived. Instead of assuming an essential human "capacity for culture," "language-using faculty," or "symbol-making behavior"—an article of faith among many cultural anthropologists and widely current in cultural studies—I prefer a *historical* analysis of this supposed "capacity," "faculty," or "behavior." Chapters 2 and 3 can be regarded as explicit attacks on this culturological assumption. In Chapter 4, "The Deconstruction of Intentionality in Archaeology," I explore another vocabulary for pursuing the point.

Paleoanthropologists and prehistorians have often taken the historical development of human toolmaking as our primary evidence for the evolution of human thought broadly conceived. I use the term "thought" advisedly here. In addition to documenting human behaviors such as foraging or making shelters, toolmaking has been understood to index human perceptual, cognitive, psychological, or symbolic skills and, more important, human thinking (or even reasoning) about the task and the tool in relation to one another. But the interrelation of toolmaking behavior and thinking *in, through,* and *about* tools has proven to be very troublesome to analyze. Archaeology tends to adopt a rigid distinction between the study of what are presented as concrete, material behaviors on the one hand (such as eating or building) and what are presented as inaccessible "ideas" or "values" on the other hand (such as desiring prestige or feeling a bond with other members in a group). In its intellectual development and in its present-day conceptual divisions of labor, archaeology has compartmentalized investigation to the extent that one influential archaeologist speaks of a "ladder of [archaeological] inference" reaching from the more "behavioral" to the more "ideational"[4] and another sees the human sociocultural universe segmented into more "technological" and more "ideational" realms.[5] The former realm is really the concrete business of survival in, and adaptation to, an environment; the latter realm, by contrast, is a superstructure of reflections on, or symbols of, this reality. The dichotomy implies that archaeology—given its supposedly material body of evidence—should focus principally on

4. Christopher Hawkes, "Archaeological Theory and Method: Some Suggestions from the Old World," *American Anthropologist* 56 (1954), 155–68.

5. Lewis Binford, "Archaeology as Anthropology," *American Antiquity* 28 (1962), 217–25, and idem, "Archaeological Systematics and the Study of Cultural Processes," *American Antiquity* 31 (1965), 203–10. After this Introduction had been written, Randall R. Dipert's *Artifacts, Art Works, and Agency* (Philadelphia, 1993) came to my attention, a book relevant not only to the concerns addressed in this section but also to the larger project of this book.

behavior. "Ideation" can be left to other scholars, such as art historians or the "traditional" archaeologists in fields like Egyptology or classical archaeology, whose forensic problems resemble archaeology's but whose interests are less naturalistic, concrete, or "scientific."

In itself, this approach is not unproductive. It would be healthy for art historians and other students of "culture" to recall that much, if not most, human (or hominid) action in history can be quite compellingly explained behaviorally. Significant work within the developing field of "material culture studies" suggests how misleading it can be to interpret production solely from the vantage point of its status in the consciousness or representation of a group. Our inquiry, the reasoning goes, should not only investigate what people think they are doing but also what they are in fact doing. "Behavioral archaeology" dramatizes the possible disjunction between these domains. In fact, some forms of cultural analysis—and especially of cultural critique—have developed a distinction similar to the archaeological one: it has been asserted that consciousness or culture arises secondarily or as an epiphenomenon in relation to the concrete forces and relations of production. (In one theory of ideology, culture is a misrepresentation of those relations.) Indeed, much of paleoanthropology—as Chapter 4 notes—seems ready to imagine "production" without *any* emergent "consciousness." To be sure, "structural Marxism," identified with French economic anthropology of the 1960s, attacked the purely behaviorist strains in social anthropology. Maurice Godelier among others argued that the forces and relations of production are not precultural facts of human social relations and of society's relation to nature, but rather constructions within human representations *of* society and nature; in Godelier's neat summation, language is the primary force and relation of production. The "structuralist" component of this account added that one could explicate "language," in turn, in terms of basic operations of the human mind in creating, transforming, and mediating categories.[6] I was very impressed with this view—with its elegant synthesis of structuralist, Marxist, and anthropological models—when I encountered it in the mid-1970s. But one should be skeptical of its real historical bite and implicit culturological bias. However compelling, Godelier's position and those like it encounter the evolutionary problem I have touched on already: at some point, we must imagine human or prehuman beings related socially to one another, and to nature, in the absence of consciousness or language. Hence, for any deep historical analysis, a behavioral—or, better, "technosocial"—bias seems preferable to an ideational or culturological one: historically and thus methodologically, relations to matter come *before* relations within meaning.

Historians usually look with equal skepticism on purely behavioral and on purely cultural analyses. Earlier in this century, the *Annales* school opened traditional forms of *Geistesgeschichte* and political-diplomatic history to essentially behavioral inquiries. More recently, behavioral inquiry in its increasingly sophisticated (for example, statistical, or "cliometric") presentation has been opened, or reopened, to a renovated cultural history indebted to structuralist and poststructuralist thinking (so-called New Historicism). Few professional historians today would assent to any recipe that asked them to jettison either behavioral or

6. Maurice Godelier, "Infrastructures, Societies, and History," *Current Anthropology* 19 (1978), 763–71; see also "Myths, Infrastructures, and Lévi-Strauss," in Ino Rossi et al., eds., *The Logic of Culture: Advances in Structural Theory and Methods* (South Hadley, Mass., 1982), 232–61.

cultural inquiry in favor of the other: none supposes that we can separate the behavioral from the ideational components of a complex human action. But prehistorians are not historians; this is both their strength *and* their weakness. The paleoanthropological proposal has been simply that the behavioral elements should be analytically privileged in studying human evolution in the deep past—for which we cannot, as I have insisted, assume human consciousness and representation.

But ironically, Chapter 4 argues, paleoanthropology so far has not been able to make good on its own interpretive urge. Its language for studying human behavior—such as human "adaptations" to natural environments—has been compromised by hidden assumptions about consciousness. Behavioral archaeology still tends to conceive material human action, such as toolmaking, to be essentially caused or driven by ideation; it shares the tendency of art history to suppose that the artist's touch of paint to the canvas (for example) is directed by guiding "intentions" to realize a plan, goal, or ideal. These animating intentions tend to be conceived as wholly stable preexisting mental blueprints for the tools; the material action merely becomes the fossil record of this blueprint. To use one of the examples discussed in Chapter 4, early human toolmaking was supposedly driven by an intention to make tools "with the least possible effort." This animating idea, or intention, this basic rationality, somehow preexisted the toolmaking itself—though tools are our only evidence for it—and accounts for the morphology of tools in the actual chain of replications of Oldowan and other very early toolmakers.

In Chapter 4, I suggest that one contemporary attempt to unsettle the analytic privilege accorded to a unitary, generative human Intentionality—"deconstruction"—has affinities with the unrealized urge of behavioral archaeology to explicate human consciousness-in-action as wholly concrete and material, requiring no necessary appeal to a domain of "meanings." Both deconstructive literary analysis and forensic behavioral archaeology, for example, claim that making a speech or shaping a stone tool are not always directed—at least wholly—by a preexisting intention to make a speech or shape a stone tool. Certainly they are not always coordinated by a stabilizing, teleologically realized image of what the speech or blade should actually sound, look, or feel like morphologically (or at the level of what has usually been called form). As Chapter 8 puts it, after Paul de Man, materiality erupts in meaning in complex, unstable, fully reversible processes of partial "formalization."

But needless to say, my approach in Chapter 4 is only one side of the coin. Later chapters explore the psychoanalytic observation, complementing the paleoanthropological one, that *meaning* erupts in materiality—in "object relations"—in complex ways. Chapters 7 and 10 offer case studies: the former asks how the possibility of "meaning" (in this case a subtle symbolic narrative) rides on, at the same time as it activates, certain properties of the morphology in use, and the latter how the possibility of "form" (in this case an intricate visual patterning) rides on, at the same time as it activates, certain properties of the meaning it replicates. The systematic question, clearly, is not either-or. My general aim in the first section of the book, however, is not to endorse a theoretical and methodological pluralism in the name of some supposed real "imbrication" of matter and meaning, or a "feedback" between behavior and intention: quite to the contrary. I want to insist that in what we must precisely call "pre-history," meanings and intentions are emergent in replications which precede and enfold them and of which they are a peculiar and particular species. This "pre-history" is evolutionarily ancient in the literal sense but has other instances as well (as Chapters 8 and 11 suggest).

REPLICATION IN ART HISTORY

Consistent with the general aim of Chapters 2–4, Chapter 5, "Beginning the History of Art," reformulates the problem of prehistory and "prehistoric art" as the problem of "pre-historicity" and "pre–art historicality." The main work of the chapter, however, is negative. Art history, I suggest, has been unable to identify an actual prehistoric art that is "pre–art historical" in the right sense, even though its ordinary narratives require such a "Figure 1." The easiest solution has been to pass "pre–art historical" art, whatever it might be, onto archaeology—just as archaeology passes "cultural ideation," whatever it might be, onto art history and other "cultural-historical" disciplines. Whereas the replications studied by art historians only occupy the last page of archaeology textbooks, the replications studied by archaeologists only occupy the first page of art-history textbooks. Chapter 5 accounts for this phenomenon in terms of fundamental disciplinary determinations; I call them aestheticist concepts and institutions. Aestheticism is not, of course, the sole motivation of art history. In Chapter 9, I consider an opposing historicism as well. But, as comparison of Chapters 5 and 9 will show, the reasons for bemoaning the lack of historicism in the aestheticism of art history are not the same reasons for bemoaning the lack of aestheticism in the historicism of art history.

In Chapter 5, I examine art history's aestheticist prejudice that for the purposes of art historical analysis the appropriate replicatory relations obtain between one art object and another or (a slight shift) between art objects and closely related replicatory structures such as artists' "intentions," which amount to a mental image of the work of art to be produced, "styles," or the "visual conventions" of a society. (In Chapter 6, I suggest that these structures are often identified on the basis of observed replicatory relations between art objects in the first place. Thus they are as much art historical constructions as features of art historical reality.) Chapter 5 employs a familiar device. If we imagine replication between art objects—for example, the historical reproduction of a "style" of making art objects—to be a real relation, then at some point in historical analysis we must ask how that relation came into existence. Chapters 1–4 provide a rough sense of how this problem can be addressed without assuming that the relation has "always" been there—that depiction and style, for example, are essential features of working matter or making marks. There I insist that depiction (or, as Chapter 6 urges, style) is historically emergent in nondepiction (or nonstyle)—a process that is visible, in principle, to our forensic and historical interpretation. But in Chapter 5, I explore a major resistance to this approach. Art objects have traditionally been defined as whole, autonomous, and self-sufficient. Many descriptive and comparative methods in art history, as well as modern philosophies of art, have embraced this conception.

Whether or not it is correct, this conception makes it difficult to remember that any art object must have substantial replicatory relations with *non*–art objects. These include other realizations of the raw materials from which the art object has also been made and, more interesting, artifacts or images in the maker's experience that are not themselves art objects. In part through a retrospectively meaningful connection established by the artist with the art object, such non–art objects (whatever kind of artifact or image they might be) can be seen as the prototype or "source" of the work of art, and the work of art as their reworking or "shadow." I am deeply interested in such possibilities—for example, in the historical role of artifacts owned or collected by artists that are not, in themselves, part of the artist's activity qua artist (for a case study, see Chapter 11). These relations of replication *between* old, ordinary, or nonartistically significant artifacts *and* art objects are erotic relations in the broad sense. They mediate what an individual consciousness has taken to be subjectively meaningful and desirable; and it is not surprising that they should enter art objects produced precisely *as* replications—repetitions, revisions, and refutations—of meaningful and desirable experience. I investigate these possibilities extensively in Chapters 9–12. As Chapter 9 suggests, because professional art history has had difficulty assimilating its *own* eroticisms—the fact that art historians often have erotic relations with artifacts, art objects or not—it has difficulty handling this feature of art historical reality.

Although it is tempting to regard art objects as partly or even largely self-sufficient replications, Chapter 5 starts to unpack this view and to develop the alternative explored in later chapters. If art history tries to write the history of such replications as wholly autonomous, self-sufficient works of art, it must fail. Once we recognize, however, that the "origin" and history of art objects lies in their replication not only of other whole, self-sufficient art objects but also of bits and pieces drawn from any and all levels of the maker's experience and consciousness, the real question can be clarified. As Chapter 5 suggests, our issue is not how an art object does or does not replicate *other* art objects, artists' "intentions," "style," or visual "codes" and conventions. This inquiry leads merely to fallacious source-hunting, whether formalistic, iconographic, or structuralist and semiotic in its details, posing as history—a mistaken aestheticism leading to a fake historicism. Rather, the issue is how, in realizing itself, an artwork emergent in a determining environment of nonartwork compares itself with itself (as I put it in Chapter 5)—how it replicates the bits and pieces of experience that it does. This approach requires an actual historicism that is nevertheless properly aestheticist. To my mind, it also enables a more realistic species of descriptive and comparative analysis than the kind that frequently organizes a professional art historical narrative.

On the account favored in Chapter 5, we can usefully imagine a "first" art object—an actual prehistoric art—when we do not need to imagine a preexisting art object for it but only the availability of bits and pieces for replication. At this point, the model presented in Chapters 2–4 would kick in, whether or not we are speaking of actual prehistoric arts: we can show logically, if not in every given case, how the stylized depiction can emerge from bits and pieces of nonstylized nondepictions. In Chapter 5 it suffices to recall this line of thinking to see why art history, in pursuing the "origins of art," or what I call its "Figure 1," a theoretical entity of great importance to its system, pursues the wrong replicatory relations. Shading into a prehistory it cannot complete, art history looks for ever earlier art objects as such—or, in the archaeological equivalent of this maneuver, ever earlier styles or symbols (see Chapter 4)—rather than for the bits and pieces retrospectively (that is, summatively and recursively) realizable, in replication of a certain kind, *as* art objects. (In Chapters 11 and 12, I strongly emphasize the importance of retrospection in replication; it is also fundamental to the view of the "activation" of meaning presented in Chapter 7.) In art history, it is, unfortunately, as if a history of a studio should begin and end with the finished products going out the door rather than with the stuff on the shelf or the garbage on the floor. Admittedly Chapter 5 does not provide a formal model for arthood (historically emergent in nonarthood) parallel to the "canonical chain of replications" for depiction (historically emergent in nondepiction) presented in Chapter 3 or for style (historically emergent in mere making) presented in Chapter 6. I am not sure that any current philosophy or aesthetics can do so; it has certainly been beyond my competence. But Chapter 5 operates on the premise that such a model should be presumed if art history is to make sense—be realistic—at all.

Within both archaeology and art history, the most important means of handling the partly summative and recursive (rather than autonomous and self-sufficient) history of morphology—what, in Chapter 8, I call the process of formalization—is the concept of style. Chapter 6, "Style and History in Art History," explores it. From the Renaissance through the eighteenth century, "style" referred to proper form—to morphology that obeys certain rules or models of form. This was, of course, a replicatory concept: a relation of reproduction, imitation, or expression supposedly obtains between the model of style and the properly stylized performances.

In the nineteenth century, however, this normative concept began to fade. Style was increasingly located in a behavioral realm. Instead of resulting from the maker's obedience to rules of form, the "stylization" of morphology supposedly results from his or her largely unconscious embodiment—placed between social conventions and personal preferences, on the one hand, and perceptual and motor habits, on the other—of a style. Style appears to be a system in the production of morphology that any maker must *necessarily* possess just in virtue of being that maker. It follows that the style must be replicated whenever this maker makes something. Obviously this relation has tremendous analytic value for a social history—at least, for a social history of making—extending from matters of simple fact (who made what when) to matters of more general sociology.

Recently, the pendulum has swung back again, especially in "postprocessual" archaeology and in "cultural studies"—two variants of antibehaviorist opinion in the social and human sciences. Here, style is seen as made (or even "performed") creatively by makers—active subjects, or "agents"—who aim at certain effects and enact, revise, and resist socially available preferences, conventions, or roles.[7] Paradoxically, this account suffers from the intentionalist fallacies discussed in Chapter 4. Despite the claims of its proponents, it embeds a traditional concept of cultural morphology as essentially aesthetic and celebrates an essen-

7. Readers may wish to read the anthology in which Chapter 6 was originally published—Margaret W. Conkey and Christine Hastorf, eds., *The Uses of Style in Archaeology* (Cambridge, 1989)—for a range of approaches, although the authors do not necessarily phrase the issues in the way I do here. Another anthology, *The Concept of Style*, ed. Berel Lang (Philadelphia, 1979), contains a number of articles that were my points of reference in writing Chapter 6.

tially creative subject. (Such conservatism may function in what appear to be progressive affirmations of the diversity of cultural production.) It also narrows the concept of style substantially. It ignores the stylization of morphology that arises, as the nonnormative forensic analysis of Giovanni Morelli had it, from nonintentional, largely motor-muscular, causes.[8] At root it is the eighteenth-century normative analysis, reversed. Where "style" once flowed from social models to agents who obeyed them, now "style" flows from originating agents to the performances that enact them.

When I began studying art history in the mid-1970s, the concept of style had fallen into some disrepute. There were, of course, many for whom so-called stylistic (or "formal") analysis was the bread and butter of art history; it was their dominant topic. Moreover, some art historians had long avoided making style the centerpiece of their enterprise. For them, stylistic analysis, though necessary, was never sufficient. Within the minority tradition of Marxist art history, for example, Meyer Schapiro approached style as a wholly indexical phenomenon. His art histories explored a number of different possibilities—from the social, or "external," to the psychic, or "internal"—for *what* style indexes.[9] But a watershed in the interests of art history seemed to be reached when, in the 1970s, stylistic analysis—mistakenly called formalism and sometimes even equated with Formalism, the philosophy of historical interpretation developed by the Vienna school (chiefly Alois Riegl)—was supposedly to be replaced by a "social history" of art. This was a terribly odd situation (labeled, by some, as a "crisis in the discipline"),[10] for stylistic analysis, as I noted above, could potentially be a most valuable tool in a social history of making.

These debates of the 1970s and early 1980s, it now appears, were as much institutional as intellectual. They exemplified a generational shift from art historians educated after

8. Ivan Lermolieff (Giovanni Morelli), *Le opere dei maestri italiani nelle gallerie di Monaco, Dresda et Berlino* (Bologna, 1886) (English trans., *Italian Painters* [London, 1892–93]). For a brief introduction to Morellian forensics and the causes of style it recognized, see Henri Zerner, "Giovanni Morelli et la science de l'art," *Revue de l'art* 40–41 (1978), 209–15. As I will show in Chapters 10–12, the psychoanalytic approach to cultural morphology must be able to move flexibly between normative, agent-centered, and nonintentionalist (behaviorist) accounts of style. I do not believe that Morelli's forensics had any historical impact on the development of psychoanalysis. But this historical fiction contains an intellectual truth. See further Jack J. Spector, "The Method of Morelli and Its Relation to Freudian Psychoanalysis," *Diogenes* 66 (1969), 63–83; Richard Wollheim, "Giovanni Morelli and the Origins of Scientific Connoisseurship," in *On Art and the Mind: Essays and Lectures* (London, 1973), 177–201; Carlo Ginzburg, "Clues: Roots of an Evidential Paradigm," in *Clues, Myths, and the Historical Method*, trans. John and Anne C. Tedeschi (Baltimore, 1989), 91–125; and David Carrier, "Winckelmann and Pater, Morelli and Freud," *History of the Human Sciences* 2 (1989), 19–38.

9. Oddly, Schapiro's comprehensive essay on style—perhaps because it was written as a neutral overview of the disciplinary consensus—does not really capture his distinctive application of the concept ("Style," in *Anthropology Today*, ed. Alfred Kroeber [Chicago, 1953], 287–312). Three great essays give a sense of the range of realities that Schapiro took to be the objective correlates of style. I designate them "depth-psychological," "affective-ideological," and "sociocultural": from, respectively, "The Apples of Cezanne" (1968), in *Modern Art, 19th and 20th Centuries: Selected Papers* (New York, 1982), 1–38; "The Sculptures of Souillac" (1939), in *Romanesque Art: Selected Papers* (New York, 1977), 102–30; and "Courbet and Popular Imagery" (1941), in *Modern Art*, 47–86. Schapiro steered well clear of a proposition that tempted and defeated other Marxist analysts—namely, that style indexes ideology because ideology, supposedly, historically causes style. He correctly recognized that all ideology is style but not all style is ideology. Indeed, as implied in Chapter 6, style can be the Marxist historian's best evidence for "material conditions" outside and determining ideology.

10. See Henri Zerner, ed., "The Crisis in the Discipline," *Art Journal* 42 (1982), 279–325.

World War II in specialized academies of art history (like the Fogg Art Museum at Harvard or the Warburg and Courtauld Institutes in London) to art historians trained in the 1960s and 1970s in university departments with little affiliation with major art collections; a new critique of the unethical complicity between academic art history and the art market; the growing unfeasibility of connoisseurship based on frequent, well-funded travel; political resistance to the elitism supposedly manifested in traditional scholarship; changes in students' mastery of literary models and in their desire, or ability, to write the discursive prose that good stylistic analysis demanded; and several other factors.

Furthermore, stylistic analysis itself had come to be conducted chiefly to produce the enormous compendia that characterized art historical scholarship from the 1920s through the 1950s—works of astounding descriptive and comparative detail like W. S. Smith's *History of Egyptian Sculpture and Painting in the Old Kingdom* (1946–49), the major work in the field of my dissertation, and similar efforts. These magisterial texts masked their fundamental conceptual instability; though consuming the resources of the discipline, they had become inattentive to principle. They confused stylistic analysis with a nonstylistic "formal" analysis—a phenomenology of morphology—which they wanted to treat *as* stylistic, that is, as revealing the historical relations of production that "social history" would, for its share, attempt to describe. Thus many such art histories treated replicatorily *unique* morphology as if it were stylistic. As Chapter 5 notes, although similarity between two objects can be seen as stylistic (at least it permits the hypothesis of a replicatory relation), in these projects *dis*similarity could *also* be seen as stylistic. For instance, a "stylistic parallel" might be evidence for objects' derivation from the same workshop, but the *lack* of a parallel might be evidence for an artist's "independence." But if everything in the pool of morphologies is "stylistic" in this way, then nothing is; and forensic analysis—it needs to assert that "style" results from real structures in production—loses its ability to identify actual scenarios in the history of art making. One will not find this error in the Formalism of Alois Riegl or the stylistic analysis of the Marxist art historian Arnold Hauser, which merely differ in the sociologies employed to interpret the styles identified. In my own judgment, the error derived in part from the involvement of academic art history with the worldwide art market; the market imposes an overriding need to find elements of uniqueness in the most standard object, warranting maximum inflation of its value. Stylistic analysis was effectively gutted: the identification of morphological dissimilarities, a necessary element of stylistic analysis, overtook its ability to suggest historical explanations for similarity, its proper business.[11]

11. One arena in art history in which this general problem was debated was pioneered in the 1970s and early 1980s by "postmodernist" art historians. They began a critique of the supposed "originality" of avant-garde and modernist arts and, more broadly, of the aestheticized commodity fetishism seemingly inherent in much traditional art history, art criticism, and art exhibition (see esp. Rosalind Krauss, *The Originality of the Avant-Garde and Other Modernist Myths* [Cambridge, Mass., 1985], and Craig Owens, *Beyond Recognition: Representation, Power, and Culture* [Berkeley and Los Angeles, 1992]; both are collections of essays published earlier). The high postmodernist approach was both theoretical (based, for instance, on a reading of structuralism and semiotics) and political (based, for instance, on a reassessment of the cultural, national, and racial politics of art dealing and art exhibition). This literature has certainly influenced the approach I adopt in Chapters 4–6. But I tend to stress matters that are more narrowly conceptual—that have to do with the internal logic or principle of art

In Chapter 6, I stress the replicatory structure of style without wholly embracing the normative, agent-centered, or behaviorist models of style. Unlike the normative concept of style, mine recognizes what is nonintentional or nondirected in style—the target of the technical (or "special") theory of style developed by Giovanni Morelli, which extended stylization from conventional to nonconventionalized morphology and employed the latter to derive a social history (namely, to make historical attributions). But unlike this concept of style, I do emphasize that style is partly "made," the product of goal-directed human action. Anthills may have styles—a function of the replicatory structure of style as such. But human artifacts have styles that are a function of human intentionality in addition to (and intertwined with) the replicatory structures that emerge *regardless* of intentions. Chapters 4 and 5 already imply that we should be skeptical, however, about an *entirely* agent-centered characterization of style. Although some style results from *intentional* making, for the purposes of nontautologous historical analysis I retain the idea (at home in Morelli's special theory of style) that style also results from the structure or material conditions and parameters of making as such. It is an entirely open question, then, whether the pyramids are more like anthills or art objects. Our view depends on our "formal" analysis (our phenomenology of form and "formalization") (see Chapter 8), our stylistic analysis (our identification of replicatory structures), and our sociological analysis (our explanation of the cause of replicatory organizations in form and style). From the vantage point of one influential historical sociology, for example, the pyramids *are* anthills—the product of a vast centrally directed mobilization of human labor power in which individual makers' habits, but not necessarily their will and desire, are reflected in the style.[12]

Chapter 6 should have insisted more strongly than it does that human making, though it necessarily generates artifacts with style, simultaneously generates their nonstylistic dimension—a complement of nonreplicated morphology threaded through the stylistic morphology. An artifact is not *wholly* stylized, just as it is not *wholly* intentional (Chapters 3–5). Thus a stylistic analysis, however subtle, always states particular replicatory relations; it is never a complete characterization of morphology. Uncertainty on this point, among others, compromised stylistic analysis in the descriptive-comparative compendia and led to a slide from a powerful historical Formalism to a weak aestheticist formalism. But despite my attraction to Formalism, I reject the use of a style, however described, to provide a history—at least, in the kind of "as if" approach in which styles themselves (such as "the Beaker Folk" or "the International Style") are historical agents. To identify a style is, as I see it, to predict a particular replicatory relationship—namely, that a group of artifacts descend from the same system of production. But nothing is said in advance about what this system of production might have been. Stylistic and historical analysis turn out to be mutually implicated. This is not, however, because styles have historical

history's most traditional and supposedly valid methods. My view of certain by-now-familiar high postmodernist approaches is presented in my review of Donald Preziosi's *Rethinking Art History: Meditations on a Coy Science* (New Haven, Conn., 1989), in *Art Bulletin* 52 (1990), 156–66.

12. See further Whitney Davis, *The Canonical Tradition in Ancient Egyptian Art* (New York, 1989).

causes, a trivial truth, but because no statement of historical cause could be made independent of a stylistic analysis in the first place. As one reader remarked, history, for me, is "stylistic analysis all the way down."[13] The question, then, is when we decide to stop describing replication (for example, a style) and assume it for the purposes of further explanation (that is, identify a history). This determination is independent of the theory of style as such. Ways of approaching it are explored in later chapters.

Chapter 7, "Narrativity and the Narmer Palette," serves as a case study of the issue occupying the first half of the book—the interpenetration, in replication, of "matter," or material conditions, and "meaning," or guiding intentions (amounting to mental images of form) and emerging expressions. The Narmer Palette, made about 3000 B.C., certainly replicates earlier palettes belonging to the complex tradition of late prehistoric Egyptian image making: it repeats, revises, and refutes these historical points of reference.[14] More important for my purposes in this book, however, is the way in which the palette's "meaning" emerges in its own *internal* structure of replication—in the way, to use the terms with which Chapter 5 ends, it "compares itself with itself." In this process, the most basic material and perceptual parameters of the artifact itself—for example, its "two-sidedness"—organize but are also reorganized by the directionalities imposed by makers and viewers, at whatever level of awareness and calculation. In active handling by makers and viewers, the narrative image, I suggest, spreads across and threads through both sides of the palette (more properly, an indefinitely extendable viewed sequence of different "sides"). In fact, this "motion" can be seen as a concrete performance (see Fig. 7.6) of the theoretical structure of images as such (compare Fig. 3.5)—the "palimpsest" created in the consolidation of repetitions of morphology.

To this extent the Narmer Palette, whatever else it might be, is an allegory of viewing an image. A (re)cognition or (re)construction of the allegory tells the viewer that *this* "motion"—a particular sequence of scanning and flipping the palette—is, in fact, the way to view and interpret what is otherwise mere morphology.[15] Needless to say, this "delayed activation" (what Freud called *Nachträglichkeit*) seems to have a peculiar temporal and causal structure (see further Chapters 11 and 12): an allegory of the viewing process that tells the viewer how to view what is viewed can only be realized at the end (a fully *open* end) of some sequence of viewing. We can suppose, of course, that the viewer knows in advance "how to view," or, more narrowly, what it is that she or he should take account of in *this particular* viewing of *this particular* morphology. This extreme culturological simplification, which asserts, for instance, that a viewer knows "conventions" or "codes," understands a "discourse," or belongs to a "culture," might be warranted in some extraordinary cases. But it is not, as I have already urged, an approach that a truly materialist and historical analysis could endorse.

13. Margaret W. Conkey, "Experimenting with Style in Archaeology," in *Uses of Style*, ed. Conkey and Hastorf, 16.

14. See further Whitney Davis, *Canonical Tradition*, chap. 6, and idem, *Masking the Blow: The Scene of Representation in Late Prehistoric Egyptian Art* (Berkeley and Los Angeles, 1992). Chapter 7 is an extremely compressed version of the account presented in the latter book.

15. In *Masking the Blow* (esp. 30–37, 148–60, 197–200) this matter is considered in slightly different ways under the headings "chasing the view" and "chasing the viewer" in the context of a general picture of "the temporality of meaning."

Close attention to the motion of *Nachträglichkeit* shows that the supposed difficulty here can be overstated. The meaning coming out of the future is the product of a replicatory process organized in the past and embedded in a material morphology that persists *from* past *through* "present" *into* future. As I have stated, the persistence of nonmeaningful morphology—morphology that cannot be consolidated as a "depiction" or "style"—confirms the *directionality* of some replications precisely by contrasting with an exponential proliferation of what increasingly will appear to be "disruptions" of form (see Chapters 3 and 6). More exactly, the sequence, direction, and pace of disruption construct *organized* disruption or emergent "meaning," for there is no such thing as "pure" disruption but only disruption constrained, quite apart from human ideas and intentions, by the parameters of the material situation.

In principle, it might be that such replicatory motion, consolidation, and self-symbolization—which transpires in relation to a material substrate that continually sustains the emerging organization of meaning—occurs entirely "in the viewer's head." It is a cognitive, not a physical, activity. (I stress again that my account, though it now begins to deal with the contents of consciousness, does not impute a *guiding* or *originating* idea to the maker or viewer [see Chapter 4]. Rather, the narrative of the Narmer Palette emerges summatively and recursively in the sequence of actions of making and viewing the palette; although the replicatory structure must have a "canonical form" to guarantee the very possibility of a meaning, it is fully open-ended.) Thus we need not believe that the Narmer Palette was *actually* "flipped" over from side to side in the "canonical" sequence of eighteen replicatorily linked views that I suggest consolidates a particular pictorial narrative built from a repetition of four scenes. Maker and viewer *might* have done this; although we have no independent historical information about it, the narrative could have been physically performed. But the narrative is entirely available to internal scanning conducted by the "mind's eye." Even this formulation probably attributes too much foreknowledge of meaning to an active agency (and thus fails to answer the deepest historical questions about the very construction of such meanings and agencies): it endows an observing internal homunculus with the power to decipher material morphology. The "mind's eye" is not the "eye's mind"—even though it might seem that we must invent the "eye's mind" to understand how the "mind's eye" could consolidate the meaning "in" the material morphology it perceives. Rather than decipher figures, the "mind's eye" excavates forms. And the excavation of form in the visible, in the visual field, provides, through its replicatory persistence, evidence of directionality and hence of intentionality.

In the broadest sense, I am shifting ground from the "physics" of replication to the "psychics" of replication—though the real job, of course, is to explicate their interanimation. A concrete performance of a visual allegory, a "motion" of pictorial understanding realized in an internal and possibly an actual act of handling, the Narmer Palette serves as a useful hinge for my larger inquiry. The internal motion of consciousness is the subject of Chapter 8, "Opticality and Rhetoricity in Paul de Man's 'Historical Materialism.'" De Man drew synthetically on Kantian, Hegelian, Romantic, phenomenological, Heideggerian, and "deconstructive" vocabularies to offer a subtle account of the process of "formalization"—of the evolution (more exactly, the devolution) from matter to meaning and, simultaneously, from meaning to matter. The transfer or montage between these domains is not smooth. But neither is it so unbounded or disjunctive that we cannot solve the logical problem of infinite regress (stated in Chapter 3) or approximately characterize the real cognitive temporality of "delayed activation." Earlier chapters suggest that we confront a series of replicatory translations—repetitions, revisions, and refusals—*within* a field of replicatory coherence.

For me, de Man's work implies that the emergence of meaning occurs in some kind of slide through the different dimensions—the *three* dimensions of spatial orientation (such as handling an artifact or the movements of walking and climbing), the *two* dimensions of optical imagery (such as the material or mental images), and the "*one*" dimension of nomination or predication (such as "rules" for behavior or form). As I have already shown, any "meaning" that has been organized in any one of the different dimensions is partly a function of what the physical parameters of material systems, encountered and represented in that dimension, will naturally permit in the context of a wider persistence of "disorganization." In this situation, "meaning" (de Man's work suggests) will partly be an *interpretation* of such organizations projected from the platform of an organization already achieved in one of the *other* dimensions; though "meaning" is simply a dimension change, for just this material reason it functions as a *representation* of experience. In itself, any provisional platform constructed in moving and handling, in scanning and viewing, or in labeling and interpreting must be subject to the same general condition: it is a representation—consisting morphologically merely in a dimension change—of disorganized, nondepictive and nonstylized, perceptual continua in other dimensions. But "delayed activation" seems more intelligible when the supposedly self-generated key that turns the lock is acquired by one mode from another: in fact, one might now say that meaning emerges in the apparent impossibility of "delayed activation" because there need be no delay, waiting for thought to catch up to itself, but rather a jump across thoughts. The connection between them is not a nonexistent, or as yet unrealized, shared meaning but, again, a more broadly replicatory one—morphological resemblance, spatiotemporal proximity, or (a matter to be explored in Chapters 10–12) common affect or converging psychic genealogy.

Needless to say, de Man's account and those like it assume that we simultaneously inhabit the different dimensions. In the terms de Man accepted, adopted in Chapter 8, the requirement is banal. (However, present-day disciplinary configurations—such as divisions between art history, film studies, performance studies, and material philology—strongly resist it.) The interesting questions, which de Man does not so much solve as order, are well within this purview. How does the mind coordinate differently dimensioned experiences? Perhaps replication of experience in another dimension, reducing or expanding it, constitutes a representation of it; and in turn, perhaps this previously unavailable interpretation edges consciousness toward rhetorical self-consolidation. But does this jump from one dimension to another require an internal homunculus that comprehends experiences in different dimensions *as* mutually resemblant (for example, on the plane of the retinal image)? Or does it merely require the material setup, for example, of the human eye, which receives the three-dimensional object world as a two-dimensional "representation"? Does the fact that consciousness has a "style"—in virtue of being *this* rather than some other consciousness—ensure that all the representations it projects will necessarily display convergent morphologies completely independent of any originary "intention"? I could not possibly answer such questions. But the fact that they present themselves indicates why our future art historical task ought to be what, in an earlier book, I called a cognitive history.[16] At the present stage of research—and in light of the gulf between archaeology, art history, and psychoanalysis, on the one hand, and "cognitive studies," on the other, despite common interest in "mental images"—we simply need to recognize their urgency.

Replication in Psychoanalysis

In Chapter 9, "Winckelmann Divided," I recognize a replicatory (a partly "psychic" or cognitive) history that earlier chapters have not systematically addressed. Although Chapters 4 and 5, for example, consider the disciplinary methods and concepts—the disciplinary consciousness—of archaeology and art history, Chapter 8 implies that the individual archaeologist's or art historian's consciousness organizes his or her multifarious encounters with artifacts and images. There are many ways to describe this relation, which is not, I insist in Chapter 9, simply a question of a scholar's choice of an archaeological or art historical "method" or "theory"—for example, a social-historical or deconstructive approach.

The relation between an archaeologist or art historian and his or her historical objects is certainly erotic in the broadest sense. Our memory and recollection of what we have "subjectively" taken to be beautiful and desirable, in sexual, aesthetic, ethical, and political terms, directs—even as it is reorganized by—our interpretation of images and artifacts. This would not be especially troublesome if we did not simultaneously suppose that archaeologists and art historians explicate the eroticism of *other* subjects, people in the past—the makers and viewers whose replications and replicatory consciousness we study according to formal models of image making or style. Chapter 9 explores the intersection of our "objective" account of others' replications and replicatory consciousnesses and our own "eroticized" replicatory consciousnesses. As a matter of historical fact, I urge, modern archaeology and art history emerged *as* disciplines in a particular, influential view of the way in which this intersection might itself be represented—largely due to the thought and writing of J. J. Winckelmann (1717–68).

Once again, the structure of "delayed activation" must be central to an understanding of replication. Winckelmann's homoerotic interest in beautiful and desirable young men partly motivated his famous rhetorical call, in 1755, for modern artists to reproduce the forms of classical Greek sculpture and painting. At the same time, his encounters with

16. Davis, *Canonical Tradition*, xvii. There I wrote that "paradoxically, a total cognitive history would, if absolutely true to its subjects-in-history, be both overwhelming and unintelligible to us as readers, for it would merely reprint their cognition." But this should not, of course, keep us from the explicatory modeling of the kind attempted in Chapter 7 or the inquiries attributed to de Man in Chapter 8.

the form (especially the contours) of Greek art organized his homoerotic yearnings. Gradually these desires issued in a distinctively modern "homosexual" subjectivity (the term itself was unknown to Winckelmann, who imagined an extension of romantic homoeroticism on the model of ancient Greek pederasty): "homosexuality" retrospectively understands itself as an "inborn" disposition to appreciate male desirability in sexual, aesthetic, ethical, and political terms, warranting a desire to produce cultural forms, the depictions and styles, and social relations that can sustain and fulfill this disposition.[17] Freud's concepts of repression, sublimation, "transference" *(Übertragung),* mourning, and "delayed activation" *(Nachträglichkeit)* provide a rich vocabulary for—as well as more tendentious implicit explanations of—this process. In Chapter 9, I use them to suggest that if art history is a coherent enterprise, it is not because its objects, whether the objects of scholarly analysis or the objects of the historian's desires, are "whole." These objects—Winckelmann's classical Greek sculptures *and* his modern German or Italian beloveds—are partial, fragmentary, and frequently unobtainable embodiments of his desires (compare Chapter 5). Rather, it is the replicatory interanimation, the stitching-up, of subjective images of and objective encounters with these objects—the beloved youths seem to replicate classical sculptures and vice versa—that consolidates an art historical self-consciousness and, indeed, I suggest, fundamentally organizes the art historical discipline.

In Chapter 5, and to a lesser extent in Chapter 6, I argue that an "aestheticist" ambition in archaeology and art history understands replication as a set of formal relations between self-sufficient wholes. This aestheticist ambition must be juxtaposed with the equally fundamental "historical," "materialist" recognition that replications are, at best, *emergent* wholes, a "canonical" structure *within* morphology (Chapters 3 and 7). Often they are nondirected, unintentional by-products of behavior (Chapter 4), "bits and pieces" available for later replicatory summation (Chapter 5), or devolving "formalizations" and "totalizations" of a continuous disruption (Chapter 8). Art history's peculiar *coordination* of aestheticist and historical procedures, Chapter 9 suggests, derives from Winckelmann's success in placing the discipline "across" the objective and subjective replicatory histories I noted in the previous paragraph. The art historian's subjective erotic objects can be consolidated, rendered whole, in the art historical object—such as an ancient sculpture—which collects together and represents them. Conversely, the art historian's disparate historical objects, the archaeological stuff surviving into and lying around the present, can be consolidated in his or her subjective image of what is desired, which collects together and represents *them* (what, in Chapter 11, I call the subjective object and what, in Chapter 12, sometimes must be seen as fetishes).

Just as a tension between aestheticist and historical-materialist ideas characterizes the "physics" of replication (Chapters 3–5), so too does it characterize the "psychics"—our

17. This understanding can be seen especially in Winckelmann's essay *On the Perception of the Beautiful in Art and Instruction in the Same* (Dresden, 1763; partial English translation in *Winckelmann: Writings on Art,* ed. David Irwin [London, 1972], 89–103). Chapter 9 does not directly consider this essay but focuses instead on Winckelmann's more specifically art critical and art historical texts. The chapter might be read with an essay that fleshes out this picture: see Whitney Davis, "Winckelmann's Homosexual Teleologies," in *Sexuality in Ancient Art,* ed. Natalie Kampen (New York, 1996), 262–76. In a full-length study, I hope to situate this history in a treatment of homoeroticism in modern arts.

supposed histories of the replicatory activity of consciousness that stitches up, in material morphology, the images and artifacts to be explicated *as* replications. And in exactly the same way that the history of physical replications risks becoming merely a history of "formal relations" among autonomous images and artifacts, the history of psychic replications risks becoming merely a history of "formal relations" between *mental* images or *internal* objects.

Chapter 10, "Pleasure and Its Contents: Bersani and Dutoit's Assyrian Reliefs," considers the crucial psychoanalytic claim that the formal dynamics of "repression" and "sublimation," the repetition, revision, and refusal of particular forms and themes, must be explicated in terms of the continuity and disruption of particular "instinctual" dispositions (for example, egoism or aggression), affects (for example, fear or envy), and contents or meanings (for example, castration or incorporation). To be sure, there is a spectrum of opinion within psychiatry, psychology, and psychoanalysis about these processes. Chapter 10 considers, for example, a tendency to neglect aggressive instincts, affects, and meanings in favor of "sexual" ones, despite Freud's acknowledgment of their interdependence. But my general point is simply that the history of replicatory consciousness cannot be understood as a play of purely "formal relations." In Chapter 10, I find this latter view, however, in Leo Bersani and Ulysse Dutoit's provocative visual and metapsychological interpretation of Neo-Assyrian relief sculpture of the eighth to the sixth centuries B.C. From one vantage point, their interest in the "formal relations" of internal objects seems to be a way to acknowledge the *materiality* (rather than ideal intentionality) of consciousness. But it also brackets the material parameters, properties, and determinations of consciousness—keeping us from identifying *what* it is that people have desired and *why* they did so. Formal relations are the indices of a history of instincts, affects, and contents (even though, as Chapter 6 urges, we cannot directly "read off" this history from the forms of its historical precipitates). When the formalist or aestheticist ellipsis occurs in an account of psychic replication, it is cut off from, or cannot lead into, a history. What passes for a history of consciousness actually is no more than a stylistic description using Freudian metapsychological terminology ("sadism," "masochism") rather than the more familiar literary- or art critical terminologies ("contrast," "blending") (see further Chapter 12). For reasons that do not need repetition here, this result would be the antithesis of the aims endorsed in this book.

Chapter 10, like Chapters 9, 11, and 12, advances my conviction that psychoanalysis is not primarily—although it might be secondarily and in many of its methods—a study of images, styles, meanings, or language as such. It is an account of their emergence in the material matrix of a historical person. More exactly, and more radically, it is an account of the emergence of a historical person in the material matrix of *non*personhood—the matrix of behavior, habit, accident, and material limitation, disruption, and evolution in the human organism. It is significant, for me, that Bersani and Dutoit have been strongly influenced by Jean Laplanche's superb investigation of the translation *from* the "vital order," the biological history of the organism, *to* the system of fantasy and consciousness. What Laplanche, following Ernest Jones, calls *anaclisis,* the "propping" of fantasy on organismic want or need, is the material matrix—the cognitive substrate, as it were—of

Nachträglichkeit, the delayed activation of the "meaning" of perception and experience. Simultaneously, it is in *Nachträglichkeit* that *anaclisis* occurs—a retrospective reorganization of bodily experiences and needs as desire and the projection of the internal fantasy objects that will fulfill it. Cases and aspects of this complex temporality of replicatory consciousness are explored in Chapter 11, in terms of an exchange between the experiences of two subjects, and in Chapter 12, in terms of an exchange between inner and outer objects.

In the context of this book, the interest of such work lies partly in the way in which Laplanche's "historicism" tempers a more culturological approach. Because it is people—if not "persons"—who make artifacts and images, psychoanalysis is one of the necessary complements of archaeology and art history. It may be objected that modern thought offers numerous accounts of people and of persons. In Chapter 8, for example, one might seem to be led by Paul de Man's work toward an eclectic psychology. Explicitly, de Man takes up insights developed in critical idealism and phenomenology; implicitly, he relies on a rough idea, to take one case, of the findings of physiological optics. Why should Freudian psychology—its metapsychological description of formal structures and relations in replicatory systems of images or texts—be preferred?

My involvement with psychoanalysis in this book should not be seen as a rejection of other psychologies—far from it. But psychoanalysis engages the broad concerns outlined in Chapter 1 in ways too close, powerful, and useful to ignore. Leave aside the narrow question of Freud's own involvement with archaeology and his substantial interest in image making (see Chapter 11). Both historically and conceptually, psychoanalysis is a translation—however peculiar and tendentious—of the evolutionary biology, psychophysics, and physiological optics that underpin, however simplistically, much of the reasoning of the archaeology and art history endorsed in this book. Crudely put, psychoanalysis attempts to reorganize this "physics" as a "psychics"—for example, by rewriting the established analysis of perceptual-motor behavior, such as the concept of the "reflex arc," in psychological terms. (Details of this terminological and theoretical reorientation are considered in Chapter 11, in my discussion of the Freudian model of repression, and Chapter 12, in my discussion of the physiological optics, psychophysics, and psychoanalysis of scotomas and fetishism.)

The point in engaging psychoanalysis, then, is not to save a psychology (let alone a culturology) of artifact or image making from more material inquiries. Quite to the contrary, because of its intimate connections with material investigations psychoanalysis should enable us to refashion the humanistic interests of archaeology and art history—for example, in the human creation of "culture"—to take account of the historical processes in which human culture is embedded. This argument should be taken at the most general level. Many of the material investigations Freud pursued, such as Lamarckianism (the theory of the inheritance of acquired traits), were utter failures. The methodological scientism he carried from existing psychophysiology into his psychoanalysis did not and could not match the psychological, intentionalist, and humanistic translation that was his own contribution. I am not asking us to push archaeology and art history toward biologisms or behaviorisms—though psychoanalysis contains a dose of both. (Moreover, as I show throughout this book, archaeology and art history already are "biologistic" or "behavioristic"—for instance, in the theory of style [Chapter 6]—to the extent that they acknowledge the material parameters, natural, bodily, *and* cognitive, of the production of morphology.) Instead, we must discover how human culture and identity have been organized in a historical process—understood, in this book, to be a process that leads to replicatory structures, such as depiction and style, that are evolutionarily *emergent* (although not immanent) in biology and behavior. As I argued in the first section of this Introduction, here we cannot assume a culturological premise but must work toward, and through, the supposed "cultural" result.

The specific interest of psychoanalysis is not so much its explicit, and by now largely discredited, scientism—though this is some evidence, at least, that psychoanalysis guards against unwarranted culturological and aestheticist claims. Psychoanalysis permits a highly differentiated, though not always precise, description of replicatory consciousness. Most important, like a powerful novel or history it is experientially adequate to the social and psychic differences between people, recognizing the specificity and diversity of their desires and fantasies. It understands their practices and productions, such as image making and artifacts, to be emergent from, as well as a coordination of, their individual histories; it does not, then, see them as the fundamentally anonymous replications archaeology and art history otherwise tend to invent, however the replications are "attributed" to historical or analytic "individuals." In Chapter 10, I consider how the "sadism" and "masochism," which according to Bersani and Dutoit formally and thematically characterize Neo-Assyrian relief sculpture, might index actual intrapsychic and intersubjective histories. I am not particularly concerned with, or worried about, the supposed problem of "psychoanalyzing" the Assyrians. The problem is much broader: we should worry about how we attribute *any* kind of intentions, plans, rules, desires, aims, meanings, or values *not only* to long-dead people *but also* to the contemporaries who supposedly inhabit our "culture." Psychoanalysis is just one of the many languages we might use to make this attribution. And in fact its effort to identify the "psychics" in the "physics" can be much more cautious than the traditional humanistic or culturalist approach; it is, for example, more likely than traditional art history to acknowledge what, in Chapter 5, I call the non-, pre-, or para-intentional dimensions and configurations of image making. An objection to "psychoanalyzing" the Assyrians is not really an objection to psychological analysis as such. It actually seems to be a resistance to acknowledging the past and present reality of sex and eroticism. Chapter 9 offers one reason for this resistance: as their means of creating internal "discipline," archaeology and art history systematically eject their own eroticism, which, as Chapters 9, 11, and 12 suggest, must itself have been intersubjectively constructed—the recognition, incorporation, and transformation of the eroticism of others, including long-dead people.

This interest in a differentiated history of replicatory consciousness is humanism rather than scientism. No contradiction obtains between it and the somewhat more abstract "cognitive" analysis explored in earlier chapters. As the underlying question of the behavioral-intentional continuum—of the material embeddedness of meaning and its "delayed activation"—suggests, cognitive and psychoanalytic approaches substantially overlap. Indeed, for me the latter just *is* the former—personalized. Psychoanalysis asserts that the material matrix of cognition is not only the body and its perceptual and motor behavior but also the person and his or her history—even as it acknowledges, consistent with the general aim of the "archaeology" pursued in this book, that persons are historically emergent, in turn, in people, in bodies and social relations.

A more subtle objection pitched against a psychoanalytic archaeology or art history is not so much that it "psychologizes" but, indeed, that it "personalizes." No doubt, for example, Freud's case histories are descriptions (and only partial, often misguided explanations) of *particular* late-nineteenth-century persons, whose bodies and social relations Freud understood quite imperfectly. Many fundamental analytic concepts, such as the Freudian concept of fetishism or of homosexuality, function best as descriptions of particular modern subjective and social structures. It has even been urged by some commentators, especially Marxists, that pursuing a psychoanalytic account of consciousness indulges "personalism" at the expense of a supposedly more fundamental *social* analysis. But this view profoundly misunderstands psychoanalysis in two ways.

First, as already seen, psychoanalysis exerts powerful pressure on the concept of persons. Even as it considers specific activities or productions of body and cognition to be derived from a person's history, it embeds a person in the material matrix of body and cognition in which he or she is emergent. Psychoanalysis is not a "personalism"—supposedly identified, in turn, with certain specific Enlightenment, bourgeois, and modernist illusions—because the person is not the unit, though it might be the principal field, of psychoanalysis.

Second, and closely related, the psychoanalytic "person" is not the "analytic individual" picked out, for example, by stylistic analysis, which identifies the unconscious, nonconventionalized behavior of the individual organism whose bodily and cognitive activities supposedly leave certain historical traces just in virtue of being that, rather than some other, organism (see Chapter 6). It may be important to identify these "analytic individuals," or "people," in history. But such "people"—they can, of course, be the nonhuman, primate, hominid, or hominoid creatures identified by paleoanthropology—are not necessarily persons. A person, the *psycho*analytic individual, is both an intersubjectivity (as Chapter 11 shows) and a set of object relations (as Chapter 12 shows)—the replication, in the material matrix of the "analytic individual" or organism, of the replications of other individuals constructed in exactly the same way. Intersubjectivity and object relations are, of course, social relations. Thus the alleged "personalism" of psychoanalysis is precisely its distinction of social persons from monadic physical individuals. In this light, the force of the Marxist objection should diminish, for all along it was really a political objection to bourgeois or liberal individualism at the expense of communitarian or socialist values.

In Chapter 11, "Sigmund Freud's Drawing of the Dream of the Wolves," I consider how Freud's most complex case history, his analysis of the "Wolf Man" in 1910–14 (published in 1918), was organized intersubjectively.[18] In the interest of misguided scientism, Freud downplayed the role of intersubjective relations in his own practice with his

18. The material in this chapter is presented in greater detail in Whitney Davis, *Drawing the Dream of the Wolves: Homosexuality, Interpretation, and Freud's "Wolf Man"* (Bloomington, Ind., 1995).

patients. With female patients, as several feminist commentators have shown, these relations were necessarily "patriarchal," perhaps "misogynistic." With a male patient, as I suggest, they were necessarily homoerotic, perhaps homosexual. Nevertheless, Freudian theory predicts that there is no reason why a person should be able fully to recognize, let alone self-consciously represent or deliberately reorganize, his or her intrapsychic intersubjectivity—all the ways in which he or she incorporates and projects other social individuals (qua bodies, qua people, or qua persons). Such recognition would require a self-historicism that by the very terms I have been exploring would require one to disembed oneself from one's material bodily and cognitive conditions—an impossibility. Thus, I, Whitney Davis, might write a partial history of Freud's intersubjective relations with the Wolf Man, but *Freud* can only be within, or enact, this intersubjectivity. In itself this is no excuse for misogynistic domination or homophobic contest. But we must acknowledge the full material and historical difficulty inherent in any call that someone be a different (supposedly better) person in the sense required here.

The replicatory history explored in Chapter 11 suggests that a person's historical experience with, and production of, images and artifacts organizes his or her interpretation of images and artifacts produced by others even as it reorganizes *their* experience and production. The same premise (hardly a novel one) animates Chapter 9, on Winckelmann's art history. Putting together the results of Chapters 9 and 11, it should be obvious—as the final pages of Chapter 11 observe—that my own intersubjective history must organize my archaeological and art historical representation of the intersubjective relation between Freud and the Wolf Man. At the same time, however, the internal "discipline" of archaeology and art history largely forbids representation of this fact on my part—even presuming I were capable of the self-historicization it would require in the first place. A supposed solution to this alleged difficulty (it seems to be a self-fulfilling double bind) has occupied recent historians, critics, and commentators. Supposedly, they say, we should "position" our own "subjectivity" in relation to—and somewhere in our pedagogical and published representations of—our archaeological and art historical projects. In Chapter 11, however, I suggest that this "positioning" can be little more than a superficial "posturing." A person is not *in* a position to be the historian of his or her own intersubjectively constructed subjectivity. More modestly, one can try to acknowledge—and "perform"—the double bind as such, or even, as I do explicitly in Chapter 9 and implicitly in Chapter 11, recognize it to be the very motivation and source of archaeological or art historical achievement.

In fact, as Chapter 11 suggests, the real issue is not whether archaeologists and art historians are willing and able to represent the "subjectivity" of their own scholarship. It is whether they are willing and able to represent the intersubjective historicity they might recognize in the scholarship of *other* archaeologists and art historians—and are willing and able to open their own scholarship *to* such historicization *by* those others. In this communal, intersubjective, obviously open-ended, and necessarily ongoing archaeological and art historical practice—Chapter 11 offers a case study of the kind of inquiry each of us could undertake regarding the scholarship of others—the double bind cannot be effaced. But it *can* be interpreted—the only cure, Freud noticed, for intrapsychic and intersubjective stasis, the repetition of the past in the present rather than its revision and refusal.

The practice imagined here—it would, of course, go far beyond the existing book review, critical essay, or historiographical study—requires no substantial transformation of existing archaeological and art historical methods. We require stylistic and iconographic analysis to unravel the replicatory history of consciousness; we might also want to consult formal theories about such history. The job, really, is simply to do art history not only on art but also on art history—discipline and practitioners. The chief stumbling block, as always, will be art history's "aestheticist" tendency to focus on "works of art" in the intersubjective history of *art historians* (as I do myself, for example, in Chapter 9, exploring Winckelmann's involvement with classical Greek art). But as Chapter 11, along with the rest of this book, urges, art historians must be prepared to encompass a much wider field of image making and artifact production. Freud's interpretation of the Wolf Man's drawing replicated his experience not only with works of fine art but also with medical and other scientific illustrations, with his own notations and doodles, with artifacts in his family's possession, with children's books, and so on. Unfortunately we shall probably never be able to become the archaeologists or historians of the whole field of human image making and artifact production that a person encounters. But the material (that is, the personal) matrix of image making and artifact production requires open-minded interdisciplinary scrutiny.

In Chapter 12, "HomoVision: A Reading of Freud's 'Fetishism,'" I consider the replicatory history that connects an intersubjectively created "internal object," a strictly mental image that is not the same as (or even a representation of) any actual historical image or artifact, with image- or artifact-making practices in a person's intersubjective environment. Images or artifacts in the intersubjective environment nonetheless provoke and sustain an internal object. In one way or another, this history is the prime concern of virtually all of the chapters in this book. It is, however, especially visible in the personal erotic practice that has come to be called "fetishism." Freud's general theory of fetishism, presented in 1927, offers, in contrast to the theories of fetishism to which he was responding, a virtually paradigmatic analysis for my interests.

One of Freud's sources, the "associationist" psychology of Alfred Binet and his followers, a forerunner of present-day cognitive psychology, explained the sexual fetish as a product of a contingent association between a highly desired image, the genitals of a female or male love object, and a proximate object (such as hair, gloves, or boots) that could serve sexually as an effective replication. A more immediate source, the psychoanalytic perceptual psychology of René Laforgue, suggested that the highly desired image had not been encountered and experienced even though the fetishist had looked directly at and for it. Hence the fetish replication itself becomes the highly desired object because it is, for all intents and purposes, what the fetishist saw when he or she looked for the highly desired love object. As Chapter 12 shows, Freud combined and reorganized these accounts by seeing them not as a model of a single perceptual situation—the fetishist looking at an object—but by setting them into an intrapsychic and intersubjective personal history. Briefly, a highly desired image seen in the fetishist's fantasy is replicatorily replaced by a concrete effigy that serves as the sign, though not the substitute, of what the fetishist had seen contingently associated with the fetish-image itself *before* eliminating the fetish-image from his or her perceptual memory. This association is activated, in the fetishist's erotic practice, *after* a delay in which the intrapsychic and intersubjective reasons (whether rational or not) for eliminating the fetish-image must be realized in further, ongoing psychic and social relations.

There is a great deal that is both obscure and tendentious in Freud's account; Chapter 12 takes these up in detail. At the most general level, however, Freud understands the history of fetishistic consciousness—granting, of course, that the *un*conscious is one of the channels of consciousness—to issue in a socially performed erotic relation to images and artifacts (even their actual production) that is, as it were, simply the tip of the iceberg. In Freudian psychoanalytic archaeology, the analyst attempts to reconstruct the submerged structures and processes. In Chapters 10 and 11, I investigate some of the procedures and pitfalls of this reconstruction. In Chapter 12, they can be taken for granted. Instead, the importance of Freud's inquiry lies in its vision of replication itself: fetishism, I suggest at the end of the chapter, simply *is* embodied vision in the broad sense—the intrapsychic, intersubjective, and optical-manual handling and movement of artifacts, images, and persons in the social field. At this level, fetishism, although it is a highly particular personal practice, is not only that. It is also the realization of our material, psychic, and social relations to images and artifacts as such, outside of which they are merely fossils or displays. Freud's "fetishism" suggests that artifacts and images are not *inherently* fossils or displays—as archaeology and art history tend to pretend—even though one result of a paralyzed, fearful, self-limiting, or self-disciplined consciousness is that it can turn images and artifacts *into* mere fossils and displays as its best or only way of going on. The "cure" for fetishism, if needed at all, is archaeology or art history—a recognition, by and for the fetishist, of the replicatory history in which his or her fossils and displays have been constituted. But this history cannot be obtained if archaeology and art history themselves remain fetishistic. Thus it is the defetishization of archaeology and art history—disentangling them from mistaken commitments to the integrity and self-sufficiency of artifacts and images—that will enable us to see the truly "fetishistic" status of artifacts and images, their material entanglement in the intrapsychic, intersubjective, and optical-manual handlings and movements that are the subject of this book.

Archaeology, Art History, Psychoanalysis

It will be obvious in this book that I am not terribly concerned to observe many of the supposed differences between archaeology, art history, and psychoanalysis. I am often interested in the boundaries only in order to find ways to surmount them in pursuit of my general theme. But this is not to say that I want to jettison the distinctive methods, modes of argumentation, or species of evidence that emerge from these disciplines conducting themselves *as* disciplines. Interdisciplinarity can only be achieved, I believe, when arguments about questions of maximum generality have been refined—both deepened and broadened—by engaging individual disciplines at their intellectual sources and in terms of their most strongly developed, closely defended concepts. Interdisciplinarity only deserves the name when it can be seen to make, by practitioners within a discipline, a substantive—if not necessarily perfect—contribution to that discipline. Thus there is no getting around the necessity, in many chapters in this book, to go fairly deeply into some of the more technical and specialized domains of archaeology, art history, and psychoanalysis. But after these investigations have been pursued, what remains of the three disciplinary boundaries that have necessarily organized my work in this book?

The first disciplinary boundary observed here is the boundary between archaeology and art history. Despite the common intellectual origin of the two disciplines in the late eighteenth and early nineteenth centuries, the boundary seems, to me, to have become institutionally somewhat impermeable. But I see no useful demarcations of principle to be made here, however convenient or practical some rough divisions of labor might be. Notably, in the work of conservators and connoisseurs art history numbers practitioners who are much more archaeological than many archaeologists, and in the work of ethnoarchaeologists and social archaeologists archaeology numbers practitioners who are much more art historical than many art historians. There are virtually no interesting *overall* differences in materials, methods, or theories to be identified, though some comparatively recent, localized developments have sometimes obscured that fact. All of the substantive issues—for example, about the status of "scientificity" in art historical and archaeological practice or about the real range and depth of their sociology—are well within a shared frame of reference and equally prominent in both disciplines.

Many shots have been fired back and forth over the second boundary, between art history and psychoanalysis. Art historians have long used or "applied" psychoanalytic conceptualizations in their cultural and historical inquiries; psychoanalysts have long attempted to interpret art historical materials. Despite complaints and resistances on both sides, there has been a considerable, often fertile exchange. But in my view art historians have been too reluctant to engage psychoanalytic concepts at their source—for example, in the clinical and interpretive writings of Freud—and too willing to suppose that their business, if any, should be simply to "apply" psychoanalysis. Psychoanalytic concepts, especially about representation and its means and about objects and their histories, should appeal to the most fundamental interests and instincts of art historians, who are, for their part, well equipped not only to "apply" but also to examine, refine, criticize, or refute them.

Although psychoanalysts commonly complain that art historians lack, and need, "clinical" experience, they forget, of course, that Freud pursued cultural and historical investigations and obviously regarded them as pivotal. More important, clinical knowledge acquired in the absence of cultural and historical interpretation would be worse than useless—it would be dangerous. Although a distinction between the world of the site or museum collection and the world of the clinic is real and important, it need not actually appear in any sensible debate between art history and psychoanalysis—for just the reason that modern art history, unlike archaeology, is not really *in* the site or the museum collection in the first place. Art history operates, rather, in a site or museum collection "of the mind"—what André Malraux, in a famous phrase, called the "museum without walls"[19]—in which an extraordinary extrapolation from the material conditions and limits of the site or collection has been attempted, to the dismay, of course, of many archaeologists. And the site or the museum of the mind is precisely the subject matter of psychoanalysis when it encounters it, embodied in a person and his or her intersubjective relations, in the so-called clinical setting. So although the psychoanalyst may be right that art historical experience is not clinical experience (as Chapter 10 acknowledges), clinical experience (as Chapter 11 suggests) is certainly art historical experience.

As these comments imply, the most profound debate obtains between archaeology and psychoanalysis. This third boundary that has organized my work in this book perhaps hardly qualifies as a boundary at all, for a boundary presupposes contiguous fields. Despite murmurings among younger archaeologists,[20] and despite Freud's interest in the deep past, there is no formal or practical relation between archaeology and psychoanalysis. But for me this feature of the disciplinary landscape traversed in this book has been the most surprising. Freud explicitly envisioned his practice in relation to archaeology. It has sometimes been urged, quite mistakenly, that Freud thought that psychoanalysis *is* an archaeology. His point, however, was to clarify what psychoanalysis is not. Psychoanalysis is a version of impossible archaeology, a not-archaeology. The defining material conditions of the archaeological situation—that strata of different ages are materially separate and some of their past realities have been utterly destroyed—are precisely the conditions psychoanalysis must imagine to be violated in a cognitive or psychic domain: all contents of the mind, of different antiquity, are supposedly preserved, though perhaps in a revised or negative form, all at once in the same stratum—namely, the present time of the psychoanalysis itself.[21] Despite superficial methodological similarities, then, there is tremendous conceptual distance between archaeology and psychoanalysis.

But it is also for just this reason—set, in turn, in the context of the two other disciplinary boundaries I have already mentioned—that art history, for me, is the necessary middle term for the relation of archaeology and psychoanalysis. Art history introduces a particular and, this book tries to show, just the right emphasis on the imaginary or imagistic coherence of replications, enabling us to begin bridging the material disjunctions that archaeology discovers and the psychic continuities psychoanalysis supposes—and vice versa: hence my subtitle, *Archaeology, Art History, Psychoanalysis.* I claimed earlier in

19. André Malraux, *The Voices of Silence*, trans. Stuart Gilbert (London, 1953), 13–131; see also Ellen Handler Spitz, *Museums of the Mind: Magritte's Labyrinth and Other Essays in the Arts* (New Haven, 1994). This feature of the wide-ranging visual archive of art history is highlighted by Preziosi, *Rethinking Art History;* David Carrier's more convincing *Principles of Art History Writing* (University Park, Pa., 1991) assumes it throughout. Both writers offer numerous thoughts about how the visual knowledge upon which art history—and several other disciplines—is based was generated, but a systematic study remains to be written.

20. For vague hints, see, e.g., Timothy Yates, "Derrida: 'There Is Nothing Outside of the Text,'" in *Reading Material Culture: Structuralism, Hermeneutics, and Post-Structuralism*, ed. Christopher Tilley (Oxford, 1990), 162, and Christopher Tilley, *Material Culture and the Text: The Art of Ambiguity* (London, 1991).

21. For Freud's disanalogy between an archaeology of the city of Rome and psychoanalysis, see Sigmund Freud, *Civilization and Its Discontents* [1930], in *Standard Edition*, 20:60–63. The passage is misunderstood by Donald Kuspit, "A Mighty Metaphor: The Analogy of Archaeology and Psychoanalysis," in *Sigmund Freud and Art: His Personal Collection of Antiquities*, ed. Lynn Gamwell and Richard Wells (Binghamton, N.Y., 1989), 133–52; see also Ellen Handler Spitz, "Psychoanalysis and the Legacies of Antiquity," in *Sigmund Freud and Art*, 153–72.

this Introduction that the "physics" and "psychics" of replication—what might seem to be the provinces of archaeology and psychoanalysis respectively—completely exhaust anything that art historians could possibly want to say about artifacts and images. This could only be a problem for art history and art historians, however, if they supposed that they should pursue the "physics" and the "psychics" as wholly independent projects—as certain misguided scientisms and humanisms sometimes suggest. As I have noted here, and as these chapters show in some detail, when we are dealing with artifacts and images it is inconceivable that either the "physics" or the "psychics" could be exclusively invoked in answering even the most elementary questions about their history. Thus, and in sum, though art history can barely claim any materials, methods, or theories of its own—and indeed should not try to do so—it grasps the historical reality that archaeology and psychoanalysis, for their part, never actually see.

REPLICATION IN ARCHAEOLOGY

Chapter 1

Finding Symbols in History

Some notoriously demanding passages in Ludwig Wittgenstein's *Philosophical Investigations* raise a skeptical puzzle any theories or histories of human symbol making will ignore at their peril.[1] Stated in one of its strongest forms (which does not necessarily capture Wittgenstein's own exact sense), it is this: although a particular overt behavior may represent (for example, denote or depict) something to you and me, having a conventional "meaning" for us in a "language" we share, there is no guarantee that, and no final test to determine whether, the same overt behavior—as we could ever perceive and study it—"means" the same thing, or anything at all, to someone else. For example, you and I might represent something by the way in which we blink our eyes and grunt. Someone else, however, is just blinking and grunting. Or, to take Saul Kripke's example, by writing the mark or sign "+," you and I "mean" the addition function, or "plus." But someone else actually means something else by the same sign "+," say, "quus," a function in which x quus $y = x$ plus y, if x and y are less than 57, but otherwise (always) = 5.[2] Obviously you and I could not even tell that

1. Ludwig Wittgenstein, *Philosophical Investigations*, trans. G.E.M. Anscombe, 3d ed. (Oxford, 1968), e.g., sec. 201.

2. Saul Kripke, *Wittgenstein on Rules and Private Language* (Cambridge, Mass., 1982), 8–9.

our "rule" for using "+" diverges from this in any (qu)adding of integers less than 57. To use Simon Blackburn's term, we do not detect that this (or our?) rule is "bent":[3] that, at a certain point in the application of the sign, this "practice" diverges from (as it were, makes a turn or bend out of) ours. We can imagine other, perhaps even more extreme, examples in which no possible test we could ever make would ever settle the question whether our practices—our intersubjective application and individual understanding of shared meanings—diverge or, more profoundly, whether one of us actually lacks "practice" altogether.

In this chapter, I do not explore all of the implications of the skeptical puzzle for art history and the anthropology or archaeology of symbols, though some of them are certainly taken up in later chapters. For my purposes here, I use the puzzle to assert that no empirical or experimental scrutiny of a behavior (like grunting) or a morphology (like a mark) "on the ground" or "in front of our noses," as it were, can definitively establish that it is a sign (a symbol or a representation) and what its referent might be for its producer. That it looks like a picture does not mean it is; that it seems to depict my dog does not mean it does. We need to know something further about it. In this and the following chapters, I interweave a specific form of the skeptical puzzle with a specific kind of answer or, more exactly, an avoidance maneuver. I hope it will be obvious, however, that my strategy, suitably rewritten, could be made fully general. It can be phrased for any symbols.

Twenty-five thousand or more years ago, someone for the first time entered the cave of Gargas, a small self-contained cavern close to the 700-meter elevation near the present-day village of Aventignan in the French Pyrenees. Within 50 meters of the entrance, the cave became fairly dark, and at 100 meters, making a turn to the left, completely so. Our visitor lighted her way with oil or fat burning in a stone lamp. Fortunately the cave was smooth and dry, though from time to time animals had inhabited it. The sharp-clawed cave bear had even scratched on its walls. Although our visitor may have known other caves in the region, we do not know what purposes animated her first visit to Gargas. But one of her actions—and, of course, perhaps one of her purposes—was to draw, or, more precisely, to make marks.[4]

Oozing from hidden fissures, water carrying fine silts of calcium carbonate had deposited panels of moist clay on many surfaces of the cave. With her fingers together, our visitor gouged straight and curving traces, or with one finger traced somewhat more complicated zigzags and swirls. We cannot say exactly how long this activity was kept up—perhaps for generations. Finally someone traced a simple line in the minimal form of a bison's forequarters—its horns, head, and muzzle (see Fig. 3.8).[5] Later the whole outline was drawn, including details of eyes, fetlocks, and hooves, incised with a sharp stone on the harder surfaces of the cave walls (see Fig. 3.10). Horses, reindeer, various species of antelope, and

3. Simon Blackburn, *Spreading the Word: Groundings in the Philosophy of Language* (Oxford, 1984), 74–92.

4. André Leroi-Gourhan, *Treasures of Prehistoric Art*, trans. N. Guterman (New York, 1967), 307–8; Claude Barrière, *L'art pariétal paléolithique de la grotte de Gargas*, British Archaeological Reports, Supplementary Series 14, 2 vols. (Oxford, 1976); idem, "Gargas," in *L'art des cavernes: Atlas des grottes ornées paléolithiques françaises*, ed. André Leroi-Gourhan (Paris, 1984), 514–22.

5. See Barrière, *L'art pariétal de Gargas*, 1:151, for such images.

other animals were depicted with increasing differentiation, detail, and modulation, and in individually recognizable styles. At least for this people in this part of the world, about 20,000 B.C., image making had been born.

It is the ring of inevitability in this narrative I wish to subvert—or, more exactly, its sufficiency in helping us to understand what it could be for image making to be born. For although I accept that some narrative of the crystallization of symbolic technologies and conventions underwrites the history of all arts (see especially Chapter 5) and by some has been regarded as the history *of* art, the status of these "first" images in traditions is puzzling.

I must make the obvious reminder that the cave of Gargas is not the origin of image making. I use it here as one example of how image making originates. Images were certainly made elsewhere and perhaps earlier, like the simple but seemingly unmistakable depictions of animals on portable limestone blocks from rock shelters in the Périgord, the earliest dated to about 30,000 B.C. (see Fig. 2.2),[6] or other animal figures painted on stone from the Apollo XI Cave in Namibia, dated at the earliest to about 24,000 B.C.[7] We cannot know whether images were made by earlier hominids in a perishable medium, like bark painting or sand drawing. In the preserved media, *Homo sapiens neanderthalensis* produced nonfigurative graphics (see Fig. 2.7),[8] and on the present view, image making is associated with the technologically "modern" Upper Paleolithic culture of *H. sapiens sapiens*. In fact, *sapiens sapiens* has often been defined as just that creature which makes images and uses other complex symbol systems (see Chapter 2). But for my purposes, the whole question of the absolutely "first" image in chronological terms is a red herring.

Although they were broadly related to and descended from earlier Upper Paleolithic people, there is no direct evidence that the people of Gargas had learned about earlier images. (They did, however, make other kinds of images; the wall engravings are in part "dated" by a tendentious association with one figure on an incised plaquette found in the cave.) Theoretically, a feral child or a Robinson Crusoe, completely cut off from society or tradition, or both, could make images; theoretically, image making inaugurates time and time again in history. Though Gargas is a useful example, the same general puzzles arise for any real inaugural image making, whenever and wherever found archaeologically.

For an inaugural image, the problem is not external—the problem of identifying its stylistic affiliations or formal sources—but rather internal. Since the first image maker had never seen one before, how did she know how to make an image? By hypothesis, no one had told her what they are or how they can be used.

Now, in this initial narrative, the visitor to the cave simply began tracing lines resembling the silhouettes of bison, horses, and other creatures. But this description fails to come to grips with two facts. First, as a projection of a three-dimensional object, a two-

6. Brigitte Delluc and Gilles Delluc, "Les manifestations graphiques aurignaciennes sur support rocheux des environs des Eyzies (Dordogne)," *Gallia Préhistoire* 21 (1978), 213–438.

7. J. D. Lewis-Williams, *The Rock Art of Southern Africa* (Cambridge, 1983), figs. 42 and 43; Alex R. Willcox, *The Rock Art of Africa* (New York, 1984), 231–37.

8. The pioneering study is Alexander Marshack, "Some Implications of the Paleolithic Symbolic Evidence for the Origin of Language," *Current Anthropology* 17 (1976), 274–82.

dimensional visual display is ambiguous. According to any standard of projective fidelity, it can correctly represent any number of different real objects.[9] What, then, accounts for the particular judgment that, for example, a square depicts a cube and not some other kind of six-sided object? (This is the kind of question the skeptical puzzle would dramatize.) Second, that a visual display happens to resemble some real object does not guarantee it depicts that object. (The skeptical puzzle also worries this point.) Shadows and mirror "images" resemble the objects that produce them, but they are not necessarily representations of those objects. All kinds of patterns, like Leonardo's mottled wall, resemble various objects fortuitously (on the vexed question of resemblance-in-representation, see Chapter 3). How is it, then, that the simple curves in the cave of Gargas, resembling animal profiles (as well as many other things), were also apparently taken to stand for just those aspects of animals? How is it, in other words, that we could recognize them to be images?

The obvious answer to both questions is that the marks in Gargas, whatever they may look like to us, were (or were not) produced as depictions of particular objects. But this answer provokes a vicious regress. It seems to imply that the image maker already knows what an image is and how to produce it. Where was this knowledge acquired? Unqualified, this "conventionalism" cannot account for the first image maker (see Chapter 3).[10]

Let us look more carefully at what was happening in Gargas. Nondepictional tracing—the "digital flutings" and scribbles made with one or more fingers in the soft clay (Fig. 1.1)—accumulated on the walls, covering long panels. The tracing has internal rhythms of its own. Although a good deal more can be said about it (see Chapter 3), for my purposes here it suffices to say that some fraction of it results in marks that can be seen as certain objects—like panels of digital tracing thought by some observers to contain animal figures.[11] Similar complex and suggestive marking can be found in other archaeological contexts, for instance, among the incised blocks of the Périgord (see Figs. 2.2, 2.3)[12] and, of course, in the scribbling of simians (see Chapter 2). That such marks in some contexts can be mistaken for real things derives directly from the fact that the perceptual system sometimes arrives at mistaken interpretations of the information it picks up in reflected light. Although it is in itself a complex phenomenon, for my purposes one can take "seeing-as" to be an automatic (autonomic) operation of the visual system responding to perceptual ambiguity.

Like any psychological event, seeing-as, if it has no overt manifestations, is inaccessible to direct observation. Whether it occurred ten seconds or ten thousand years ago, it is, as it were, "outside" history—that is, lacking the material evidence of overt human behavior preserved in a fragmentary way in the archaeological record of actions performed and things made. Although it took place in history, seeing-as often has no history.

Recall now that someone's momentarily seeing a mark as an object is not enough for the mark to depict that object. In the flickering semidarkness, our visitor to the cave may have

9. Margaret Hagen, *Varieties of Realism* (Cambridge, 1986), provides the best survey.

10. For a potential solution to the paradoxes and regresses of conventionalism, see David K. Lewis, *Convention: A Philosophical Study* (Cambridge, Mass., 1967).

11. E.g., Barrière, *L'art pariétal de Gargas*, 1:136, pls. 23, 35, 39.

12. Delluc and Delluc, "Les manifestations graphiques," and idem, "De l'empreinte au signe," *Dossier de l'archéologie* 90 (1985), 56–62.

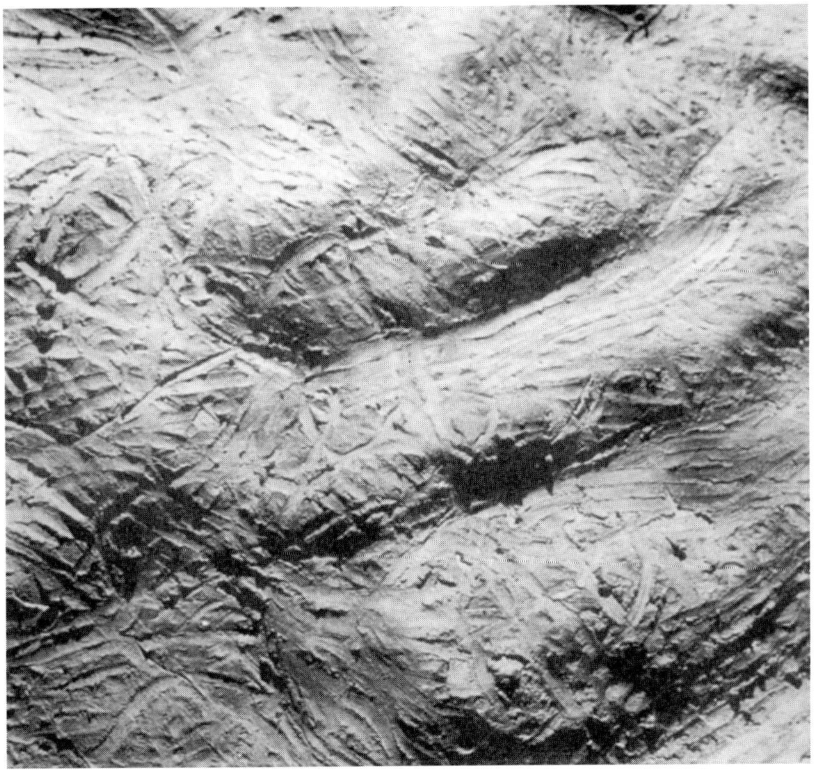

Fig. 1.1. Polydigital tracing in the cave of Gargas, French Pyrenees, about 20,000 B.C. (?).

momentarily mistaken some of the marks—whether made by her or by anyone else—as animal forms, but they were not necessarily representations of animals for just that reason.

Still, if our visitor looked again, she could at least learn that what she took to be something else was just and only a mark, morphologically indiscernible as it might be from any of the marks she (or anyone else) had been making all along, for whatever purpose or lack of purpose. In this, she would already learn that she could make the mark not just and only as a mark but also as a mark that could be seen as an object. If and when she *remade* that or that kind of mark for seeing-as—knowing it was just a mark but interested, now, in its object-resembling properties—then she made an image. Mark became remark. And insofar as this marking and remarking is a kind of making and remaking, it has a history: in principle, we can find it archaeologically.

We shall never know, then, whether many of the tracings in Gargas were ever seen as objects. Their recognizability to us as images (or not) is—as the skeptical puzzle reminds us—no evidence one way or another; our seeing-as may have nothing to do with someone else's. Furthermore, we do not even know why the marks, seen-as or not, were being made in the first place. Perhaps, as Claude Barrière and others have supposed, they were merely a kind of "spontaneous graffitomania."[13]

13. Barrière, *L'art pariétal de Gargas,* 2:364.; see further Robert G. Bednarik, "Parietal Finger Markings in Europe and Australia," *Rock Art Research* 3 (1986), 30–61.

But for some tracings, we can observe the continual replication of an object-resembling mark. At Gargas, drawn vertically, a double S curve can be seen as the curving horns, forehead and muzzle, and neck of a bison (see Fig. 3.8). Drawn horizontally, the same curve can be seen as the horns, humped back, and rising tail or descending hindquarters.[14] Gargas exhibits a good deal of replication and variation of this particular form. (I use the last term advisedly in order not to prejudge whether the *form* is a *figure;* see further Chapter 8.) The curves are repeated in the whole or in part of their length to give two horns; two curves are placed at angles to each other to produce a half or two-thirds-complete outline; the final flips of each curve can be neatly fitted together or superimposed on one another; finger holes establish an "eye"; a few strokes create "legs" or a "tail"; the whole contour may be finished off by a second horizontal (ventral) curve below the first (dorsal) one (see Chapter 3). As marks, these elaborations are indiscernible from what had already appeared in (hypothetically) nondepictional or even nonsemantic tracing. But we can infer that they were in fact being made for seeing-as—that is, as images—because in replication the object-resembling properties were preserved in the transition from surface to surface or in the translation from one tool and medium to another. (Similarly, we could infer they were being made as nondepictive "notations" if other properties, like the discreteness and disjunction of "characters," were held constant in use and reuse, in replication [see Chapter 3].)[15] But to reiterate, the very first mark in this and the other replicatory sequences was not made as an image but only as a mark.

This analysis solves the logical paradox of regress. But it has potentially troublesome implications. Because of the possibility of ambiguity, fortuitous resemblance, and the variability of seeing-as, no amount of study of the visual properties of a mark can definitively tell us whether it is an image and precisely what it is an image of. Despite the apparently bizarre consequences of this result (surely we just know, for example, that the Sistine Chapel paintings are images—otherwise what in the world could they be doing up there?), an interpreter must know the whole chain of replication and variation of all the properties of the mark right back to the initial moment of seeing-as in her or in someone else's "psychological" experience. For depiction, this claim is a close (but not exact) parallel for so-called causal or historical theories of the reference of proper names and natural-kind terms;[16] in the successful production and perception of symbolic reference, an interpreter does not so much have a correct and complete "description for" or "belief about" a sign, as Bertrand Russell had suggested,[17] as a more or less hazy understanding of its history of first application ("baptism"), transmission, and change. To oversimplify hideously, the inter-

14. E.g., Barrière, *L'art pariétal de Gargas* 1, fig. 43, nos. 10 and 11.

15. See Alexander Marshack, "The Meander as a System: The Analysis and Recognition of Iconographic Units in Upper Paleolithic Compositions," in *Form in Indigenous Art*, ed. Peter J. Ucko (Canberra, 1977), 286–317, and idem, "Concepts théoriques conduisant à de nouvelles méthodes analytiques, de nouveaux procédés de recherche et catégories de données," *L'Anthropologie* 88 (1984), 85–100.

16. Hilary Putnam, "The Meaning of 'Meaning,'" in *Mind, Language, and Reality: Philosophical Papers II* (Cambridge, Mass., 1975); Stephen Schwartz, ed., *Naming, Necessity, and Natural Kinds* (Ithaca, N.Y., 1977); Gareth Evans, *Varieties of Reference* (Oxford, 1979); Saul Kripke, *Naming and Necessity,* 2d ed. (Cambridge, Mass., 1980); and Michael Devitt, *Designation* (New York, 1982).

17. For crucial essays, see Bertrand Russell, *Logic and Knowledge,* ed. R. C. Marsh (London, 1956).

preter does not so much decipher as excavate a language. The point applies both to someone within and to someone outside a particular community of language users or sign makers.

Now, sometimes we can study this whole closed cycle of production, from "baptism" on, in an experimental setting—with simians in a laboratory, infants in a playpen, or draftsmen in a workshop. Most important, we can observe ourselves at work: we can see our own images (or notations) for what they are images (or notations) of, irrespective of someone else's ability to pick this up. Otherwise, however, it would be difficult to identify the sequence and structure of the relevant chains of replication.

For one thing, each variant in a chain is necessarily separated from preceding and following variants by some span of space or lag of time. An interpreter's archaeological survey of sign production has to be extremely comprehensive to pick them all up. For another, some properties of the morphology are reproduced in succeeding variants, often becoming inextricably incorporated (drawn over or built into the latest variant), whereas others, not reproduced, are abandoned or destroyed. We are left archaeologically with a complex morphology, presenting itself as a single unitary "artifact," that is simultaneously a selection and palimpsest of many variations—and the garbage of the studio contains a good deal of what we would like to know.

It would be the task of an "archaeopsychology" or a "paleosemiotics" to sort out these relations: archaeopsychology is the interpretation of both dimensions of the artifact-sign, and especially of the interrelation or identity of artifactuality and representationality. Although it is obvious that this task requires rigorously formulated and empirically or theoretically defensible theories about both representation (for example, semiosis, interpretation, reference) and artifactuality (for example, morphology, style, sequence and distribution), it will be enormously complex. Admitting both evolutionary and culture-relativistic premises, perhaps no fully general assertions will be possible.

At any rate, at Gargas and in other unusual art historical or archaeological cases we can sometimes circumvent the immediate difficulties. Because the Paleolithic engraver was removing matter from a surface rather than adding to it, she could not easily change or erase her work; thus it tends to accumulate in one place. We can therefore watch a chain of replications forming as a palimpsest with an internal "stratigraphy"—all the way back to the initial variation of a nondepictional trace. For instance, in the deepest chamber of Gargas, the Panel of the Great Bulls (see Fig. 1.2)[18] exhibits many complete and incomplete animal forms superimposed on one another. Individual lines have been reused to establish new images. Several images can share a single line. (We would not predict such morphologies if superimposition were "random," that is, if the later engraver had taken no account of the work of the earlier.) A number of more complete forms can be resolved, but some seem to be arrested in replicatory development—an elk with a subtly modulated contour; horses with forehead or muzzle apparently attempted twice, or redrawn by a later artist; two bison; a heavily worked ibex with outline deeply scraped and interior filled in, with three "versions" of its head; and the Great Bull itself, created partly by a carved line

18. Barrière, *L'art pariétal de Gargas*, 2, pl. 56.

and partly by a much finer incised line, perhaps preliminary to heavier cutting (see Chapter 3).

Replication is simply the sequential production of similar artifacts substitutable for one another in some specific context of use. The general notion of a chain of replications, somewhat parallel to linguistic philosophers' concept of a "history of reference" or "designation chain,"[19] goes by various names already in art history and archaeology. For example, George Kubler called it a "form class," descending from a "prime object," an artifact with no formal antecedents.[20] It is perhaps equivalent to what some art historians mean by style, a set of similarities between artifacts explained by their common historical descent, although style encompasses artifacts that do not represent (reference necessarily has a style, but not vice versa) (see Chapter 6). A variety of sophisticated formal, comparative, and statistical methods are required to understand these chains, classes, or sets.

Often we assume, circularly, that some property of a visual display does or should signify something, perhaps because similar-looking properties in other displays do. We make up a psychological event—a perceptual episode, a belief or intention or rule—to account for it. But as the possibility of ambiguity and of fortuitous resemblance entails, we cannot know in advance which property of the display will be seen as something else and what this something exactly will be. On my analysis, depiction occurs within a chain of replications. Therefore the interpretation of any image is necessarily historical: it requires that the interpreter know how the mark or sign was produced and its various properties seen or interpreted. Surely in a sense this is good news for art history: it provides a strictly logical justification for the very existence of art history itself.

However, there is bad news built in here. The epistemic conditions for the interpretability of images are extremely strict, and the evidence generally poor. Without full archaeological knowledge of the history of a mark, the interpreter cannot be certain what it signifies. More worrying still, the initial moment of seeing-as itself, which invests the whole chain with that particular significance, as a psychological event is actually inaccessible to direct archaeological investigation. It can only be reconstructed inferentially as that perceptual episode (whether or not it is *our* episode or recognizable to us) which would best explain the whole package of formal and contextual properties of the chain. In psychoanalytic studies of image making and its replication this need to reconstruct or even to imagine an originary or "primal" perceptual episode has been placed at the center of the historical enterprise (see especially Chapters 11 and 12).

Emile Durkheim complained that we are in trouble whenever we have to offer a psychological explanation of anything—and indeed there has been a tendency in modern anthropology to see "rules" or "codes" of interpretation as somehow suprapsychological, in "culture" or some other reified supraindividual entity. Without worrying the metapsychological questions, however, one can see that in ordinary social situations people do readily infer or learn the relevant archaeological knowledge about making marks—just as they learn how the words of a language have been and are to be used. Images are labeled; their properties are pointed out; particular denotations and connotations are socially discussed.

19. Kripke, *Naming and Necessity,* 95; Devitt, *Designation.*

20. George Kubler, *The Shape of Time: Remarks on the History of Things* (New Haven, Conn., 1962).

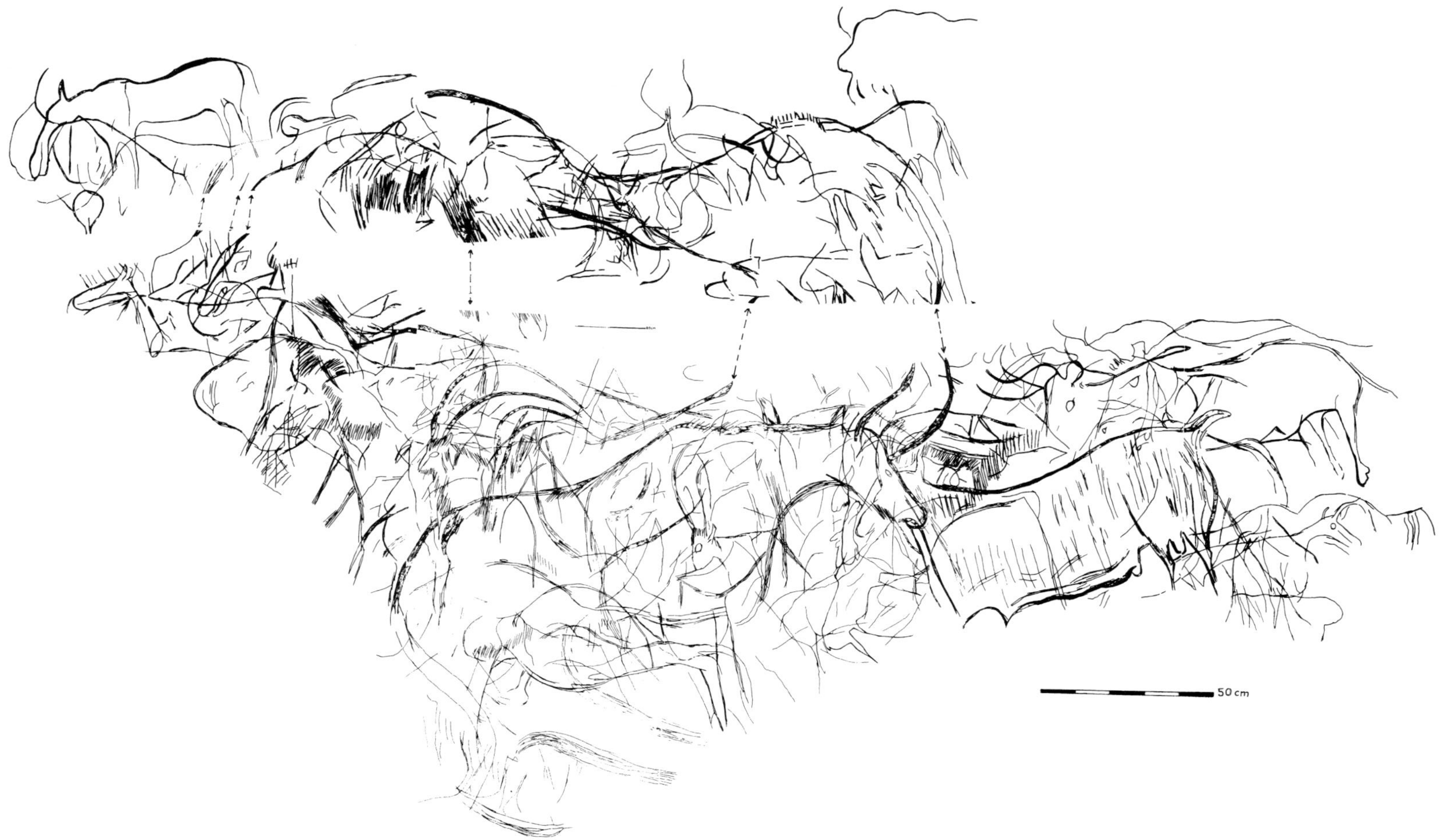

Fig. 1.2. “Panel of the Great Bulls,” cave of Gargas.

Supposedly this knowledge becomes conventional or institutional. The social group takes it for granted that certain properties of a visual display are to be interpreted in a certain way; "rules" and "codes," as it were, come to replace actual historical understanding and investigation. It follows that the task of art historians is simply to reconstruct that local common knowledge about images. One strand in the so-called social history of art—although not explicitly Durkheimian—has set out to do just that.[21]

I have been using the example of a Paleolithic cave in part to suggest that if conventional knowledge about images and the archaeology of their production is vastly removed from us, then our interpretive task is just that much harder and the results that much less complete. Despite intriguing speculation, we really have no idea exactly in what sense the cave drawings and paintings represented aspects of their makers' world.[22] The images made by folk, "outsider," or "eccentric" artists, by other cultural marginals, or by the mad are similarly detached, in varying degrees, from conventional routines of interpretation; their significance is equally hard to reconstruct (I do not claim, of course, that their significance is at all like that of prehistoric art). But these are platitudes, pointing only to the practical limitations of art historical or other "archaeological" evidence. Insofar as such images are images at all, they are part of a chain of replications; in theory, they have some history establishing some signification. But I have been making a stronger claim. With a first image, wherever and whenever we find it, there is no preexisting history of replication to anchor it, no history of interpretation in which it is deciphered. It is, as it were, a novel remark in an unknown language.[23]

Paleolithic images on portable blocks or cave walls may be the first images in some absolute historical sense (see Chapter 5), but this is inessential to the argument. Throughout history, chains of replication are continuously inaugurated in novel episodes of seeing-as. Many of these chains are firmly embedded in existing practices, guided by rules such as those applied in the modern West for perspective projection. These are undoubted realities of social life—about the power of institutions—to be explained in a variety of ways. But there is no logical restriction on when and where seeing-as will take place—no restrictions on the morphology of the mark or on which object-resembling properties can be replicated, or even, of course, on how resemblance itself is judged. Wherever and whenever people make marks, or work matter in any way, a visual form may inaugurally take on semantic significance of any kind. (A visual form is always, however, accompanied by morphology that has no such significance.)

To recap: Art historians often assume that images are readily recognizable as such, somehow in advance of art historical research *on* and interpretation *of* them. However, it

21. Although it now has literally hundreds of versions, the *locus classicus* of this approach remains Michael Baxandall, *Painting and Experience in Fifteenth-Century Italy: A Primer in the Social History of Pictorial Style* (Oxford, 1972).

22. See, e.g., Leroi-Gourhan, *Treasures,* and Margaret W. Conkey, "On the Origins of Paleolithic Art: A Review and Some Critical Thoughts," in *The Mousterian Legacy: Human Biocultural Change in the Upper Pleistocene,* British Archaeological Reports, International Series 164, ed. Erik Trinkaus (Oxford, 1983), 201–27.

23. Although I do not develop the point here (see Chapter 6), it seems to me that all accounts of images in a "tradition," which in a way postpone the diachronic problem of origins for a synchronic or structural analysis, are exposed to the skeptical puzzle and the concomitant difficulties of conventionalism.

is a kind of art history—the archaeology of replication—that establishes them as images in the first place. To understand what an image signifies, an interpreter must know exactly in what way the properties of a visual display were produced for seeing-as. Because of the possibility of ambiguity and of fortuitous resemblance, no amount of inspecting the display itself, empirically recording its attributes, can possibly provide this information. The interpreter must have what I call "archaeological" knowledge (it is, obviously, also a social or intersubjective knowledge) about the replication of seeing-as. Such knowledge is often coordinated conventionally and passed on institutionally, though this is hardly even a reliable generality and there are no promises about how easy it will be to reconstruct any part of the history. It might be enough to determine that the physical properties and context of the artifact (its apparent morphology, distribution, mode of manufacture, deposition, or preservation, and so on) are most compellingly and comprehensively explained by supposing that it is a sign, and even a sign with such and such a representational value. Of course, without knowing the precise meaning of the sign, we can still make useful, pointed statements, or collect information, about the "archaeological" place of apparently representational activity in a society—for example, about its chronology, frequency, distribution, socioeconomic or other behavioral correlates, and so forth. But however it is codified by its users or reconstructed by us, knowledge about images is inaugurally anchored in a psychological event "outside," the moment of taking a mark for something in the world, forever inaccessible to us archaeologically.

I do not feel threatened by this result and hope for an archaeology vigorously embracing rather than avoiding it. By phrasing the problems of art history or of an anthropology of symbols as I do in this book, I am merely questioning a conception of art history as a fully empirical enterprise—the usual positivism awkwardly accompanying a final mysticism. We can certainly gather the facts about the making of marks, and image making is something people do with the marks they have made; the more empirical precision about both, the better. But when mark first becomes image, when a mark remarks, there is no fact of the matter to be located archaeologically.

What kind of history or archaeology is it that could never dig up and display its central event? It is, I think, a history that necessarily offers not only the facts about its objects but also a theory about itself—a systematic organizing hypothesis, like those of Darwin or Freud, about how the present inherits its form from the past and why the past is—or is not—coherent. On my account, symbolic meaning is a particular function of how the present inherits its forms—it is a form of the archaeological coherence of making. "Seeing-as" and "replication" might remind us in various ways of mutation and selection (see further Chapters 4 and 6) or trauma and repetition (see further Chapters 10–12). My own hunch is that this hypothesis, whatever its final form, will arise for art history from the study of perception and visual cognition, and for other marking and sign systems from the study of other cognitive domains. Be that as it may, symbols without history are a puzzle only when history is without a theory. In the following chapters I attempt to present the general outlines of this theory.

Chapter 2

The Origins of Image Making

Image making is often considered one of the unique and quintessential competences of *Homo sapiens sapiens,* differentiating the subspecies, for example, from *H. sapiens neanderthalensis* and from earlier hominids. Some controversial chronologies even identify the emergence of *H. sapiens sapiens* with the cultural transition to the Upper Paleolithic, about 45,000–35,000 B.C., signified archaeologically, at least in part, by the appearance of items of personal adornment and of image making, or "art."[1]

In many accounts, "art" supposedly appears as an autonomous domain of human activity of relatively recent vintage and extraordinary sophistication. A commitment to this proposition perhaps underlies the whole discipline of art history, as traditionally pursued; it certainly contributes to all manner of ideological claims about humanness and human evolution in biology, anthropology, and psychology (see further Chapters 4 and 5).[2] Although often mythologized as sudden, primal, and spontaneous, image making is a pre-

1. See reviews in Peter Mellars, "The Character of the Middle-Upper Paleolithic Transition in Southwest France," in *The Explanation of Culture Change,* ed. Colin Renfrew (London, 1973), 255–76, and Randall White, "Rethinking the Middle/Upper Paleolithic Transition," *Current Anthropology* 23 (1982), 169–92.

2. See further Donald Preziosi, "Constru(ct)ing the Origins of Art," *Art Journal* 42 (1982), 320–25.

dictable adaptation that should be coherently situated in the overall trajectory of hominid evolution. To be sure, image making is a distinctive and specific social achievement. But it can be derived logically from simple and archaic perceptual and cognitive processes. An account of its origins does not require speculative or transcendental psychological, anthropological, or aesthetic assumptions about "cognitive evolution" or "artistic sensibility" that have no hope of being tested experimentally or confirmed archaeologically.[3]

In developing this point, one must observe strict distinctions between the different varieties of what cognitive psychologists and philosophers have called Representation (here capitalized to indicate its very generalized sense).[4] In the wide sense, Representation includes both somatic and extrasomatic modes of acquiring, preserving, and manipulating knowledge. For my purposes, the important variety of somatic Representation is visual perception. Extrasomatic Representation has several varieties, and they have been variously defined. Unfortunately for the interests of interdisciplinary clarity, art historians, semioticians, and others have reserved the term "representation" for only one of them, namely, image making.[5] An image refers to its object iconically or nonarbitrarily. (This common definition requires refinement but is adequate for preliminary purposes.) I follow established usage in art history and aesthetics by calling other extrasomatic modes of knowledge *nonrepresentational*. Unlike the image, they do not refer to their objects iconically (Fig. 2.1).

The evidence for which I wish to provide an account begins with the images of the early Aurignacian period in southwestern Europe (about 32,000–26,000 B.C.). These are engravings and paintings in outline only, with no interior details (for example, Fig. 2.2).[6] (Evolutionarily or historically earlier images or even "traditions" of images have been proposed, but these cases are sufficiently doubtful and their replicatory status and relations remain so uncertain that one does best to err on the side of caution and begin with the Aurignacian [see further Chapters 3–5].) The lines are simple—near straight, or simple, single C curves—and have been incised very deeply or pecked with a stone point. Most of the outline drawings represent only parts of animals—horns, foreparts, dorsal lines, or legs. The only complete outline engraving of an animal that survives from the Aurignacian period, to be found on the block from the Abri du Renne (Belcayre) on the banks of the Vézère River, seems to represent a herbivore with a very short tail, probably a stag or an ibex (Fig. 2.2*b*).[7] It is not certain whether the drawings are incomplete, intentionally abbreviated, or self-sufficient representations of interesting features. They appear on the

3. My discussion is confined throughout to figurative representation. Other "artistic" phenomena, such as ornament or architecture, are not considered explicitly. It is unlikely that Upper Paleolithic societies maintained a concept of "art." At any rate, it is unproductive to assimilate different conceptualizations and technologies as if they all had a common cognitive source such as an "aesthetic" sense.

4. For instance, Jerry Fodor, *The Language of Thought* (Cambridge, Mass., 1973).

5. For instance, Meyer Schapiro, "On Some Problems in the Semiotics of Visual Art: Field and Vehicle in Image-Signs" [1970], in *Theory and Philosophy of Art: Style, Artist, and Society* (New York, 1994), 1–32; Umberto Eco, *A Theory of Semiotics* (Bloomington, Ind., 1976).

6. L. Capitan and D. Peyrony, "Les origines de l'art à l'Aurignacien moyen: Nouvelles découvertes à la Ferrassie," *Revue Anthropologique* 31 (1921), 92–112; Brigitte Delluc and Gilles Delluc, "Les manifestations graphiques aurignaciennes sur support rocheux des environs des Eyzies (Dordogne)," *Gallia Préhistoire* 21 (1978), 213–438.

7. Henri Breuil, *Four Hundred Centuries of Cave Art*, trans. Mary Boyle (Montignac, 1952), 281; André Leroi-Gourhan, *Treasures of Prehistoric Art*, trans. N. Guterman

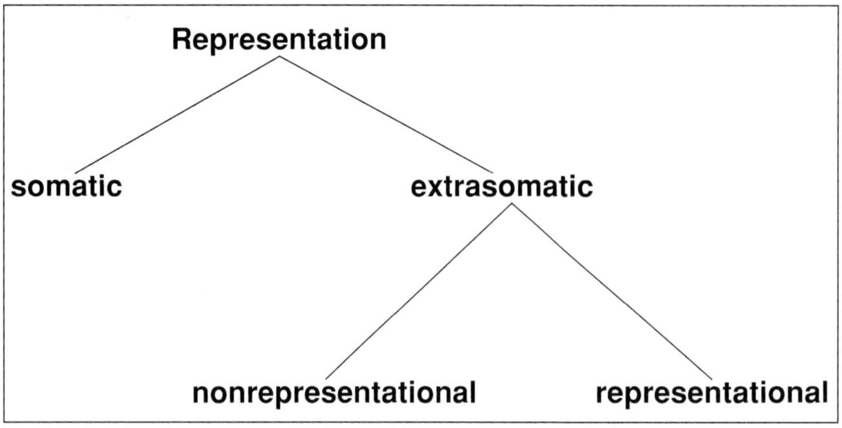

Fig. 2.1. Varieties of representation.

same blocks as do what are often called female genitals; the blocks also bear short series of linear strokes and small hollows (cupules) of various sorts (see Fig. 3.3). Possibly all or at least a substantial portion of these marks were meant to be jointly significant.[8]

Between 23,000 and 17,000 B.C., a more common (or at least better documented) tradition of depiction seems to have derived organically from the earliest Aurignacian. The bison from the open-air entrance room at the cave of La Grèze (Fig. 2.3), dated to the Lower Solutrean period,[9] seems strongly reminiscent of earlier figures in the simple, deeply engraved line, profile silhouette, and selective attention of the engraver (as in earlier figures, no interior details or feet are shown), although the line here actually does far more work. At Los Hornos de la Peña in Santander, the surviving parts of the horse in the open-air section of the cave are depicted with five simple, sweeping lines; the curve of the neck, dorsal line, and flowing tail are rendered with a single S curve.[10] Compared with a simple Aurignacian curve, a continuously modulated double, or S, curve has far greater descriptive power.

In fact, sometime between 32,000 and 17,000 B.C. a continuous technology underwent one profound conceptual alteration. Image makers discovered (and could henceforward deliberately manipulate) the essential feature of the representational line—its analogical, continuously modulated, semantically "dense" quality.[11] This property was apparently recognized initially in that first turn or flip of the simple C curve and then in the S curves that represent multiply linked and ever-changing features of reality in a single, continuous, controlled statement. Form appeared for the unformed, the unformable (see further Chapters 3 and 8). How are we to account for this transformation?

In my view, image making originated in the discovery of the *representational capacity* of

(New York, 1967), fig. 256; Delluc and Delluc, "Les manifestations graphiques," fig. 95, no. 16.

8. Leroi-Gourhan, *Treasures*, 150, 206.

9. F. B. Naber, D. J. Berenger, and C. Zalles-Flossbach, *L'art pariétal paléolithique en Europe romane*, pt. 1, *Inventaire des sites*, 2 vols. (Bonn, 1976), 107–8.

10. Leroi-Gourhan, *Treasures*, fig. 288.

11. For "density," see Nelson Goodman, *Languages of Art: An Approach to a Theory of Symbols*, 2d ed. (Indianapolis, 1971); Kent Bach, "Part of What a Picture Is," *British Journal of Aesthetics* 10 (1970), 119–37. The concept is examined further in Chapter 3 (and see Chapter 3, note 18, for bibliography).

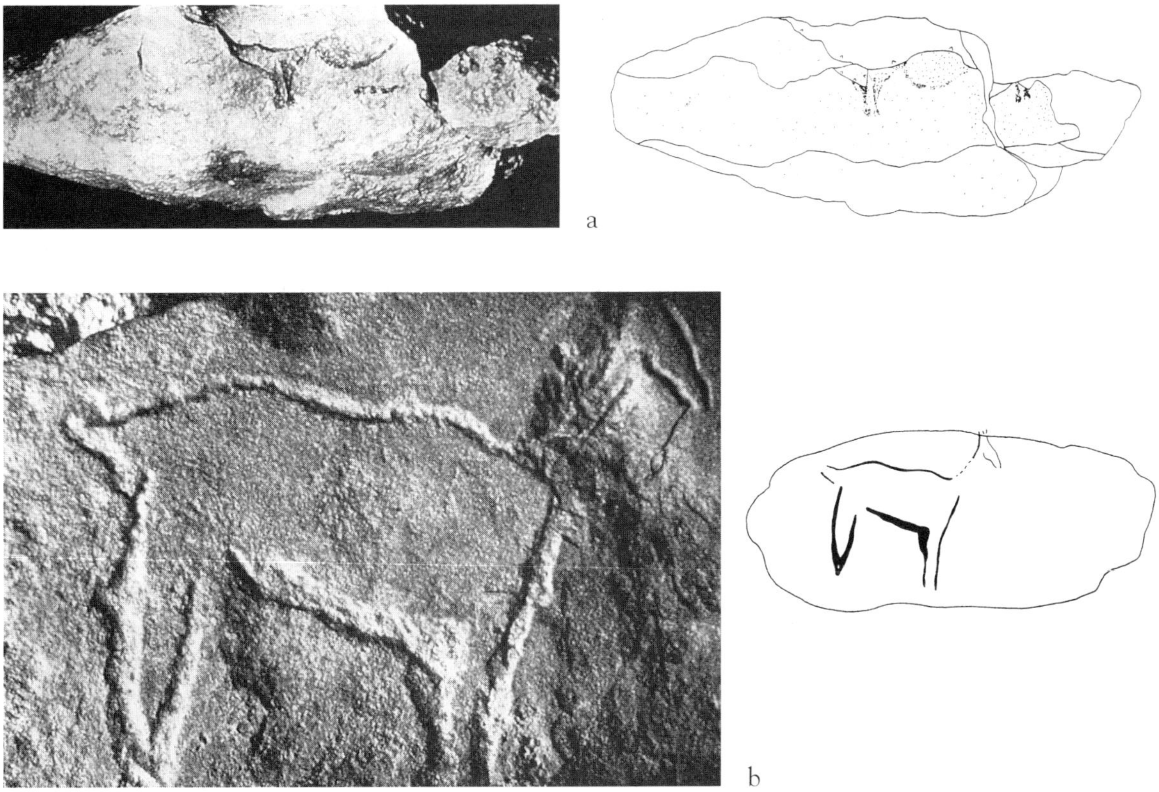

Fig. 2.2. Aurignacian images on limestone blocks from rock shelters near Les Eyzies, Dordogne, France, about 32,000–26,000 B.C. *a.* Blocks 11–12, Abri Blanchard (painted legs and underbelly of a herbivore). *b.* Block 1, Abri du Renne, Belcayre (incised outline of a stag or ibex).

lines, marks, or blots of color that *need* not and often *do* not have a representational—a semantic, semiotic, or significative—status. This claim requires some exposition, and some of its implications deserve to be specified.

Image making may be powerful and convincing, but not necessarily because it is a generalized or deeply rooted activity. Since it emerged so late in human evolution, it is probably a highly specialized technology. It is important to insist on this point. Much of our confusion about its origins stems from assimilating image making to other modes of information transmission, symbolism, or Representation broadly interpreted, to which it may bear only a distant likeness.

One confusion is relatively easy to clear up. Despite what some artists, art historians, and aestheticians have metaphorically asserted, and in the face of complications generated by the concept of "mental images," images in the sense interesting me here are not percepts. Images are extrasomatic; visual perception is somatic. Visual perception, the exploitation of optical information, has an exceedingly archaic history in primate and hominid evolution. Crucial "cultural" achievements like the emergence of toolmaking depended upon sophisticated binocular, stereoscopic visual processes (see further Chapter 4). But for our purposes, the human visual system—its mode of constructing a Representation of the three-

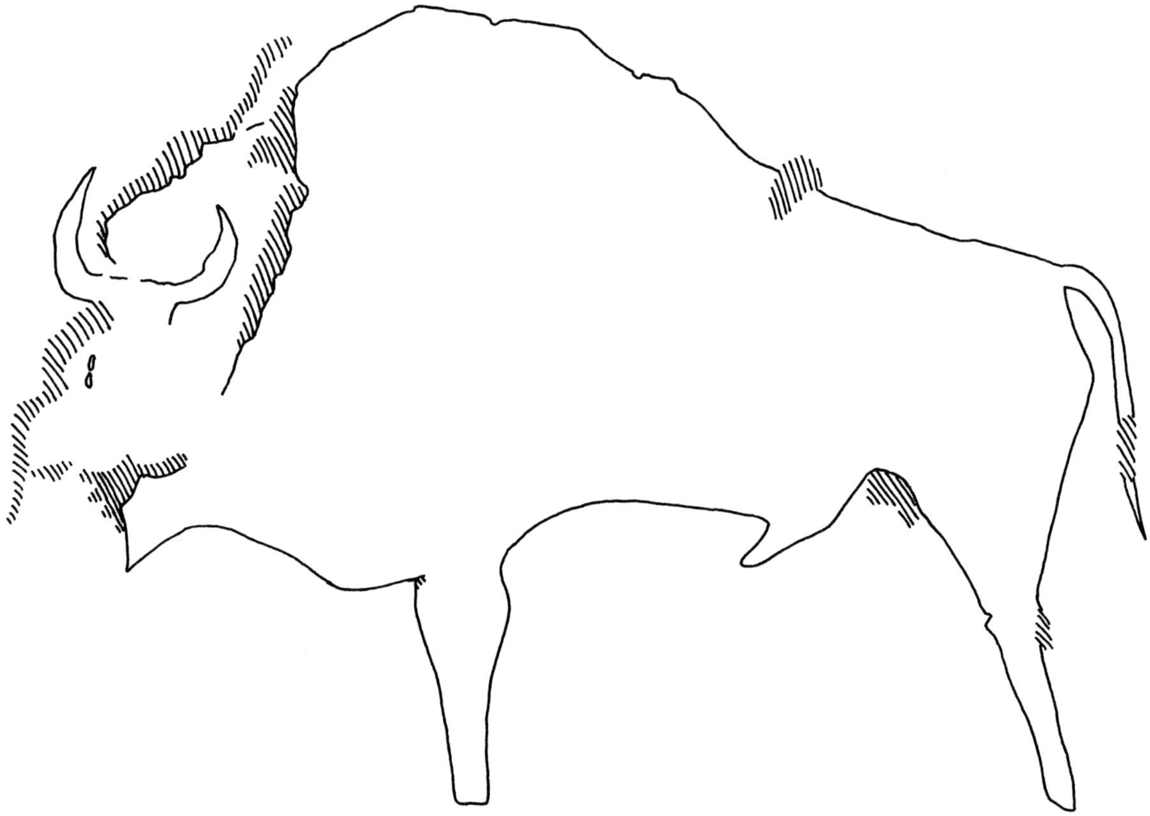

Fig. 2.3. Incised bison, cave of La Grèze, Marquay, Dordogne, France, about 20,000 B.C.

dimensional object world from intensity variations in the reflection of light from surfaces[12]—was fully in place by the Upper Paleolithic.

In relation to visual perception, representation is a specialized process because it is, in a sense, the reduction or *de*composition of human vision—which, at least as consciously experienced, immediately delivers a full-color, three-dimensional view of a constant object world (see further Chapter 8). Images could not have been produced for visual inspection before the evolution of the visual system itself. Therefore the origins of image making might lie in the discovery, conscious or unconscious, that visual perception is insufficient for some specialized purposes. In other words, image making might be regarded as a *further* stage in the *continuing* evolution of the modern visual system, much as archaeologists think of the emergence of toolmaking technologies as a phase in the continuing evolution of hominid manual adaptations (see Chapter 4). For the moment, however, let us keep to the distinction between somatic Representation, including visual perception, and extrasomatic Representation, including images.

12. See especially James J. Gibson, *The Perception of the Visual World* (Boston, 1950); idem, *The Senses Considered as Perceptual Systems* (Boston, 1966); and David Marr, *Vision: A Computational Investigation into the Repre-*

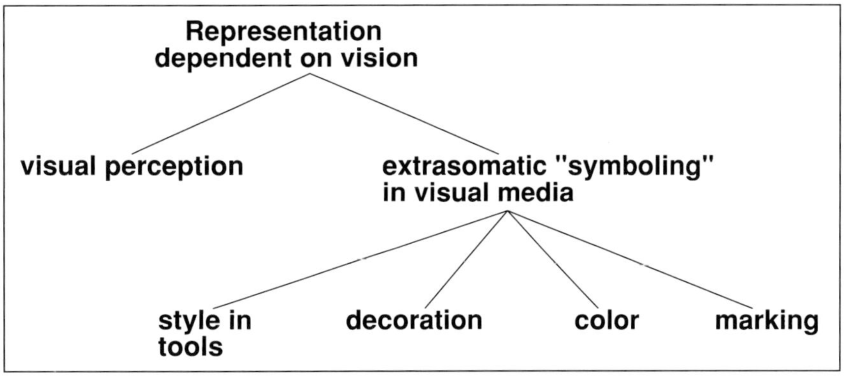

Fig. 2.4. Modes of representation dependent on vision.

It is also important to avoid confusion between images and other forms of extrasomatic Representation also depending upon vision (Fig. 2.4). All of these forms may depend upon the human capacity for what Leslie White called symboling.[13]

Determining exactly what human activities or artifacts count as "symboling" or "symbolic"—that is, as Representation—has been notoriously difficult. For example, although toolmaking surely evolved from unplanned practical discoveries, the definition of a symbol might be stretched too far if it were made to include such concrete solutions to immediate material problems (see further Chapter 4).[14] However, in addition to toolmaking, hominids long before the emergence of an image-making *Homo sapiens sapiens* probably exploited at least three other kinds of "symboling" technology—decorative stylization, color symbolism, and marking. In one way or another, each of these activities has been thought to constitute the root, origin, or primal condition of image or art making (see also Chapter 5).

The first of these, decorative stylization, can be defined and detected only vaguely, above and beyond the necessary "stylization" of any organized form of labor (for style, see Chapter 6). There are some puzzling instances of an interest among hominids in "decoration" affixed to a functional form or revealed in its manufacture and intentionally preserved and elaborated. Kenneth Oakley has discussed very early stone tools with "decorative" incrustations or inclusions, such as fossils in the stone, apparently preserved intentionally. Nonetheless, only a long, insecure chain of inferences will lead from these manifestations to "aesthetic sensibility," or, as Oakley would have it, the "roots of art."[15]

---

sentation and Processing of Visual Information (New York, 1982).

13. Leslie White, "The Symbol: The Origin and Basis of Behavior," *Philosophy of Science* 7 (1940), 451–63. White's concept was very broad. He included somatic and extrasomatic, visual and nonvisual modes of Representation as examples of "symboling." Although the term is useful as a synonym for Representation, it would be misleading to believe that some *deeper faculty or competence of the mind*—a "symboling" faculty—really exists, uniquely characterizing *H. sapiens*, and accounts for the evolution of the various modes. Each mode evolved as a distinctive adaptation. Hence I am considering one for which we have at least *some* archaeological evidence. The problem is to specify exactly what the mode is, how it operates, and why it should have been successful.

14. Cf. Thomas Wynn, "The Intelligence of Later Acheulean Hominids," *Man* 14 (1979), 371–91.

15. Kenneth P. Oakley, "Emergence of Higher Thought 3.0–0.2 Ma B.P.," *Philosophical Transactions of the Royal Society of London* B292 (1981), 205–11. Other examples have sometimes been proposed; Oakley's paper, however, is paradigmatic of the general approach.

Second, Neanderthal people colored certain sites, such as burials, with red ochre.[16] It is not immediately relevant here whether this characterization of the Neanderthal deposits is sustainable—whether, for instance, the ochre indicates the status of the site, somehow already preconceived as special. For my purposes, one may ask whether the use and manipulation of pigments was continuous with the emergence of image making. Is the manipulation of pigments the "origin" of image making?

In considering this question, it is important to note that a color patch does not necessarily have a status as a representation: that a surface is colored does not necessarily mean that the color stands iconically for something.[17] Moreover, even when used representationally, color marking is only one element of a whole package of techniques used to make images. Finally, color seems to have been a subsidiary element in the Aurignacian period. Although we cannot be completely sure—given the fugitive nature of some pigments—it seems that color helps the maker of an outline to distinguish figure from ground.[18] At the moment, the record suggests that color (at least in the Paleolithic traditions of southwestern Europe) came to have a truly representational use *in itself* only in the Magdalenian period, some ten or more millennia after the emergence of the representational line. At this point, in Lascaux, Pech-Merle, and the other Magdalenian painted caves (about 15,000 B.C.) color was sometimes used to represent the three values of surface, texture, and volume. In the Magdalenian, then, color became one representational—analogical, semantically "dense," continuously modulated—means of reference, of creating meaning.

In sum, like line, color marking is very ancient, long antedating the manufacture of images in the Aurignacian. It can be used in the manufacture of images. But image making is not equivalent to the use of color and apparently before the Magdalenian was not significantly dependent upon it.

A third variety of extrasomatic Representation, or "symboling" technology, marking, bears the closest relation to image making. Image making is obviously a *kind* of marking. In theory, however, the distinctions between various kinds of marks deserve to be rigorously observed (Fig. 2.5).

Nonsemiotic marks may be important archaeological documents—for instance, as incisions made to test the cutting power of a tool—but are not immediately relevant to this discussion (but see Chapters 3 and 4). Semiotic marks signify in some way. They can be divided into self-sufficient marks and marks (as ordinary usage has it) with semantic value, that is, marks possessing some kind of reference.[19]

16. S. W. Edwards, "Nonutilitarian Activities in the Lower Paleolithic: A Look at the Two Kinds of Evidence," *Current Anthropology* 19 (1978), 135–37; E. Wreschner, "Red Ochre and Human Evolution: A Case for Discussion," *Current Anthropology* 21 (1980), 631–44; Alexander Marshack, "On Paleolithic Ochre and the Early Uses of Color and Symbol," *Current Anthropology* 22 (1981), 188–91.

17. Even if the ochre stood for "death," "danger," or "difference," it would not be an *iconic* symbol; ochre iconically might stand for blood. It is hard to see how we could prove that Neanderthals maintained any of these possible symbolic associations.

18. Delluc and Delluc, "Les manifestations graphiques," fig. 95, no. 8, here Figure 2.2*a*.

19. The usages adopted here highlight an important distinction for my purposes, although other categories are certainly available. The term "semiotic" is rather loosely applied to admit any marking produced deliberately and for its own sake, and therefore in a sense meaningfully. A semiotic mark only has semantic value, is referential, if it stands for an object besides or beyond

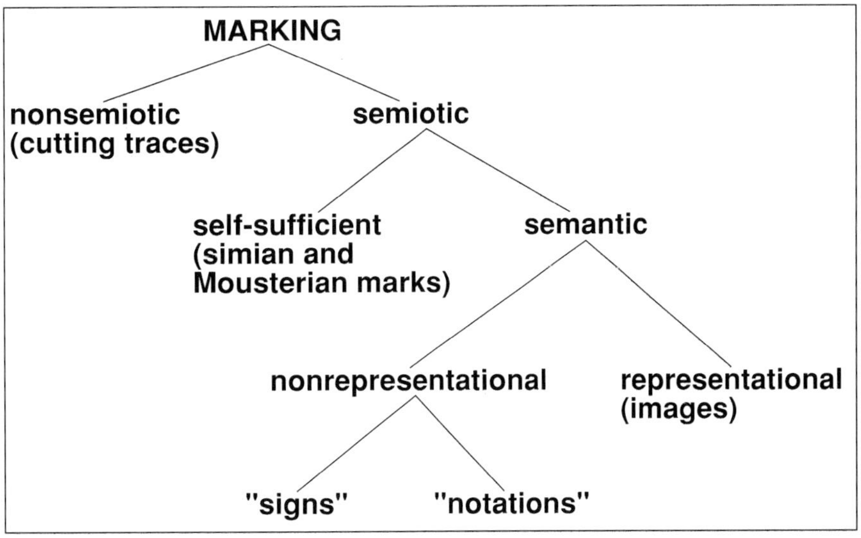

Fig. 2.5. Types of marking.

Self-sufficient marks appear to have a long if somewhat obscure history in primate and hominid evolution. Apes (chimpanzees and gorillas) and some monkeys can be induced to scribble.[20] The scribbling seems to exhibit an awareness of the self-sufficient graphic qualities of the mark, such as its "balancing" against the edge of a surface or in relation to another form (Fig. 2.6), and some developmental elaboration, possibly due merely to the mastery of a precise grip on the instrument. Although an ape apparently can recognize objects in both black-and-white and full-color photographs, subsequently identifying the real object it has only seen pictured, it is not known whether this training could be made to lead to an ability to correlate marks the ape could produce with the traces of objects it saw in photographs or to any similar response that might result in the "spontaneous" production of representation.[21] There is little evidence that the ape ever attaches

itself. Simian scribbles probably fall to one side of this division (they may even be nonsemiotic, but this is a primatologist's worry); "signs," "notations," and representations—what current theory often calls writing, in an extended sense of the term (see Chapter 4)—fall to the other side. Arguably, some simian markings "stand for" pleasure or a reward; some abstract "representations" operate self-referentially. I do not take up these complexities here.

20. Influential early studies include Paul H. Schiller, "Figural Preferences in the Drawings of a Chimpanzee," *Journal of Comparative and Physiological Psychology* 44 (1951), 101–111; Desmond Morris, *The Biology of Art: A Study of the Picture-Making Behavior of the Great Apes and Its Relationship to Human Art* (New York, 1962); D. A. Smith, "Systematic Study of Chimpanzee Drawing," *Journal of Comparative and Physiological Psychology* 82 (1973), 406–14; A. Whiten, "Primate Perception and Aesthetics," in *Beyond Aesthetics: Investigations into the Nature of Visual Art*, ed. Don Brothwell (London, 1976), 18–40; J. M. Brewster and R. K. Siegel, "Reinforced Drawing in *Macaca mulatta*," *Journal of Human Evolution* 5 (1976), 345–47.

21. For the initial research on apes, see R. K. Davenport and C. M. Rogers, "Perception of Photographs by Apes," *Behavior* 39 (1971), 318–20; R. K. Davenport, C. M. Rogers, and I. S. Russell, "Cross-Modal Perception in Apes," *Neuropsychologia* 11 (1973), 21–28; and idem, "Cross-Modal Perception in Apes: Altered Visual Cues and Delay," *Neuropsychologia* 13 (1975), 229–35. On monkeys, see R. R. Zimmerman and J. Hochberg, "Responses of Infant Monkeys to Pictorial Representations of a Learned Visual Discrimination," *Psychonomic Science* 18 (1970), 307–8; see also various doubts expressed in E. Winner and G. Ettlinger, "Do Chimpanzees Recognize Photographs as Representations of Objects?" *Neuro-*

semantic value to the marks it produces. To date, no image making has ever appeared in the careers of primate markers.[22]

Self-sufficient marks produced by prehistoric hominids include the clusters of scratches found on objects made by Neanderthals (Fig. 2.7, and compare Fig. 5.17) and the "meanders," or finger-paintings, traced by *Homo sapiens sapiens* on parietal surfaces.[23] Like modern telephone-pad doodling, these marks do not initially or necessarily possess but may quickly acquire meanings, either representational or "notational." But we should not assume that just because a creature produces self-sufficient marks or scribbles, it will inevitably begin to make marks that refer, notations or images. The consolidation of a semantic value for a scribbled or doodled mark is a distinct event.

Efforts to interpret Neanderthal scratches semantically have been frustrating and unconvincing. By contrast, some of the Upper Paleolithic marks thought to have been made by *Homo sapiens sapiens* are much more plausibly considered to have meaning. In my terminology, this meaning is nonrepresentational. These markings include the "notations" identified by Alexander Marshack and perhaps some of the "signs" in Aurignacian and later graphic work thought by André Leroi-Gourhan and some of his followers to be sexual symbols.[24] The "female genitals" in some Aurignacian engravings (see Fig. 3.3) may be not images but rather some kind of sign; their form seems to be highly standardized. A substantial literature has been devoted to these puzzling manifestations and to the difficulty of distinguishing them—assuming that we even wish to do so (see Chapters

psychologia 17 (1979), 413–20, and review, advances, and further references in J. C. Tolan, C. M. Rogers, and D. R. Malone, "Cross-Modal Matching in Monkeys: Altered Visual Cues and Delay," *Neuropsychologia* 19 (1981), 289–300.

22. The Gardners' chimp Moja attached "word" labels to what we would judge as nonrepresentational scribbles (R. A. Gardner and B. Gardner, "Comparative Psychology and Language Acquisition," *Annals of the New York Academy of Sciences* 309 [1978], 37–76). Did she see her scribbles as objects? Observed by Premack in an ingenious study, the chimp Sarah "put together a face" from "primitive elements" provided by the experimenter. Although this study deserves careful attention, the chimp was not engaged in semantically "dense" production (D. Premack, "Putting a Face Together," *Science* 188 [1975], 228–36).

23. Pioneering studies include François Bordes, "Os percé moustérien et os gravé acheuléen du Pech de l'Azé," *Quaternaria* 11 (1969), 1–6; Alexander Marshack, "Some Implications of the Paleolithic Symbolic Evidence for the Origin of Language," *Current Anthropology* 17 (1976), 274–81; and idem, "The Meander as a System: The Analysis and Recognition of Iconographic Units in Upper Paleolithic Composition," in *Form in Indigenous Art*, ed. Peter J. Ucko (Canberra, 1977), 286–317.

24. For Marshack's analysis, see esp. his "Cognitive Aspects of Upper Paleolithic Engraving," *Current Anthropology* 13 (1972), 445–77; *The Roots of Civilization: The Cognitive Beginnings of Man's First Art, Symbol, and Notation* (New York, 1972; 2d ed., New York, 1992), and "Upper Paleolithic Symbol Systems of the Russian Plain: Cognitive and Comparative Analysis," *Current Anthropology* 20 (1979), 271–311. Quotation marks are used here because the logical requirements for a notation are quite strict (see Goodman, *Languages of Art*); many symbol systems, although not representational, do not fulfill them, Marshack's marks perhaps among them. Unfortunately, we do not have a good descriptive term for such systems. For Leroi-Gourhan's analysis, see esp. his *Treasures;* "Les signes pariétaux comme 'marqueurs' ethniques," in *Altamira Symposium* (Madrid, 1980), 289–94; and *The Dawn of European Art* (Cambridge, 1982). For other accounts, see Joachim Hahn, "Aurignacian Signs, Pendants, and Art Objects in Central and Eastern Europe," *World Archaeology* 3 (1972), 253–66; F. Collot, M. Boumokra, and R. Cassé, "Les signes dans l'art pariétal: Mode d'étude des representations non animalières," *Etudes Préhistoriques* (Société Préhistorique de l'Ardèche) 2 (1972), 22–26.

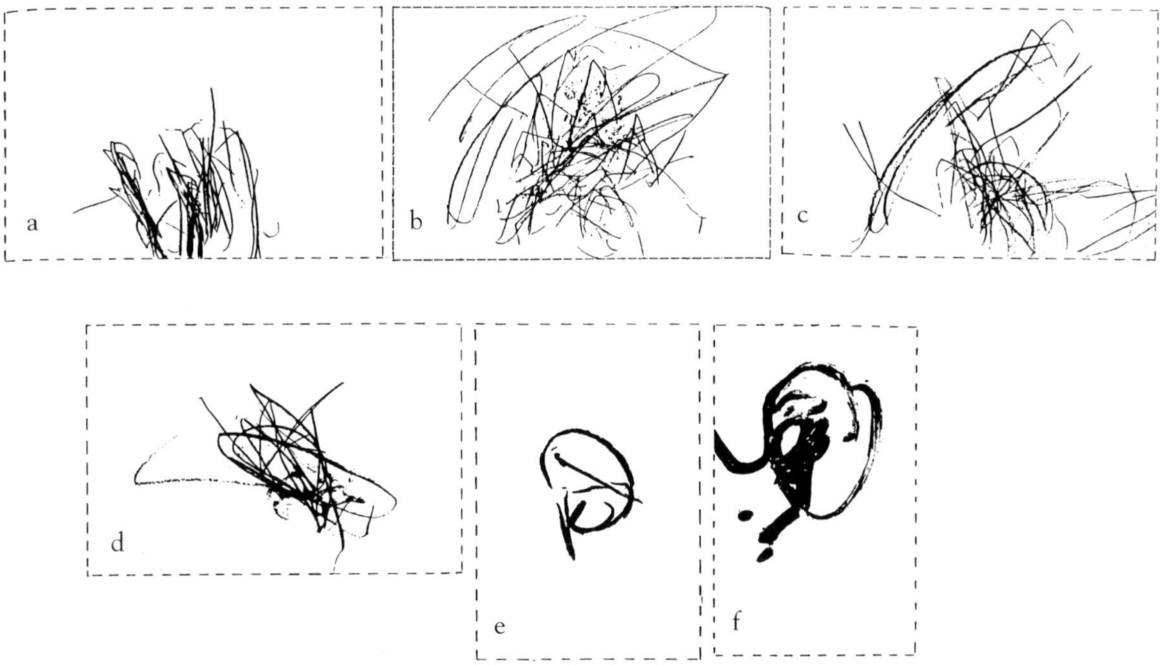

Fig. 2.6. Drawings by chimpanzees. *a–d.* Typical clusterings and strokes. *e.* "Advanced" control over mark making. *f.* Image of a face by a human infant, about thirty months old.

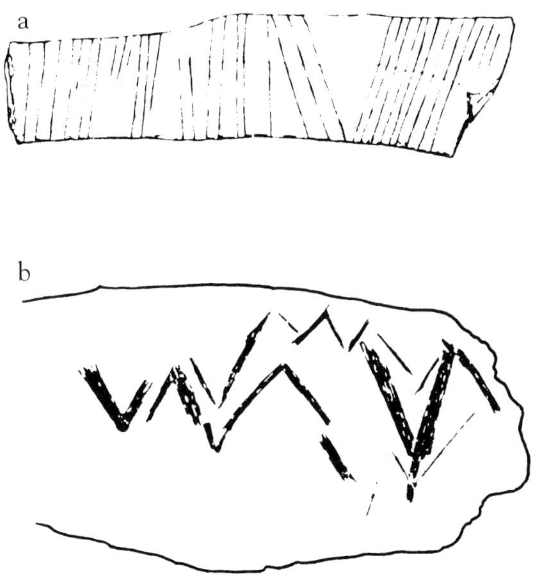

Fig. 2.7. Nonfigurative, "self-sufficient" marks of the Mousterian (Neanderthal) period. *a.* Incised bone from La Ferrassie, France. *b.* Engraved bone from Bacho Kiro, Bulgaria.

4, 5, and 8)—from an amorphous mass of similar-looking but probably self-sufficient scratchings, doodles, or "ornaments." The question now, however, is rather different: among marks with semantic value, how do we distinguish between representational and nonrepresentational?

At the extremes, the difference between an image and a notation seems clear enough. In one standard definition, the image is analogical, the variables of line and color continuously varying.[25] A notation is digital; its characters are discrete. But there are well-known problems with this definition, true enough as far as it goes. Images certainly can be produced using a thoroughly "digital" technology. An image produced by pecking out separate marks, like some Aurignacian and later engravings, is digital in this sense. Furthermore, images can be used as characters in a notational system, as in the classic ideographic or hieroglyphic writing systems of the ancient world (for one example of relations between pictures and pseudohieroglyphic characters with pictorial forms, see Chapter 7). Perhaps less commonly, a notational system can be represented in an image. For such cases, only contexts of use or knowledge of certain conventions—or, better yet, information about the history of the mark—will tell us precisely what we are seeing (see Chapter 1).

Many commentators want to draw the distinction completely otherwise. The image *looks like* its subject, whereas the notational sign is associated with its object in a purely arbitrary way. Leaving aside many logical pitfalls in this solution (for instance, the perception of relevant similarity is administered by "arbitrary conventions"),[26] it is troubling in its potential for ethnocentrism. Since we know little about the subject matter of Paleolithic markings, how do we know that a marking refers "arbitrarily" except by relying on what seems representationally unintelligible *to us?*

A rough-and-ready approach finds some middle ground. First, we assume tentatively that similarity between sign and object was much the same for Aurignacian people as it is for present-day users of signs. Second, we assume that most early markings were not deviously sophisticated notations using images or pictures of extremely unlikely visual appearances we could never expect to identify. However plausible, these *are* very strong assumptions, and they *may* mislead us in dealing with very alien marking practices.

Iconicity, then, is the most common *test* for representation (although it is not its only property).[27] In the image, in contrast to nonrepresentational varieties of reference, the "form," the physical character of the sign, is inseparable from its "content." Thus, in linguistic notation, A is acceptably A, a, *A*, *a*, and so on; in an image, the apple is always no more and no less than *this particular* apple. In an approximation of the case, representation works through rule-governed, arbitrary similarities between properties of things and properties of the learned representational repertory. In representation, form is the site of the

25. Bach, "Part of What a Picture Is."

26. Paul Ziff, "On What a Painting Represents," *Journal of Philosophy* 57 (1960), 647–54; Patrick Maynard, "Depiction, Vision, and Convention," *American Philosophical Quarterly* 9 (1972), 243–50; T. G. Roupas, "Information and Pictorial Representation," in *The Arts and Cognition*, ed. D. Perkins and B. Leondar (Baltimore, 1977), 48–79.

27. Here it is impossible to undertake a rehabilitation of the notion of iconicity. Iconicity is a far broader phenomenon than the "realism" of a representation, narrowly conceived as a resemblance to the visual or natural appearances of objects. A sign may be iconic to spatial relations on a plane or to many nonvisual orders. See further Chapter 3, note 24.

creation of meaning, for potentially, at any rate, every modulation in form to the minutest degree has a meaning and a similar in the world. Iconicity is not a formula for getting denotation "just right"; it is a program for adjusting reference to "just-just right," "just-just-just right," and so on, ad infinitum. Therefore it can be expected to be well suited to the transmission of certain kinds of information and limited or even confusing for the transmission of other kinds.

These considerations suggest that the varieties of Representation and of extrasomatic "symboling" technology should be kept quite distinct. We need a specific argument—call it an origin myth—to show how the diagrams of the logical relations between modes of Representation, or "symboling," and of marking (Figs. 2.1, 2.4, 2.5) might be converted into a *history*. We need an origin myth for representation *as such*.

The most widely influential origin myth is the argument from projection, stated in archaeology and art history by E. H. Gombrich and found in one form or another in many other psychological, anthropological, and aesthetic studies. This account proposes that images emerge—presumably continuously in history—when human beings impose semantic values upon vaguely suggestive shapes preexisting in nature, like the cracks and stains on the aged wall cited by Leonardo da Vinci as the most instructive study for a young artist. At some point in prehistory, this supposedly occurred for the very first time; "the animal shape," Gombrich claims, "had been discovered somewhere in a rock." Supposedly these projections were then copied, "matched" or tested against reality, and incorporated into artistic traditions.[28]

Largely a hypothetical construction, the origin myth of projection really rests upon only one empirically observed fact of Paleolithic image making. Almost every study of cave marking notes the incorporation of "natural" features of the rock surface into some finished representations. What should be made of this fact? For Gombrich, the implication is clear: the image was *suggested by* the natural features—it was imposed upon them as their organic completion, as the *projection* of what the artist had seen in the vague outlines.

This view ignores a great deal. First, there are all kinds of irregularities on the surfaces that did *not* suggest particular images to Paleolithic draftsmen. The argument from projection totally fails to account for the peculiar selectivity of the early image maker's projects. Stains, cracks, and humps in the surface should suggest all manner of similars and result in an endlessly diversifying representational practice. Instead, however, we find only a few themes rendered, over ten or more millennia, in a comparatively consistent style.

Second, the account conveniently ignores the obvious truth that *any* representation anywhere must always accommodate the qualities of its surface. If for as yet unknown reasons the image maker desired to work in deep caves, he necessarily worked with the surfaces he could find. If a surface was irregular, then as a matter of course his representation would incorporate irregularities. Presuming that the image maker knew what it was he wished to represent, he very reasonably made occasional use of natural features that could assist him in his project.

28. E. H. Gombrich, *Art and Illusion*, 2d ed. (Princeton, 1961), 107–9, 188–89.

The argument really requires a convincing proof that Paleolithic image makers made an unpredictably intensive and intentional use of underlying surfaces *and* that they could not have made images *without* the stimulation of underlying features. It is, however, not at all clear how this proof could plausibly compare the completely unmeasurable fact that image makers did *not* use any number of "suggestive" natural features with any visual conviction that they did, in limited but striking instances, use some of them. In fact, in the Upper Paleolithic period in southwestern Europe the exploitation of features of the natural rock surface is principally a characteristic of later Magdalenian representations (about 15,000 B.C.). By contrast, earlier Aurignacian engravers selected relatively smooth and unblemished surfaces. The exploitation of surface features in Magdalenian image making seems to be associated with the general Magdalenian elaboration of the representational values of variables other than the simple line—of color, volume, space, and, here, surface texture. Like line and color, a natural feature of the rock could be made to have a representational status.

In sum, the hypothesis that images were projections onto surfaces is unsustainable. Nevertheless, one fundamental intuition of Gombrich's idealist and intentionalist history—with which the materialist approach favored in this book must be contrasted (see further Chapters 4 and 8)—does not necessarily collapse under these objections. For idealism, the mind imposes representation on a disorder of prerepresentational potentialities, whether clusters of nonrepresentational lines scratched for other reasons, qualities of a blot of color, or an appealing stretch of surface. The mind finds forms for meanings: it sees the possibility of similarity between natural or human-made form and something else in the world and determines to realize this insight in a permanent medium. Therefore an explanation for the emergence of representation must lie in some capacity or intention of the mind. Idealist history and archaeology are committed to seeing the emergence of representation as due inevitably to the progressive evolution of cognition, most usually of "aesthetic" intelligence and sensibility—even though these cognitive capacities cannot be identified archaeologically apart from the very representational practices I am seeking to explain (see further Chapter 4). Idealist writers have not usually attempted to show how such capacities were ever constructed historically.

In Gombrich's account, the mind is supposed to see objects, natural or human-made forms, *as images* (not, in fact, merely as other objects) and to find a means of marking down this experience. It is not clear where the Aurignacian mind suddenly derived or developed this remarkable capacity of projecting, of "abstracting" from the seeing of objects, if not in the learning of representation itself. When they assume these capacities as existing from the beginning, in a fundamental sense Gombrich and many other psychologists and historians with similar views simply wave away the real problem of the origins of representation: image making is just something the human mind is capable of doing.[29] In my view, it is useful to reverse the standard idealist claim, immediately simplify-

29. Although it need not do so, this view usually goes along with other views about human "creativity" or the ineffability of invention. For example, in George Kubler's account in *The Shape of Time: Remarks on the History of Things* (New Haven, Conn., 1962) the infinitely inventive human mind intervenes in material history to deliver itself of free, creative, mysterious "prime objects." The complex relation between intentionalist accounts of the history of consciousness and formalist, aestheticist interests in the history and criticism of rep-

ing it and rendering it psychologically and historically credible. Objects are not seen as marks; rather, *marks are seen as objects.* (In both cases, of course, "seeing-as" plays a role, and I shall return to an analysis of its structure in making marks and seeing objects in them.)

For many hundreds of millennia before the emergence of image making, hominids had been making marks and recognizing degrees of similarity (as close as perceptual identity) between them, and examining things in the object world, including manufactured things, and recognizing degrees of similarity between them as well. My account requires only the following four simple terms:

1. mark = mark (one mark is perceptually identical to another);
2. mark / mark (one mark is perceptually similar to but not identical with another);
3. thing = thing (perceptual identity);
4. thing / thing (perceptual similarity).

Because of the unpredictable possibility that information in the structure of the light array presented to the eye is ambiguous,[30] a mark can readily be taken for a thing:

5. mark = thing.

We can imagine hundreds of variations upon this chance: a blot is taken for a hole, a line for an edge, and so forth. By (1) and (3), this chance happening is repeatable in different, later contexts:

6. where $\text{mark}_1 = \text{thing}_1$, if $\text{mark}_2 = \text{mark}_1$, then $\text{mark}_2 = \text{thing}_1$.

Furthermore, the nature of the mark can be slightly varied in contexts of repetition. Thus a new mark may be identical with or similar to a new thing:

7. where $\text{mark}_1 = \text{thing}_1$, if $\text{mark}_2 / \text{mark}_1$, then $\text{mark}_2 = \text{thing}_2 / \text{thing}_1$.

Several marks can also be made at the same time in a series, only one of which is perceptually identical to anything:

8. $\text{thing}_1 = \text{mark}_1 / \text{mark}_2$ ($\neq \text{thing}_2$)

resentation has been made clear by Paul de Man (see Chapter 8), among others.

30. Excellent accounts of various relevant phenomena can be found in Gibson's *Perception of the Visual World* and *The Senses Considered as Perceptual Systems*, Gombrich's *Art and Illusion*, and Marr's *Vision*. For important general reflections on "seeing-as," see Michael Polyani, "What Is a Painting?" *British Journal of Aesthetics* 10 (1970), 225–36; T. E. Wilkerson, "Seeing As," *Mind* 82 (1973), 481–96; Richard Wollheim, *Art and Its Objects*, 2d ed. (Cambridge, 1980), 205–26; Malcolm Budd, "Wittgenstein on Seeing Aspects," *Mind* 96 (1986), 1–17. A wider context can be approached in David Michael Levin, ed., *Modernity and the Hegemony of Vision* (Berkeley and Los Angeles, 1993), and Stephen Mulhall, *On Being in the World: Wittgenstein and Heidegger on Seeing Aspects* (London, 1990).

or

9. $thing_1 = mark_1 / mark_2 / mark_3 = thing_2$,

and so forth and so on. In other words, a series of marks may be partly dependent upon perceptual identities with things and partly detached; this is a crucial feature of representations, which are usually much more than trompe l'oeil illusionistic replicas of the simplest seeing-as. The whole series is, of course, repeatable and also variable in later contexts:

10. $mark_1 + mark_2 + mark_3 = mark_4 + mark_5 + mark_6$;
11. $mark_1 + mark_2 + mark_3 / mark_4 + mark_5 + mark_6$, where $mark_3 / mark_6$.

All proportional, transformational, and topological variations—such as rotations in the positions of identical marks in a series—are relevant here. Although the series of marks (that is, the image) may be generated initially in the experience of perceptual identities between certain marks and certain things, in a series of repetitions the initial identities may fade away, and new ones may become established. Where $mark_1 = thing_1$, and so forth, we have a possible progression:

12. $mark_1 + mark_2 + mark_3 = thing_1 + thing_2 + thing_3$;
13. $mark_1 + mark_2 + mark_4$ $(/mark_3) = thing_1 + thing_2 + thing_4$ $(/mark_4$ [by (7)]);
14. $mark_1 + mark_4 + mark_5$ $(/mark_4) = thing_1 + thing_4 + thing_5$ $(/mark_5)$;
15. $mark_4 + mark_5 + mark_6$ $(/mark_5) = thing_4 + thing_5 + thing_6$ $(/mark_6)$ . . .

Many related progressions are possible. Starting from one set of perceptual identities and similarities, internal variations lead one to the possibility of other sets—which are now experienced not *in relation to the outside world* as such but only in and by the image. In such processes, a series of marks may become similar to but not identical with things in the world:

16. where $mark_1 = thing_1 / thing_2 / thing_3 = mark_2$, $mark_1 / thing_2 / mark_2$.

One may seek out satisfactorily identical or similar marks for these things, which then become *merely represented* things (they have *no* perceptual identicals in the world):

17. $mark_1 = thing_1 / thing_2 / thing_3 = mark_2$;
18. $mark_1 = thing_1 + mark_2 =$ (or /) $thing_2 + mark_3 = thing_3$.

We do not need to investigate all of the complex variations we could play on these formal progressions to see, in sum, that the image can be derived from simple identities and similarities between marks, things, and the chance perception of marks as things.[31]

31. That the relevant identities and degrees and respects of similarity must be intersubjectively (conventionally) specified does not tell against the argument at all. I could build into terms 1 through 4 qualitative or

By the Aurignacian period, hominids had been making marks for hundreds of millennia. If we accept Marshack's controversial assessment of the scratchings on and punctations of Mousterian and Upper Paleolithic artifacts, marking already depended significantly upon the *intentional regulation* of similarity relations between marks for the purposes of symboling or "notation."[32] In principle, the similarities and differences between marks in a series could be made to signify the similarities and differences between groups of extensions (for instance, groups of different kinds of days, animals, or celestial phenomena). We do not need to enter the detailed debates over Marshack's claims. Semantic *or* nonsemantic marks must have been recognized as identical or similar within a recognized tolerance of variation.

For thousands of millennia, the primate and hominid visual systems had experienced perceptual ambiguity (as we know from evolutionary responses like stereoscopic vision) and had recognized identities and similarities. (Notice, of course, that "recognition" can be taken to be an intentional act [see further Chapters 4 and 8]; in the present chapter, the term is used merely to designate perceptual disambiguation in a context of environmental action requiring information appropriate to completing tasks in and surviving the dangers of that environment.) The toolmaking habits of at least a million years show that hominids planned action with the advance "knowledge" that similar actions similarly performed would reliably result in similar effects (for problems, see Chapter 4). The history of toolmaking could be described in a very generalized way as the gradual introduction of variation through shifting occasionally from relations of identity to relations of similarity in production. Contexts of use determined whether it was worth shifting back to relations of identity, that is, whether it was worth preserving a new form introduced in an earlier shift. The real tree of development, then, was not a simple bifurcation program but a complex program of identities and similarities reproduced differentially. The history of image making could be written in much the same way.

The conceptual logic of representation requires only the perception of identities and similarities between marks and marks and between things and things ([1]–[4] above), abilities possibly documented in the earliest toolmaking horizons (see further Chapter 4). In addition, however, the *probability* of seeing marks as things varies directly with the quantity of available marks. The more one marks, the more likely one will be to produce at some point a mark that will be seen, by him or by someone else, as a thing.

Although it is not the topic of this book, this finding should be associated directly with the psychophysics of light and visual perception. Information about edges and depth is potentially transmitted very ambiguously in perception (not to speak of "psychological" constructions, such as the supposed "scotomas," which interfere with a complete or exact

---

quantitative specifications of relevance and degree—providing a logical account of "style" (see Chapter 6)—that are avoided here for the sake of simplicity. In fact, the argument implies that information transmission in the image channel is almost infinitely plastic (partly because an image/mark series depends upon recursive and combinatorial operations) and could be (historically has been) developed in many directions. Preserving particular identities, reproducing them, and varying the degrees and respects of similarity is the conventionalized, or "cultural," work of representation—the province of art history in its traditional form.

32. See Marshack's "Cognitive Aspects of Upper Paleolithic Engraving," *The Roots of Civilization*, and "Some Implications of the Paleolithic Symbolic Evidence for the Origin of Language."

pickup of visual information [see further Chapter 12]). Therefore the addition of edge shifts and depth changes to a visual field increases the probability that perception will construe ambiguous information erroneously—will see edges or depth where edges and depth do not exist, and not see them where they do. Marks can seem to establish edges that do not exist, such as a texture change on a surface or the existence of a corner. In general, marks add ambiguous edge shifts and depth changes to a visual field.

It follows that continually marking the world will continually increase the probability that marks will be seen as things. Eventually, very complex clusters of marks—it does not matter whether they have been deliberately clustered or just happen to be seen together—will result in occasional perceptual interpretations of marks as very complex things, such as the closed contours of natural objects. The manufacture of marks on surfaces and all manner of other activities, from body ornament to building, potentially add marks and color patches to the world. In sum, the emergence of representation is the predictable logical and perceptual consequence of *the increasing elaboration of the human-made visual world*.

By the Aurignacian period, I suggest, the visual world of southwestern Europe had become organized in precisely the right way—had accumulated complex clusters of complex marks—for the initial interpretations to occur regularly and predictably. (The "canonical" matrix for depiction, one might say, is the replication of human-made visual ambiguity; see further Chapter 3.) The interpretations most likely to occur and to be preserved, reproduced, and varied were construals of complex marks as animals or features of animals.[33]

The effort to investigate the primal experience of seeing-as is quite predictable from the

33. Why anyone wanted to record the experience of seeing-as, why it happened (among other times) in the Aurignacian and (among other places) in southwestern France and Spain, and why its earliest efforts were images of animals are, strictly speaking, matters for the social and "cultural" history of a particular replicatory tradition (see note 31 above). Particular users of images investigate particular relations of perceptual identity and similarity. Whether their investigations are "culturally determined" or whether their culture is "constructed" according to the nature of their Representational activity is still an open question. At any rate, these investigations into the potentialities of a single information channel have not ceased in the entire long history of representation since the Upper Paleolithic. In my view, these questions cannot be solved unless the conceptual logic of representation is understood along the lines suggested here. In itself, the analysis may not answer them; it is not primarily an account of particular historical images. This is, however, an analytic advantage; ultimately we need not be committed irrevocably to the idea that the elaboration of the human-made world and conceptualization of representation occurred specifically in southwestern France and Spain in the Aurignacian period. Since evidence to the contrary has not appeared, I have written here as if this were so. We can most productively attempt to answer a question that is archaeologically accessible: what did the conceptualization of representation involve? Analysis of when, where, and why requires a set of extra assumptions (for instance, images are likely to depict qualities of things not readily denoted in other semiotic channels). Although not uninteresting, these cannot be developed here. From an anthropologist's point of view, the question is really being posed, not solved. For possible Mousterian Aurignacian scenarios, see Margaret W. Conkey, "On the Origins of Paleolithic Art: A Review and Some Critical Thoughts," in *The Mousterian Legacy: Human Biocultural Change in the Upper Pleistocene*, British Archaeological Reports, International Series 164, ed. Erik Trinkaus (Oxford, 1983), 201–27; idem, "To Find Ourselves: Art and Social Geography of Prehistoric Hunter-Gatherers," in *Past and Present in Hunter-Gatherer Studies*, ed. Carmel Schrire (New York, 1984), 253–76; Clive Gamble, "Interaction and Alliance in Paleolithic Society," *Man* 17 (1982), 92–107; and John Pfeiffer, *The Creative Explosion: An Inquiry into the Origins of Art and Religion* (New York, 1982).

initial ambiguity of seeing marks as things. Usually almost immediately, the visual system detects that it has failed to resolve ambiguity correctly. A movement of the head or refocusing of foveal vision (highly developed in the higher primates and humans) will immediately reveal that a shape in the distance is really a mark on a nearby surface or that a texture gradient such as fur or some other natural substance is really just a blot of colors. (It is also possible, of course, for a movement of the head or refocusing of foveal vision to *eliminate* a perception of a mark or of a thing; this process, opposite to the one considered here, might have an equally important role in the construction of significance [see further Chapter 12].) The visual system usually discovers the *dis*similarity of things, marks, and marks-as-things, occasionally ambiguously conflated. However, though the "illusion" vanishes and ambiguity is resolved, one has already learned that the nearby surface mark can stand for the distant thing or quality. The ambiguity can be investigated and the "illusion" confirmed as such by repeating the mark and the viewing conditions as far as possible—and by varying the mark and the conditions. In other words, we can predict the relatively swift elaboration of complex representational conventions.

Up to this point, I have avoided discussion of the semantic values of Paleolithic images, often the prime focus of studies of Paleolithic "art." In my opinion, the "meaning" of Paleolithic images will not—by the logic of the case, cannot—tell us about the constitution or origins of the image channel itself; "meaning" exists only *in* an information channel. Switching an information channel on is, by definition, a semantic affair; by definition, messages in the channel have semantic values. But we must describe the emergence of the image channel, its switching on, without at all assuming preexisting "meanings" or that the organism "knows" what it will represent before being able to represent it. I have tried to avoid assuming that the prehistoric mind already possessed certain "meanings" and imposed them upon brute matters, whether stones or marks or reflexes or sound waves, thereby transforming matter into symbols.

It is more desirable to work up to this point—the possibility of a semantic, of symbolic knowledge, of "mind"—on the basis of entirely different premises. I focus on the conceptualization of the image channel. If we are to avoid absurdity, we must assume this conceptualization could not have been that of determining in advance what the channel would inform its users about and then of building the channel itself (that is, of using language$_2$ to design language$_1$, and language$_3$ to design language$_2$, ad infinitum). I claim that this conceptualization is thoroughly predictable in a certain physical context; we do not need to invoke new capacities or creativities to explain it, and conversely, in itself it cannot be used as evidence for the emergence of new capacities or creativities. As I have suggested, the structure of the image channel and the properties of images can be generated from seeing marks as things, an automatic response of the hominid visual system in certain kinds of relation to the structure of light energy in the world. The user immediately acquires a semantic system, the possibility of using the mark to stand for the thing, as he automatically resolves ambiguity. In the repetition and variation of seeing marks as things, the particular semantic values of the image channel will automatically be "discovered," according to the particular relations of identity and similarity the channel user investigates.

The story of origins I have sketched has several advantages over the traditional argument from projection. First, we do not need to assume that representation emerges because of the appearance of aesthetic sensibility or other mental capacities that cannot be observed archaeologically. We can document the perception of identities and similarities in toolmaking and other concrete human activities. We avoid the idealist tautology of supposing that the mind somehow knew what it wanted to represent before it learned to represent—because all it had to do was "project." This is not to say that projection is not a real and vital cognitive activity; in the intersubjective human lifeworld, the lifeworld of our "cultures," it is both the source and the mechanism of meaning. But projection, as I suggested in the last section of the Introduction, is historically emergent in—rather than an essential capacity of—human thought.

Second, we can make sense of the evolutionary record as we have it. The technology of representation—the scratching of lines, the manipulation of pigments—has a long history in primate and hominid evolution before its conceptualization as such. Mark making occurred long before the Upper Paleolithic. But it was the total accumulation of marks in the Upper Paleolithic—as I have put it, the elaboration of the human-made visual world—that predictably resulted, through humans' seeing marks as things, in the emergence of the specifically representational mark.

Third, we can account for the features of the earliest representational material as we know it. The Aurignacian outlines (Fig. 2.2, and see Figs. 3.2, 3.3, 3.4), near straight lines and simple C curves, were only a step away from nonrepresentational marks. The majority of the "figure" parts could be construed nonrepresentationally as easily as representationally; they may or may not be signs, and the difference may or may not matter. Once marks were perceived as things, however, the full analogical, expressive power of the line could be quickly and logically derived and even detached from mere experiences of perceptual ambiguity. When representation was activated in this way, it quickly proliferated: it was a powerful adaptation. As soon as *one* complex of lines could be interpreted representationally, potentially all lines could; all lines became either representational or not. The emergence of images was, then, a "threshold discovery," like several others in human evolution.[34] Where before nothing was possible, a single conceptualization made possible everything in a very extended domain whose limits are not even known today. If meaning "is not everywhere, it is nowhere."[35] Form appeared for the unformed.

Fourth, we remain sensitive to the logical differences between representation and other marking strategies or sign systems. The whole "figurative system" of Paleolithic symbolism probably depended upon the simultaneous use of several sign systems, many of which may be older than the image system, but we can begin to understand their relationship and offer decodings only if we know what each system is capable of doing and how it evolved.

If we do not equate the origin of representation with other, related problems in the much larger and longer development of human ordering behavior, "symboling" tech-

34. Glynn Isaac, "Chronology and Tempo of Cultural Change During the Pleistocene," in *Calibration of Hominoid Evolution*, ed. W. W. Bishop, J. A. Miller, and S. Cole (Toronto, 1972), 381–430; H. Martin Wobst, "Stylistic Behavior and Information Exchange," in *For the Director: Research Essays in Honor of James B. Griffin*, Museum of Anthropology Anthropological Papers 61, ed. Charles E. Cleland (Ann Arbor, Mich., 1977), 317–42.

35. Claude Lévi-Strauss, *Totemism*, trans. Rodney Needham (Boston, 1963), 91.

nology, or marking, and do not assume that *Homo sapiens sapiens* was suddenly and mysteriously gifted only 30,000 years ago with a uniquely new projective, aesthetic faculty, the question of the "origins of art" probably reappears as a question about the biological and conceptual history of image making—about certain historical replications.[36]

36. Since this book was prepared for publication, three important publications relevant to the topics of this and the next two chapters have appeared; unfortunately, I have not been able to take account of them. See Francesco d'Errico, "A New Model and Its Implications for the Origin of Writing: The La Marche Antler Revisited," *Cambridge Archaeological Journal* 5 (1995), 163–206; James Elkins, "The Impossibility of Close Reading: The Case of Alexander Marshack," *Current Anthropology* 37 (1996), 185–226 (with a comment by the present author, pp 204–7, sketching an overall perspective on Marshack's approach); and Alexander Marshack, "A Middle Paleolithic Symbolic Composition from the Golan Heights: The Earliest Known Depictive Image," *Current Anthropology* 37 (1996), 357–64.

Chapter 3

Replication and Depiction in Paleolithic Art

Since we overcame the error of supposing that the forgetting we are familiar with signified a destruction of the memory-trace—that is, its annihilation—we have been inclined to take the opposite view, that in mental life nothing which has once been formed can perish, that everything is somehow preserved and that in suitable circumstances (when, for instance, regression goes back far enough) it can once more be brought to light.

—Sigmund Freud, *Civilization and Its Discontents*

What textbooks of art history ordinarily call Paleolithic art—the "cave art" of southwestern Europe in the Upper Paleolithic period (from about 32,000 to about 10,000 B.C.)—is interesting for my purposes not so much as such but for what we might learn from it about a general problem, namely, the context in which and the conventions by which a graphic pattern is taken to be an image of some reality. The problem is familiar to art historians in their day-to-day business of interpreting images and through their reading of methodological mentors—E. H. Gombrich, Nelson Goodman, Richard Wollheim, and others.[1] Image making was a distinctive "cultural" achievement, but it can be derived logically from simple and archaic perceptual and cognitive processes (see Chapter 2). This is not to say, however, that image making was caused *by* or is the product *of* culture or of perception and cognition *in* culture. It is one of my fundamental premises—though I advance an

1. E. H. Gombrich, *Art and Illusion*, 2d ed. (Princeton, 1961); Nelson Goodman, *Languages of Art*, 2d ed. (Indianapolis, 1971); Richard Wollheim, *Art and Its Objects*, 2d ed. (Cambridge, 1980). Although these are perhaps the most important, they are not the only works that have shaped my views here; see notes 20 and 21 below.

argument for it as well—that cognition and culture simply *are* networks of representational systems, each with its particular biology, neurology, psychology, and history.[2] The problem is to account noncircularly for the history of these representational systems that constitute cultures.

If this problem is so familiar and has been so extensively debated, why do I choose to address it with such unfamiliar historical and archaeological evidence? For one thing, I want to know whether the familiar arguments are workable when extended to more alien, or even the most alien, conditions. More important, and without giving away too much in advance, Paleolithic art has some special archaeological features that make it a helpful test case, both in stating and in attempting to solve the general problem. These features are not exhibited by *all* of Paleolithic art (that is, by all Paleolithic representations), nor are they unique to it: they can be found, for example, in other prehistoric image making, like the rock art of aboriginal Australia. But those traditions are likely to be even more unfamiliar to historians of Western art than European cave art. These features can also be found in the art of the West—in the painting, say, of Michelangelo, Manet, or Jackson Pollock—but in such a familiar way as to be unhelpful.

Paleolithic Depiction

I shall introduce the problem by reintroducing Paleolithic image making very briefly (see also Chapter 2).[3] The earliest two-dimensional images recognizable in the archaeological record are found incised on small limestone blocks from rock-shelter sites near the village of Les Eyzies in the Dordogne River valley of southern France, assigned to early and later phases of the so-called Aurignacian culture, the earliest identifiable subculture of the Upper Paleolithic in southwestern Europe (Fig. 3.1).[4] These incised—or, in the parlance of Paleolithic archaeology, "engraved"—blocks are dated stratigraphically or by cultural association to between 32,000 and 26,000 B.C., toward the very beginning of the Upper

2. Among many studies in psychology, anthropology, and other social sciences, I feel most sympathetic to Dan Sperber, "Anthropology and Psychology: Towards an Epidemiology of Representations," *Man* 20 (1985), 73–89.

3. Basic sources for a detailed study of Paleolithic art must include Henri Breuil, *Four Hundred Centuries of Cave Art,* trans. Mary Boyle (Montignac, 1952); André Leroi-Gourhan, *Treasures of Prehistoric Art,* trans. N. Guterman (New York, 1967); idem, *The Dawn of European Art,* trans. S. Champion (Cambridge, 1982); Peter J. Ucko and Andrée Rosenfeld, *Palaeolithic Cave Art* (New York, 1967); Alexander Marshack, *The Roots of Civilization: The Cognitive Beginnings of Man's First Art, Symbol, and Notation* (New York, 1972; 2d ed., New York, 1992); F. B. Naber, D. J. Berenger, and C. Zalles-Flossbach, *L'art pariétal paléolithique en Europe romane,* pt. I, *Inventaire des sites,* 2 vols. (Bonn, 1976); André Leroi-Gourhan, ed., *L'art des cavernes: Atlas des grottes ornées paléolithiques françaises* (Paris, 1984) (hereafter *Atlas*).

4. Leroi-Gourhan, *Treasures,* 206, 300–302, for his "Style I"; Brigitte Delluc and Gilles Delluc, "La Ferrassie, Abri Blanchard, Abri Castanet," in *Atlas,* 214–19; and idem, "Les manifestations graphiques aurignaciennes sur support rocheux des environs des Eyzies (Dordogne)," *Gallia Préhistoire* 21 (1978), 213–438, the essential reference for Aurignacian materials. I have followed Delluc and Delluc in their evaluation of the stratigraphic or other means of dating the individual blocks.

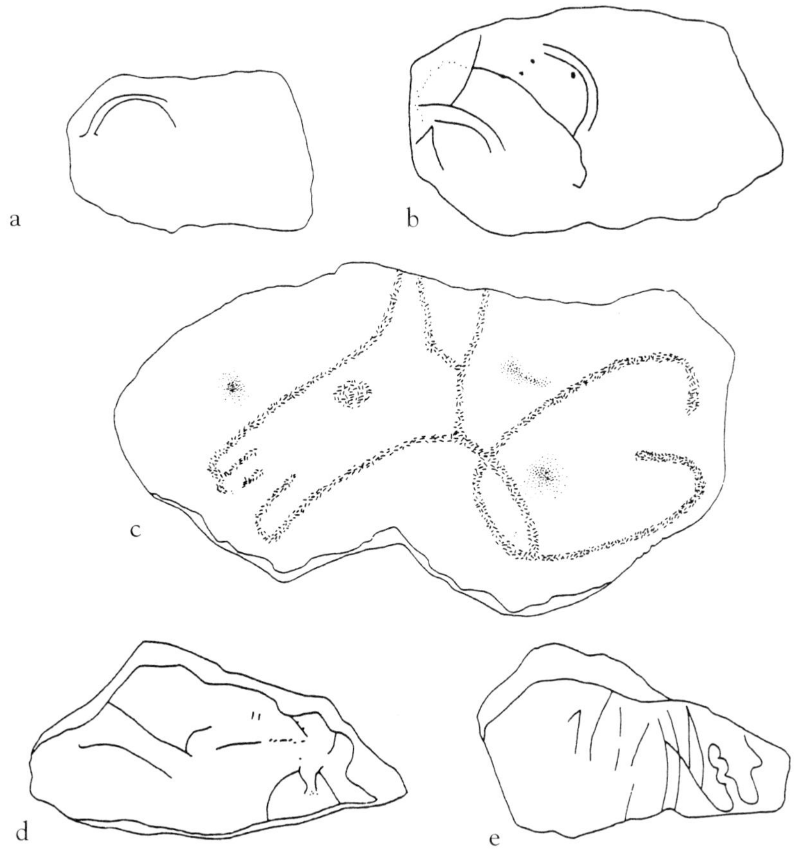

Fig. 3.1. Aurignacian images on limestone blocks, from rock shelters near Les Eyzies, Dordogne, France (about 32,000–26,000 B.C.). *a.* Block 1, Abri Cellier (animal horns?). *b.* Block 5, Abri Cellier (horns and head of an animal). *c.* Block 2, Abri Cellier (head of a horse?). *d.* Block 1, Abri Blanchard (horns and head of an ibex?). *e.* Block 5, Abri Blanchard (forepart of animal head?).

Paleolithic sequence and among the earliest cultural remains of "fully modern man," *Homo sapiens sapiens*, in this part of the world. In fact, *H. sapiens sapiens* is sometimes diagnostically distinguished from *H. sapiens neanderthalensis*, *H. erectus*, and other hominids at least in part by the very presence of "cultural" remains of this kind.[5]

The images are quite minimal, incised very deeply, pecked out with a stone point, or painted in simple strokes. Blocks 1, 2, and 5 from the Abri Cellier (Figs. 3.1*a–c*),[6] plausibly associated with an Aurignacian I level, can be considered the earliest in the group. Blocks 1 and 5 depict only what appear to be the horns and parts of the heads or backs of ibexes.

5. This element of the "normal science" of paleoanthropology is probably best stated in the writing of the late Glynn Isaac; see his "Aspects of the Evolution of Human Behavior: An Archaeological Perspective," *Canadian Journal of Anthropology* 3 (1983), 233–43, and see further Chapter 4. For specific treatments of the Middle-to-Upper Paleolithic transition, about 40,000–35,000 B.C., and emergence of "culturally" modern human populations in this part of the world, see, for example, Randall White, "Rethinking the Middle/Upper Paleolithic Transition," *Current Anthropology* 23 (1982), 169–92, and Erik Trinkaus, ed., *The Mousterian Legacy: Human Biocultural Change in the Upper Pleistocene*, British Archaeological Reports, International Series 164 (Oxford, 1983). A more radical perspective is represented by Antonio Gilman, "Explaining the Upper Palaeolithic Revolution," in *Marxist Perspectives in Archaeology*, ed. Matthew Spriggs (Cambridge, 1984), 115–26.

6. For Block 1, see Delluc and Delluc, "Les manifestations graphiques," 337–39 and fig. 71. For Block 2, see ibid., 339–42 and figs. 72–73. For Block 5, see ibid., 350–51 and figs. 61–62, and Leroi-Gourhan, *Treasures*, pl. 23 and fig. 253.

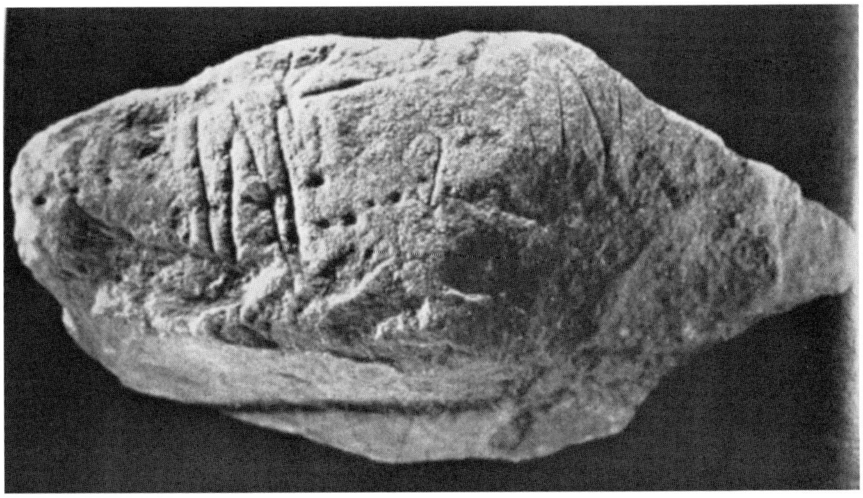

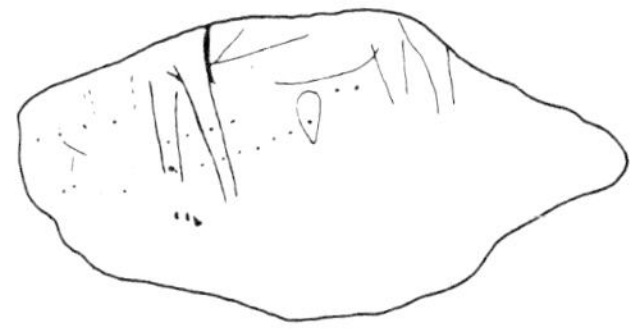

Fig. 3.2. Block 16, La Ferrassie (incised legs and underbelly of a herbivore).

Block 2 is thought to represent a horse's head. Block 16 from La Ferrassie (Fig. 3.2),[7] dated to the end of the Aurignacian sequence (Aurignacian IV), represents the four legs, without feet, and part of the underbelly of an ibex or other herbivore.

The other blocks are not closely datable to any subphase of the Aurignacian, although they probably all belong to this general culture period. Block 1 from the Abri Blanchard (Fig. 3.1*d*) seems to show the head and part of the back or neck of a horse or cervid.[8] Block 5 (Fig. 3.1*e*) represents an animal's head with open jaws.[9] Block 11 (see Fig. 2.2*a*) depicts the hind legs and underbelly of an animal variously described as a horse or bison, painted in black lines, with the ground, or perhaps the interior parts of the animal, in red.[10] Block 12 is thought to join this block. At the moment it shows only the two legs of an animal—the front legs of the animal depicted on Block 11 or another creature. Finally, from the Abri du Renne (Belcayre), the only complete outline engraving of an animal securely dated to the Aurignacian period (see Fig. 2.2*b*) seems to represent a herbivore with a very short tail, possibly a stag or an ibex.[11] If we are feeling liberal, we could expand this exceedingly short list to include a few other examples. For example, Block B from the Abri Castanet, now lost, was sometimes described as a fragmentary painting of an animal, and another block from the same site, also lost, was described as representing the legs of a mammoth. A limestone block from the Abri Labatut, found between two Upper Perigordian levels at the site (about 23,000 B.C.) and sometimes thought to have fallen from the wall of the shelter through natural exfoliation, may represent the continuity of the Aurignacian tradition of making images—either on portable blocks or, as may be here,

7. Leroi-Gourhan, *Treasures*, fig. 254, and Delluc and Delluc, "Les manifestations graphiques," 313–17 and figs. 61–62.

8. Delluc and Delluc, "Les manifestations graphiques," 225 and fig. 67.

9. Delluc and Delluc, "Les manifestations graphiques," 232–34 and fig. 12.

10. Delluc and Delluc, "Les manifestations graphiques," 247–56 and figs. 22–24.

11. Delluc and Delluc, "Les manifestations graphiques," 327–32 and figs. 67–68; Breuil, *Four Hundred Centuries*, 281; Leroi-Gourhan, *Treasures*, fig. 256.

translated to the surfaces of walls. It represents a horse, but apparently, as before, relies solely on deeply incised, or "sculpted," outline.[12]

It is difficult to say much about any of these representations without building in prejudicial assumptions about significance or style. With the exception of the Belcayre figure (see Fig. 2.2*b*) and of the later figure from Abri Labatut, all of the drawings depict only parts of the animals—such as horns, foreparts, dorsal lines, or legs.[13] The identifications of the species depicted are very insecure. In addition, stylistic assessment is problematic. Since indices of style depend upon comparative measures (see further Chapter 6), the very earliest material is, in a sense, stylistically unmeasurable. Possibly it is legitimate to say, with many commentators, that the drawings are "schematic," "simplified," or "stiff." We do not really know, however, what standard of performance could be relevant in this context.

Many of the Aurignacian blocks also bear engravings of what are often thought to be female genitalia, and other marks or "signs" resembling short series of linear strokes and hollows (Fig. 3.3).[14] Possibly these markings were all jointly significant. Several observers have remarked a systematic order in some of them.[15] At this point, it is important only to draw attention to the possible association between image and nonimage in these early works.

Moving on from 26,000 B.C., the better preserved and more frequent images of the succeeding Gravettian through Solutrean eras—that is, down to about 17,000 B.C.—seem to derive organically from the earlier Aurignacian. For instance, a bison from the cave of La Grèze (see Fig. 2.3) seems strongly reminiscent of the early engravings in the simple, deeply engraved line, profile silhouette, and selective attention of the engraver.[16] As I noted in Chapter 2, the line here is beginning to do more work: the continuously modulated double, or S, curve has greater descriptive and expressive power, and the images appear to be more elaborate and authoritative.

The so-called archaic and classic styles of the later Solutrean and Magdalenian, after

12. Delluc and Delluc, "Les manifestations graphiques," 277. For Abri Labatut, see Delluc and Delluc, "Abri Labatut," in *Atlas*, 220–21, and Jan F. Simek, "A Paleolithic Sculpture from the Abri Labatut in the American Museum of Natural History Collection," *Current Anthropology* 27 (1986), 402—7.

13. Leroi-Gourhan, *Treasures*, 206, writes that the "starting point of [the] stylistic evolution [of Paleolithic art from the Aurignacian through the Magdalenian periods] is not a primitive realism—this latter idea was a pure invention by nineteenth-century prehistorians—but a mode of representation that focuses first on the traits that particularize an animal species, disregarding the rest." There is no reason to expect that we should be able to attach labels from our natural language(s) to these "parts," or that they were metonymically related to any "wholes." They could be no more and no less than the depiction of unnamed bits, patches, and fragments of the world (see further Chapters 5 and 8).

14. Delluc and Delluc, "Les manifestations graphiques," 243–47 and figs. 19–21. The identification of these marks as female genitals has been challenged. Brigitte Delluc and Gilles Delluc, "De l'empreinte au signe," *Histoire et Archéologie* 90 (1985), 56–62, have suggested some of the marks may depict footprints. For this question and others, see Paul G. Bahn, "No Sex Please, We're Aurignacians," *Rock Art Research* 4 (1986), 99–120.

15. For instance, Leroi-Gourhan, *Treasures*, 150, 206, has argued that the "thematic" relation or equation between "vulvae and dots" persists throughout the Paleolithic period and that the Aurignacian material gives first evidence of this "figurative system."

16. Leroi-Gourhan, *Treasures*, fig. 286; *Atlas*, 164–66. On stylistic grounds (Leroi-Gourhan's "Style II"), the image is generally assigned to the Lower Solutrean, about 20,000 B.C. For this and other guides to dating, see Naber et al., *L'art paléolithique*, 107–8, and *Atlas*, 164–66.

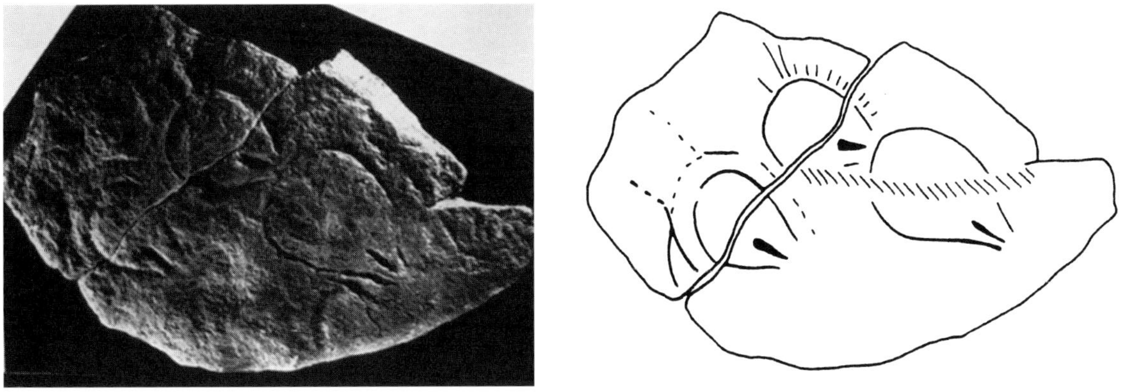

Fig. 3.3. Block 10, Abri Blanchard (incised "signs," including parallel scratches, hollows, and punctuations, and "female genitals").

17,000 B.C., are best known in the remarkable cave paintings of Lascaux, Pech-Merle, Altamira, and other sites, datable to around 14,000 B.C.[17] In these works, the analogical, continuously varying, or (to use Nelson Goodman's terms) semantically "dense" quality of the representational *line* has been generalized to *all* of the other representational variables—for example, to colors and surface textures, used to establish volumes, interior details, effects of light, and so forth.[18] Although sometimes placed at the very beginning of art-history textbooks (see Chapter 5), the Magdalenian paintings are best regarded as skilled and sophisticated performances in what was, by this point in time, a 15,000-year-old tradition.[19]

17. See, e.g., Arlette Leroi-Gourhan and J. Allain, eds., "Lascaux inconnu," *Gallia Préhistoire,* suppl. 12 (1979); Denis Vialou, *L'art pariétal en Ariège magdalenienne,* Mémoires de la Laboratoire de Paléontologie Humaine et de Préhistoire 13, 3 vols. (Paris, 1981); idem, "Niaux, une construction symbolique magdalenienne exemplaire," *Ars Praehistorica* 1 (1982), 19–45; and a special issue of *L'Anthropologie,* 88, no. 4 (1984).

18. On "density," see Goodman, *Languages of Art,* 127–76. Helpful expositions and elaborations are provided by David Carrier, "A Reading of Goodman on Representation," *The Monist* 58 (1974), 269–84; Geoffrey Hellman, "Symbol Systems and Artistic Styles," *Journal of Aesthetics and Art Criticism* 35 (1977), 279–92; and Catherine Z. Elgin, *With Reference to Reference* (Indianapolis, 1983), 97–126. For "density" as "continuous correlation," see Kent Bach, "Part of What a Picture Is," *British Journal of Aesthetics* 10 (1970), 119–37. However, I believe this direction of analysis ultimately fails to provide room for invariances of human perception in the production and reproduction of pictures. It is exposed also to serious internal or logical objections. See, e.g., Anthony Savile, "Nelson Goodman's 'Languages of Art': A Study," *Journal of Aesthetics and Art Criticism* 11 (1971), 3–27; Paul Ziff, "Goodman's Languages of Art," *Philosophical Review* 80 (1971), 509–15; Richard Wollheim, "Nelson Goodman's Languages of Art," in *On Art and the Mind* (Cambridge, 1974), 290–314; Kendall Walton, "Are Representations Symbols?" *The Monist* 58 (1974), 236–54; and Jenefer Robinson, "Some Remarks on Goodman's Language Theory of Pictures," *British Journal of Aesthetics* 19 (1979), 63–75. Working out a naturalistic (nonsemiotic or preconventionalist) account of representation, such as the one adopted here, has fundamental consequences for art historical practice. It must have clear advantages over the competition—such as Goodman's or any simple illusion theories.

19. Although I am primarily interested in a theoretical difficulty with this narrative, it is appropriate to enter some historical caveats. First, extremely early dates are available for two-dimensional images outside the Franco-Cantabrian area and not associated with the Aurignacian culture as defined there (for a recent comprehensive survey, see Paul G. Bahn and Jean Vertut,

Criteria for Depiction

Our problem is simply this: how do we know that the Aurignacian engravings and the other early productions are in fact *images* or *depictions,* terms I have used extremely loosely up to this point? It is worth pinpointing why art historians have been uncomfortable with this question. A survey of the literature—not only the literature of Paleolithic art—shows that art historians hardly ever do ask directly whether in any given historical instance they *are* working with images. Usually they assume instead that images are unproblematically recognizable as such and somehow are so in advance of beginning art historical research *on* and interpretation *of* them. If I can establish anything in this chapter, it should be that the question must be asked and reasked at every turn in art history. (I develop a precise notion of what these "turns" might be.) In fact, it is a kind of *art history*—a kind of *archaeology*—that must establish images as images in the first place. To assume image is to shut our eyes to a real historical process.

The Paleolithic graphics underline the question nicely. Some of the usual approaches to the question, "*Is* this an image?" do not work quite well when applied to material like this. One approach is to say whether we recognize the objects depicted by the marks. Here, however, we are not really certain what the objects might be—"abbreviations" of animal figures, or just *parts* of animals, and exactly *what* animals or *what* parts? Another approach would say that the material looks sufficiently like material already accepted to be an image. Here, however, if we want to avoid anachronism, there *is* no material before the Aurignacian period already and unequivocally accepted as image. (As I show in Chapter 5, prehistoric marks have been accepted as works of art on the basis of their similarity to much later works

---

Images of the Ice Age [London, 1988]). Second, however, equally early or even earlier dates have been established for three-dimensional "sculptural" imagery. For the sake of simplicity, my detailed considerations later in this chapter are confined to marks. But the account could be applied straightforwardly to lumps or to any other medium. Third, it may be that two-dimensional images of the Aurignacian could be a simple genetic continuation of a two-dimensional image-making tradition developed far earlier in another medium that has not been preserved; certainly images could have been produced in wet sand, soft clay, or grease paint or tattooing on the body. In itself, this does not establish that the Aurignacian engravings descended genetically from such images—in what I describe later in this chapter as a "chain of replications." In the account I favor, taking the *first* image *as an image* depended crucially on the physical character of the first medium itself and on a particular perception of it—conditions that might *or might not* be generalized to any other media in any later productions. Even if the image maker used the same tools and motions, the transfer from one medium to another might have eradicated the image; at each significant shift the producer could fail to take the new mark as an image. In replication, genetic continuity of the image is not guaranteed. Therefore to assert that images might have been produced before is not enough to show why we have *these* particular images before us. Of course, if a particular mark *were* taken to be (still) an image after transferring it from one surface to another or varying how it was produced, we would then have to ask about the origin of making that image in the very first of its contexts of production and perception. Aurignacian engravings could stand somewhere far down the line in a genetic sequence. However, there is really no need to venture this speculation at all. The Aurignacian engravings conform to what an explicit formal definition predicts the "first" images in a particular chain of replications should be like (Chapter 2), a moment that is archaeologically (formally and contextually) identifiable, although it occurs *throughout* history in both phylo- and ontogenesis (see further Chapter 5). It is not merely out of archaeological parochialism or even archaeological necessity that I focus on Aurignacian materials as evidence of origins.

accepted as works of art; although accepting the marks as images does not wholly depend on this parallel, it probably influences the attribution.) Furthermore, it is surely fair to say that these graphics *also* look sufficiently like material we would *not* accept as image. These are only intuitive approaches, and only somewhat damaging, not fatal, objections. But they do suggest that we must think again about how we recognize some visual patterns as images.

Although it is going to be difficult to do even the minimum justice to some arguments, let us assume that we apply an a priori notion of an image to new evidence as it is discovered archaeologically. In one standard definition, the image looks like or resembles its object. Any simple mimetic theory of representation is easily demolished and should not detain us here. Many things resemble many other things without being images of them. How do we know how to distinguish an image from any chance resemblance?[20]

In another definition, the image is analogical, the variables of line and color continuously varying. By contrast, a notation is digital; its characters are discrete.[21] Still, an image can be produced using a digital technology—like the Aurignacian engravings produced by pecking out separate holes, Seurat's pointillism, or a television transmission, to take obvious cases. Apparently the separate marks are not taken as separate marks but rather as continuously correlated in a single pattern perceived all at once. But how would we know that we are looking at such an analogical pattern, "morphologically indiscernible"—to borrow Arthur Danto's term[22]—as it might be from a pattern of *merely* separate marks? How do we know to take it analogically and not digitally? Images may appear as characters in a notational system, like Egyptian hieroglyphs (see further Chapter 7). How do we know how to distinguish images from nonimages here?

Such problems with these and other standard formal definitions suggest that it is only knowledge of certain contexts of use or of so-called conventions that tells us precisely what we are looking at. Simplifying and synthesizing a good deal of debate, and presenting a somewhat personal view, I propose that there are two fundamental conditions for a lump of matter or a two-dimensional pattern to be an image.

The first condition can be called the *constitutive criterion* (CC): some particular features of the pattern must be determinable as signifying. There are no essential or universal features of a pattern that will necessarily establish that it is a sign; conversely, there are no features that cannot establish it as a sign. Consequently, the particular signifying features of the mark must be determinable in practice for the pattern to be constituted as a sign at all. We need to know how this determination is made.

20. The classic arguments can be found in Goodman, *Languages of Art*, 3–43, and idem, "Seven Strictures on Similarity," in *Problems and Projects* (Indianapolis, 1972), 437–46. The upshot is that "resemblance is always asserted and assumed relative to a variable purpose or point" (David Novitz, "Pictures, Fiction, and Resemblance," *British Journal of Aesthetics* 22 [1982], 227); here, resemblance is within representation. But resemblance certainly figures in my account, and can be built into various suitably inflected analyses: see, from various points of view, the arguments of James Q. Knowlton, "On the Definition of 'Picture,'" *AV Communication Review* 14 (1961), 157–83; James W. Manns, "Representation, Relativism, and Resemblance," *Journal of Aesthetics and Art Criticism* 11 (1971), 281–87; Robert Schwartz, "Representation and Resemblance," *Philosophical Forum* 5 (1980), 499–51.

21. See Goodman, *Languages of Art*, 159–64; David K. Lewis, "Analog and Digital," *Nous* 5 (1971), 321–27; and John Haugeland, "Analog and Analog," *Philosophical Topics* 12 (1981), 213–25.

22. Arthur C. Danto, *The Transfiguration of the Commonplace* (New York, 1981), 1–5, 33–39. See note 36 below.

Recall that a pattern must resemble many things in many respects but is not apparently an image of all of those things. The second condition can be called the *criterion of specific resemblance* (CSR): some particular resemblances between the pattern and things in the world denote what they resemble.[23]

These two conditions are often casually collapsed in the single formula, correct as far as it goes, that in an image particular resemblances signify. For my purposes, however, it is absolutely critical to keep the two conditions as separate as possible (Fig. 3.4). Although the mark has features that establish that it signifies an object (CC), some of these features must also resemble that object for the mark to be an image (CSR); however, the features of the image that resemble the object (CSR) may not exhaust the features that establish that the image does so depict (CC).[24] The criteria CC and CSR classify the features of a pattern in different and somewhat crosscutting ways. CC sorts signifying from nonsignifying features. CSR sorts resemblant features as signifying or nonsignifying. When CC and CSR are operating simultaneously (that is, in an image), some features will necessarily be sorted as both signifying and resemblant. However, not all features picked out by CC and by CSR will fall into the intersection $CC \cap CSR$ (namely, the nonresemblant signifying features). Moreover, some features do not have a status at all in the sorting $CC \cup CSR$ (namely, the nonsignifying features, resemblant or not). The features of a pattern that are *both* signifying *and* resemblant, by definition to be found in images, should not distract us from the fact—intuitively obvious—that any so-called image *also* has these other, nonsignifying or nonresemblant features, or both, and that there are important orders of resemblance that are not pattern-to-object but rather pattern-to-pattern (this order is what we mean by style, considered in greater detail in Chapter 6).

The two conditions operating simultaneously can be regarded as the criteria for the interpretation of marks as images. (An analysis of this process as a cognitive algorithm is presented in Chapter 2.) Under interpretation, certain resemblances between marks and things are taken as depictions of objects. We need to recognize that this identification is not unproblematic; it is quite special and contingent—context-bound.

For one thing, an interpreter need not always perceive the same pattern of marks in the same way. At one moment we might perceive a pattern as merely a pattern; at another as

23. This condition clearly rules out a mark in which a thing-resemblance denotes, but not that particular thing the mark resembles. But it does not imply that there are no further interesting and important resemblances, for example, between features of the mark and features of other marks. In fact, mark-to-object "denotational resemblance" is actually a specialized function of mark-to-mark resemblances, or replication.

24. Since I have indulged semiotic language here to some extent (and register my distress with it only later), I shall go all the way. In Peircean language, an image is not a "pure" iconic sign, for it cannot iconically exhibit the fact that it is a sign and that particular relations of iconic resemblance to an object also signify that object (see Arthur W. Burks, "Icon, Index, and Symbol," *Philosophy and Phenomenological Research* 9 [1949], 673–89, and Arthur K. Bierman, "That There Are No Iconic Signs . . .," *Philosophy and Phenomenological Research* 23 [1962], 243–49, for full discussion in Peircean terminology). For this reason, as A. J. Ayer notes (*The Origins of Pragmatism* [San Francisco, 1968], 140), no actual sign could be a pure icon; it is rather what Peirce sometimes termed a hypoicon, a sign incorporating iconic resemblances specified "symbolically" as signifying what they resemble as well as other sign relations not immediately relevant to its iconic signification (for instance, it is an index of the procedures used to manufacture it and a symbol that someone had an intention so to manufacture it).

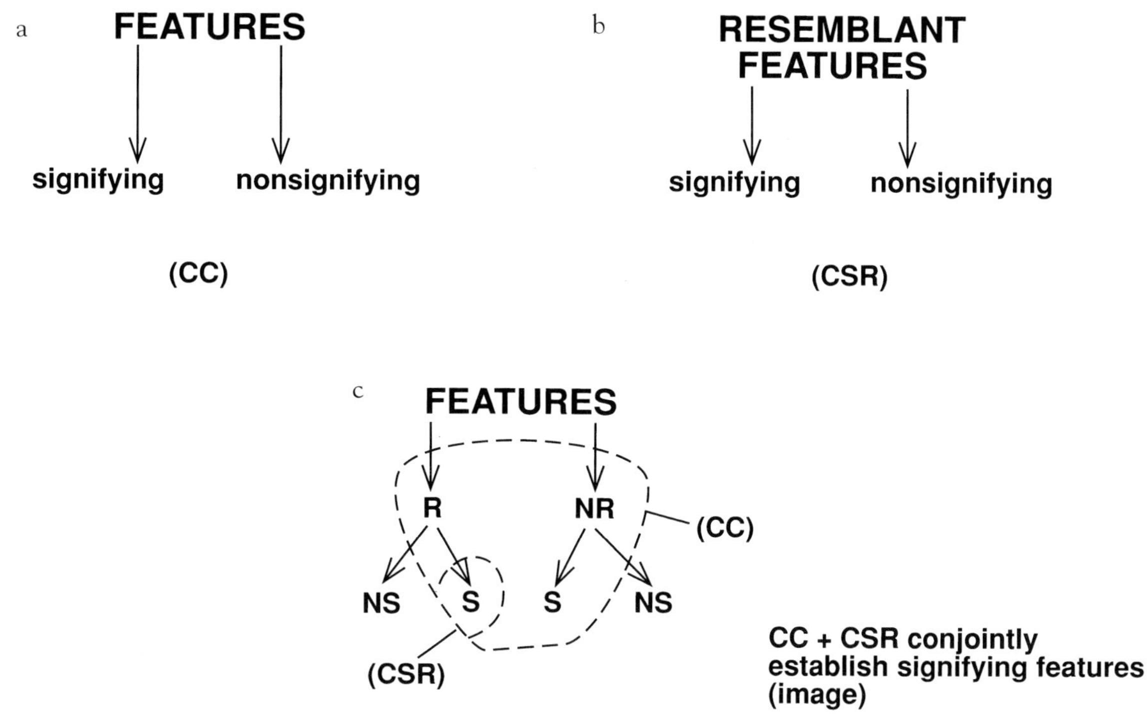

Fig. 3.4. The sorting of features of marks. *a.* The Constitutive Criterion (CC): Some particular features of the visual display must be determinable as signifying. *b.* The Criterion of Specific Resemblance (CSR): Some particular resemblances between features of the visual display and "reality" denote what they resemble. *c.* The joint sorting of CC and CSR: CC and CSR each classify different features of the visual display but conjointly establish the image.

resembling but not denoting a face, or denoting but not resembling a face; or, finally, as an image of a face, both resembling and denoting it. The context in which image interpretation occurs is evidently a specific one.

Furthermore, a second interpreter may also perceive this same pattern as an image but, in this case, as a *different* image—say, an image not of a face but rather of an animal. Therefore the context in which image interpretation results in specifying *this particular image*—of a face and not an animal—evidently is a specific one also.

In sum, interpretation is fundamentally "correctable," to use A. J. Ayer's apt phrase.[25] Different interpreters can take marks as being images *or* not and as having the same *or* different objects. Since an interpreter could fail to see an image at all or could see several different images, taking a pattern in some context as *this particular image* seems to be "arbitrary" and "conventional" to the very extent that it *is* contingent and variable in that context.

Although I do not consider art history's various expressions or versions (such as debates about "natural" or "conventional" signs by writers like Goodman, Gombrich, or

25. Ayer, *Origins of Pragmatism*, 130.

J. J. Gibson), here I have reached the founding argument of much of contemporary art history. The argument certainly provides a specific subject matter for art history to take as its own. An interpreter must learn the "convention" (namely, CC ∪ CSR) that in a particular context particular features of a mark establish it as an image. Therefore the initial business of art history would be, in Umberto Eco's words, to identify "the cultural procedures and operative processes that go to make up the predication of homology between mark and object."[26] Far more insidiously, and on a tendentious understanding of conventions, the argument also suggests that *only* an art history—or, more broadly, a cultural history—could provide an account of any substance, for supposedly the learning of the convention could only take place socially, by induction or actual instruction.

Actual instruction in the interpretation of images might take place in some literal sense, leading to unfortunate metaphors for culture as a school to be attended, a theater to be witnessed, or a text to be understood. Learning about images, however, minimally requires only consistently successful induction: the observed social uses of a pattern as an image of a particular object is all an interpreter needs to perform, to use it, in the same way. However we find it, learning requires another interpreter or group of interpreters to establish the use of images, examples of acceptable images from which to learn, and so forth: it seemingly requires culture.

But something has gone badly wrong here somewhere. An account of learning how to interpret images by induction or instruction in a given cultural setting ultimately begs the question by landing us in an infinite regress. If interpreter_1 is instructed by interpreter_2, did interpreter_2 in turn learn from yet another person, interpreter_3? Ultimately we would have to know by whom the first teacher was instructed: we end in paradox. Alternatively, interpreter_2 learned the interpretation of marks as images by induction before instructing interpreter_1. Here, though, he must have observed interpreter_3 using images, in turn picked up by induction or instruction—and so on.

Any regress of this kind can be minimized by focusing on the performance of a single individual in a given cultural setting—as it were, absorbing, transforming, and passing on culture. Not surprisingly, methodological solipsism is deeply entrenched in art history. Furthermore, art historians can always leave it to others—anthropologists or historians—to determine what the "given setting" amounts to, despite the likelihood that commonality of culture is best defined, in the first place, as the mutually intelligible use of various representational systems. But wished away or not, the regress is profoundly unsatisfactory from a historical point of view.

Again, the regress may not seem to be too troublesome in some historical contexts: the conventions are supposedly ancient and widely shared. But when Willibald Sauerländer argues that the apparent homogeneity of style in the classic tradition is an artifact of what he calls aesthetic historicism, or when T. J. Clark wonders why literate bourgeois critics could not interpret the painting of Manet,[27] we are no longer relegating the strong effect of

26. Umberto Eco, *A Theory of Semiotics* (Bloomington, Ind., 1976), sect. 5.2.

27. Willibald Sauerländer, "From Stilus to Style: Reflections on the Fate of a Notion," *Art History* 6 (1983), 253–70; T. J. Clark, *The Painting of Modern Life: Paris in the Art of Manet and His Followers* (New York, 1985).

the regress—the puzzle of how and where to terminate it (see further Chapter 5)—to the obscurity of origins or to the dramatic conflict of revolutions. Instead we are seeing induction and instruction as somehow always and everywhere unreliable and incomplete. The infinite regress may not, then, really be so infinite. In my case, the puzzle of the regress is pure and unadulterated: Aurignacian engravers (in my thought experiment) had no previous images to consult, no previous image interpreters to observe, no conventions to learn. How, to use Saul Kripke's words, did an "initial baptism" somehow "fix the reference" of the patterns on the blocks?[28]

THE CANONICAL CHAIN OF REPLICATIONS FOR DEPICTION

A genuine solution, I think, requires rethinking what the so-called convention or conventions of image making amount to. Shifting out of semiotic and iconological doctrine—that image is a code, is learned, is inaugurally ruled or stipulated, is culturally conventional, and so forth—we can say that making an image is not something we learn about a pattern but rather something we *do* with it. An image is a tool or, more broadly, a "form of life."[29] In this, I want most of all to preserve art historians' vivid impression that the *history* of the image has something to do with its intelligibility.

To avoid infinite regress (and related circularities in what might be put forward as an intentionalist or neo-Gricean analysis of pictorial meanings), the interpretation of images can be regarded as a program or sequence of steps none of which individually assumes the operation of CC and CSR in advance.[30] At the end of the sequence, all of the relevant operations of CC and CSR are in place; the program is image interpreting. In brief, the

28. Saul Kripke, *Naming and Necessity,* 2d ed. (Cambridge, 1980), 96–97, 135–40.

29. See Wollheim, *Art and Its Objects,* 104–5.

30. In a Gricean account, a picture maker would in or by a picture try to get a picture viewer to recognize the maker's intention that the viewer have a certain response. Although I have never seen the account rigorously formulated for pictures, something like it seems central to art historians' talk about pictures and viewers. See H. P. Grice, "Meaning," *Philosophical Review* 66 (1957), 377–88; idem, "Utterer's Meaning, Sentence-Meaning, and Word-Meaning," *Foundations of Language* 4 (1968), 225–42; and Stephen Schiffer, *Meaning* (Oxford, 1972). I am sympathetic to the Gricean effort to (re)construct semantic notions from nonsemantic primitives. However, the Griceans cannot seem to pull themselves up by their bootstraps over what Neil Tennant calls the "Gricean hump," the emergence of intentions and meanings in representation and communication ("Intentionality, Syntactic Structure, and the Evolution of Language," in *Minds, Machines and Evolution,* ed. Christopher Hookway [Cambridge, 1984], 73–103). The circularity and regress of an independent determination of a speaker's "intention" to mean something are nicely expressed by J. I. Biro, "Intentionalism and the Theory of Meaning," *The Monist* 62 (1979), 238–58, although Grice himself ("Meaning Revisited," in *Mutual Knowledge,* ed. N. V. Smith [London, 1982], 223–43) seems untroubled. Dan Sperber and Deirdre Wilson have claimed to break out of the circularity or cut the regress by analyzing (neo-Gricean) conversational standards sufficient for reasonable comprehension (in the absence of full "mutual knowledge"); see *Relevance: Cognition and Communication* (Cambridge, 1986). John R. Searle's more radical solution—to make the "intention to communicate" dependent on a prior sense of "meaning," that is, the representation of information, rather than the other way around—seems more promising in making fewer assumptions about the sociality and communicativeness of the creatures manipulating representations; see "Meaning, Communication, and Representation," in *Philosophical Grounds of Rationality: Intentions, Categories, Ends,* ed. Richard E. Grandy and Richard Warner (Oxford, 1986), 209–26.

program builds depiction from more primitive—that is, evolutionarily preceding and cognitively anterior—judgments of similarity and substitutability between features of a mark and things in the world (including other marks). Although no features of a mark are necessarily privileged in the beginning and none are inherently perceived to resemble or denote anything, in the continuous replication of marks some of them will be specified as denotationally resembling objects.[31] Let us proceed briefly through the stages of this argument.

To summarize the approach presented in Chapter 2, we start from the simple perceptual experience of taking a two-dimensional mark for something else—perceiving a blot as a hole, a line as an edge, and so forth. Our interpretation of the mark is an instance of the general experience of what is usually called *seeing-as*. For my purposes, seeing-as is erroneous perceptual interpretation, a simple equivalence equation in which mark = thing; it is involuntarily erroneous, and predictable given how information is structured in light presented to the eye, that is, ambiguously.[32] Usually the perceptual system detects that it has made a mistake. A movement of the head will show that a shape in the distance is really a mark on a nearby surface. The correction is often called *disambiguation,* and like seeing-as is involuntary and automatic. It requires no instruction, and the inductions are, as it were, built into the human nervous system. Now, after successful disambiguation, examination will show the mark to be very similar or even perceptually identical to the thing in some respects, at least in part the respects perceived in seeing-as, but different in others, at least in part the respects perceived in disambiguation. If and when the mark is replicated, *for whatever purpose or lack of purpose,* these respects of resemblance and nonresemblance in relation to the thing perceived in seeing-as can be reproduced or varied.

Assume, then, that we have such a chain of replications before us.[33] In this chain (the critical point for the present chapter) reproducing and varying both resemblant and non-

31. Both similarity and substitutability are relative to a function and to a theory. Replication is a special case of the production of similars and substitutes in which similarity is the grounds for substitutability. One can produce a string of merely substitutable marks without similarity (for example, labeling an entrance for the seeing and the blind) and a string of merely similar marks without substitutability (for example, nervously tapping the page with a pencil).

32. See esp. J. J. Gibson, *The Perception of the Visual World* (Boston, 1950), and David Marr, *Vision: A Computational Investigation* (New York, 1982). On seeing-as and his alternative "seeing-in," see Wollheim, *Art and Its Objects,* 205–26. To my mind, seeing-in is not a unitary, simple perceptual process but a description of what we do when we experience seeing-as and disambiguation in relation to marked surfaces. However, Wollheim's account has many advantages, and I reserve the option to rewrite elements of my own in its terms. In my use of seeing-as, note the following: (1) The general distinction between ambiguous stimulus (mark) and erroneous perceptual interpretation (thing) should not be collapsed into the particular distinction between a possible two-dimensional projection and a three-dimensional solid. Thinghood must be widely defined to include three-dimensional solids, illuminated surfaces with reflectance gradients (like a shadowed wall), and fields of color (like a patch of sky). (2) A single mark may be seen as two or more different things in successive viewings, or even during successive instants of the same viewing punctuated by a "Gestalt switch" (so-called ambiguous figures like the duck/rabbit or other figure/ground "illusions"). This type of ambiguity is not that of seeing-as in my usage, that is, the confusion of a mark with a particular thing. But the fact that a single mark can support an indefinite number of distinct episodes of seeing-as (duck, then rabbit, then . . .) lies behind the interpreter's need to have historical knowledge of the particular episode inaugurating the production of an image.

33. In Chapter 2, I offer a formal characterization of these chains, only some of which could ever be images. For other relatively formal accounts of variation in repli-

resemblant features, the thing perceived in the mark can be held constant. More precisely, the features perceived to resemble that thing in an episode of seeing-as can be reproduced or varied in replication without variation in the judgment of resemblance. The fundamental chain of replications, for my purposes, has a "canonical form" (Fig. 3.5). In this chain, some features of the marks are constantly judged to resemble the same thing (Fig. 3.5*a–e*), although the marks, compared mark to mark, might be judged resemblant (Fig. 3.5*a–b*) or nonresemblant to some degree or in some respects (Fig. 3.5*b–e*). In a chain of replications, mark-to-mark resemblance, mark-to-thing resemblance, and thing-to-thing resemblance are intertwined but potentially bifurcating.

Simple enough—but note that the whole chain need not be made with the advance "intention" to hold the thing resemblance constant or even the advance knowledge (cultural, conventional knowledge) that thing resemblance *can* be held constant. Although I do not go into this matter at length, for it is logically and perhaps historically anterior to the problem of image making, the chain may be the simple product of replicating *particular marks* that are "worn out" or otherwise requiring reproduction in another time, place, or medium than their first production, or, even more simply, of scribbling or rhythmic repetition. Not every chain, of course, will take the canonical form for even part of its length. Perhaps the mark maker makes no replications at all. More important, presuming a mark maker is not initially replicating marks *for* their thing resemblance, in replication the resemblant features could be too quickly erased for their constancies to be discovered.

Despite the special replicatory conditions that give rise to it, a chain of the canonical form—or derived and complex forms—is all that is required to give depiction. Consider that an artifact is ordinarily replicated in order to preserve and modify certain of its features in and for further use. In an ordinary tool, the functional features are preserved throughout a chain of replications and varied within certain limits—else the function changes or the tool becomes altogether functionless. The tool is replicated *for* the function. Similarly, and on this model, depiction is not the replication of an intrinsically special or unique kind of mark, or the application of special and unique interpretations *to* otherwise mundane marks, but rather and much more simply the replication of marks for the purpose of reproducing and varying features that resemble the thing initially encountered in seeing-as. More briefly, an image is a mark replicated for seeing-as.

Phrased this way, the "convention" or "conventions" of interpreting a pattern as an image and the so-called arbitrariness or correctability of this interpretation amount to recognizing that the convention is not a code to be cracked but a historical function to be discovered: a pattern has been produced and reproduced for some particular resemblance to things it had in a moment of seeing-as.

How do we distinguish replicating the mark *for seeing-as* from other replications that merely preserve thing resemblance? After all, the mark maker might just set out to reproduce particular resemblant features (that is, just *those* features, irrespective of their resemblance). Here, however, he would hold those particular resemblant features constant

cation, see George Kubler, *The Shape of Time: Remarks on the History of Things* (New Haven, Conn., 1962), whose internal "rule of series" fails, and David L. Clarke, *Analytical Archaeology*, 2d ed. (New York, 1983).

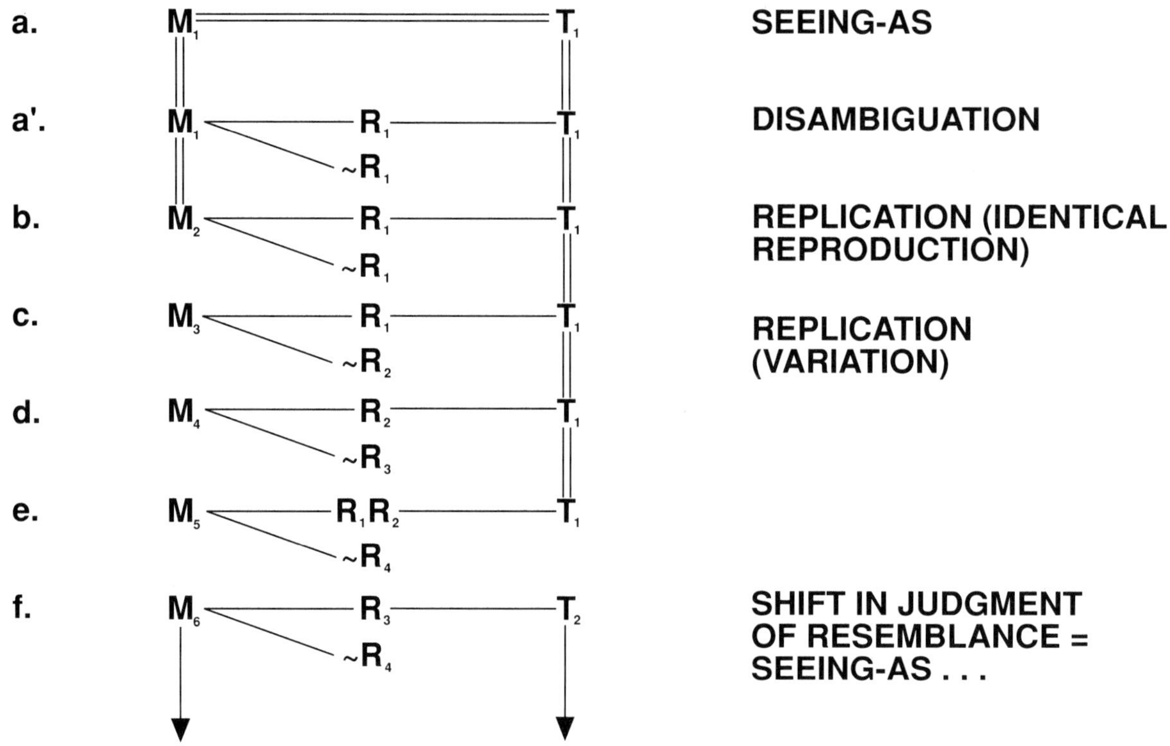

Fig. 3.5. Canonical form of the chain of replications necessary and sufficient for depiction. M = mark; R = features resembling object initially perceived in seeing-as; ~R = features not resembling object initially perceived in seeing-as; T = object perceiving in seeing-as ("thing"); ‖ = judgment of perceptual identity.

throughout a chain of replications. But, as I have shown, particular resemblant features do *not* have to be held constant for the judgment of resemblance *to the thing* to be held constant. In one "image" the curve of the animal's back is established by a shadowed incised line, in the next the same curve is established by a black painted line, and so forth.

The catch, clearly, is that no amount of morphological analysis of the mark alone will tell us it is an image. The question is precise: confronted with a mark produced for its particular thing resemblance, that is, as an image, how does an interpreter *know* that this is indeed its status, that the purpose of its production was the preservation of seeing-as? (We can, I believe, safely assume that in many cases the interpreter is provided with this information in advance, but in my view this is not a penetrating historical analysis, simply because it begs the question of the ultimate source of this information.) And the answer seems precise enough: the very variability of nonresemblant morphology throughout a canonical chain of replications indicates that a particular resemblant morphology has been preserved for its thing resemblance, subject to the condition just noted, that from mark to mark the resemblant morphology may itself be variable. This is a complete translation of what is understood by CC and CSR: particular resemblances "denote" what they resemble in the sense that in relation to other and all features of the mark particular resemblant features are determinably produced for their thing resemblance or as having a thing-resembling function, else the chain of replications would not have the (canonical) form it does. But by these terms, an interpreter cannot know a priori or from the mark alone *which* conceivably resemblant morphologies of the mark, conceivably being held constant in a chain of replications, he should identify as depictional. *He must know the whole chain of replications* back to the initial moment of seeing-as and disambiguation, that is, the whole field of resemblant and nonresemblant morphologies and their indifferent or different substitutability in a chain of replications.

This condition is extremely strict. An interpreter must be very well informed about mark making and about judgments of resemblance rendered (or renderable) on marks. It may be that he can be instructed in parts or in the whole of the relevant chain. Moreover, on the basis of "archaeological" evidence or observation and experience, he might be able to infer what the chain actually happens to be. Without the whole chain, however, he cannot be completely certain what he is recovering from the mark. Interpretation becomes necessarily historical.

As my account implies, even within a given culture—whatever we might accept this puzzling entity to be—an interpreter must become an archaeologist of the marks with which he is presented. The business of art history would be, then, to reconstitute chains of replication. Putting together these claims, art history is a vastly removed or alienated version of what art historians ordinarily and automatically do in interpreting the familiar marks of their immediate culture. Conversely, to recapture their culture as a culture—produced, reproduced, and varied—they must become its archaeologists.

The Stratigraphy of Depiction

When we cannot observe the whole closed sequence or cycle of production itself, it is very difficult to identify the canonical chain of replications. Two unavoidable features of replication are responsible for this central problem of symbolism.

First, if it is a material artifact at all, each variant in a chain is necessarily distinguished spatially and temporally from preceding and following variants. In theory, there is no limit to the span of space or lag of time that might separate two variants. What we can call the interpreter's "archaeological survey" would have to be extremely comprehensive to pick up all the variants. In general, as Freud made abundantly clear, the archaeological resolution an interpreter requires to interpret symbols is not necessarily deep and specific enough (see further Chapters 10 and 12).

Second, insofar as some features of a pattern of marks are *reproduced* in succeeding variants, for whatever purpose, they may become inextricably incorporated—drawn over or built into the latest variant. And insofar as some features are *not* reproduced in later variants, they may be abandoned or destroyed. The interpreter is left archaeologically with a single pattern that is really at one and the same time a complex filtering and palimpsest of many variations—and the garbage of the studio contains a good deal of what he would like to know.[34]

At the beginning of this chapter I noted that some Paleolithic art presents special features that make it a useful case for analysis. Because the Paleolithic engraver was using a subtractive technology, removing matter from a surface with his gouging fingers or an incising tool rather than adding to it,[35] he could not easily change or erase his work. And because for several reasons we believe he was working solely in the restricted confines of the cave, his productions accumulate more or less in one place. We can therefore watch a chain of replications piling up as an enormous palimpsest of variants that potentially has an internal stratigraphy all the way back to (although not materially encompassing) the initial episode of seeing-as and disambiguation. If images are produced in the way the general account suggests, then in favorable contexts there should be archaeological evidence of this. Conversely, it is this "archaeological evidence" interpreters use in determining whether any pattern is an image, what it is an image of, and so forth—reconstituting the replication of seeing-as as having been produced as such.

The Aurignacian Replication of Depiction

If a trace of an origin was preserved at all, then the archaeological record should contain graphic patterns that (1) are "morphologically indiscernible" (a term given new life by Arthur Danto)[36] from patterns produced nonrepresentationally, (2) are nonetheless capable of supporting seeing-as, and (3) were determinably replicated *for* the seeing-as rather than for any nonrepresentational purpose (or lack of purpose). How do the Aurignacian engravings hold up when these simple tests are applied?

We can best explore the grounds for the powerful conviction that in examining these "outlines" we are indeed examining images by trying to suppress seeing-as as much as possible. Any familiar art school technique will do the trick. Examine the pattern of marks

34. Despite the approach of many archaeologists and art historians, the problem of archaeological resolution is not that of identifying the work of actual individuals in a sequence of artifacts (see also Chapter 6). The interpreter's task, in the face of the two inherent difficulties, is simply to establish the association between different marks, produced whenever by whomever, within which an episode of image-interpretation (seeing-as, disambiguation, recognition, and canonical preservation of thing-resemblance) occurred for interpreter$_n$. This is very likely but not necessarily a matter of examining marks produced by one person at one time.

35. For the use of fingers, see the detailed examination by Robert G. Bednarik, "Parietal Finger Markings in Europe and Australia," *Rock Art Research* 3 (1986), 30–61; for the subtractive technologies of incising on bone, rocks, and so on, see an early, underappreciated work by G.-B.-M. Flamand, *Les pierres écrites (Hadjrat-Mektoubat): Gravures et inscriptions rupestres du nord-africain* (Paris, 1921).

36. Danto, *Transfiguration,* 1–5, 33–39. In this chapter I have made considerable use of the powerful device of imagining "morphologically indiscernible" phenomena that are nevertheless psychologically or categorially distinct and discernible in some contexts (say, semantic, aesthetic, or institutional). In his famous argument about the perceptual and aesthetic relevance of our knowledge about the authorships of apparently "indiscernible" orig-

with one eye or through a peephole, with unfocused eyes, or with foveal focus on a point somewhat to the right or the left of the pattern. Seeing the outlines *as marks* in this way shows them to be nearly straight lines and simple C curves, often doubled or repeated in a rhythmic series. Block 16 from La Ferrassie (Fig. 3.2) has eight parallel, short, nearly straight lines in two sets, with the inner lines in each set touching at one end, and two "connecting" lines at right angles to and between the sets. Seen in this way, they are morphologically indiscernible from anything produced in the earlier history of mark making by incising aimlessly, rhythmically, or with a nonrepresentational interest in simple pattern, balance, and direction, like some scratchings on Mousterian (Neanderthal) or even earlier artifacts (see Figs. 2.7, 5.17).[37] The first test is satisfied: the marks have no inherent features dramatically distinguishing them.

Yet the marks can certainly support a minimal episode of seeing-as. We know from the past history of interpretation itself that an interpreter *can* see the lines as (say) the legs and underbelly of an animal. The second test is satisfied.

Although the marks therefore *could* be emergent inaugural images, what counts as evidence, finally, that they were produced *for* seeing-as, that they were *in fact* images? This is a much trickier point.

The general account states that, in image making, thing resemblances must be held constant, whereas nonresemblances can be indifferently substituted or even eliminated throughout a chain of replications, for marks are being replicated *for* thing resemblance as such. Moreover, the constancy of thing resemblance in replication can be independent of *just those particular features* initially seen as a thing: the resemblant features are not being replicated as just *those* features, for whatever purpose, but, again, only for their thing resemblance, which could be obtained through *other* features. These requirements of the general analysis imply that there should be different kinds and rates of variation for resemblant and for nonresemblant features of the marks. Specifically, and first, in replication nonresemblant features do not change in continuous correlation with the resemblant and may even be differentiated and eliminated (barring some considerations to be taken up later), ultimately leaving "image" against "ground." Second, resemblant features should survive (to some limit) a variety of translations in medium or technique.[38] A concise, if metaphorical, way of putting the point is to say simply that in replication the image is detached from nonimage. We should be able to identify this archaeologically.

inal and forged works of art, Goodman (*Languages of Art*, 99–123) seems to suggest that if we are talking about separate artifacts, then there are no morphological indiscernibles (no perfect fakes): there is always some feature we could isolate (if we knew to look for it) serving to distinguish them. At its core my argument is closer to Danto's than to Goodman's.

37. See, e.g., Alexander Marshack, "Some Implications of the Paleolithic Symbolic Evidence for the Origins of Language," *Current Anthropology* 17 (1976), 274–81, and, for the archaeological problems of this material, Leslie G. Freeman, Lewis R. Binford, and Randall White, "More on the Mousterian: Flaked Bone from Cueva Morin," *Current Anthropology* 24 (1983), 366–77.

38. The first in a sense includes the second, for indifferent substitutability or eliminability of nonresemblance includes (but is not limited to) the fact that in a translation of technique or medium features once resemblant can become nonresemblant and are therefore as susceptible to substitution or elimination as any initially nonresemblant features.

Again, the Aurignacian engravings seem to satisfy the kinds of expectations of the third test. First, *in any one variant,* like Block 16 from La Ferrassie (Fig. 3.2), what we *could* take as the resemblant features are visibly isolated from other markings, like the various strokes and punctuations. Furthermore, the whole of any single mark in the "image" group can be seen as simply and coherently resemblant: the full curve of the line is "continuously correlated" with the curve of the animal's belly.[39] Second, *across or among variants* of Aurignacian engraving on blocks, the lines resembling (say) a quadruped are maintained more or less invariantly—whether incised on the single Block 16 from La Ferrassie (Fig. 3.2), painted across the two joining blocks from the Abri Blanchard (see Fig. 2.2*a*), or gouged and hammered out on the block from Belcayre (see Fig. 2.2*b*). These marks were evidently being replicated for the quadruped resemblance (shape and perhaps color), evidently in these cases indifferent (to some limit) to dimensionality or depth of mark, to position on a surface in relation to its edges, to scale, and so forth (these nonresemblant features of the mark being indifferently substitutable across variants). Resemblance survives translations that nonresemblance does not.

In sum, despite the marks' morphological indiscernibility from many other marks, we are entitled to describe the Aurignacian outline engravings as inaugural images, for their particular morphology in replication can be most simply and comprehensively explained (and best predicted) as having been produced in the replication of marks for thing resemblance as such.

We have arrived here at (a sketch of) an objective, non- or preconventionalist means of identifying an image as an image. But the logical consistency of the demonstration has been obtained at a high price—although no higher a price than is paid in *all* interpretation. For one thing, I have assumed all the Aurignacian engravings to be variants in a single network or chain of replications. Although this assumption may be archaeologically plausible—for the blocks come from the same small region at broadly the same time and are technically and stylistically quite similar—it was not established independently.[40]

Worse, at a crucial point I have relied on the recognizability of the object *to us*—namely, in pointing to the differential variation of resemblant and nonresemblant features. Surely, one might say, we could not classify features as resembling or not resembling a particular object at all unless we already assumed an image, although this is precisely what we are trying to establish we are entitled to assume about the marks (morphologically indiscernible from nonimage) in the first place. Remember, however, that if we accept the critique of simple mimetic theories of representation, thing resemblance as such is often independent of and certainly not sufficient for depiction. Our tests have to show *which* conceivable thing resemblances of a mark also *depict* (that is, were replicated *for* their resemblance). We do not assume an image to get at relevant thing resemblance, but we

39. As I show momentarily, these characteristics of the engraved blocks cannot be found on many of the cave wall panels, where the image is deeply embedded in nonimage. To avoid complexity, I do not treat the cave wall panels here, for the blocks may be related to or even derived from them.

40. In Chapter 6, I consider style (mark-to-mark resemblance) in part as an interpreter's evidence for the archaeological identification of chains of replication.

assume this or that thing resemblance to get at the image. Since we cannot observe the whole chain of replications all the way back to the initial moment of seeing-as, we must assume *our* judgment of relevant resemblance to be identical with the seeing-as that *actually* produced the chain. The consistency of our result, comprehensively accounting for the whole structure of replicatory variation that we are able to observe archaeologically, is indeed our only evidence that we have succeeded. But on my analysis this is the necessary fate of interpretation.

Image and Nonimage

With some minimal idea of how we go about identifying an image as an image, let us turn to the longer and more complex chains of replication in which images are actually embedded if the whole process of producing them is preserved. I take as my example here the engraved and painted cave at Gargas near Aventignan in the French Pyrenees, datable on the best evidence to the Solutrean period, about 20,000 B.C.[41] With the exception of the famous hand stencils in the cave and a few paintings of animals (thought by some authorities to be later than the engravings), all of the marks in Gargas were produced subtractively. Barring some vandalism by modern tourists and some decay, all variations have been preserved or absorbed, or both, in any later variations in the chain(s) of replication.

The cave contains many "digital flutings" made with three, four, or five fingers held together and dragged through the soft clay (Figs. 3.6, 3.7, and see 1.1). The flutings often meander quite far with little modification in the direction or pressure of the line. However, a few are curved, limited, or terminated in a way that would support the seeing-as of a fragmentary outline. As one excavator says, "[S]ome of them suggest animal figures, or offer a striking design."[42]

Curves made with one finger only are more various and complex than the polydigital curves (Fig. 3.7). Many of them seem to be variations on *one particular* initial moment of seeing-as, a particular form, as it were, filtered out of the many forms produced in polydigital tracing—namely, a double, or S, curve drawn horizontally (left-right) or vertically (up-down). Drawn vertically, the S curve can be seen as the out-curving horns, forehead, muzzle, and neck of a bison (Fig. 3.8*a*);[43] drawn horizontally, the S curve can be seen as the out-curving horns, humped back, and rising tail or descending hindquarters of a bison

41. Leroi-Gourhan, *Treasures*, 307–8 and figs. 77, 93, 289–304; Claude Barrière, "Gargas," in *Atlas*, 514–22; and comprehensive publication in idem, *L'art pariétal paléolithique de la grotte de Gargas*, British Archaeological Reports, Supplementary Series 14, 2 vols. (Oxford, 1976). The dating depends on one tendentious association between some engravings on the walls and one face of one decorated pebble found in a stratigraphic context by early excavators at Gargas. The questions I wish to raise—and perhaps to settle—are somewhat independent of the matter of absolute (that is, actual chronological) dating.

42. Barrière, *L'art pariétal de Gargas*, 1:136 (e.g., pls. 23, 35, 39).

43. Barrière, *L'art pariétal de Gargas*, 1:151 and pl. 36 (fig. 40, no. 1).

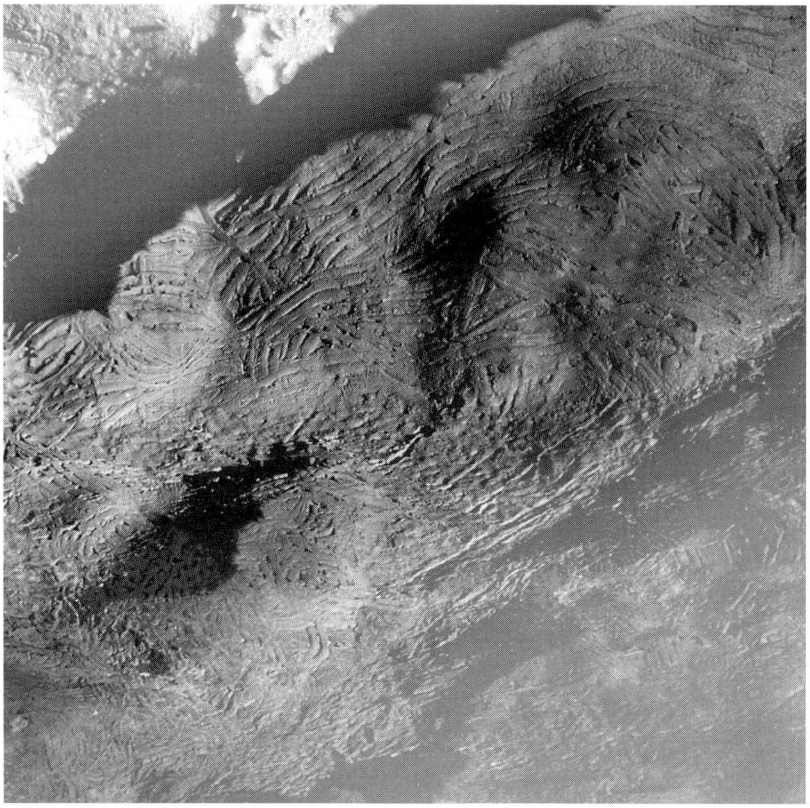

Fig. 3.6. Polydigital tracing in the cave of Gargas, French Pyrenees, about 20,000 B.C. (?).

(Fig. 3.8*b*).[44] These curves can be repeated in the whole or in part of their length to give *two* horns, and so forth. Moreover, *two* double S curves can be placed at oblique or right angles to each other to give an outline of a figure that is half or two-thirds complete (Fig. 3.8*c*).[45] The treatment of this angle is of special consequence for the whole outline, and one may observe considerable deliberation in constructing it, an intensive effort of replication and variation for this feature—for example, fitting (Fig. 3.8*d*),[46] superimposition (Fig. 3.8*e*),[47] or elimination (Fig. 3.8*f*)[48] of parts of the curves. A few additional dots or strokes flesh out the basic outline (Fig. 3.8*g*).[49] All of these details—since they are just holes or strokes—are in themselves, as marks, morphologically indiscernible from various finger marks embedded in the polydigital meanders.

More elaborate images (for example, Fig. 3.9) are engraved, rather than traced, further in the cave and may possibly represent a further stage in the accumulating palimpsest of

44. Barrière, *L'art pariétal de Gargas,* 1:151 and pl. 39 (fig. 43, no. 10).

45. Barrière, *L'art pariétal de Gargas,* 1:151 and pl. 40 (fig. 43, no. 11).

46. Breuil, *Four Hundred Centuries,* fig. 276; Leroi-Gourhan, *Treasures,* fig. 24 (color); *Atlas,* 517 (no. 8); Barrière, *L'art pariétal de Gargas,* 1:151 and pl. 37 (fig 41, no. 8).

47. *Atlas,* 517 (no. 9); Barrière, *L'art pariétal de Gargas,* 1:164 and pl. 43 (no. 18).

48. Barrière, *L'art pariétal de Gargas,* 1:151 and fig. 44 (no. 15).

49. Barrière, *L'art pariétal de Gargas,* 1:151–64, nos. 5, 8, 9(?), 15(?), 18, 20.

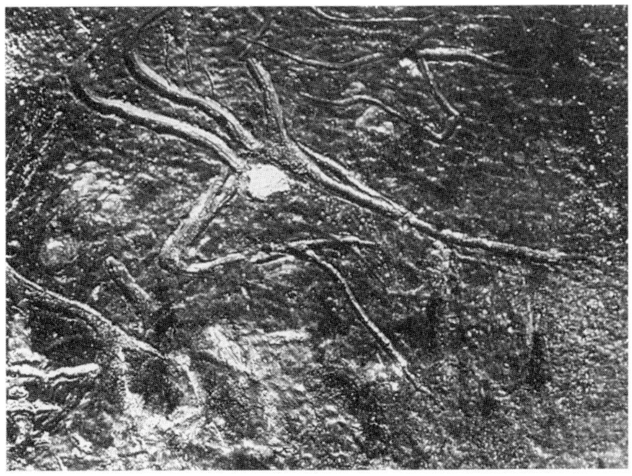

Fig. 3.7. Polydigital tracing in the cave of Gargas, French Pyrenees, about 20,000 B.C. (?) (head and horns of an animal?).

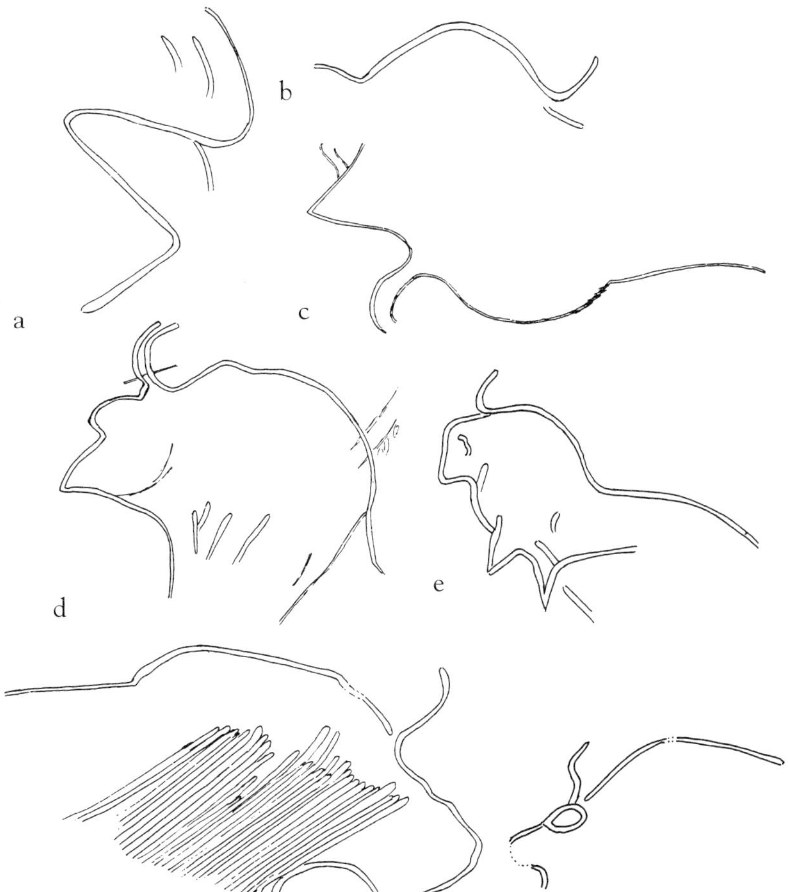

Fig. 3.8. Monodigital tracings depicting aspects of bison, in "Les Crevasses," Room 3, cave of Gargas. *a.* Double S curve (head). *b.* Double S curve (horns, dorsal line, and tail). *c.* Two double S curves (dorsal and frontal outlines). *d.* Two fitted double S curves and strokes (outline; modern damage to the head). *e.* Three superimposed double S curves and strokes (outline). *f.* Abbreviated and double S curves and strokes (outline). *g.* Abbreviated and double S curves and circular stroke (dorsal line, head, and eye).

replications.[50] On one engraved panel (Fig. 3.10),[51] several animal heads have been extracted; particularly around the turn of the muzzle and mouth, the lines often falter and skip, as if the engraver were proceeding slowly, changing his mind, or testing his direction. Series of parallel hatches and other, longer, single lines lie beneath or above many of these images, but occasionally they have been caught up in the image as part of the outline. In fact, a very large percentage of all the lines in the panels can be brought into association with one or another of the recognizable images, many of which blend into each other or depend on the same lines. In the chamber of the cave known as the "Camarin," many finely detailed images are associated with numerous other apparently nonrepresentational marks, including animal scratches. In many cases the line is firm and subtly modulated, particularly in the "Panel of Mammoths" and "La pierre noire" (Fig. 3.11),[52] containing at least three nearly complete outlines of whole figures as well as several fragmentary outlines.

What are we to make of a tangle like the "Panel of Mammoths" or many comparable clusters? Although it is often thought to occur in Paleolithic art and can, I think, be identified in some later caves, *completely random superimposition*—where the later artist takes no account of the work of the earlier—cannot explain some striking features of the palimpsests in Gargas. In Gargas, two or more images may depend upon a single shared line. Both representational and nonrepresentational forms are quite clearly "filled in" by hatchings or marked around by short series of strokes. The outlines of two or more images are fitted into each other. The whole palimpsest "spreads out," isolating image from nonimage (to some degree) and separating different individual images. Later lines modulate the underlying forms in regular ways, taking nonimage into image or, for established images, taking the form (in a series of re- or overmarkings) in the direction of greater completion, detail, modulation, and so forth. Although some of these formal structures could be produced fortuitously in completely random superimposition, we could not predict the regular repetition of all of these few structures.[53] At Gargas, superimposition of image on nonimage, nonimage on image, and so on, seems to be taking place *within a single system* or chain of replications or very closely related chains. Furthermore, the

50. We have no independent means of dating the engravings as any later than the digital tracings. It is probable that whether earlier, contemporary, or later, they were not solely derived from the tracings, for then we would expect them to exhibit only the forms and formats of the "later" stages in the replication of digital tracings, from which they were supposedly translated. They have been published and discussed in Leroi-Gourhan's topographical analysis of the cave (*Treasures,* 307–8), the *Atlas* (514–22), and in the comprehensive publication (Barrière, *L'art pariétal de Gargas*) as a separate set or system of marks and images in themselves. By my terms, this is an analytic convenience. We cannot determine whether the engravers themselves applied a distinction between engraving and digital trace (as we could if they were obviously "earlier" and "later" in a chain). In other words, we could be looking at a single network or chain of replications in which the medium and technique of the mark itself (tracing or engraving) was of no consequence compared (say) to its shape, or we could be looking at two self-sufficient but structurally parallel systems (tracing versus engraving). For my purposes here the difference can be set aside. As with tracing, in engraving image emerges palpably from nonimage.

51. Breuil, *Four Hundred Centuries,* fig. 284; *Atlas,* 516 (no. 3); Barrière, *L'art pariétal de Gargas,* 1:129 and fig. 30.

52. Barrière, *L'art pariétal de Gargas,* 1:200–201 and figs. 52, 57–63.

53. Conversely, in completely random or nonmeaningful superimposition, later marks should overlie the earlier in all kinds of unpredictable ways, since for all intents and purposes the earlier marks are not there. Moreover, we should expect to find regularly repeated

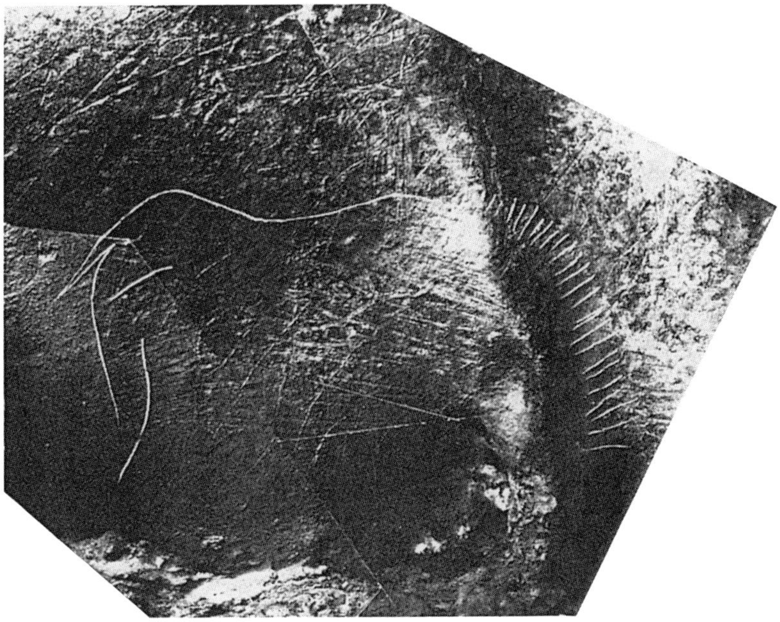

Fig. 3.9. Incised outline of a horse with surrounding linear incisions, "Chambre du Camarin," cave of Gargas.

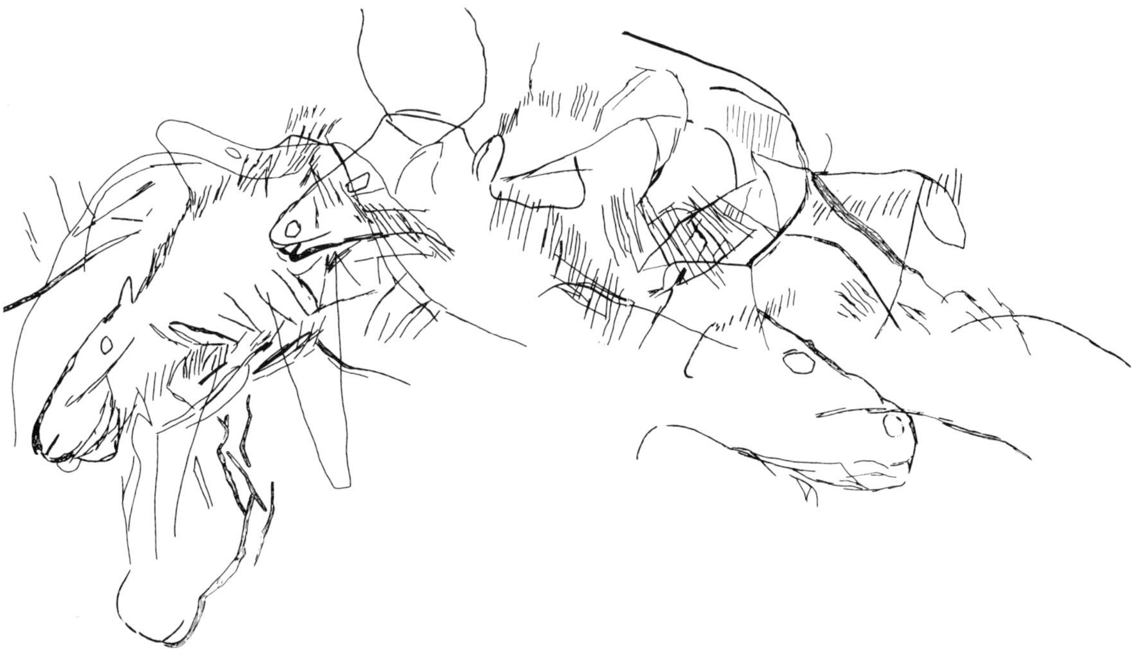

Fig. 3.10. Incised panel with bovids, horses, and mammoth (not shown), in "Le Baldaquin," cave of Gargas. (Drawing shows left two-thirds of panel.)

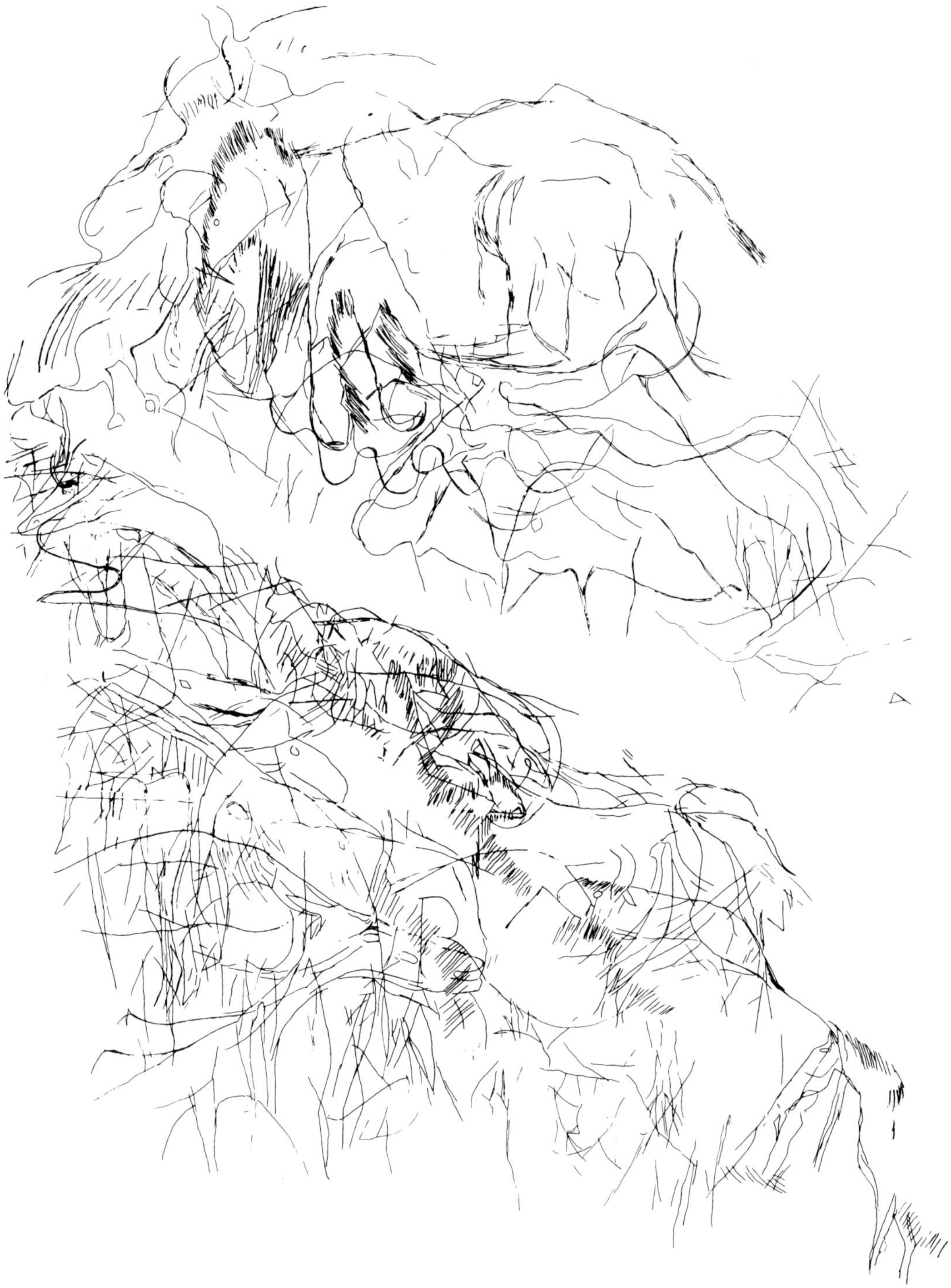

Fig. 3.11. "Panel of the Mammoths" (top of figure), cave of Gargas, incised palimpsest with several bison, a mammoth, serpentine form, and other marks, above "La pierre noire" (bottom of figure), incised palimpsest with two bison, two ibexes, two horses, and mammoth. Both panels have many additional markings. (Drawing shows right and larger portion of panels, separated from each other by a flow of calcite.)

palimpsests exhibit a morphology predictable only if the later artist were taking account of earlier marks and producing the palimpsest as such.[54] The artist takes account of his taking account of earlier marks, ad infinitum throughout a chain of replications.

This finding is quite compatible with whatever empirical determinations might be made about the absolute chronology of superimposition, a question that often bogs down in inconclusive debate about the *actual* time lag between the production of variants. There is necessarily some lag between variants, but whether it is five minutes or five hundred years is really less consequential for interpretation than whether the variants belong to a single chain or closely related chains of replication or to entirely unrelated chains. If they belong to a single chain, whatever the lag, the producers are taking account of past work and the accumulation as such; if they are unrelated, whatever the lag, this taking account does not occur.

Why, then, are nonimage elements, "early," minimal or fragmentary outlines, and "later," complete, detailed, modulated, and differentiated images produced in complex palimpsests, exhibiting the constant use and reuse of forms and formats of many different "logical ages" in the chains of replication? Why did the artist deliberately thread his latest work through the tangled fabric of his earlier, and his firm, resolved images through and among his fragmentary or tentative efforts or into the ground of nonimage altogether?

Some elements of a solution can be derived straightforwardly from my general analysis of image making. We cannot assume that the artist was *just* producing images, derived from the nonimage that happens to be preserved. Those features of a pattern *not* implicated in an image may perfectly well have a variety of *other,* nonrepresentational semantic values. (If we accept Charles Sanders Peirce's analysis of pictures as "hypoicons," then they necessarily have other values.) In a single pattern, several referential systems could be

formal (morphological and compositional) relations between the later marks themselves or between the later marks and the context, since placement is not being determined by an underlying mark but by other factors. Finally, we should expect to find regularly repeated formal relations between the earlier marks not picked up and repeated between the later. All of these characteristics of the palimpsest would count as evidence that earlier and later marks were produced completely independently. Note that we can investigate questions about the meaningfulness of superimposition as questions about the morphology, structure, and context of a palimpsest, without knowing in advance which marks are in fact earlier or later. (Although here we do, of course, have the evidence of literal superimposition to guide us, the literal data are underdetermining, for in a single chain it might be that earlier and later marks never physically touch.)

54. Note that an artist's taking account of earlier marks in theory is not enough to establish that he produced the palimpsest as such. The mark maker could produce his later marks on the basis of his experience of earlier marks, but being just the unavoidable by-product of the fact that he makes unerasable marks, the palimpsest as such may have no interest for him; he could be interested at any given moment only in his latest marks—produced as they are on the basis of past experiences—and the fact that the earlier are still there would be of no account. I have no space to present a full demonstration that at Gargas the mode of production required the mark maker to take account both of earlier marks *and* the ongoing production of a palimpsest of the earlier and his latest marks. The demonstration investigates archaeological expectations about the replication of marks: for example, if the mark maker is interested only in his latest marks, then he should gradually fill up a surface (unavoidably creating a palimpsest), move to another surface, and start there with his latest variants, building a new but developmentally later palimpsest there. At Gargas it seems that the mark maker skipped from surface to surface and returned to previously marked surfaces.

operating simultaneously: a notation may be commenting upon or labeling an image, an image may be an element in a heraldry, and so forth. Alexander Marshack's analysis of the alterations, reuse, and overmarking of Paleolithic images by nonimage features strongly suggests the nonimage elements were significant—produced nonrandomly as such, regularly repeated and varied in a few limited formats. Sometimes the strokes and marks seem to lead the viewer from one cluster of marks to another or signify points of transition; they could be signposts of sorts. They might even have semantic value as a notation accompanying the images—perhaps to be paralleled with the puzzling symbolism of the famous red, black, and white hand stencils also produced in the cave at Gargas—or as a symbolism denoting the presence of certain people, the performance of certain activities, and so forth, or even as a kind of signature, caption, or "audience response."

A meaningful representation does not always and only derive from, replicate, and vary a ground of absolutely meaningless stuff (lumps, marks, sound waves) but also derives from, replicates, and varies a ground *with other meanings*. For images, the depictive mark derives from seeing-as in relation to a nonimage mark, that is, a mark that has not already been interpreted and replicated as an image of a particular object or even has been so interpreted unbeknownst to a later interpreter. Specifically and positively, the "nonimage" mark may be a naturally produced mark, a semantically meaningless human-made mark (such as an incision made to test the cutting power of a tool), a semantically meaningful but nonrepresentational mark, and so forth. Similarly, semantically meaningful nonrepresentational graphics and glyphs, like heraldic emblems or "hieroglyphic" notations, might derive from a context that is nongraphic or nonglyphic in terms of the constitutive criteria of *those* representational schemes (a case of this kind is described in Chapter 7).

If we could completely interpret the palimpsest at every level—requiring penetrating analyses of notation, decoration, and so on, in addition to an analysis of images—then all marks might be seen to be necessary in replication and for "total signification": the palimpsest as such is the sum, a figurative system of astonishing range. The replication of the system as a whole will exhibit a complex structure of variation not entirely predictable by the replicatory requirements or trajectory of any one embedded representational scheme. For instance, although in the replication of images the nonimage elements might "fade out," precisely those nonimage elements might be required in the replication of a nonrepresentational scheme—a notation, "decorative" or heraldic design, and so forth.

The figurative system of image and nonimage may be a necessary feature of production in a final sense as well, a sense more directly relevant to image making as such than our recognition that nonimage marks might be representational.

To produce an image is to hold thing resemblance constant throughout a chain of replications. But this is only the most minimal characteristic of many chains in which marks depict an object: most chains have further characteristics. For one thing, chains of replication do not merely establish one stable image. In an actual chain, thing resemblance need not be held *forever* constant once an image has been established but can be varied considerably. Inaugural images become in turn the ground for further seeing-as (for a formal statement of such possibilities, see Chapter 2). The chain of replications will montage over time into a new image (that is, marks with thing resemblances preserved as such and derived from but not judged as identical to initial thing resemblances). Throughout this potentially continuous process of replication of the same and into a different image, the balance of resemblant and nonresemblant features is continuously shifting. For example, even in the replication of the same image (a chain of the canonical form), nonresemblant features are indifferently substitutable, and the resemblant features may change as long as their thing resemblance is judged to be constant. And in the establishment of a new image, the resemblant features of the old may become nonresemblant in the new, and the new may use nonresemblant features of the old as resemblant. Of course, if at any point after the image is established in a chain of the canonical form *no* thing resemblances are seen and preserved as such in a further canonical chain, then the whole pattern of marks reverts to nonimage. In sum, if replication goes further than simply the continuous reproduction of the same image by identical marks (which would appear to be materially impossible), whatever the further work might be (leading to a new image or to none at all), *then it will necessarily and constantly generate nonimage.*

In a complex palimpsest, nonimage never completely falls away, because the *images* themselves are continually varying in replication, moving away from an initial moment of seeing-as but (allowing a teleological phrasing) moving toward other moments of seeing-as, refinding the founding possibility of nonimage at every turn (turn of the line, turn of the page . . .). Although I shall not try to demonstrate this here, it is probably not too much to suppose that the artist ultimately takes control of what is initially presented simply as an inherent and necessary fact of making marks. Just as seeing-as is an automatic response of the perceptual system to a certain pattern of marks, so too, of course, is *not seeing-as*—and both processes can be recognized as such, preserved, and varied in replication. The image maker is necessarily master of both; it is the art historian—all too often seeker after iconological meaning or the securities of signification—who privileges the one over the other.

It may seem odd to speak of nonimage or not seeing-as as a vital positive element of image making with vivid direct consequences. Nonimage is fundamentally implicated in image at many levels; it is the most immediate and most important context of the image. It is required to establish image, as the very marks to be seen-as and as part of the interpreter's very test that thing resemblance has in fact been produced as such. It is the unavoidable by-product of replicating the image. It is constitutive of other symbolic schemes with which image is ordinarily (and perhaps necessarily) associated. It is the very ground or possibility for change in the image or, at the limit, for its decay altogether. In fact, nonimage is simply mark making as such—historically of far greater antiquity and with far broader functional application and cultural consequence than the particular technology of depiction I have looked at here. Image making is something we do with marks we have made, but the marks have a life of their own: they assert themselves literally and in all their intractable materiality at every turn. The fundamental and problematic truth for the production and interpretation of images is simply that it is only the mark that is literally and really there.

The Necessity of History

As a pattern that can be taken by different interpreters as being representational or not and as having the same or different objects, an image certainly requires interpretation under the constitutive and specific resemblance criteria—that is, in a particular conventional context. A good deal has been made of conventions and contexts in modern art history. In fact, conventions and contexts seem to be the stuff of history itself—painting a Virgin in the fifteenth century, exhibiting a pile of felt in downtown New York, or carving a bone in the last Ice Age. But as the very stuff of history, conventions and contexts cannot easily be made into the *explanation for* or the *grounds of* history. Here we experience puzzling regresses and crippling circularities. These paradoxes can be swept under the rug, or, in the modern urge to describe conventions and contexts completely and accurately, their resolution can be indefinitely postponed.

What might be called a preconventionalist and precontextualist account seems to be required to show why conventions and contexts would ever have the configurations they do. I have offered only a sketch of a small element of such an account. I have suggested that images are generated in the replication of seeing-as as such, a process that, at least inaugurally, can occur automatically and involuntarily and—although I did not stress this element of my analysis—in the total absence of a preexisting cultural or social structure. In fact, when pressed for their hard-cash analytic value, the conventions and contexts of depiction simply amount to the replication of seeing-as. But in saying this, I have not forgotten about history in a reckless embrace of the image as beyond constraint, before deliberation, or above prediction, as somehow emptied into history by the inexplicable transcendental authorities going by various names—genius, creativity, or what-have-you. As I have stressed, the interpretation of an image as this particular image is the archaeology of its replication—and an adequate archaeology is a historical project par excellence. Replication begins from a specific and, from my point of view, possibly a determinable point and has a specific and determinable trajectory. What more could a historian want?

Certainly there is much more. With tremendous labor and good luck in our archaeology we could determine that we have before us an image of a particular object. On my analysis, this determination is totally equivalent to describing it conventionally and contextually. But we could still wonder why this image is there at all. We could, in other words, justifiably want an account of *replication itself,* the ongoing human practice of making and remaking the world as perception delivers it, preserving what we perceive or elaborating, revising, reversing, or suppressing it, repeating ourselves with accruing differences: in short, the human fate *to have history.* But that is another question, not unhistorical in itself.

Chapter 4

The Deconstruction of Intentionality in Archaeology

At present, the figure of archaeology is the funerary monument; its concern is death and its methods are commemorational and reconstructive—like the embalmer who takes the rotting corpse to reverse and fill in its decay. But archaeology could take its own name seriously. Instead of mourning an irreducible "logos" in its funereal condition as *archē*, it should accept the irreducibility of *archē as* the condition of logos. An original intention is lost not because evidence for it may not exist for us today but because it never existed in stability and purity in the first place. Archaeology should not be the mourning and denial of this loss but rather its endless acknowledgment (see further Chapter 9), for archaeology is most properly the study not of the original logos, now *archē*, but of the logos *as archē*, then, now, and forever.

Archaeology and Logoi

If we follow the etymology of its name, archaeology conceives itself as the study of the logoi, or "words"—more broadly, the meanings—made by people in the past, *archē logoi*. As the object of archaeological inquiry, the logoi themselves have been variously defined throughout the history of archaeology. In the twentieth century alone, a traditional archaeologist like Grahame Clark understands them to be values and beliefs: on his account, the archaeologist attempts to reconstruct the value systems or belief systems of people in the past.[1] A "New Archaeologist" like Lewis Binford identifies the logoi as reasons and strategies. In his view, the archaeologist identifies past peoples' decisions about and strategies for living.[2] (Sometimes, however, the past conceptual activity of "strategizing" is partially obscured in New Archaeological writing by conflating it analytically with "behavior" or "adaptation" strictly speaking.) An "anthropological" archaeologist like Guy Gibbon specifies the logoi as "cultural norms," "models," or "rules."[3] Finally, a "postprocessual" archaeologist like Ian Hodder—coming closest to the root connotations of the Greek concept—defines the logoi as symbols or semantic structures or, more recently, as ideologies or rhetorics. For Hodder, an archaeological investigation should attempt to "read" the past symbols or symbolic systems—there are many ways to characterize them—preserved in the archaeological record and open to interpretation in the present.[4] Even "postmodernist," "critical" archaeologists are interested in logoi. It is just that they find them as much in the present—in archaeologists' *own* values and beliefs, reasons and strategies, norms and rules, or ideologies and rhetorics (compare Chapter 9)—as in the past.[5]

For my purposes here, the logoi, *however* they are defined, make an appearance in practically any archaeological analysis in a particular fashion. Not all archaeologists produce what I call, following Jacques Derrida, logocentric analyses all of the time. Almost all of them do so, however, almost all of the time. Archaeologists use archaeological materials as the "records," the "remains," or the "traces" (even the "signatures")[6] of formerly existing logoi, the values, strategies, norms, or ideologies of people in the past (if sometimes only past archaeologists), now supposedly represented, expressed, or embodied in the texts or inscriptions, the images, and the other kinds of artifacts like lithics, ceramics, shelters, costumes, architectural forms, and so on, which have survived into the present.

The logoi seem to provide the guarantee of, and explanation for, regularity in the archaeological record. To that degree they create whatever deserves to be called a "record" in the first place—for "records" are always "records of . . . something," namely, logoi. Thus, for example, similarity between artifacts might be explained on the grounds of their common derivation from the same underlying logos, conceived as a value system, as a strategy of life, or as an ideology, each with an expression in ways of doing or making things. (Such explanation should be contrasted with, though it often rides on, stylistic analysis, which,

1. E.g., Grahame Clark, *Symbols of Excellence: Precious Materials as Expressions of Status* (Cambridge, 1986).

2. E.g., Lewis Binford, *In Pursuit of the Past: Decoding the Archaeological Record* (New York, 1983).

3. Guy Gibbon, *Anthropological Archaeology* (New York, 1984), 139–40, 150.

4. E.g., Ian Hodder, *Symbols in Action: Ethnoarchaeological Studies of Material Culture* (Cambridge, 1982), and idem, "Post-Processual Archaeology," *Advances in Archaeological Method and Theory* 8 (1985), 1–26.

5. Fundamental studies in this vein have been offered by Mark Leone, "Symbolic, Structural, and Critical Archaeology," in *American Archaeology, Past and Future,* ed. D. Meltzer, D. Fowler, and J. Sabloff (Washington, D.C., 1986), 415–38, and M. Shanks and C. Tilley, *Reconstructing Archaeology: Theory and Practice* (New York, 1987).

6. R. A. Gould, *Living Archaeology* (Cambridge, 1980), 113.

of course, has an important role in archaeology; as I show in Chapter 6, stylistic analysis does not necessarily attribute values, strategies, or ideologies to the style makers.) This underlying logos is often regarded as a stable, preexisting reality, a specific mental event or process. Thus it is independent of the artifact forms in which it is embodied. Especially in traditional archaeology and conservative disciplines like Egyptology and Sinology, the logos is often regarded as the typical or essential habit of thought—the so-called perspective, mind-set, or worldview—of people who can be categorized as belonging together on geographic, biogenetic, linguistic, or historical grounds. (In branches of archaeology that have been influenced by modern cultural anthropology, these idealist concepts of agents' "perspective" or of a people's worldview are restated in culturological jargon. The underlying logos is said to be "culture," "cultural meaning," "meaning in context," and so on. As I shall show, these formulations cannot escape logocentrism without considerable qualification.) For example, people who are supposed to share a habitat or an ethnicity are thereby understood to share a logos—a value system, strategy of life, or ideology—which we encounter re-presented or ex-pressed in their artifacts. Conversely, if we apply certain "archaeological methods" in studying their artifacts, then we should be able to read off their values, strategies, or ideologies and recover their essential historical, ethnic, or other identity.

Simply put, if there were no logoi, then there would be no "archaeological" record; there would *just* be an array of artifacts lying around in the present in various spatial distributions and encountered by us in various temporal sequences. It is only by believing in the reality, the stability or specificity, and the recoverability of the *archē* logoi—the values, strategies, or ideologies of people in the past—that things lying around in the present can become "traces."

Deconstruction and Logoi

Let us now recall a contemporary challenge to the "archaeological" ambition. Deconstruction denies the autonomous, transcendent reality, stability, and retrievability of logoi lying beyond or behind material cultural forms. By now, deconstructive arguments have been broadly applied in many different fields and in many ways; they have been widely accommodated in theoretical work in many of the social and human sciences. In this chapter, however, I stick to the deconstructive assault, by now classical, on what underlies the archaeological ambition as I just sketched it, namely, an entrenched view of human consciousness and the way in which it is directed at the world.[7]

7. Jacques Derrida, *L'origine de la géometrie*, 2d ed. (Paris, 1974 [1962]); idem, "La forme et le vouloir-dire: note sur la phénoménologie du langage," *Revue Internationale de Philosophie* 81 (1967), 277–99; idem, *La voix et le phénomène: introduction au problème du signe dans la phénoménologie de Husserl* (Paris, 1967); and idem, *Writing and Difference*, trans. Alan Bass (Chicago, 1978). For commentary, see Rodolph Gasché, *The Tain of the Mirror: Derrida and the Philosophy of Reflection* (Cambridge, Mass., 1986), and Judith Butler, *Subjects of Desire: Hegelian Reflections in Twentieth-Century France* (New York, 1987).

Specifically, deconstruction offers a revised, perhaps even an inverted, conception of the relation between human thought and its manifestations, including the stream of consciousness itself, script, image making, and other media of expressing thought. According to the entrenched view, a metaphysics of consciousness propounded by many Western philosophers and harking back to Platonic themes, thoughts precede their particular material representation, expression, or embodiment. The material embodiment is merely a stuff or medium of some kind supplementing and relaying thought itself. If you like, writing or other embodiments of thought, such as pictures, are the archaeological records of thought.

If writing is the material mediation of thought, then thought itself must be unmediated or immediate. Whether or not it is represented, expressed, or embodied in script, pictures, or other artifacts, according to the entrenched view thought suffuses the consciousness of the thinker. To use terms taken up from phenomenology, thought is immediately "given" or "present" to the thinker. This transparency of thought to the thinker—its original, irreducible "presence" for her—is the taken-for-granted of the traditional view. All else flows from this starting point, including, for example, personal and social identity: *cogito, ergo sum*.

By contrast, deconstructive writers—they work from insights gleaned from psychoanalysis and linguistics as well as from movements in phenomenology and philosophy itself—insist upon the distance of thought from itself, its lack of full immediacy or presence. Most simply put, the thinker's relation to her thought must contain some kind of lag, most easily conceived as a temporal lag (see further Chapter 8). Thus in making herself aware of the content of her thought, the thinker is necessarily moving beyond that thought precisely by making it the object of her "current," "present" thought. Self-consciousness, in the traditional view the epitome of thought present-and-immediate-to-itself, becomes, then, the epitome of thought chasing and supplementing itself—thinking about itself thinking about itself thinking . . .—in what would seem to be a continuous repetition, review, and perhaps revision. On this view, *thought itself* becomes "writing" *(écriture)*—that is, an ongoing material mediation, an ongoing "writing-out" or "writing-down," whether it transpires in the supposed privacy of the stream of consciousness or in public activities of producing inscriptions, making pictures, or fashioning artifacts of other kinds.

In the entrenched, traditional view, the value systems, strategies of life, cultural norms, or ideologies investigated by archaeologists would all be thoughts, immediately "present" to the thinker, supposedly re-presented or ex-pressed in merely material media, which thus become the traces of thought. The entrenched account does allow the thinker's values and norms to be tacit, her reasons to be unarticulated, or her ideology to be unconscious. But these thoughts—tacit or explicit, unarticulated or enunciated, unconscious or conscious—are always taken to be suffused with a full presence of the values, reasons, or ideology that centers the thinker as thinking in accord with those values, reasons, or ideology in the first place. By contrast, in the deconstructive revision of the entrenched account, value systems, strategies of life, or ideology are "written." They are constituted only *in* the activity of thinking them out or, more accurately, thinking them down *in some medium or other,* from the stream of consciousness through toolmaking to script itself. Thus the logoi are not "in the heads of" the makers and then, like a Word made Flesh, somehow emptied into matter. Rather, they are made, "written," by the makers neither before nor after but only always in the ongoing, temporally and spatially ramified structure of making, "writing," as such.[8]

ARCHAEOLOGY AND DECONSTRUCTION

From this brief outline, one might conclude that there must be a strong tension between "archaeology," the study of ancient logoi "in the heads of" and "present" to their original thinkers, and deconstruction, a variety of skepticism about the very existence of logoi. We certainly need to explore this tension. For example, if—as a deconstructive extremist might conclude—the logoi do not actually exist (except as a fiction of an entrenched metaphysics of human consciousness centered in its primordial, pure Thought), then what is the object of an archaeological inquiry hoping to be material, not metaphysical? Unlike some commentators, however, I do not believe that deconstructive arguments entail the dissolution of archaeology. As Derrida has pointed out on several occasions, "[T]here is no sense in doing without the concepts of metaphysics in order to shake metaphysics."[9] I argue not that archaeology is *not* deconstructive but rather that archaeology is *always already* deconstructive. In other words, I wish to make a deconstructive argument about the relationship between archaeology and deconstruction.

In practice, the best archaeology has never *assumed* Intentionality—my summary term for all possible logoi like values, strategies, and ideologies—and has never *concluded* with Intentionality.[10] At its most fertile and productive, archaeology maintains a deep, perhaps even defining uncertainty about, as well as a painstaking empirical scrutiny of, the very reality, locatability, and recoverability of the sites of Intentionality in the material traces supposedly constituting the archaeological record. Unfortunately, archaeology does often degenerate into so-called methods for *reconstructing* supposedly original Intentionalities from traces, which, once their diagnostic status as "trace of . . ." has been understood, are disregarded or even literally destroyed in the act of excavation and reconstruction itself. For example, in the study of prehistoric and ancient art we can find a logocentric effort to specify what has been called "the meaning of the art," in which the material properties of

8. On Derrida's concept of writing, a group of commentaries published soon after Derrida's work became widely known in the English-speaking world remain most useful: E. Casey, "Origin(s) in (of) Heidegger/Derrida," *Journal of Philosophy* 81 (1984), 601–10; Tom Conley, "A Trace of Style," in *Displacements: Derrida and After,* ed. Mark Krupnick (Bloomington, Ind., 1983), 74–92; E. Donato, "'Here, Now'/'Always, Already': Incidental Remarks on Some Recent Characterizations of the Text," *Diacritics* 6 (1976), 24–29; R. Platt, "Writing, *Différence,* and Metaphysical Closure," *Journal of the British Society of Phenomenology* (1986), 234–51; Gayatri C. Spivak, "Revolutions That As Yet Have No Model: Derrida's *Limited Inc.*," *Diacritics* 10 (1980), 29–49.

9. Derrida, *Writing and Difference,* 280; and see also his *Positions,* trans. Alan Bass (Chicago, 1982).

10. I capitalize to distinguish the broad, technical definition of Intentionality as mental directedness (see further John R. Searle, "What Is an Intentional State?" *Mind* 88 [1979], 74–92, and idem, "Intentionality and Its Place in Nature," *Diacritics* 38 [1984], 87–99) from colloquial definitions of intentionality as consciously willed planning and the like. For recent art historical controversies about intentions and Intentionality, see Michael

the writing-out, the image (for an extended example, see Chapter 7), are merely used as a platform for the reconstruction of something, thought or Intentionality itself, allegedly lying behind the images themselves—such as the Egyptians' "perspective" or the Maya's "worldview." By contrast, in its deconstructive moments archaeology is skeptical about such sites of Intentionality; it questions the real cash value of trying to characterize them. It is alert to the metaphysical implications and to the possible logical fallacies of reading from script, images, or artifacts, "writing" broadly construed, to mind—to values, strategies, or ideologies. Most important, it is interested in the material evidence precisely *as* material, that is, as a material structure of writing, of traces and spaces between them or of spaces with traces between.

Ascribing Intentionality

Before I illustrate this general argument, recall how archaeology, along with many other disciplines, characterizes Intentionality, the sought-after logos, whether defined as value and belief, as reason and strategy, as norm or rule, or as ideology and rhetoric. Broadly speaking, Intentionality is understood to be *mental directedness,* the way in which the mind directs itself toward its objects—for example, in perceiving something, referring to it, imagining it, desiring it, believing in it, or commanding it. Logically, Intentionality is the relation of mental "aboutness." The perception, reference, imagination, and so on, is about its object.[11]

According to a perspicuous analysis by George M. Wilson, statements taking the form "A intends B"—as in "Barbara designed a tool," "Jasper copied a picture"—ascribe Intentionality to someone, or to someone's action, only if four conditions are satisfied.[12] These conditions, as they obtained in the past, then, can be taken as necessary discoveries of any archaeological identification of Intentionality as well.[13] First, the behavior is performed by the agent and not by another agent or by some natural process. In some cases, it may be difficult to make this elementary discrimination. Second, the behavior occurs at the time of the ascribed intention. As ordinary usage has it, the intention is right there in the

Baxandall, *Patterns of Intention: The Historical Explanation of Pictures* (New Haven, Conn., 1985), and Donald Preziosi, *Rethinking Art History: Meditations on a Coy Science* (New Haven, Conn., 1989), with a review by Whitney Davis, *Art Bulletin* 72 (1989), 156–66.

11. See further W. Bechtel, *Philosophy of Mind: An Overview for Cognitive Science* (Hillsdale, N.J., 1988), 40–50; M. Brand, *Intending and Acting: Toward a Naturalized Action Theory* (Cambridge, 1984); Michael Bratman, *Intentions, Plans, and Practical Reason* (Cambridge, 1987); Daniel C. Dennett, "Intentional Systems in Cognitive Ethology: The 'Panglossian Paradigm' Defended," *Behavioral and Brain Sciences* 6 (1983), 343–90; and Searle, "What Is an Intentional State?" and "Intentionality and Its Place in Nature."

12. George M. Wilson, *The Intentionality of Human Action,* rev. ed. (Stanford, Calif., 1989), 121–22.

13. Much of what must be said about the "archaeology of intentionality" would apply to the "archaeology of action" as well (see esp. Brand, *Intending and Acting*). For instance, Gibbon identifies as minimum units of archaeological analysis the "individual act" and the "activity area," "the smallest spatial unit of patterned social behavior in a community where a specific task was carried out by an individual" (*Anthropological Archaeology,* 21, 141).

behavior and can be "seen in" or "read off" it. Third, the behavior is under the agent's "direct, sentient control," conscious or unconscious. (In Wilson's scheme, the behavior is also "voluntary." However, a behavior under the agent's "control" nonetheless might be involuntary because it is not motivated by the agent's own desires or beliefs. For example, in the official image making of ancient Egypt, the behavior of making an image was fully controlled but was not necessarily "voluntary" in the modern sense.)[14] Finally, in contrast to the "sentient directionality" of animals, human Intentionality involves "reflexivity," or "reference back" to the agent's "self-consciousness"—for fourth, that the behavior exists at all *and* that it is the agent's, that it is occurring now, and that it is controlled are all matters about which the agent is directly aware without any need for further observation or evidence.[15] For the agent, these four conditions are irreducible and incorrigible. The four conditions, then, converge on the conclusion that Intentionality is apparently established in a single unitary "site" characterized by self-possession, immediacy, control, and self-awareness. Debate may rage, of course, about just what site has these properties—for example, is it the brain, the mind, language, consciousness, or the soul?—but this question is subsidiary to the principal conclusion that *some* site of unitary Intentionality must be identifiable.

At least three substantial puzzles arise, however, when we consider an Intentionality that is *archē*, archaic or even "lost"—most properly, when it is not *our own* irreducible, incorrigible Intentionality-at-the-moment that is in question. Among other things, these puzzles may require the "decomposition" of Intentionality into more primitive components—such as memory, motivation, and "prospective" and "immediate" interests—and they underlie the more extreme "deconstruction" of the entire archaeological attempt to locate past Intentionalities.[16]

First, not all action can be described as Intentional. Some behavior is automatic or habitual rather than planned or "scripted."[17] The extent of Intentionality in human action is very debatable—even though, according to the formula, we incorrigibly know the extent of our own Intentionalities. Therefore a methodological problem arises for any inquiry that can directly see or infer something about the action of another person—for example, by witnessing it or by encountering its effects—but not the presence or absence of any Intentionality in it (see Chapter 1). Where is the Intentionality in (what) action? Note that it is not simply that *some* actions are habitual, whereas *other* actions are Intentional. Instead, many, or perhaps all, actions *interweave* habitual and Intentional elements. Thus we must somehow pick out the Intentionality in the action, the siting of values and beliefs, reasons and strategies, ideologies and rhetorics. But in picking it out we cannot neglect the habitual element, somehow peeling it away in order to reveal the kernel of Intentionality. There is nothing inherent in Intentionality itself—independent of any metaphysical claim about it—guaranteeing that the Intentionality of an action is necessarily its most determining element, compared, for example, with the "practical,"

14. Whitney Davis, *The Canonical Tradition in Ancient Egyptian Art* (New York, 1989), 108–15.

15. Wilson, *Intentionality of Human Action*, 122–24, 146–48, 175–80; compare Bechtel, *Philosophy of Mind*, 55, and Brand, *Intending and Acting*, 211.

16. Brand, *Intending and Acting*, 38–47.

17. See Brand, *Intending and Acting*, 108–10, 183–85, for a careful dissection.

"natural," non-Intentional active orientation of the organism in its "lifeworld."[18] At the very least, the "thinking" is only in the material acting, the "writing"—and the writing, just because it is writing, inextricably contains non-Intentional, automatic or habitual, elements.

Second, there is no Intentionality that is not a mental phenomenon. Therefore to recognize an Intention in an action or an artifact is to recognize a mind at work. But the converse is not true. There are mental phenomena that are not Intentional, such as hallucinations. (I set aside ingenious efforts to characterize such mental events as fully Intentional; some aspects of these phenomena may be Intentional, while others may not be.) Therefore recognizing Intentionality might not be the *only* way to recognize a mind, and conversely, there might be aspects of the mind that cannot be recognized by identifying Intentionality.

Third, and most important, consider the problem of archaeology when the *archē* logos in question is one's own Intentionality. Self-awareness about one's mental events or mental acts could only be an Intentionality directed at, or "about," one's Intentionality. One is thinking about oneself thinking about the world. To that extent, a multileveled, nested, distributed Intentionality seems to feature in any possible specification of Intentionality we might make about ourselves. To specify our Intentionality "now" is to make it the object of our present Intentionality in the "now +," the moment just beyond the "now" in which we direct our thought at what we had just been thinking in the immediately past "now." Thus, contrary to the entrenched account, thought could never be fully "present" to itself in an irreducible "present tense." Instead, it always seems to be outside itself, going on with itself, going beyond itself. Again, as deconstruction puts it, thought is more like an ongoing writing, or *écriture,* than an original, irreducible Word. Put another way, the logos is always *archē* insofar as it can only be specified *as* logos by being past itself.[19]

Logocentric and Deconstructive Archaeologies of Intentionality

There are methodological problems, then, with the siting of Intentionality in action, in mental life, and in relation to itself. In each case, as I have noted, the placing and the timing of the Intentionality turns out to be uncertain, decentered, or "lost" in relation to the apparent certainty, centeredness, and immediate self-presence it would seem to have when we set out to ascribe Intentionality in the first place. Two contrasting archaeological

18. For the terms as they have been conceived in phenomenology and cognitive studies, see Hubert L. Dreyfus, ed., *Husserl, Intentionality, and Cognitive Science* (Cambridge, Mass., 1982).

19. For deconstructive approaches to Intentionality, see Derrida's essential "La forme et le vouloir-dire" and especially fine studies by J. R. Boly, "Nihilism Aside: Derrida's Debate over Intentional Models," *Philosophy and Literature* 9 (1985), 152–65, and L. Lawlor, "Temporality and Spatiality: A Note to a Footnote in Jacques Derrida's *Writing and Difference*," *Research in Phenomenology* 12 (1983), 149–65.

paradigms wrestle with this result in two quite different ways. Neither paradigm can be identified with any particular approach within the professional discipline of archaeology. Rather, they are modes of archaeological metaphysics put to use throughout most varieties of archaeology, disciplines like professional archaeology, art history, cultural anthropology, and so on.

The first paradigm, "logocentric" in its approach, tries to preserve or reconstruct the priority, irreducibility, and centeredness of Intentionality in the face of the three puzzles I have sketched. It relegates the areas of ambiguity and inconsistency in identifying an *archē* logos to the mere stuff, the "medium" or "trace," that supposedly re-presents or ex-presses the otherwise unadulterated self-sufficiency and self-consistency of the Intention itself. According to this paradigm, then, behind all of the ambiguity or diffuseness of representations and expressions—themselves understood as manifestations of uncertainty or loss precisely requiring a "reconstruction" in terms of logoi—there subsists the original Intentionality that generated them even though they have somehow, through myriad processes of degeneration, fallen away from it.

In practice, the logocentric paradigm typically works with basic distinctions between a term for the original Intention and a term for the mere trace in which the Intention appears in its degraded form. Throughout archaeology, logocentrism maintains dichotomies like Idea/Expression, Intention/Artifact, Form/Matter, Concept/Statement, Rule/Practice, Competence/Performance, Spirit/Body, Signified/Signifier, Meaning/Enunciation, Perception/Representation, or Plan/Action. In each case, in the quest for the *archē* logos the archaeologist is supposed to get behind the expression, matter, statement, practice, and so on, to the idea, form, concept, or rule.[20]

The logocentric paradigm is not the exclusive province of traditional, New, or anthropological archaeologists prone to posit unifying values, strategies, or norms at work in the past. Although postmodern or poststructuralist archaeologists supposedly recognize the instability and decenteredness of such things, the relevant question is not *whether* the shiftiness of Intentionality is recognized—a traditional archaeologist often sees this as clearly as the postmodernist does—but *where it is sited and to what it is attributed.* If the instability of Intentionality is identified only in the instability *of representation and expression,* then postmodernist archaeology would be just as logocentric as other archaeologies: the logocentric paradigm includes a variant in which representation can be as unstable, contested,

20. In some cases, the relation of the two terms can be reversed, but logocentric relationship and hierarchy is preserved. For example, in the traditional dichotomy of Spirit and Body, the body has as good a claim as anything to be regarded as the true logos. As Aron Gurwitsch put it, because the "body is the only material thing at our immediate disposal," it becomes the "privileged mundane object" (*Marginal Consciousness,* ed. L. Embree [Athens, Ohio, 1985], xxv, 33, 62). In some writing in the archaeology of gender (e.g., John Boswell, *Christianity, Social Tolerance, and Homosexuality: Gay People in Western Europe from the Beginning of the Christian Era to the Fourteenth Century* [Chicago, 1980]) it is thus the body that has been conceived analytically as an ultimate ground of essential identity. It becomes the logos that is expressed by Spirit, understood as *Zeitgeist,* cultural form, or representational practice. Within New Archaeology, it may be the human body rather than the human mind that is the logos, because it is the body that preeminently "adapts" to its environment according to the principles of natural selection. But for other writers, the body—certainly its gender or sexual identity, and perhaps even its basic "rationality" and "biological" performance—is not logos but must be written.

or "writerly" as one likes so long as it is conceived *as* representation with a signifying system, ideology, "power/knowledge regime," or similar logos behind it. Poststructuralism, as such, is no guarantee of nonlogocentrism. The more a secondary term in the logocentric relation—representation, expression, performance—is described as mediated, unclosable, contested, and so forth, the more a need may be felt to understand the primary term, the underlying idea, norm, or rhetoric, suffusing the field of writing as its governing Intentionality. And needless to say, when postmodernists insist that all expressions or performances are intrinsically mediated and contested, they have simply added a new species of governing essence, a new logos, to the old list.

By contrast, in the "deconstructive" archaeological paradigm, there is no special value (and a real risk of incoherence) in looking for the priority, irreducibility, and centeredness of *any* originally pure but now degraded Intentionality—whether it is a past belief system or worldview, adaptive foraging strategy, cultural convention, play of signification, regime of power and knowledge, "contested," "contextual" meaning, or even the archaeologist's own moral and political agenda. The deconstructive paradigm admits the three problem areas in the ascription of Intentionality in all their force and without any hesitations deriving from any form of the humanistic metaphysics—from Enlightenment/rationalist through Marxist/modernist—it aims to question. In fact, the problem areas are recognized to be the only coherent area *of* or *for* inquiry. That is to say, one does not assume but rather *investigates* the distribution of Intentionality in behavior, in mental process, and in relation to itself. The relational, ramifying, and recursive structures of Intentionality are not understood as messiness in the record to be overcome so that we can talk about what we really want to talk about; rather, they are the material itself, beyond which there *is* nothing else to talk about. Thus in the deconstructive paradigm one takes the secondary, devalued categories in the first paradigm as the material of Intentionality as such. Expression, matter, statement, practice, performance, proposition, body, signifier, and representation become the objects of study. The challenge, of course, is that each of these terms must be disentangled from its traditional relationship with a logos.

In practice, most archaeological inquiries display a clash between the logocentric and deconstructive paradigms, weighting now in favor of one, now the other. In the remainder of this chapter, I consider four examples in which the issues as I have sketched them so far have figured with particular clarity and force. As I have noted, my interest is not just in the absence but specifically in the presence of the deconstructive paradigm within archaeology.

Binford and the New Archaeology

The most credible metaphysician of the New Archaeology, Lewis Binford, offers two telling metaphors for archaeology. First, archaeology, he says, is supposedly like etiology, the discovery of connections between symptoms and the underlying disease causing them. Characteristically, Binford writes that the "cumulative character" of the "archaeological landscape" carries "diagnostic information" about "systems of origin."[21] Second, archaeology is supposedly like decipherment, the retrieval through a script of the meaning of a statement. Characteristically, he says that archaeological evidence is like "an ancient language which has not yet been deciphered." Later in the same discussion, he even calls the archaeological record a kind of Rosetta stone. (But unlike the actual Rosetta stone, with its Greek, demotic, and hieroglyphic inscriptions, in prehistoric archaeology *all* of the traces, or "scripts," are undeciphered at the time of observation. Thus the prehistorian's work is actually *not* like that of moving from a translated to an untranslated script. Binford's Rosetta-stone metaphor for archaeology conceals the real difficulty of inference from a trace to its *archē* logos.) Indeed, Binford suggests that archaeologists investigate "how mobile peoples 'mark' their environment." Whatever the "mark" might have been for the people who made it (Binford's quotation marks imply that it need not have been intended literally as a mark), the archaeologist tries to "read" it.[22]

Although his terms have varied in his many publications, for Binford the sought-after logoi indexed or inscribed in the record are past peoples' "decisions." In Binford's lexicon, "decisions"—and some of his other complementary terms, like "planning," and perhaps "adaptation"—should not necessarily be conflated with "ideas, mental configurations, or even culture in the strict sense,"[23] that is, with the value or belief systems, such as cosmologies or worldviews, investigated by traditional archaeologists. "Decision" can include nonconventional episodes of directing one's action to a goal in response to a problem.[24]

Working within this framework, the New Archaeologist confronts the question of the status of the symptoms or the script themselves, the traces through which we are supposedly going to identify the *archē* logos—the "decision" making of past peoples. On the one hand, deeply influenced by the logocentric paradigm, the New Archaeologist wants to relegate the traces to secondary status or even ultimately to disregard them. Supposedly one must work through the symptom or script to find the disease or language behind it. New Archaeological writing is filled with quasi-philosophical discussions of what it calls "archaeological inference"—methods for carrying out the tasks of etiology and decipherment in the face of the empirical problems confronted by all forensics and for justifying it in the face of the theoretical problems of induction.

On the other hand, the symptoms or script through which the archaeologist identifies

21. Lewis Binford, "Searching for Camps and Missing the Evidence? Another Look at the Lower Paleolithic," in *The Pleistocene Old World: Regional Perspectives*, ed. Olga Soffer (New York, 1987), 18.

22. Binford, *In Pursuit of the Past*, 11, 14, 20, 24.

23. Binford, *In Pursuit of the Past*, 28, 31, 75.

24. By a nonconventional act, I mean an action that has not been formulated as a solution to a problem of *social coordination* in the terms of the theory of convention (David K. Lewis, *Convention: A Philosophical Study* [Cambridge, Mass., 1967]). In America, driving on the right side of the road *because* other people are so driving is a (social) convention. But driving on the right side of the road (merely) because it allows one to get to one's destination would be nonconventional. *Both* acts are "arbitrary," often confused with conventionality as such: each probably could have been conducted in a different way, given the "natural" parameters of the problem to be solved, driving on the road to reach a destination. There are usually two or more such "coordination equilibria" for the problem, even though it is not always possible to compare them on an absolute scale of optimality. The possibility of pre- or nonsocial (nonconventionalized) actions is a central issue for any theory of the very evolution of social networks of conventionalized action, that is, of "cultures." It is one of the New Archaeology's most fundamental interests, although often not articulated as such.

past "decisions" cannot be tossed aside completely. The New Archaeology must make use of them in getting to what it really wants to talk about, namely, the "decisions" embodied in them. "From the standpoint of archaeological inference," writes Michael Schiffer, "the problem is that of 'partitioning' the traces according to the specific activities and processes responsible for them."[25] In other words, a complex activity of reading the writing of the past—the *whole* past, including the "later" life of an artifact—necessarily becomes part of archaeologocentrism even when its final aim is to put the archaeologist into contact with what lies behind the writing.[26]

Binford himself has generally maintained an unyielding allegiance to his logoi of human rationality, decision making, and planning. These are, of course, the predictable logoi of a post-Enlightenment, bourgeois Western view of what human beings (always) are and how they (always) think—namely, as adapting, planning, self-directing, maximizing organisms. As such, these views of the fundamental character of human Intentionality are open to deconstructive criticism in themselves. They derive as much from the spirit of capitalism, the twentieth-century technocratic culture of management, and universalizing claims about rationality as from any demonstration that adaptationalist explanations apply to all historical traits of organisms or social systems. But I shall not pursue these fairly banal matters here. Since I am interested in the *deconstructive* dimension to be found in archaeology, for me the challenge of Binford's approach is not the all too familiar ring of his logocentrism as such.

Unlike some of his epigones, Binford has been subtle and flexible in investigating the symptoms or the script, the traces, *as such*. First, he does not regard the traces as being suffused with Intentionality in every respect. Rather, for Binford—and for writers developing the study of "site formation processes"—Intentionality is always threaded through with non-Intentional processes leaving their *own* deposits in the overall network of traces in the record. Thus, for example, Binford frequently raises the possibility of, and the challenge posed by, non-Intentional traces in an archaeological landscape, such as natural processes or animal behaviors. When such traces mimic the morphology of Intentional traces, the archaeologist can misidentify logoi, usually by finding them where they do not exist. In this regard, Binford acknowledges that no finite list of universal correlations between symptoms and disease or between script and language can be established, even though he seeks "diagnostic" linkages where possible. "In studying past human behavior," he argues, "we must develop criteria which go beyond simple conventions [of correlating

25. Michael B. Schiffer, *Formation Processes of the Archaeological Record* (Albuquerque, N.M., 1987), 14, but cf. 266.

26. In addition to its emphasis on what we could call the holomorph—the whole history of an artifact or site from its "original" constitution to the present day—Schiffer's investigation of "site formation processes" potentially contributes to deconstructive archaeology in other ways. For example, in principle the archaeologist should consider "designed-in" transformation, decay, or obsolescence as part of an "original" Intentionality and certainly as the Intentionality of the holomorph as such. Did Michelangelo intend (expect) that the Sistine Chapel paintings would get darker over the decades, and thus intend (plan) to paint, in the "original" context, with overly bright colors? In "restoring" his paintings, do modern archaeologists reconstruct Michelangelo's "original" intentionality without considering this aspect of his holomorphic Intentionality? Schiffer himself tends to treat site formation processes as something to be stripped away, like grime on a painting, to reveal an autonomous, original intentionality. But original intentionality is always in part an intentionality that there shall be site formation processes of a particular kind.

trace and original behavior], such as the 'meaning' attached to the coincidence of high densities of artifacts and bone remains."[27]

Second, in addition to recognizing the possible disjunction between Intentionality and the *total* morphology of the trace, Binford puts pressure on the Intentionalities themselves. At a certain point, human Intentionalities disappear; they cease to have the irreducible centrality of Intentionality as such. For instance, Binford recognizes, even insists, that hominid societies may have possessed forms of life different from our own.[28] Despite its etiological or deciphering activities, the New Archaeology is not attempting to identify "our" diseases or "our" languages behind the traces.

But what, then, could it be identifying? If people in the past reasoned and decided in ways *unimaginably* different from our own, then Binford's constant return to rationality and decision making as if we could immediately recognize them when we see them, so long as their traces have been purified of their non-Intentional elements, risks collapsing from within. How do we deal with Intentionality as it indefinitely shades off from "our" form of Intentionality into species of different Intentionalities?

Binford has been tempted to polarize the continuous historical permutation and transformation of Intentionality—what Derrida calls *différance*[29]—into two neat categories. For lack of better terms, I shall label them "zero-degree Intentionality" and "variable Intentionality." Zero-degree Intentionality is not just like ours as healthy, adult human beings, nor is it, in fact even (modern) human: it is precultural. By contrast, variable Intentionality is just like ours: it embodies human modes of reasoning and deciding even though it is culturally variable. (Strictly speaking, in variable Intentionality decision making is conventionalized in limited social interactions.) In fact, then, belying his famous formulation that "archaeology is anthropology or it is nothing," Binford considers only *some* archaeology "anthropology," namely, the archaeology of variable Intentionality.[30] Some archaeology—the rest of archaeology—is ecology, zoology, taphonomy, social or population biology, and so on, namely, the archaeology of zero-degree Intentionality and of completely non-Intentional processes. The recognition that in dealing with the full material morphology of the trace, archaeology cannot wholly be anthropology is Binford's enduring deconstructive contribution to archaeology. Like all deconstructive dimensions of a text, it runs against the grain of the writer's manifest statements even as it undergirds some of his most important analyses.

Despite the hopes of some Binfordians, however, we cannot draw clear lines of demarcation between mutually exclusive non-Intentional, zero-degree Intentional, and variable Intentional artifacts or sites. Recognizing that "early humans were probably not very much like us," Binford does distinguish between "tool assisted direct adaptation to the environment" and the "construct[ed] cultural environment from which one exploits [the] natural environment," that is, between what he also calls "niche" and "cultural" geography.[31] In methodological terms, then, Binford must identify traces in which Intentionality *does not*

27. Binford, *In Pursuit of the Past,* 75; see also Schiffer, *Formation Processes,* 267.

28. Binford, "Searching for Camps," 18–19.

29. See David Wood and Robert Bernasconi, eds., *Derrida and Différance* (Evanston, Ill., 1988).

30. Lewis R. Binford, "Archaeology as Anthropology," *American Antiquity* 28 (1962), 271–75.

31. Binford, "Searching for Camps," 18, 22, 29.

appear, the zero-degree Intentionality of "direct adaptation," and traces in which Intentionality *does* appear, the variable Intentionality of human reasoning and decision making in culture. However, a zero-degree Intentionality, such as "direct adaptation" by hominids making tools, is not the same thing as a non-Intentional process, such as natural events interacting with the tools. Non-Intentional processes could interact with *both* zero-degree and variable Intentionality. Moreover, notice that zero-degree Intentionality ("direct adaptation") could continue to be threaded through variable Intentionality ("culture"). As Binford puts it, "[T]here is [often] no need to discover the ideas responsible for the artifacts," for they should be explained as "direct adaptation" rather than as cultural convention.[32] Therefore non-Intentional, zero-degree Intentional, and variable Intentional traces *are likely to coexist with one another in or as a single artifact or site*. It is this characteristic of the "archaeological landscape" that, whatever his statements about the etiology and decipherment of "decisions," both interests and troubles Binford the most, leading to his most exciting contributions. As a practicing archaeologist, Binford interrogates the material nature, or "writerliness," of the trace. As a methodologist, he assumes that the trace, as a trace, always escapes or exceeds reduction as being wholly suffused with a single, irreducible human Intentionality.

But we should not go too far. Binford points mostly to the ways in which the morphology of the trace is not to be straightforwardly correlated with what I am calling variable Intentionality. In most New Archaeological writing, non-Intentional processes are still something to be cleared away or to be deciphered for information about the environment within which people *were* Intentional. In fact, for the New Archaeologist non-Intentional traces index what amounts to the "thought" of animals or of nature itself. They are treated just like an *archē* logos that does not happen to be a *human* logos: one examines the non-Intentional trace in order to recover the originating presence of a natural or animal event suffusing the morphology of the artifact or site. Since both zero-degree and variable Intentionality manifest all four conditions for the ascription of Intentionality, they too are treated as *archē* logoi indexed by the trace. Despite New Archaeology's laudable attention to non-Intentional processes, the *overall* result, then, has been that it actually *extends* the reach of archaeologocentrism from its traditional concern with logoi like cultural values or beliefs into the domain of natural adaptation itself. Indeed, in the New Archaeology "adaptation" is handled as if it were the purest, most original thought of all—a thought that does not think through or think with anything at all but directly orients the organism to its world in an irreducible moment of immediate "biological" rationality.

Summing up, New Archaeology's virtue has been to reconstruct not only the originating fullness and presence of Culture in past human life but also the originating fullness and presence of Nature. Thus it generates a subtle metaphysics of the siting of specifically human Intentionalities in the archaeological trace as such. As I have noted, for Binford the trace is partly a non-Intentional and partly an Intentional thing, with its Intentional-

32. Binford, *In Pursuit of the Past*, 31; and see Schiffer, *Formation Processes*, 73.

ity, in turn, partly natural, or zero-degree ("adapting," "reasoning," "deciding"), and partly cultural ("valuing," "believing"). But the drawback has been that when all these cards are on the table, the New Archaeology is comfortable with an absolute distinction between the traces and whatever it is that is their logos, their originating presences. It has no way to see that what one excavates, by way of the trace, is already a trace.

Isaac and Paleoanthropology

In principle, paleoanthropology confronts the problem of the siting, extent, and centeredness of human Intentionality. According to its evolutionary framework, it recognizes a domain of indeterminate duration "before" the emergence of modern human thought. In this prehistory, creatures like us—according to crude measures of biogenetic similarity—did not act in the world or interact with one another on the basis of a stabilizing inner *cogito*. Instead, they *just* acted as organisms and interacted as social animals. Of course, there may be very little way—and thus no theoretical need?—to tell the difference between these two forms of life. Indeed, one *de*construction of "human nature" would be the *re*construction of human beings as organic systems—the achievement of paleoanthropology, social biology, and related disciplines. Unfortunately, however, paleoanthropologists sometimes resist this deconstructive insight. They reintroduce logocentrism by projecting a narrative of the evolutionary rise and triumph of Intentionality precisely *as* the "chronology and tempo of human evolution," to use the words of Glynn Isaac.[33]

In Binford's hands, as the logos of archaeological forensics Intentionality is distributed synchronically or spatially on or in a particular artifact or site without necessarily being fully present throughout it. At any given temporal moment or for any given spatial distribution, Binford finds a complex intersection and interaction of non-Intentional, zero-degree Intentional, and variable Intentional processes in the traces. In Isaac's hands, another dimension is added. Intentionality is also distributed temporally and spatially as an evolution *between* artifacts and sites. By far the greatest of these transitions, of course, was the evolution from toolmaking in the "direct adaptation" of prehuman hominids to toolmaking in the cultural lifeworld of modern human beings.

As in Binford's New Archaeology, the challenge for paleoanthropology becomes that of "partitioning" the traces according to their originating presences. Following Isaac's "method of residuals," the archaeologist strips away the non-Intentional processes that shaped and interacted with the artifact or site, supposedly permitting her a progressive identification of the underlying ideas, planning, design, style, tradition, culture, value, and ideology animating the technocultural transformations of the traces.[34]

33. Glynn L. Isaac, "Chronology and Tempo of Cultural Change During the Pleistocene," in *Calibration of Hominoid Evolution*, ed. W. W. Bishop, J. A. Miller, and S. Cole (Toronto, 1972), 381–430, and see idem, "Stages of Cultural Elaboration in the Pleistocene: Possible Archaeological Indicators of the Development of Language," *Annals of the New York Academy of Sciences* 380 (1976), 275–88.

34. See further Richard Potts, *Early Hominid Activities at Olduvai* (New York, 1988), 141–43.

As Isaac insists, his method requires its so-called "least effort prediction," the hypothesis that the past thinkers or toolmakers both thought and made things with the least expenditure of effort.[35] But the resulting logical problem is obvious. One cannot generate a non-tautologous evolutionary narrative on these grounds. On the one hand, if the way of "least effort" *is not* in itself something the maker thought or made, "wrote," then the narrative assumes an underlying optimizing behavior, a stable logos present-and-immediate-to-itself, to begin with. As a result, the narrative cannot be showing how human Intentionality evolved *as* such an irreducible Thought. We have a historical scenario that accommodates Intentionality but does not deal with evolution. But on the other hand, if the way of "least effort" *is* in itself something the maker thought or made, "wrote," then it can only be the result of the maker's Intentionality—her recognition, imagination, and so forth, that "this is the way of least effort"—and thus equally cannot serve as the *foundation* for the very emergence of such Intentionality. We have a historical scenario that accommodates evolution but does not deal with Intentionality.

Isaac tacitly recognizes the force of this difficulty. In his own writing, he struggles to find intelligible, self-consistent descriptions for the evolution of a stable, unified, centered Intentionality in hominid and human history. At every turn, however, he and other paleoanthropologists working within the same framework fall into irresolvable uncertainties and paradoxes.[36]

For instance, consider how Isaac imagines the evolution from zero-degree Intentionality—the irreducible rationality of "direct adaptation"—to culturally variable Intentionality, that is, the evolution from *Australopithecus* to *Homo sapiens sapiens.* Binford can avoid a direct answer to this question, regarding zero-degree and variable Intentionality, along with non-Intentional processes, as temporally simultaneous but different logoi behind spatially contiguous but different traces. Isaac takes on the further problem of *deriving* culturally variable behavior from zero-degree Intentional and entirely non-Intentional behavior.[37] He does so by imagining a complex, culturally variable Intentionality to be

35. See Merillee H. Salmon, "Efficient Explanations and Efficient Behaviour," in *Critical Traditions in Contemporary Archaeology,* ed. Valerie Pinsky and Alison M. Wylie (Cambridge, 1989), 10–13, and R. Torrence, ed., *Time, Energy, and Stone Tools* (Cambridge, 1989), for doctrinal disputes.

36. In general, in articulating its deconstructive awareness archaeological writing tends to deconstruct itself. But this textual turmoil should not necessarily be erased in the name of logical purity. In fact, it is the memory of what paleoanthropology (in this case) is really doing. Textual contradiction is the trace of the irreducible trace forgotten by the logocentric narrative precisely in its manifest interest in reducible traces—traces to be erased through the "method of residuals" in order to reconstruct the original logos, "planning," "design," or the way of "least effort" itself. Isaac lets contradictions persist, awaiting further evidence: in theory, some trace yet to be found will resolve the problem of the (non)traceliness of all existing traces. But, of course, such evidence will never be found as anything but a trace in itself. Therefore the temporary stability of a paleoanthropological analysis—the analytic *cogito* of paleoanthropology—can be established only by distributing the traces not only in the time of human evolution but also in the time of forensic analysis itself. The originating presence of Intentionality at the *beginning* of human evolution will be stabilized by the discovery of its irreducible trace at the *end* of paleoanthropological analysis—even though what we have *now,* in the present tense of paleoanthropology, is only a series of gaps, disjunctions, and leaps of inference. The analytic temporality of this process can be compared with the temporality of psychoanalytic archaeology: the "primal scene" of meaning will be repeated in, and constructed by, the psychoanalysis itself (see Chapter 11).

37. For example, Glynn L. Isaac, "Foundation Stones: Early Artifacts as Indicators of Activities and Abilities," in *Stone Age Prehistory,* ed. G. N. Bailey and P. Callow (Cambridge, 1986), 221–42.

already present, or *immanent,* in the earliest, zero-degree Intentionality of Oldowan toolmaking, his evolutionary baseline. An earlier baseline, of course, might be designated in the tool use of apes or in their alleged use of "signs." But whether the baseline is specified as Oldowan toolmaking, Gombe tool use, or anything else, logocentrism must nonetheless inject its logos.

On the one hand, Oldowan tools are, Isaac says, as "absolutely simple as they could be": they show no "distinct, arbitrary imposed design" (Fig. 4.1). As "fossilized habits" rather than "carefully conceived and executed tools of a specific type," they might be completely non-Intentional. Yet on the other hand, Oldowan tools—Isaac says in the same breath—display "orderly, purposive ways of flaking stone."[38] The problem here is that there is nothing more thoroughly Intentional, as well as culturally variable, as an "orderly, purposive" way of doing something: Isaac surely knows that order and purpose *is* design, at least in the cultural lifeworld of modern human beings. (Along the same lines, Richard Potts suggests that the Oldowan toolmaker merely followed "paths of least resistance" rather than predetermined goals.[39] One wonders what he would make of someone's "predetermined" goal to follow a path of least resistance.) Thus Isaac seems to be presenting an analysis of a *different* lifeworld, an earlier but determining one in relation to our own. In this prehistoric world, "orderly, purposive ways" of doing things are somehow *not* by "design."

How can this be? As Isaac puts it, although the Oldowan *technology* may be as "absolutely simple" as it could be, the Oldowan maker's *ability* is complex.[40] Orderliness and purposiveness is presumably in the "ability," while the lack of "arbitrary, imposed design" and "absolute" simplicity is presumably in the "technology" (or perhaps the tool). But what a strange proposal! To be consistent, Isaac should argue that the lack of "distinct, arbitrary imposed design" in the Oldowan tool is the trace of the *in*distinct, *un*arbitrary, and *un*imposed (that is, natural and inherent) quality of the maker's ability; however that ability might be characterized, it is precisely *not* a "design" ability. Doesn't the tool show no design simply because the toolmaker doesn't or can't design tools? Yet Isaac adopts the much more implausible claim that *despite* the orderliness and purposiveness of the maker's "ability," the tool shows nothing of it, being as "absolutely simple" as it could be.[41]

We can only conclude that Isaac is having things both ways. In fact, the attribution of immanent, if nonactualized, design "ability" to the Oldowan toolmaker turns out to be necessary for Isaac's narrative of the unfolding of human Intentionality suffusing *later* toolmaking: Isaac wants to tell a much larger story about the gradual actualization of human

38. Isaac, "Foundation Stones," 225, fig. 13.5, 227.

39. Potts, *Early Hominid Activities at Olduvai,* 235.

40. Isaac, "Foundation Stones," 225.

41. In part because he is more sensitive to the "length and interaction of operational chains," J.A.J. Gowlett ("Culture and Conceptualization: The Oldowan-Acheulian Gradient," in *Stone Age Prehistory,* ed. Bailey and Callow, 247) modifies Isaac's account of Oldowan tools to see them as a "well-defined set of ideas and routines." However, in his identification of "idealized morphological forms imposed on stone" in Site DK, Lower Bed 1, at Olduvai ("Culture and Conceptualization," 250), his logocentrism, more consistent than Isaac's, is fully evident. Still, it is worth noting that he discovers *two* such original "intended forms"; Gowlett's Oldowan logos is, it seems, not unitary. For Potts (*Early Hominid Activities at Olduvai,* 236), it is not the simplicity of Oldowan tools that indicates the zero-degree nature of Oldowan Intentionality but rather the "continuum of [their] form and [the] apparent transformation of one tool type into another." Nonetheless, Potts speaks of "types."

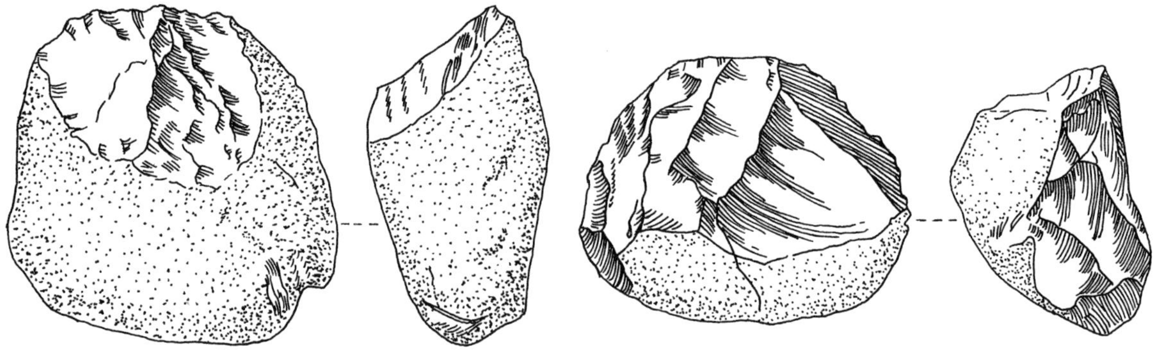

Fig. 4.1. Oldowan bifacially flaked pebbles ("pebble-tool culture"), Olduvai Gorge (Tanzania), Bed 1, early Middle Pleistocene.

Intentionality, which must, then, initially exist somewhere outside its actualization, namely, in Oldowan "ability." The "absolutely simple" logos is *always there from the beginning* in sufficient "complexity"—with sufficient purposiveness—to underlie all further developments. It is just that it is hidden in the "ability" in the head of the maker rather than manifest in the trace, which exhibits only simplicity and designlessness. But paradoxically such a trace (the tool) cannot, in fact, *be* the trace of what it manifests (the ability), for Isaac contends that the technology and the ability are different not only in site (one is physical, the other mental) but also in kind (one possesses something the other does not). In turn, this disjunction gets disguised by finding the hidden, original logos progressively emerging in the further, later evolution of toolmaking—in which, of course, one *can* link up an "orderly" or "designed" tool neatly to the design-purpose precisely as its manifest trace. Thus Acheulean tools, Isaac says, exhibit "deliberate" or "rule-bound design," "careful control," and perhaps the "arbitrariness" of "form." Despite his recognition of the role of "ad hoc," "opportunistic" activities in "intentions in action," they show "predictability and predetermination." Continuing in the same vein, the Levalloisian technique displays a "specific elaborate cognitive structure" and the "strength of culturally ordained rule systems."[42]

Isaac's initial dichotomy between "technology" and "ability"—between matter and mind, writing and thought, trace and logos—fuels a history in which practice can be as variable and changing as one likes without putting the absolute originality of the underlying competence into question. Although Isaac's history is supposed to be the history of the evolution of Intentionality, it is never more than a history of the development of an already existing Intentionality. Indeed, the logocentric master narrative *requires* an originating—here, Oldowan—moment of irreducible simplicity and centeredness, of "orderly purpose" that preexists but is not embodied in the trace, is not "written": if the Oldowan tool shows no design yet the maker's "ability" is orderly and purposive, then, it would

42. Isaac, "Foundation Stones," 231, fig. 13.11, 233–36; compare Clive Gamble, *Palaeolithic Settlement of Europe* (Cambridge, 1986), 120.

seem, it must be by the maker's order and purpose that the tool shows no design. It is, as it were, by design—presumably the orderly, purposive recognition of "least effort"—that the tool shows no design. Such nonactualized Intentionality is the paradigmatic *archē* logos, a lost logos that could never be recovered in the trace precisely because it is never actualized in matter. This logos never leaves a trace.

As I have noted, Binford, in his conception of zero-degree Intentionality, "direct adaptation," imagines human thought *with no contact with culture*. Isaac, in his Oldowan design-to-be-without-design, imagines human thought *with no contact with matter*—a preserve in which Intentionality is present unto itself alone in its direct and immediate but nonactualized orientation toward the world. In these terms, Isaac's logocentrism is more extensive than Binford's. Whereas Binford supposes that human thought, although it might not be mediated by culture, is at least mediated by matter, Isaac finds that the mediation of thought by matter is, itself, supplementary to a pure logocentric moment in which the thinker intends to stand apart from matter. In both cases, no coherent account of thought can be given. In Isaac's case, one cannot imagine how the Oldowan toolmaker recognizes that not imposing design on matter could be the design of "least effort" before matter has actually been shaped and the associated Intentionalities turned into the object of a retrospective (and thus not a primary) "rational," "optimizing" Intentionality.

But the portrait of Isaac's logocentrism should not overshadow his deconstructive insight. Isaac phrases his aim as "seek[ing] methods for assessing the *balance point* between minimizing mechanistic indications and maximizing mentalistic ones."[43] His work offers an elaborate forensics, similar to that of Binford's, for investigating this question as an analysis of archaeological traces as such. Whatever his logocentric preferences, Isaac does not simply *assume* "mentalistic" explanations but explicitly entertains "mechanistic" ones as well. The problem is simply that there never is, never was, and never will be any kind of a "point," either a place or a time, when matter and mind "balance" in steady state or fixed proportion—for instance, in Isaac's Oldowan relation between a mind that knows not to "impose" design and a tool that is "absolutely simple" as could be (see further Chapter 8). Isaac is comfortable with specifying a series of different absolute balance points in the past. Most notably, these include the originary "balance" of a total separation between raw thinking ability and undesigned matter. This balance is rebalanced in a progressive suffusion of matter by ability—the Word made Flesh as the story of human evolution. As I have shown, Isaac has no way to see that what one excavates is the balancing of a balance: the balance, as such, only exists "in balance" because someone balances it that way, "writing" the balance. More exactly, cultural evolution since the Oldowan can be understood as rewriting the balance between thought and medium, but its very origination, as a writing, is not questioned despite the founding hypothesis of an absolute initial *gap* between unactualized raw ability and wholly undesigned matter, a writing zero degree. But note that this question—the very existence of writing in the deconstructive sense, of the mediatedness of human thought—is a question *for and about deconstruction*. "Writing," of course, is deconstruction's logos. The fact that Isaac raises the question, despite the logocentric turn of his own solution, is his deconstructive archaeology.

43. Isaac, "Foundation Stones," 234, emphasis added.

The Reduction Sequence

Binford's trouble with the spacing of Intentionality and Isaac's trouble with its timing converge in recent studies of lithic "reduction sequences," the events and actions by which raw materials are "reduced" to stone tools. Although doubtless they would disavow the affiliation, some lithic archaeologists have adopted what amounts to a potentially deconstructive approach. As usual, two archaeological paradigms, logocentric and deconstructive, figure in a single archaeological enterprise.

Needless to say, lithic archaeologists do pursue logoi, such as tool types, styles, and the archlogos, the elusive "mental template" that J. P. White and Harold L. Dibble would like to disentangle from what they identify as the "five components to artifact variation," or what I have been calling "writing," namely, "material, function, mental template, technology and skill."[44] Most of this work has been carried out within New Archaeological and paleoanthropological frameworks—that is, the study of "traces of changing behavioral systems."[45] Therefore it includes a Binfordesque identification of optimizing decisions as the privileged past Intentionality and an Isaacesque narrative of the evolutionary rise of "fully cultural" toolmaking by the Upper Paleolithic period.[46]

Given this background, the reduction sequence tends to be overly logicized in analyzing the distribution of Intentionality in the making of tools. In the literature, preexisting logoi seem to be pressing in on the reduction sequence from all quarters (Fig. 4.2). At the beginning of a reduction sequence, the core supposedly must be "selected"—amounting, perhaps, to a "cultural decision" to use a thin or thick blank or "to retouch with a given intensity."[47] At this stage, conceivably some further "choice" about morphology and procedure is exercised, even though, as James Sackett observes, "choice" might be vested in the ultimate "typological result" as much as in the "technological beginning."[48] During the sequence, the maker supposedly "decides" what to do or where to go. And at the end of the sequence, the "type," "style," "intended use," or "mental template" constitutes the *telo*-logos, the Intentional idea or form supposedly realized in the making as its goal.

Close scrutiny of such accounts will quickly lead us to deconstructive skepticism. For instance, B. Bradley and C. G. Sampson describe the reduction sequence as a "*master* decision about [the toolmaker's] shaping objectives," followed by a "sequence of flakes," "each reflecting *preceding* intentions" (emphasis added).[49] But there is no reason, beyond

44. J. P. White and Harold L. Dibble, "Stone Tools: Small-Scale Variability," in *Stone Age Prehistory*, ed. Bailey and Callow, 47.

45. Isaac, "Foundation Stones," 221.

46. For example, Anta Montet-White, "Raw-Material Economy Among Medium-Sized Late Paleolithic Campsites of Central Europe," in *Upper Pleistocene Prehistory of Western Eurasia*, University Museum Monographs 54, ed. Anta Montet-White and Harold L. Dibble (Philadelphia, 1989), 360, and A. Jelinek, "Technology, Typology, and Culture in the Middle Paleolithic," in ibid., 209; but see Anthony Marks, "The Curation of Stone Tools During the Upper Pleistocene: A View from the Central Negev, Israel," in ibid., 276.

47. Marks, "Comment on Dibble," in *Upper Pleistocene Prehistory*, 195; Harold L. Dibble, "Reduction Sequences in the Manufacture of Mousterian Implements of France," in *The Pleistocene Old World*, ed. Soffer, 42.

48. James R. Sackett, "Comment on Dibble," in *Upper Pleistocene Prehistory*, ed. Montet-White and Dibble, 196.

49. B. Bradley and C. G. Sampson, "Analysis by Replication of Two Acheulian Artifact Assemblages from Caddington, England," in *Stone Age Prehistory*, ed. Bailey and Callow, 29–30.

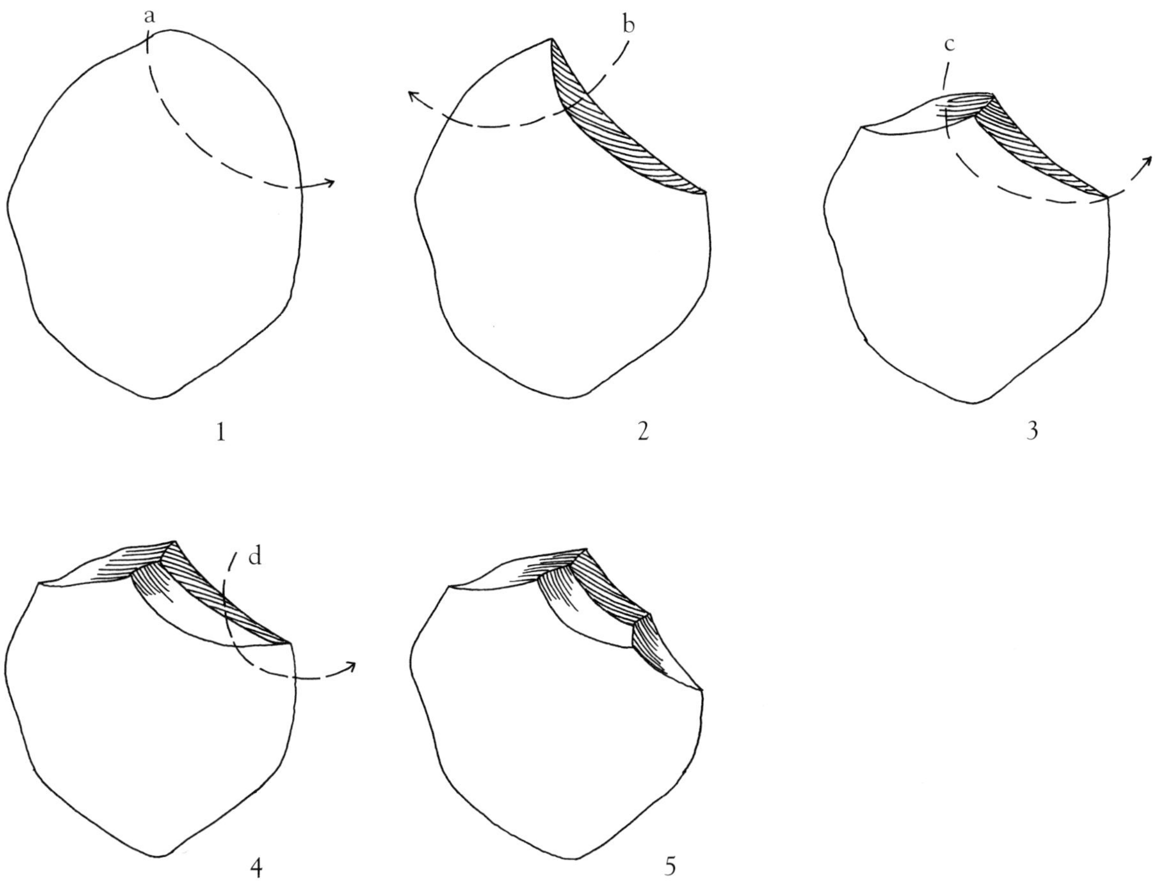

Fig. 4.2. Simplified schema of a reduction sequence, from raw material ("blank") (1) toward "finished" tool (5), an "idea" possibly motivating "reduction" *(a–c)* also incorporating "changes of mind" *(d)*.

logocentrism, to privilege an initial "decision" and "preceding" intentions rather than subsequent but obviously determining ones. Most important, there is no reason, beyond logocentrism, to suppose that a resolved Intentionality precedes manufacture itself rather than is actively written within it. Bradley and Sampson do recognize that toolmakers could "continue towards an end-product different from the first or master decision." Nevertheless, they want to describe this perturbation as the makers' "changing their minds." But we could equally say that there was no mind, no stable logos, *to be* "changed." Rather, the maker "finds" an object(ive) in pursuing and finishing the reduction precisely as "making up his mind." On this view, it would be the *end* of the sequence, as much as the beginning, that must be the "master decision," if such a notion is at all intelligible in the first place.

But despite the logocentric bias, although the lithic archaeologist may be investigating the roles of selection, choice, decision, and intended use or goal in toolmaking, she need not *assume* these Intentionalities in any given segment of the sequence—for example, at its beginning, midway through it, or at its end. Two of the primary contributions of these studies have been to demonstrate that supposedly Intentional structures thought to underlie toolmaking do not necessarily exist at all and to account for what otherwise would be regarded as "unexplained or residual variability."[50] For example, whereas a toolmaker might be thought to possess a preexisting concept of a type or style she aims to reproduce in her making of the tool, examination of the reduction sequence may suggest, by contrast, that she merely encounters specific "reduction constraints and effects" delivering up the tool according, at least in part, to their inherent material parameters.[51] To use the jargon of deconstruction, we could say that the tool writes the toolmaker as much as the toolmaker writes the tool.

Indeed, the very notion of a reduction sequence enforces a substantial deconstruction of Intentionality. As I have noted, Binford and Isaac deconstruct Intentionality by investigating its temporal and spatial extension. Like them, the lithic archaeologist cannot assume that a morphology results from the maker's Intentions, but must investigate its alternative material origins. Even further, the lithic archaeologist also wonders about the centeredness and unitariness of Intentionality *even in those times and places it seems to be present.* As Dibble seems to recognize, the toolmaker's Intentionality, if it is sited anywhere or directed at anything, does not reside only in a "mental template" of a particular tool "type" or "style."[52] Although such an image might be involved in the making of the tool, it would be far too impoverished to account for the phenomena of reduction entirely on its own: a preexisting image of a completed tool cannot, in itself, help the maker to get from core through reductions to finished product, for it is just a picture, a "template" to be imprinted or copied, not a how-to manual. Thus it would be more exact and penetrating, as some lithic archaeologists have done, to consider the toolmaker's Intentionality to be distributed or disseminated in, although not wholly identical with, the entire reduction sequence itself, the entire complex of preexisting goals, ongoing comparisons between goals and achievements, modifications of direction, corrections of error, accidents, and so on. No one element of the sequence should be privileged, for each one is fully determining on the following elements in a particular, limited, but unalterably material way.

The notion of a reduction sequence, then, replaces notions of a simple two-step Intentional movement like Idea/Expression or Template/Product with a more inclusive concept of multistep, serial, recursive Intentional relations. Instead of assuming that the performance is always less important than the initial idea, this more inclusive view notes that a later decision, or error, can render an earlier "goal" obsolete. In principle, it can handle Intentionality as a phenomenon in which no particular center or unity is privileged. What do we have here but a displacement of a view of the tool as a word spoken out with a view of the tool as an ongoing writing?

50. Harold Dibble, "Comment on Marks," in *Upper Pleistocene Prehistory*, ed. Montet-White and Dibble, 285.

51. Harold Dibble, "Typological Aspects of Reduction and Intensity of Utilization of Lithic Resources in the French Mousterian," in *Upper Pleistocene Prehistory*, ed. Montet-White and Dibble, 193; Gamble, *Paleolithic Settlement of Europe*, chap. 6.

52. Dibble, "Typological Aspects," in *Upper Pleistocene Prehistory*, ed. Montet-White and Dibble, 189.

The Archaeology of "Contextual Meanings"

Suppose we granted, as suggested in the preceding three sections, that Intentionality is not wholly present within an artifact or site or throughout a history and that when it is present it is only as a compound, recursive rather than unitary, centered phenomenon. All this still leaves plenty of room for an archaeology of Intentionality: in a comprehensive discipline, it would simply be conjoined with the archaeology of all non-, pre-, and para-Intentional phenomena. A division of labor of this kind has already occurred in contemporary archaeology. Some archaeologists study ecological or technological "parameters" and "constraints," non-, pre-, and para-Intentional, while others investigate "culture" or "meaning," the Intentional. If you like, one group examines the "physics" of the material, the other its "semantics";[53] professional archaeology regards both approaches as valid but different in kind. In a sense, the division is supported by the very deconstructions of Intentionality I have considered so far. But the division itself should be deconstructed. An archaeology of Intentionality will never find an autonomous, stable object that is, as it were, purified of the non-Intentional, will never arrive at a pure "semantics," just as the archaeology of the non-Intentional, as I have already noted, will never find an autonomous object purified of the Intentional, will never establish a pure "physics."

Consider the archaeology of meaning, the study *par excellence* (one might think) of past Intentionalities. I defer distinguishing between the "archaeology of contextual meanings," "cognitive archaeology," or "cognitive history" and "the archaeology of thought."[54] Directly or indirectly, all of these approaches employ or at least echo standard accounts of meaning—Lévi-Straussian "structuralism" in the case of Ian Hodder, iconography in the case of J. D. Lewis-Williams, and the philosophy of reference in my own case.

Considering what has been seen of its ambitions, a *deconstructive* "archaeology of meaning" would dispute aspects of these accounts, such as their formalist or structuralist procedures, and extend others, such as their distinction between reference and sense or their emphasis on replicatory change. I turn to this response momentarily in light of an example. In general, deconstruction characterizes any effort to identify *the* meaning of a form or a practice for people in the past as an idealist, logocentric enterprise. Above all, deconstruction urges, "meaning" cannot be "present" to the meaning maker as her irreducible, incorrigible, immediate Intentionality. Thus, in turn, it cannot be a stable object for logocentric historical reconstruction.

Nevertheless, as one of the very consequences of its nonidealist approach, a deconstructive account regards "meaning" as a material phenomenon with a particular history. Some

53. See Searle, "Intentionality and Its Place in Nature."

54. See Ian Hodder, ed., *The Archaeology of Contextual Meanings* (Cambridge, 1987); J. D. Lewis-Williams, *The Rock Art of Southern Africa* (Cambridge, 1983) ("cognitive archaeology"); Davis, *Canonical Tradition*, xvii ("cognitive history") (and cf. Chapter 2); idem, "Towards an Archaeology of Thought," in *The Meanings of Things: Material Culture and Symbolic Expression*, ed. Ian Hodder (London, 1989), 202–9.

features of this history—especially the context dependence and disjunctiveness of "meaning"—were identified long ago by nondeconstructive writers.

A deconstructive archaeology of meaning would hope to be an archaeology without logocentrism and teleology. But because "meaning" is an essentially logocentric notion, logocentrism and teleology still tend to dominate the existing archaeology of meaning: material forms or practices are thought to fulfill—represent, express, or perform—fully "present" meanings. Indeed, it is not clear that an archaeology of "meaning" (as opposed to an archaeology of cognition, thought, or even reference) could ever escape logocentrism. As I have argued throughout this chapter, the logocentric and deconstructive paradigms jostle one another for room within the selfsame house.

As an example, consider Ian Hodder's *Domestication of Europe*. On a superficial reading, Hodder seems to adopt a deconstructive stance—at least, a "postmodernist" self-reflexivity—as well as to offer some substantive deconstructive proposals. For instance, he draws attention to the writerliness of his own presentation, evinces skepticism about the "pastness" of the past and the "presentness" of the present, and regards his own "scientific meanings" to be uncertain. Within his positive archaeology as such, he understands the so-called agricultural revolution, a historic shift in production and subsistence, to be an "epiphenomenon" dependent upon an underlying *symbolic* (re)configuration of experience—a "deconstruction," if you will, of an economistic interpretation. More generally, he understands social forms as "written" in symbols (in his book, they are the domestic architectures and related practices of Neolithic European societies). Social change should be seen, on this view, as the ongoing "reading" of such writings, for example, in the quasi-developmental millennia-long sequence he charts from the Near East and southeastern Europe through central Europe and southern Scandinavia to Britain. Most important, he insists that the "meanings" he identifies for these symbols—for instance, the "control" of "danger," "death," and "the wild" within Neolithic houses—were "used strategically and contextually" or were "performed" in actual practices of using the symbolic forms, including all the pragmatic variations and unintended consequences of such uses.[55]

But Hodder's deconstructive gestures do not really go very far. To recognize the "contextual," "strategic," or "performative" nature of meaning is not somehow to avoid logocentrism. Although his jargon sometimes beguiles one into supposing that he has replaced the idealism of traditional *Geistesgeschichte* with a historicizing or deconstructive account, in its substantive claims his archaeology is closest to that of earlier *Strukturforscher* like Friedrich Matz or Guido von Kaschnitz-Weinberg.[56]

First of all, in itself "contextual meaning" is not a special variety of meaning in history newly identified by the alert postmodernist archaeologist as *lacking* that irreducible "presentness" of Intentionality characterized by entrenched metaphysics. By definition, the

55. Ian Hodder, *The Domestication of Europe: Structure and Contingency in Neolithic Societies* (Oxford, 1990), 28, 31, 38–40, 44, 202, 247, 278; and cf. *Symbols in Action*, 217.

56. Friedrich Matz, *Geschichte der griechischen Kunst I* (Frankfurt am Main, 1950); idem, "Strukturforschung und Archäologie," *Studium Generale* 17 (1964), 203–19; and Guido von Kaschnitz-Weinberg, *Mittelmeerische Kunst* (Berlin, 1965).

meanings of a term exist in a social and historical "context," namely, the context of just those people who assign sense *(Sinn)* to a reference *(Bedeutung)* or who belong to a community's "chain of designations."[57] In the same way as "contextual" adaptation would just be adaptation as such, "contextual" meaning is just meaning as such.

Second, it follows that to recognize "context" is not, in itself, to recognize the variability and open-endedness of meaning that deconstruction emphasizes. It remains to be shown for any given case that the "context" of meaning—of people assigning sense to reference—is characterized by variability rather than invariance or by openness rather than closure. In some cases, the material properties, production, and social history, or "use life," of artifacts suggest that, in its "context," sense for reference remained relatively stable—for instance, in the canonical tradition of ancient Egyptian image making, in which the sense of reference (I have argued) precisely *is* invariance.[58] In fact, such stability can apparently be found in the Neolithic symbolism reviewed by Hodder himself. In other cases, meaning did not remain stable—for instance, in the disjunction between late prehistoric and dynastic Egyptian art,[59] or at the far conceptual and historical horizons of Hodder's Neolithic domus, namely, the polis and the state.

Now, deconstruction does propose that meaning is unstable; its claim here is not novel. But instability is not *caused by* the dependence of meaning on its context. This explanation would be completely empty (or, to put it another way, a vacuous essentialism): meaning just *is* "contextual meaning," and thus we would be saying that the instability of meaning is caused by meaning's being meaning. The instability of meaning derives from a specific, well-defined *property* of meaning, namely, as I wish to put it, the potential and perhaps inherent slippage between reference (roughly, what is denoted by a term in a language) and sense (roughly, what the denotation connotes for the speaker).[60] Even so, for all pragmatic purposes of "performance" or use itself, this slippage may be inconsequential. We need not accept the vulgar deconstructive view, rejected by Derrida, that meaning is entirely or only characterized by slippage. Thus, in turn, a deconstructive analysis is not carried out simply by recognizing meaning's "performance" or use. Performance may be a performance of a meaning's slippage *or* nonslippage, to be identified and measured on other grounds *in* (but not *as*) the "performance."

In fact, as I noted earlier, performance or use has frequently been conceived as the secondary embodiment of a logos, the re-presentation or ex-pression of someone's irreducible, immediate sense for reference. In a logocentric account, this performance can be as unstable, contested, or "writerly" as one likes so long as it does not disturb the essential presentness of the meaning suffusing it and that it enacts.

For Hodder, what is performed "strategically and contextually" is, finally, the "struc-

57. Gottlob Frege, "On Sense and Reference" [1892], in *Translations from the Philosophical Writings of Gottlob Frege,* 2d ed., ed. Peter Geach and Max Black (Oxford, 1960), 56–79; Saul Kripke, *Naming and Necessity,* 2d ed. (Cambridge, Mass., 1980); and Michael Devitt, *Designation* (New York, 1981).

58. Davis, *Canonical Tradition.*

59. Whitney Davis, *Masking the Blow: The Scene of Representation in Late Prehistoric Egyptian Art* (Berkeley and Los Angeles, 1992); see Chapter 7.

60. See esp. H. P. Grice, "Meaning," *Philosophical Review* 66 (1957), 377–88, and idem, "Utterer's Meaning, Sentence Meaning, and Word Meaning," *Foundations of Language* 4 (1968), 225–42.

ture" of meaning.[61] Since he repeatedly characterizes this structure as the "underlying theme," "underlying logic," "structural tendency," or "principles" of the production of meaning, it clearly serves as Hodder's logos: as he recognizes, a metaphor of depth (structure) and surface (performance) organizes much of his account. In relation to the occasionally "surfacing" logos itself, "performances" in history can be as variable as several thousand years of Neolithic house-building "events" imply they must be—so long as an event's performance of the underlying structure can still be identified and analyzed as such, as an artifact-token of the meaning type. Indeed, in Hodder's account, Neolithic house-building events are intelligible not wholly in their own irreducible "contexts," whatever these might have been, but chiefly in terms of the structure, "the large-scale [Neolithic] context in which similar meanings are assigned to similar objects"—even though, for the Upper Paleolithic at least, it would be "dangerous to assume any similarities of meaning on the basis of formal similarities across such great expanses of time."[62] For Hodder, the structure of meaning *is* the "context" of meaning; he proposes an archaeology purporting to have a nonessentializing thrust but that continues to regard history, event and contingency, as a secondary term.[63]

Belying the deconstructive grafts, Hodder's unreconstructed structuralism, then, is the real engine of his archaeology of meaning. On the basis of morphological similarity and difference, he relentlessly pursues "associations" and "oppositions" between symbols, presented as orthodox Lévi-Straussian statements of homology between sets of differences. The procedure enables him to generate claims about the supposed centrality and centeredness of certain symbols within the physical space of Neolithic houses, within social space, and within the overall field of meaning itself. For the last, he offers diagrams supposedly mapping the structure of meaning, again literally centered around the two principal logoi—the "house" (or what Hodder calls the domus) and the "cultivated area" (or what Hodder calls the agrios)—that Neolithic house building and related "performances" supposedly make present in historically contingent ways.[64]

To the extent that Hodder's "context" of meaning has become identified with meaning's

61. See further Ian Hodder, "The Contribution of the Long Term," in *Archaeology as Long-Term History,* ed. Ian Hodder (Cambridge, 1987), 1–8.

62. Hodder, *Domestication of Europe,* 21, 68, 220, 228, 244, 287.

63. Nicholas Thomas's superb analysis of how a "social or cultural system or structure" can be treated as an object "out of time" (*Out of Time: History and Evolution in Anthropological Discourse* [Cambridge, 1989]) applies neatly to Hodder: "Codes of meaning or arrays of behavioral rules are [seen in the discourse of anthropology as] not immediately 'caused.' They are expressive in a circular way, or functional and mutually determining. If events are discussed at all, they lack the singular character of the historical deed or accident. In the notion of a speech act or in some other cultural enactment we find the event much reduced in relation to the generative scheme. What takes place has no life as an intrusion with a loose and partly unfixed causality, but is rather the expression of a structure, the manifestation of a cultural order or a set of notions about behavior. . . . If one sets aside the fact that things are never the same again, the event collapses into the enactment of context" (*Out of Time,* 117–19). If one abandoned the logocentrism introduced in the structuralist premise, then "in another way of writing, 'context' might equally take the form of historical system or productive accretion" (*Out of Time,* 136 n. 1). However, although "'history' or 'a historical perspective' can apparently be added to or discussed at the same time as 'culture' and 'the social system' . . . in fact no serious integration [of the two] is possible unless the exclusions [of history] which constitute the latter objects are broken down" (*Out of Time,* 95).

64. Hodder, *Domestication of Europe,* e.g., 10, 27, 36, 38–39, figs. 3.5 and 4.6, and so on.

"structure," the sense of the symbols in question remains unspecified. They are oddly contentless except as they are, themselves, the contents of a structure. As in Lévi-Strauss's treatment of symbols,[65] one of Hodder's "favorite figures [of speech] is a fairly rare form of 'abstract for concrete' substitution or synecdoche whereby a quality is used as an equivalent for the person or thing which possesses it." For instance, despite our complete ignorance of their iconographic values, the paintings of vultures or leopards at Çatal Hüyük (Fig. 4.3) become, for Hodder, symbols of "death" or "the wild."[66] In turn, "these abstract synecdoches become the instruments of a second favorite figure of speech: antithesis," sometimes "to be further developed into a chiasmus, or 'symmetrical inversion,' in Lévi-Strauss's terms":[67] in Neolithic houses with their associated decorations and fittings, death and the wild is "opposed" to life and domestic nurture, if sometimes "controlled" by it.

Spinning out this web of symbolic associations in the structure of meaning, Hodder homogenizes the material to an extreme degree. Throughout his text it is striking to see how symbols are continually identified as meaning "*the* dead," "*the* wild," "*the* individual," "*the* social," "*the* female," "*the* cultural," and so forth, throughout a vast spatiotemporal continuum (the italics are mine, the quotation marks only sometimes Hodder's). Labeling symbols with the definite article and singular noun held constant in this way empties them of any specificity of sense they might have. They become independent essences of reference entered into an abstract semantic structure[68] rather than terms implicated in continually shifting, truly context-bound *grammatical* relations within historically specific episodes of writing—writings like "a wild," "this wild," "her wild," "not . . . wild," "wildly," "wild?" and so on. Although it may be "in the head" of a thinker, meaning must be materially mediated by symbols characterized by indefinitely complex, variable syntactic and semantic *inflection* in addition to their mere structural "association" with or "opposition" to one another. For Neolithic writers, "the wild" could well have been the fully "social" or "cultural" worlds of hunting and gathering—hardly "wild"—that agriculturalism replaced. Granting Hodder's own argument that in building houses Neolithic people were beginning to "write" a form of life, the early house builders did not necessarily understand their former, progressively rewritten world as "wild" even though, retrodictively, what they finally wrote would apparently so refer to it. The point is that "the wild"—like the "peripheral," the "classic," the "private," the "legitimate," the "original," and other categories investigated by an archaeology of meaning—must be an indefinitely retreating presence; it is "*the* wild" only in a place and time that is never reached. Thus the archaeology of writings like "the wild" is not well served by seeing them as the "performance" of a fixed variable in a stable semantic "structure," a writing of the selfsame word by separate hands. Rather, at some point different writings are not comparable. Because they are not necessarily instances of the same character in a fixed notation, they should not be subsumed in a unitary "structure."

To be fair, in a fluctuating practice in his own text Hodder sometimes places quotation marks around the labels for the symbols he identifies. Presumably he wants to mark them as

65. Dan Sperber, *On Anthropological Knowledge* (Cambridge, 1985), 67.

66. Hodder, *Domestication of Europe*, 8–9.

67. Sperber, *On Anthropological Knowledge*, 67.

68. Hodder, *Domestication of Europe*, e.g., figs. 3.5, 4.6.

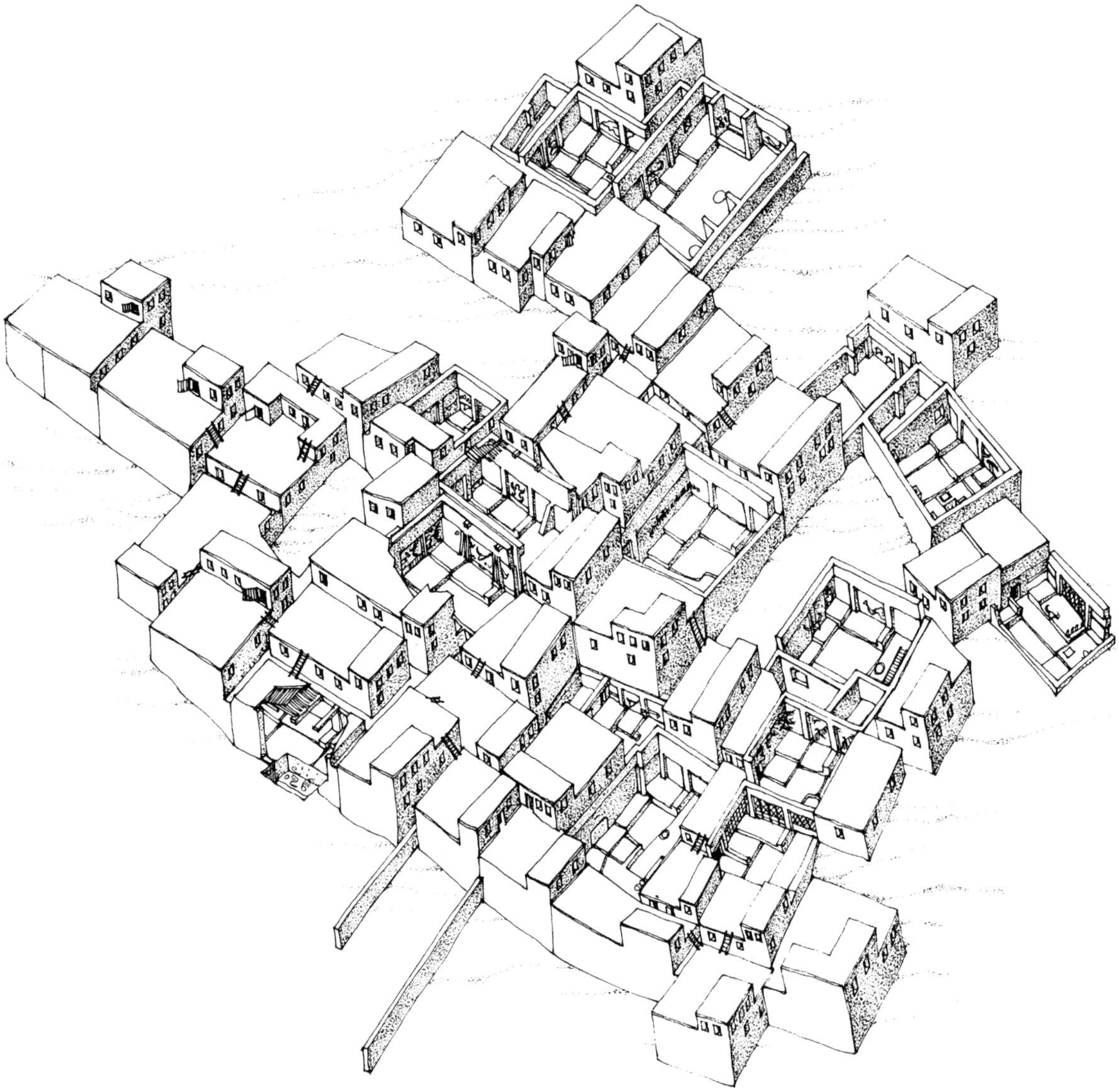

Fig. 4.3. Reconstruction of the excavated area of Neolithic houses and shrine at Çatal Hüyük VII, Anatolia.

“cultural categories” in themselves or perhaps even to indicate their preliminary status as placeholders invented by an archaeologist unable to excavate sense itself. But he still understands cultural categories as “constructed” in relation to others in a stable structure.[69] And as in orthodox structuralism, they all ultimately resolve into an overarching, irreducible opposition between “nature” and “culture,” in which culture—a similar logocentric narrative obtains in other archaeologies—suffuses the human lifeworld, becomes the meaning spoken in people’s writings, and underwrites economic, political, or other forms of

69. Hodder, *Domestication of Europe*, 61, 288.

value. In this structuralist framework, what could ever interrupt or displace culture but another culture, or more exactly, what could ever rewrite cultural structure but cultural structure? The "wild," the unstructured, is not conceived as being *in* writing, *in* a structure, as one of its material conditions and properties, in the way that psychoanalysis or deconstruction would have it. Instead, as structuralism has it, wildness remains outside, writing's other side; it becomes that which is spoken of but which never, itself, speaks.

In sum, "structure" is Hodder's logos, his way of centering, clarifying, and even erasing the *différance* of writing as such, of meaning making as such, and of characterizing its "context" and evaluating its "contingency." Because Hodder grafts explicit poststructuralist claims into his text, I have devoted space to this point. The general arguments of deconstruction against structuralism are too well known to labor further here.[70] At this point, what interests me more than Hodder's logocentrism is the deconstructive dimension of his work. If what I have said so far holds good, then this is not quite what he explicitly claims it to be—for example, in reminding us that his book has its own archaeology. Deconstruction does not take place when one *asserts* one is being deconstructive; like the other cases I have reviewed, deconstruction occurs against the grain of the manifest text.

As an example, note that Hodder ranges from the meanings of the house and its structural transformations at Çatal Hüyük to Carnac and the British henge monuments, and over equally vast chronologies, as the story of "the domestication of Europe." Why, then, does he consistently stop short of considering the meaning of *villages* as such? After all, at both Çatal Hüyük and Lepenski Vir, two of his most important examples, the "house" seems to be dependent upon or subordinated to a larger organization and meaning. At Çatal Hüyük, despite James Mellaart's reconstruction of a "typical house" abstracted from its built context, the village is obviously an architectonic whole; "houses" are subcomponents, sharing walls with each other (Fig. 4.3). And at Lepenski Vir, Hodder's own sources indicate that houses were laid out in relation to one another in order to guarantee transdomestic "communication routes" (Fig. 4.4).[71]

Hodder's stated justification for *his* focus is that "the domus was the focus" in Neolithic life. In turn, other meanings revolve around it, if only as "oppositions" to it. But why should the house be seen as the "centering" when supra- or transdomestic organizations are equally evident? For example, a village might be the "focus" of a domus in the very decision to build a house there. In part, I suggest, the truly structuring opposition of Hodder's archaeology is not the domus and agrios of his manifest narrative, or even its "domesticated" and "wild," but rather—deconstructing itself—a tacit opposition, not directly addressed, between the domus and the polis, that is, between two differing species of domesticity.[72]

In Hodder's text, the domus is an unquestioned, essential "centering" because it supposedly expresses human needs, fears, and motivations that are, themselves, unquestionably basic, natural matters—namely, "joy in life [and] the comfort of home" versus "the natural

70. See esp. Derrida, *Writing and Difference,* chap. 10. For another effective antidote to meaning idealism, or "cryptological semiology," see Dan Sperber, *Rethinking Symbolism* (Cambridge, 1975).

71. Hodder, *Domestication of Europe,* 1–4, and figs. 1.3, 1.4, 2.1.

72. Hodder, *Domestication of Europe,* 85, cf. 54.

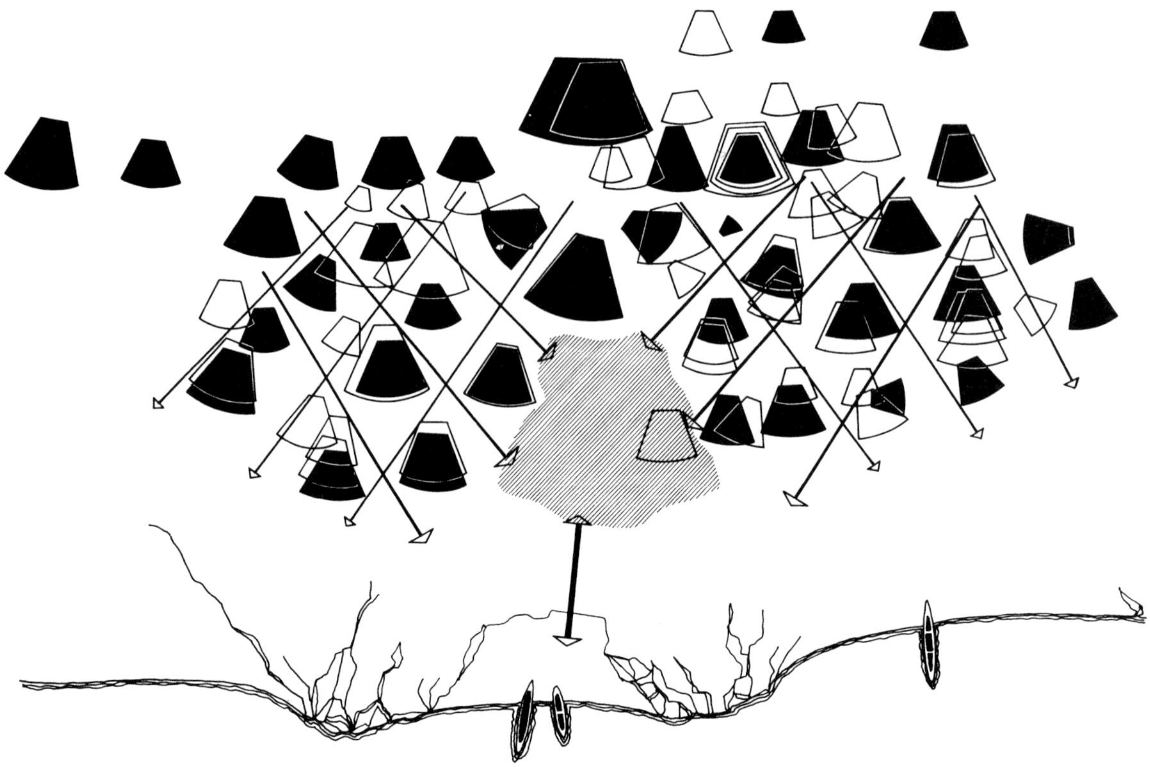

Fig. 4.4. Plan of Neolithic houses with hypothetical circulation and communication routes at Lepenski Vir.

fear and danger of death" or "the danger of the wild." (For the difficulties in making any such attributions of affective significance on the basis of formal or structural relations, see Chapter 10.) "The house," Hodder supposes, "was always a safe haven, providing warmth and security, the focus of a child's early life, and the centre of domestic production." Indeed, the house "provides a basis for loyalties that cross-cut societal-wide interests." Why the house should be the site of joy, comfort, warmth, security, children, loyalty, and so forth, rather than, as might be the case, discipline, subordination, conflict, concealment, abuse, and so on, is never explained. A house is not necessarily a home; it might just be an oven or a bed.[73]

In fact, belying his Victorian view of Neolithic houses, Hodder recognizes that houses "serve the interests of actors within the social fabric" or even "self-interest."[74] Now, exactly this link between the house and self-interest underlies Plato's famous argument that the guardians of the ideal polis "must not possess houses of their own or land or any other property."[75] Needless to say, within the city-states of Greece a house was not a male citizen's home. His "center" was the street, agora, or gymnasium. (For other reasons, it

73. Hodder, *Domestication of Europe,* 29, 37, 40.

74. Hodder, *Domestication of Europe,* 281.

75. Plato *Republic* 464b.

would be equally difficult to see the Athenian house as a "home" for women or slaves.) Whereas the domesticity of the Victorian home is associated with joy, comfort, children, and loyalty, in the modern bourgeois imagination the domesticity of the polis has become associated with argument, contest, homosexuality, politics, and spectacle. Since these cannot (according to the same imagination) be natural, their material symbols—village and urban clusters; streets and passages; fields, docks, baths, parks, or other public spaces—are left out of archaeologies in which it is the house that naturally "centers" life. They are merely secondary forms, agglomerations of or gaps between the essential "domestic" building blocks. But despite everything, they return to the house through its back door. For Hodder, ultimately "power," "prestige," and "self-interest" do fuel the structure of Neolithic house building.[76] Such forces are constructed, of course, not only "at home" but also in social relations in the public, transdomestic arena of the village, polis, or state—in the material settings that have only secondary status in Hodder's depictions.

In its actual architectonic and social setting at Çatal Hüyük or Lepenski Vir (Figs. 4.3, 4.4), then, the domus might have been the "focus" only because the village provided a regulation and measure of its meaning and value. By contrast, in Hodder's text the domus is the focus precisely because it is not the village: it has meaning and value on its own. In Neolithic European societies, villages might write their houses; but in Hodder's text, the house is logos: because it is natural, it writes itself. It gives itself "structure." But such a house deconstructs itself.

Hodder sometimes abandons his structuralist image of a "large-scale context in which similar meanings are assigned to similar objects," of houses as "homes" and "centers." In its place, he offers a historical narrative of the disjunctiveness of meaning. The structuralist concern for "a clear social and conceptual opposition or distinction" between meanings,[77] its ambition to identify "centers" of meaning, actually creates room for a deconstructive intervention. If meanings are centered, autonomous entities entered into an abstract "structure" and if the "context" of their production is principally the "structure" itself, whence could a shift in meaning derive except from within these "centers"? Thus, to the extent that an archaeology of "contextual meanings" recognizes the shift of meaning at all, it *requires* the deconstruction of the centeredness of meaning.[78] Put another way, once structuralism admits any history, it is consumed by history: and the history always consists of the evacuation of centers.

Hodder's account of the tombs, barrows, and henges of Britain, one of his most suggestive

76. Hodder, *Domestication of Europe,* 281.

77. Hodder, *Domestication of Europe,* 21, 271–72, but cf. 232.

78. Note, however, that disjunction is quite different from the "polysemousness" of meaning Hodder also identifies. As the standard distinction between a reference and its senses implies, the "meaning" of any term is inherently "multiple and ambiguous" (to use Hodder's words, *Domestication of Europe,* 99). But if there is no such thing as monosemy, then to identify polysemy could not be an interesting historical discovery about meaning! (See further Whitney Davis, "Interpretations of Meaning in African Art," *African Arts* 22 [1990], 24–32.) *Disjunction* denotes not the inherent slippage between reference and sense but the contingent slippage between meaning (ambiguous reference *and* multiple sense) and morphology—for example, between the depicted form of a beardless, heroic young man and his "meanings," ambiguous and multiple in each case, as Apollo or as the Good Shepherd (see Erwin Panofsky, *Renaissance and Renascences in Western Art* [Stockholm, 1960]). In the simplest case, morphology remains constant, while meaning shifts, or vice versa. In complex cases, both morphology and meaning are partly constant and partly shifting over time.

analyses, is deconstructive history in just this sense. In Neolithic Britain, he says, houses themselves were "small and dispersed." Tombs "provide[d] the channel for transforming the domus into the agrios," involving an "internal transformation": a "new emphasis on individuals, males, warring, and hunting, although in principle opposed to the domus, begins to emerge from its very centre." In henges, "the concerns with defence and the wild have been brought [even] closer to the centre."[79] All in all, in Neolithic Britain the centered domus Hodder has earlier introduced is traversed with its own immediate outsides or frames, what Derrida has considered as the *parerga* of centered forms (and see Chapter 8).[80] As Hodder puts it, the British Neolithic is "turning things inside out."[81]

In fact, these frames are not only the outsides or frames of the domus as depicted in Hodder's image of its meaning. They are also the frames of his analysis itself. It is not surprising that Hodder ends his depiction of Neolithic Britain by raising the question of public monument building, of society-wide control, and, indeed, of the emergence of states.[82] The domus is now so empty in its supposed "center" that the archaeologist finally turns to what was always his subtext—the trans- or supradomestic forms and meanings I have already noted as as the object of Hodder's most conspicuous silence.

Mapping disjunction can become a specifically *deconstructive* dimension of the archaeology of meaning (for examples, see Chapters 7, 8, and 10). This might seem more obvious when we recall that such archaeologies—they need not be structuralist—often assume a long-term homogeneity of meaning, conceived, in itself, as univocal (no polysemy *or* disjunction). For example, in his self-styled "cognitive archaeology" of southern San rock art, J. D. Lewis-Williams projects his iconographic decipherments of San images, based upon historical sources and ethnographic analogies of nineteenth- or twentieth-century vintage, as much as two millennia back into the southern African past. Elsewhere, he is suitably cautious about the very oldest images, with archaeological dates of at least 19,000 B.C.[83] Perhaps, then, he feels that the more recent centuries of this apparently continuous tradition can safely be assimilated. But straightforward archaeology shows that the so-called Brandberg Culture (ca. A.D. 1400 to 1900) exhibited substantial change in settlement pattern over its whole five-hundred-year duration, as well as cultural transformations due to European colonization and other influences in the second half of the nineteenth century. Moreover, this cultural phase does not even extend to the period 500 B.C. to A.D. 1400, to which some rock art must certainly be dated.[84] When the social context itself has changed so markedly, it is inconceivable that synonymies of meaning should somehow have been preserved.

At the most general level, an archaeology of meaning that principally does iconography—the identification of the external source and reference of a symbolic form—without

79. Hodder, *Domestication of Europe*, 244, 255, 257, 261, 264.

80. See especially Jacques Derrida, *The Truth in Painting*, trans. Geoff Bennington and Ian McLeod (Chicago, 1987).

81. Hodder, *Domestication of Europe*, 258.

82. Hodder, *Domestication of Europe*, 269–72.

83. J. D. Lewis-Williams, "Ideological Continuities in Prehistoric Southern Africa," in *Past and Present in Hunter-Gatherer Studies*, ed. Carmel Schrire (Orlando, 1984), and idem, *Rock Art of Southern Africa*, 26.

84. P. Breunig, "Archaeological Investigations into the Settlement History of the Brandberg," in Harald Pager, *The Rock Paintings of the Upper Brandberg*, pt.1, *Amis Gorge* (Cologne, 1989), 1:17–45.

"iconology," an examination of disjunctive sense and use, will remain logocentric. It is not surprising that the problem bedevils the study of the very origin of symbolism, one of the prime concerns of recent archaeologies of meaning. The appearance of depiction (for example) does, or could, betoken a cognitive transformation. Some writers have argued that depiction copies a mental image with various contents, such as perceptions, entoptics and hallucinations, or gestures.[85] Alternatively, depiction might be the *deconstruction* of copying as such, for example, in the continuous disambiguation and remarking of previous judgments (see Chapters 2 and 3). In either case, at least depiction is an example of Intentionality going beyond itself: consciousness takes its own contents as the object of its directedness. But here, logocentrism will try to get back through the palimpsest of re-vision and re-mark, the image as "written," to the underlying presence of pure percept, hallucination, meaning, or what-have-you from which the image supposedly derives as a copy or translation. Such accounts lose sight of the image as consciousness-directing-itself-at-itself to focus on the supposedly *underlying* mental direction of a supposedly preexisting Intentionality toward objects in the world. In falling into this trap, although they may make incidental discoveries about the sources of an iconography in perceptions, entoptics, gestures, or what-have-you, they fail to tell us anything about depiction as such, as a material writing.[86]

But we can safely bypass logocentric investigations. In depiction, we find a distribution of Intentionality in a timing and spacing of traces and spaces that are themselves re-vision and re-mark.[87] A logos is not the "origin" of the process as such. Reducing and supplementing, and taking reductions and supplements as objects for further reducing and supplementing, the image "originates" when a logos, the supposedly preexisting and underlying perception, hallucination, or what-have-you, temporarily crystallizes as a retrodictive interpretation of the sequence. In this, the logos can be no more and no less than yet another reduction and supplement. It is always *archē-* or *telo-* in relation to spacing and tracing, to the materiality of writing, as such.

85. For an account of (and attack on) the theory of copying perceptions, see Norman Bryson, *Vision and Painting* (Cambridge, 1979); for copying entoptics, see Robert G. Bednarik, "Parietal Finger Markings in Europe and Australia," *Rock Art Research* 3 (1986), 30–61, and J. D. Lewis-Williams and Thomas Dowson, "The Signs of All Times: Entoptic Phenomena in Upper Paleolithic Art," *Current Anthropology* 29 (1988), 201–36; for copying gestures, see Iain Davidson and William Noble, "The Archaeology of Perception: Traces of Depiction and Language," *Current Anthropology* 30 (1989), 125–55 (see further Chapter 5, note 41).

86. Whitney Davis, "Comment on Lewis-Williams and Dowson," *Current Anthropology* 29 (1988), 222–24.

87. See further Michael Podro, "Depiction and the Golden Calf," in *Visual Theory: Painting and Interpretation,* ed. Norman Bryson, Keith Moxey, and Michael Ann Holly (New York, 1991), 63–89.

REPLICATION IN ART HISTORY

Chapter 5

Beginning the History of Art

Opening many textbooks of art history, one finds "prehistoric" images like the Paleolithic paintings from Lascaux or Altamira standing for the history of pictorial art from its hypothetical inception about forty thousand years ago until about 10,000 B.C.—that is, for the first half or three-quarters of the entire preserved duration of human image making. For instance, the substantive historical narrative in the latest edition of H. W. Janson's well-known *History of Art* is introduced by a painted bison from the Spanish Magdalenian cave of Altamira and a view of the so-called Axial Gallery at Lascaux (Fig. 5.1), with its great painted horses and engraved bison.[1]

There is much to puzzle us in these devices. First, despite various speculations about the meaning or function of Paleolithic images, the textbooks never really address the problem of their historical origins. This blindness can be found both in conservative and more recently in so-called new art history. For conservative historians, there simply will never

1. H. W. Janson, *History of Art*, 4th ed., rev. Anthony F. Janson (New York, 1991), vol. 1, 1st color plate ("Key Monuments in the History of Art"), and also 74–76, figs. 30–32.

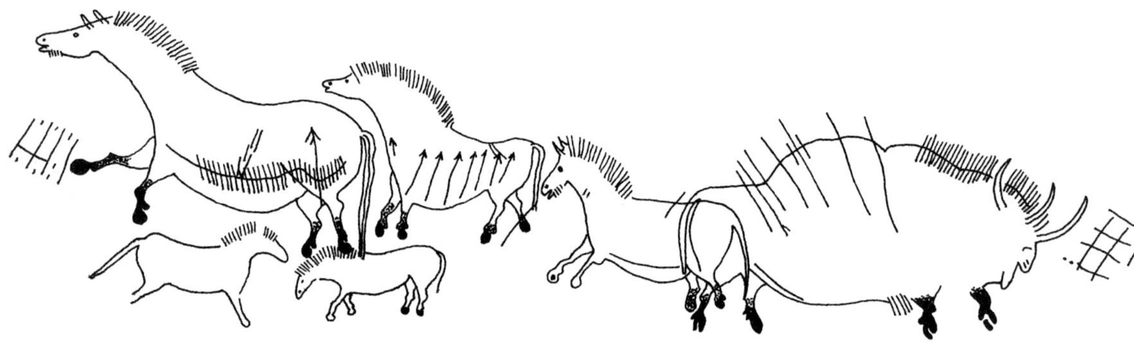

Fig. 5.1. Painting of horses (left horse is 3' 8" long) and engraving of bison (4' 5" long), entrance to the Axial Gallery, cave of Lascaux, about 15,000 B.C.

be enough archaeological evidence in the matter. The issue, then, is condemned as inherently and supposedly fatally theoretical. For many "new" historians, although theoretical discussion is admissible, questions of origins are still banned. For them the notion of an origin cannot be reconstructed in terms of the founding assumption semiotics and structuralism require about language or languagelike systems, namely, that such systems are conventional. Whether conventionality can be God-given or must rather be produced in a historical and social process, and whether this process must have its own history that cannot in itself assume conventionality, are questions logically prior to and thus outside of the strict antirealism and strong conventionalism of orthodox semiotics and structuralism.[2] It is thus in spite of a strong professional disposition to distrust questions of origins that our textbooks do go ahead and attempt to identify them at all.

Identify origins, maybe; but analyze, explain, or debate them, certainly not. For second, it is obvious that a single received view has dominated the "Figure 1" slot in the textbooks, namely, the Axial Gallery (including the Rotunda, into which it leads) at Lascaux. Views of this site appear yet again in three other widely used texts, *Gardner's Art Through the Ages*, Lawrence Cunningham and John Reich's *Culture and Value*, and William Fleming's *Arts and Ideas*.[3] Lascaux has been nominated for this obsessive regard, to use Jerrold Levinson's term,[4] in part because the circumstances of its discovery were accidental and dramatic, confirming two of our long-standing intuitions about what an "origin" should feel like—in 1940, boys chasing their dog stumbled upon an entrance to the cave.[5] Moreover,

2. For a powerful statement of the "antirealist" position in "new" art history, see Mieke Bal and Norman Bryson, "Semiotics and Art History," *Art Bulletin* 73 (1991), 174–209; for a "naturalistic" alternative, see Chapter 1.

3. Horst De la Croix, Richard G. Tansey, and D. Kirkpatrick, eds., *Gardner's Art Through the Ages*, 9th ed. (New York, 1991), 29, fig. 1.1; Lawrence S. Cunningham and John J. Reich, *Culture and Values: A Survey of the Western Humanities*, alternate volume, 2d ed. (Fort Worth, 1990), 12, fig. 1.1; and William Fleming, *Arts and Ideas*, 8th ed. (Fort Worth, 1991), 2, fig. 1.

4. Jerrold Levinson, "Defining Art Historically," *British Journal of Aesthetics* 29 (1979), 232–50; see now his "Refining Art Historically," *Journal of Aesthetics and Art Criticism* 47 (1989), 21–33.

5. For the latest photographs, see Mario Ruspoli, *The Cave of Lascaux: The Final Photographs* (New York, 1986); the essential archaeological account is Arlette Leroi-Gourhan and J. Allain, eds., "Lascaux inconnu," *Gallia Préhistoire*, suppl. 12 (1979).

the story is easily narratable as one that modern audiences have heard many times before—for instance, for Heinrich Schliemann at Troy in 1871 and Howard Carter at the tomb of Tutankhamen in 1923. Lascaux alleviates the paradox of how the "beginning" of the history of art will be told, by locating its narratability not in its *own* historical beginnings but in its historical beginning *for art historians*.

Indeed, the textbooks' standard view of the Axial Gallery predisposes readers to understand it as an intelligible origin. Lascaux has been reproduced as an artwork possessing several very familiar properties of artworks as recent tradition—that is, tradition long after Lascaux—has established them. With its long cumulating frieze of apparently interrelated figures, which the viewer encounters all at once in an initial view and then moves along, the Axial Gallery resembles Egyptian tomb paintings, Greek pedimental reliefs, medieval nave mosaics, or the Sistine Chapel—making the appropriately "primitive" exception that animals occupy the places of human figures. Never mind that Paleolithic viewers could not see Lascaux this way, with their small lamps illuminating very short stretches of wall surface at a time.[6] Even if we recognize the unrolled, evenly illuminated frieze as a modern photographic artwork, the individual figures themselves seem to us almost complete in outline, monumental, and vividly realistic in many details. To our eyes, they are fully resolved images—formal, iconographic, and aesthetic wholes. Never mind that some of them were heavily reworked or scratched over by Paleolithic makers or viewers.[7]

Even though they are seen as wholes, the images also seem to spring from the living rock itself. Like the circumstances of discovery, this fact can be construed to alleviate the burden of explicating origins, allowing Lascaux self-evidently *to be* an origin. As one influential argument would have it, pictorial image making began as a human-made response to and elaboration of natural forms seen to look like other things (for this "argument from projection," see Chapter 2). Never mind that any image must reflect some of the properties of its supporting medium, which can always be seen in it; that a rock looking like a bull is not, as such, a picture of a bull; and that it was Leonardo da Vinci who recommended apprentice artists should seek out suggestive resemblances in lichen stains on a wall, not the painters at Lascaux, who mostly avoided the really bumpy bits and whose solutions to painter's block are unknown.

Now, none of the textbooks is so naïve as to offer a painting in Lascaux as being, in itself, the "first" picture or the beginning of the history of art. It is widely known that the caves of Lascaux and Altamira, at approximately 15,000 B.C., appear late in a long history, perhaps to be understood as a developed tradition. The earliest known examples, whatever they imply about broader historical and philosophical questions, are dated to about 35,000 to 32,000 B.C., the period during which *Homo sapiens sapiens*, anatomically modern humans, are thought to have achieved adaptive dominance over Neanderthals in hominid ecological

6. Ruspoli made a striking attempt to reproduce this effect (*Cave of Lascaux*, cover, 102 [top left], and 108 [bottom left]). For the original lighting system, see Brigitte Delluc and Gilles Delluc, "L'éclairage," in "Lascaux inconnu," ed. Leroi-Gourhan and Allain, 121–42.

7. This is fully apparent in any good reproductions (e.g., Ruspoli, *Cave of Lascaux*, 51, 136–37). The phenomena of reworking, overmarking, and so on, have been variously interpreted; for a review, see Paul G. Bahn and Jean Vertut, *Images of the Ice Age* (London, 1988), 184. For reasons that emerge later, I shall consider them as partially constitutive of the "origins" of image making itself (see also Chapters 2 and 3).

niches.[8] In Hugh Honour and John Fleming's *Visual Arts*, one of the most sophisticated textbooks on the market, Lascaux's bulls do make their ritual appearance, but only in sixth place after several earlier "sculptures" dating back to 30,000 B.C..[9]

Nonetheless, the organization of the art historical chronicle, and especially its narrativization, seems to require some "Figure 1." Whatever it is, "Figure 1" has a complex status. On the one hand, it is tied to art history's conception of artworks as essentially historical. It asserts not only that art making somehow begins or emerges in time and space—that it is a historical object, like a species or a person, open in principle to classificatory analyses and historicizing accounts of all stripes (such as stylistic analysis, for which, see Chapter 6). "Figure 1" also implies a "Figure 2," "Figure 3," and so on. It establishes that art making is inherently a matter of replication, of ongoing, accruing, or compounding repetition and variation. In these terms, "Figure 1" is understood by all to be a placeholder. As a discursive convenience, a narrative or pedagogical necessity, it is open to change with new historical discoveries about beginnings or replications.

On the other hand, however, "Figure 1" is also tied to art history's counterthrusting conception of artworks as essentially ahistorical, leaning on certain definably modern but apparently inescapable aesthetic doctrines and critical conceptions. According to this conception, there must be some time and place at which an artwork is *irreducibly* first, originary, or emergent. Accordingly, any history of secondary, repetitive, or derivative replications—such as the art historian's typical mosaic of sources, influences, quotations, audience responses, and the like—is ultimately beside the point. Moreover, to interpret the artwork's "beginning" historically would be to misrecognize the absolute originariness of the beginning—the sense in which what the artwork begins is history itself. What remains to us here, then, must be our inaugural confrontation with the artwork as such.

The historical and the ahistorical Figure 1 may not be the same actual artwork. Lascaux has certainly been established as a historical Figure 1. The textbooks use it to exemplify actual historical beginning, the emergence of and basis for replications. But, equally clearly, it is not the ahistorical Figure 1. What motivates its selection as the historical Figure 1 is a prior commitment to a history of Greek sculpture, or Michelangelo's, and of Leonardo's creativity—in which Lascaux is actually understood as a replication, admittedly retrochronologically. In art historical aesthetics, Lascaux is at best a Figure 2, with an ahistorical Figure 1, the great bronze "Zeus" from Artemísion or Michelangelo's *David*, coming before it—literally on the covers of the textbooks, where they serve not as an "Artwork Number 1" but as the "Artwork" to or for which a history of artworks, Figure 1 through the rest, will be appended.[10] In this sense, the actual prehistoric image is thor-

8. For the two-dimensional Aurignacian images, see Brigitte Delluc and Gilles Delluc, "Les manifestations graphiques aurignaciennes sur support rocheux des environs des Eyzies (Dordogne)," *Gallia Préhistoire* 21 (1978), 213–438; for the Vogelherd figurines, see Alexander Marshack, *The Roots of Civilization: The Cognitive Beginnings of Man's First Art, Symbol, and Notation* (New York, 1972), 246–56. For other early Paleolithic arts, see Bahn and Vertut, *Images of the Ice Age*, 26–40, 53–60.

9. Hugh Honour and John Fleming, *The Visual Arts: A History*, 4th ed. (Englewood Cliffs, N.J., 1995), 4–13, figs. 1.1–1.6.

10. Janson's Artwork, in this sense, is the "Zeus" from Artemísion; Gardner's is the palace at Persepolis; Cunningham and Reich's is Poussin's *Landscape with the Burial of Phocion;* Fleming's is Manet's *Portrait of Emile Zola;* Honour and Fleming's is Michelangelo's *David*.

oughly historical, and the actual historical image is outside or before history, the standard, motivation, and frame for a history that easily invents and enfolds its self-fulfillingly legible prehistory.

Let us now suppose, however, that the historical Figure 1 and the ahistorical Figure 1 are the same pictorial artwork, namely, an actual prehistoric work, presumably a very early one, that can be said to be outside or before art history. This artwork would not just be the historical inauguration of a particular chain of replications. It would also be the historical origin of the very possibility of any art historical replication as such, of art making as such, or of art history as such. Can we make sense of this supposition? Do we or could we have such "pre-historic" artworks, and what could be their properties? Is there an artwork that historians should ever put on the cover of an art history?

Art Beyond Compare

In considering the possibility of artworks that stand as Figure 1 in the strongest sense, we could define them simply as artworks with no art historical comparisons. Such artworks are outside and before art history in the straightforward sense of art history as that which simply gives substantive historical explanations for the possibility of comparison between artworks—such as Camille Pissarro's and Richard Estes' paintings of a street in Paris (Figs. 5.2, 5.3), dated 1897 and 1972 respectively. Crudely put, an art historian is just someone who shows two slides at the same time.

Of course, my characterization is simplistic. For one thing, comparisons are not made only by academic art historians. Artists, critics, philosophers, and other viewers often function as "art historians" in my sense. Indeed, possibly one cannot even function as a critic or philosopher of the arts, or even as an artist, without necessarily functioning, at least in part, as an "art historian."

For another thing, comparison as such between artworks does not art history or an art historian make. The comparison must be interpreted in terms of a historical explanation for its possibility. There are many such explanations. In addition to familiar claims about "influences" running from one artwork to the other, it might be a good historical explanation of the comparison to say how the person showing the slides has been able to find them in a slide archive in the first place. Recent art history, in the professional sense, has been divided about how statements about art history's history should be related to apparently very different statements about art's history.[11]

A Figure 1 with no art historical comparison would be "pre-historic" in the strong—and, I argue, the only coherent—sense because the comparisons of art history have always been undertaken out of the awareness, more or less obscure, that the history of art, the past of art making, is essentially continuous with art history. To put it another way, the events of mak-

11. For one view, see Donald Preziosi, *Rethinking Art History: Meditations on a Coy Science* (New Haven, Conn., 1989), with Whitney Davis, *Art Bulletin* 72 (1990), 156–66. See also Chapters 9 and 11.

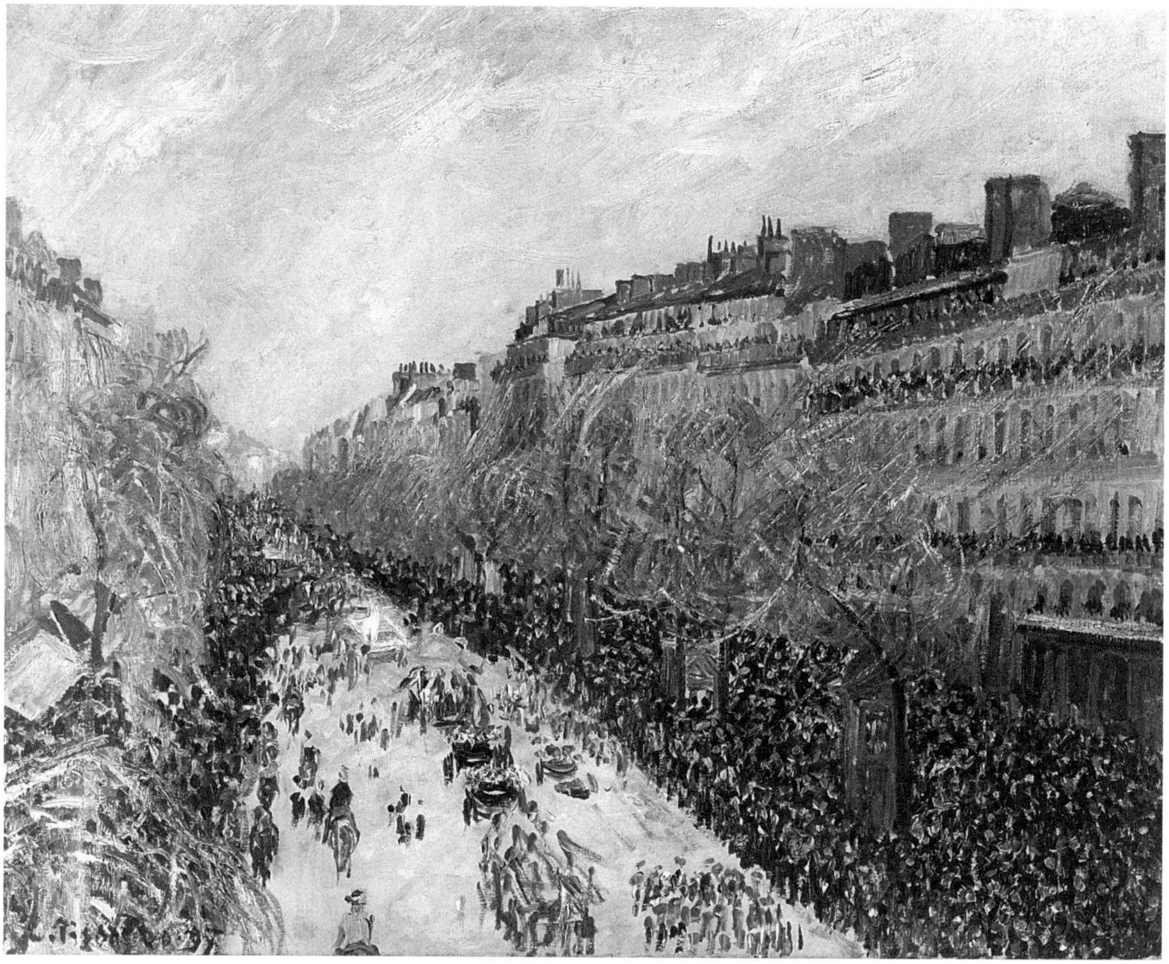

Fig. 5.2. Camille Pissarro, *Mardi-Gras on the Boulevard Montmartre, Paris,* 1897. Collection of the Harvard University Art Museums, by permission.

ing an artwork in the past themselves involved an art history—a taking account of, a making reference to, and a comparing with other objects and images, some of them artworks, as historical in relation to, and to an extent explanatory of, the artwork being made. Art historians' comparison—their juxtaposition of Figures 1 and 2, 2 and 3, 3 and 4, and so forth—is supposed to model this past art historical activity within art making, typically an artist's use of and reference to the work of other artists. (In Chapters 2 and 3, I offer a formal account of the morphologies that result from this process. The notion that an artwork is established *entirely* on the basis of its legibility in terms of other artworks' previous legibilities would be too limited. The artist might also be taking account of other objects and images not legible as artworks at just that, or any, moment [see Chapter 11].) Thus I might say that Estes, in working out his picture of an empty, lonely Parisian street (Fig. 5.3) viewed at street level by someone who is standing outside the buildings, took account of—and expected his viewers to recognize—Pissarro's or many similar Impressionist portrayals of a Paris populated, colorful, and excited (Fig. 5.2). Estes' "realism" consists not only in his

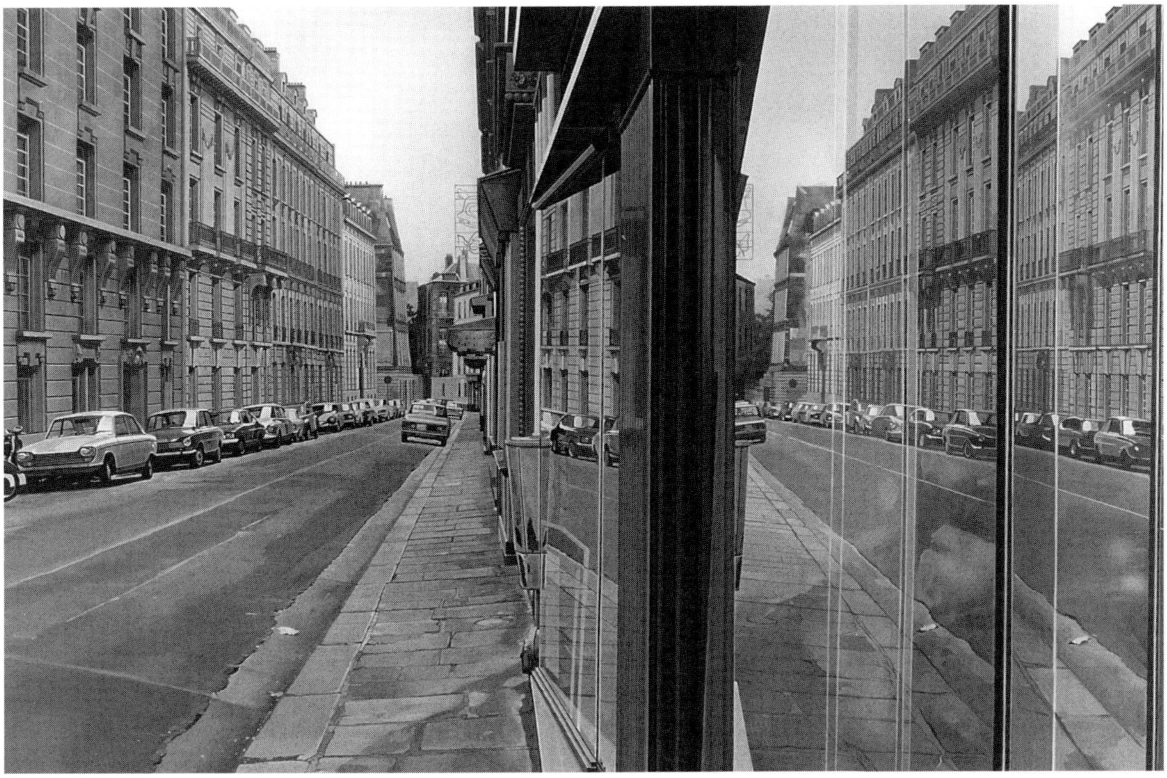

Fig. 5.3. Richard Estes, *Paris Street Scene*, 1972. Virginia Museum of Fine Arts, Richmond.

trompe l'oeil technique but also in his attempt to express what might be the actual, perhaps disappointing "reality" of Paris for a modern American viewer imbued with an image of Paris inherited from the Impressionists.

As everyone recognizes, many forensic and hermeneutic obstacles stand in the way of successfully identifying the art historical relations intrinsic to artworks. We might not have direct testimony from Estes or other traces of his working practices; even these would be open to historical criticism. The historical explanation of the comparison might be an inference from purely "formal" facts. For example, to establish Estes' presumed historical relation to Pissarro, we could note that Estes organizes his composition, like Pissarro, around a deep receding diagonal. Furthermore, he seems to play with the very theme of images and reflections that a viewer thinking about Pissarro, or Paris, might entertain: the art historical relation not only is a condition of the work's conception but also seems to have been staged, by Estes, in order that its presence as a condition be legible.[12]

On the basis of formal observations alone, art historians cannot show their model of art historical relations, embodied in a comparison, to be an adequate representation of the

12. We might assert, further, that an artist took account of an earlier artist's work to the extent that the later practitioner apparently worked in the "style" of the earlier (though this is not the case with Estes in relation to Pissarro). Unfortunately, however, the historical category of "style" (which, in art history, usually refers to a production system from which many artifacts, by different makers, commonly descend) is inferred from formal similarities between the artifacts hypothetically thought to belong to it (see Chapter 6).

art historical relations in past art making. But despite this difficulty, art history is supposed to model, among other things, the art historicity of artworks in the past. (The pastness of the artwork, of course, is not the whole story. The artwork must exist in our historical present as well, otherwise its historicity could not be modeled in the first place. And art history—for example, in "formal analysis" conditioned by art-market demands—might serve the present histories of artworks as much as their past.) When the art historicity of artworks *cannot* be described and explained, comparisons between them remain comparisons whose possibility or basis has not been accounted for. Such works are, I say, "pre–art historical." My special term here is really not that different from the usual. Because archaeologists define the "historical" as the "literate," actual "prehistoric" arts are professionally defined as just those arts for which no written evidence can be adduced—barring at least one major avenue for the art historical explication of comparisons between them.

Some basis for the very possibility of the comparison can always be articulated; we can say, at least, where we got our two slides. For this reason actual individual artworks are never completely pre–art historical. They have a rooting in our art historical reality (see further Chapters 9 and 11). But conversely, because the art historicity of artworks cannot be fully revealed by all of the comparisons our art historical reality allows us to make, artworks are always partly pre–art historical. We cannot fully root them in their art historical reality. Put another way, at times or in some places we just live with artworks as part of the brute furniture of our world. Our encounter with them is ahistorical. At other times or in other places, we grasp them as having histories. Moreover, according to the intuition underlying our art historical reality, the condition of our art historical reality as partial and fluctuating must be continuous with artworks within history. At times, artifacts and images were just in the world as part of its brute furniture, and people lived with them as such. At other moments, people grasped them as having histories. All of this is only to say that art historicity and its prehistoricity are interpenetrating and variable phenomena, historical in themselves. They are never wholly present in but never wholly absent from an actual individual artwork. Thus it might be a mistake—and a major source of the apparent insolubility of the question of art's origins—to look for a beginning in actual individual artworks, chronologically prehistoric or otherwise. A Figure 1 that can actually be dug up and exhibited will never be found. In earlier chapters, chronologically prehistoric art was used to advance some theoretical discussions, but the "originariness" or "originality" of the works of art cited, as I stressed, lies only in the place they hold in chains of replication with certain formal and contextual properties.

The Gaps Between the Works

Art historical comparisons frequently leave the impression that the historicity identified by the comparison lies somewhere in the space between the two artworks compared, in the art historical chronicle, narrative, or other discourse filling the printed page between a Figure 1 and a Figure 2. After all, in themselves the two artworks are two wholly separate physical objects made at different times and places. Indeed, because anyone can compare two wholly separate artworks, art historians seem to be just those people who are able to write up a discursive justification of the comparison conforming to certain canons of reasoning. This labor seems, as it were, to be a supplementary, specific operation art historians "do" to the artworks themselves.

Thus a typical text might compare Eric Fischl's *Power of Rock and Roll* (Fig. 5.4), of 1984, to Jan Vermeer's *Young Lady Standing at a Virginal,* of about 1670, in the National Gallery in London (Fig. 5.5).[13] Both paintings situate a young person in domestic interiors, in a sensual or even erotic relation to music, at the intersection of a strong exterior light on the left and a recognizable image depicted hanging on the wall above and to the right of the figure. Most art historians, or critics functioning as art historians, would probably say that Fischl strongly alludes to Vermeer. Vermeer, then, must be placed somehow within Fischl's very near experience in painting the *Power of Rock and Roll,* for example, in a visit by Fischl to the National Gallery, the narrative of which will bridge the gap between the two works.

But part of the point of the comparison is precisely to suggest that there is not a "gap" between Vermeer and Fischl, a temporal and spatial separation between two autonomous artworks to be "filled in" by history. Instead, the comparison models Fischl's taking account of and making reference to the Vermeer not as "separate" from Fischl but precisely *for* Fischl and *as* Fischl encountered it. Both Vermeer's *Lady at a Virginal* and Fischl's emerging *Power of Rock and Roll* are "in" the single, continuous but differentiated historical process of Fischl's painting his painting, what Richard Wollheim would call Fischl's painting "as an art."[14] Like Estes staging his relation to Pissarro, Fischl does seem to stage the way art history (or at least a dominating image of our culture, like Andy Warhol's *Marilyn*) is "in" his painting process as well as an element of the final explicit theme of the painting itself. But the staginess, as such, is not the issue—or even whether Fischl and his viewers consciously recognize the presence of the earlier in the later replication. It would be impossible to know how many viewers of Fischl's *Sheer Weight of History,* of 1982, identify the Hellenistic sculpture placed on the left side of the depicted space and thus to a degree literally "in" the painting (Figs. 5.6, 5.7). But this surprising marble hermaphrodite—the *Borghese Hermaphrodite,* now in the Louvre—is thoroughly threaded through Fischl's identity and art as a painter. It does not stand apart from, completely outside and before, *Sheer Weight of History* but, instead, is the weight of history in and for that painting—one of the very conditions, perhaps the motivation, of its ability to represent this history for the depicted person *within* the painting in the first place (see further Chapters 9, 11, and 12).

Between two separate artworks in a comparison, Figures 1 and 2, the chronicle or narrative text, then, is actually the historical justification for understanding Figure 1 *as* Figure 2, or vice versa, or both together, at least in part. Each figure in a comparison is a palimpsest, a differentiated structure of the taking-account and making-reference-to

13. See Peter Schjeldahl, *Eric Fischl,* ed. David Whitney (New York, 1988), pl. 66, and Ludwig Goldscheider, *Jan Vermeer: The Paintings, Complete Edition* (London, 1958), pl. 78.

14. Richard Wollheim, *Painting as an Art* (Princeton, 1987); and see also Michael Podro, "Depiction and the Golden Calf," in *Visual Theory: Painting and Interpretation,* ed. Norman Bryson, Keith Moxey, and Michael Ann Holly (New York, 1991), 163–89.

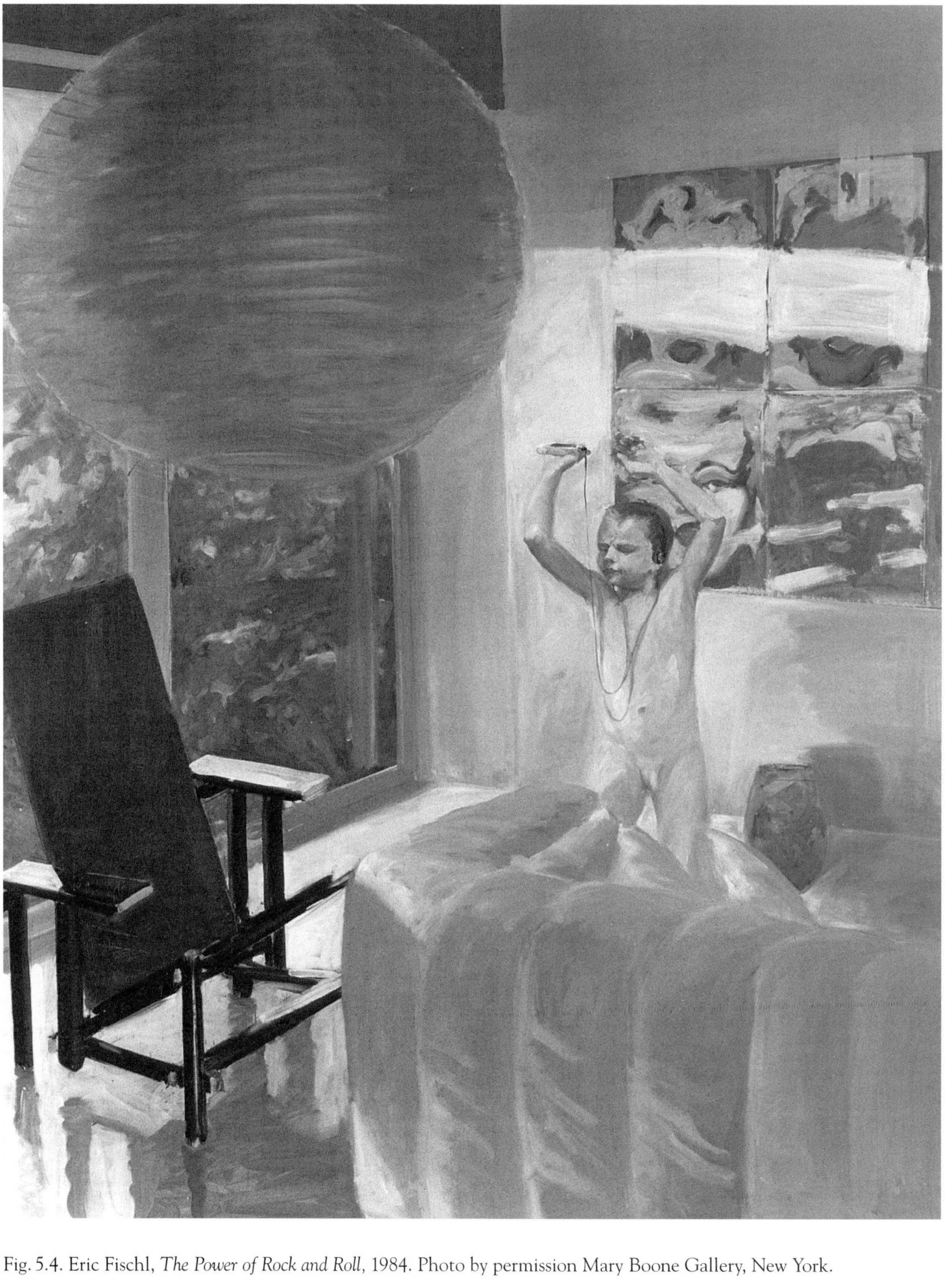

Fig. 5.4. Eric Fischl, *The Power of Rock and Roll*, 1984. Photo by permission Mary Boone Gallery, New York.

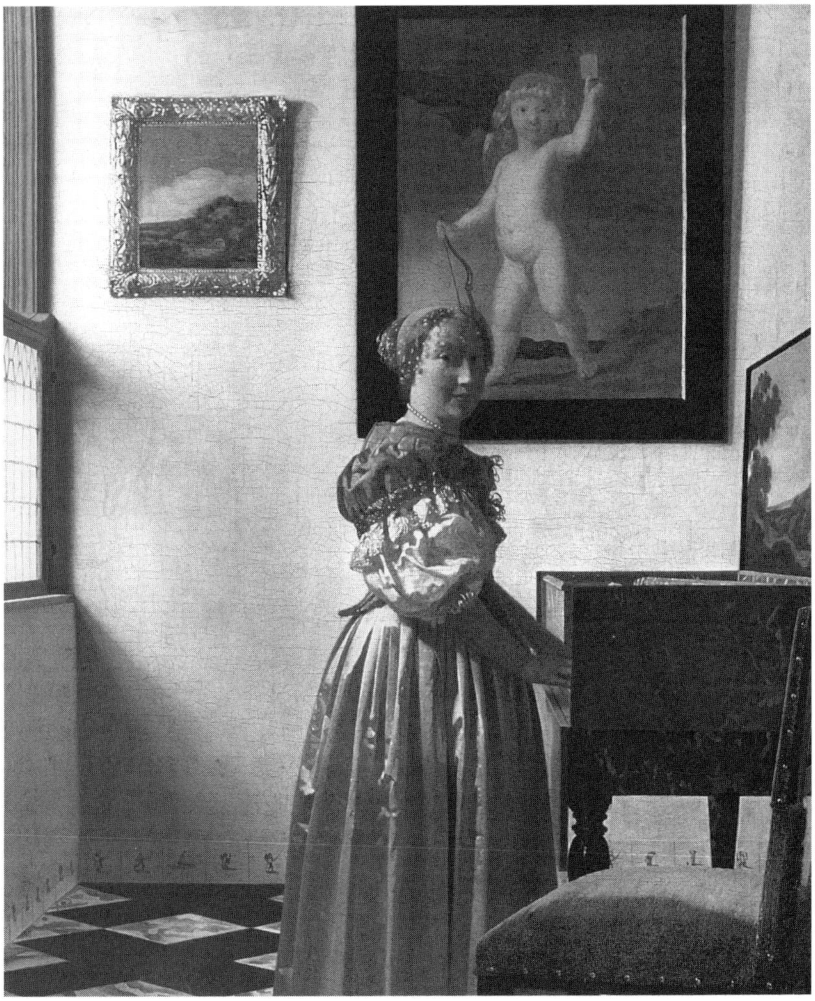

Fig. 5.5. Jan Vermeer, *Young Lady Standing at a Virginal,* about 1670. Collection of the National Gallery, London, by permission.

constituting the artist's Intentionality, disentangled *by* the comparison for narrative and pedagogical convenience. Thus the appropriate historical object to which we are led by the comparison is not, or not just, that of real historical routes of association between separate artworks. Rather, it is a mental entity, the art historical Intentionality of each maker.

Hence the paradoxical quality of the comparison. On the one hand, it says that two different artworks go together, connected by some real route of historical association—as we can infer if we compare them. But on the other hand, it says that two artworks transcend comparison, or, more properly, do not need it "done" to them, for they already belong together as elements in an individual artwork's art historicity. Therefore comparisons, in trying to take the pre–art historical and make it art historical, end up invoking both actual history, a replicatory sequence and relationship, and prehistory, the enfolding of every replication within the emergent intentionality of a single artwork. In turn, by eliminating the gap between the artworks, since they are "in" one another, comparative art history must somehow reinstitute the gap at the absolute limit of all artworks: if art historicity is a whole, then it is, of course, separate from non–art historicity.

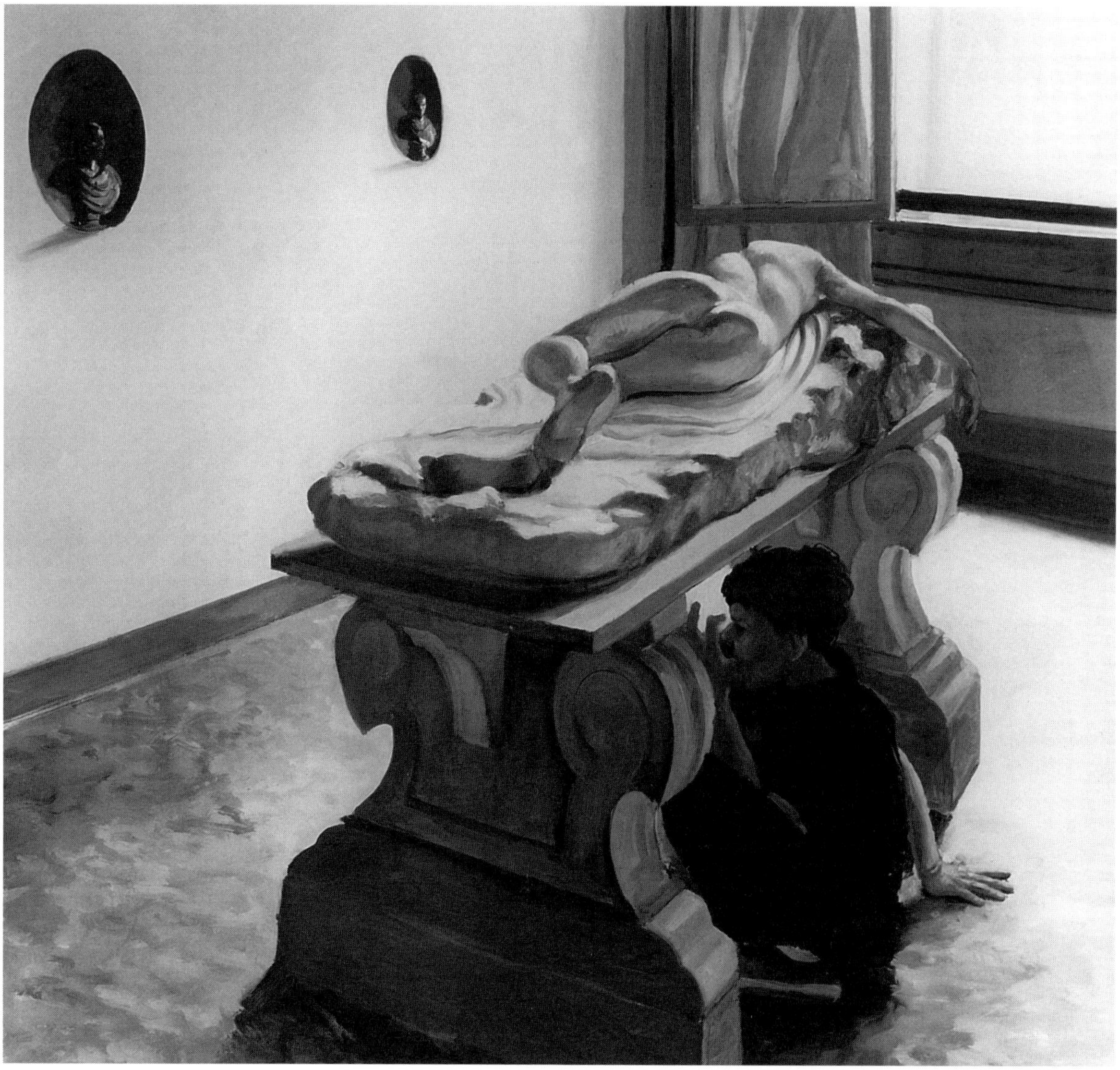

Fig. 5.6. Eric Fischl, *The Sheer Weight of History*, 1982. Photo by permission Mary Boone Gallery, New York.

The Impossible Link

Art history tends to consider pictorial artworks as finished wholes, suffused through and through in their making with the maker's Intentionality, which consists at least in part of art historicity. On this account, the work to be identified as our hypothetical Figure 1 could only be imagined as a replication and summation. As such, how could it also be a beginning?

I do not want to deny replicatoriness and summativeness as the art historicity of artworks; indeed, one of the principal aims of this book is to affirm the point. But strictly speaking, only the chains of replication and summation themselves, the art histories to which individual artworks partly belong, are replicatory and summative. Within these

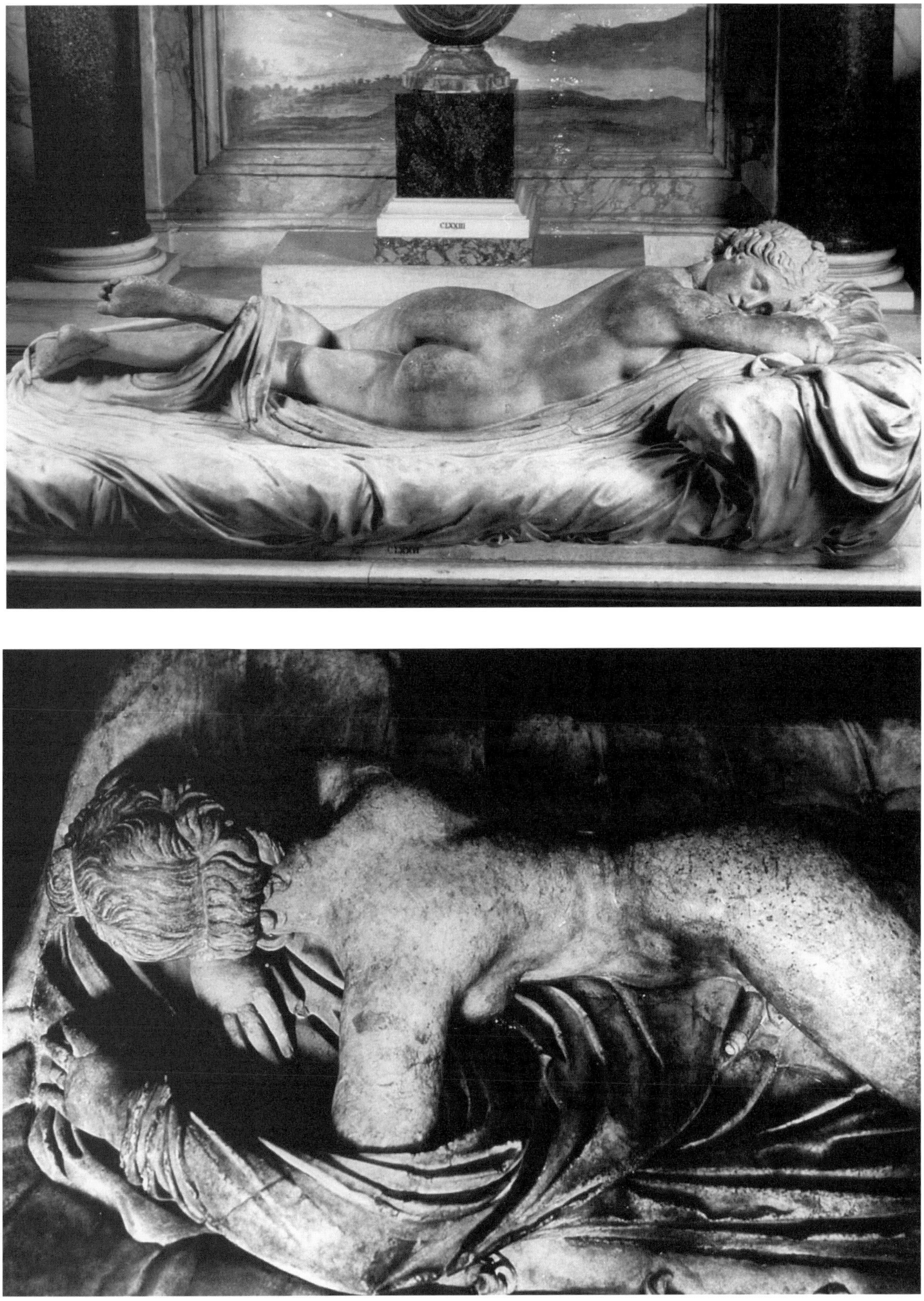

Fig. 5.7. Sleeping hermaphrodite (the "Borghese Hermaphrodite"), now in the Louvre, Paris, about 150–100 B.C.

chains, an individual artwork is only a link, discovered to be such through the method of comparison. Taken out of a chain, a link is either broken apart or it can be soldered up as a self-contained, closed unit. Art historical aesthetics has opted for this latter conception as the essence of artworks, what we might call the "impossible link." The artwork, this aesthetic asserts, is a self-contained, autonomous object. Perhaps it can be an available "link" for the attachment of the currently broken, unrealized, or unmade bits of *later* links, but, in itself, it is already a whole. At the same time, however, art historical archaeology in its modern, forensic form can at least conceive all of the links as available, merely "broken" bits, no one of which is whole or finished, lying around for the possibility of a later linking up in or as a chain. The tension between these two perspectives—what I have just distinguished as the "aesthetic" and the "archaeological" or "forensic"—derives from the beginning of art history as a chain of disparate events in itself.

The full intellectual and social history of the "impossible link" in art history and its antecedents has yet to be written. In the broadest terms, the supposed wholeness of artworks might be a condition or a consequence of the larger Western aesthetic intuition, imbibed even by Marx, that artworks transport or redeem us from the vague, unresolved, merely material and human chaos of history (or delude us with claims to do so). More to my specific purposes in this chapter, aesthetic wholeness has persistently been identified with the *spatiotemporally discrete physical object of art* rather than with the art historicity of the maker's Intentionality as it is distributed—or "disseminated"—among both elements of many artworks and elements of the maker's nonartwork activities.

For example, to take an early stage in the beginning of art history, Livy tells us that the "craze" for Greek art began with the robbing of the Greek temples in Sicily in 211 B.C.; it was advanced by the annexation of Greece in 148 B.C. and of Pergamon in 130 B.C.[15] A Roman collector of Greek art did not just want to display Greek culture in a "linguistic" sense—for example, by learning the *koinē* or, like the emperor Hadrian, adopting Greek coiffure. He also wanted Greek culture as an independent, whole thing, a material trophy identifying his sophisticated, luxury tastes and international connections, and to that end imported sculptures by the shipload to be exhibited in his salon or garden. Despite his various errors and prejudices, in the *Natural History* Pliny served these purposes well by writing an art history in which discrete, labeled sculptural works were classified under the names of historical Greek sculptors.[16] In discussing oratory and rhetoric, a major concern for the Roman public man, Cicero and Quintilian added stylistic judgments on long-dead Greek artists and their artworks (see Chapter 6). Thus the physical thing within one's grasp became the currency for art historicities definitively beyond it. Its value was constructed in the admixture of nostalgia, fear of inferiority, vulgarity, pragmatism, and remorseless colonization, commodification, and selective homogenization that was bourgeois Roman culture.

To take a later stage, in early modern Europe it was possible to give, sell, transport, dis-

15. Documentary information is collected by Cornelius C. Vermeule, *Greek Sculpture and Roman Taste* (Ann Arbor, Mich., 1977); fine interpretive essays, which I depend upon here, are Paul Zanker, "Zur Funktion und Bedeutung griechischer Skulptur in der Römerzeit," *Entretiens sur l'Antiquité Classique* 25 (1979), 283–314, and J. J. Pollitt, *Art in the Hellenistic Age* (New York, 1986), 150–63.

16. The clearest picture of Pliny's approach to recording Greek art emerges from Andrew Stewart's comprehensive and exacting analysis of the literary and epigraphic sources for Greek art in his *Greek Sculpture: An Exploration* (New Haven, Conn., 1990), 1:237–310.

play, or collect a discrete physical thing while that thing's art historicity, the maker's art historical Intentionality, remained largely unknown. The identification and exhibition of art historicity as such—the way in which makers took account of and made reference to other objects and images—would only become the social function of archives and museums, developing well after the advent of large-scale European collecting, and of art advertising, art history, and art criticism (what David Carrier calls "artwriting"),[17] whose origins for me lie not so much in Vasari's *Lives* (1550, 2d ed. 1568) as in Winckelmann's writing, in the 1750s and 1760s, again long after the rise of big-time collecting and, most important, coincident with the first real art dealing (see further Chapter 9). Seventeenth- and eighteenth-century "dealers" were mostly diplomats, travel guides, belletrists, and secretaries or librarians to the nobility or the church. Also moving private correspondence, gossip, aristocratic trinkets and gifts, boys, and wives, they moved whole collections of works often only vaguely tied to known history, such as Cardinal Alessandro Albani's first collection of antiquities, acquired, with the help of Baron LePlat, in the great purchase of 1728 by the king of Poland for his new antiquarium in Dresden. Here young Winckelmann saw it, as well as Raphael's *Sistine Madonna,* shaping the basic idea of his seminal essay of 1755, *Thoughts on the Imitation of Greek Art in Painting and Sculpture.* After the first sale, Albani went on to rebuild his collection—partly with the help of Winckelmann himself, now transplanted to Rome and employed as the cardinal's librarian, house designer, and confidant. But until arriving in Italy and visiting Herculaneum, Winckelmann's actual familiarity with Greek art was based in large measure upon the unparalleled collection of small ancient gems and coins, sometimes bearing images of lost major works, in the hands of the Baron Stosch, a peripatetic nobleman and spy. The 1760 sale catalogue for Stosch's holdings constituted Winckelmann's first major scholarly work, setting the stage for his great *History of Ancient Art* of 1764, rightly regarded, I think, as the first "true" art history.[18]

To take a still later stage in the development of art history, the forensic interests of nineteenth- and twentieth-century art history can be understood in part, I believe, as a response to a crisis in the autonomous artwork. The growth of art historical galleries and museums tied to competing German, British, and French nationalisms, the opening of seemingly insatiable art markets in America, and other factors dramatized the limited availability as well as the increasingly stupendous cash value and potential equity of artworks. A hundred years after Winckelmann saw Raphael's *Madonna* in Dresden, it was clear that the Dresdeners, for example, would not likely be able to acquire such a work again, even though artworks of the second rank and below were now pouring from tomb robbing, excavations, and colonial enterprise.[19]

17. David Carrier, *Artwriting* (Amherst, Mass., 1987).

18. For the Dresden collection, see Paul Herrmann, *Verzeichnis der antiken Originalbildwerke der Staatlichen Skulpturensammlung zu Dresden* (Berlin/Dresden, 1925); for Winckelmann's knowledge of it in the 1750s, see Konrad Zimmermann, ed., *Die Dresdener Antiken und Winckelmann,* Schriften der Winckelmann-Gesellschaft 4 (Berlin, 1977). For a general interpretation of Winckelmann's knowledge of Greek art, see Alex Potts, "Winckelmann's Construction of History," *Art History* 5 (1982), 377–407; for the Villa Albani, see W. O. Collier, "The Villa of Cardinal Alessandro Albani, F.S.A.," *The Antiquaries Journal* 67 (1987), 338–47; for Winckelmann's life and publications, Carl Justi, *Winckelmann und seine Zeitgenossen,* ed. Walter Rehm, 5th ed. (Cologne, 1956), despite gaps, is still indispensable.

19. An adequate history of these matters remains to be written, although aspects are reviewed in Heinrich

However, the crisis could be circumvented, and relative values secured, by minutely identifying and discriminating traits that could be found in some measure in many lesser works as well as the greater. Applying his forensics to the galleries in Dresden and elsewhere, Giovanni Morelli, in his art history of the 1890s and its successors, differentiated not only separate artworks but also separate styles, manners, schools, traditions, and periods. These were now interpreted as collectable wholes in themselves, with the organicist cultural histories of Jakob Burckhardt and Heinrich Wölfflin producing the text of comparisons between them.[20] Through the work of Bernard Berenson and other early twentieth-century art historians, *more* styles and periods—primitive, exotic, "medieval," archaeological, "modern"—were added to the list. Even when the artwork could be found only as a broken and mysterious fragment, fragments themselves were often interpreted as aesthetic wholes, rather than energetically restored, as in the seventeenth and eighteenth centuries, to an "original" whole. Finally, living artists were constructed not only as the authors of autonomous individual artworks but also as the engines of an open-ended art historicity known as a "career," also constituted as a whole. Following intimations in Vasari's biographies, and in the connoisseurship of Berenson, Sir John Beazley, and other art historians, "careers" were retroactively conferred on long-dead art producers in remote historical contexts. The discovery of the wholeness of "artists" in the past, and their analogs in styles, periods, and careers, came to obsess scholarly art history.

In sum, the palpable wholeness of the physical objects of art has conferred wholeness—boundaries, suffusions, and finishes—on their supposed art historicity. In today's art market it might seem to be aesthetic value tied to the ineffable creativity of the maker's intentions that inflates the raw material worth of the mere things of art. But in the history of art history it was, in fact, the autonomy of the mere things of art that inflated aesthetic value and the art historicity of artworks or, more accurately, packaged them as wholes.

However, if art history's origins lie partly in recounting and securing artworks—and their analogs in styles, periods, and careers—as autonomies, its paradoxical result, increasingly obvious by the turn of this century, was to attenuate the ways in which artworks can plausibly be conceived to be such wholes. At the same time as forensic scrutiny will pick out underlying essences—the origin, cause, or regularity in diversity—it will simultaneously identify the irregular and variable. In principle, variability should be ruled out as irrelevant to the underlying essence. But in practice, the more underlying wholes one picks out—not only autonomous artworks but also styles, periods, and "careers"—the more likely an irregularity can be analytically "discovered" as an index of some supposed historical essence or other.

There thus arose the fatally unsystematic character of the magnificent descriptive-

Dilly, *Kunstgeschichte als Institution: Studien zur Geschichte einer Disziplin* (Frankfurt am Main, 1979).

20. Although his *Civilization of the Renaissance in Italy* (1860) is often cited as the best expression of his approach, Burckhardt's specifically art historical conceptions are more visible in *The History of Renaissance Architecture and Decoration* (1867) and his last, little-read, four-volume work, *History of Greek Civilization* (1898–1902). A persuasive deconstruction of Wölfflin's work suggests how unstable his comparisons really were: Marshall Brown, "The Classic Is the Baroque: On the Principle of Wölfflin's Art History," *Critical Inquiry* 9 (1982), 374–404.

comparative compendia forming the vast bulk of art historical scholarship in the twentieth century. For example, consider William Stevenson Smith's *History of Egyptian Sculpture and Painting in the Old Kingdom,* prepared just before World War II at Harvard under the supervision of F. R. Grace and G. H. Chase, classical archaeologists deeply influenced by Sir John Beazley, whose own treatises on Greek vase painting best embody this scholarship within the study of prehistoric and ancient art.[21] When Smith scrutinizes a work of Egyptian art, like a wooden relief of the royal official Hesire dated about 2700 B.C. (Fig. 5.8), through comparison he finds close parallels with other works, like the earlier Palette of Narmer, about 3000 B.C. (see Fig. 7.4). For him the parallel indexes one aspect of the work's art historicity, namely, its period style associated with particular high-status patrons. But sometimes Smith *cannot* find a parallel. For example, he identifies several unique features of the relief of Hesire in small details like the arrangement of the thumb. Nevertheless, this irregularity becomes an index, for him, of just another aspect of the work's art historicity—namely, here, the supposed "inventiveness" of its maker.[22] Forensic method, pressed to identify regularities between Figures 1 and 2, 2 and 3, 3 and 1, and so on, simultaneously ensures that every figure will become partially a Figure 1—as I have put it, beyond compare—in order to handle the parallel fact of irregularity observed between Figures 1, 2, and 3: of course, Smith needs some occasional "invention" in his period style to account for the variability his own forensic comparisons reveal to him. Such scholarship appears to generate descriptive-comparative histories revealing the rich art historicities of whole artworks and their analogs. But one suspects that in many cases its dubious methods—like Smith's observation of the absence of a parallel turned into an argument for the presence of inventiveness—stitch up a largely fictitious account. Overly ambitious in establishing wholes through any means, it is often grossly underdetermined by forensic standards themselves. Nowhere does Smith evaluate alternative scenarios, such as the possibility that Hesire's sculptor was not especially inventive but simply could not draw thumbs.

Putting my point the other way around, we must search hard through the literature of art history—with some exceptions in the last fifteen years—to find an adequate forensics, let alone any historical interpretation, of the unfinishedness or overall half-bakedness of artworks. For example, art historians can usually provide only a garbled, severely qualified account of what would have counted as outright error for the artists or in the styles and periods they know best. They are predisposed to reconstruct what seems to be an error precisely as a whole intention suffusing that supposed error and fulfilled in it—for example, an ambition to do it differently from predecessors or, like Hesire's sculptor, to be "inventive," or the like.[23]

21. William Stevenson Smith, *A History of Egyptian Sculpture and Painting in the Old Kingdom* (Cambridge, 1945); J. B. Beazley, *Attic Red-Figure Vase-Painters* (Oxford, 1942). Beazley's procedures, however, can be difficult to reconstruct because he often merely listed his results without providing a discursive narrative or justification.

22. Smith, *History,* 139–41.

23. No doubt "reader response theory," "deconstruction," and other interpretive methods in art history and criticism have increased our sensitivity to phenomena like "constitutive blanks" (Wolfgang Kemp, "Death at Work: A Case Study on Constitutive Blanks in Nineteenth-Century Painting," *Representations* 10 [1985], 102–23), "disfigurations" (Michael Fried, *Realism, Writing, Disfiguration: On Thomas Eakins and Stephen Crane* [Chicago, 1987]), "failures to signify" (T. J. Clark, *The Painting of Modern Life* [New York, 1985], esp. chap. 2),

It is not as if candidates for a forensics of half-bakedness do not exist. For example, if Hesire's thumb is not error but inventiveness, then consider the artist's slip on the top zone of the obverse (saucer) side of the Narmer Palette (see Fig. 7.4), Hesire's most important art historical predecessor. Working left to right and top to bottom, the sculptor needed to turn the palette at right angles to draw the ten decapitated enemies of the king. He placed the first small enemy in the top row against the side edge, drawing the enemy's two feet both facing right. Doing the same thing for the next enemy, second from the left in the top row, he recognized the "error" he had just made, that is, the compositional difficulty he was creating for himself. With the third enemy in from the left, he turned the two feet to face inward; now he could be sure to fit in all ten enemies. In one sense, the making is driven by a forward-looking intention to include ten enemies, but in another sense the making, though threaded through with this intention, is not suffused with it. Instead, the making is a loose tissue of partially realized intentions, of matter escaping form or artifact sliding out from underneath image (see further Chapters 4 and 8).

An "error" belongs to a complex continuum of pre–art historical phenomena. They range from what forensic interpretation construes as a rendition just barely missing an evident intentional target, such as the enemies' feet on the Narmer Palette, to works manifesting so little apparent emergence of an intentional target that we cannot say what, if anything, has been targeted and missed in the first place. Many actual prehistoric artworks would have to be included here (see Chapters 2 and 3). "Errors" and other formations are not without their own histories, but they are rarely written as the text bridging art historical comparisons: histories of non-, of pre-, and of para-intentional phenomena would not recount a taking-account-of and making-reference-to other artworks but rather some uniquely contingent circumstances of the maker's concrete situation and history.

To sum up, art historical aesthetics has conceived the artwork, as an autonomous whole thing, to be one or a whole with the inherent art historicity of its maker's intentions, with no remainder or disruption. At the same time, however, art historical archaeology, a forensic inquiry in part dedicated to identifying art historical wholes, constantly discovers such remainders and disruptions.

"subversions," and the like. However, all too often these properties of an artwork are made over into its supposed whole intentionality to constitute itself *as* blanked, disfigured, and so forth. As Jacques Derrida ironically notes, "[T]he hypothesis of a rigorous, sure, and subtle form is naturally more fertile" (*Dissemination*, trans. Barbara Johnson [London, 1981], 67). Present-day "social art historians" often consult initial critical responses to artworks in part because these are thought to tell us about canons of performance (for example, for the "finish" of a work) from contemporary points of view. But just because a salon critic, for example, tells us that something is wrong in a painting does not mean that the work had this status in the Intentionality of the maker; for the maker, the painting could be completely suffused with some particular resolved art historicity. To complicate matters a bit, it is perhaps part of the particular whole art historicity of modern painting that it must fail to represent the truth about modernity's own real blurring or mystification of social boundaries (see esp. Clark, *Painting of Modern Life*). But this could be only to say that the art historicity suffusing such paintings assumes a different form than it had for the makers of the traditional descriptive-comparative compendia. At any rate, a tradition of subsequent critical response does not automatically say anything about the art historicity of makers' intentions. Using it as historical evidence requires anachronistic reasoning, however rationalized by an appeal to a maker's own supposed prospective intention to make something for an expected audience. In fact, this research assumes yet another art historical whole without remainder or disruption, namely, the whole of artistic "production-and-reception."

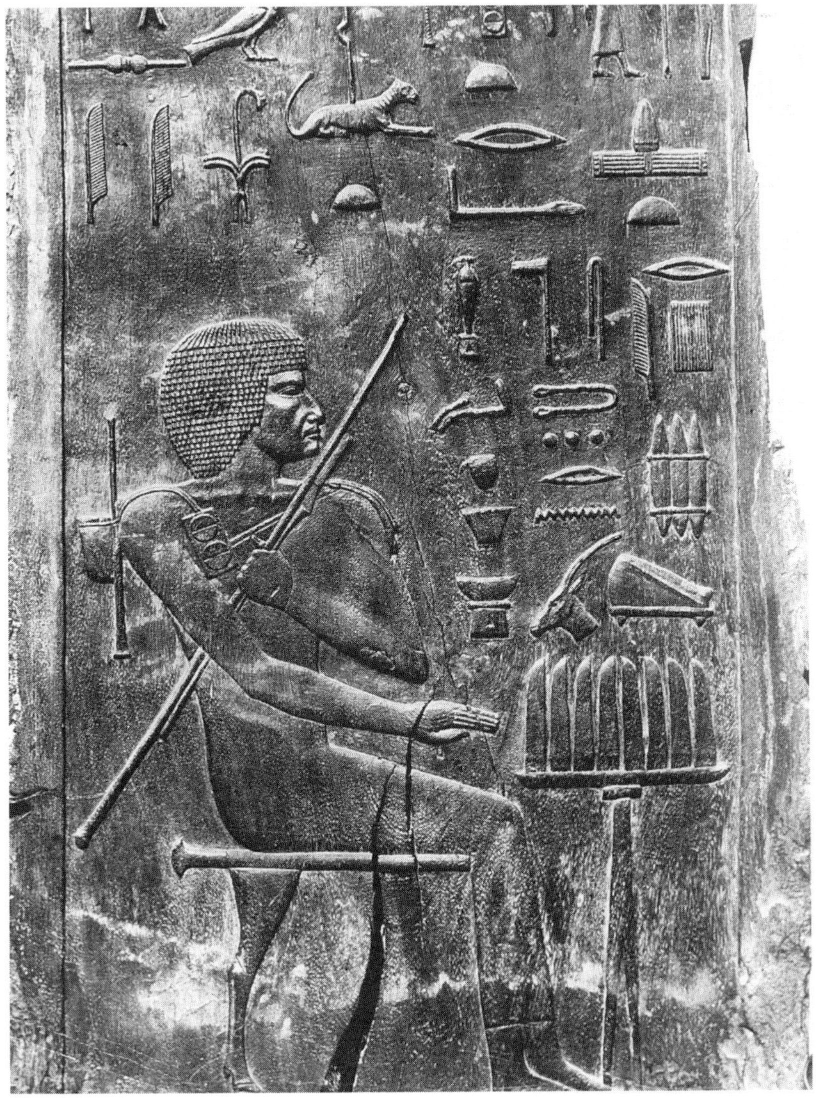

Fig. 5.8. Detail of wooden tomb relief of vizier Hesire, from Tomb of Hesire, Sakkara, Third Dynasty (about 2700 B.C.).

The Broken Link

Works of prehistoric art, as I noted in Chapters 2 and 3, often cannot be related to artists or even to periods and styles. Thus they could be pre–art historical, beyond or, more exactly, before compare. Even though many of them are intensively understood in forensic terms, the inquiry seems to be going nowhere—or, at least, nowhere art historical. But art history has not rested content, of course, with the pre–art historicality of prehistoric art. Art history necessarily seeks out whole art historicities in the mosaic of regularities among comparisons even though some prehistoric art seems to include art history's equally necessary pre-historic artwork, its ahistorical Figure 1.

From the beginning, forensic evidence implied that the first cave paintings to be discovered were Paleolithic in date. The evidence, in fact, did not depend wholly or even substantially upon art historical comparison. Altamira, the first painted cave known to modern scholarship, was discovered in 1879 by Don Marcelino Sanz de Sautuola on his estate in Santander in northern Spain. Don Marcelino was struck by the resemblance between the paintings in his cave and engravings on bone objects he had seen exhibited in the Exposition Universelle in Paris in 1878, already well known from a monograph by the antiquarians Edouard Lartet and Henri Christy, their *Reliquiae Aquitanicae* of 1875. In turn, these objects were accepted as prehistoric because several of them had excavation contexts in prehistoric strata, including Lartet's own 1864 excavations at La Madeleine, datable through the forensic means established in Jacques Boucher de Perthes' *Celtic and Antediluvian Antiquities* (1846) and Sir John Lubbock's *Prehistoric Times* (1863). But, as critics pointed out, the resemblances were not complete: whereas the engravings were small and frequently somewhat abstract, the paintings at Altamira were large, vivid, and mostly naturalistic. In fact, then, comparison between the decorated caves and the portable objects was not fully accepted until 1902. However, in his 1880 publication of Altamira, Don Marcelino did not rest his case on a comparison that was, itself, pre–art historical, since the art historicity constituting it—namely, the existence of a Paleolithic style common to the portable objects and the caves—did not yet exist for art history. Instead, he related his discovery of middle Magdalenian tools, hearths, and debris at the entrance of Altamira, some meters away from the paintings, urging that the archaeological deposits provided a firm forensic date independent of the possible comparison between artworks.[24]

In response to Don Marcelino's non–art historical forensics, professional archaeology and art history (they were not wholly distinguished at the time) mobilized art historical comparison to deny the possibility of a whole Paleolithic art historicity established by forensic means outside strictly art historical comparison. Altamira's paintings, it was said, best resembled modern art in their lack of darkening, in their realism, and in their skillfulness.[25] It was even put about that Don Marcelino had been duped by a contemporary French painter who had visited his estate. Taken to its logical conclusion, this self-fulfilling blindness would prevent the very possibility of an art history that could ever adopt such strictures against a possible "prehistoric" art in the first place.

For the next twenty years, forensic historicities like Don Marcelino's deposits at Altamira became tighter. However, even when engravings were found on the ceiling of the cave of Chabot right above Magdalenian deposits on the floor, in 1878,[26] and Emile Rivière opened the totally sealed decorated cave of La Mouthe, in 1895,[27] for many observers the

24. Marcelino Sanz de Sautuola, *Breves apuntes sobre algunos objetos prehistóricos de la provincia de Santander* (Santander, 1880). A relatively complete early description was widely disseminated by Salomon Reinach, *Répertoire de l'art quaternaire* (Paris, 1913), 7–19. Useful accounts of the discovery of cave art can be found in Bahn and Vertut, *Images of the Ice Age*, 17–25, and Peter J. Ucko and Andrée Rosenfeld, *Palaeolithic Cave Art* (New York, 1967), 31–36.

25. See esp. Edouard Harlé, "La grotte d'Altamira, près de Santander (Espagne)," *Matériaux pour l'Histoire Primitive et Naturelle de l'Homme* 12 (1881), 275–83.

26. Emile Rivière, "Sur les gravures de la grotte de Chabot," *Bullétin de la Société d'Anthropologie de Paris* (1897), 319; L. Chiron and C. Gaillard, "L'industrie et la faune des grottes Chabot et du Figuier sur les bords de l'Ardèche," *L'Homme Préhistorique* 9 (1911), 129–37, 202–12.

27. Emile Rivière, "Les parois gravées et peintes de la grotte de la Mouthe (Dordogne)," *Bullétin de la Société d'Anthropologie de Paris* (1897), 302.

proper comparison remained the known, whole art historicity of modern painting technique. The cave painters, it was said, must have used artificial light, steel tools, and the like. As we would expect, to preserve an established, whole art historicity this forensics reconstructed apparently non- or para-intentional phenomena, those elements of image making beyond compare, to fit its scheme. For instance, the fact that Altamira's aurochs sometimes exhibit features not to be observed in "real" aurochs supposedly implied that the modern painter did not understand the anatomy of the beast, now extinct, whereas a prehistoric painter surely would have. Ironically, then, the paintings of Altamira were compared with the art historicity being denied, what a Paleolithic cave painter would have done (if such a person had ever existed), in order to preserve the comparison with the art historicity being promoted, what modern painters do. Thus the cave paintings' status as "beyond compare" was erased: no matter how one cut it, the cave paintings are comparable within art historicity, it being the case merely that the Paleolithic art historicity, one possible comparison, did not exist. Here art history found a temporary solution to the problem of origins. The beginning of art history is recognized as a logical necessity precisely to serve the claim that it does not historically exist in this case: if we compare Altamira, the artwork we have, to what the beginning of art history would be like, we can see that the artwork we have is not that beginning.

Nonetheless, by the turn of the century the art historicity of prehistoric art became possible. In a magisterial 1907 work, Edouard Piette fully accepted the formerly banned comparison between dated Paleolithic decorated objects and the undated cave art.[28] Two general concerns motivated Piette and his immediate contemporaries. First, French archaeology became more receptive to the idea of prehistoric art as more cave art began to be discovered in France, especially around the village of Les Eyzies in the Dordogne heartland. A Paleolithic art could potentially root the whole art historicity of French national culture well before Carolingian and Celtic art—shared, unfortunately, with the Germans and others—and prove its pre-Roman vitality and glory, outshining British standing stones or the "eoliths" from southern England now displacing Boucher de Perthes' Somme valley flints for pride of place in paleontological research.[29] Second, the anti-Darwinians—resisting any history whatsoever before 9 a.m., 23 October 4004 b.c., Bishop Lightfoot's date for the flood—had been defeated by Thomas H. Huxley and others, in part invoking the new evidence provided by prehistoric archaeology. Advancement within scientific culture now required evolutionist opinions; and evolution required an ever longer human prehistory.

But for my purposes the real turning point came in 1895 at the newly opened cave of La Mouthe outside Les Eyzies. Here adventurous boys discovered an engraved bison, soon seen to be part of an enormous panel. Prehistoric tools had been found earlier at the cave entrance, but they had been swept aside; and at any rate the engraving was deep within the cave, raising the old objection that there was no connection between tools and artworks.

28. Edouard Piette, *L'art pendant l'âge du renne* (Paris, 1907).

29. For Boucher de Perthes, see Glyn Daniel, *One Hundred and Fifty Years of Archaeology* (London, 1975), 58–59; on the English discoveries, see esp. John Evans, *The Ancient Stone Implements, Weapons, and Ornaments of Great Britain* (New York, 1872).

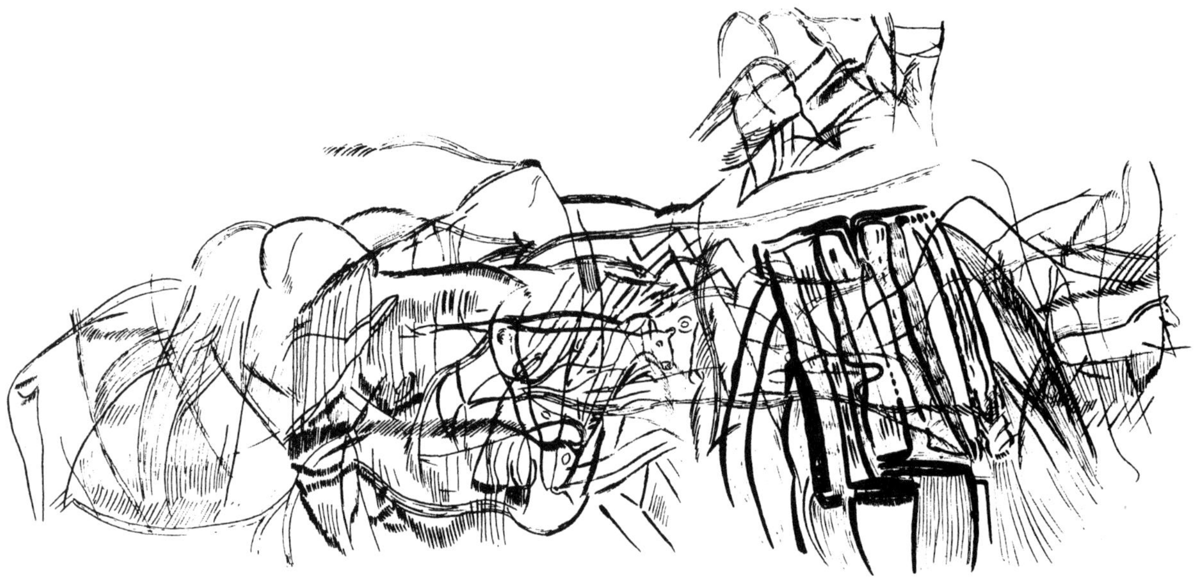

Fig. 5.9. Henri Breuil's line copy of wall paintings and engravings ("Panel of the Hut"), cave of La Mouthe, Dordogne, France, about 15,000 B.C.

Nonetheless, the excavator of the interior galleries, Emile Rivière, clearing back through the cave to about 130 meters, invited Emile Cartailhac, a leader of French archaeology, to visit the site. Although he had earlier written on prehistoric portable objects in his comprehensive *La France préhistorique* of 1889, Cartailhac had long refused to admit the Paleolithic antiquity of cave art, leading the charge against Altamira. However, at La Mouthe it was Cartailhac himself who removed untouched soil of Paleolithic antiquity to uncover painting underneath—establishing an absolute stratigraphic association, the only kind of evidence for date admitted in the strictest archaeological forensics, not quite achieved at Altamira (Fig. 5.9). Within a week of each other in September 1901, two impressive caves were discovered, and soon they were visited by Henri Breuil—Font-de-Gaume, with beautiful painted bison like those in Altamira (Fig. 5.10), and Les Combarelles, with thirteen engraved mammoths, an extinct animal, and many other figures (Fig. 5.11).[30] In 1902, with Breuil and Gabriel de Mortillet, author of an influential *Prehistoric Antiquity of Man*, Cartailhac returned to La Mouthe and other caves, preparing his famous "'Mea culpa' d'un sceptique" for the *Revue Anthropologique* in order to declare his acceptance of the Paleolithic antiquity of cave art: "I have been an accomplice to an error committed twenty years ago [at Altamira] that I must confess to openly and rectify."[31]

In his surprise find, Cartailhac established the art historicity of pre–art historical artworks. The forensic evidence for history—for a date and technological context—was liter-

30. See Henri Breuil, *Four Hundred Centuries of Cave Art*, trans. Mary Boyle (Montignac, 1952), 75–106.

31. Emile Cartailhac, "Les cavernes ornées de dessins: La grotte d'Altamira, Espagne: 'Mea culpa' d'un sceptique," *L'Anthropologie* 13 (1902), 348, translated by the author.

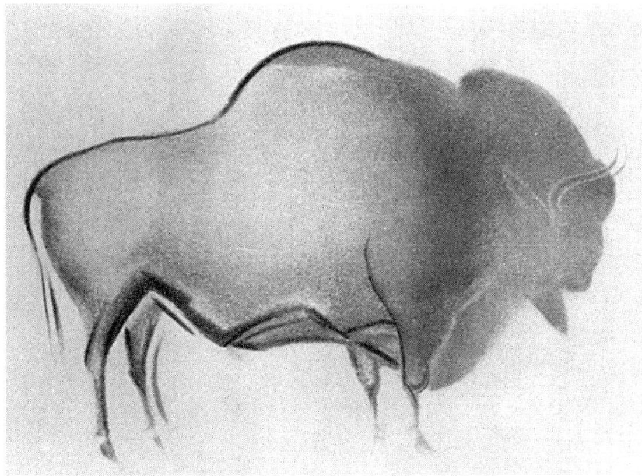

Fig. 5.10. Henri Breuil's line copy of bison, cave of Font-de-Gaume, about 15,000 B.C.

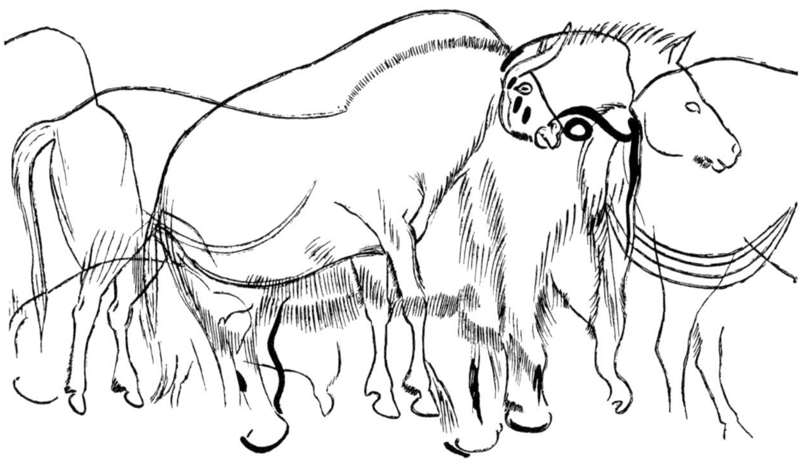

Fig. 5.11. Henri Breuil's line copy of mammoths and other animals, cave of Les Combarelles, about 15,000 B.C.

ally *superimposed* upon the artwork in the layer of prehistoric soils covering it, justifying a comparison between cave art and the tools or other objects from such strata. To revert to terms I used earlier, the historicity of the cave artwork at La Mouthe, like Hellenistic sculpture or Vermeer within Fischl, was literally "in" the artwork; the cave artwork was part of a palimpsest directly exhibiting its historicity. Moreover, quite unlike what could be seen at Altamira, the artworks found by archaeologists at La Mouthe, Font-de-Gaume, and Les Combarelles were literally palimpsests, accumulations of several images superimposed in complex ways upon one another (Figs. 5.9–5.11). Although a systematic analysis of what Alexander Marshack has called the "periodic," "time-factored" properties of Paleolithic image making did not emerge until the 1960s, it was immediately understood, by Breuil above all, that the superimpositions combined with the stratigraphic associations provided the key to the internal historical chronology of Paleolithic image making from the early Upper Paleolithic to the Mesolithic, a 30,000-year span. Minute scrutiny would

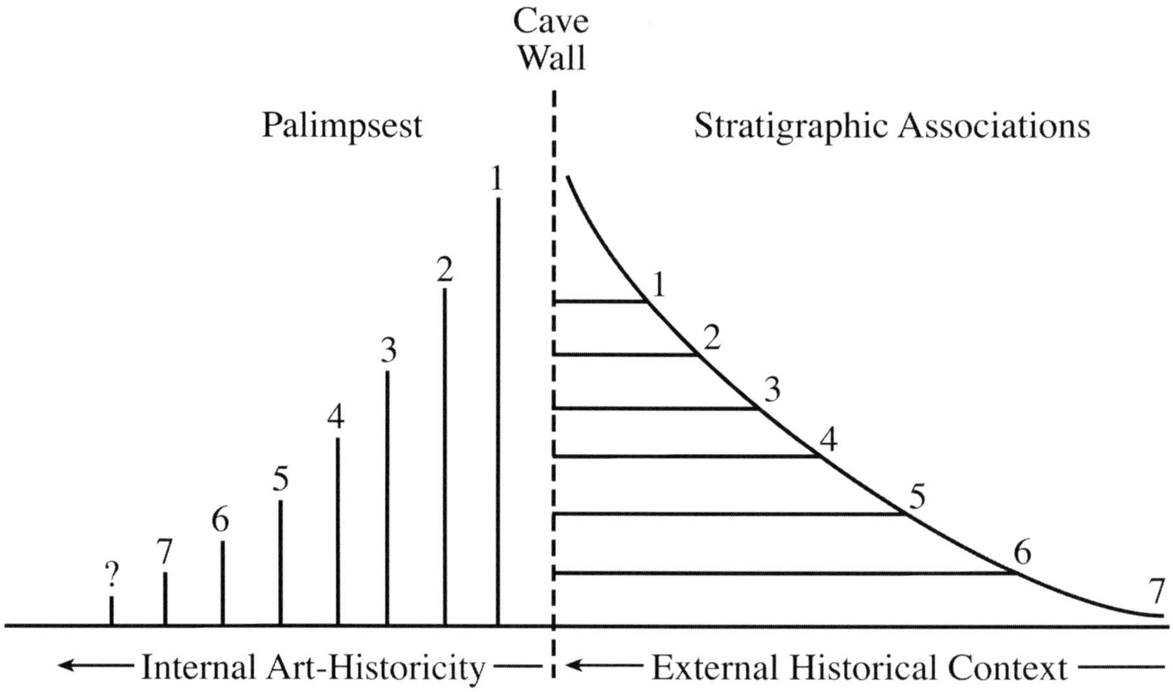

Fig. 5.12. Cartailhac's palimpsest.

show which lines and pigments lie on top of others and thus in what temporal sequence the elements of the images had been laid down. In sum, "Cartailhac's palimpsest" (Fig. 5.12) provided the archaeologist with a directly exhibited, continuous correlation between the external historical context of the artwork and its internal art historicity. Links usually sundered seemed available for forensic analysis precisely as linked.

Indeed, Cartailhac and Breuil's discoveries forged such an apparently complete art historicity for cave art that forensic analysis overestimated its own success. After 1902, cave art became suffused with art historicity, quickly assimilated to familiar forms of art making. In the 1910s and 1920s Breuil worked out an elaborate art history in which prehistoric art making went through two major "cycles" of development, a scheme replaced in the 1950s, in its turn, by André Leroi-Gourhan's identification of four separate sequential styles.[32]

In general, the pre–art historical artwork became prehistoric art; art historians transformed the pre-historical Figure 1 that could not exist into a historical Figure 1 that did exist, precisely by finding it to be suffused with whole art historicities. But obviously a

32. In his *Four Hundred Centuries*, 37–41, Breuil provided his final scheme; Leroi-Gourhan's stages were explained in his *Treasures of Prehistoric Art*, trans. N. Guterman (New York, 1967). For evaluations of these chronologies, see Ucko and Rosenfeld, *Palaeolithic Cave Art*, 195–213, and Bahn and Vertut, *Images of the Ice Age*, 58–64. Both chronologies complemented complex interpretations of cave imagery, extracting various whole art historicities, which I do not have space to consider here.

problem was sidestepped. What about the pre–art historical prehistoric artwork, the prehistoric artwork remaining outside and before the art historicities discovered for prehistoric art? What happened to the beginning of the beginning of art?

At the Bottom of the Palimpsest

On first glance, the question seems to have an obvious answer. Even with their growing paleontological knowledge about the evolution of the human species, it would not have occurred to historians before 1900 to seek the beginning of art before the "Reindeer Age," the Upper Paleolithic. As the controversies over cave art suggest, the Upper Paleolithic—only recently classified as such by de Mortillet and others—was pre–art historical in itself, despite Louis Figuier's belief, in 1870, that the "precursors of Raphael and Michelangelo" had worked the small objects accepted, by the time he was writing, to be actual prehistoric works (Fig. 5.13). Before the opening of La Mouthe in 1895, there was no need to consider anything *pre*–pre–art historical. However, once artifacts and images of the Upper Paleolithic had been reconstructed as fully art historical, as replicatory and summative, the prehistory of this art history would have to be found before it—namely, in the Middle Paleolithic, before 35,000 B.C., or even before.

Prehistoric archaeology has still not resolved this possibility to its own satisfaction. Among other things, art historians are still working with a very short list of possible candidates for an actual Figure 1 conceived as a physical artworklike object. In a recent review, Iain Davidson and William Noble list only thirteen candidates for "documented early [pre–Upper Paleolithic] objects with deliberate marks," to be updated to about twenty or so with the more recent publication of the supposed "deliberate engravings" on the four Middle Paleolithic bones from Bilzingsleben and a few other candidates.[33] The list could be broadened to include instances of coloring artifacts or soils by Neanderthals and of so-called ritual decoration associated with supposed Neanderthal burials, but not in such a way that the coloring or supposed decoration could serve as an art historical beginning for the supposed deliberate marking.[34]

As Davidson and Noble have observed in relation to the thirteen candidates they cite, we cannot easily identify what they call "tradition" or "shared meaning" in this material,

33. Iain Davidson and William Noble, "The Archaeology of Perception: Traces of Depiction and Language," *Current Anthropology* 30 (1989), 125–55.

34. For Neanderthal coloring, see discussion and references in Chapter 2; the Bilzingsleben bones are discussed below. For broad discussions of other possible evidence, see P. Chase and Harold L. Dibble, "Middle Paleolithic Symbolism: A Review of Current Evidence and Interpretations," *Journal of Anthropological Archaeology* 6 (1987), 263–96, and an opposing view by J. M. Lindly and G. A. Clark, "Symbolism and Modern Human Origins," *Current Anthropology* 31 (1990), 233–61. Neither article clarifies the interpretive issues. A convincing criticism of Neanderthal burial by Robert H. Gargett, "Grave Shortcomings: The Evidence for Neanderthal Burial," *Current Anthropology* 30 (1989), 157–90, suggests how a careful forensic analysis can undermine the quest for apparent art historicities or other whole semiotic historicities, a matter I pursue below.

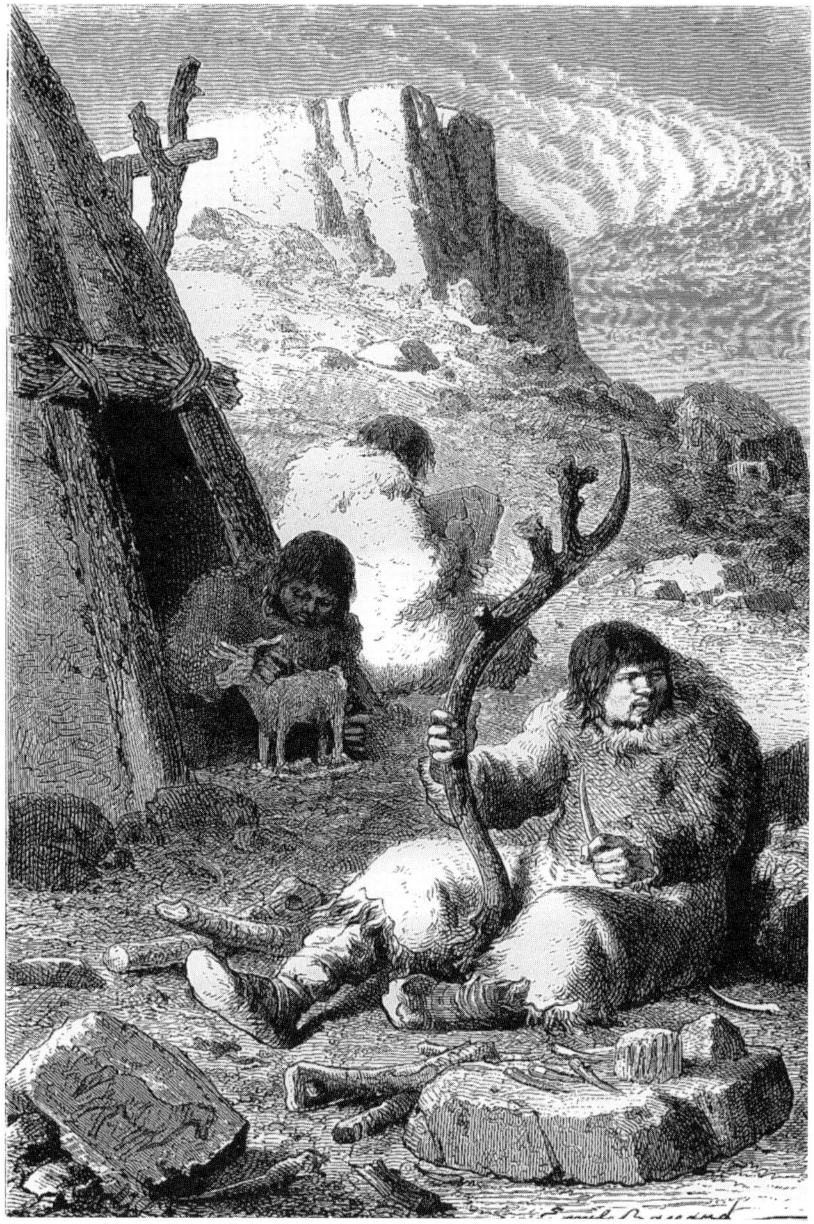

Fig. 5.13. Emile Bayard, *The Precursors of Raphael and Michelangelo, or The Birth of the Arts of Drawing and Sculpture in the Reindeer Age*, 1870, lithograph to illustrate Louis Figuier, *L'homme primitif* (Paris, 1870).

what I have been calling replicatoriness and summativeness.[35] In itself, strictly speaking, this does not tell against the thirteen candidates as possible Figure 1s in my strong sense, for a Figure 1 in my strong sense cannot be art historically replicatory or summative in the first place. But it would be difficult to discover art historical replicatoriness or summativeness in *any* selection of only thirteen dispersed objects anyway—so the fact that it has not been identified does not imply that the candidates were not art historical. Whether

35. Davidson and Noble, "Archaeology of Perception," 132–34.

pre-historic in my strong sense or not, then, the thirteen candidates are at least pre–art historical.

More important, just because the debate about art historicity has shifted from the Upper to the Middle Paleolithic does not, in itself, insulate forensic interpretation from its desire to identify whole art historical intentionalities. Once identified, these will institute regress all over again, ensuring that the beginning of art historicity *cannot* be identified. In principle, forensic interpretation should be forced to displace its quest for the beginning of art from the Middle Paleolithic to a yet earlier history—for instance, to much earlier hominoids like *Australopithecus* or even to the great apes. In fact, this displacement began to occur by the 1950s, in Paul Schiller's studies of chimp marking. It was well under way with the publication of Desmond Morris's *Biology of Art* in 1962 and E. H. Gombrich's attempt, in 1963, to root depiction in the responses of animals and even fish to substitute perceptual stimuli.[36]

In order to take the Middle Paleolithic materials as beginning art history they have inevitably been reconstructed as art historical wholes. But this reconstruction exerts much greater strain on forensic adequacy than with the Upper Paleolithic materials already examined in this respect. In fact, so far art history has been unable to frame the archaeology of this period. In turn, then, the Middle-to-Upper Paleolithic transition might index a real evolutionary transformation. It is best characterized for my purposes by saying that art historical aesthetics cannot be applied to history before this threshold, however that history should be written in its own right—for example, in terms of the replacement of Neanderthal populations by *Homo sapiens sapiens,* of the emergence of language, or of other large-scale biological and historical factors.[37] The regress seems to terminate; there is indeed a "beyond compare" for art history.

The Missing Link: Depictions

The Acheulean grooved pebble from Berekhat Ram in the Golan Heights (Fig. 5.14), dated 230,000 B.C. at the youngest, has been thought to exemplify one of the cherished dramas of art historical aesthetics, the story of the beginning of art in the "seeing-as" of natural shapes resembling other objects. According to the excavator, "It seems that the occupants of the site selected a pebble that bore some characteristics of a female body. These were enhanced by adding the incised grooves delimiting the head and arms."[38] Here

36. For the early studies of chimp marking, see discussion and references in Chapter 2; Desmond Morris, *The Biology of Art: A Study of the Picture-Making Behaviour of the Great Apes and Its Relationship to Human Art* (London, 1962); and E. H. Gombrich, "Meditations on a Hobby Horse," in *Meditations on a Hobby Horse and Other Essays on the Theory of Art* (London, 1963), 1–11. Arthur Danto's views on animals as "masters of the 'standing for' relationship" can be found in his interesting reflection "Description and the Phenomenology of Perception," in *Visual Theory,* ed. Bryson, Holly, and Moxey, 201–15.

37. Paul Mellars, ed., *The Emergence of Modern Humans* (Edinburgh, 1990), contains many proposals.

38. Naama Goren-Inbar, "A Figurine from the Acheulian Site of Berekhat Ram," *Mitekufat Haeven* 19 (1986), 7–12.

I shall not question whether the grooves are human-made (although no forensic evidence is cited). I shall not even question whether to us the pebble might look something like a female figure. Note, however, that this "looking like" is probably influenced in part by an anachronistic art historical comparison with Upper Paleolithic images of women, recalled by the excavator at the end of the publication of the pebble, and by a long-standing discursive association in both Neolithic and industrial societies between femininity and origins.[39]

What is notable for my immediate purposes is that the excavator's forensics takes the *un*worked pebble to have *naturally* looked like a female body. There is no evidence whatsoever that this was so, apart from the later (re)working itself. (Just as nothing is cited to prove the grooves are human-made, nothing is cited to prove that *only* the grooves are human-made.) Thus it is the art historicity of the final product, as it were, that tells us what the original material looked like—as if, paradoxically, the wholeness and finish of the final product were not so whole and finished that the original material condition could not be recognized in it.

Strictly speaking, an account of depiction as seeing-as, or seeing-in, does not require that what is seen-as *already* resembles what it is then seen in it. In depiction the maker shapes brute materials, not necessarily resembling what will be seen in them, into patterns that can then be so seen. In other words, in the case of depiction in general the maker must already know what a depiction is, and how to make one, in order to shape materials so that they resemble something or support seeing-in. It begs the question to *derive* this ability from one of its particular expressions, namely, the narrow case in which the maker makes a depiction using preresemblant materials—for how, from this narrow case, could the general condition be achieved, when in the general case the preresemblant material, the supposed required basis for depiction, is not present? At the very least, the depiction-from-preresemblant-materials stage in evolution would have to be supplemented by a copying-of-that-depiction-in-nonresemblant-materials stage of development. But then, of course, we would have a replicatory and summative sequence, an art historicity *as* the beginning rather than a beginning *for* art historicity.

Even setting aside the fact that "enhanced" naturally resemblant shapes would have to be copied to yield depiction in the general case, interpretation suffuses the Berekhat Ram pebble with an art historicity in another way as well. Any depiction anywhere must always accommodate the qualities of its surface or medium. If an Acheulean sculptor wanted to work with pebbles, he or she necessarily worked with pebbles to be found; if their surfaces were irregular, then the depiction would incorporate irregularities—although, in the general case, the irregularity as such might not depict anything. Presuming that the sculptor already knew how to depict, then he or she reasonably made use of natural features aiding the project, perhaps threading the discovery of preresemblant shapes seen in the material

39. For the later female figurines, see Henri Delporte, *L'image de la femme dans l'art préhistorique* (Paris, 1979). The broader association between femininity and origins is explored in an important paper by Margaret W. Conkey and Sarah Williams, "Original Narratives: The Political Economy of Gender in Archaeology," in *Gender at the Crossroads of Knowledge: Feminist Anthropology in the Postmodern Era*, ed. Micaela di Leonardo (Berkeley and Los Angeles, 1991), 68–89.

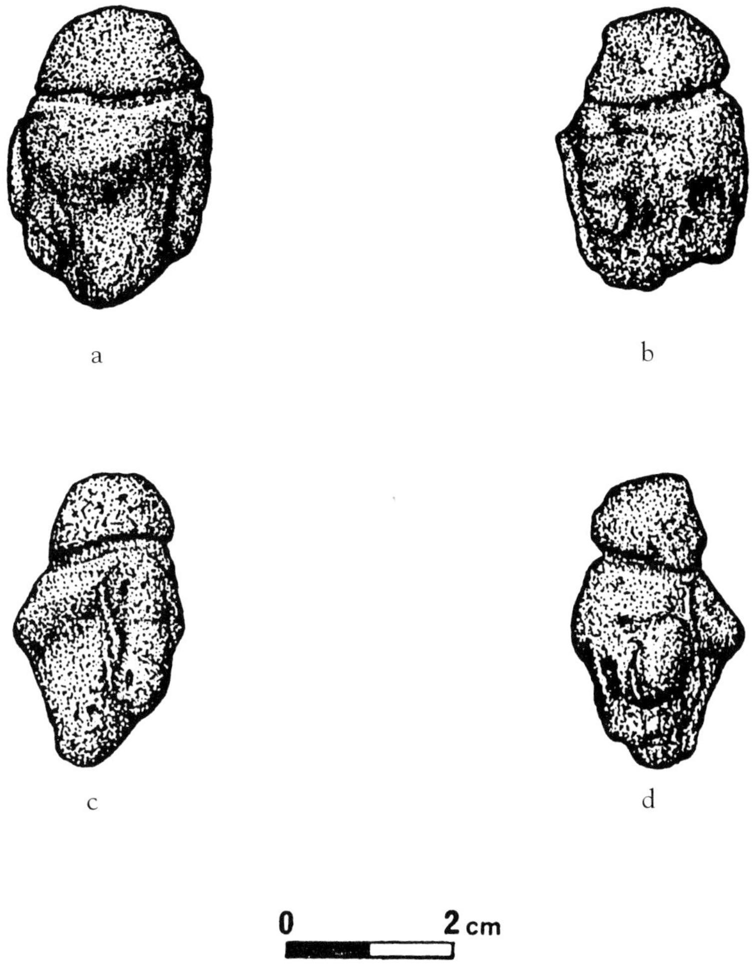

Fig. 5.14. "Figurine" from Berekhat Ram, Golan Heights, Acheulean period, about 230,000 B.C.

through the ongoing intention to depict something. In other words, an art historicity intervenes between the mere perception of the object-resembling properties of the natural shape and the intention to "enhance" them or incorporate them (or not) in depiction.

Thus, however we cut it, in the excavator's forensics the pebble exemplifies an art historical Intentionality—either a prior knowledge of depiction transferred onto the pebble in order to make it depict, or a prior belief that "enhancing" the pebble would make it into a depiction of what it already resembled. In both cases, *depictiveness* serves as the art historical whole sewing together the otherwise broken links of preresemblant natural shapes, the human-made enhancement of materials, and the final so-called figurine, no one of which requires, implies, or generates the others in any particular material sequence.

Depictiveness as such has materialized out of nowhere in this account. More precisely, it emerges not out of the past of the pebble but out of its future, where the art historicity of depiction already fully suffuses—indeed, constitutes—image making. Depictiveness is the missing link, discovered in the present tense of art history, which has the power to turn the broken links into the impossible link of an artwork at the beginning of the history of art. Within the history of art, such a missing link—identified in the art historical present—always retroactively forges broken links into the impossible link of an artwork, the link that the broken links cannot be in themselves but will only be seen to be from a later replicatory and summative vantage point. Becoming whole, as both Darwin and Freud knew, is a matter of *Nachträglichkeit*, or "delayed activation." But needless to say, for biological species, for human persons, or for artworks, we have great difficulty in conceiving how *Nachträglichkeit,* the meaning coming out of the future, can literally be the historical process of origin itself as the possibility coming out of the past.

The Missing Link: Signs

Despite the lack of forensic evidence for the scenario of origins it supposedly exemplifies, the pebble from Berekhat Ram has been taken as a plausible missing link because the whole of depictiveness—of seeing-as, shaping, copying, and seeing-in as an art historicity—is so well established in art historical aesthetics, along with the complementary art historical whole of each artist's identity and intention, style and period, and production and reception. Since we shall likely never recover artists' identities, styles, or reception histories in the Middle Paleolithic, in recent archaeology depictiveness has become the most attainable sought-after originary whole. And if not depictiveness (the Berekhat Ram pebble, as I have noted, might not do the job), then, of course, a more general symbolicity.

Once we have symbol making in the Middle or Lower Paleolithic or among primates, then it is apparently a quick step to the history of different proliferating producers, modes, styles, and periods of symbol making in the Upper Paleolithic and later.[40] No doubt it is inconvenient that the material relation between modes of sign making like gesturing, speaking, or building and picturing has often not been well defined. (And it is even more inconvenient that when the relation *is* well defined—for example, in Charles Sanders Peirce's "semeiotic," his general theory of signs, or Nelson Goodman's typology of notation—strong logical differences between pictures and other signs must be observed, for example, in the degree and role of so-called iconicity, nondiscreteness, or "continuous correlation.") Nevertheless, within art history, archaeology, and anthropology we find an easy elision between sign making *sui generis* and picturing, such that the former somehow serves as the historical *origin* of the latter—not just, as in Peirce's theory of signs, its typological context in a theoretical model of human knowledge.

Sometimes this relation is achieved by sleight of hand. For example, in deriving from hand gestures pictures made of marks, the question of the derivation of pictorial reference as such is sidestepped: what Davidson and Noble have called "imitative gestural signalling" as the evolutionary first step *toward* depiction is, in fact, *already* depicting, namely, by waving one's hands in the air.[41] Sometimes the relation is achieved through conflation,

40. See notes 33, 34, 36, 37 above.

41. Davidson and Noble, "Archaeology of Perception," 148. More recently, Davidson and Noble have added an uneconomical and implausible "evolutionary sequence" in explanation of their unsatisfactory earlier proposal that the supposed "imitative gesture" becomes

for example, when archaeologists or art historians deny the very typology that motivates them to derive pictures from other signs by assimilating pictures to signs like pointing. And sometimes the relation is secured simply by assuming its wholeness, in what we can call pansemiotic essentialism. As an influential movement in recent art history would have it, once we have semiosis, we necessarily have art history: the question of the historical status of reference, conventionality, and semiotic arbitrariness as such is avoided by taking them as essential in and throughout the history we write. Here, semiotics is made to be the beginning of art history—the study of the art historicity of reference, convention, and arbitrariness in pictures—by assuming, but not explaining, it to be the beginning of the history of art.[42]

According to this general logic, because picturing can be dated to the very early Upper Paleolithic, about 32,000 B.C., sign making must be assigned to the Middle Paleolithic or before as essential for the later art historicity. Consider, for example, the Acheulean archaeological scatter at the site of Terra Amata, about 220,000 B.C., dug by Henry de Lumley in 1966–69. De Lumley reconstructed an "ovoid hut" at this site; the hut was supposedly maintained for several seasonal occupations by its inhabitants (Fig. 5.15).

Although de Lumley does not quite show us the neat clothesline Louis Figuier had included in his 1870 imagination of a Paleolithic hut (Fig. 5.16), his depictions certainly express archaeology's wish to locate a "whole" site—a site in which no disjunction exists between the traces and the unified Intentionality responsible for them—in order to fill a gap in prehistory, which in the 1960s knew little about Acheulean living arrangements.[43]

"trace" becomes "sign" (or picture). They now propose that the "one-handed aimed throwing" of hominids hunting becomes "pointing" (at the hunted target) and finally becomes the "initially iconic signs" of the supposed "imitative gesture," which ultimately "depicts" the animal when the gesture, "frozen" as a trace, gets taken as a "sign" (see Iain Davidson and William Noble, "The Evolutionary Emergence of Modern Human Behaviour: Language and Its Archaeology," *Man* 26 [1991], 245). But, as with the first sequence (see Whitney Davis, "Comment," *Current Anthropology* 30 [1989], 140–41), they continue to smuggle symbolic reference into this sequence. As Peirce showed, there are no pure "iconic signs," and the "initially iconic" resemblances of an "imitative gesture" could only be secured through a "symbolic" or other complementary semiotic criterion (see esp. Arthur K. Bierman, "That There Are No Iconic Signs . . .," *Philosophy and Phenomenological Research* 23 [1962], 243–49). This matter would not be a problem for an account that allowed the "symbolic" specification of an "icon"—what Peirce called a hypoicon (see A. J. Ayer, *The Origins of Pragmatism* [San Francisco, 1968], 140)—to be carried out in spoken language. But Davidson and Noble are trying to show that "imitative gesture" *precedes* language in an evolutionary sequence! Moreover, they earlier claimed that the "perception of resemblance"—what they would have to assume for a supposed pure "iconic sign"—should actually be the "'cognitive result' of depiction" ("Archaeology of Perception," 129–30), which "imitative gesture," again, supposedly precedes. As I have shown, depictiveness is the whole that sews together the otherwise broken links of behavior or practice; in Davidson and Noble's account, this whole takes the form of a pure, autonomous "iconicity" somehow underlying both depiction and language.

42. See Bal and Bryson, "Semiotics and Art History." For a perspicuous analysis of the logical flaws in Saussure's concept of semiotic "arbitrariness," see David Holdcroft, *Saussure: Signs, System, and Arbitrariness* (New York, 1991).

43. Henry de Lumley, "Les fouilles de Terra Amata à Nice," *Bullétin du Musée d'Anthropologie Préhistorique de Monaco* 13 (1966), 29–51; idem, "A Paleolithic Camp at Nice," *Scientific American* 220, no. 5 (1969), 42–50; Henry de Lumley and Yvonne Boone, "Les structures d'habitat au paléolithique inférieur," in *La préhistoire française*, ed. Henry de Lumley, vol. 1, *Les civilizations paléolithiques et mésolithiques de la France* (Paris, 1976), 625–43. Louis Figuier, *L'homme primitif, avec 39 scènes de la vie de l'homme primitif* (Paris, 1870) is an extraordinary visual embodiment of many of the issues I consider in this chapter.

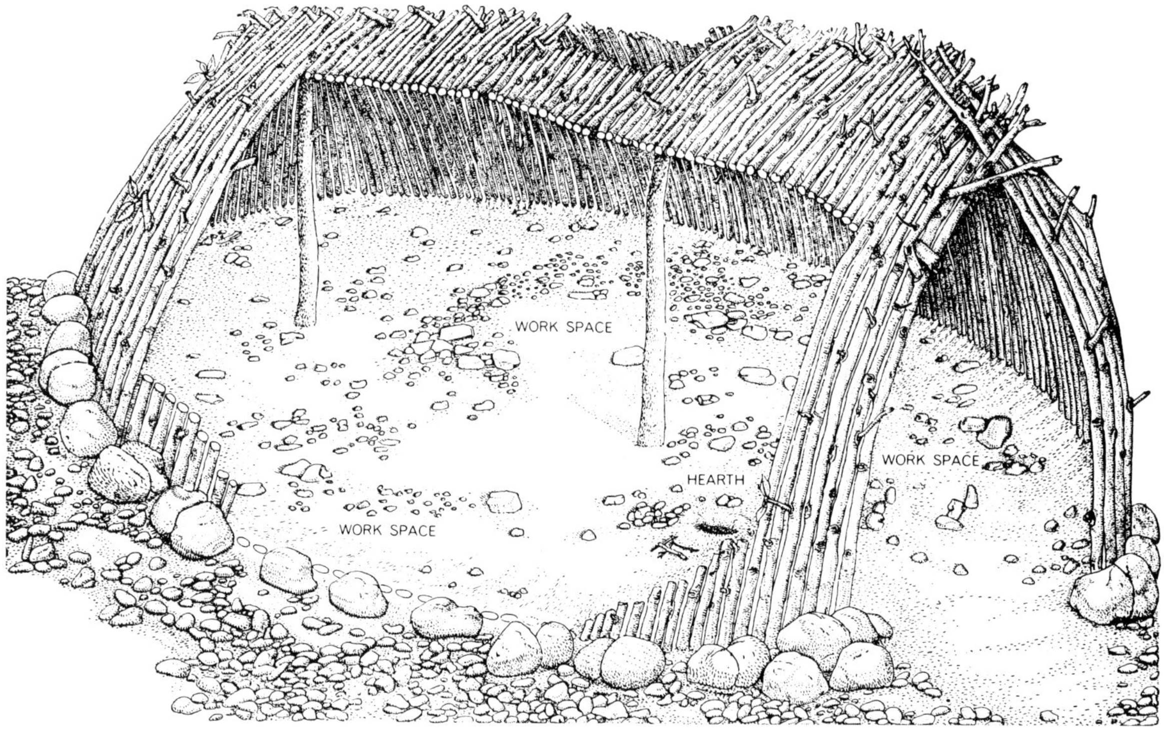

Fig. 5.15. Henry de Lumley's reconstruction of an "ovoid hut" at Terra Amata (Nice), Acheulean period, about 220,000 B.C.

Donald Preziosi, promoting semiotic treatments of art, has recently gone a step further. For him, Terra Amata is "no random aggregate of materials . . . [but] a highly complex, regular, systematic object," "a building essentially identical in form to many found today in various parts of the world," a "carefully organized," "complex sign." As a sign, it is shot through with sign historicity. Specifically, as a "mark" in its environment, it is not just a whole hut but also the ongoing sign for a particular livability to which Acheulean hunters were supposedly returning season after season and to which the hut materials refer. Like depictiveness sewing up the broken links of the Berekhat Ram pebble and at the same time supposedly being the forensic evidence for the beginning of such depictiveness, for Preziosi a general symbolicity sews up the broken links of Terra Amata and at the same time becomes the forensic evidence for the very beginning of such symbolicity in "remarkably advanced artifactual behaviors" like Terra Amata.[44] Terra Amata serves as the semiotic equivalent of "Cartailhac's palimpsest" (Fig. 5.12), a conjunction of external history and the art historicity of the work, because it is a historical semiotic whole, established on independent forensic grounds, that contains its own internal sign historicity.

Lest his readers wonder what Terra Amata, as a living place and its sign at 220,000 B.C., has to do with pictorial art at 32,000 B.C. and later, Preziosi hastens to assert "a certain

44. Preziosi, *Rethinking Art History,* 128–30.

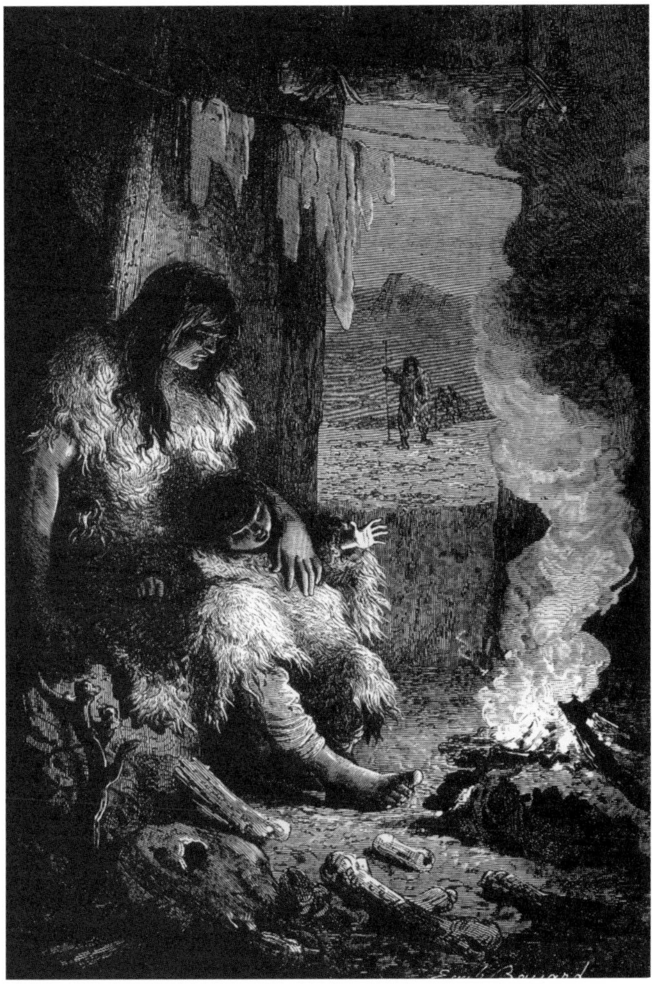

Fig. 5.16. Emile Bayard, *Interior of a Hut of the Reindeer Age*, 1870, lithograph to illustrate Figuier, *L'homme primitif*.

conceptual resemblance between the structure [of the hut] and the imagery [of the caves]." Advancing the hypothesis of semiotic wholeness, both the hut and the pictures, he says, "are built up out of elements whose meaningfulness is a function of a total system"[45]—sticks and stones in the case of Terra Amata, lines and blobs of paint in the case of cave art. In yet a further sewing-up, then, Terra Amata becomes "Cartailhac's palimpsest" for cave artwork in the dubious move of establishing the "complex sign" of Terra Amata as the relevant external history with which the art historicity of cave artworks is continuous. This can only be accomplished by threading symbolicity through the two sets of objects as if it were the *same* symbolicity, a whole. And a very general symbolicity it has to be. If Terra Amata qualifies as an art historical beginning for pictorial cave artworks because its elements are only

45. Preziosi, *Rethinking Art History*, 130.

"meaningful" within a "total system," why not say language, cuisine, or games—or the making of fires, fashioning of tools, or DNA—are the beginning of pictorial artwork?

But the question is moot. Decoupled from the urge to establish art historical wholes, careful analysis shows that the archaeological landscape at Terra Amata, with many broken bits of many objects mixed through several levels, cannot be resolved as de Lumley's scenario must have it. Terra Amata is probably just an array of stuff never linked up to be broken in the first place, at least as a seasonally rebuilt "hut."[46]

The Missing Link: Marks

The four marked bones from Bilzingsleben, a *Homo erectus* site dated 300,000 B.C. at the youngest, have taken center stage in recent discussions. Forensic inspection shows that all the lines on each bone were cut by "the same tool," probably "in the course of one single process" (Fig. 5.17). Among the four bones, however, different tools were used and there are several differences in the number, orientation, lengths, and apparent pattern of the supposed "rhythmic sequences of linear marks."[47]

For the excavators, the bones imply that *Homo erectus* had "gained the faculty of abstract thinking" and spoke a language, supposedly because "verbal communication is a prerequisite for the creation of deliberate markings which must have conveyed information of some form,"[48] such as a counting or coding scheme. As most observers have stressed, these inferences are unnecessary. Nothing shows that the marks counted or encoded anything; they could just be marks in sequences or patterns. Moreover, spoken language is not a prerequisite for other kinds of communication.

Nonetheless, even skeptics have wanted to say that the bones provide a relevant historical context—an evolutionary precursor—for the specifically pictorial artwork of the Upper Paleolithic. In other words, although the bones are not, in themselves, the impossible link of the first symbolic, let alone depictive, marking, they are possibly the suitable *broken* links—a necessary raw material of what would later become pictorial image making. But why should this be? Why are the bones of Bilzingsleben, materials that could and supposedly would later be linked up as a whole sign or picture, not just like the stones of Terra Amata, materials that cannot be linked up as a whole artifact or sign except through wishful thinking?

Two intuitions underlie even the skeptics' sense that Bilzingsleben says something about the beginning of sign and art making. First, whereas other Middle Paleolithic supposedly "symbolic" markings turn up as unique specimens, the four bones as a group might document precisely that replicatoriness or art historicity thought, in art historical aesthetics, to

46. Paola Villa, *Terra Amata and the Middle Pleistocene Archaeological Record of Southern France* (Berkeley and Los Angeles, 1983), esp. 69–75, 79–82, 165–70.

47. Dietrich Mania and Ursula Mania, "Deliberate Engravings on Bone Artefacts of Homo Erectus," *Rock Art Research* 5 (1988), 91–107.

48. Mania and Mania, "Deliberate Engravings," 95.

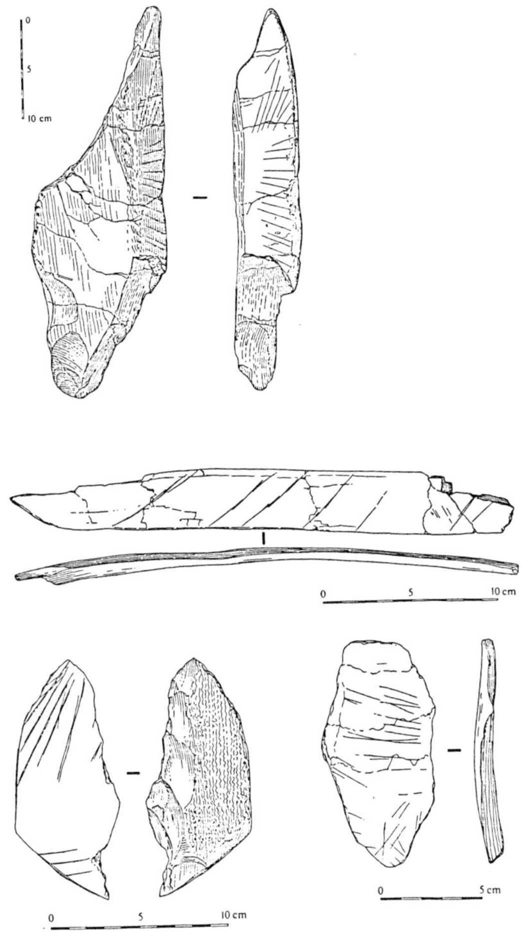

Fig. 5.17. Marked bones from Bilzingsleben, Germany, Acheulean period, about 300,000 B.C.

be essential to the wholeness of artworks or signs.[49] The four bones together possibly index a particular "tradition" or "style," whether or not it is a tradition or style of making meaning such as counting or encoding, as the excavators would have it.

In order to take the bones as a replicatory whole, however, the argument requires "Cartailhac's palimpsest": the wholeness of the *external* historicity, the site of Bilzingsleben as a whole, has to be threaded through the four individual objects—for, of course, the marks themselves are not an actual palimpsest of accumulated marks taking account of or making reference to one another. As far as we can see, the marks are just next to each other. And in themselves, just as four individual objects with marks, the bones are as different from one another as they are similar. Now, according to the logic of art historical comparison, such

49. The point is well made by Davidson and Noble, "Archaeology of Perception," 127–28.

differences must somehow index an art historical whole—in this case, the replicatory nature of the mark making. Thus the palpable differences between the marks could be explained by claiming that the tradition had internal distinctions or developments, as might have been the case with Hesire's sculptor, who does not just carve in his own utterly nonconventional way but supposedly does it differently—say, "inventively"—in relation to the images he took account of in making his own version. But there is no forensic evidence that the bones constitute a replicatory class or sequence apart from their having been found together at the same whole site. Several scenarios could account for the properties of each bone, scenarios that do not assume makers at this site intended anything at all in relation to the other bones, even if *each* bone's markings are "deliberate" or "symbolic." Putting the point metaphorically, the whole of the Upper Paleolithic palimpsest (such as Figs. 3.11, 5.11) has been overlaid on the group of bones in order to constitute them as the broken links *for* such later palimpsests.

Crosscutting this concern for the bones as a replicatory whole is the status of the supposed "deliberateness" of the marks. Forensic analysis decoupled from art historical comparison and its search for wholes quickly implied that the markings could be the nondeliberate by-product of other processes, either natural processes or hominid activities such as defleshing the bones or using them as cutting platforms.[50] Indeed, the Bilzingsleben bones do not even pass the easy test of formal similarity to accepted instances of deliberate symbolic marking of the very early Upper Paleolithic. As the marks on the side of the Aurignacian Hohlenstein-Stadel figurine (approximately 32,000 B.C.?) show, in deliberate marking spacing and length tend to be much more consistent one mark to the next and throughout the set than on the Bilzingsleben bones. Moreover, in deliberate marking each of the visually discrete marks is often produced by multiple rather than by single tool cuts: we might say that the replicatoriness literally "in" the mark is good forensic evidence for its having been made deliberately as just that mark (or, at least, as what can finally be seen as the re-marked palimpsest). No such over- or re-marking occurs at Bilzingsleben.[51]

Needless to say, these findings fatally compromise the Bilzingsleben bones—not, however, as the broken links of some "deliberate," "symbolic," replicatory whole—just as the broken links of the mark making, as such, taken *as* that whole. The marks could have been produced nondeliberately in the course of a deliberate, symbolic, replicatory activity in which the bones, or what was cut on or from them, were employed. For example, the bones could be the forensic index, the broken links, of the fashioning of animal skin costumes for ritual use. Perhaps they were even its symbol, since they could be recognized as standing for the ritual, or its meaning, through an indexical connection to its preparations.

However, such speculations encounter the problem I have already noted at Terra Amata. Nondeliberate or deliberate, natural or human-made, the bones at Bilzingsleben might be forensic evidence for a Middle Paleolithic sign making. But the bearing of such sign making

50. Iain Davidson, "Bilzingsleben and Early Marking," *Rock Art Research* 7 (1990), 52–56, is the most exacting analysis.

51. These observations are due to Davidson, "Bilzingsleben," 55 and photo; see also Bahn and Vertut, *Images of the Ice Age*, 85 and fig. 49.

on pictorial artwork remains to be demonstrated. And at any rate, little forensic evidence locates any particular symbolic activity in the Middle Paleolithic, let alone how it should be attached to pictorial artwork.[52] One had wanted to see the Bilzingsleben marks, as such, *as* symbolic replication precisely because a causal or genetic connection can be assumed between something like sequential, patterned marking and specifically pictorial marking.

Or can it? The second argument for the relevance of the Bilzingsleben bones—deliberate and symbolic or not—is based on the feeling that the historical emergence of pictorial artwork presupposes a history of nonpictorial marking that picturing can inherit, replicate, and transform. (In Chapters 2 and 3, I assumed this condition for the sake of convenience; now it must be challenged.) According to such a history, the marks of Bilzingsleben (as well as all other pre–Upper Paleolithic marks) are necessary conditions, part of the required raw materials, of depiction. They are, then, genuine broken links.[53] In turn, the very existence of broken links promotes the view that a missing link can transform them into the impossible link of the pictorial artwork, by definition suffused with its own art historicity—in the case of our absolutely inaugural Figure 1, an art historicity of the inheritance, replication, and transformation of preexisting nonpictorial marks.

The broken links, the nonpictorial marks, and the impossible link, the art historical artwork, are physical objects. The missing link that sews them together, however, is an intentional object. It is the psychological and social measure of the difference between what otherwise could be physically similar and perceptually indiscernible sets of marks. As some have argued, this intentional structure might be the "institutional" relations in which pictorial artworks are identified as such by a group. If this specification begs the question, then the missing link might be, as others have argued, one of several kinds of mental processes in which nonpictorial marks are taken to depict: the acceptance of substitutes;[54] the discovery of similarity between marking and depictions in another medium, such as gestures indicating objects by outlining them;[55] the disambiguation of perceptual ambiguity according to established expectations;[56] or a complex episode of seeing-as and seeing-in, that is, of simultaneously seeing the object "in" the mark (or what Wollheim

52. See notes 33, 34, 41 above.

53. In addition to the Bilzingsleben bones, of particular interest are the Mousterian (Neanderthal) marks from Bocksteinschmiede, Germany, discussed by Alexander Marshack, "La pensée symbolique et l'art," *Dossiers de l'Archéologie* 124 (1988), 80–90; various other examples have been proposed. For each case, the questions discussed here do arise—are the marks a "replicatory sequence"? "symbolic"? "deliberate"?—but might be differently answered. In Chapters 2 and 3 I assumed that *any* preexisting mark(s) would do the trick. In her interesting essay "On the Origin and Significance of Paleolithic Cave Art," Maxine Sheets-Johnstone (*The Roots of Thinking* [Philadelphia, 1990], 233–74) takes me to task for ignoring the "experiential dimensions of the original acts of [pre- or nondepictive] drawing" (234), such as the "digital fluting" I took to be the most immediate prior context of marking for Upper Paleolithic cave art (see Robert G. Bednarik, "Parietal Finger Markings in Europe and Australia," *Rock Art Research* 3 [1986], 30–61). However, it is precisely my point that such nondepictive markings can come in all sorts of graphic, or "experiential," varieties so long as they can support a (later) moment of "seeing-as" (or seeing-in). In Chapters 10 and 11, I explore the "experiential," or affective and erotic, dimensions of graphic replication.

54. E.g., Gombrich, "Meditations on a Hobby Horse."

55. E.g., Davidson and Noble, "The Archaeology of Perception" (although this is not their interpretation of the scenario they sketch).

56. E.g., E. H. Gombrich, *Art and Illusion* (Princeton, 1960).

calls "twofoldness") and seeing the mark "as" having been made as a particular mark (or seeing the style "in" the mark).[57]

Without evaluating the cogency of any of these scenarios, note that none of them actually requires marking *preexisting* those marks which do, themselves, become depictive. A "substitute" need not have been made before its actual use. Although a stick formed by nature could be picked up by a child and used as a substitute horse, the horse-substitutability could be produced in the child's very cutting and whittling of a block of wood without its being whittled *as* a horse. A mark supposedly "freezing" a preexisting depiction, such as a gestural picture of an object, need not have been made before the "freezing" takes place. (In making a mark for the very first time, one could notice its visual or kinesthetic similarity to the depictive gesture. In the most literal version of this scenario, a depictive gesture accidentally leaves a trace in a permanent mark; here, "freezing" occurs at the very moment of making both gesture and mark.) Finally, the disambiguation of ambiguous marks or their seeing-as/seeing-in can be encountered in the initial making of a mark for whatever reason. In each case, preexisting marks might be turned into depictions. But the process can transpire simultaneously with the manufacture of the marks that are its very material basis and one of its intentional objects. These or anything like them need never have been made before.

Even if no marks had ever been accidentally or deliberately made by Middle Paleolithic peoples, then, depictive marking could begin in the Upper Paleolithic; and even if Middle Paleolithic marks had been accidentally or deliberately made by Middle Paleolithic peoples, specifically depictive marking of the Upper Paleolithic might not have begun. Thus, even though Bilzingsleben might be reconstructed in its own context as a whole symbolicity at a whole site, in relation to the beginning of depictive marking in the Upper Paleolithic it is not even a broken link. Like Terra Amata, it is just an array of stuff that happens to be archaeologically contiguous in a broad sense with later depictive marking.

Comparison with Itself

To avoid instituting regress and circularity or chasing red herrings in ever more ancient histories, such as Middle Paleolithic sign making, and diffuse contexts, such as undocumentable scenarios about signaling, gesturing, and the like, we should conceive the beginning of depiction, as I have suggested, as a complex palimpsest of intentions directed at a mark made at the same time as, although not caused by, these intentions. The mark could have been made long ago, even, like Leonardo's stains of lichen, by nature itself. Forensic historical analysis might establish that this mark was the initial target or support of the relevant intentions turning it into a depiction. But this kind of preexisting link is not

57. Richard Wollheim, *Art and Its Objects,* 2d ed. (Cambridge, 1980), Supplementary Essay 5.

required. The mark need have no history of replications outside the very history of intentions in which it becomes a depiction, and these intentions do not require anything but the replication of just that mark being made at the moment. Unique in many properties and "beyond compare" with any other marks, but a spatially and temporally persisting object to which people direct themselves nonetheless, a single mark develops in its own internal cognitive history for someone—through *Nachträglichkeit,* or "delayed activation"—as broken link, missing link, and impossible link. In its intentional constitution as an artwork, a single mark is always a palimpsest.

So much should, I think, be clear to a forensics of aesthetic cognition, although here I have not discussed this inquiry as such. For my purposes in this chapter, *being comparable* and *being historical* are crosscutting matters that specifically art historical aesthetics has conflated. For art history, since being in history is being comparable, what is *without* comparison could not be *in* history, and what is in history must be comparable at all costs. Art history thus cannot easily conceptualize what is without comparison but within history, that is, its Figure 1s—phenomena such as the error, half-bakedness, or general unwholeness of replications, and processes such as the beginnings of styles, periods, receptions, or art history itself. By the same token, though I have not considered the issue here, it equally cannot conceptualize what *is* comparable but *without* history—namely, "Figure 0s," those objects which have yet to be rendered art historically interesting to art history (see further Chapters 11 and 12). Forensic comparison has gradually been approaching some popular, folk, and "outsider" arts. But the art of the mentally ill or of children remains well outside. Although everyone knows that children's drawings have styles, traditions, and receptions, and even though historical study of such materials might reveal far more about processes of signification and communication, ideologization, gender formation, or class consciousness than self-conscious art products made in the art world, their art histories remain unwritten.

Strictly speaking, depiction begins as a palimpsest of intentions, however they are to be characterized, directed at a single persisting mark. Art historical comparison, however, sets out to distribute this palimpsest among *different* marks in time and space. Thus the pebble from Berekhat Ram (Fig. 5.14), the scatter at Terra Amata (Fig. 5.15), or the bones of Bilzingsleben (Fig. 5.17) are constituted as broken links for Upper Paleolithic artworks in almost the same way that Hellenistic sculpture (Fig. 5.7), Jan Vermeer (Fig. 5.5), and Andy Warhol seem to be the historically preexisting broken links for the art historicity of Eric Fischl's painting (Figs. 5.4, 5.6). The difference, however, is that Berekhat Ram, Terra Amata, or Bilzingsleben are supposed to provide evidence for the very origin of such art historicities in addition to merely exemplifying them. Thus art history distributes even originary art historicity among the whole objects of a corpus of supposedly comparable works, for art historical wholeness requires a whole object linked to other artworks. But, as I have shown, to begin such art historicities without regress, tautology, or other fallacies, wholeness must be found elsewhere—namely, in the intrinsic material historicity of objects neither whole nor comparable in the art historian's sense. Here, "Cartailhac's palimpsest," an ongoing internal historicity continuous with the external history of the context of making, is all we need. In all cases of a Figure 1 for art history—of error or other unwholeness within an artwork and of origins for art historical wholes or for art history itself—the historicity of the artwork is a matter of the whole produced in the work's comparison not with other whole artworks, the possibility of which cannot be assumed, but only with itself. At the end of an artwork's becoming whole, art history begins. Before that point, there is only the beginning of the history of art.

Chapter 6

Style and History in Art History

Most working art historians probably believe that "style is an indispensable historical tool; it is more essential to the history of art than to any other historical discipline."[1] Many, however, are also intrigued by the possibility that "style descriptions can be written and rewritten unconstrained by anything except prevailing art historical interests."[2] There would be no need to worry about this possibility if art historians had a clear idea of their "interests," historical and theoretical—but they do not. As I shall show in this chapter, the concept of style itself does not and should not commit art historians to any particular way of writing history. Moreover, consensus about the proper concerns and central concepts of art history seems difficult to achieve today. Perhaps it would even be undesirable.

In this chapter I cannot pretend to offer a complete statement of the concept of style in art history, or even of an art historical concept of style, like the treatments by Meyer

1. James S. Ackerman, "Style," in *Art and Archaeology*, by James S. Ackerman and Rhys Carpenter (Englewood Cliffs, N.J., 1963), 164.

2. Richard Wollheim, "Pictorial Style: Two Views," in *The Concept of Style*, ed. Berel Lang (Philadelphia, 1979), 140.

Schapiro, James S. Ackerman, or E. H. Gombrich.[3] Instead, I pursue an argument I take to be intrinsically important. It leads to some descriptive and some prescriptive claims about art history and related disciplines, but also suggests some necessary skepticisms about any such claims.[4]

Style in History

The definition of style offered in this chapter is intended to capture some aspects of the practice of working art historians. More important, however, I suggest how the concept of style ideally or logically should function. That in practice it sometimes cannot function this way is not a problem for the theory of style itself; it is a problem of evidence or interpretation. A definition should be built to take account of some matters of special interest to art historians. But it must also be able to comprehend many phenomena, some of them hardly ever studied by art historians. Art historians may want to be able, for example, to talk about the "style" of chimpanzee scribbles (see Chapter 2), the monolith in *2001: A Space Odyssey*, driftwood, Polyclitus's *Doryphoros*, forged Vermeers, Duchamp's bottle-racks, ordinary bottle-racks, rocks in a Japanese garden, or Mousterian scratchings.

For the art historian's purposes, *(a)* "style" is a description of a polythetic set of similar but varying attributes in a group of artifacts, *(b)* the presence of which can only be explained by the history of the artifacts, *(c)* namely, common descent from an archaeologically identifiable artifact-production system in a particular state or states. In the discussion that follows I shall refer to these elements of a definition of style in the shorthand form *(a)*, *(b)*, and *(c)*.

This definition requires a good deal of explanation and clarification of its several ambiguities. The key elements—for example, polythetic classification, similarity relations, phylogenetic explanation, and production systems—are independent of one another but are brought together here in a single statement. Although the definition seems general, flexi-

3. Meyer Schapiro, "Style," in *Anthropology Today*, ed. Alfred L. Kroeber (Chicago, 1953), 287–312 (quoted here), reprinted in his *Theory and Philosophy of Art: Style, Artist, and Society* (New York, 1994), 51–102; Ackerman, "Style"; E. H. Gombrich, "Style," in *International Encyclopedia of the Social Sciences*, ed. David Sills (New York, 1968), 15:352–61.

4. In writing this chapter, I have learned from (and sometimes take issue with) the following works, noted in order of date of publication: Schapiro, "Style"; Thomas Munro, "Style in the Arts: A Method of Stylistic Analysis," in *Toward Science in Aesthetics* (New York, 1956), 192–226; Alfred Kroeber, *Styles and Civilizations* (Ithaca, N.Y., 1957); Ackerman, "Style"; Gombrich, "Style"; James R. Sackett, "The Meaning of Style in Archaeology," *American Antiquity* 42 (1977), 369–80; H. Martin Wobst, "Stylistic Behavior and Information Exchange," in *For the Director: Research Essays in Honor of James B. Griffin*, Museum of Anthropology Anthropological Papers 61, ed. Charles E. Cleland (Ann Arbor, Mich., 1977), 317–42; Nelson Goodman, "The Status of Style," in *Ways of Worldmaking* (Indianapolis, 1978), 23–40; George Kubler, "Towards a Reductive Theory of Visual Style," in *The Concept of Style*, ed. Lang, 119–27; Kendall Walton, "Style and the Products and Processes of Art," in ibid., 45–66; Wollheim, "Pictorial Style"; Jenefer Robinson, "Style and Significance in Art History and Art Criticism," *Journal of Aesthetics and Art Criticism* 40 (1981), 6–14; and Willibald Sauerländer, "From Stilus to Style: Reflections on the Fate of a Notion," *Art History* 6 (1983), 253–70. Philosophical aesthetics suggests, among other matters, the importance of authen-

ble, and circumspect, the concept of style is significantly restricted. In particular, it makes no statements or predictions one way or another about many aspects of artifacts and works of art—like sequence, distribution, rates of change, or causes of variability—that are of great interest to art historians and to archaeologists.

The Art Historian

The art historical concept of style (clauses *a–c*) is derived from a more inclusive concept, that of *(a)* alone, or the concept of "format," maintained by critics of the arts, teachers, artists, and others and enshrined in most dictionary definitions of style. (For the concept of form and "formalization," see further Chapter 8.)

Under the more inclusive definition *(a)*, historical statements are not the only substantive or permissible statements about style. Thus, a critic points to the striking similarity between an ancient Egyptian drawing of a house and a modern architectural blueprint, and remarks—contrasting them with an isometric projection—that they are "in the same style." Inclusive statements like this often serve as a prolegomenon or provocation for art historical or archaeological research, for similarities are not always due to chance factors but may result from relations of influence, shared methods, and so forth.

Strictly speaking, statements of the inclusive form *(a)* are inadmissible in art historical discourse unless and until they can be shown to satisfy the further clauses *b* and *c*. In a great deal of writing about artifacts, however, this specification is never actually carried out. The visible validity of *(a)*—the recognition of similarities in the "format" of artifacts—is often used as a *proof* of *(b)* and *(c)*.

"Style"

Although style is a primary classificatory concept in art history, it is obviously not the only one. Stylistic descriptions are often coupled with nonstylistic classifications of artifacts, for example, by the date, technique, function, or "meaning" of a work. In particular,

---

ticity, of indiscernibility and similarity, of the symbolic nature and institutional context of artifacts, and of the criteria of identity of works of art. See esp. George Dickie, *Art and the Aesthetic* (Ithaca, N.Y., 1974); Nelson Goodman, *Languages of Art: An Approach to a Theory of Symbols*, rev. ed. (Indianapolis, 1972); Richard Wollheim, *Art and Its Objects*, 2d ed. (Cambridge, 1980); and Arthur C. Danto, *The Transfiguration of the Commonplace* (New York, 1981). Classic studies in the methodological foundations of art history must be constant, if implicit, points of reference. See esp. Alois Riegl, *Late Roman Art Industry*, trans. Rolf Winkes (Rome, 1985); Heinrich Wölfflin, *Principles of Art History*, trans. M. D. Hottinger (London, 1932); Erwin Panofsky, *Studies in Iconology* (Oxford, 1939); idem, *Renaissance and Renascences in Western Art* (Stockholm, 1960); E. H. Gombrich, *Art and Illusion* (Princeton, 1960); and idem, *Meditations on a Hobby Horse and Other Essays in the Theory of Art* (London, 1963). For orientation and commentary, see Michael Podro, *The Critical Historians of Art* (New Haven, Conn., 1981), and W. J. T. Mitchell, *Iconology: Image, Text, Ideology* (Chicago, 1986). Formal studies of taxonomy and phylogenetic explanation provide exact analytic tools. See esp. Willi Hennig, *Phylogenetic Systematics*, trans. D. D. Davis and R. Zanger (Urbana, Ill., 1979); George Gaylord Simpson, *Principles of Animal Taxonomy* (New York, 1961); and Peter H. Sneath and Robert R. Sokal, *Principles of Numerical Taxonomy*, 2d ed. (San Francisco, 1973). See also Whitney Davis, "Periodization" and "Taxonomy," in *The Dictionary of Art*, ed. Jane Shoaf Turner (London, forthcoming).

the "fateful interconnection of *Stilus* and *Chronos*"[5]—the real underpinning of art history—does not derive wholly from the theory of style but also from theories of change, evolution, or progress.

Logically, taxonomies founded on nonstylistic statements about artifacts may vary independently of stylistic description. The label "Greek sculpture," for example, may be taken as a monothetic statement—a classification based upon a single trait—about the date and the medium of an artifact rather than as a stylistic description, which must classify a complex of overlapping traits. However, in practice, attributions of date or function are sometimes *derived from* stylistic descriptions. Conversely, stylistic descriptions are often *produced for* "a group of artifacts" preclassified by chronological, technical, or other criteria. Although the informativeness of a stylistic description will be strongly affected by any coupled and sometimes crosscutting classifications, the theory of style is not committed one way or another to any coupling.

Statements about style are very different from other kinds of descriptive or historical statements art historians make. To ask whether a painting is by Velázquez is very different from asking whether it is in Velázquez's style. The one question can be answered directly and empirically; the other requires a complex polythetic description. Stylistic statements are related to these nonstylistic statements in many ways. Statements about morphology, similarity, and synonymy are preliminary to stylistic analysis. Statements about representation, "meaning," or value may be but are not *necessarily* involved in stylistic descriptions. Statements about tradition and fashion follow upon stylistic analysis.

A Description

Style is not "in" the material, the physical matter of artifacts or works of art. Style must be discovered and written up by someone. No rigid protocols seem to be available for writing stylistic descriptions. Art historians prefer densely descriptive expository prose, perhaps impressionistic or subjective but often more subtle, flexible, and informative than simple checklists of attributes.[6] Metaphorical description ("warm," "fluid") may suit continuously varying attributes not easily broken into units or quantified. Noninitiates may be puzzled by the logical structure, weight, or value of the complex art historical descriptions coupling stylistic and nonstylistic classifications.

A Polythetic Set

In a fully polythetic group of artifacts, (1) each artifact possesses a (large) number of the attributes of the group; (2) each attribute may be found in a (large) number of the artifacts in the group; and (3) no single attribute is found in every artifact in the group. It follows that no single attribute is both necessary and sufficient for membership in the group.[7]

5. Sauerländer, "From Stilus to Style," 266.

6. Schapiro, "Style," 289; Alfred Kroeber, *Toward Definition of the Nazca Style* (Berkeley and Los Angeles, 1956), 330–31; Frank N. Sibley, "Aesthetic Concepts," *Philosophical Review* 68 (1959), 421–50; Michael Baxandall, "The Language of Art History," *New Literary History* 10 (1979), 453–65; and idem, *Patterns of Intention: The Historical Explanation of Pictures* (New Haven, Conn., 1985).

7. For the general definition of polythetic aggregation,

The polythetic character of stylistic description is one of its most important features. Therefore it is worth making three supplementary points.

First, the numerical quantities in (1) and (2) above are unspecified. But by definition they must be greater than one and less than the total. Art historians often tend to prefer high average quantities—that is, groups in which *many artifacts share many attributes*. This preference can be justified by a secondary assumption, namely, that many of the artifacts assigned to the same category in monothetic classifications (by date, author, and so on) tend to share many attributes. However, this assumption sometimes breaks down: "being by Picasso" does not automatically give us "being in Picasso's style," and conversely, "being in Vermeer's style" does not automatically give us "being by Vermeer." This possibility strikes a fatal blow at correlations between stylistic descriptions and historical, cultural, or chronological entities and phases unsupported by an independent archaeological argument.

Second, in practice many stylistic descriptions can only be pseudopolythetic. They must describe some attributes as being possessed by all artifacts in the group as it has been constituted for analysis. Some of these "universal" properties—for example, objecthood or materiality as such—are not usually meaningful and need not be treated as taxonomic characters. However, some may be treated operationally as diagnostic when they are discovered (or believed) not to appear beyond the group. But insofar as diagnostic attributes are used to define a single style or discriminate between different styles, the power and flexibility of polythetic classification has been forfeited. An artifact might always be discovered that does not possess the diagnostic attribute but which clearly belongs to the polythetic group by virtue of its other attributes.

Third, by my definition it is not possible to write a *stylistic* description of *one* unique attribute of an artifact. In theory, style is a description of a set of attributes distributed in a certain way in a set of artifacts. In practice, however, art historians may not explicitly cite the whole distribution or group, although stylistic analysis of single artifacts is implicitly informed by it.

The polythetic nature of stylistic description implies that ultimately it is fruitless to look for neat or absolute boundaries for and between styles. "Almost any style," Gombrich notes, "can be convincingly described as transitional."[8]

Furthermore, it is fruitless to hope for stylistic descriptions of uniform scale, complexity, and resolving power. Focusing on individual clusters of attributes, we can always extract subsets from any polythetic set, and a polythetic set can always be nested within larger sets; and conversely, any well-defined polythetic set can be derived from sub- or suprasets. The principles and procedures of stylistic description do not in themselves tie us to any particular level of historical or other particularity. To reveal historical particulars—for example, artists' identities, workshops, traditions—the resolving power of stylistic description must be carefully regulated. The criteria used here have to be defended on independent

---

or a polythetic set, see M. Beckner, *The Biological Way of Thought* (New York, 1959), 22; Simpson, *Principles of Animal Taxonomy*, 94–96; Sneath and Sokal, *Principles of Numerical Taxonomy*, 21–22; Rodney Needham, "Polythetic Classification," in *Against the Tranquility of Axioms* (Berkeley and Los Angeles, 1983), 36–55; and David L. Clarke, *Analytical Archaeology*, 2d ed. (New York, 1983), 36.

8. Gombrich, "Style," 357.

grounds. Unfortunately they are not often stated in the text of a stylistic description itself. In art history, "explanation" is often the expansion, contraction, nesting, and mutual derivation of stylistic descriptions of varying scales: style has been regarded as its own cause, history, and context.

Similar but Varying

The attributes of different artifacts in the group cannot be identical. In a material sense, no action can be repeated in exactly the same way every time. There will always be minor and sometimes major variations in the morphology of a type of artifact as it is repeatedly made. In a logical sense, even two identical or "indiscernible" morphologies may have different stylistic values. Therefore, the attributes studied in a stylistic description are not identical but similar.[9]

The definition and measurement of similarity poses as many problems in the study of style as it does in the study of perception, biological species, and elsewhere.[10] Art historians have evolved a complex vocabulary for this element of their work. Here only a few comments are possible.

First, as a statement about the distance of the relation between two attributes, similarity has many degrees. "Mass-produced" artifacts, "duplicates," "replicas," "copies," "quotations," and "forgeries" are very close to each other or to the template, original, master, or prototype. "Parallels" and "allusions" are more distant, as are many productions separated by literal distance, that is, by a chronological hiatus or spatial barrier. It is important, however, to note that similarity is not necessarily a good measure of the *distance* of the relation between two attributes, as cases of "negative influence" (such as an artist responding immediately and closely to another's work by doing exactly the opposite) or "antithetical similarities" suggest.[11]

Second, although many of our similarity terms ("copy," "quotation") prejudge the case, a similarity relation of whatever degree does not in and of itself necessarily reveal the *cause* of the relation between two attributes—for example, parallelism, convergence, analogy, mimicry, and so forth.[12] From the presence of a similarity relation alone, it is not possible to determine which of two artifacts might be an original and which a copy, or whether an artifact distantly alludes to or quotes from another or merely resembles it fortuitously. These judgments must be rendered on independent grounds.

Third, in the inclusive definition of style *(a)* above, similarity relations can be used to propose nonhistorical statements about the relatedness of artifacts. Moreover, although the presence of a similarity relation may be evidence of the historical relatedness of artifacts (a matter proved independently), the *absence* of a similarity relation is *not* evidence of their historical *un*relatedness. For this reason, stylistic description alone can always miss historical relations between artifacts.

9. See further Danto, *Transfiguration*, for the dynamic discernibility of indiscernibility.

10. See Nelson Goodman, "Seven Strictures on Similarity," in *Problems and Projects* (Indianapolis, 1972), 437–46.

11. Discussion in Göran Hermerén, *Influence in Art and Literature* (Princeton, 1975), 45, 50–89.

12. Simpson, *Principles of Animal Taxonomy*, 78–79.

Fourth, because of the polythetic character of stylistic description, analysis of similarity relations between *whole* artifacts, each with many attributes, becomes a matter of finding the relative weight perceivers give to (1) the proportion of shared to unique attributes and (2) the degree or strength of similarity between the shared attributes—for if a very small number of shared attributes, compared to a much greater number of unique attributes, are judged to be strongly similar, the whole artifacts may be judged to be quite similar even though each possesses many unique attributes. An overall measure of the intensity of similarity between artifacts with some identical, indiscernible, or very similar attributes and some very different or unique attributes has proved to be quite elusive. Art historians often employ intuitive judgments, although some formalizations have become available (such as Amos Tversky and I. Gati's "weighted difference of the measure of the common and distinctive features").[13]

Fifth, like style itself, similarity is not "in" the material. All artifacts are similar to all other artifacts in some respects, and a well-defined statement about similarity must be a statement about the nearness of the positions of attributes *in a particular order* set up by the observer. Art historians sometimes do not make explicit statements of quality orders and their measurement in digital or analogical units. Descriptions produced by different writers therefore become very difficult to compare, and new observations cannot be easily integrated into the existing body of descriptions.

Furthermore, art historians often favor the study of certain particular quality orders using certain particular measures—namely, visible surface qualities using the unaided eyes, hand, and body as measuring devices and anthropocentric and highly social or cultural categories as units. These preferences have led variously to the drift of stylistic analysis toward what might be called visual or optical formalism, connoisseurship, and metric historicism. Justification for these preferences has not been highly articulate. These visible qualities, simple unscientific devices, and special metrics are often assumed to have been those self-consciously manipulated by artisans in the past. In and of itself, however, stylistic description cannot be a proof of such assumptions; they must be confirmed by independent archaeological and anthropological knowledge of production. Although anthropologists suggest that art historians should try to use the relevant original "cultural" categories in their analysis, it is often stylistic analysis that enables art historians to see what these categories might have been and not the other way around.

Strictly speaking, *no* particular quality orders or metrics of and for similarity are uniquely inherent in the definition of style. Advances have been achieved precisely by abandoning one quality order or metric for another.

Attributes

In keeping with the polythetic character of stylistic description, "no fixed catalogue of the elementary properties of style can be compiled."[14] *All* attributes of an artifact are potentially stylistic; however, in any single artifact in a polythetic classification, not all attrib-

13. Amos Tversky and I. Gati, "Studies in Similarity," in *Cognition and Categorization*, ed. E. Rosch and B. Lloyd (Hillsdale, N.J., 1978), 79–98.

14. Goodman, "The Status of Style," 32.

utes *are* stylistic in practice. The several implications and difficulties of this statement should be outlined.

Which attributes of an artifact are picked out for inclusion in a stylistic description? Art historians tend to use visible, material, "formal" attributes, like line, color, or surface texture, which are supposed to be "intrinsically expressive" and form a coherent whole, "apart from denoted meanings."[15]

Nevertheless, despite occasional assertions that it is "something essentially concerned with form,"[16] style should not be reserved just for optically visible morphology or just for those perceptible or palpable attributes we believe to be "nonfunctional," "aesthetic," and so forth. (As I show in Chapter 8, a helpful way to understand style, in fact, is as a "totalization" of an accumulating "formalization" of the perception of material morphology. Style, then, is emergent in form—and never wholly absorbs it.) Not only visible formal properties but also "unexhibited" functional, symbolic (for example, denotational, expressional, or exemplificational), and institutional properties of the artifact are *potentially* stylistic.[17] To represent the Virgin Mary "in the style of Raphael" in 1500 would be to use an already somewhat conservative, deeply spiritual, idealizing or classicizing style; to represent the Virgin "in the style of Raphael"—that is, with the visible morphology of a Raphael—in 1996 would be to use some kind of radical, perhaps even ironic or satirical style. A description encompassing only formal attributes would group the visually indiscernible Virgins of 1500 and 1996 together. A description encompassing the contemporary connotations of subject matter, the institutional functions of the artifacts, and so forth, might group them in different categories—although, of course, it might not.

Although material morphologies can be stable, social functions, attributed meanings, and other unexhibited properties of the artifacts might be volatile. Conversely, artifacts might possess closely similar functions or meanings and yet appear to be formally remote—for example, because of decay, because we do not possess a chain of variants connecting them, or because they were once used together in a single context now lost to us. (Who would know from visual inspection alone that caterpillar and butterfly belong to the same species?) Evidently different classes of formal and unexhibited attributes may vary independently of each other. We know very little about the full range of these relations.

Just as with material formal attributes, the functions and meanings of different artifacts—the unexhibited attributes—are not identical but only similar in varying degrees. Although all formal and unexhibited attributes are potentially stylistic, we want to know how to *recognize* the stylistic attributes of any single artifact or within any single group of artifacts. As Goodman says, "not all differences [between artifacts] . . . are differences in style."[18]

Briefly, a stylistic attribute is one for which a match or similar can be found elsewhere in the group. By the terms of my definition, style is always a relational, comparative, or statistical description (clause *a*). Moreover, this match or association must be explained by

15. Schapiro, "Style," 291, but cf. 304, 309.
16. Kroeber, *Styles and Civilizations*, 26.
17. See Dickie, *Art and the Aesthetic*; Goodman, *Languages of Art*, distinguishes between denotation, expression, and exemplification.
18. Goodman, "The Status of Style," 23.

the history of the artifacts (clauses *b, c*). Although any attribute may enter into the "functioning of the work as a symbol or as such,"[19] if it cannot be matched or associated with attributes of other artifacts, a description of it remains a purely morphological, rather than a stylistic, characterization. Therefore all formal and unexhibited attributes of an artifact are also potentially *non*stylistic (morphological) insofar as they may not be entered into a polythetic classification.

By this definition, an attribute may be without style, or styleless, but no artifact can be without style, or styleless, for an artifact for which *no* matches or associations can be found anywhere for any attributes is unthinkable. Although some attributes remain unmatched or unassociated, all artifacts can be brought under a stylistic description of some kind. Strictly speaking, there is no need to prefer a high number of matches or associations for the attributes of our artifacts: "[M]any objects we deal with," Sauerländer remarks, "are not as uniform, not as patterned, briefly not as stylized, as our notions of style would like to have them."[20] Although to my mind this comment is one of the truest statements in the discipline of art history, its lesson is rarely heeded—probably because it has radical methodological and disciplinary implications.

All stylistic description requires morphological characterization but certainly is not identical with it. The residuum of "unique" morphology that cannot be taken up in a stylistic description may be the result of decay, or "random" (if nonetheless informative or even diagnostic) variation in motor or manufacturing habits.[21] More important, some proportion of it *must* be generated just because the most vigorous and penetrating stylization cannot touch every attribute of the artifact (compare the analysis of the necessary interpenetration of image and nonimage presented in Chapter 3). Insofar as some morphology is unique, it can serve as a defining description of the artifact or a defining trace of the artifact's particular history. Interartifactual style, then, might be successfully anchored to a specific history or historical situation of production through infra-artifactual morphology, some proportion of which is always nonstylistic. However, in the absence of independent evidence it is often difficult to recognize truly nonstylistic morphological variation, for potentially all kinds and levels of variation can be stylistic.

A great deal clearly depends upon the morphological—and therefore potentially the stylistic—description of attributes. The difficulties of decomposing a whole artifact into its component attributes are well recognized. Continuously varying attributes are particularly problematic. They are potentially infinitely divisible. For example, every morphological variation in a pictorial sign potentially has semantic meaning (so-called continuous correlation)[22]—so it would seem impossible to be sure of capturing all semantic nuances in a descriptive metric for the sign. However important to the art historian, strictly speaking, these are all problems in the analysis of (attribute) morphology—logically prior to all derived stylistic *and* nonstylistic taxonomies.

Of more immediate consequence for the theory of style are the problems not of

19. Goodman, "The Status of Style," 35.

20. Sauerländer, "From Stilus to Style," 167.

21. James N. Hill, "Individual Variability in Ceramics and the Study of Prehistoric Social Organization," in *The Individual in Prehistory*, ed. James N. Hill and Joel Gunn (New York, 1977), 55–108.

22. Kent Bach, "Part of What a Picture Is," *British Journal of Aesthetics* 10 (1970), 119–37.

attribute but of artifact morphology. Searching through the group only for similar instances of attributes produces only a polythetic classification of attributes. However, the total composition of all attributes may be quite individual in each artifact. An appropriate terminology for this composition—for the "look" or "feel" of whole pieces, what Wollheim calls the "coordinating rules"[23]—has proved hard to find, despite the massive investment art history has made in sustaining the concept of whole artworks (see Chapter 5). Notwithstanding the difficulty of describing the artifact (rather than its attributes) stylistically, art historians tend to focus on the whole artifact as such—taking it to be a cluster of attributes mutually correlated in a specific sequence or coordination.

Typical art historical preferences do not invalidate the fact that stylistic description proceeds equally legitimately at the level of unities, pairs, or other subartifactual clusters of attributes, of whole artifacts, or of clusters of artifacts (for example, in buildings or rituals). The study of style is not ineluctably tied to the study of single discrete "objects." In fact, although "the object of classification should be what Hennig calls the *holomorph,* all the characteristics of the individual throughout its life,"[24] in practice no art historian ever handles *all* of the attributes of an artifact in their full coordination. Operating stylistic descriptions are almost always subartifactual, building from certain attributes. Therefore in my definition of style the attribute is the analytic primary.

A Group of Artifacts

In my definition, stylistic descriptions apply to artifacts. The definition of an artifact is not entirely a problem for the theory of style. Although sufficient for most purposes, the usual definition of an artifact as a human-made physical object is theoretically too restrictive. At the extreme, an artifact is anything—object, process—any attribute of which was produced or assigned by human agency, including unexhibited symbolic or institutional attributes not actually manufactured by anyone wielding tools and working matter. This broadened definition allows us to include natural or "found" objects (often used in rituals), buildings, physical processes, human persons or personalities, and so forth. In some circumstances, all of these entities can be said to have, to be in, or to be part of a "style," however minimal, broad, or uninteresting.

Although the preference easily reaches its limits, especially in the study of the contemporary scene or the very remote past, art historians tend to study heavily worked, deeply meaningful, and socially valuable artifacts—in a phrase, *highly stylized* artifacts or "works of art." Needless to say, then, the theory of style must be able to accommodate anything we take to be a work of art, in which many attributes are manipulated at many levels in many ways. The material attributes are often wholly produced by human manufacture, constrained by the physical properties of the medium and technology. Its symbolic and institutional attributes are extremely complex: a painting may depict complex objects, and even simple nonrepresentational artifacts, such as a Japanese teacup, may require

23. Wollheim, "Pictorial Style," 137.

24. Hennig, *Phylogenetic Systematics,* 7; Simpson, *Principles of Animal Taxonomy,* 71.

elaborate interpretation or have a role in substantial social activities. The traditional fine and decorative arts—drawing, painting, sculpture, gem- and metalwork, and so forth—provide some paradigmatic examples of artifacts of this kind. Further transcendental descriptions of these artifacts—in terms of aesthetic quality, good, significant, or perfect form, beauty, and so forth—in practice do little work for art history and need not be considered here; "there is nothing inherent in the notion of style itself," Svetlana Alpers comments, "that encourages such distinctions being made."[25]

Beyond the traditional "fine" arts, we can certainly find many further examples of "highly stylized" artifacts (such as machines or vehicles, weapons, and costume) studied at the moment by archaeologists, historians of science and technology, and others (for one example, see Chapter 7, which deals with an object made to be used in a personal, if probably ritual, toilet). Furthermore, considerations of style and therefore art historical research, as I have suggested in Chapters 2 and 3, need not be limited to "highly stylized" artifacts.

A somewhat stronger case can be made for art historians limiting themselves to artifacts—"highly stylized" or not—that possess symbolic attributes, that is, that function as denotations, depictions, expressions, or exemplifications.[26] These concepts all seem to entail a theory of style: symbols are such relationally (syntactically and referentially), and therefore a description of shared or similar attributes between instances must be available by definition. Goodman claims, in fact, that stylistic attributes are "properties of the functioning of the work as a symbol," which rules style out of any artifact we do not take to be symbolic.[27] As is obvious from Chapter 3, I reject this view. It is fully conceivable that utterly nondepictive marks could be thoroughly stylized. But no depictive marks could be thoroughly *non*stylized. In other words, depiction is a subset of style, emergent in a "canonical chain of replications" that must be understood to have a style in the sense of the definition presented here.

Why Style?

We may now ask what stylistic description in art history—both "taxonomic" *and* "generative"[28]—is supposed to do for us. "Why," Goodman asks, "should style matter more than some quality that might be discerned, with enough study, as characteristic of works in a random selection?"[29] (For myself, I doubt that style matters *more* than, for example, certain properties of material morphology, some proportion of which are nonstylistic. But style certainly does matter.) The question admits either a simple answer or a complex and still controversial one.

Simply, style can be seen as *the explanation for* the similarities between the attributes of artifacts. The attributes are similar because they have, are in, or are part of a single style.

25. Svetlana Alpers, "Style Is What You Make It: The Visual Arts Once Again," in *The Concept of Style*, ed. Lang, 97.

26. Goodman, *Languages of Art* and "The Status of Style."

27. Goodman, "The Status of Style," 35.

28. Wollheim, "Pictorial Style"; Sauerländer, "From Stilus to Style," 260–65.

29. Goodman, "The Status of Style," 39.

Therefore style matters simply because it has explanatory value. Statements based on this reasoning are frequent in art historical and archaeological writing. But by the terms of my definition, they are obviously tautological—for style simply is a description of the similarities between artifacts.

The truth of the matter, then, is really more subtle. The tautology can be seen as a convenient shorthand for another, more difficult analysis, indicated in clauses *b* and *c* in my definition above. Style—the similarity between artifacts—is explained by the history of the artifacts. Therefore style matters as the *explanandum* for art history or archaeology. Without style, art historians have nothing to talk about, no problem to solve.

Reading from Style to History

Since its modern inception in the work of Jakob Burckhardt, Alois Riegl, Heinrich Wölfflin, and others, art history has flirted with and often embraced the idea that the "history" explaining style is revealed or made available to us in and by style itself. In the frequent absence of any other information about artifacts apart from their stylistic descriptions, we might nonetheless find in them their histories—their authors, dates, values, and significances. "Style is the mirror which makes all the buildings, the statues, the images of the past accessible to aesthetic historicism, for its dreams and for its files."[30]

Although reading from style to history and back again to style is ultimately a great circularity, it is important to consider the justification of the procedure. If we make certain assumptions in addition to those adopted in stylistic description itself, both the *internal structure* of styles and their *external correlations* might in a sense be given directly in stylistic description. These structures and correlations are often thought to be all that we require to explain styles historically.

The Diachronic Reading: The Internal Structure of Styles

A purely stylistic description of artifacts is an unwieldy affair unless and until it is structured by crosscutting information, particularly about sequence and distribution. Ideally, the sequence and distribution of artifacts can be established by independent archaeological evidence about the time and place of production of different artifacts in the group. Less ideally, sequence and distribution can also be established by hypothesis—by granting assumptions about variations in production over time and space not necessarily inherent in the theory of style itself. Unfortunately, art history has not paid much attention to developed theories of sequence (for example, seriation) or distribution (for example, deposition) in archaeology.[31]

30. Sauerländer, "From Stilus to Style," 254.

31. But see George Kubler, *The Shape of Time: Remarks on the History of Things* (New Haven, Conn., 1962), and idem, "Towards a Reductive Theory of Visual Style."

Armed with both archaeological and hypothetical information about sequence and distribution, many art historians and anthropologists have claimed to find regular temporal and spatial structures in styles. These structures have commonly been conceived as connected series of slightly varying artifacts—lines of variation or evolution connecting two or more fixed temporal or spatial points, such as a line between a point of "origins" and a point of "fulfillment," or a line between a point at a "center" and a point at a "periphery." As art historical analysis became more complete and elaborate in the first half of this century, recurrences or cycles of these simple structures were described, resulting in detailed accounts of the life history of styles.[32] Any artifact could be positioned, described, and in a sense explained in terms of the life-historical structures of style: an artifact is archaic or classic, cosmopolitan or provincial, inventive and authoritative or degenerate and derived, and so forth. Although many statements of this kind incorporate actual archaeological dates or contexts, many of them are also partly or wholly stylistic.

For critical purposes, it is enough to observe that many of the life histories of style were erected on a slight base of independent dates and contexts. They depended frequently upon dubious procedural prescriptions not inherent in the theory of style itself—for example, the rule of thumb that it is best to begin the search for similarities to the attributes of an artifact with the very next artifacts (in either or any direction) in sequence or distribution. In fact, in the absence of archaeological evidence, sometimes artifacts were initially positioned next to each other in sequences or distributions on the basis of morphological similarity, making possible, by definition alone, a coherent stylistic description with a satisfyingly regular structure. Teleological notions—"the fine arts spend much of their course evolving toward their ideal or goal,"[33] ultimately "attained" and then "exhausted"—at the extreme gave rise to almost mystical conceptions, like Riegl's *Kunstwollen*, or "will-to-form."[34] In evolutionist or diffusionist enthusiasm for regular lines of temporal and spatial variation, especially when further and closely crosscut by narrative biography and chronicle, much of the power and flexibility of polythetic classification was forfeited.

None of these difficulties at all proves that regular temporal or spatial structures cannot be found in styles or will not be confirmed archaeologically in some instances. That they exist is something we may find out about some styles. However, they are certainly not uni-

32. See further Munro, *Evolution in the Arts* (Cleveland, 1963), and Ackerman, "Style," 170–74, 177–81. An early opposition to these views was the archaeologist-historian-philosopher R. G. Collingwood's stress on historical periods, cycles, and patterns as artifacts of the observer ("The History of Historical Cycles," *Antiquity* 1 [1929], 311–25, 435–46, and *The Idea of History* [Oxford, 1946], 205–334). Although Jane Richardson and Alfred Kroeber's study of fashion is still perhaps the best-known empirical examination of cycles (*Three Centuries of Women's Dress Fashions: A Quantitative Analysis*, Anthropological Records, University of California 5 [Berkeley and Los Angeles, 1940]), Kroeber also voiced skepticism about the treatment of cyclical or other periodicity in art history (Kroeber, *Styles and Civilizations*, 137–49). See also Pitirim Sorokin, *Social and Cultural Dynamics*, vol. 1, *Fluctuations of Forms in Art* (New York, 1937). For the relations between supposed "centers" and supposed "peripheries," see Whitney Davis, "Writing Culture in Lower Central America," in *Prehistory of Lower Central America*, ed. Mark Miller Graham (Boulder, Colo., 1992), 253–76.

33. Kroeber, *Styles and Civilizations*, 21.

34. Riegl, *Late Roman Art Industry*. It must be said, however, that Riegl's "Formalism" issued in a reasonable historical approach precisely because he practiced stylistic analysis in its strictest terms, never conflating stylistic analysis (in the sense defined here) with a merely formal one, a phenomenology of morphology.

versally or essentially immanent. The representation of matched or similar attributes in a population does not always change in any single linear direction but may oscillate or fluctuate in complex ways. In fact, the theory of style makes no inherent predictions about the rate, pace, direction, or degree of change.[35] Erected a priori or by hypothesis alone, the life-historical structures of style do not reliably make available a history of style from within.

The Synchronic Reading: The External Correlations of Styles

Any artifact can be anchored to its historical context—its time and place of production, its maker, and so forth—in a variety of ways. Ideally, we have independent archaeological or documentary evidence for these details (what, in Chapter 5, I called Cartailhac's palimpsest): the artifact was unearthed in a sealed deposit, was described in a contemporary letter, and the like. The procedures for critically evaluating this evidence are not part of the theory of style itself.

Somewhat less ideally, the nonstylistic morphology of an artifact may be the unique product and therefore the trace of its context. (In Chapter 3, I considered a parallel situation: nonresemblant morphology is part of the evidence an interpreter uses to determine that he or she is, in fact, interpreting an image resembling objects in the world.) For example, a stone can be traced by archaeologists to a single quarry. Or again, a photograph is in part a representation of just those objects before the camera when the shutter closed. However, neither stylistic nor nonstylistic morphology is invariably the product of anything as specific as a particular historical instant or individual. The sputtering of my pen might be due to my illness in a given month, but it also might be due to built-in features of a type of pen in use for generations. Only independent experimentation will settle the point.

These possibilities are greatly complicated by the fact that *all* morphology is potentially stylistic by my definition. Therefore the traces of past contexts could be imitated (preserved or revised) in an artifact, as an element of its style. If I arrange objects before my camera in a certain way, I am at least in part working in the style of, say, Stieglitz, and the unique nonstylistic trace of my own context must be sought in different attributes. Giovanni Morelli, Bernard Berenson, Sir John Beazley, and other great connoisseurs proceeded on the assumption that in an artifact it will always be possible to locate nonstylistic morphology directly due to the habit or preference of an individual producer (see further Chapter 5). However, as any morphology might instead be either stylistic or nonindividual, or both, the matter can only be pursued on an ad hoc empirical basis.[36]

35. The "constancy" of form so central to Schapiro's concept of style is not a necessary feature of style by my definition (Schapiro, "Style"; see also Kubler, "Towards a Reductive Theory of Style"). Various interesting attempts have been made to demonstrate the "inherent unity and continuity of the development of art" (Jerrold Levinson, "Defining Art Historically," *British Journal of Aesthetics* 19 [1979], 232–50)—for instance, in studies of influence (review in Hermerén, *Influence in Art and Literature*), in emphasis on stylistic *traditions* or *fashions* (by my definition, special cases of style, adding further detailed specifications of the rate, pace, direction, degree, and regularity of change), or in relatively formal theories like Kubler's "rule of series" (in his *Shape of Time*). The theory of style certainly accommodates but does not inherently call for "continuity."

36. See Hill, "Individual Variability in Ceramics," with references, for experimental investigation of morphological variation.

Perhaps least ideally of all, context can be established by hypothetical correlation alone. A *stylistic* grouping is held to be coextensive with actual *historical* entities—with artists, workshops, "periods" or "phases" of cultural and social history. In our stylistic description, then, we can be given history—for we can read from style to the presence of an artist, a workshop, a social convention, instruction, or institution, a cultural preference, outlook, or way of life, and so on. If sustainable, the possibility of such a reading would be the most important contribution of stylistic description, for it would show stylistic description, as Ackerman and many other art historians hope, to be an "indispensable historical tool."[37] But however deeply entrenched in art history, reading from style to history in this way seems to falter badly on two counts.

Style Coextensive with What?

First, the mapping between stylistic and historical entities must actually be stronger than a mere correlation, for correlation could be due to sheer chance and therefore cannot always be counted on to do the work we want. If the relation is not a mere chance correlation, then how should it be construed?

Art historians apparently often assume that style is the *expression* of a historical entity, such as an individual's idea or emotion (that is, the mind of the maker in a particular state) or a society's way of life or worldview (that is, the consensus or consciousness of the community in a particular state). Although style regarded as having coextensive historical correlations may seem to require a theory of expression, theories of expression can be defended independently of a theory of style. In fact, for Richard Wollheim and other commentators style is a precondition of expressiveness.[38] For my purposes, expression, considered solely as the alleged *cause* of style, is an uninformative concept. If expression is by definition made identical with all stylistic attributes, then we have not gained anything or established any causes at all. But if not all stylistic attributes are expressive or expressional—for example, if some of them are exemplificational instead—then the correlation between style and expression is not one-to-one; expression is *not* the (only) cause of style.

Moreover, in the absence of independent archaeological and historical evidence, an "expression" cannot be easily identified with any well-defined historical entities. Where and what are the ideas or emotions *x*, *y*, and *z*, the ways of life or worldviews *p*, *q*, and *r*, that are supposedly expressed by the style? Logically, further correlations have to be established on independent evidence between an entity-of-style-as-expression-of-idea-*x* and whatever historical entity it was that expressed that idea—one person at one point in his or her life? a group of persons in agreement? Since historical individuals and social groups potentially can express many ideas or emotions, stylistic description alone cannot lead us necessarily and invariably to find historical individuals or groups. But if in stylistic description we can only find "individuals"-expressing-ideas-*x*-*y*-or-*z*, then again we have not gained anything beyond the definition of style as expression.

37. Ackerman, "Style," 164.

38. Wollheim, "Pictorial Style," 133; see also E. H. Gombrich, "Expression and Communication," in *Meditations on a Hobby Horse,* 56–69.

It may be that we do have independent evidence for the ideas or emotions expressed in a style and for the entities—individuals, groups, cultures—carrying out the expression. We might have a letter by or an interview with an artist declaring his or her aesthetic or other aims; we might have sociological data informing us that everyone making artifacts within a well-bounded temporal and spatial region was a Christian and professed Christian values in thought and action. However, using this evidence in effecting correlations between a stylistic and a historical entity would be reading *from* history *to* style—a procedure that might just as well turn out to disconfirm as to confirm any correlations established the other way around.

To avoid some of the difficulties noted in the last three paragraphs, the correlations between stylistic and historical entities need not be interpreted as a relation of expression but rather as an *indexical* or *symptomatic* relation. According to this view, style is necessarily the index or symptom of the presence of a historical entity. This approach has been characteristic of some recent archaeology that does not use the humanist's language of expression and intentions and avoids interpreting archaeological entities like artifact types, style areas, or culture phases as ideas, emotions, or worldviews. However, we have really gained nothing beyond our stylistic description itself if we do not specify precisely *what* historical entity *is* represented, in fact, by an artifact type, style area, or culture phase. When such a specification is thought to be "given" in the stylistic classification, it is exposed to all of the trivialities and circularities noted already.

An indexical or symptomatic correlation does not have the advantages of a truly coextensive, let alone causal, correlation. Indexically, the stylistic description does *point to* a historical entity, but does not *map* it and is not necessarily caused by it. The real entity could be much larger and very different from the respects singled out by a stylistic description. The description sees the entity behaving in a particular way at a particular time, but knows nothing more about the whole of the entity in its other respects. Among other things, it risks partitioning the entity into falsely independent entities. These matters have been much debated by Lewis Binford and other archaeologists (see Chapter 4).

In sum, the first problem with historical correlations established solely on the basis of or directly given by a stylistic description is simply the fact that we cannot know, without independent evidence, whether the description has picked out a real historical entity, a fragment of an entity, or a conflation of entities. We may not care, of course, that we happen to be studying fragments or conflations—one artist's "mood" or "phase," the production of many artists sharing a plan—*as long as we know that this is what they are.* But a stylistic description alone cannot give us this knowledge.

Perhaps the problem can be minimized by employing several parallel or superimposed stylistic descriptions. As I have noted, stylistic description may proceed at any level or particularity. Therefore a description tuned to pick out an individual's lifelong mannerisms, overlaid with descriptions of more momentary or more stable attributes, might provide a valid picture of a group of makers, each with some transient and some stable mannerisms, working over a period of time. Art historical writing usually consists of such complex grids of descriptions. Nevertheless, the historical validity of the most complex grid still cannot be confirmed from within.

A Pure Nonhistorical Stylistic Description?

The second problem with the external historical correlations of style cuts much deeper. To lead us to valid historical correlations, in addition to technical and formal characterizations of artifacts, stylistic description, as I noted earlier, incorporates statements about "unexhibited" attributes. These are necessarily historical statements about the use and significance of artifacts in a particular context (such as the "Virgin in the style of Raphael" in 1500 or in 1996). Therefore, to avoid fatal circularity or illegitimate correlations obtained by artificial stipulation, valid statements about these attributes must be obtained prior to and independently of the completed stylistic description.

This problem figures in much art historical and archaeological analysis. For example, the connotation of a representation cannot be read off directly from the appearance of the figures, however precisely described. Pictorial meaning must be fixed through detailed study of representational and iconographic conventions. In his remarkable studies of iconographic "disjunctions," Erwin Panofsky stressed how stable classical forms often shifted significance profoundly in the long development from antiquity itself through the formative centuries of the Christian "late antique" into the Middle Ages and on to the Renaissance revivals.[39] George Kubler has offered a similar treatment for pre-Columbian Mesoamerica.[40] Their research does not necessarily show that we should reject descriptions of remarkably stable "classic styles" in the Hellenized West or certain Central American polities. Stylistic description may be legitimate at many levels of historical particularity. Nevertheless, at the limit we will find formally similar artifacts produced by people entirely unrelated to or uninfluenced by one another and employing their own unique symbolic conventions and institutions.[41] From a formal description alone we cannot differentiate disjunctions and diffusions from true discontinuity or dissimilarity; we must refer to context.

In addition to considering unexhibited symbolic or institutional attributes, knowledge of production methods, authorship, and other historical aspects of artifacts will be used to inflect a stylistic description. The description will be crosscut by these independent monothetic classifications. For example, two works produced by an Inuit carver and Henry Moore respectively might look very similar (a valid statement in the inclusive concept of style *[a]*), but they were probably made in altogether different ways, especially if we discover, as we might, that Henry Moore knew nothing about Inuit sculpture. Knowledge of production methods could lead us to assign the Inuit and the Moore work to different styles. Or again, a stylistic description might pick out a group of "artifacts in the style of Vermeer," although it turns out that Vermeer himself made only about thirty-four of these artifacts. Although strictly speaking it is an independent problem of monothetic classification (that is, attribution), individual or cultural authorship (or authenticity) seems to be such a necessary element for the historical correlation of style that in practice it is often treated as an unexhibited or even an exhibited stylistic attribute of artifacts.

39. Erwin Panofsky, "Renaissance and Renascences," *Kenyon Review* 6 (1944), 201–36, and idem, *Renaissance and Renascences*.

40. Kubler, "Towards a Reductive Theory of Visual Style."

41. See George Kubler, "Polygenesis and Diffusion," in *Collected Essays of George Kubler*, ed. Thomas F. Reese (New Haven, Conn., 1985), 251–55.

In sum, the second problem with historical correlations established solely on the basis of, or directly given by, a stylistic description is simply the fact that a full stylistic description of potentially relevant attributes is not something independent of and prior to history, which leads into, makes available, or correlates with history. In brief, history has already entered into the stylistic description that is supposed to be "giving" history.

From Style to History?

The two problems above show that the hope of reading from style to history is unintelligible. A stylistic description that does not employ historical statements about the attributes of artifacts cannot prove from within that it is validly correlated with any real historical entity, or any fragments or conflations thereof. But a stylistic description that *does* employ historical statements about the (often unexhibited) attributes of artifacts, although it may be validly correlated, is already assuming some prior knowledge of the history to which it will be correlated.

Most art historians would not ordinarily depend wholly on reading from style to history. In some respects, the procedure might be more common in archaeological disciplines, where nothing is known about the past except what can be said about its artifacts. A full-scale art historical analysis is often a bewildering, jerry-built maze of purely morphological characterizations, purely archaeological facts, interpretive statements, and stylistic descriptions, some of which, it is true, are not supposed to be revealing historical structures or correlations. Nevertheless, a survey of the whole domain of art history would probably show how few independent contexts and confirmations are used and how frequently arguments invoke stylistic structures and correlations suffering from some or all of the difficulties noted here.

Reading from History to Style

In construing the critical clauses *b* and *c* of my definition of style, I have shown that a stylistic description itself cannot reveal the history that explains style. As the *explanandum* of art history, no matter how sophisticated the integration of one level of "directly given" internal structure or plausible external correlation with another, style does not explain itself. We need to read *from* history *to* style—and this history is not style itself.

This "history" has been specified in a number of ways. Clause *c* attempts to characterize it specifically and positively; style in the art historian's sense is the result of the common descent of a group of artifacts from an artifact-production system. But it is not immediately clear what an "artifact-production system" might be and how artifacts "descend" from it.

Modern art history employs two important accounts of artifact-production systems, or, more briefly, of production. According to the first account, production is the use of a "language." According to the second, it is an activity or process of making. The central metaphors and arguments of both accounts have much to recommend them as well as obvious drawbacks.

Production as the Use of a "Language"

All current concepts of style have deep roots in the classical rhetoricians' treatment of style as a normative prescription for oratorical, epistolary, or other verbal practices aimed at desirable effects, like the persuasion of audiences or elaboration of philosophical arguments.[42] The various contemporary accounts of production as a "language" share with the ancient analysis the view that style involves choosing and following norms or rules for obtaining specific effects, of which the bare minimum is intelligibility or communication. This "language" requires a choice between two or more and up to an infinity of alternatives—it has informational value. Furthermore, it is a competence its users possess and employ in particular circumstances—it has psychological or social reality.[43] Insofar as artifacts are produced "linguistically"—as a rule-governed selection from alternatives—they have style.

At the simplest and most general level, the linguistic model requires only the elementary terms of information theory. In a language with three possible elements, +, –, and !, always to begin a message with + and end it with ! is consistently to convey particular information (in the middle variables) or, in my metaphor, to use a particular style. E. H. Gombrich has devoted several influential papers to working out the implications of this insight for art history, and the analysis need not be repeated here.[44] For my purposes, ignoring their actual intellectual histories, more sophisticated versions of the linguistic model may be regarded as building from this level.

In archaeology, James Sackett's "isochrestic" model for style proposes that "style resides in the specific context-determined variants ('choices') assumed by functional form." The model requires that function could be fulfilled by any one of a set of alternative forms—that there are "isomorphic functional equivalents."[45] Therefore the form that we actually find must represent a "selection" from these alternatives. Furthermore, the model assumes that the selection must be determined in or by a well-defined context. By all my earlier arguments, the nature of the selection or style itself will not tell us directly what this context actually involved, its scale or particularity, and so forth. Conceivably, the "selection" was made by some individual or group acting in a certain way, for certain purposes, and with certain habits, knowledge, and values. However, this possibility cannot be confirmed from within the stylistic description itself.

42. See Jan Bialostocki, "Das Modusproblem in den bildenden Künsten," *Zeitschrift für Kunstgeschichte* 24 (1961), 128–41; Gombrich, "Style," 353–54; and Sauerländer, "From Stilus to Style."

43. Wollheim, "Pictorial Style," 138.

44. E.g., Gombrich, *Meditations on a Hobby Horse* and "Style."

45. James R. Sackett, "The Meaning of Style in Archaeology," 371, 374. See also idem,"Approaches to Style in Lithic Archaeology," *Journal of Anthropological Archaeology* 1 (1982), 67–80, and idem, "Style and Ethnicity in Archaeology: The Case for Isochrestism," in *The Uses of Style in Archaeology*, ed. Margaret W. Conkey and Christine Hastorf (Cambridge, 1989), 32–43.

Sackett associates two further and logically quite independent proposals with the isochrestic model itself. (1) Apparently as a "highly specific and characteristic manner of doing something," namely, selecting from functional isomorphs, a style is "always peculiar to a specific time and place." (2) "The degree of similarity among the choices that are made in two historically related loci depends upon the intensity of social interaction shared by their occupants."[46] In these senses, "form is an index to history." By this reasoning, the isochrestic model of style, like any other, might be put to use in attempts to read from style to history.

I have already noted the difficulties of this kind of correlation. The claims of (1) above are clearly invalid: people at a specific time and place may not make use of or determine a "peculiar" style, that is, a *single* characteristic manner of doing something that is *also* not to be observed at other times and places (either within society or among societies). To establish a one-to-one correlation, in theory we would need at least two further assumptions—namely, that the use of different alternatives at a given time and place (for example, in a given activity) is mutually exclusive in some well-defined temporal, spatial, or other sense, and that "an object of its precise form and design is most unlikely to recur in any locus other than the one in which we have actually found it."[47] These two assumptions are much too unreliable to include among the necessary assumptions of a theory of style.

Although, like (1) above, it might be confirmed on independent evidence in some instances, the necessity or logic of (2) is also open to question. A similarity relation of whatever kind does not in and of itself necessarily reveal the cause of the relation between the two attributes. Furthermore, although the presence of a similarity relation may (or may not) be evidence of the historical relatedness of artifacts, and therefore of their producers, its *absence* is *not* evidence of their *un*relatedness. A description of similarities alone not only might erect false histories of relations between artifacts but also might miss relations. On independent evidence, we might actually discover "intense social interaction" between the producers of artifacts. Even so, intense interaction could also lead to stylistically divergent production by very closely related producers. Therefore, and in sum, we need an *independent* characterization of interaction—as, for instance, of producers sharing a plan, quoting a model, imitating a master, revising an ancestor, rejecting a competitor, and so on, also admitting such possibilities as reversing oneself or forging another. Although often contaminated by purely stylistic inference, such "ethnoarchaeological" analysis is the bread and butter of many art historical studies of schools and workshops, academies, movements, and traditions of art, and so forth.[48]

Although the isochrestic model of style, like any other, should not be put to use in reading from style to history without independent supports, for my purposes here its true

46. Sackett, "The Meaning of Style in Archaeology," 371; cf. idem, "Approaches to Style in Lithic Archaeology," 73. For the role of this claim in recent archaeology, see the reviews and criticisms by Ian Hodder, "Economic and Social Stress and Material Culture Patterning," *American Antiquity* 44 (1979), 446–54.

47. Sackett, "The Meaning of Style in Archaeology," 370; but cf. idem, "Approaches to Style in Lithic Archaeology," 73.

48. Although almost any traditional and much revisionist art history could be cited, see the classic studies by Erwin Panofsky, *Early Netherlandish Painting,* 2 vols. (Cambridge, 1953); G.M.A. Richter, *The Sculpture and Sculptors of the Greeks,* 4th ed. (New Haven, Conn.,

usefulness is simply as a specification of the *nature of production*. The isochrestic model simply states that style is the process—however distributed or institutionalized—of selecting from functional isomorphs and employing the chosen variant(s) in a given context.

In theory, selection is "context determined." No particular specification of an *actual historical context* is necessarily implied in a pure information-theoretic or isochrestic account of the "linguistic" production of style. The selection could be made by a machine responding to certain frequencies of external stimulation (for example, output + if high, – if low, ! if middling). The "selection" could be due to a natural process in which one alternative state of the possible outcomes appears with a frequency greater than chance. Such possibilities lead to the difficulty—much underlined in recent archaeology—of differentiating, in the absence of independent evidence, between "style" produced by robots (a technology acting automatically and leaving certain by-products), by nonhuman creatures, and by human beings (see further Chapter 4).

However, in the definition of isochrestic style we can certainly include a specification of the context of selection. In art history and the other humanities, selection from alternative states of a function or message is variously defined as a human being (1) using a code, (2) following a rule, (3) indulging a preference or fulfilling an intention. Codes, rules, or intentions are things that a human being uses, follows, or fulfills only in certain contexts. Therefore it is possible to assert definitionally that style is generated only by a system in those contexts or having those states. Unfortunately all of these specifications tend to force archaeological and art historical analysis toward an unjustified idealism or intentionalism (see Chapter 4)—unjustified in the strict sense that stylistic variability could, by the terms of my general definition, have thoroughly nonintentional causes—and hence to specify, definitionally, that style derives from intentional processes would be precisely to ignore a good proportion of the "styles" produced in hominid and human history.

(1) A semiotic account of visual and verbal production would be impossible to outline here. In general, from a semiotic point of view a visual or verbal representation—using the term in its widest sense—is an individual message within a complex code. The code has particular units and imposes a structure upon the message; it consists of paradigmatic and syntagmatic levels of articulation (see further Chapter 8). In verbal language, the units are the phonemes, and the structure is the syntax of the language. Although the issue is controversial, in semiotic analysis of graphic displays the units are usually thought to be basic graphic means (like points, lines, and fields of color), and the structure the means of combining them to construct forms or figures and compose a design or scene. In theory, any

1970); and Meyer Schapiro, *Modern Art* (New York, 1979). Polly Wiessner—in "Style and Social Information in Kalahari San Projectile Points," *American Antiquity* 49 (1983), 253–76, and "Reconsidering the Behavioral Basis for Style: A Case Study Among the Kalahari San," *Journal of Anthropological Archaeology* 3 (1984), 190–234—provides a review and provocative extension of work on style conducted by archaeologists and anthropologists, especially on the problem of "deriving social information from style" ("Reconsidering the Behavioral Basis for Style," 191). The relevant literature includes central studies by Nicholas David and Hilke Henning, *The Ethnography of Pottery: A Fulani Case Seen in Archaeological Perspective* (Reading, Mass., 1972); Wobst, "Stylistic Behavior and Information Exchange"; Margaret W. Conkey, "Style and Information in Cultural Evolution: Toward a Predictive Model for the Paleolithic," in *Social Archaeology*, ed. Charles Redman et al. (New York, 1978), 61–85; and Ian Hodder, *Symbols in Action* (Cambridge, 1982).

particular message in the code can be located precisely on the paradigmatic and syntagmatic axes, making possible a precise—a uniquely defining—description for every message. Many topics—for example, syntactic hierarchy, intertextuality, and modality—can be considered in this framework.

(2) The tendentious notion of following a rule is as suggestive as the semiotic notion of using a code. Notions of style as "ruled originality or originality bound by rules" are at least as old as the eighteenth century.[49] From this point of view, we specify the rules of manufacture, use, and interpretation that gave to the original makers and users (or would give to the modern typologist) all and only those artifacts brought together in a polythetic classification. As a historical assertion, following the rule produces artifacts in the style.

The algorithm itself can be written at any level of particularity and complexity. Some writers claim to have isolated the rule—of so-called intellectual realism, or aspective (nonperspective surface-attending representation)—that produces the nonnaturalistic, "conceptual" images of children, of many pre-Greek (preperspective) societies, and so forth.[50] This rule has to be exceedingly general and specifies an extensive global style. Within this style, the conventions of particular cultures can be isolated. An ancient Egyptian draftsman apparently followed a complex set of at least four interrelated "canonical" rules of drawing, each with dependent subrules. Within Egyptian culture itself, we could write algorithms—now of extraordinary complexity—that would give the styles of individual workshops or craftsmen. Even in the absence of independent historical evidence for the rules, their encoding, and their transmission, the formal adequacy of all these proposals in a sense can be tested directly. A suitably programmed computer should be able to produce all and only the artifacts brought together in a stylistic description.[51]

(3) Despite the success of some semiotic and algorithmic analyses of image-making traditions, the humanist's traditional and eclectic talk about having and fulfilling intentions probably still constitutes the richest vocabulary for verbal and visual production.[52] One intends or means to say what one says. The limits and paradoxes of this claim—must one say what one means? is what one means what one says?—are too well known for review here (see Chapter 1): however tendentious the description, style is the result of meanings one intends, and in selecting from alternatives, one uses or chooses that which is one's meaning or intention.

Needless to say, reading *from* a stylistic description alone *to* a code, rule, or intention (supposing that we should try to do so in the first place) may go badly wrong. The stylistic description itself is grossly underdetermined. *Many* kinds of codes, rules, or intentions could produce just, and only those, artifacts brought together in a polythetic classification. For my purposes here, the true usefulness of these models is *only* as a specification of the nature of production. Clearly, codes, rules, or intentions are not easy historical entities to work with: they can be anything from innate response systems of the human organism

49. Sauerländer, "From Stilus to Style," 255–57.

50. Georges Henri Luquet, *Le dessin enfantin* (Paris, 1927); Heinrich Schäfer, *Principles of Egyptian Art,* trans. J. R. Baines, 4th ed. (Oxford, 1974).

51. Whitney Davis, *The Canonical Tradition in Ancient Egyptian Art* (New York, 1989); Gay Robins, *Proportion and Style in Ancient Egyptian Art* (Austin, Tex., 1993).

52. E.g., Baxandall, *Patterns of Intention.*

(see Chapters 1–4) through highly social conventions and "languages" in the everyday sense to the affective states of individual personalities (see Chapters 10–12). However, although independent evidence for these entities may be hard to come by, clause *c* of my definition instructs us to search for it archaeologically; found, it is the source and explanation of style.

Some suspicions must be voiced about all accounts of production as the use of a "language," at whatever level. First, no satisfying explanation of the origins of rule-governed selection has ever been provided. Why should we have style at all in this sense? If, for instance, there are functional, formal, or semantic alternatives from which choice is made by code, rule, or intention, why should this procedure be any better or more common in human culture than simply adopting the first or only alternative to hand—or does this occur as well? A stylistic description cannot tell us from within whether variants were "selected" or just brought together randomly or under complete constraint. Furthermore, even when "selected," the information value or information content of a style must fluctuate from artifact to artifact. Although an initial selection will have full value, repetition and variation will be redundant to some degree. And at the limit, if a producer has no choice in production whatsoever, strictly speaking her work is completely lacking in information value. Implicitly or explicitly, the linguistic model asserts that style *communicates;* it must go on, then, to assume or to provide a theory of the nature and evolution of communication. Did *Australopithecus* have style because she communicated, or did she communicate by style—or both (by definition), or neither (in fact)? Bees and porpoises communicate; do they have style? Such questions suggest that style and communication may vary independently—so how, then, should a concept of communication be built definitionally into a general theory of style?

Second, a fully satisfying account of the "alternative" states of a function or message also has yet to be provided. A stylistic description encompasses only the variant state actually selected and recovered archaeologically. Where, then, are the alternatives? Should we be able to find them archaeologically, or perhaps picked out in another description? Although it may make sense to assert that something could have been done differently, in many cases this is merely an argument from silence. In fact, because a stylistic description cannot tell us from within whether a selection was random, rule governed, or completely constrained, how do we know that things could have been done differently?

Furthermore, the very notion of a formal, functional, semantic, or other isomorph is logically problematic. Although form, function, and content are not neatly separated, we have to say that two forms could fulfill the same function or have the same content, that two functions could have the same form, and so on, in order to envision selection from alternative states. This notorious doctrine of synonymy is not easily defended.[53] For instance, the "continuous correlation" of form and content in depiction implies that if any formal detail of an image is altered, its meaning necessarily alters correlatively.[54] In

53. See Nelson Goodman, "On Likeness of Meaning," *Analysis* 1 (1949), 1–7, and idem, "The Status of Style"; see also the suspicions of Schapiro, "Style," 303, and the defense by Gombrich, "Style."

54. Bach, "Part of What a Picture Is."

speaking, one cannot really choose between two ways of saying the same thing; rather, one chooses to say one of two somewhat different things. Moreover, *any* aspect of an artifact—formal or functional, exhibited or unexhibited—can be stylistic. We cannot have it (for example) that function will *always* be invariant, with form varying: cutting may be performed by shears or knives, but two formally indiscernible knives might be stylistically differentiated in a polythetic classification by functional or semantic criteria—one used at the table, the other in warfare, or one connoting political authority, the other servitude. In sum, the "alternatives" selected seem necessarily different or unequal—noncomparable in ways that prejudge the rationales and procedures for selecting from them.

None of these suspicions necessarily invalidates all accounts of style as the use of a "language." They remind us that specifying the artifact-production system—here, as a system in which selection from alternatives has information value and some kind of psychological and social reality—supports many interpretations and requires supplementary assumptions not inherent in the theory of style itself.

Production as an Activity of Making

An account of production as an activity of making is more general than an account of production as the use of a language. It may therefore escape some of the difficulties of the linguistic models.

Making does not necessarily involve communication. In a description or explanation of making, there is no necessary place for a spectator, audience, or receiver. Making does not necessarily imply that the artifact will have public intersubjective meaning, that it will represent, express, or exemplify anything intelligible to anyone, including its maker, or that it will "signify" at all; nonetheless, the artifact has style. Making does not necessarily imply that the artifact will end up being used in any particular way, if it is used at all. Making does not necessarily imply that the producer selects from alternative possibilities; the making might be completely constrained, always limited to one procedure or sequence of procedures. Making generates style insofar as certain actions have certain exhibited or unexhibited effects. Repeating the actions will result in a repetition of the effects, within some tolerance of variation—resulting in the set of similarity relations between artifacts picked out in a polythetic stylistic description. As a historical assertion, reading from history to style, the necessary condition of style is that the artifacts must have been made in the same way.

This very general account requires considerable fine-tuning, especially to meet some special cases in which archaeologists and art historians tend to be interested. For instance, if completely constrained making still results in products with style, then ants building a hill are working in a style. From a social scientist's or humanist's point of view, this implication may be counterintuitive or unacceptable, but only if we feel we have to build into a theory of style various further assumptions about rule-governed selection, intention, communication, and so forth. From a biologist's point of view, this implication may be unexceptionable. Although she might not say that ant hills have a style, nevertheless she may use ant hills diagnostically or as one element in a polythetic taxonomy to differentiate one species of ant from another, to recognize changes in the responses of ants to their environment, and so forth. She will here be extracting all the classificatory and historical information a stylistic description provides. To rule out cases of this kind, but now confronting difficulties we have already reviewed, we must say that the qualified necessary condition of style is that artifacts must have been made in the same *but, for the maker, potentially variable* way.

The account also has the consequence that a Vermeer and an extremely successful forgery of it might belong to different styles, insofar as they were made in different ways. The consequence is also unexceptionable. The Vermeer is in the style "Depicting Dutch landscapes and interiors with great sincerity using mid-seventeenth-century oils"; the forgery is in the style "Copying Old Masters with considerable cynicism using twentieth-century paints." The forgery is polythetically similar to the Vermeer in some formal respects, but also to other modern forgeries. Here, we are merely recognizing once again that the stylistic attributes of artifacts may be exhibited or unexhibited, formal, functional, symbolic, or institutional, and so forth. Moreover, polythetic classification might always end up judging an original and a copy to be polythetically very similar in many relevant attributes, grouping them together stylistically—as when we are studying not forgeries but a student's copy of a master's drawing, an artist's homage to an ancestor, or other productions.

Although it must be one of the prime desiderata of archaeology and art history, a fully satisfying account of making itself has yet to be worked out (compare Chapters 4 and 8). We must avoid relying on assumptions about making those artifacts we ordinarily believe to have style, for here style is our *explanandum*. Strictly speaking, our account of making, as of language, must be established independently of a theory of style.

At the limit, our concept of making must extend to natural substances left materially unaltered by human craft but constituted symbolically and institutionally. We want to include rocks brought into a Japanese garden (in the style of Buson) or a pile of felt assembled in a New York gallery (in the style of Robert Morris). Among other things, the "making" in such cases is simply transporting and exhibiting—not, in some instances, a negligible task. Even if materially worked by human hands and tools, alteration can be slight: early statuary might have derived from a tree trunk gouged by a few rough blows of the axe. Representation itself might derive from the ambiguity, for the human perceptual system, of a completely happenstance clustering of marks and scratches on a surface: the "making" here can simply be the inaugural phenomenon of "seeing-as" (see Chapters 2 and 3). The ordinary (and for most purposes comprehensive) art historical concept of making seems to require the partial or whole manufacture, transport, exhibition, symbolic interpretation, and institutional affiliation of a thing, but it is not clear that these are all and always necessary or sufficient criteria.

Interesting formulations have been put forward by Richard Wollheim, for whom the stylistic features of an artifact are just those dependent on the "processes of acting as a painter" (sculptor, builder, and so on), and Kendall Walton, who suggests that in style "we 'see' in the work the action of producing it."[55] "Acting as a painter" or the "action of producing"—making—must be highly variable by time and place. Much stylistic description in art history might be (and often is) taken as a rich historical description of variable ways of making artifacts. Needless to say, by all my earlier arguments, we cannot read securely from the stylistic description to the history of making: "acting as a painter" may not be so easily or at all correctly "seen in" the artifact.

Walton opens the Pandora's box by reminding us that how an artifact *appears* to have been made may be sufficient for critical purposes, generating description in my inclusive sense of style *(a)*. Under the inclusive definition, an observer writes up his "vivid impressions of the physical behavior of the artist as well as perhaps more ambiguous impressions of his motivations and personality," generally construing the artifact as an "apparent intentional act."[56] However, problematic cases are easily located (and see Chapters 4 and 10). The forged Vermeer appears to have been made by a Dutch painter using mid-seventeenth-century oils. The metopes of the Parthenon appear to have been made so as to present the velvety white surface of crystalline marble. The marked bones from Cueva Morin appear to have been made by the cutting tools of a Neanderthal. Only independent evidence will tell us that the Vermeer was actually made by a modern criminal, that the metopes were once fully painted, or that the bones were gnawed by carnivores.

Our new evidence about authenticity, condition, or artifactuality itself could certainly lead us to see other attributes in the artifact, that is, to a substantial revision in the stylistic description. Nevertheless, this possibility does not establish that we will always eventually see the real history of making from an (endlessly revisable) stylistic description, but only that stylistic description could be underwritten by any number of coherent scenarios for "apparent" acts of making—none of which can be seen from the description itself to be a historical specification. "We need to be careful," Walton rightly concludes, "about in what sense the property of appearing to have been made in a certain manner is to be 'located' in the work in which it does so appear."[57]

Read in the other direction, from history to style, an archaeologically identifiable system of making artifacts (clause *c*) is the explanation for style (clause *a*). Evidently this account includes but is not limited to a notion of making as the use of a "language"; making may or may not require selecting from alternative states. In an adequate account of making, some steps in the sequence might be regarded as completely constrained by the physical nature of the medium, the maker's knowledge and skill, and so forth, some steps as requiring rule-governed selection, and some steps as completely unconstrained (see Chapters 3, 4, 7, and 8). Making at any of these levels may be stylistic or nonstylistic, for polythetic classification may or may not be able to locate any repetitions in or similarities for some elements of production. However, insofar as making cannot be entirely unique,

55. Wollheim, "Pictorial Style," 134; Walton, "Style and the Products and Processes of Art," 51. See also Guy Sircello, *Mind and Art* (Princeton, 1972), and Hermerén, *Influence in Art and Literature*, 21.

56. Walton, "Style and the Products and Processes of Art," 52, 54.

57. Walton, "Style and the Products and Processes of Art," 56.

every time a new artifact is produced, any balance or permutation of these possibilities results in an artifact with style.

History as Privileged Stylistic Description

Little has been said so far about how an artifact-production system might be "archaeologically identifiable" (clause *c*) without using inferences from stylistic description. My theory of style states only that an archaeology of production—of language, of making—will be the context for, control upon, and explanation of style. "In the study of the arts," Ackerman asserts, "works—not institutions or people—are the primary data."[58] Data they certainly are, but it is the archaeology of institutions and people that, in the logic of the theory of style, must be primary.

However, "independent evidence" for production—a notion relied upon heavily so far—is in a sense a contradiction in terms. Insofar as archaeology provides evidence of institutions or people at all—a chronicle or archive, a letter or interview, a manual or contract, a tool kit or workshop—it cannot be evidence independent of style, for as I have noted, all documents and artifacts of whatever kind can themselves be brought under a stylistic description. When we refer to seasonal technology to account for a taxonomy of Mousterian tools, or to Jackson Pollock's interviews to account for a pictorial interpretation of his paintings, we are simply underwriting one stylistic description (the taxonomy or interpretation) with another (the technology or document). For the moment, in a given analysis one description is "style," the other "history." But both, as archaeological evidence, are no more and no less than stylistic descriptions.

From this point of view, "history" is therefore a stylistic description specially privileged, in a given archaeological analysis, according to theoretical commitments beyond any possible reach of evidence. (In Chapter 10, I explore one set of ways in which "formal relations" can be translated into statements about causes and contents. But the analysis does not escape the stricture stated here: psychoanalytic theory, like other theories [compare Chapter 8], simply offers a scheme for privileging certain stylistic descriptions—certain observations of morphology and style—as the manifestations of history.) Any stylistic description can become "history," the privileged description, by theoretical stipulation. We could, by stipulation, explain the "style" of Mousterian seasonal technology by a taxonomy of Mousterian tools or the "style" of Pollock's interviews by a pictorial interpretation of his paintings.

My theory of style implies only that we must *choose* which description of archaeological evidence will be used in a given analysis as the privileged description, as the "history" by which all and sundry other stylistic descriptions will be explained. Once we have made this choice, throughout the analysis we are completely constrained by it. However we

58. Ackerman, "Style," 164.

specify our history—as technology, as intention, as institution, as unconscious motivation—we cannot read back to it by or attempt to find it through any other stylistic description. We must choose the description that we stipulate gives history to us, and proceed from there. For the moment, the historical description has become irreducible and incorrigible: it is the source, guarantor, and test of any styles it underwrites.

The theory of style says nothing one way or another about *which* stylistic description of whatever archaeological evidence should be privileged as "history" in a given analysis. That decision, as I suggest elsewhere (for example, Chapters 3, 8, and 10), is taken and defended on other grounds.

Chapter 7

NARRATIVITY AND THE NARMER PALETTE

The hypothesis of a rigorous, sure, and subtle form is naturally more fertile.

—Jacques Derrida, *Dissemination*

In this chapter, I consider one well-known example of ancient Egyptian image making, the great carved schist cosmetic palette of "King Narmer" (Fig. 7.4), probably made about 3000 B.C., from the point of view of aspects of contemporary narrative theory. I do not consider "narrative in Egyptian art" in general. Our understanding of the rules and practices of Egyptian image making is not yet powerful enough to handle complex questions of metaphor, allegory, and narrative in the tradition as a whole.[1] I prefer to attend closely to one work. At any rate, narrative theory requires us to investigate individual representational productions at a very specific level. Indeed, the Narmer Palette poses special problems. As an early, if not the first, "canonical" image in the Egyptian tradition, it should not be assimilated to later Egyptian practices of narrative representation. Instead, there are good reasons to regard it as a typical "prehistoric" work, belonging to a tradition of image making in the Nile valley dating back to the eighth millennium B.C. and possibly before, for it clearly belongs to a small group of decorated palettes made in the late fourth

1. For such general attempts, see H. J. Kantor's contribution to the well-known Archaeological Institute of America symposium on ancient pictorial narration (*American Journal of Archaeology* 61 [1957], 43–91) and

millennium B.C., or "late prehistoric" period, such as the Oxford, Hunter's, and Battlefield Palettes (Figs. 7.1–7.3), and some associated works.[2] The boundaries of this group of artifacts are not well defined. Some palettes usually included in it do not belong to the pictorial system exemplified on the four palettes just mentioned; thus, although they are tokens of a single, general artifact type, the decorated cosmetic palette, they are not tokens of the same *meaning* type. Moreover, some of the objects are probably forgeries; some are too poorly preserved to interpret. Finally, relations between the palettes within this group are, in themselves, disjunctive; and the Narmer Palette stands somewhat apart from the others.

Date, Context, and Function

Sometimes called "predynastic," "precanonical," or "Pre-Formal," late prehistoric Egyptian art—to which the Narmer Palette belongs—has a double historical relation with the "canonical" art of the dynastic "Great Tradition" of the third, second, and first millennia B.C.[3] On the one hand, the Great Tradition derived techniques and motifs from many prehistoric sources, tracing back to early rock art and to the material culture of the Nagada I period (about 4700–3700 B.C.)[4] as well as to the pottery decoration and relief sculpture of the Nagada II/III periods (about 3700–3000 B.C.).[5] On the other hand, dynastic image makers and their patrons forged a new administrative apparatus and developed a mode of representation appropriate to it. The emerging bureaucratic, patrimonial state of the early Old Kingdom (about 3000–2700 B.C.) approached the prehistoric legacy with actively selective interests. At the very least, in the emergence of the canonical tradition some aspects of earlier image making were avoided or suppressed, while others were adopted and refined.[6] These developments are important processes in their own right. However, and as we would expect (see Chapter 3), neither the earlier prehistoric sources for nor the later

G. A. Gaballa, *Narrative in Egyptian Art* (Mainz, 1977). Although interesting reflections of Egyptological approaches, neither makes the minimally necessary narratological distinctions. Elizabeth Meyer, "Component Design as a Narrative Device in Amarna Tomb Art," in *Pictorial Narrative in Antiquity and the Middle Ages*, ed. Herbert L. Kessler and Marianna Shreve Simpson (Washington, D.C., 1985), 35–51, seems to consider, to some extent, the relations between story and text in Amarna art as well as some extraneous matters. Roland Tefnin has produced the fundamental semiological studies; see his "Image et histoire: Réflexions sur l'usage documentaire de l'image égyptienne," *Chronique d'Égypte* 54 (1979), 281–44; "Image, écriture, récit: A propos des representations de la bataille de Qadesh," *Göttinger Miszellen: Beiträge zur ägyptologische Diskussion* 47 (1981), 55–76; and "Discours et iconicité dans l'art égyptien," *Annales d'Histoire de l'Art et d'Archéologie* 5 (1983), 5–17.

2. The best comprehensive photographic publication of the palettes is Henri Asselberghs, *Chaos en Beheersing: Documenten uit aeneolithisch Egypte* (Leiden, 1963), and see also W. M. Flinders Petrie, *Ceremonial Slate Palettes* (London, 1953). For further references and a framework for the history of late prehistoric Egyptian art, see Whitney Davis, *The Canonical Tradition in Ancient Egyptian Art* (New York, 1989), chap. 6.

3. For the term "precanonical," see Davis, *Canonical Tradition*, chap. 6, esp. 119–20; for "Pre-Formal," see Barry J. Kemp, *Ancient Egypt: Anatomy of a Civilization* (London, 1989), chap. 1. For the "Great Tradition," see Bruce Trigger, "The Rise of Egyptian Civilization," in *Ancient Egypt: A Social History*, ed. Bruce Trigger et al. (Cambridge, 1983), 1–70.

4. Davis, *Canonical Tradition*, 116–26.

5. Davis, *Canonical Tradition*, 135–71; Bruce Williams, *Decorated Pottery and the Art of Nagada III: A Documentary Essay*, Münchner Ägyptologische Studien 45 (Munich, 1988).

6. See note 3 and Bruce Williams and Thomas Logan,

canonical legacies of late prehistoric image making necessarily tell us anything about the meaning of individual late prehistoric representations in their own historical, "cultural," and semiological contexts.

The striking homogeneousness of dynastic Egyptian art was probably produced by artists following a systematic set of sophisticated rules in an "academic" setting. By contrast, late prehistoric image making is characterized by considerable stylistic and iconographic heterogeneity. Many works cannot now be associated with academic contexts of production or even with elite contexts of patronage (although our lack of archaeological evidence does not prove that such contexts did not exist). It is not surprising, then, that the late prehistoric works are different both from canonical productions and among themselves.

The sequence of routine, mostly undecorated funerary palettes discovered in dated prehistoric graves establishes a relative chronology possibly applicable to the decorated examples.[7] It seems likely, on these grounds, that of the four decorated palettes mentioned above, the Oxford Palette (Fig. 7.1) is the earliest (probably Nagada IId, about 3300 B.C.) and the Narmer Palette the latest (probably Nagada IIIa–b/early First Dynasty, about 3000 B.C.). The Hunter's and Battlefield Palettes (Figs. 7.2, 7.3) may fall in between, although there is nothing in their pictorial systems that would prevent the Hunter's Palette from being contemporary with the Oxford, and the Battlefield with the Narmer. Indeed, a chronology of the images should be based upon study of their pictorial systems rather than upon a typology imposed from the outside, in this case, from the series of routine funerary palettes. However, here, for convenience, I will abide by the conventional dating.

Several of the canonical rules of image making were not fully codified until the Third and Fourth Dynasties. However, the most critical phase in the formulation of the canon was the Nagada III/early First Dynasty period, the period in which the Narmer Palette likely was made. In this period, a potentially national state structure—with its associated administrative, military, commercial, and liturgical instruments—was emerging in Upper Egyptian polities like Hierakonpolis and perhaps Nagada, even though the activities of the earliest rulers of these polities cannot at present be documented in full detail.[8] In itself, the chronology does not prove that the palettes were made *for* the rulers by artists working for them, perhaps in the rulers' centers of residence, as some interpretations—such as those attributing a "propagandistic" function to the images—seem to require. Although court-affiliated artists can be identified in the early dynastic period, somewhat later, we cannot say whether the late prehistoric palettes were manufactured by such specialists.[9] Some of the palettes could have been produced in a traditional village craft economy by artisans unattached to the growing, if still small-scale, centralized administrations.

Unfortunately, then, the relative chronology of the late prehistoric palettes cannot be

---

"The Metropolitan Museum Knife Handle and Aspects of Pharaonic Imagery Before Narmer," *Journal of Near Eastern Studies* 46 (1987), 245–84.

7. Petrie, *Ceremonial Slate Palettes;* H. J. Kantor, "The Final Phase of Predynastic Culture: Gerzean or Semainean (?)," *Journal of Near Eastern Studies* 3 (1944), 110–36; Werner Kaiser, "Zur inneren Chronologie der Naqadakultur," *Archaeologia Geographica* 6 (1957), 69–77.

8. See Trigger, "The Rise of Egyptian Civilization"; Michael Hoffman, *Egypt Before the Pharaohs* (New York, 1979); Fekri Hassan, "The Predynastic of Egypt," *Journal of World Prehistory* 2 (1988), 135–88.

9. Whitney Davis, "Artists and Patrons in Predynastic

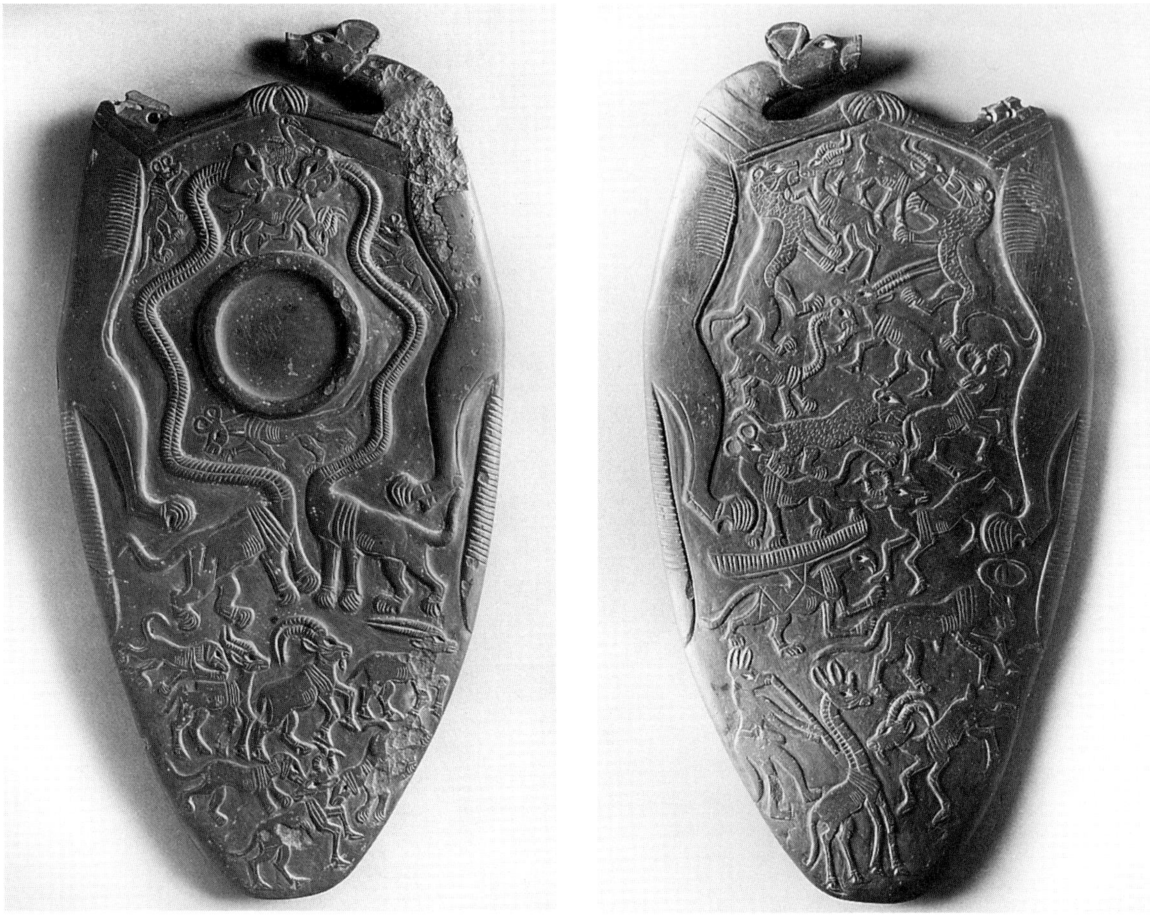

Fig. 7.1. The Oxford Palette (left: obverse; right: reverse), late predynastic period (Nagada IIc/d), about 3200 B.C. Courtesy the Visitors of the Ashmolean Museum, Oxford University.

backed up by extensive independent archaeological evidence about their contexts—a desideratum, I have suggested (Chapter 6), for any historical explanation of style. Unlike routine funerary palettes from prehistoric graves, two of the larger, decorated palettes, the Oxford and Narmer Palettes (Figs. 7.1, 7.4), were unearthed in the "Main Deposit" at Hierakonpolis, a much later collection of heterogeneous earlier artifacts deposited as late as the end of the Old Kingdom. As a "secondary" archaeological context, the Main Deposit provides no direct information about the "original" date, function, audience, or meaning of either palette. All it tells us is that later viewers valued the earlier palettes—for whatever reason—and determined to deposit them, along with a number of other objects, perhaps in order to hide or preserve them (we do not know).[10]

and Early Dynastic Egypt," *Studien zur Altägyptischen Kultur* 10 (1983), 119–39.

10. See J. E. Quibell and F. W. Green, *Hierakonpolis*, 2 vols. (London, 1900–1901); Barbara Adams, *Ancient Hierakonpolis Supplement* (Warminster, 1975).

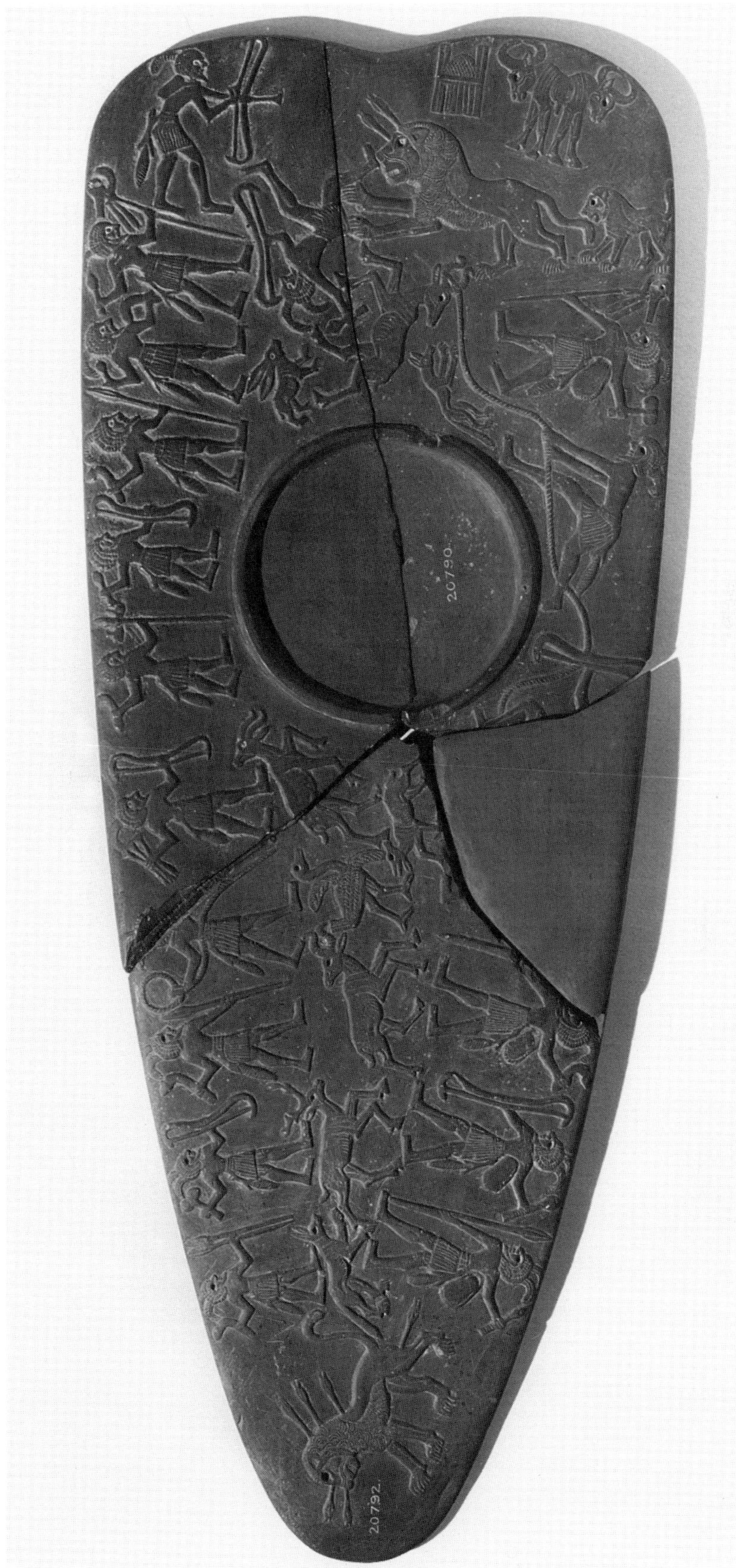

Fig. 7.2. The Hunter's Palette, late predynastic period (Nagada IId?), about 3200 B.C. Courtesy the Trustees of the British Museum.

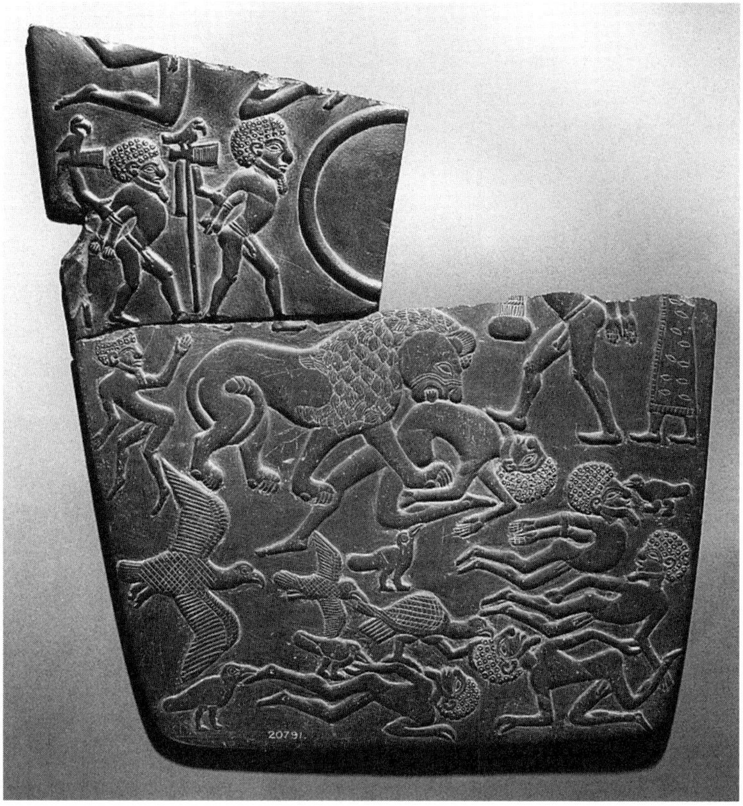

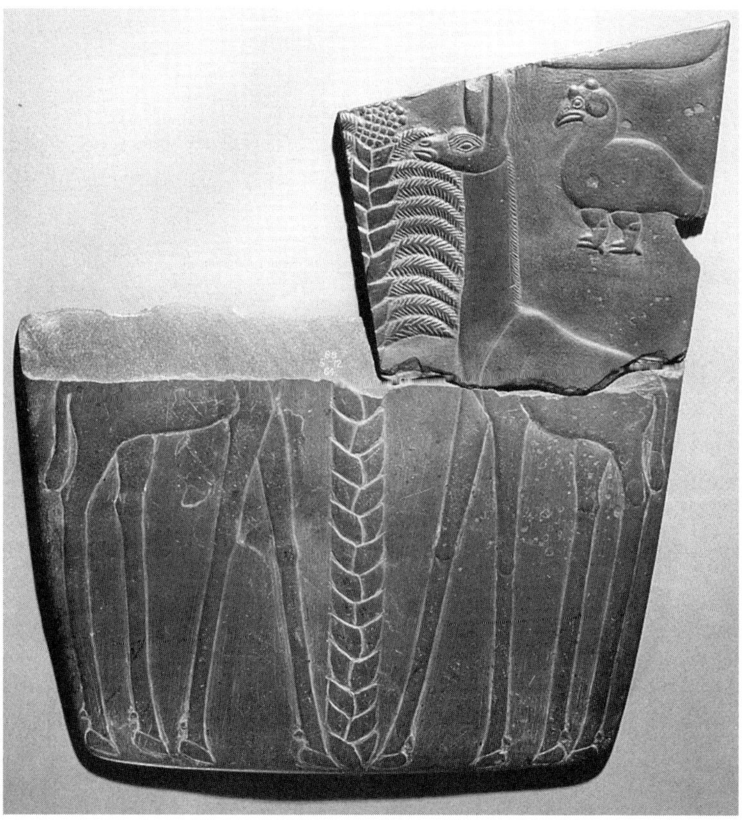

Fig. 7.3. The Battlefield Palette (top: obverse; bottom: reverse), early First Dynasty (?) (Nagada IId/III?), about 3000 B.C. Collection of the British Museum (large fragment) and Ashmolean Museum (small fragment). Courtesy the Trustees of the British Museum.

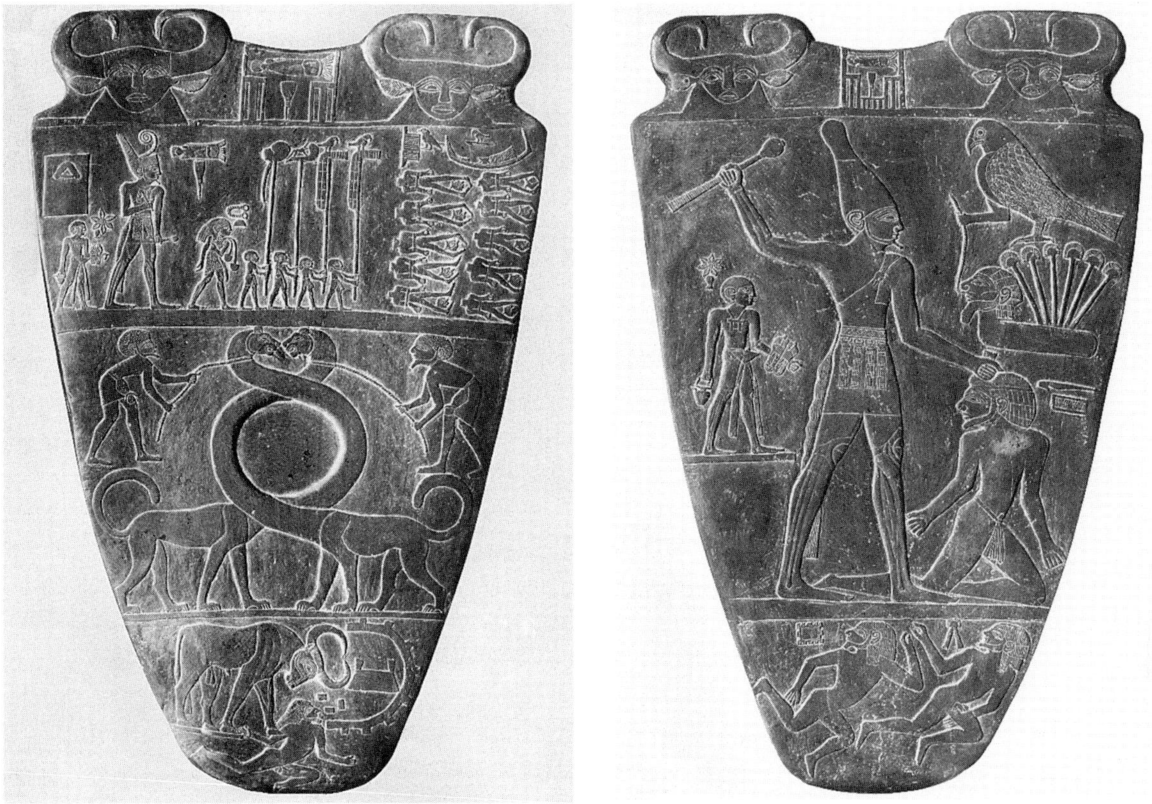

Fig. 7.4. The Narmer Palette (left: obverse; right: reverse), early First Dynasty (Nagada IIIa/b or Horizon A/B), about 3000 B.C.

Earlier commentators on the palettes wrongly supposed that the Main Deposit was, in fact, a late prehistoric assemblage. Considering the objects found in it, they regarded it as a dedication at an early temple of Horus (for instance, a gold hawk, a typical later emblem of the god, was discovered in the deposit) or Hathor (for instance, according to a common misreading of the iconography of the Narmer Palette from the deposit, the cows' faces on its top edge depict Hathor). Thus they reasoned that the palettes were temple dedications to divinities made by "royal" patrons, for the iconography of both Horus and Hathor was later associated with the pharaoh.[11] However, although it is logically possible that the objects had a dedicatory or votive function in a temple, we now know that we have no actual evidence to this effect for the two palettes from the Main Deposit. Therefore I do not assume a connection between the palettes from the Main Deposit and temple cult, temple furniture, or temple dedications—even though my interpretation is not incompatible with a such a connection.

Contextual information on the other late prehistoric palettes and associated objects usually grouped with the Narmer Palette is equally hard to come by. The Hunter's and

11. For such interpretations, see Asselberghs, *Chaos en Beheersing*, and Elise J. Baumgartel, *The Cultures of Prehistoric Egypt II* (Oxford, 1960), 81–105.

Battlefield Palettes (Figs. 7.2, 7.3), the two images most closely related to the theme of the Narmer Palette, have no reliable recorded provenances. In view of this, it is surprising that assertions about the function, audience, or meanings of the palettes can be found throughout the literature.

Some scholars have confidently assumed the "ceremonial" or "liturgical" use of the palettes, implying that they were set up for display in a residence, temple, or public place or were stored and used on special ritual occasions. It is logically possible that the Narmer Palette had a "ceremonial" nature; my interpretation is not logically incompatible with the thesis. But there is not a shred of independent evidence in the matter. Even if correct, the hypothesis of "ceremonial" function is not helpful when we do not know what the "ceremony" itself was all about. Perhaps some late prehistoric images document ceremonies known from later textual sources, although the anachronism is dangerous. For example, for Siegfried Schott and Jacques Vandier the Narmer Palette commemorates a celebration of victory over defeated "northern" enemies or a royal jubilee celebration later known as the *Sed* festival.[12] Nicholas Millet has interpreted the decorated macehead of Narmer as depicting, or even documenting, a festival of the "Appearance of the King of Lower Egypt" stated on the Palermo Stone (a Fifth Dynasty chronicle describing earlier "history") as having occurred in the First Dynasty.[13] But even if the images do, in fact, depict or document particular ceremonies, it does not necessarily follow that the objects or images themselves were also used in or made for those very ceremonies. (Although the reliefs on the Ara Pacis Augustae in part depict a ceremony conducted at that altar, J.-L. David's *Tennis Court Oath* was painted for exhibition, not for the swearing of the oath itself.) And certainly nothing at all is discovered about the way in which the images, qua images, represent the supposed ceremonies—that is, about the particular metaphorical or narrative way in which they "document" or otherwise imagine them.

Possibly contradicting the "ceremonial" hypothesis, other writers have urged that the decorated palettes had a "magical" function. The palettes could have promoted success in the hunt or battle or secured the favor of a totem or divinity, rendered "magically" efficacious by the images themselves, by "ritual" use of the object, or by both together. The diversity and vagueness of these accounts indicates that they are implausible.[14] There is no archaeological evidence that the palettes or the images carved on them had a "magical" function. Although some Egyptologists have cited the "magical" properties of funerary statues or liturgical implements in later dynastic art and cult, it is gross anachronism to suppose that meanings so closely tied to the canonical theology and iconography of the hierocratic state were present in the late prehistoric context.

12. Siegfried Schott, *Hieroglyphen: Untersuchungen zum Ursprung der Schrift*, Akademie der Wissenschaften und der Literature (Mainz), Abhandlungen der Geistes- und Sozialwissenschaftlichen Klasse 24 (Wiesbaden, 1950); Jacques Vandier, *Manuel d'archéologie égyptienne*, vol. 1, *Les époques de formation* (Paris, 1952), 594–96.

13. Nicholas B. Millet, "The Narmer Macehead and Related Objects," *Journal of the American Research Center in Egypt* 27 (1990), 53–59; see also Patrick Gautier and Béatrix Midant-Reynes, "La tête de massue du Roi Scorpion," *Archéo-Nil: Bullétin de la Société pour l'Étude des Cultures Prépharaoniques de la Vallée du Nil* 5 (1995), 87–127.

14. For versions of this interpretation, see Petrie, *Ceremonial Slate Palettes*, and the treatments of the earlier (Nagada I and II) decorated palettes by Baumgartel, *The Cultures of Prehistoric Egypt II*, and Asselberghs, *Chaos en Beheersing*.

Finally, some recent writers have argued that the palettes might have served, as Michael Hoffman puts it, as "symbols of power generated as political propaganda."[15] However, the possibility that the objects were literally used as "propaganda" does not exhaust the ways people could have attached sense to images with the pictorial system I identify below. This functional specification, like any other, needs to be secured on independent archaeological grounds. Unfortunately the evidence is not compelling. "Propaganda" is usually addressed by a particular, often elite group to an outside, often mass audience. But we do not find the palettes in wide circulation, mass production, or public display, or in any contexts of nonelite or popular reception, consumption, and use, as we would expect to do if they functioned literally as elite "propaganda" aimed at the population. Perhaps the evidence is simply unavailable, as it is for the "ceremonial" or "magical" hypotheses; but if this is so, we should not simply assume the possibility as the very basis for a historical interpretation.

We cannot determine whether the objects were viewed by a public circle wider than that of the maker and his or her immediate or initial beholder. Of course, since we have no direct evidence for external "elite" or other patronage, even these identities could have been the same actual individual—for "maker" and "beholder" are simply "positions" within the field, or scene, of representation that anyone, who may not literally or physically possess that position, can potentially imagine himself or herself to occupy.[16] Despite their sometimes unwieldy bulk, even the largest palettes were made, we might suppose, to be inspected by at least some viewers, however few in number or restricted their access to the viewing situation. The images seem to be organized, as images, to be "read" in a specific way, if not by actually handling the object then at least by moving around it, possibly just in the "mind's eye." The physical reality of this situation and activity of beholding is totally unknown. Did it transpire in a ritual setting? Was the object set up for display so people could see its two sides, or could one actually take it in one's hands? Could people

15. Hoffman, *Egypt Before the Pharaohs,* 299; cf. Kemp, *Ancient Egypt,* chap. 1, and Elizabeth Finkenstaedt, "Violence and Kingship: The Evidence of the Palettes," *Zeitschrift für Ägyptische Sprache* 111 (1984), 107–10.

16. This phenomenon, essential to any understanding of pictorial narrative, is the subject of brilliant essays by Michael Fried: "Representing Representation: On the Central Group in Courbet's *Studio,*" in *Allegory and Representation,* ed. Stephen Greenblatt (Baltimore, Md., 1981), 94–127, and "The Structure of Beholding in Courbet's *Burial at Ornans,*" *Critical Inquiry* 9 (1983), 635–83. Fried's analysis suggests that among other things the perimeter, or boundary, of the image should not be located at its ostensible, physical, or literal boundary—for example, the manufactured frame of a painting or the actual "edge" of a decorated palette. In a more important sense, the "boundary" of the image extends to, and even beyond, the place "outside" the image where the "beholder" interprets it, for example, by narrativizing it; and the beholder's body is "in" the image itself to the extent that, for example, he or she must approach, inspect, and perhaps even manipulate the image in order to interpret it. For the dynamic and "deconstruction" of the frame in representation, see Jacques Derrida, *The Truth in Painting,* trans. Geoff Bennington and Ian McLeod (Chicago, 1987), 15–148. Art historians' typical insistence that the "frame" of an image is coextensive with the physical perimeter of an artifact is one reason the narrative dimension—the textually organized spatial and temporal dimension and duration—of pictorial image making has been so difficult to identify and interpret, for such a frame, so literally understood, cuts through the continuous interaction between the visual text and its "beholder," the place in or process by which metaphor, narrative, or any other species of textual meaning is constructed (cf. Wolfgang Iser, *The Act of Reading* [Baltimore, 1978]). As Derrida shows, the "frame"—that middle term between the "content" of the image itself and its ostensibly surrounding social "context"—can be regarded as a fully permeable membrane or even as what constitutes, by separating, "content" and "context" themselves. As I show below, narrative—or, more properly, narrativization—occurs in, or as, the frame.

see what the palette depicted, or, like stained glass windows high in the wall of a medieval cathedral, was the image largely unreadable in its details?[17]

All of these questions about possible functions and uses are somewhat beside a point that, surprisingly, still needs to be made; although they are not irrelevant questions, we need to address a prior consideration. Irrespective of the possible votive, ceremonial, commemorative, ritual, magical, documentary, exchange, propagandistic, or other functions of the decorated objects, they have a *representational* function. In some ways this conclusion is obvious. However, it is both broader and more penetrating than the specifications I have noted—for all of these must be seen as specifications of a possible function of what is already functioning as representation. In fact, most of the specifications I have noted are too general. Other activities or artifacts apart from images, as well as other sorts of images, could have served successfully in ceremonial, ritual, magical, or propagandistic ways, and probably did. Therefore we still have to offer an account of *these* objects as fulfilling *these* functions by way of *these* images. How could we expect to determine what the function, social use, or cultural meaning of the images might have been if, as I suspect, we have not even identified the properties or system of representation in the images themselves?

Along with the Oxford, Hunter's, Battlefield, and possibly several other decorated palettes, the Narmer Palette, I suggest, functions as a complex narrative representation. Since we have no independent archaeological information about this, or any other, function and meaning of the images, this hypothesis can be evaluated only by examining its power to account for the images themselves better than the competing hypotheses (see Chapter 3). A narrative analysis is compatible with any of the general functional hypotheses I have already noted; a "ceremonial," "ritual," or other image can certainly also be a narrative one. In particular, then, the narrative analysis must account for the properties of the images more adequately than the most popular interpretive method adopted in the literature. This procedure claims to identify what an image "means" by comparing its motifs with motifs in other, earlier or later images, some of which supposedly can be deciphered on the basis of independent evidence or associations (for the history and general procedure of this approach, see Chapter 5). And indeed, the narratological analysis, whatever its own flaws and uncertainties, fares much better than this crudely "iconographical," source-hunting and parallel-quoting method—for this method fails not only on empirical but also, and more important, on theoretical grounds.

Several writers have investigated the possible "sources" of and parallels for the decorated palettes in earlier and contemporary media, like rock art, pottery design, wall painting, or textile decoration.[18] Since these were, apparently, ancient and rich traditions, it is not surprising that we can discover apparent antecedents and analogs for many elements of the late prehistoric images, for they form just part of a larger, longer history of visual production in the Nile valley. This tradition might even have derived some mannerisms

17. Of course, we should not assume that what seems visually illegible to us was indeed illegible to viewers familiar with the established conventions of the iconography. For the narrative dynamics of apparently "illegible" images, see Richard Brilliant's discussion of the upper registers of Trajan's Column in his *Visual Narratives: Storytelling in Etruscan and Roman Art* (New York, 1984).

18. E.g., see Kantor, "The Final Phase of Predynastic Culture," and Williams, *Decorated Pottery and the Art of Nagada* III.

and motifs from older or contemporary Near Eastern sources, perhaps mediated by small Mesopotamian seals (although to date such seals found in late prehistoric Egyptian contexts do not themselves actually document the diffusion of the motifs in question).[19]

However, it is not at all clear what any of this painstaking research really manages to discover. Since all cultural practices necessarily have some kind of cultural heredity (just as biological individuals have a biological heredity), in principle we can always find a stylistic or iconographic "source" for an element of an image. We could continually extend the parallels to other and yet further associations. But to identify a source or a parallel is not thereby to understand the role of the element in any one of its immediate semiological contexts. Although an image maker derives a motif from another's work or even from another culture, he might put it to quite independent use, altering its established meaning by inserting it into a new formal or semantic setting; as I urge in Chapter 6, there are no true stylistic or depictive "synonyms." For example, some commentators have suggested that the intertwined "serpopards" on the Narmer Palette symbolize the "unification" of Upper and Lower Egypt—a signification that presumably had nothing to do with the "original" Mesopotamian prototype of serpent-necked beasts.[20] Source hunting alone will not expose such disjunctions. Indeed, unqualified by attention to the formal (for example, compositional) and semantic (for example, metaphorical or narrative) coherence of each image, source hunting based on ramified comparison among the disparate elements of many images, taken out of their immediate contexts, distracts attention from the meaning of any single image (see Chapter 5). The possibility of an earlier origin for some late prehistoric Egyptian motif tells us nothing one way or another about the symbolic function—for example, the metaphorical or narrative status—of this motif *as it was replicated by a late prehistoric image maker.* It would be interesting to find that the image maker expected his viewers to recognize the earlier instances as an aspect of the motif he used, and thus as an element of its connotation. But we can only establish this pictorial possibility by scrutinizing the entire mechanics of his image, not just by identifying the earlier analog. A sign made according to the criteria of one symbol system is a different sign from that made according to different criteria, even if the morphology of the two signs is formally indiscernible. But only scrutiny of each image, as a semiological whole, will tell us what kind of symbol system it might be.[21]

19. See Henri Frankfort, *Studies in Early Pottery of the Near East* (London, 1925), 1:93–142; idem, *The Birth of Civilization in the Near East* (Bloomington, Ind., 1951), 121–37; H. J. Kantor, "Early Mesopotamian Relations with Egypt," *Journal of Near Eastern Studies* 1 (1942), 174–213; idem, "Further Evidence for Early Mesopotamian Relations with Egypt," *Journal of Near Eastern Studies* 11 (1952), 239–50; R. M. Boehmer, "Orientalische Einflüsse auf verzierten Messergriffen aus dem prädynastischen Ägypten," *Archäologische Mitteilungen aus Iran (DAI Teheran)*, n.s., 7 (1974), 15–50; Markus Mode, "Frühes Vorderasien und frühes Ägypten: Motivgeschichtliche Berührungspunkte in der Kunst," *Halle'sche Beiträge zur Orientwissenschaft* 6 (1984), 11–35; and Beatrice Teissier, "Glyptic Evidence for a Connection Between Iran, Syro-Palestine, and Egypt in the Fourth and Third Millennia," *Iran* 25 (1987), 27–53.

20. See Finkenstaedt, "Violence and Kingship," and Pierre Gilbert, "Fauves au long cou communs à l'art égyptien et à l'art sumérien," *Chronique d'Égypte* 22 (1949), 38–41.

21. On the nonsynonymy of formally similar semiotic entities—a phenomenon with obvious implications both for "vulgar" iconographic comparison and for the more rigorous procedures of structuralist analysis—see Nelson Goodman, "On Likeness of Meaning," *Analysis* 1 (1949), 1–7, and idem, *Languages of Art: An Approach to the Theory of Symbols* (Indianapolis, 1972). For the dynamics of indiscernibility, see Arthur C. Danto, *The Transfiguration of the Commonplace* (New York, 1981).

Exactly the same considerations apply when we consider the replications of late prehistoric motifs in later, canonical art. By definition, the late prehistoric images form one part of the context for this subsequent production. But the late prehistoric image maker could hardly have intended all of the selections canonical image makers would make from particular aspects of his production (for example, they drew what I have called the "core motifs" of canonical iconography from the prehistoric repertory).[22] To use George Kubler's term, the late prehistoric image maker could not have been fully aware at the time of the "serial position" he occupied in a continuous art history.[23] But despite the obvious anachronism, it has been extremely tempting for many writers to take what we know of canonical art, hieroglyphic script, or Egyptian ritual, mythology, and cult and apply it back to images produced in an almost wholly preliterate, less complex prehistoric society. The procedure is completely unsound methodologically. In every case, independent evidence would be required to show that the earlier and the later images did refer to their objects, as images, in the same or very closely similar ways, but in most cases, the only evidence adduced for this is the "parallel" itself (for such dubious use of formal and stylistic parallels, see Chapter 5). Luckily, it turns out that little of real interest hinges on information gleaned from canonical iconography. Here or there a motif might be more precisely identified or a glyph deciphered. But by and large, and as we would fully expect, the late prehistoric image maker's practices were intelligible to him, and presumably to his audience, in their own terms. In fact, these terms were strikingly disjunct from the terms ultimately adopted in canonical representation. Late prehistoric narrative images, including the Narmer Palette, cannot be assimilated easily either to what came before or to what came after.

Late Prehistoric Narrative Images

Whatever their order of manufacture may have been, and despite their common status as the background for the canonical tradition, close scrutiny of major late prehistoric palettes—the Oxford, Hunter's, Battlefield, and Narmer Palettes (Figs. 7.1–7.4)—reveals that they are related to one another in Erwin Panofsky's "iconographic" sense. That is, they are related "disjunctively": although certain motifs might be morphologically constant throughout the series, comparable with instances in earlier or later art production, each image exhibits a distinctive metaphorics. Thus, while form remains relatively stable, meaning is disjunct from one image to the next. Although each image depends upon, or "works with," earlier images, it also "works away from" them in an evolving discourse, what Panofsky meant by an "iconography" as a continuous history of repetition and revision. The specific meaningfulness of each image is a matter of its own coherence within its own particular context, its social horizons, of manufacture and use, what Panofsky meant by its "iconological" context.[24] Unfortunately, although considerable attention has been paid to

22. Davis, *Canonical Tradition*, 64–82.

23. George Kubler, *The Shape of Time: Remarks on the History of Things* (New Haven, Conn., 1962), 54–61.

24. Erwin Panofsky, *Studies in Iconology* (Oxford, 1939), chap. 1, and idem, *Renaissance and Renascences in Western Art* (Stockholm, 1960). An excellent discus-

"iconographical" constancies in prehistoric and canonical Egyptian art, little attention has been paid to the defining disjunctiveness of iconography in its "iconological" contexts. Late prehistoric Egyptian images are disjunct from earlier prehistoric and later canonical representation precisely in the fact that they seem to require a particular form of narrativization as the condition of their iconological intelligibility.

Here I cannot consider the disjunctive metaphorics of the two dozen or more late prehistoric images constituting the Narmer Palette's immediate iconographical and iconological context.[25] Many of the works are simply too fragmentary to permit a properly detailed analysis of their pictorial structure. However, in order to understand the specific dynamics of the Narmer Palette, we must look briefly at the general characteristics of the Oxford, Hunter's, and Battlefield Palettes (Figs. 7.1–7.3). Despite their textual variety, all four palettes evidently project a common "fabula" (a useful narratological term for the underlying causes and spatiotemporal relations of event and action). In various ways, each depicts the human hunter's or ruler's presence in and mastery of the natural and social worlds. The hunter on the Oxford Palette (Fig. 7.1, reverse bottom left) and the Hunter's Palette (Fig. 7.2) disjunctively becomes a lion on the Battlefield Palette (Fig. 7.3) and the human person of the ruler himself on the Narmer Palette (Fig. 7.4). In the latter two images, human enemies replace wild animals as the ruler's antagonists. At the most general level, this fabula of the ruler's mastery will become the central concern of canonical representation as well.[26]

More important for my purposes, no matter how each image relates a common, general fabula, at the levels of both "story" (the sequential presentation of those causes and relations) and visual "text" (the morphology and style in which the story is formatted by the image itself) each image masks the blow of the hunter or ruler. In every case, the viewer does not directly behold the ruler's decisive violence; it is not presented in the pictorial text for the story related, although it is logically required in its fabula. Instead, the viewer sees certain of the preconditions of the blow, like a hunting expedition (Fig. 7.2), or certain of its consequences, like a battlefield strewn with corpses (Fig. 7.3). Nevertheless, despite the ellipsis the pictorial story and text take the viewer as "close" as possible to this logically central event in the fabula without literally presenting it.

To take a simple example, on the Hunter's Palette (Fig. 7.2) the viewer encounters a hunter at the top and "beginning" of the image. Possibly the leader of the hunting expedition (he is taller than all of the other figures), he is fitting an arrow to his bow, about to

sion of the "iconological" moment in Panofsky's "iconography"—Panofsky historicized what would otherwise be a purely "formal" analysis, and thus permitted a genuine hermeneutics of meaning—can be found in Silvia Ferretti, *Cassirer, Panofsky, and Warburg: Symbol, Art, and History*, trans. Richard Pierce (New Haven, Conn., 1989), 207–20. Disjunction has interested the principal post-Panofskyan iconographical theorist, George Kubler, especially in classic essays like "On the Colonial Extinction of the Motifs of Pre-Columbian Art," in *Essays in Pre-Columbian Art and Archaeology*, ed. Samuel K. Lothrop et al. (Cambridge, Mass., 1961), 14–34.

25. A fuller analysis of the problem can be found in Whitney Davis, *Masking the Blow: The Scene of Representation in Late Prehistoric Egyptian Art* (Berkeley and Los Angeles, 1992), which also takes up aspects of the Narmer Palette—for example, its figuration of the ruler's violence as well as its manifestation of that violence in the representation itself—which I pass over here (although see Chapter 10).

26. See Davis, *Canonical Tradition*, chap. 4, and Emma Swan Hall, *The Pharaoh Smites His Enemies*, Münchner Ägyptologische Studien 44 (Munich, 1988).

shoot a lion attempting to protect its cub. But we do not literally behold the flight of the arrow—that is, the fact that in the fabula, the causal and spatiotemporal logic of events, the hunters succeed in hitting the lion several times, an event leading from one state of affairs to another, namely, the death of the lion after being struck by six arrows, presented at the bottom of the image. In fact, this ellipsis in the pictorial text is even greater than might first appear. At the top of the image, the hunter seems to stand in front of the lion to shoot directly at him. The confrontation of the pair is face to face. However, at the bottom of the image, we discover that the lion has been struck by one arrow in the anal-genital region. In order to synthesize the story and fabula from the text of the image, then, the viewer must reconstitute the moment of the kill itself as having involved the hunter's sneak attack from behind. In unfolding this narrative, the viewer goes back—in the light of a later passage of depiction (the dead lion)—to an earlier passage of depiction (the lion about to be killed) in order to discover its incompleteness; the viewer experiences the movement, or filling out, of the story by interpreting what fabula must be implied in the material presented or elided by the pictorial text. All four palettes (Figs. 7.1–7.4) work in this fashion, although the Narmer Palette does initially seem to present a full pictorial textualization of the fabula of victory. But even here an ellipsis between the story and text and the logic of the fabula itself has a central role to play in the Narmer Palette's construction of narrative meaning.

As the example of the Hunter's Palette suggests, it would be misleading to isolate individual figures, groups of figures, motifs, or signs and try to identify their meaning independent of their metaphorical and narrative context within a particular image. By definition, an image is a concatenation of passages of depiction functioning for a viewer as a referential whole. No detail in or compositional zone of the pictorial text can be ignored, for almost all details and zones are related to the others as structures of metaphor and narrative. In the example of the Hunter's Palette, if a viewer ignores the arrow plunging into the lion's anal-genital region, then it is not possible for him or her to reconstruct the developments in the fabula (for instance, the sneak attack) that, once the viewer realizes their necessity, alters any total understanding of the story and its textualization: the sequencing of episodes in the story has been set up to give us a textual surprise, a communication of a transformation in what is otherwise just the "static" depiction of states of affairs. Thus, although the lion on the Hunter's Palette (Fig. 7.2) may be formally comparable to the lion on the Battlefield Palette (Fig. 7.3), its narrative "meaning" is specifically constructed in relation to other figures in the image in their particular compositional arrangement. Taken out of this context, the lion "means" nothing—and certainly does not mean what it seems to signify on the Battlefield Palette (Fig. 7.3), where the beast is not the antagonist and victim of the ruler.

In order to understand all of these images, the viewer must observe several general conditions that render them pictorially intelligible. First, each image requires the viewer to begin with the "top" of the "obverse" side of the palette, namely, the zone of pictorial text above the cosmetic saucer. Although we have no independent archaeological evidence about the actual handling, use, or display of the palettes, it is reasonable to suppose that the "obverse"—or "first" or "beginning"—side of the image was specified as the side for carrying the cosmetic grounds, which would spill if and when the palette were turned over. The only one-sided image in the group, the Hunter's Palette (Fig. 7.2), has this saucer on its decorated side; and in the whole corpus of predynastic palettes there are no palettes with saucer on one side and images on the other. The "top," or the "beginning" in the top-to-bottom axis of the story, is specified by the fact that the routine funerary palettes from which the decorated palettes typologically derive[27] oppose an emphasized, three-dimensionally sculpted edge—often ornamented with double birds' heads, or "heraldic" animals in our group (Figs. 7.1, 7.4)—to a plain, tapering edge. The cosmetic saucer (Figs. 7.1, 7.2, 7.4) is usually closest to the sculpted edge, which, in predynastic graves, is usually aligned with the head of the dead body. However, notice that "top" and "bottom" are always relative to a viewer's orientation, which need not be constant. Since the palette can be turned in the hands, "top" can become "bottom" and vice versa. A narrative can unfold through this reorientation. Notice, too, that the narrative experience as a whole would not be greatly compromised if a viewer were to begin with the "bottom" or the "reverse" rather than with the "top" or the "obverse." The fabula eventually can be reconstructed from the story sequence however it is ordered. Of course, as distinct from the interpretation of the fabula, the viewer's experiences of the story and text vary with his or her point of entry, for example, at the "top obverse" and "beginning" or at the "top reverse" and "halfway through." Pictorial narrative can play on this fact. On the Narmer Palette, only by "reading through" all of the pictorial material does the viewer discover that, in the logic of the fabula, the "beginning" of the story on the "obverse top" is actually the logical *end* of the fabula.

Second, on either side of the palettes the image presents either three or four distinct groupings of figures arranged in visually discrete zones or bands of depiction. In canonical representation of the dynastic period, register lines and other independent framing devices will be used to distinguish such zones. By contrast, in late prehistoric images the zones are distinguished by the fact that each typically contains one or more pairs of actors—the several animal or human figures in the whole image—engaged in some kind of mutual action or interaction. (The Narmer Palette, of course, uses both the canonical and the late prehistoric means of dividing and sequencing the story.) These zones form the several episodes of the story from which the fabula can be projected. They tend to have quite different textual qualities one from the next (for example, in compositional arrangement, pictorial detailing, or use of complementary "hieroglyphs"), but they are all linked with one another as the episodes in the story of the narrative, or the poles of a metaphor, in particular top-to-bottom, left-to-right, and side-to-side or obverse-to-reverse relations.

Third, within each story zone or band, the nature of the mutual relation between the individual actors in the narrative is established in several ways working together simultaneously: by the animals' or human figures' placement (at the sides or in the center, bottom or top, right or left, of the zone); by their bodily orientation (moving toward, moving beside, or moving away from one another, from or toward an edge of the zone, from or

27. Types 76–80 in W. M. Flinders Petrie, *Ceremonial Slate Palettes and Corpus of Protodynastic Pottery* (London, 1953), and see also his *Prehistoric Egypt Corpus* (London, 1921). For the derivation, see Davis, *Canonical Tradition*, 138–40.

toward the center of the palette, and so on); and by the directions of their glances (looking at one another or looking elsewhere).[28] These relations may be repeated or revised (for example, reversed or inverted) in other zones on the palette. That is to say, the placement, orientation, and directionality of zones establish the mutual relations between story episodes just as the placement, orientation, and directionality of figures establish the mutual relations between actors within a story episode. Such infrazonal interrelations generally establish that any two zones should be taken together as a continuous segment of the story, whatever its chronological arrangement (for example, as before to after).

Fourth, in order to identify and inspect all of these relations within and between zones, the viewer is generally required to twist, rotate, or flip the whole palette in order to obtain a series of views of its surface. For example, the viewer can twist the object from "left" side up to "right" side up or flip it from obverse to reverse. Many of these views could also be generated by the viewer moving around the object placed, displayed, or held in a fixed position. In fact, such movement could be carried out in a viewer's imagination. For convenience of exposition, I write as if the beholder's action on the palette were physical. Depending, then, upon where the viewer's hands grasp the object, upon what can be seen as upright in holding it from that angle, upon what disappears from view, and so on, the individual figures within the zones and the relations both within and between zones will have changing aspects in the activity of viewing. The viewer narrativizes the depictions by moving and scanning them in a particular order.

This concept of the active narrativization of an image through its real or notional manipulation and transformation is central to an understanding of late prehistoric Egyptian image making. Unfortunately, as I have noted, we have no independent information about the way in which the palettes were actually manipulated or displayed. If they were "ceremonial" objects, then they might have been handled infrequently; people's access to them might have been quite restricted. If exhibited in a "liturgy" (in later periods, eye paint was applied to cult statues), then they could have been carried or displayed by handlers in such a way that viewers could see both sides of the image. For simplicity, I suppose that the palette could, in principle, be handled by one person examining the several zones of depiction in a sequence of twists, rotations, or flips—whether or not anyone actually did so. Of course, at least one person did indeed handle the object this way: its maker's conceptualization of his "position" in relation to the image articulated the narrative in the first place.

Whether or not we can suppose that people physically rotated or flipped the palettes, the plain fact of the matter is that with the exception of the Hunter's Palette (Fig. 7.2) the objects present depictions on both sides (Figs. 7.1, 7.3, 7.4). Any interpretation of the images must accommodate this obvious morphological property of the artifacts—the fundamental material condition (in Chapter 3, I call it the "nonimage" condition of the replication of depiction) that any pictorial handling had to take into account. Indeed, we may

28. Extending and revising the fundamental work of Gérard Genette, Mieke Bal, "The Narrating and the Focalizing: A Theory of Agents in Narrative," *Style* 17 (1983), 234–69, has offered a theory of narrative "focalizers" that could provide one way of handling these phenomena. Although the term might refine my analysis, to avoid overburdening it with narratological terminology I do not apply it.

suppose it to have been a constitutive one. In theory, it is not incidental but intrinsic to the significance of a visual narrative that it requires a "transposition" or "mobility of its internal elements," some "summation in time" of a "combination of an initial stable state with a subsequent movement," which Juri Lotman has identified as the essential feature of narratives in nondiscrete texts such as pictures.[29]

One might object that if the palettes were used, in practice, to grind eye paint, then they could not have been rotated or flipped without spillage. It would follow that the palettes either were not actually flipped or were not actually used for their ostensible "practical" purpose. However, it is risky to proceed as if we knew what late prehistoric Egyptian viewers would have regarded as practical given their own understanding of the functions of their images. To suppose that the images could for "practical" reasons not be rotated or flipped supposes that any narrativization of the images derived from these motions was an "impractical" action. But we have no grounds for this supposition because we have no independent evidence for the function of the objects or the images on them. In fact, I have already noted that the representational function of the images is not incompatible with, and is actually required by, the "functional" hypotheses themselves. Consider the parallel of a decorated chair. Of course, when a person is sitting on the chair, using it for its literal or practical function, any decoration applied to the back of the chair cannot be seen without great difficulty, the chair cannot be tipped over, and the sitter cannot simultaneously move around it. But certainly none of this, in itself, implies that the decorations on the chair cannot be systematically structured as narratives or other complex representations. It certainly does not entail that the images cannot be related to the "practical" function of the chair—for example, as symbols of the person displayed on the chair or as metaphors for "sitting" (being settled, being in the seat, and so on). In fact, the representations both specify and universalize the merely practical function of an otherwise inert object by symbolically stating what its ostensible practical function "means," deploying the natural, social, cosmic, or other terms of an iconography: one can say that "sitting in the seat" is as much a metaphor

29. Juri Lotman, "The Discrete Text and the Iconic Text," *New Literary History* 6 (1975), 335. There are numerous differences between narrative potential in a visual text and that in a spoken or written text; for one account, see Davis, *Masking the Blow*, 234–55. However, the narratological triad of fabula, story, and text in principle applies to narrative in any medium—spoken, written, depictional (in pictures, gestures, or dance), and so on. In a spoken or written text, the narrative must accommodate the sequential, discrete, "linear" arrangement of the semiotic elements in the medium. But notice that *just because* a verbal text is sequential (a visual text, like a comic strip, can display this property as well) does not in itself guarantee that the text is narrative, for it may simply juxtapose scenes that are not related as the texts of story episodes in a common underlying fabula. Conversely, *just because* a visual text is nonsequential and nondiscrete, or "iconic," does not in itself imply that the picture cannot be a narrative, so long as through an "internal transformation" of the elements a viewer can interpret several views of the visual text as the story episodes of a fabula. Since all pictures necessarily require scanning the surface of the image, back and forth, all pictures potentially permit a narrative organization of their material. Art historians who insist on the sequential character of a pictorial narrative—supposedly one discrete "scene" in the visual array must follow another, paralleling the sequence of story episodes for the fabula—fail to recognize the multiple ways in which a *single* scene has a narrative dimension to the extent that viewing it has both spatial and temporal extension: clearly, we want to be able to say that single, unified compositions, like many nineteenth-century "history" paintings, have a narrative quality. In sum, the discreteness or sequentiality of the elements of the spoken, written, or visual text is a matter crosscutting its narrative organization.

as a use (see further Chapters 3 and 8). So, too, with the Narmer Palette: both the "practical" and the representational dimensions of the object are interconnected aspects of the use and meaning of a complex artifact that also happens to be an image, an artifact representing something, and of a complex image that also happens to be an artifact, an image to be handled.

Narrativity and the Narmer Palette

The Narmer Palette (Fig. 7.4) takes the general structure and conditions of intelligibility of late prehistoric image making to an extraordinary level of complexity, ingenuity, and calculation. (I cannot say, however, whether such calculation was wholly directed, from the beginning, to make a narrative image with precisely these ingenious properties; as Chapter 8 suggests, the "formalization" of the figurative system was emergent in a temporally and spatially extended relation—even contest—with matter.) It can hardly be understood except as the product of several generations of cultural practice. As I have already stressed, however, despite its continuities with earlier examples of prehistoric art in Egypt, the Narmer Palette is disjunctively related to these origins.

The top edges of both sides of the Narmer Palette are decorated with two frontal heads of bovids. (In some commentaries, the bovids are identified as Hathor, divine mother of the Egyptian pharaoh, or as the cow-goddess Bat, but they could equally be heads of the bull that stands, in the main image, for the ruler himself.) They flank a "palace façade," or *serekh*, containing the *nar*-fish and the *mer*-chisel, signs also attached to the largest figure on the top zone of the obverse, apparently naming the ruler himself. This decorated top edge is sometimes interpreted as depicting a roof or canopy for a (palace) façade with bucrania. Although not necessary for my purposes, the reading is not incompatible with other features of the image. The top edge is divided from the zones below it by a thin register line.

Below the decorated top edge, the two sides of the palette are each divided into three horizontal zones. Excepting the "rebus" (reverse top right), each zone on the Narmer Palette containing a representation of the ruler has been provided with a register groundline—namely, the obverse top, with the ruler and his retainers and standards inspecting the corpses of enemies; the obverse middle, with the ruler's retainers mastering "serpopards"; the obverse bottom, with the ruler as bull vanquishing an enemy; and the reverse middle, with the ruler smiting his enemy. By contrast, zones depicting enemy personages do not possess a groundline—namely, the obverse top right, the obverse bottom, and the reverse bottom. In each of these zones, the enemies are depicted as defeated, twisted on and from their baselines and upright axes. The special place of the enemy chieftain on the ruler's groundline in the reverse middle zone concerns me later.

The registers therefore mark the different status of figures within the image either as being part of or associated with the ruler or as being outside or not associated with the ruler, two different grounds. However, in addition to maintaining distinctions indicated in earlier images in the group, the registers on the Narmer Palette also divide each zone from the others on that side of the palette. As elements of composition, passages of visual text, they separate the zones—and thus presumably the elements of the story—in a way never presented on the preceding late prehistoric narrative images (Figs. 7.1 to 7.3).

Each side of the palette presents a zone depicting the aftermath, at the top, and the beforehand, at the bottom, of the ruler's blows of victory, with the obverse depicting the aftermath and the reverse the beforehand of the ruler's most decisive blow, the killing of the enemy chieftain. Thus, the story is arranged in the four top and bottom zones, top-to-bottom/obverse-to-reverse, as consistently after-to-before (Fig. 7.5). A few commentators have almost recognized this structure;[30] otherwise, however, the Narmer Palette is usually described in very general nonnarrative terms as a symbolic or allegorical image.[31] It is even reproduced incorrectly—for example, as if the obverse side with saucer should "come after" the reverse side with its picture of Narmer smiting,[32] and sometimes showing just one side, equivalent to reproducing one-half of a narrative painting sliced down the middle.[33] As distinguished from the fabula and story, the pictorial text also includes elements relating material in the other temporal direction, from before to after (strictly speaking, a counternarrative), as well as elements breaking out of the narrative sequencing altogether. In view of this complexity, it is useful to go through the zones one by one before considering their metaphorical and narrative interrelations.

Beginning with the obverse top, flanked on the left by his sandal bearer and on the right by a "priest" bearing scribal equipment, the victorious ruler (wearing the Red Crown of Lower Egypt) is preceded by four standard-bearers. The whole group of ruler and followers inspects two rows of five decapitated enemies, each spread on the ground, without groundlines, at right angles to the progress of the victors. Signs, or "hieroglyphs," above this group—it is not clear whether they should be understood in the way later canonical hieroglyphs can be—depict or designate a door on its pivot (= the hieroglyph "great door"), a falcon (= the ruler?) carrying or vanquishing a harpoon (= the enemy on the reverse side, labeled with a harpoon?), and the "sacred bark" of the ruler.[34] The pictorial text on the Narmer Palette begins, then, with the final achievement of the king, the celebration of his victory.

The beforehand of this episode is related in the top zone on the reverse of the palette. Here, a "rebus" depicts the "enemy" or enemies brought to the ruler by a falcon—an aspect, double, or representation of the ruler's identity or perhaps his divine protector. (On the basis of an anachronistic comparison with canonical Egyptian iconography, we could con-

30. E.g., Vandier, *Manuel d'archéologie égyptienne,* 1:596.

31. E.g., Heinrich Schäfer, "Das Niederschlagen der Feinde," *Wiener Zeitschrift für die Kunde des Morgenlandes* 54 (1957), 168–76; Finkenstaedt, "Violence and Kingship"; Kemp, *Ancient Egypt,* chap. 1.

32. E.g., H. W. Janson, *History of Art,* 4th ed., rev. Anthony F. Janson (New York, 1991), 1:99, figs. 72, 73.

33. E.g., Trigger, "Rise of Egyptian Civilization," 59, fig. 1.8.

34. For the possible hieroglyphic decipherments, see Williams and Logan, "The Metropolitan Museum Knife Handle"; Walter Fairservis, "A Revised View of the Na'rmr Palette," *Journal of the American Research Center in Egypt* 28 (1991), 1–20. For interesting speculations on the visual organization of the Narmer Palette—partly challenging my conception of the "zones" and their relations—see James Elkins, "Before Theory," *Art History* 16 (1993), 647–53.

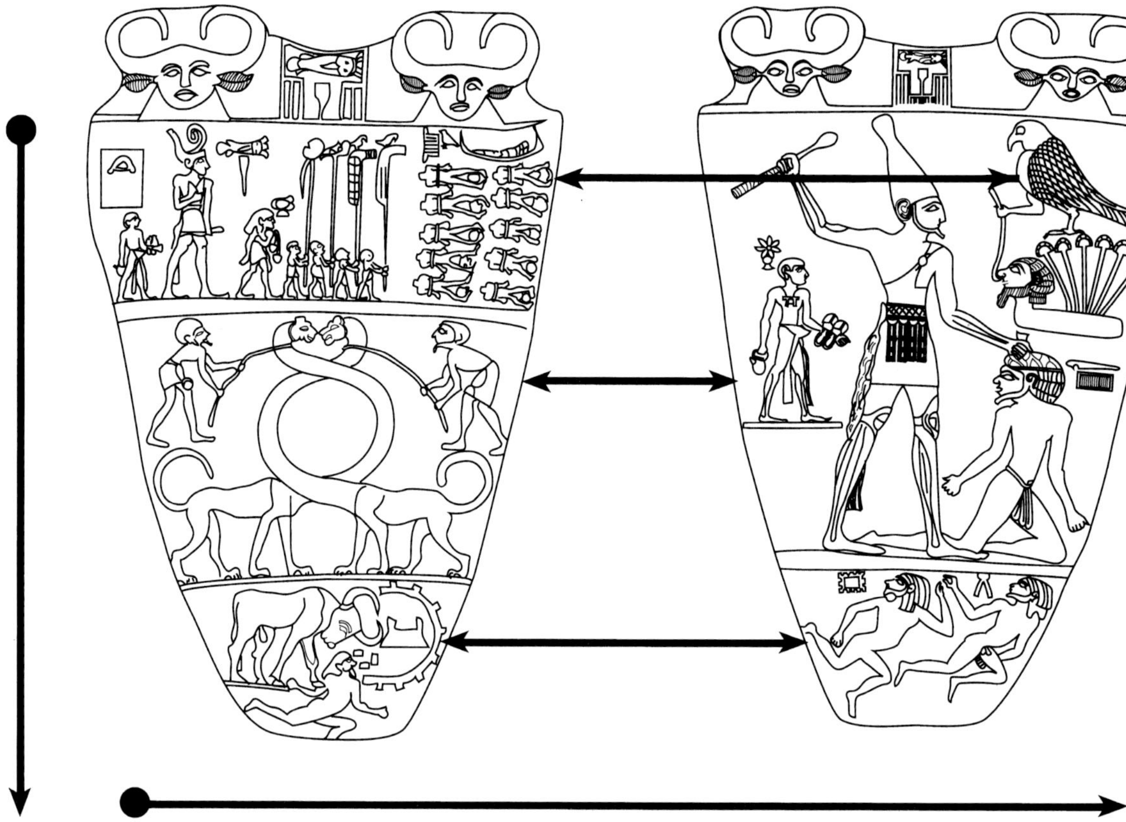

Fig. 7.5. Story structure of the Narmer Palette.

clude that the falcon is the god Horus; but this inference is methodologically unsound.) The falcon inserts a hooked cord into an enemy's nose in order, it seems, to prepare him for the beheading whose aftermath is related in the obverse top zone, where the ruler inspects decapitated corpses. The papyrus stalks growing from the enemy's body probably denote the enemy's home territory, "Papyrus Land." However it should be interpreted, in a general sense, the rebus indicates that the ruler—in his aspect as or with the protection of "Falcon"—has defeated his enemies and prepares them for their judgment and destruction.

On the obverse bottom, the beforehand of this episode—storying backward in the fabula—is related. Here, a great bull uses its horns to break down the walls of a fortress evidently inhabited by the enemies, one of whom is thrown to the ground, facing away from the bull, and trampled. We can take the bull as an aspect, double, or representation of the ruler, although he should not be identified with the human person of the ruler as such. This zone seems to depict the moment in the battle itself when the enemies' defeat was secured. In his aspect as, or with the protection of, "Bull," the ruler enters their citadel.

Finally, on the reverse bottom, the beforehand of this episode is related; in the storying of the narrative, the "beginning" of the fabula comes at the "end" of the text. Here, two enemies are depicted as fleeing toward the right, that is, if one looks back through the text to the preceding stage (obverse bottom), toward the citadel in which they plan to take refuge (without avail, as even later episodes in the story have already told us in the text). They look back over their shoulders; they are being pursued by the ruler. Although the ruler does not appear in the pictorial text of this zone of the image, the text of the image as a whole is quite clear about his presence. The viewer already knows (obverse bottom) that "Bull" will break down the enemies' citadel, a building that the text depicts as a broken and inverted version of a sign labeling the left enemy figure. Furthermore, the enemies' glances over their shoulders are directed "up" to the figure of the ruler smiting his enemy, presented immediately above this zone. Although coming last in the story, the fabula "begins," then, with the ruler pursuing his enemies.

Almost all commentators agree that the sign labeling the left enemy depicts or denotes a fortress with bastions. The denotation of the right sign is more obscure. In one interpretation, the signs label the towns of Memphis and Sais in the Lower Egyptian delta.[35] If all three signs labeling the enemies on the Narmer Palette, in the obverse and reverse bottom zones, refer to their actual hometowns, then the Palette could document a contest between "Nar-Mer" of Upper Egypt and a delta coalition in which a principal "Enemy," the town of Buto or the "Harpoon" of the enemy on the reverse middle, was assisted by Memphis and Sais.[36]

But I doubt that trying to force the Narmer Palette into serving as a document for actual historical events can be justified. At any rate, it cannot be the end of the matter in understanding the image. Even if a specific reference for the whole image could be found in actual events, this finding would not, in itself, be enough to show why they are represented in the particular symbolic, metaphorical, or narrative fashion that they are in the image as such. For example, the maker decides to use "Bull" to stand for the ruler, an intention probably determined in part by earlier or other representations of the ruler in the aspect of a great animal (see Fig. 7.3).

If we invert the order in which the image arranges the fabula as a story, the four episodes can readily be reconstituted: the enemy flees and resists the ruler, who pursues and conquers them, leading to their presentation to the victor and his celebration of their death (Fig. 7.6). In turn, although not literally presented in any of the relevant passages of depiction, each of these episodes in the story must be linked one to the next, in the chronological and causal logic of the fabula, by the success of a direct blow by the ruler. As read from the "beginning" of the fabula (the "end" of the pictorial text), between the first two episodes of the story the ruler must successfully track the fleeing enemies, locate their citadel, and scale or undermine its walls; we behold the enemies fleeing (Fig. 7.6, Episode One) and the citadel, already taken, with the enemies already being trampled (Fig. 7.6, Episode Two). Between the second and third episodes of the story, the ruler or his army must round up the conquered inhabitants and prepare them for judgment and imprisonment; we behold the town being overrun just after the walls have been demolished (Fig. 7.6, Episode Two) and "Falcon" already mastering the captives taken (Fig. 7.6, Episode Three). Between the third and fourth episodes of the story, the ruler or his executioners

35. Werner Kaiser, "Einige Bemerkungen zur ägyptischen Frühzeit, III: Die Reichseinigung," *Zeitschrift für Ägyptische Sprache* 91 (1964), 90; Peter Kaplony, *Kleine Beiträge zu den Inschriften der ägyptischen Frühzeit* (Wiesbaden, 1966), 159.

36. Percy E. Newberry, "The Petty-Kingdom of the Harpoon and Egypt's Earliest Port," *Liverpool Annals of Archaeology and Anthropology* 1 (1908), 17–22.

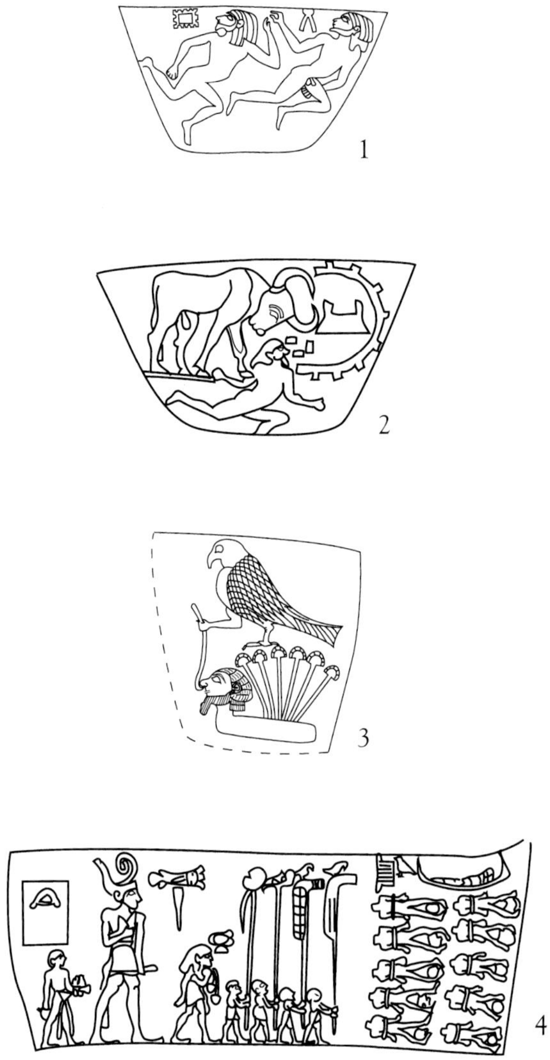

Fig. 7.6. Episodes of the story of the Narmer Palette.

must lop off the heads of the enemies condemned to die or to be sacrificed in the victory ceremonials; we behold "Falcon" lifting an enemy's head (Fig. 7.6, Episode Three) and the ruler already inspecting the decapitated corpses (Fig., 7.6, Episode Four).

The ruler's decisive blow, then, occurs several times or throughout the fabula. It is that transition, the event or process, that takes the story inexorably from one state of affairs to another. In the text, when we flip the palette from obverse top to reverse top (Fig. 7.6, Episode Four to Episode Three), despite the expectation and requirement that we inspect the rebus (reverse top zone), we cannot help initially noticing the picture of the king smiting his enemy, the picture occupying the reverse middle zone. Here, accompanied by his sandal bearer and wielding the mace, the human person of the ruler himself—wearing the

White Crown of Upper Egypt and other regalia—is about to strike an enemy labeled "Harpoon" (or coming from "Harpoon Land"). The figure of Narmer is presented at larger scale than any other figure in the composition of the image; in fact, he appears at larger scale than any other figure in the whole known group of late prehistoric images of the ruler's victory. The rebus in the reverse top zone is almost squeezed in beside him. In the flip from reverse top to obverse bottom (Fig. 7.6, Episode Three to Episode Two), that picture is removed from view but replaced, in the same compositional position, by what seems to be its metaphorical equivalent—namely, the picture, in the obverse middle, of the ruler's two retainers mastering two serpopards. Finally, in the flip from obverse bottom to reverse bottom (Fig. 7.6, Episode Two to Episode One), the picture of Narmer smiting his enemy, removed from view after the first flip, reappears. Thus, no matter how the viewer flips the palette to determine the relation between the zones of depiction spread across it, reconstructing the fabula on the basis of the story sequence, Narmer smiting his enemy continually appears in the text.

The text provides the viewer with a key to the cipher of the narrative image at exactly the place where the palette itself would be both grasped and flipped, namely, the depiction of the ruler's two retainers mastering the two serpopards. As well as representing the ruler's, they represent the viewer's own blow in viewing the image: The two serpopards are the two sides of the palette to be twisted around one another in the viewer's own two hands. Whatever their role as metaphors for the ruler's victory, the figures of the retainers, textually associated with the viewer's own hands, are depicted as moving in a clockwise circle (from obverse flipping right hand over left hand toward reverse), gradually twisting together the long necks of the beasts from their heads down to their bodies. The palette, then, must be viewed by starting with the obverse top scene and always flipping the palette right hand over left in the same direction (that is, obverse to reverse to obverse) and always scanning top to bottom.

If the viewer adopts and without interruption continues to follow this means of reconstructing the narrative fabula, then a simple, continuous twist will be generated. It can be summarized as follows:

OBV TOP	to	OBV BOTTOM (flip)
REV TOP	to	REV BOTTOM
(complete top-to-bottom scan for each side)		
REV TOP (flip)	to	OBV TOP
OBV MIDDLE (flip)	to	REV MIDDLE
REV BOTTOM (flip)	to	OBV BOTTOM (flip)
(complete side-to-side scan, top to bottom for each side)		
REV TOP (flip)	to	OBV MIDDLE
OBV MIDDLE (flip)	to	REV BOTTOM
(complete side-to-side, top-to-bottom, one-strand twist)		
OBV TOP (flip)	to	REV MIDDLE
REV MIDDLE (flip)	to	OBV BOTTOM
(complete side-to-side, top-to-bottom, other-strand twist)		

The full twist takes the viewer through all the available sequences of all zones of the depiction. On completing this twist at the obverse bottom, the viewer could only repeat the twist all over again. Therefore, this simple, continuous twist allows the viewer to construct what I call the basic form of the narrative image available in the Narmer Palette (it is visualized in Fig. 7.7). The basic narrative incorporates all possible forms of sequencing available within the context of the general conditions of intelligibility of late prehistoric image making and apparently leaves nothing out and nothing in excess. Returned to the obverse side whence the construction of the narrative began, in the progress through this basic pictorial narrative the viewer makes ten complete flips of the two-sided palette, metaphorically equivalent to the two rows of five decapitated enemies, ten in all, depicted in the obverse top zone where the text "begins."

I have been looking so far, of course, at the arrangement of the fabula in the story presented by the image simply in terms of the sequencing and connectedness of the four episodes it logically requires. But the properties of the pictorial text invest the basic sequence with particular accumulating properties, a textual "tone," such as the continual reappearance—as it were, the underlining—of the ruler standing firm on his groundline and stabilizing the center of the image on a horizontal axis, the place of pictures of the ruler's blow, as the palette continually rotates around its vertical axis (Fig. 7.5). Moreover, although the top and bottom zones on the two sides are all episodes in the story (Fig. 7.6), they are not all, of course, textually alike.

For example, consider the textual qualities of and relation between just the first two logically closest episodes in the image's inverted storying of the fabula (that is, in Fig. 7.6, Episode Four, the obverse top zone, and Episode Three, the reverse top zone). In the inverted storying of the fabula, Episode Four precedes Episode Three. In fact, in the basic form (Fig. 7.7) and any other sequencing that still obeys the general rule of beginning with the obverse, Episode Four, the obverse top zone, "begins" the text, and Episode Three, the reverse top, turns up later and necessarily after a flip of the palette. Already, then, the text of Episode Four, the depiction on the obverse top zone, must prepare the viewer for the text of Episode Three, the rebus on the reverse top. In the text of Episode Four, the ten decapitated enemies, depicted frontally, and the ruler's retinue, depicted in profile, literally and jointly ground the viewer's point of view: the viewer has been placed above and looking down on the enemies while being on the same level as and at the side of the ruler's group. The picture itself is highly descriptive. It graphically depicts the human person of the ruler, with crown, costume, and regalia, his chief retainers, and his standards or army, as well as the specific fate of the enemies, with all attributes of costume, individual gesture, and so forth, carefully rendered. Some of this ekphrastic detail has a narrative status. For example, the decapitated heads of the enemies must be connected with the depiction in the rebus—"later" in the viewing of the narrative (Figs. 7.5, 7.7), if "earlier" in the fabula (Fig. 7.6)—of "Falcon" lifting up an enemy's head in order for him to be executed. However, some of the description is superfluous for the purposes of the narrative. Just compare the textualization of quite similar narrative material in the rebus, pictorially the least explicit of all the zones of the image. Here ekphrasis is at a minimum. To represent the "many enemies," the maker uses a single enemy head, without details of body, and plants

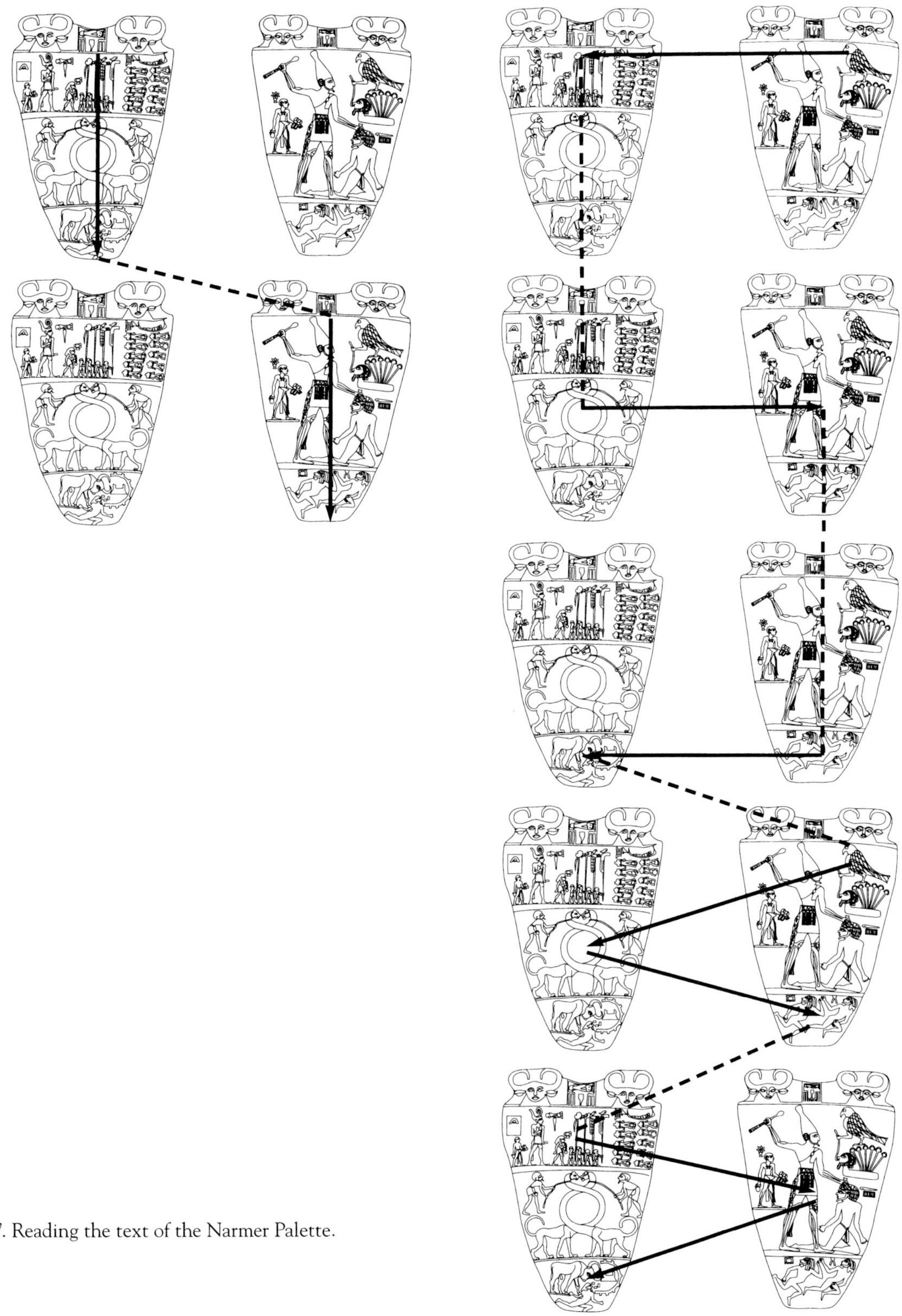

Fig. 7.7. Reading the text of the Narmer Palette.

possibly symbolizing the enemy homeland, "Papyrus Land." In fact, as a rebus, pictorial textuality in this passage of the image has been modulated into another species of textuality altogether, quite close to, if not identical with, ideographic script.

Other zones in the depiction stand somewhere in between these two relatively extreme possibilities of greater or lesser descriptive richness in the pictorial notation. Three "hieroglyphic" zones of pictorial textuality (the obverse middle, obverse bottom, and reverse top) can be readily distinguished from three "descriptive" zones (the obverse top, reverse middle, reverse bottom). The descriptive zones supplement pictorial text with the addition of actual symbolic labels ("Nar-Mer," "Harpoon," left and right enemy "towns"), that is, with nonpictorial text, but the "hieroglyphic" zones (cipher key, "Bull" and citadel, rebus) do not need to do so, for they are already quite close to or have completely modulated into nonpictorial text anyway.

These and other textual differences between passages of depiction play out in the way the narrative image is interpreted by the beholder. For example, in the basic form of the image (Fig. 7.7), the viewer encounters Episode Two, in the obverse bottom, *after* the descriptive Episode Four, the obverse top, and *before* the "hieroglyphic" Episode Three, the reverse top. In this midway position, the obverse bottom seems pictorially more descriptive than a group of hieroglyphs or a rebus: its figures of "Bull" and an enemy are visually separated one from the other, and the hieroglyphs labeling the home towns of the enemies on the reverse bottom are treated here as actual pictures of their citadel itself. But the obverse bottom is less pictorially descriptive than the picture on the obverse top. Therefore, in this first segment of the entire basic sequence (obverse top to obverse middle to obverse bottom to reverse top), the narrative image begins with a very graphic, vivid look at the "end" of the story (obverse top), gives the viewer the key required for unfolding the story leading up to it (obverse middle), goes back in some sketchy detail to a much earlier episode, the taking of the town (obverse bottom), quickly telegraphs the connection between the taking of the town and execution of prisoners, should the viewer fail to infer it, and simultaneously anchors further material it will introduce (rebus), and so forth. To use the (possibly misleading) parallel of many modern novels and films, the viewer-reader progresses through paragraphs of dense description for and briefer summaries of events nested in an armature of foreshadowings and recapitulations—the montage editing of long or short takes in close-up, deep focus, zoom, and so on, with greater or lesser clarity, color, and the like.

It would consume too much space to describe all of the textual properties of every possible segmentation and sequencing of the basic narrative image on the Narmer Palette (Fig. 7.7). However, take note, at least, of the way in which the four episodes of the story at the top and bottom of the two sides of the palette (Fig. 7.6) are related to the two central passages of text, the obverse middle and the reverse middle. Both of these passages seem to have the narrative function of picturing the ruler's blow that the fabula requires throughout the story—from pursuing the enemies to taking their town, to rounding up prisoners, to executing them—even though the former adopts a more "hieroglyphic" and the latter a more descriptive textualization. Both zones have been singled out textually, appearing at larger scale and in the center of the composition on either side, precisely because of their relatively greater narrative significance, that is, the fact that they continue to reappear in the image. But neither zone, of course, literally denotes or describes the very moment of the ruler's blow. Consistent with the overall organization of the image obverse-to-reverse/top-to-bottom as after-to-before (Fig. 7.5), the obverse middle depicts the moment just *after* the decisive blow has fallen (here, the serpopards have just been caught and their heads begun to be twisted together), and the reverse middle depicts the moment just *before* it (here, Narmer throws back his right arm, carrying his mace, just about to smite his chief Enemy down). The blow itself as it strikes its target, after the beforehand of the blow and before the aftermath of the blow, is not depicted as such. It must be *in the center of the middle of the image*—namely, in the cosmetic saucer, where the beholder, a holder or user or even the owner of the palette, reaches down to mix the eye paint.

As they twist together the necks of the serpopards, the ruler's retainers are also depicted as tightening a noose around the cosmetic saucer, where the ruler's blow at the instant it strikes its target must be placed in the center of the middle of the image. In continually flipping the palette to retrieve the image caught and recaught up in its twist (Fig. 7.7), the viewer, then, seems to come closer and closer to beholding the falling of the blow, to pulling the noose tight around it with his or her own two hands.

But in fact, although the picture of Narmer raising his mace reappears again and again in the basic form of the image (Fig. 7.7), the blow escapes depiction and the image continues to mask it. Although there is no need to describe all of its textual properties and relations (I have looked briefly at the first segment), the full viewing sequence through all ten flips gives the narrative image on the Narmer Palette a complete text of eighteen zones—that is, the three sets of possible ways of scanning the six zones on the two sides according to the general conditions of intelligibility of late prehistoric image making, these sets sequenced in turn to accord with the same conditions and with nothing left out, no overlap, and no excess. This complete text can be listed as follows:

1. OBV TOP (Episode Four)
2. OBV MIDDLE (cipher/after the blow)
3. OBV BOTTOM (Episode Two)—(flip)
4. REV TOP (Episode Three)
5. REV MIDDLE (before the blow)
6. REV BOTTOM (Episode One) [completes top-to-bottom set]
7. REV TOP (Episode Three)—(flip)
8. OBV TOP (Episode Four)
9. OBV MIDDLE (cipher/after the blow)—(flip)
10. REV MIDDLE (before the blow)
11. REV BOTTOM (Episode One)—(flip)
12. OBV BOTTOM (Episode Two) [completes side-to-side set]—(flip)
13. REV TOP (Episode Three)—(flip)
14. OBV MIDDLE (cipher/after the blow)—(flip)

15. REV BOTTOM (Episode One)—(flip)
16. OBV TOP (Episode Four)—(flip)
17. REV MIDDLE (before the blow)—(flip)
18. OBV BOTTOM (Episode Two) [completes double-twist set]

Several features stand out in this text. First, the rate of flipping "speeds up" as the text progresses. In fact, it literally becomes three times faster at the end of the text than at the beginning. By the end of the text, casual viewers may long since have abandoned it; but viewers accepting the general conditions of intelligibility and following the whole narrative—the handling visualized in Figure 7.7—will experience its accumulating excitement, as a physical sensation, to be something like a roller-coaster ride, which begins slowly and rockets through the final stretch.

Second, in the first set of flips (top to bottom, zones 1–6), the enemies' execution (Episode Four) and the enemies' flight (Episode One) begin and end the segment, or "chapter" (as zones 1 and 6). In the fabula, these episodes are separated by the greatest temporal span, namely, between the very beginning and the very end of the war or conflict.[37] In the second set of flips (side to side, zones 7–12), the enemies' capture (Episode Three) and the taking of the town (Episode Two) begin and end the segment (as zones 7 and 12). In the fabula, these episodes are separated by a lesser temporal span (namely, as episodes within the war). In the center of this segment, and of the text as a whole (zones 9 and 10), the viewer seems as temporally close to the blow as it is possible to get, insofar as the blow itself is not directly depicted (zones 9 and 10 depict "after the blow" and "before the blow," the least temporal span of all). But in the third and final set of flips (double twist, zones 13–18), that temporal closeness is forced open again. The enemies' capture (Episode Three) and the taking of the town (Episode Two), as they had earlier (for zones 13 and 18 = zones 7 and 12), enclose the after of the blow and the before of the blow (zones 14 and 17 = zones 9 and 10); but they, in turn, enclose the *greatest* temporal span in the fabula, namely, the enemies' flight (Episode One) and the enemies' execution (Episode Four) (zones 15 and 16). In sum, despite the increasing pace of the viewing, or precisely because of it, the image relates the greatest possible temporal span of the fabula as entirely caught up within the king's blow, the central, focal moment. The viewer, then, cannot be led closer and closer to the blow, for the blow is outside and around whatever the viewer's viewing unfolds. In the way it interrelates the many details and zones of the image, the storying works to establish the image's principal metaphor, an expression of the continuousness of the ruler's blow.

Third, the viewer, in fact, does not only fail to behold the ruler's blow. The ruler's blow also comes at the viewer from precisely the direction in which the viewer is not looking. Whereas in the pictorial text (obverse middle), the ruler's retainers are twisting the serpopards together clockwise in the ten obverse-to-reverse flips of the palette, the ruler with his mace raised to strike (reverse middle) is poised to begin precisely on the side opposite the viewer's place of beginning. In the flips of the palette, Narmer is always about to strike counterclockwise in the reverse-to-obverse direction. Therefore—like the lion on the

37. On the concept and problems of narrative "span," see Mieke Bal, *Narratology: Introduction to the Theory of Narrative*, trans. Christine van Boheemen (Toronto, 1985), 61–63.

Hunter's Palette (Fig. 7.2)—the viewer fails to see the ruler coming up around "behind." The noose will twist off the head of the viewer before it is ever tight enough to capture the ruler's blow; in the viewer's cumulative and dizzying viewing of the image, the ruler pulls the noose tight *as* his blow, and it is the viewer who becomes its victim. At the beginning of the text, then, the viewer has been invited by the image to enter the scene like the ruler executing his enemies (obverse top, zone 1): the viewer marches beside the ruler and looks down upon the decapitated corpses. But at the end of the text (by zone 18), the viewer understands the real import of the scene initially viewed, for it was, after all, the "last" scene (Episode Four): the viewer leaves the text as yet another victim caught up in the ruler's blow.

In sum, it is not surprising that although in viewing the image the viewer may seem to unmask the ruler's textual appearances and to come ever closer to seeing the blow taking place throughout the fabula, in the ten flips of the palette the ruler is finally remasked. The ruler is always escaping the depiction of the identity the viewer thinks to behold wielding the actual blow. As I have noted, the six zones of the two sides of the palette (eighteen in all in the basic form of the image visualized in Figure 7.7) are presented in two quite visibly different modes of pictorial textuality, a descriptive, or ekphrastic, mode (D) and a "hieroglyphic" (H) mode. In the basic form of the image, the sequence of appearance of these modes can be outlined as follows:

D H H H D D (top-to-bottom set, zones 1 to 6)
H D H D D H (side-to-side set, zones 7 to 12)
H H D D D H (double-twist set, zones 13 to 18)

The viewer begins with a graphic description of the final episode, Episode Four, the enemies' execution (zone 1). In the first set of flips (top to bottom), the preceding episodes are presented in less descriptive, "hieroglyphic" pictorial text (zones 2 to 4), only to be reviewed again in more descriptive terms (zones 5 and 6). For the viewer setting out to view the image, it would seem that the "masked" depictions of the ruler—as "Bull" and "Falcon"—are going to be unmasked, and his human person smiting down his Enemy revealed.

The lure of unmasking the ruler, and of finding the real climax of the fabula, sets the viewer off on a further series of flips, only to be caught up in the ruler's noose (zones 7 to 18). A parallel device can be found in other late prehistoric images—for example, on the Oxford Palette (Fig. 7.1), a victim moves toward the lure of the hunter's presence only to be attacked from behind—but the Narmer Palette, disjunctively related to the earlier work, handles this arrangement as a metaphor in its own turn: the viewer is now a "victim." After a dizzying exchange of maskings and unmaskings (zones 7 to 12), in which the viewer can never be certain who or where the ruler really is in the narrative (although he appears to be throughout it), the viewing ends with the three most descriptive depictions of the ruler (zones 15 to 17) enclosed by the three most "hieroglyphic" (13, 14, and 18). Because the arrangement of episodes of the story embeds the greatest temporal span within the least temporal span, the textualization of this story embeds descriptive specificity within "hieroglyphic" generality. In other words, it turns what would ordinarily be a simple inversion of spatiotemporal and causal logic for the purposes of presenting a story into a metaphor for the narrative, an expression of the universality of the blow paralleling its continuousness.

The depiction of the ruler about to smite his Enemy (reverse middle zone) is insistently repeated. In the fabula, it appears between Episodes One and Two, Two and Three, and Three and Four. In the basic form of the narrative story as constructed in the ten flips of the palette, it turns up as zones 5, 10, and 17. Finally, the pictorial text strongly highlights it by magnifying its compositional scale. The picture of Narmer smiting his Enemy is strongly visible every time the viewer flips to the reverse side of the palette (flips 1, 3, 5, 7, and 9); it is therefore textually present in a full half of the narrative.

For these reasons, the picture of Narmer smiting his Enemy becomes not only an element in (to be sure, a major, focal element) but also a symbol of the narrative in which it is embedded. In fact, it advances into a single passage of text (reverse middle zone) the pictorial dynamics of the whole narrative image as it is spread out in or spread over a whole series of passages of depiction segmented and sequenced in various ways. In other words, the reverse middle zone directly depicts the metaphor that is not directly depicted in any one of the zones but rather constructed by the concatenation of all the zones. It is the pictorial symbol of the metaphorical content of the narrative.

In what Heinrich Schäfer called the main "symbolic image" of the Narmer Palette, the rebus (reverse top right zone) is not divided from the picture of the ruler smiting his Enemy by a register line like those separating the zones elsewhere on the palette.[38] Whereas the late prehistoric narrative image on the Narmer Palette constructs the reverse top and the reverse middle zones as distinct passages of pictorial narrative text, the pictorial symbol of the narrative—a second, complementary text readable in the whole text of the Narmer Palette—does not so distinguish them.

As I have noted, the rebus indicates that "Falcon" rounds up and presents the enemy captive or captives to the ruler. In the symbolic image, in which reverse top and reverse middle zones are not separated, the depiction explicitly shows that "Falcon" lifts the enemy's face to gaze directly at the face of the human figure of the ruler, Narmer. Unlike the fleeing enemy on the Battlefield Palette (obverse, third zone), who looks behind him to see and acknowledge the victorious lion-ruler facing away from him (Fig. 7.3), Narmer's enemy, already subdued by "Falcon," here faces the master who takes possession of his town.

However, just below, a less compliant Enemy is depicted, grasped by Narmer himself: although his body faces away from Narmer, the ruler twists his head completely around. Narmer stands fixed to a solid groundline drawn below the group from side to side of the whole palette. But the blow he is just about to strike, of course, cannot actually curve in or on the picture plane, indicated by that groundline, to land on top of his Enemy's skull or between his eyes. Because the end of the mace points up rather than down, and considering the way in which Narmer's arm, wrist, and hand are rendered, the blow, when it

38. Schäfer, "Das Niederschlagen der Feinde."

comes, must swing forcefully to the side of the Enemy's head, caving it in or knocking it off. The ten decapitated enemies on the obverse top zone are the aftermath of such a blow. Narmer's decisive blow, then, must arc through a wild, unrepresented space—an ellipsis in the image's specification of "place"—from the point of view of the figures ranged along the depicted groundline. The ruler's deadly force enters the world from outside, where it cannot be seen. In this case, his force enters directly from the place—like the cosmetic saucer on the obverse—where the real viewers of the palette must be standing, invited to view the narrative image as followers of the ruler, and where the ruler himself must be standing behind, for his blow, in the full unfolding of the narrative, will take them too. In the depiction, the doomed Enemy seems about to slump on the groundline. Since the ruler is holding him up by the topknot of his hair, when the blow falls—the aftermath of this before—his broken body will collapse forward along the groundline or at right angles to it, in any case "falling off" the groundline and "out of" the picture into one or more unrepresented place. But again, in the full unfolding of the narrative image, all of these places, in "back," "beside," or "in front of" the palette, have already been mastered by the ruler in the counterclockwise direction of his blow.

In addition to the rebus (reverse top right zone) and the figure of Narmer smiting "Harpoon" (reverse middle zone), the symbolic image also contains a third element (reverse left zone). Behind the ruler and placed on his own small solid groundline, the ruler's personal and evidently favored servant waits on the sidelines to perform his services. The viewer has already met him in the introduction to the narrative image (obverse top zone), where he comes up "behind" Narmer. In both passages, he carries the ruler's sandals, a water jug, the ruler's seal in a case around his neck (?), and slung around his waist what seems to be a bowl with two long hanging flaps of cloth for washing. Above his head, two "hieroglyphs"—a "royal" rosette and what is probably the bulb of the liliaceous plant that produces the flower—give his title as "sandal bearer of the ruler."[39]

In the obverse top zone, the sandal bearer has a relatively straightforward place in the highly detailed description of the enemies' execution. On the reverse of the palette, matters are by no means as clear. Because he stands "below" the ruler's upraised right arm clutching the mace, he appears to be part of the reverse middle zone; he appears to be accompanying the ruler just before the moment of his decisive blow. And yet, because he has his own groundline placed in the left portion of the composition, he could also belong to the reverse top zone, facing and completing the group of the rebus. On this view, the whole passage of pictorial text above the principal groundline on the reverse (reverse middle *and* reverse top zones) presents a "close-up" but also more "hieroglyphic" view of the scene depicted on the obverse top, that is, the ruler, accompanied by his personal servant and other companions (represented by "Falcon"), executing his enemies.

Why, then, should the sandal bearer be the only one of the ruler's retainers, of the several depicted in the introduction to the narrative image (that is, at the end of the fabula), to stand near the ruler just before the decisive blow? Although on the obverse top he has an obvious, if limited, place in the narrative image by filling out the ekphrasis at the

39. See further Schott, *Hieroglyphen*, 22.

beginning of the story, why should he be included in the text that symbolizes the narrative as a whole? Why, in the symbolic image, does he occupy the place, walking "beside" or "behind" the ruler, that the viewer initially occupies in the beginning of the narrative and by its end discovers as being struck by the ruler's blow? Finally, if we treat the whole reverse side of the palette as part of the symbolic image, then why do the fleeing enemies below the groundline look over their shoulders not only at the ruler but also at the sandal bearer? No other such glances "across" register lines appear on the Narmer Palette. Are we looking simply at the compositional and iconographic ambiguity necessarily inherent in a passage of text that functions simultaneously as part of a narrative image and as a symbol of the narrative whole? Or are we looking at the maker's, or viewer's, difficulty in extracting a symbolic whole out of a narrative image?

If the symbolic image on the reverse of the palette extracts the same metaphor for the sandal bearer as it extracts for the group of Narmer and his Enemy, then the sandal bearer's position as "coming up behind" spatially might be interpreted as his continuous, universal temporal place. Like Narmer smiting his Enemy, he too must be before, after, and throughout the story of the blow—with the difference that throughout he is masked from the sight of the Enemy, for Narmer stands before and between them. On these grounds, the sandal bearer might, I think, be regarded as Narmer's own son and successor. There is no independent evidence, of course, to back up this iconographic hypothesis. On another image of approximately the same date, the sandal bearer does appear below and to the right of the seated ruler, facing or moving toward him.[40] On yet another, the rosette labels the ruler himself, perhaps implying that Narmer's sandal bearer has succeeded to the ruler's position.[41]

The pictorial text places the sandal bearer directly below the ruler's raised arm, clenching its mace. In the text, then, after the blow falls, he will be given a place to grow. With the text of the symbolic image placing the heir apparent on the left and "future," or after, side of the blow, the two enemies depicted "below" Narmer's groundline (reverse bottom zone) are correlatively placed on the right, forward side of the ruler, looking back in the very direction the blow will be coming toward them. Like the son of the ruler, in the symbol they too seem to have a place in both the befores and the afters of the ruler's blow. In the before of the blow—in the forward direction of the narrative image—they flee the ruler's deadly wrath, are pursued, and are destroyed (Fig. 7.6). In the after of the blow—and in the message of the narrative image extracted by its symbol—they acknowledge Narmer's heir: while the left enemy raises his left hand and looks back over his right shoulder, the right enemy reverses direction, raising his right hand and looking back over his left shoulder. In either case, the pictorial text depicts them as able fully to see what is behind them, the power and danger of the ruler, only with a firm twist of their heads back even further to their left (that is, twisting off their heads) or completely around to their right (that is, changing their "point of view").

40. For this object, the so-called Narmer Macehead, see Adams, *Ancient Hierakonpolis,* no. 1.

41. Elise J. Baumgartel, *The Cultures of Prehistoric Egypt I,* 2d ed. (Oxford, 1955), 116; for reconstruction of this object, see Davis, *Masking the Blow,* 224–31, and Gautier and Midant-Reynes, "La tête du massue du Roi Scorpion."

Considering its place in the composition of the narrative and its composition as an independent text, the symbolic image on the reverse side of the palette presents the continuity of the blow, plaited through and tightening a noose around history, both an order outside and a precondition of that history as a continuous cycle of afters-to-befores and befores-to-afters. In all of history itself, the ruler—as well as his dynasty—is always coming around behind his enemy.

Henceforth, this pictorial mechanism and ones like it become the canonical narrativity of the art of the dynastic Egyptian state, which literally subordinates the viewer of its representations to and by those representations themselves.[42] Despite the two sides and several zones of depiction, and the possibility of different ways of scanning, segmenting, and sequencing them (though Figure 7.7 is the basic narrative image, it is not the only image on the palette), the insistence of the Narmer Palette's narrative image cannot be ignored: in the text, it regulates the story sequence by the use of register lines and repeatedly introduces or inserts and magnifies the scale of the ruler; in metaphor, it expresses the continuousness and universality of his blow; and in symbol, it represents and reduces the narrative. One cannot look away when the ruler is always there, everywhere. In fact, it is possible that many viewers of the Narmer Palette did not, in fact, pursue the narrative image all of the way through its complex, complete form (Fig. 7.7), despite the fact that the palette derives from and replicates the established conditions of intelligibility of late prehistoric narrativity. Instead, the symbolic image on the reverse side of the palette—the choice of a single striking picture to stand for the whole narrative image—became the dominant meaning in reading the pictorial text. Singled out by its compositional scale and framed by register groundlines, the symbolic image of Narmer about to strike his Enemy literally pushes the other zones of depiction to the side. In the constitution of the canonical tradition in the early dynastic period, later artists selected the symbolic image for replication as such, that is, as an independently meaningful visual text that could be applied in new scenes of representation the image maker of the Narmer Palette could never have anticipated. Moreover, as far as we can tell, these later image makers also suppressed the replication of the late prehistoric narrative image from which this symbol derived and in which it was initially embedded.[43]

In sum, considering both the narrative image and the symbolic image metaphorically related to it, the pictorial text on the Narmer Palette—the viewer's experience of the representation of the ruler's blow—has become the homolog of the fabula itself. Beholding the Narmer Palette is, in itself, an example of the ruler's victory.

42. See further Davis, *Canonical Tradition*, 192–224.

43. Hall, *Pharaoh Smites His Enemies*; Davis, *Canonical Tradition*, 64–82, 159–71, 189–91.

Chapter 8

Opticality and Rhetoricity in Paul de Man's "Historical Materialism"

The difference has been spread out over a temporality which is exclusively that of the poem and in which the conditions of error and wisdom have become successive. This is possible within the ideal, self-created temporality engendered by the language of the poem, but it is not possible within the actual temporality of experience. The "now" of the poem is not an actual now, which is that of the moment of death, [and which] lies hidden in the blank space between the two stanzas.

—Paul de Man, "The Rhetoric of Temporality"

As all linguistic idealists have done, Paul de Man insists that the way language points at the world is also the way human consciousness posits, or creates, the world. Such idealism of the word generally resists a material analysis, a material history, of the word itself. More exactly, material history of the word—such as the remarkable attentiveness of de Manian criticism to the "temporality" of linguistic construction and "inscription" usually turns out to be *within* a history in which the constituting power of the word is given from the beginning of the time of human consciousness. In semiotics, for example, or in "cultural studies," dogmas of the supposed "arbitrariness" of signification or of the constitutive role of "meaning" in social relations must construe language as God-given. These systems cannot say exactly how language evolves or emerges in a historical process in its own right (see Chapters 1–3).

De Man wanted to think himself, however, to be engaged in a material history—that is to say, a *non*theological one. He recognized that yearning for an all-constituting Word lands material history in logical paradox. In this chapter, I do not conclude that de Man resolves the paradox. But I suggest—making a de Manian point in itself—that he has a means of representing the problem, even of turning it to his advantage. As a preliminary formula, I say that de Man came to *visualize language*—that is, to identify the fully reciprocal relations between the light *in* the world, what gives the world to us in vision, and the light we throw *on* the world in speech. Needless to say, this is a metaphor: if the "light" of speech evokes, even as it replaces, the "light" in the world, and if the "light" in the world passes into, even as it is reconfigured by, the "light" of speech, these are not at all the same lights. De Man's metaphorical operation, however, enables a philosophical one—what I characterize as a metaphorics (if not quite a theory) of materiality in the history of consciousness, otherwise construed as linguistic through and through. In brief, de Man suggests a "historical materialism." Thus he was not blind—to use terms that he made famous—to the blindness of linguistic idealism, even though his insight runs against the very project he made so much his own. My reading proceeds chiefly from passages in de Man's late essay "Phenomenality and Materiality in Kant," first published in 1984, but where appropriate I briefly indicate how my observations might extend to other writings.

Syntagmatic Sequence and Paradigmatic Totalization

Shortly after midnight on a clear night in 1785, a French Egyptologist, Claude-Etienne Savary, and his assistant, an engineer, set off across the desert plain to the west of the village of Giza outside the city of Cairo. "Scarcely had we proceeded a quarter of a league," wrote Savary in his account of their journey,

> before we perceived the tops of the two grand pyramids. We were but three leagues from them, and the moon shone on them with full splendour. They appeared like two pointed rocks, with their summits in the clouds, and the aspect of these antique monuments, which have survived nations, empires, and the ravages of time, inspired veneration. . . . We approach the pyramids, which, with aspect varying, according to the windings of the plain we traverse, and the situation of the clouds, become more and more distinct.[1]

Savary hoped to settle the old question of the size of the pyramids. "Far from removing doubt," he noted, the many calculations made by Greek, Roman, and modern observers "have but augmented" it (194). As Savary discovered, there was good reason for the confusion. Because the faces of the pyramids had been largely stripped in antiquity of their outer limestone casings, and sand had later drifted all around the bases, one had to move toward and away from, back and forth beside, and completely around the structures in order to render a scientific judgment. More important, the very possibility of an exact survey was continually disturbed by one's tendency—we can call it "aesthetic"—to judge the

1. Claude-Etienne Savary, *Letters from Egypt* [Amsterdam, 1787] (London, 1798), 1:189. Further page references in the text are to this anonymous translation. Savary refers to the two "Great Pyramids" now known as the pyramids of Cheops (Khufu) and Chephren (Khafre), erected about 2500 B.C.

pyramids to be *unmeasurably* large. Approaching the pyramids, "the mind," Savary admitted, "shudders with involuntary awe!" (190). Sure enough, his own calculations were wrong despite his best efforts. The pyramids were not measured correctly until Flinders Petrie's surveys of 1880–82.[2]

Indeed, we do not quite know what it would be to measure the pyramids correctly. Even if Savary or Petrie had managed to determine the objective size of the pyramids, what we might call their "material" dimensions, their judgment would have had to employ a human metrology. Here there seems to be a difference in "sense"—if not of reference—between saying that the Great Pyramid measures "*x* feet" at the base, as Flinders Petrie might say, and saying that it measures "*y* cubits," as an ancient Egyptian might say. The human language of judgment changes the very "size" of the pyramids for its observer. And no measurement captures the subjective or "phenomenal" dimensions of the pyramids—their apparent size for us, and possibly for an ancient Egyptian—as unmeasurably vast.

For Immanuel Kant, Savary's experience was a paradigm of sorts. The objective parameters of material extensions such as the Great Pyramids—or, in Kant's other example, the interior of St. Peter's in Rome—are uncertain.[3] They are ambiguously small or large and far or near, even though these dimensions are given to us phenomenally in a series of visual and other impressions of them.[4] By seeing and moving around them, the imagination does obtain an "apprehension" of them. Sometimes it is possible to attain a further rational "comprehension" of these extensions—what de Man calls a "paradigmatic totalization of the apprehended trajectory" in an image that can be measured or otherwise surveyed as a summation of the "phenomenal" experience.[5] But there is always a potential

2. W. M. Flinders Petrie, *The Pyramids and Temples of Gizeh* (London, 1883). Some accurate measurements had been obtained in 1836–38 and 1864–65, "but the great scientific expedition of Napoleon [at the end of the eighteenth century] was only a little more precise than the travelers who preceded it" (George A. Reisner, *The Giza Necropolis* [Cambridge, Mass., 1943], 1:21).

3. By "extension," I mean the three dimensions of length, breadth, and thickness (the continuation of which is spatial extension as such, or three-dimensional "space"). By "material extension," I mean a body—solid or not—that has these dimensions. Notice that such a body necessarily *also* presents plane surfaces in *two* dimensions. For a pyramidal body, the plane surfaces of four sides are triangles and of the fifth side a square. (More exactly, triangles and square are the "plane figures" of the plane surfaces, portions of the planes terminated on all sides by lines. A plane surface contains an infinitely large number of possible plane figures.) A surface is defined such that if any two of its points are joined by a straight line, that line will be wholly in the surface. Any point on such a surface, or at the intersection of such surfaces, is in *one* dimension. These technical concepts of geometric topology are important in unraveling the metaphorics of de Man's "historical materialism." The "materiality" of light, regarded as material extension, requires special attention later.

4. Immanuel Kant, *Critique of Judgment* [1790; 2d ed., 1793], pt. 1 ("Critique of the Aesthetical Judgment"), lst div. ("Analytic of the Aesthetical Judgment"), bk. 2 ("Analytic of the Sublime"), sect. 26 ("Of that estimation of the magnitude of natural things which is requisite for the idea of the sublime"). All further references in the text are to these brief paragraphs in the widely available, if inelegant, English translation by J. H. Bernard, *Critique of Judgment by Immanuel Kant* (New York, 1951), 89–95. Kant used Savary in the original French edition of 1787. It should be stressed at this point that I do not attempt to explicate Kant as he may have intended to have been read or as he has been read by his modern philosophical commentators. Much more narrowly, I am interested in a certain texture of terms and ideas in the Kantian text that de Man seems to have thought he had discovered there and that seem to be required, as a "Kantian" point of reference, for de Man's further, distinctive speculations in his reflections on "Kant." Whether de Man's text is an adequate reading of Kant is not my concern here; see recently Jean-François Lyotard, *Lessons on the Analytic of the Sublime (Kant's 'Critique of Judgment,' Sects. 23–29)*, trans. Elizabeth Rottenberg (Stanford, Calif., 1994).

5. Paul de Man, "Phenomenality and Materiality in Kant," in *Hermeneutics: Questions and Prospects*, ed. Gary Schapiro and Alan Sica (Amherst, Mass., 1984), 129.

disjunction between the phenomenal apprehension of materiality—de Man's term for all material extensions, including the ground plane of the earth, the vault of the sky, and (as I shall show) the structure of reflected light—and its rational "totalization" and "comprehension." As Kant (91) points out, at the Great Pyramids or in St. Peter's (or, as romantic aestheticians had it, standing by the ocean in a storm or on a mountaintop at sunrise) one has "a feeling of the inadequacy of [the] imagination for presenting the ideas of a whole, wherein the imagination reaches its maximum, and, in striving to surpass it, sinks back into itself."

Striving for generality, Kant (90) had described this disjunction as the difference between distinct cognitive "operations"—namely, "apprehension" *(apprehensio)* and "comprehension" *(comprehensio aesthetica).* De Man connects other distinctions with Kant's cognitive one. Apprehension *sequences* phenomenal impressions of materiality, creating what de Man calls a "phenomenality." At the pyramids, for example, we walk around them or climb up them. This activity might be seen (de Man uses the jargon of linguistics) as a "syntagmatic" operation, a "consecutive motion along an axis" (129)—the route of our walking or climbing. By contrast, for de Man comprehension supposedly *sums* the sequence of impressions. It produces a representation that is not identical with any one impression but rather collates them. Thus it might be seen as a "paradigmatic" operation (129). The "axis" of this representation is not the route of our walking or climbing as such. Rather, it is the trajectory of our judgment as it retrospectively sums what we have phenomenally apprehended throughout our taking this route (compare Chapter 7).

Whereas apprehension (syntagmatic succession) can be extended indefinitely, comprehension (paradigmatic collation), as Kant had noted, seemingly has a "maximum." If measuring the pyramids or depicting a storm at sea are any evidence—in both cases, we *fail* to comprehend—we reach this limit relatively quickly. In every succession of phenomenal impressions, as Kant (90) had put it, "the partial representations of sensuous intuition at first apprehended begin to vanish in the imagination, while this ever proceeds to the apprehension of other [sensory appearances]." At a certain point, de Man says, the "vanished" or forgotten sensory appearances cannot be included in an emerging "paradigmatic totalization." For de Man, "as the paradigmatic simultaneity substitutes for the syntagmatic succession, an economy of loss and gain is put in place" (130). The totalization "gains" its clarity, simplicity, or efficiency precisely by "losing" part of the phenomenal richness of the sensory impressions it represents.

If we suppose that "totalization" represents a certain subset of our impressions, there is no cognitive problem here. But if we suppose that totalization at least tries to represent *materiality itself*—to refer to the world—then its "gain" is apparently undermined by its "loss." "The exchange from part [impressions] to whole [totalization]," de Man concludes,

---

Further page references in the text are to this essay. See also de Man's remarks on the "enigma of the relationship between the aesthetic and the poetic" ("Reading and History" [1982], in *The Resistance to Theory* [Minneapolis, 1986], esp. 68–70, on the symbolism of pyramid and sphinx in Hegel and Baudelaire). It would be fair to describe de Man's later work—from the late 1970s on—as an analysis and "deconstruction" of aesthetics "just before and with Kant" and "since Kant" (*Resistance to Theory,* 7, 25). As I shall show, de Man tries to excavate a Kantian "materialism" that post-Kantian aesthetics supposedly ignores. In his published essay on Kant, de Man (130) follows Kant on Savary; it is not clear whether he read the original text.

"generates wholes that turn out to be *only* parts" (130; emphasis added). Consequently, as de Man notes, "when the sublime [the apprehended and potentially uncomprehendible materiality] is translated *back* . . . *from* language *into* cognition [the first "translation" was from apprehension into language] . . . it loses all intellectual coherence and dissolves in the aporias of intellectual and sensory appearance" (130; emphasis added). Our "intellectual" measurements or notations—produced in the "paradigmatic" axis—are merely fragmentary, troubled reminders of the loss of "sensory" syntagmatic variety. This supposed fact of our cognitive history is the immediate starting point for a de Manian "deconstructive" formal and thematic criticism, for a de Manian history of the production of "totalization."

For de Man, we must distinguish between continuous sensory perception and the emergence of memorable, cognitively manipulable mental images. In principle, these images might be *complete* totalizations of *single* impressions. It is theoretically possible that when we look fixedly at an object without moving our eyes, head, or body, there need be no division between the content of the syntagmatic and paradigmatic forms apprehended and comprehended: our "totalization" of what we see is identical with what we do, in fact, see.[6] But for de Man, we do not know immediately whether our calibration of syntagmatic succession and paradigmatic summation *is* a "totalization" or not. Therefore meaning in language must be the acceptance of functional *part* images for sequences of appearances that, quite possibly, are partly missing (compare Chapter 12). To use the terms de Man prefers, linguistic meaning is "a tropological system," an "economy" of *metonymic* apprehension (phenomenal part for material whole) and *metaphoric* comprehension (linguistic part for phenomenal whole). The metaphor is never a perfect translation of the metonym (compare Chapter 7 on narrative sequence and emergent symbol). Or, more exactly, we cannot know, immediately and incorrigibly, that it is.

"Radical" Materiality and the Materiality of Phenomenality

The deeper problem, however, is not so much that a metaphor might not be a completely adequate label for metonymic relations. A phenomenal connection between A and B might be perfectly represented by saying that A *is* B. For Savary traversing the plain of Giza, for example, the tops of the pyramids in the distance were "like two pointed rocks" (189)—his metaphor is meant to evoke a particular impression made on him by the

6. One important project in contemporary painting and sculpture traded, albeit unsuccessfully, on this theory—more exactly, on the possibility that an object (often a simple cube or other regular solid) could be made to solicit and support this complete viewing. See esp. Robert Morris, "Notes on Sculpture, I," *Artforum* (February 1966), and idem, "Notes on Sculpture, II," *Artforum* (October 1966), both reprinted in *Minimal Art*, ed. Gregory Battcock (New York, 1968), 222–36. For a counterproject that acknowledges the "de Manian" problem of seeing *that* what we see *is* what we see, compare Whitney Davis, *Pacing the World: Construction in the Sculpture of David Rabinowitch* (Cambridge, 1996).

human-made structures—but in fact the tops of the pyramids *are* (or once were) two pointed rocks. More fundamental, for de Man, the metaphor cannot sum the metonym *other than* phenomenally: metaphor cannot reach beyond what the metonym makes available as an *internal, cognitive "materiality."* This "materiality" of phenomenality—the cognitive substance of the "metonymic" sequence of phenomenal impressions—*stands between* "metaphorical" representation and what de Man calls the "radical" materiality of material extensions as such (137). In this respect, "it would be unfortunate," de Man declares, "to confuse the materiality of the signifier with the materiality of what it signifies."[7]

Deconstructive criticism would scrutinize this gap between the "materiality" of metonym and its "phenomenality," uncertainly totalized in metaphor (compare Chapter 4). This is a gap *in* representation—as opposed to the gap between representation and the world, between the "materiality" of external extension and its "phenomenality" as apprehended by metonym. As I have been urging, these are not the same gaps. The gap between world and metonym, between materiality and phenomenality, is caused by our failure to see all of the world. Most of the world is dark to us most of the time; our eyes do not receive its reflected light. The gap between metonym and metaphor, between the materiality of phenomenality and its "meaning," is caused by our failure to see all of the light that has been reflected to us—for representation is not an *independent* source of light capable of illuminating what has not been reflected to us in the metonymic succession.

And yet we hardly need to recall that there tends to be a moment of linguistic "idealism" in the deconstructionist attention to "materiality." "Creation," de Man asserts in a closely related context, "is purely verbal, the imperative, pointing, and positing power of the word"—certainly if the first words were *fiax lux*, "let there be light." At the interior terminus of reflection, then, it would seem that consciousness reflects the world out of itself; certainly de Man himself is partly swayed by the "fundamental epistemological metaphor of

7. De Man, *Resistance to Theory*, 11. And further: "This may seem obvious enough on the level of light and sound, but it is less so with regard to the more general phenomenality of space, time or especially of the self" (*Resistance to Theory*, 11). See further idem, "The Epistemology of Metaphor," *Critical Inquiry* 5 (1978), 13–30. Among other things, this essay seems to have prepared the ground for de Man's work of the early 1980s on Kant and Hegel. It would take me too far from my interests here to examine the relation of de Manian "allegory" to metaphor. Whereas "metaphor" is bound by the pattern of resemblances emerging in phenomenality, "allegory," de Man says, "has lost confidence in the effectiveness of the substitutive power generated by resemblance" and "states a proper meaning . . . by using a literal sign which bears no resemblance to that meaning" (*Allegories of Reading: Figural Language in Rousseau, Nietzsche, Rilke, and Proust* [New Haven, Conn., 1979], 74). From this vantage point, allegory is either a sovereign metaphor—because it evolves an independent, nonphenomenal totalization—or, as Rodolphe Gasché suggests, it is a "disfigured" one, because it "permanently disrupts the totality specific of the figure of metaphor" (that is, the totalization of resemblance) (Rodolphe Gasché, "'Setzung' and 'Übersetzung': Notes on Paul de Man," *Diacritics* 11 [1981], 48). For my purposes, it is enough to see that de Manian allegory lies *further* from phenomenality than metaphor. But for just that reason, as the most complete act of comprehension or understanding, it must inevitably exemplify the most extensive ambiguity—for the allegorical sign can always sustain "at least two mutually exclusive readings and [thus] asserts the impossibility of a true understanding, on the level of the figuration as well as of the themes" (*Allegories of Reading*, 72; compare 10–12). As his example, de Man recalls John Ruskin's reading of Giotto's *Charitas* in the "Virtues and Vices" at the Arena Chapel in Padua. According to Ruskin, the female personification of charity gives corn and flowers (or fruit) to men, while God's angel (or Christ) gives her a heart (*The Stones of Venice*, in *Works of Ruskin*, ed. E. T. Cook and A. Wedderburn [London, 1906], 10:397, and *Fors Clavigera: Letters to the Workmen and Labourers of Great Britain*, in ibid., 27:130); *or* she gives her heart to God (*Fors Clavigera*, index, s.v.

understanding as seeing" that he identifies in the writing of Marcel Proust.[8] In the actual, material world, however, it is only at the *exterior* terminus of reflection—illuminated by the light source itself, such as the "full splendour" of the moon that Savary observed over the plain of Giza (189)—that the world is reflected to us. Thus the "reflection" supposedly inaugurated by the word, by consciousness *as* an act of naming or labeling, must be, as it were, an act of training light on the dark world of unreflected (that is, unthought) materiality. The overarching paradox, then, is that when, in this darkness, we illumine a world in our consciousness, we can no longer see what is there. The materiality of the *world* is utterly cleaved from us, exchanged for the materiality of the *word*.

In considering these relations, as de Man recognizes, we seem to be making a subtle shift from "considerations on vision . . . to the order of discourse" (130). The shift is troublesome not least because the "order of discourse" seems to have been metaphorically conceived by de Man *as* a species of vision. The logos, language, is an interior *source* of the visibilization of the world—a "virtual focal point" emitting light, even if it is really a "nothingness"—competing with and ultimately replacing actual light sources.[9] Thus de Man's reading of Kant's lines on the "analytic of the sublime"—that is, de Man's consideration of the passage *from* exterior "materiality" *to* interior "phenomenality"—seems continually unsure whether, and exactly where, to linguisticize. If light reflects the world into our consciousness at the same time as consciousness reflects the world out of itself, where is "pure materiality" overtaken by "pure phenomenality," the world by the word? How can we imagine a moment when, in the darkness of the full light of the world, *fiat lux* is spoken to illuminate it—if, in darkness, we cannot speak? These questions are unanswerable—outside of a theological ontology in which the Logos is God—because they are structured by paradox.

Despite de Man's linguistic idealism and his critical interest in the ordinary gap "in" language—the failure of its own "materiality" (or, better, "literality") to be comprehended in its manufacture of meaning—he realizes that there remains the *other* materiality to be faced. Whether we see the world *as* anything or not, and however partial and disturbed such labeling must be, we continue, nonetheless, to *see* it (compare Chapters 2 and 3). An

"Charitas"). The image—the gesture of giving a heart to or receiving a heart from God—is, de Man says, "ambivalent rhetoric" (*Allegories of Reading*, 75–77), although it is perhaps too strong to say that the two meanings necessarily "denounce" one another (*Allegories of Reading*, 12). The two "mutually exclusive readings" of the gesture—the visual *metaphor*—can readily be reduced: whether Charity gives her heart to God or God gives Charity a heart, Charity is Charity—she still gives gifts to men. But the "mutually exclusive readings" of the visual *allegory* as such, the understanding that Charity *is* Charity, cannot finally be reduced (perhaps Charity is really "Invidia," *taking* corns and fruit *from* men? [see *Fors Clavigera*, in *Works of Ruskin*, 27:126, 28:518]). Giotto's inscription of her name at the top of the painting, "KARITAS," ultimately does nothing to help, for the "literal sign [i.e., the form of the inscription] . . . bears no resemblance to that meaning" (*Allegories of Reading*, 77).

8. Paul de Man, "Hegel on the Sublime," in *Displacement: Derrida and After*, ed. Mark Krupnick (Bloomington, Ind., 1985), 146; idem, *Allegories of Reading*, 60.

9. Paul de Man, *Blindness and Insight: Essays in the Rhetoric of Contemporary Criticism*, 2d rev. ed. (Minneapolis, 1983), 19. These are de Man's metaphors and problems, not Kant's. In Kant's text, sublimity marks the far horizon, not the center, of teleological judgment. Savary's experience at the pyramids is the *extreme*—it is precisely for this reason that Kant recalls it—and we are not to imagine that most cognition subsists in such extremis. See further Lyotard, *Lessons on the Analytic of the Sublime*.

ordinary "deconstruction" of *language* does not necessarily engage our material being in the world as it is organized by the world's intrinsic materialities. The entire "tropological system" could be in the dark. But poetical or rhetorical criticism cannot necessarily discover any trace of this materiality—for what such criticism discovers can only be literality disturbing meaning, a trace of the word in its "materiality" and not of the world in *its* materiality. But a "history"—or critical "archaeology"—of the full passage from "radical" exterior "materiality" to interior meaning would enable us to avoid linguistic idealisms, the stock-in-trade of semiotic and cultural analysis of all kinds. Such "materialism"—one that "Kant's posterity has not yet begun to face up to" (143)—is the most interesting project of the late de Man. The elements of the "materialist" history he has in mind—partly following Kant—can, I think, be identified in his metaphorics.

The Materiality and the Phenomenality of the Sublime and Sublimity

In de Man's reading of Kant, the Great Pyramids or the interior of St. Peter's are "sublime" because comprehension is overwhelmed by the task of collating a judgment of their magnitude. In these examples, however, apprehension certainly anticipates a "paradigmatic totalization," the production of an adequate metaphor, that comprehends the experience *as* purposely sublime. Before we approach the pyramids or enter the doors of St. Peter's, we already comprehend that they have been *made for* us to be overawed by them. In such cases, we cannot easily disentangle our comprehension of "sublimity" from our *initial* experience—later to be labeled "sublime"—in which we are overwhelmed *simpliciter*. On approaching the pyramids, Savary noted, "the mind shudders with involuntary awe" (189). But Savary and his companion were already well on their way toward ascending the Great Pyramid and "engraving our names at the top" (194), as many earlier travelers had done: Savary fully expected to master the overwhelming exterior materiality in (his own) word. "Once more safe at the bottom," he continues, "we made the tour of the pyramid, contemplating it with a kind of terror" (194). But whatever "kind of terror" they experienced at this point was quite different from their initial "shudder of involuntary awe": after climbing the pyramid and signing their names at the top, their "kind of terror" is a metaphor, whereas their "shudder of awe" on approaching the pyramid is metonymic.

Kant hoped to distinguish teleologically manufactured "sublimity"—phenomenality comprehendible as "sublime"—from the "sublimity" of materiality in its *un*comprehendible phenomenality. According to de Man, Kant claimed, for example, that the sight of the "starry heavens" or the stormy ocean is sublime "merely by what the eye reveals *[was der Augenschein zeigt]*" (133). At the Great Pyramids or in St. Peter's, this inaugural visual sublimity cannot really be experienced, because we must already see them—give them meaning—*as* "sublime." But Kant imagined a "savage" who lives in the open air seeing one of our houses for the first time; supposedly this creature does not know the purpose of the material extension. If so, then he merely sees whatever properties of the material extension are phenomenally received by him in sequence. As de Man puts it, "[T]he link between seeing and dwelling, *sehen* and *wohnen,* is teleological and therefore absent in pure aesthetic vision" (134).

De Man rightly implies that we do not know in advance if, and where, this "link" exists (compare Chapter 5). Kant's "savage," for example, must be a creature who cannot even comprehend the materiality of the "house" as a manufactured one, for to apply the most minimal labels here would be to convert materiality to meaning. In seeing the heavens or the ocean, as de Man points out, *we* might see them as an "architectonic construct," taking the "vault" of the sky and "ground plane" of the earth to be the "space" in which we "dwell." Meaning would be introduced into materiality by the very fact that we live in it. But who is to say whether we are not *also* frequently "savage"—I would prefer the term "wild"—in the "Kantian" sense de Man picks out, *just* seeing as well as seeing-*as?*[10] De Man credits the possibility that we experience "how things are to the eye, in the redundancy of their appearance to the eye and not to the mind, as in the redundant word *Augenschein*" (135).

However, to ask about "merely what the eye reveals" is already to tip the balance in favor of the emergence of language over the exteriority of materiality. (The very use of the phrase, then, is consistent with the linguistic idealism that countercuts de Man's incipient "historical materialism.") In its many permutations, the concept already metaphorically represents the application and construction of meaning. "The eye reveals," for example, that we live underneath the "vault" of the sky: totalizing metaphor necessarily emerges in the sequence of apprehensions indicated here because we assume "the eye" effects *some* predication or other, however minimal, partial, and unstable it might or must be.

But in fact "the eye" does not "reveal" anything at all (Kant's term, *zeigen,* "to share or display," is perhaps a little less strong). It simply receives light reflected off surfaces in the world (see Chapter 2). Predication is not an operation of the eye; the active agency is less "the eye"—metaphor for the mind or language—than light itself.[11] And *without* predication, the appearance of materiality to the eye is "redundant," to use de Man's term (135): if the "link" between apprehension and comprehension, eye and mind, the phenomenality of materiality and the literality of meaning does not exist—or has been severed—then we "merely" experience endlessly repeated ("redundant") instants of light shining into the eye. But again, if we accept the metaphor that the eye does "reveal" the world to us—that it beams light off the surfaces of the world and back to itself (another kind of

10. In *Masking the Blow: The Scene of Representation in Late Prehistoric Egyptian Art* (Berkeley and Los Angeles, 1992), I try to characterize the nested relations of being-in-representation and being-in-the-"wild" in a particular system of pictorial metaphors (see also Chapter 7). For obvious reasons, the topic has been interesting not only to philosophers but also to prehistorians. See, for example, Ian Hodder's analysis of the fundamental structure of pre-state-level (Neolithic/peasant) European thought as the opposition between "house" (domus) and "wild" (*The Domestication of Europe: Structure and Contingency in Neolithic Societies* [Oxford, 1990]), discussed in Chapter 4.

11. As de Man says, "'light' names the necessary phenomenality of any positing *(setzen)*" ("Hegel on the Sublime," 147). He might have said more accurately that "light is the necessary materiality for positing." See further John McCumber, "Derrida and the Closure of Vision," in *Modernity and the Hegemony of Vision,* ed. David Michael Levin (Berkeley and Los Angeles, 1993), 234–51.

"redundancy")—then we build in the desired "link" from the beginning. The historical problem—now definable as the material determination of literality (compare Chapters 3 and 6)—can be waved away.

For de Man, "wild seeing," the reflection of exterior materiality into the eye, can "hardly be called literal, which would imply its possible figuralization or symbolization by an act of [teleological] judgment" (135). It is utterly nonlinguistic—the sheer visual phenomenality of radical exterior materiality.[12] I have suggested that de Man is willing to credit this theoretical possibility, a recognition of the materiality of the body in the world. But clearly the gap identified here must be analyzed. Just as meaning is not God-given, an eye-mind positing *fiat lux* for itself, but instead emerges in a bodily history containing the ongoing ("wild") possibility of its nonreflection (and hence the continuous possibility of nonfiguration), so too does meaning emerge as the reflection of the bodily history *into* the troubled sequence of metonymic impressions and metaphoric representations. The gap exists, then, but it is also bridged in a historical process. What is the nature and temporality of this process?

"Formalization"

"The only word that comes to mind" for "pure aesthetic vision," or "wild seeing," de Man says, is "material vision"—"but how this materiality is then to be understood in linguistic terms is not, as yet, clearly intelligible" (135). We have already seen that "wild seeing" does not have a linguistic organization. It is reflected into language *once it crosses* the gap between the phenomenality of materiality ("material vision") and the materiality of metonymic apprehension ("the eye reveal[ing] the world"). But de Man still tries to discover linguistic organization on the "prehistoric," "savage" side of the gap, where it is logically and historically nonexistent, though obviously it is "not clearly intelligible" how this analysis might be accomplished.

"Wild seeing," by definition, is "purely material, devoid of any reflexive or intellectual complication" (136). But for de Man it "is *also* purely formal, devoid of any semantic depth and *reducible to the formal mathematization or geometrization* of pure optics" (136; emphasis added). The "place and function of formalization in this intricate process" explains the "gap" of language—what criticism studies as the "intricacy and wealth of movements triggered by the original chiasmus." But at the same time, "formalization" potentially *bridges* the "radical materiality of sublime vision," or "pure ocular vision" ("wild seeing"), on the one hand, and metonymic and metaphoric literality, the "concrete representation of ideas" (136–37), on the other hand. Thus in principle criticism could identify the "chiasmus" as such, "the hidden relays . . . that appear to reconcile the incompatibilities of the inner with the outer world." It seems, then, that what de Man calls "formalization" *is* the

12. It is worth stressing, again, that "phenomenality," here, does not mean how things appear to us as predicating agents but rather how to us, a nonpredicating bodiliness, things appear. The role of affect or "desire" in "wild seeing"—as well as in figuralization—is not clarified by de Man (compare Chapters 10 and 12).

"reflexive or intellectual" moment as such. When "formalized," "wild seeing" passes from the phenomenality of materiality into its metonymic apprehension, to language and meaning.[13]

Now, "formalization" is metaphorically represented in the de Manian text—whether de Man explicitly considered the problem or not—as a descent from surface to depth. Apparently, for example, it is or involves a "reduction" from "pure ocular vision" to its "mathematization or geometrization," which achieves "semantic depth" where none initially existed (136). (Compare my comments in Chapter 4 on the "reduction sequence.") Several complex maneuvers seem to be embedded here.

Consider, first, de Man's slide from the "purely formal" to the "formal*ized*" or the "process of formal*ization*." In "wild seeing" as such, the world is not reflected to us *as* a "mathematization or geometrization" of itself. It is surely not "formal*ized*." As Savary indicated, although the Great Pyramids appeared to be "like two pointed rocks" from a distance, their "aspect" was "varying according to the windings of the plain . . . and the situation of the clouds," becoming "more and more distinct" as the beholders moved closer (189). This very approach triggered "doubtful" calculations about the size of the pyramids. Some doubts—Kant's most specific reason for citing Savary in the first place—are based on uncertainty about its *shape*. For example, as one approaches the structures, their "tiers" become visible: the pyramids do not, in fact, exhibit flat, smooth faces. As one climbs the vast steplike structures, the lower tiers cannot be held in the "imagination" at the same time as the upper ones; "the first tiers," Kant says (90), "are always partly forgotten before the imagination has taken in the last." Finally, some of the lowermost tiers are completely buried in sand, leading us to ask about the height and overall shape of the structure. In all of this, where does the material extension materialize cognitively—where is it "formal*ized*"—as a "pyramid"? When do we pass from the "wild seeing" of the materiality as such to its "reduction" to a geometry in a "process of formal*ization*"? This must be an operation applied to "pure ocular vision" by an active agency that is not identical with it.[14]

13. See de Man, *Allegories of Reading*, 43, 60. Again, such "meaning" is always troubled by its historical condition as a reflection and diffraction—by the gap between metonym and metaphor. Having assumed the cognitive metaphysics I am considering here, deconstructive *criticism* takes this secondary finding as its special matter (see further Chapter 4).

14. We should proceed carefully here. Savary's experience is not a pure instance of *inaugural* "formalization"—emerging from the condition of sheer "material vision." As already seen, the two investigators went to the "two grand pyramids" (189)—the material extensions on the plain of Giza—predicating that they were, indeed, geometrical pyramids, for they were already thinking, for instance, about the problems of measuring a pyramid's height and volume. For Kant, the interest of Savary's account lies in the visitor's attempt to reconcile an accepted predication with phenomenal difficulties actually experienced at the site and in his implicit textual acknowledgment of the ambiguous back-and-forth between sensation and judgment. Indeed, at least one of Savary's actions at the site—he tells us that he engraved his name on the "top" of the "pyramid"—presumes that the "pyramid" is *not*, in fact, a "geometrical" one, because the "literal" geometrical apex could only be a vanishingly small materiality. Kant's example of the "savage" is intended to give us the pure instant of "material vision"—for de Man also supposedly an instant of "purely formal" cognition. But there is nothing in Kant that suggests the "wild" sight is formal*ized;* Kant's point is precisely that it is not. De Man's textual shift from "formal" to "formalized," then, gives an appearance of *explaining* the process that Kant's distinction implicitly identified. Without the further specifications I consider momentarily, however, the purported explanation is empty.

If "wild seeing" does not, itself, "formalize," what accomplishes the necessary "reduction"? The answer cannot be that the "eye-mind," the agency of "linguistic" apprehension and comprehension, deciphers the phenomenality of extension *as* a mathematically or geometrically "formal" order, such as a measurable size or a particular shape. This would be the very tautology we hope to avoid. At this point, in addition to the shift from "purely formal" phenomenality to "formalized" phenomenality, we need to notice a second slide in the de Manian text.

"Material vision," or "pure ocular vision," de Man says, is "reducible to the formal mathematization or geometrization of *pure optics*" (136; emphasis added). In this sense, the passage from "vision," or ocularity, to "pure optics" obviously must be the passage to or process of "formalization." But this operation does not require—does not historically presuppose—a predicate-forming or labeling agency that construes, that *re-cognizes*, phenomenal impressions *as* "houses" or "pyramids."

"Optics" exist in exterior "materiality" whether or not human minds predicate anything about the geometric structures reflected *by* light—for because it travels in straight lines, light is itself reflected *in* or *as* geometries. (The incidents of reflection of light from surfaces constitute the "lines" of the geometry, and the angles of incidence its "points.") The material extension that could be recognized as the "Great Pyramid" is given to us optically by the pyramids of light that reflect from it, pyramids at least partly reflected into the eye.[15] Thus the *materiality of light*—rather than the "materiality" of the material extensions from which it is reflected—guarantees that the phenomenalities of material extensions available within it are "purely formal" (136). No mind need *predicate* geometries of light for that light to be reflected geometrically into that mind.

I have suggested that de Man's metaphorical terminology for the history of consciousness enables him to build across the "gap" between materiality and meaning. Notice, however, that he constructs his bridge simultaneously from both sides of the divide—hoping, it seems, that they will somehow meet in the middle. From the side of meaning, assuming a consciousness that "formalizes," he builds *toward* "material vision" located in the domain of "radical materiality" itself—because "material [pure ocular] vision" is supposedly *also* "purely formal," and thus implicitly "formalized." From the side of materiality, assuming a

15. The fact that the Great Pyramids are also a *symbolization* of these pyramids of light—a feature of their "meaning" understood by Greek observers (see Savary, *Letters from Egypt*, 1:390–94) and generally recalled by later commentators—I take up later. The pyramid's seemingly double identity as the materiality of an unreflective or unreflected cognition, on the one hand, and as the concretization of emergent ideas in a symbol, as literality, on the other hand, is the principal reason for its continuing reappearance in the symbolism of eighteenth-, nineteenth-, and twentieth-century philosophies of consciousness—from Kant and Hegel to Derrida and de Man. "In the symbolic imagination," de Man writes, "no disjunction of the constitutive faculties takes place, since the material perception and the symbolic imagination are continuous" ("The Rhetoric of Temporality," in *Blindness and Insight*, 191). There is no space here to explore the social and racial dynamics of the allegory—most notoriously, its more or less explicit theory of a developmental history of consciousness that necessarily moves from Native American or African ("savage") thought and pre-Greek ("Egyptian") preliminaries to Greek and Western rationality. The usual late-twentieth-century response to this tradition has been to assert that "early" or "non-Western" societies do not lack history. But in light of what is, nonetheless, the fundamental interest of Kant's and de Man's allegory, the more appropriate point would be that modern, Western societies do not lack pre-history (see further Chapters 1, 5, and 11).

geometry of light that "forms" phenomenality "reducible to the formal mathematization or geometrization of pure optics," he builds *toward* "its possible figuralization or symbolization by an act of judgment" (135)—because apprehension (the first step toward metaphoric totalization) is supposedly *also* the reception of "formal" geometries reflected from the world into the syntagmatic sequence of sensory impressions.

Form and Figure

According to de Man's metaphorics, the reflected phenomenality of "radical" exterior materiality gives us "forms," and the linguistic materiality of pure interior phenomenality gives us "figures." But if these two processes are, in fact, to pass into one another, if radical materiality is to be "re-cognized" as meaning in an actual cognitive history, "form" must somehow shade into "figure" and vice versa. If they become identical, a stronger thesis, then the *historical criticism of figurality*—the method of de Manian "deconstruction," or "rhetorical criticism"—correctly takes itself to go all the way from the "depth" of consciousness, the site of figurality, to the surface of the body in materiality. In fact, the method might fully absorb, even supersede, other scientific or historical criticisms of human materiality such as epidemiology, archaeology, sociobiology, or some species of social history. But if something is lost in the translation from "form" to "figure," then the criticism of figurality remains at least partly unhistorical. As its supposed historical object, criticism will have constituted a "freestanding *anaclisis*"—figurality *as* materiality even though "figure" does not wholly absorb or create "form" but is not wholly propped on it either *(anaclisis)*. ("Poetic language can do nothing but originate anew over and over again; it is always constitutive, able to point regardless of presence but, by the same token, unable to give a foundation to what it posits except as an intent of consciousness.")[16] The method of rhetorical criticism as "historical materialism" would be limited, perhaps fatally, by this paradox.

Thus the major burden of de Man's metaphorics turns out to be a translation back and forth between—the implicit, if tendentious, identification or mutual absorption of—"form" and "figure."[17] In fact, in the "intricate process" of "formalization" imagined by

16. Paul de Man, *The Rhetoric of Romanticism* (New York, 1984), 6.

17. Needless to say, there are numerous analogs and, more important, conceptual pseudosyntheses of "form" and "figure" in de Man's work as a whole. The concepts of "style," "image," and "aesthetic formalization" often function, for example, as means of holding together these profoundly disjunct but necessarily conjoined domains. In his long-standing dispute with "formalism," for example, de Man repeatedly urged that both the links of and the gaps between form and figurality have been critically misrecognized (see esp. *Blindness and Insight*, chaps. 1, 2, 6, 10 ["The Dead-End of Formalist Criticism," 1954], and 11 ["The Rhetoric of Temporality," 1969]). His central critical-historical interest in the troubled "imagism" and "(dis)figurality" of Romantic poetries of sublimity, as well as in the claims of Romantic aesthetic theory as such, is fully consistent with this. In Romantic poetry, imagination supposedly "restores to language the material substantiality that had been partially lost," so that it "becomes difficult to distinguish between object and image, between imagination and perception, between an expressive or constitutive and a mimetic or literal language" ("The Intentional Structure of the Romantic Image" [1960], in *Rhetoric of Romanticism*, 1, 7). Here, "questions of definition and of temporal

de Man the necessary translation from "form" to "figure" actually occurs *twice*—once in the domain of materiality (that is, "before," or outside, language) and once in the domain of meaning ("after," or within, language). In both cases, it consists in a reduction of dimensions. The dimensions in question, however, are not the same in the two domains.

In the domain of materiality, "form" passes into "figure" in the passage from material extensions as such, the "radical materiality" of pyramids of light (reflected from pyramids of stone), to their "optical" phenomenality, their "geometry" reflected into the eye. The illuminated world of three-dimensional objects is reconstituted as the *two*-dimensional "image" on the retina. And in the domain of meaning, "form" passes into "figure" in the passage from phenomenal impressions, the "syntagmatic" sequence of "images" registering on the eye, to their "paradigmatic" totalization in predication—"images" in the rhetorician's sense, or "figures of speech." The two-dimensional cinema of phenomenal images in the "mind's eye" is reconstituted as the *one*-dimensional meaningfulness—the name or other sense—presumed or attributed by the "eye's mind."

In principle, this "intricate process" is fully reversible. In an actual cognitive history, presumably it operates in both directions simultaneously. (Unfortunately, however, the weight of our existing critical vocabularies—broadly "materialist" *or* broadly "idealist"—tends to be placed on critically tracking one privileged direction.) This process is, in fact, "deconstruction"—not the critical method of that name but rather the "mental functions" themselves, the material cognitive history of "tropological transformations" (141). Here de Man's play on "topological transformations," the rotation or other geometric translation of plane figures or solids, is intended to evoke the "purely formal" operations of "pure optics." In de Manian "deconstruction," tropology *is* the topology of our knowledge of the world.

In principle, "formalization" is the "reduction" of full materiality to utter *im*materiality. Forms pass from three dimensions to two (in the domain of materiality) and from two dimensions to one (in the domain of meaning). Climbing the "pyramid," for example, Savary tells us that he finally engraves his name at the "top" (194), or apex, of the pyramid: the word comprehends material extension precisely by surveying it from a place essentially outside it, an *im*material "point" of understanding that surmounts materiality. In Hegel's history of consciousness, de Man points out, "the word" is the "first and only phenomenal manifestation of the idea." The Egyptian pyramids and "other monuments

situation" and "questions of shape and of figure" are fundamental to understanding the poetic reference or image; "whenever this self-receding scene [of meaning] occurs, the syntax and the imagery of the poem tie themselves into a knot which arrests the process of understanding" ("Shelley Disfigured" [1960/1979], in *Rhetoric of Romanticism,* 94, 98). (See further the essays on "image" and "emblem" in Yeats, based on de Man's 1960 Harvard dissertation, and on Kleist's "attempt to articulate the phenomenal particularity of a spatial entity . . . with the formalized computation of number" [266] in *Rhetoric of Romanticism;* and compare de Man's study of "rhetorical agitation" in the "picture postcard" lyrics of Rilke [*Allegories of Reading,* chap. 2] and his slide between "image" and "figure" in examining Proust [*Allegories of Reading,* chap. 3, esp. 71].) In this general context, de Man's late works on "phenomenality and materiality" in Kant and Hegel on sublimity appear to be a partial *Aufhebung,* as Jacques Derrida noted soon after they appeared (*Mémoires: For Paul de Man* [New York, 1986]). The de Manian project partly deconstructs itself by closely scrutinizing the claim—hitherto taken largely for granted in polemical and critical contributions—that "form" and "figure" translate one another; these late essays, I am suggesting, try to write the material cognitive history implied in the earlier writings. Manifestly, however, both texts resist their own insights, for both, at the end, reinstall pure and original figurality.

and statues made of stone and metal" are "sensory appearances all right, but not, or not yet, appearances of the *idea,*" which "appears only as written inscription." As soon as "such a notation has occurred, the inside-outside metaphor of experience and signification can be forgotten, which is the necessary (if not sufficient) condition for thought *(Denken)* to begin."[18]

Notice, however, that in materiality the "top" of the Great Pyramid is a plateau, a finite horizontal extension formed by the tops of the last tiers taken in by the imagination as the observer climbs the structure. These topmost tiers truncate the notional "pyramid" observed from a distance, although they cannot be seen *from* a distance—where the pyramids, for Savary, seemed to be "like two pointed rocks" (189). Thus the final act of signing one's name to the pyramid or, more accurately, to the act of approaching and climbing it—the final act of totalizing comprehension—is still "within" the material extension of the pyramid, the constraints of its materiality: to sign one's name at the apex of a *geometrical* pyramid, the complete "reduction" from materiality to metaphoricity imagined in de Man's linguistic idealism, is materially impossible. (Like sexuality, then, meaning *is* anaclitic.)[19] In fact, from our vantage at the "top" of the pyramid we need not even comprehend what is "inside" or "underneath" it, though Savary did include a narrative of the observers' grueling investigation of the interior shafts. Eruptions of materiality might readily disrupt the totalizations of the word organized within them. At its best, deconstructive criticism returns to this possibility, not resting content with the more predictable *glissage*—the metonymic sliding of image to image—in which naming emerges.

De Man struggles against himself to recognize that figuration is within and propped on, rather than outside and transcending, radical materiality.[20] Overall, his metaphorics deny that either terminal dimension in the history of consciousness—the three dimensions of radical materiality, the space of material extensions given by light, and the one dimension of pure nomination or predication, writing a name on/at/as the "top" of the pyramid—can be any kind of historical origin for the other. Instead he tries to build away *from* each terminus *toward* the other. Thus the two *remaining* dimensions become, for de Man, the dimensions of historical reality: the *second* dimension, "figurality," and the *fourth* dimension, "temporality," must be the props of materiality and meaning; de Man insisted early on that "the temporal factor . . . should remind us that the form is never anything but a process on the way to its completion" (compare Chapters 3 and 7). Needless to say, the second and fourth dimensions, their reciprocal relations or mutual absorption, are the

18. De Man, "Hegel on the Sublime," 142–44.

19. A project parallel to de Man's "historical materialism" is Jean Laplanche's effort to explicate the bodiliness of sexuality in a supposed material history in which desire is propped on biological instinct and "need" (see esp. *Life and Death in Psychoanalysis,* trans. Jeffrey Mehlman [Baltimore, 1983], chaps. 1 and 2). Not surprisingly, the most suggestive recent work in psychoanalysis concerns the "unconscious"—repository of forgotten figurations—at the surface, or integumental envelope, of the body (see, e.g., Didier Anzieu, *The Skin Ego,* trans. Chris Turner [New Haven, Conn., 1989]). On this model, repression can be conceived as the intersection of rationality (the defensive adaptation of the ego) and all varieties of social-political "repression" striking at bodily realities (see further Chapters 10 and 11). Whether de Man's concept of a passage between or translation of materiality and meaning takes full account of repression—a filter between the domains—is a question I cannot explore here.

20. See esp. Paul de Man, "Hypogram and Inscription," in *Resistance to Theory,* 27–53.

dimensions of "writing" and "reading" (or "making" and "viewing"). They are de Man's "bottom line," as he puts it—specifically, the "prosaic materiality of the letter" (143).[21]

Motion and Motivation

How could the two-dimensional "figure" that can be "reduced" from the materiality of light in the "mathematization or geometrization of pure optics" be the *same as* the two-dimensional "form" of phenomenal impressions that can be "reduced" in "paradigmatic totalization" to a "figure of speech"? It is here that the domains of materiality and meaning would pass into one another in an actual cognitive history. Indeed, it seems, they are the same—but in different dimensions.

The optical "figure" is a pure image, a two-dimensional "reduction" of three-dimensional materiality. And phenomenal "forms" are its *temporalized equivalent*—the *series* of optical images or the "metonymic," "syntagmatic" array that will be reduced to what I call one dimension in the "paradigmatic totalization" of "figuralization or symbolization in an act of judgment" (129, 135). (As Chapter 7 implies, "paradigmatic totalization" appears in the emergence of a narrative in the beholder's moving of a *static* image. Indeed, as Chapters 3 and 5 assert, every image—to become meaningful—"compares itself with itself"; replication is *within* each image, in our viewing of it, as much as in a sequencing of separate images.) The necessary conversion—from material form/optical figure to phenomenal form/linguistic figure—transpires when *motion* occurs. The static "image" in the "mind's eye," registering the geometry of the optical organization, becomes the continually shifting montage or blur of phenomenal impressions that the "eye's mind" registers as best it can in a rhetorical image, or "figure of speech."

21. See de Man, *Blindness and Insight,* 31. "No degree of obfuscation or ideology," de Man asserts at the end of his essay on Kant, "can transform this ['prosaic'] materiality into the phenomenal cognition of aesthetic judgment" ("Phenomenality and Materiality in Kant," 143). In other words, for de Man "wild seeing" antecedent to language, supposedly identified by Kant (at least in the "Analytic of the Sublime"), is *not* the "bottom line," despite the fact that he is simultaneously attracted to Kant's hypothesis of "a materialism that Kant's posterity [that is, idealism] has not yet begun to face up to" (143). This hypothesis tempers de Man's own occasional temptation, as a literary critic, to discover language as the "bottom line"—that is, to privilege the poetic figurality of metaphor, allegory, or symbol over the metonymic (prosaic) materiality of phenomenality. Such "prosaic materiality of the letter," writing-and-reading or figurality-in-temporality, should not be understood as "language" in the traditional sense. De Man's invocation of a prosaics as opposed to a poetics—the "priority of lexis over logos" (*Allegories of Reading,* 45) or an interest in the currency of figuration as "mere metal, not coins" (*Allegories of Reading,* 111)—is meant to be a radical criticism of traditional literary-critical interests. Because the metonymic sequence is supposedly linked back to the reflection of materiality itself, de Man's approach has the added cachet of possibly entraining a slew of "materialisms"—from the Bakhtinian to the Marxist—that seem more compatible with prosaics than with poetics. Nevertheless, one remains a linguistic idealist if the "prosaic materiality of the letter" is imagined as a reduction of language rather than a construction of materiality. See further a fine essay by Jan Rosiek, "Source, Writing, (Dis)figuration: Martin Heidegger and Paul de Man," in *(Dis)continuities: Essays on Paul de Man,* ed. Luc Herman, Kris Humbeeck, and Geert Lernout (Amsterdam, 1989), 85–97, esp. 90–96. I do not think, however, that Rosiek is correct in asserting that de Man's thought "terminate[s] in the canonization of 'the prosaic materiality of the letter' as the only conceivable sublimity" (96).

As de Man carefully points out, Kant's "material vision," or "wild seeing"—the "pure" phenomenality of radical materiality—requires "tranquility" (140). Visual impressions become "image"—not, of course, the *rhetorical* but the *radically material* "image"—as one somehow settles quietly into the materiality of light itself. Such "tranquility" can properly be called the "reflexive moment" (139) for Kantian "aesthetic vision"—the process when we fall, or return, out of the *materiality* of our phenomenality, the metonymic blur, toward its *pure* phenomenality in the optical image, a registration of absolute exterior materiality.[22] Conversely, movement (although de Man does not say so explicitly) can properly be called the "reflexive moment" for comprehension—the process when we fall, or return, out of phenomenality, forms apprehended in light, toward the *rhetorical* image, the naming or figure of speech.

Needless to say, the general argument continues to hold: as Kant pointed out, Savary's movement up, down, and around the Great Pyramid—constituting his act of "comprehension"—did not enable an easy judgment of its size. The metonymic blur overwhelmed calculation even though it was organized by a foreknowledge of the supposed formal geometry of the material extension. Correlatively, then, we would expect phenomenal impressions to overwhelm the supposed stabilization of an optical image in "aesthetic" vision, or "wild seeing." Nevertheless, the "stabilized optical image" remains one of the great metaphorical dreams of modern optics, ophthalmology, and neurology and some of their associated or derived psychologies. It can sometimes be induced experimentally or artificially.[23] There is no evidence that de Man was familiar with this research. But there is considerable evidence that de Man regards Romantic poetic figurality as "imagism," or pictorialism—an idea leading him to install the optical image (and its inevitable reflection and diffraction) at the very cognitive *origin* of the rhetorical figure and to discover the optical image, in the strongest self-reflective Romantic poetry, to be one of the most common rhetorical figures or "allegories of reading."[24] Perhaps seduced by the example of metaphors that seem to replicate the stabilized optical image—paintings, for example—de Man, like Freud and others, is tempted to give it a fundamental role in a material history of consciousness.[25] But a painting, of course, is precisely the "figure" rather than the "form" of a stabilized optical image—and this image remains a largely hypothetical entity.

To return to the metaphorics of de Man's history, in the domain of materiality movement of the optical "figure" creates the "metonymic" blur. And correlatively, in the domain of

22. The correlation between solitude, tranquility, stasis, and so forth, and the sublime—our encounter with "radical materiality"—is a staple of Romantic poetry, painting, and aesthetics. One suspects that in a roundabout way de Man extracts from this poetics the very theory of vision and consciousness that he uses to explicate it.

23. For a succinct account, see R. W. Ditchburn, "Retinal Images, Stabilization," in *The Oxford Companion to the Mind*, ed. R. L. Gregory (Oxford, 1989), 682–84, esp. fig. 5. See further Chapter 12.

24. See esp. "Intentional Structure of the Romantic Image" [1960], in *Rhetoric of Romanticism*, 1–17; "Symbolic Landscape in Wordsworth and Yeats" [1962], in ibid., 125–43; "Image and Emblem in Yeats" [1960], in ibid., 145–238; and "Shelley Disfigured" [1979], in ibid., 39–73. See also note 17 above.

25. Overtly, of course, de Man knows perfectly well that paintings are "pseudo-synchronic structures" that have no "stability of meaning" (*Blindness and Insight*, 133). In Freud's theory of fetishism a stabilized image of a traumatic event is inferred to be at the beginning of an intrapsychic history of its later blurring, refocusing, or occlusion; see Chapter 12. As I show momentarily, there is a parallel to this idea in de Man.

meaning, *arresting* that movement—the act of "paradigmatic totalization"—must create the rhetorical "figure." More exactly, the domain of meaning simply *is* the domain of arrested optical figurality: the instant of positing, pointing, or picking out is a punctuation of the temporality of figurality. As such, rhetoricity is a purely *theoretical* instant in the strict sense. As a punctuation of the materiality of cognitive time it is nothing and nowhere, a "point" (or, to revert to earlier terms, the "one dimension" of the name signed at the "top" of the pyramid). The *reality* of rhetoricity—its materiality—is the ongoing temporality of figurality sliced by its theoretical "formalizations" in figuration.[26]

What, then, causes the movement of optical figures? And what causes their arrest as rhetorical figures? ("The entire scene of the shape's apparition and subsequent waning [in Shelley's "Triumph of Life"] is structured as a near-miraculous suspension between these two different forces whose interaction gives to the figure the *hovering motion* which may well be the mode of being of *all* figures.")[27] The answers to these questions, it should be clear, would designate the substance of a de Manian history of inscription—an identification and explanation of the movement of material "form," optical "figure," phenomenal "form," and linguistic "figure" from *material* beginnings to *theoretical* endings and vice versa. In this "intricate process," any points of relative stabilization, optical and rhetorical figurality, are not to be privileged over any passages of relative mobility and mutation, "materiality" and "phenomenality" as such.

From an idealist vantage point, we can suppose that the mind *intends* to move optical figures—to inspect the world by moving through it—and to arrest rhetorical ones, to select its labels and descriptions. On this view, both phenomenal impressions and linguistic "totalizations" are the productions of a mind seeking information about and order in its world. Cognitive movement, then, is *motivation*.

For some purposes this idealist account, in its many versions, is perfectly satisfactory. It is consistent with de Man's point that mental activity partly proceeds *from* meaning *to* materiality—an element of the "Kantian" insight that Kant's posterity presumably has "faced up to" (143). But from a materialist vantage point, the account is incomplete. It assumes preexisting "linguistic" formalizations, "paradigmatic totalizations" or rhetorical figures, that launch our observation of and action in the world. In other words, "motivation" is actually the cause of *arresting* phenomenality: seizing phenomenality coming toward it, motivation punctuates the continuous "metonymic" flow and transforms it into a "formalization." But whence the movement that originally—we might say in the last instance—constituted these "formalizations" that subsequently constitute the arrests of phenomenality? When is cognitive movement *un*motivated?

As de Man puts it, when we imagine an instant of "material vision," or "wild seeing," the pure phenomenality of the optical "figure," our "assumption [must always be] that the

26. See esp. Paul de Man, "The Resistance to Theory," in *The Resistance to Theory*, 3–20. Here de Man urges that our "resistance to theory"—that is, to de Manian and closely related "deconstructive" and "rhetorical criticism"—is a resistance to literary language itself, for rhetoricity is the theoretical moment, or point in the time, of perception and judgment. But at the same time, literary language in the de Manian sense is a "resistance to theory"—that is, to the moment of its own figural theorization—just to the extent that it is material, that is, literal, imagistic, and metonymic rather than figurative and metaphoric.

27. *Rhetoric of Romanticism*, 109, emphasis added.

person is not directly threatened, or at the very least [is] separated from the immediate threat by a reflexive moment" (139). The absence of "threat" provides the "tranquility" in which the optical "figure" is reduced from the "radical materiality" of the forms of stone and of light. And therefore the "threat" must *also* create the mobility in which materiality is apprehended as *un*reduced pure form—that is, as a blur of phenomenal impressions. Our utter fear of "radical materiality"—our terror at a danger coming directly at us from the outside—prevents us from stabilizing an optical figure in Kantian "aesthetic vision": we simply will not stay long enough to allow the lunging reality of a danger to become its mere geometric reflection, its stable image on the retina. But once we are "separated from this immediate threat by a reflexive moment," when there is sufficient distance between us and the danger, "aesthetic vision" can occur.[28] The optical "figurality" of materiality can be inspected—"observed," "viewed," or "beheld"—at leisure and in detail, creating the sequence of *phenomenal* forms ultimately reduced to ("totalized" as) a rhetorical "figure." If we do *not* attain such distance, of course, the entire question of "formalization" is moot: the forms of materiality destroy all possible figures of sight and of speech (compare Chapters 7 and 10).

To escape the destructiveness, including the threats of other persons and of our own bodies, located in the material world is to achieve the distance in which danger or threat might be rendered meaningful. Savary proceeded more or less readily, for example, from his "shudder of involuntary awe" (190) to observing the "varying aspect" of the pyramids, then to his visual inspections (creating the purely phenomenal "doubt" that Kant identifies, rather than the material terror de Man notices must be assumed to be lacking), then to his calculations, and finally to engraving his name on the topmost level of one pyramid. After his descent his "contemplation" of the pyramid had a "kind of terror" for him (193), to be sure—but it was substantively different from his initial "involuntary awe." Judgment is achieved and a language, a system of metaphors, is formed under the threat of the Other's blow—if, however, it only hits hard enough to create a "shudder." The initial mobility induced by the terror in materiality gradually (re)settles into a figurality that absorbs it as the motivation of rhetorical description (compare Chapters 7 and 10).

Savary's pyramids clearly did not possess utterly destructive power. They could not induce utterly overwhelming terror. In fact, even upon Savary's approach the pyramids were less material—awe-inspiring material extensions with totally unknown, potentially dangerous properties—than metaphorical. For him, the pyramids were merely "antique monuments which have survived nations, empires, and the ravages of time" (189). As such they "inspire veneration" (189)—"the mind, casting a *retrospective glance* over the ages that have passed by these mountains, shudders with involuntary awe" (190; emphasis added). The involuntary shudder is a trace of the extreme terror latent in exterior materiality. But it is organized "retrospectively": its meaning and the appropriate metaphors ("these antique monuments" upon which we can sit "as upon a throne" [191]) have already been securely established.

28. "Disinterested" or "defamiliarizing" aesthetic perception, to use two of the most popular characterizations, is *distancing* or *distanced* perception; de Man may be taking the metaphor and striving to rediscover its material bodily reality.

Indeed, de Man implies that the examples of supposedly greater sublimity adduced by Kant—they must be more terrifying and dangerous than Savary's pyramids—have also been drained of their radical materiality and exteriority, their real "threat." Formalizing operations of figuration transform the unimaginable vastness and remoteness of the starry heavens into the "vault" of the sky; the stormy ocean stretching to the horizon becomes part of the "house" of nature in which we "dwell." The *Verwunderung* ("surprise") of materiality has been absorbed and retrospectively organized by the *Bewunderung* ("admiration") of metaphor (144): de Man is correct to notice this subtle but telling shift in Kant's terms.[29]

But none of this shows, of course, that reality, the material world of nature, other people, and our own bodies, does not contain utterly destructive powers that, when they strike us with full force, erase our language completely—obliterating the very possibility of motivation, metaphor, and meaning. It is only to say that in de Man's history of consciousness the topology of death is the negative force that constitutes the tropology of living. It is the materiality that meaning must have escaped.

Meaning might well include *figurations* of death. What is the pyramid but a symbol of the dying king's hope—as well as his material means—to ascend on ladders of light to the skies, where the stars are the souls of the dead?[30] But precisely because these images evolve in the domain of meaning rather than emerge from the domain of materiality, they offer, as Savary put it, nothing more than a "kind of terror" (193). Moreover, death might continually strike life a glancing blow. It must do so, in fact, to cause the "shudder" absorbed *by* language in its "intricate process" of "formalization"; the "shudder" is not only the mind teasing itself with figuration of its own mortality but also destabilization introduced by the threat or violence of the Other. By contrast, the full materiality of death is antithetical to the materiality of language. The one always renders the other immaterial.

Doubt and Terror

If flight from death creates the mobility and ultimately the motivation of language, then the emergence of an optical "figure" measures the distance traveled between the threat and our consciousness. In its "reduction" of material forms to the figures of "pure optics," an optical "figure" marks, for de Man, our "separation" from danger—the moment when we

29. According to de Man, Kant supposedly hopes to construe the visions of *Verwunderung* as "emphatically not tropological, entirely distinct from the substitutions and exchanges between faculties [i.e., between 'apprehension' and 'comprehension'] or between mind and nature [i.e., between language and the world it represents]" (142). De Man wants to correct Kant: he thinks we can only construe the results of seeing in terms of the fact of our living (see 134). For de Man, it is not possible, following the Heideggerian and phenomenological traditions, to see the world as it would be if we were *not* living in it—for this would be a *return* to materiality from metaphor, a particular figuration of materiality. Such "realism"—the stance, for example, of an omnipresent but invisible narrator—contrasts with the paradoxically greater de Manian "materialism" achievable in an overt narrative of an individual narrator's consciousness. See further Paul de Man, introduction to Gustave Flaubert, *Madame Bovary*, trans. and ed. Paul de Man (New York, 1965), vii–xiii, and idem, "Reading (Proust)," *Allegories of Reading*, 57–78.

30. See Whitney Davis, "The Ascension-Myth in the Pyramid Texts," *Journal of Near Eastern Studies* 36 (1977), 161–79.

can leave behind the three dimensions of actual moving bodies. (But it is, of course, one of my chief points in this book that we can *never* leave behind actual moving bodies—our own or those of any signifiers themselves [see Chapters 4, 7, 9, 12].) At this distance, whatever it is, we can safely turn about and quietly face materiality. And thus materiality becomes a two-dimensional image spread before us instead of the three-dimensional vortex in which we are being pursued. In turn, this "figure" can be inspected in detail and at length. We can even move back *into* it as a three-dimensional world fully available for our observation. But this fictively material world remains "two-dimensional" just to the extent that it is now apprehended by us *as* a sequence of images, the visual and physical unpacking or unfolding of the inaugurally safe "figure."

At the same time, however, the sequence of images or phenomenal forms does preserve something of the mobility provoked by the inaugural terror. And the emergence of a rhetorical "figure," the reduction of the sequence to its sign, marks our "separation" from *this* danger. (Because there is supposedly an "inherent tendency to gain momentum" in *irony,* this particular rhetorical figure is the most complex and literally unsettling, threatening, or "mad" rhetorical figure.)[31] Instead of being overwhelmed by the radical materiality of dangerous Otherness, we fear being overwhelmed by the materiality of its phenomenality *for us* (frightened of being frightened by the image that depicts our destruction [see Chapter 7])—even though this is only an *un*threatening image of the actual dangers. Metaphoric "totalization" arrests this motion.

The passage from optical "figure" to phenomenal "form," then, is a passage from safety achieved in a dangerous situation to danger discovered in a situation of safety. But the dangers in question are considerably reduced in the translation, for example, from sheer "terror" to mere "doubt." Optical "figure" and phenomenal "form" might be *formally* identical—at least for an instant—in an actual cognitive history, permitting reciprocal passage between the domains of materiality and meaning in the process of "formalization." But they are not, for all that, *psychologically* identical. For this reason among others, a study of the "formal relations" of and between images, including thematic (figural) relations, cannot in itself identify their affect, or psychic "content"; historical scrutiny of the actual role such images have played in the movements and motivations of a person's life in its intersubjective and natural contexts must be attempted (see further Chapters 9–12).

It is here, then, that a de Manian cognitive history based on the de Manian metaphysics of consciousness—or, running in the other direction, a de Manian textual criticism—could make its most misleading elision. Tropology, the metaphorical landscape of doubt and representation, perfectly supersedes topology, the material landscape of danger and safety and of threat and desire,[32] *if* opticality is fully absorbed by rhetoricity. The translations of dimen-

31. De Man, *Blindness and Insight,* 215.

32. If "threat" drives us *away* from materiality until we can pause in "tranquility" to observe it in "aesthetic vision," "desire," it would seem, drives us *toward* materiality (see further Chapter 10). Desire would have the same structural effect, however, on the subsequent history of consciousness: according to Nietzsche, according to de Man, "only the artist who can conceive of the entire world as appearance [i.e., phenomenality] is able to consider it without desire: this leads to the feeling of liberation and weightlessness that characterizes the man freed from the constraints of referential truth, what Barthes, in more recent times, has referred to as *'la libération du signifiant'*" (*Allegories of Reading,* 114). (As I have shown, "materiality" is the materiality of three-dimensional objects and of light in spatial extension; therefore it

sions, from three to two and from two to one and back again, might well be "purely formal," equally accessible to tropological *or* to topological descriptions. To the extent that both materiality and meaning are wholly "immaterial" in relation to the supposed constituting powers of the other—de Man makes the argument continually—there will be endless debate about which is more actual or real in human history. But the terror that destabilizes an optical "figure" is not the same as the doubt that destabilizes the phenomenal "form" that could be its perfect reflection. One protects us from the "radical" materiality of absolute Otherness. The other protects us from the materiality of phenomenality—the way in which Otherness has been reflected to us and observed by us as a safe reduction of danger, available as a sequence of "forms" and finally as a depiction or figure of speech.

Any history that fails to make this distinction—indeed, to place it at the center of an account of the temporal emergence (and aporias) of a consciousness or a text—will mistake the central historical phenomenon that de Man, in his late work and against himself, struggles to recognize: however "deconstructive," textual analysis too readily assumes "that the person is not directly threatened." A de Manian history that acknowledges the "materialism that Kant's posterity has yet to face up to" (143) is not a history of "wild seeing," of a mythical "savage" seeing the world as it is in its substantial illuminated materiality. It is a history not of *our* "savagery" but of the *world's*.[33] Its savagery punctures the stability in which we speak of the world as if it were an image—"the pyramids appeared like two pointed rocks"—and places us suddenly in the real time in which there is no time to make a picture.

has "weight" and potentially imposes it on consciousness—the "weight of history," "body weight," gravitational weight, or "referential truth" in the "weight of an argument"; by contrast, pure nomination, predication, and figuration are *im*material, "one-dimensional," "weightless.") If the de Manian history imagines consciousness to be determined, in the last instance, by reflections of violence and of desire, one still casts about for a developed characterization of these primary conditions. "We have moved on to the question of reading," de Man says, "as the necessity to decide between signified and referent, between violence on the stage and violence in the streets" (*Rhetoric of Romanticism,* 280).

33. De Manian "historical materialism" is emphatically *not*, however, Marxist historical materialism. De Man cannot accept the Marxist history of consciousness, because it is "bound to the necessity of a reconciliation [between materiality and meaning] scheduled to occur at the end of a linear temporal development." By contrast, a "truly historical poetics would attempt to think the divide in truly temporal dimensions instead of imposing upon it cyclical or eternalist schemata of a spatial nature"; "such a poetics promises nothing" (*Blindness and Insight,* 242).

REPLICATION IN PSYCHOANALYSIS

Chapter 9

Winckelmann Divided

Winckelmann's *History of Ancient Art* is often taken to be the first true "history of art." Of course, Winckelmann also produced focused descriptions of works of art as they appear to us; so represented, these apparitions can serve both aesthetic-ethical evaluation and historical analysis (see Chapter 5). Winckelmann *integrated* the twin methods of what later became the professional discipline of art history—namely, "formalism" and "historicism." He explored the form of Greco-Roman art, and all the facts, as far as climate, he took to be relevant to explaining it historically.

It is well known, however, that major aspects of the *content* of classical art—for example, its inherence in the social practices of ancient homoeroticism—were not usually acknowledged by Winckelmann. He employed an elaborate euphemism: for him, Greek art is about and depends on "freedom"—although the freedom to be or to do exactly what is left vague. It would be a misreading of German Enlightenment discourse to suppose that Winckelmann's *Freiheit* means political freedom alone; freedom—of movement, of figuration—is a cognitive condition. Recent commentators, chiefly Alex Potts, have explored Winckelmann's republicanism and the later reception of his "historicist" determination of the form of Greek art in the civic freedom of the Greek polis.[1] But this aspect of Winckelmann's account hardly exhausts the matter. It is precisely the manifest formal-historical analysis Winckelmann offers—determining artistic production, somewhat uneasily, in the political structures of civil society—that we should go beyond.

The history of art history, from the 1760s to the 1990s, has produced an approach in which art history is often reductively equated with the objective historicist explanation of artistic form. As is often said, this paradigm constitutes a discipline. But what it disciplines are not primarily the "facts" of the history of art; rather, it inaugurally disciplines *itself*—for example, by cleaving "aesthetics" from "history" (but see Chapter 5); by suppressing the subjective reality of the historian's own place and taste (but see Chapter 11); and by claiming to comprehend history through chronological and causal analysis without simultaneously acknowledging its own status as narrative (see further Chapters 5 and 6). I want to look at this defensive splitting—this *Ichspaltung im Abwehrvorgang*—in Winckelmann's *History*.[2]

At points, Winckelmann's understanding of the "freedom" of Greek art does shine forth—but in code. For example, the naturalistic beauty of Greek statues derives, he says, from the sculptors' close observation of beautiful boys naked in the gymnasium. But why the boys are "beautiful" is not represented as a hallucination of the historian-observer himself, who cannot actually *see* them; instead it is said to result from the "favorable" Greek climate (another hallucination) and practice of training men for war—facts that must somehow determine forms of natural beauty and of art. In general, such objective "historicist" explanation overrides the "subjective" aesthetic, political-sexual response, sited in sensory apparitions, that motivated it in the first place.

Many contradictions derive from this transposition of subjective desire into objective belief. For example, according to Winckelmann's explicit standards, the Hellenistic hermaphrodites (Fig. 5.7), let alone the Flavian portraits of Antinous, were contemporary with the decline of political "freedom" in Greece—and thus could not embody the essence of Greek art. But nonetheless they are cited as great classical works, indicating that the real determination of "freedom," for Winckelmann, is not—or not only—in civic politics but in erotic-ethical culture present in both democratic and authoritarian society.

As Potts has noted, Winckelmann's chronology exhibits a general *disjunction* between the time of political freedom in the Greco-Roman world and the period of its great, or classical, art. I should add that Winckelmann defines classicism itself in relation to formal and historical precursors—Egyptian, archaic Greek, Etruscan, and late Roman arts—which he cannot quite disentangle *from* classicism, supposedly the autonomous expression of history peculiar to the fifth- and late-fourth-century Greek city-states. For example, because

1. See esp. Alex Potts, "Political Attitudes and the Rise of Historicism in Art Theory," *Art History* 1 (1978), 191–213; idem, "Winckelmann's Construction of History," *Art History* 5 (1982), 377–407; and idem, "Beautiful Bodies and Dying Heroes: Images of Ideal Manhood in the French Revolution," *History Workshop Journal* 30 (1990), 1–21. Cf. Michael Embach, "Kunstgeschichte und Literatur: Zur Winckelmann-Rezeption des deutschen Idealismus," in *Ars et Ecclesia: Festschrift für Franz J. Ronig zum 60. Geburtstag*, ed. Hans-Walter Stork (Trier, 1989), 97–113.

2. Sigmund Freud, "Splitting of the Ego in the Process of Defense," in *The Standard Edition of the Complete Psychological Works of Sigmund Freud*, 24 vols., ed. and trans. James Strachey et al. (London, 1953–74), 23:275–78.

Greece in the sixth century possessed the same climate and militarized competitiveness of Greece in the fifth, for Winckelmann's historicism its art should be classically beautiful. Greece before Kleisthenes lacked political freedom; but if Winckelmann is willing to admit the unfree, if Hellenized, art of Hadrianic Rome or Justinian's Ravenna as producing great classicism, how can he exclude the *kouroi?* (Winckelmann did not know the great free-standing stone sculptures of the Archaic period now known as *kouroi,* images of nearly naked young men, but he did know the small-scale metal figurines of *kouros* type; he even understood the formal similarity between this tradition and Egyptian sculpture.) The real distinction must lie in other aesthetic or ethical responses to the *kouroi* and naturalism respectively, but Winckelmann does not provide his criteria. Instead the objective chronology of political history—with its statement of causes and sequences—is supposed to render the distinction intelligible *ex post facto*. Despite their unfreedom, Rome and Ravenna preserved a memory of Greek classicism sufficient to engender a classical art, while earlier Greece, although historically closer to the zenith, did not. As Winckelmann's reasoning implies, identifying the classical evidently turns on the presence of memory and retrospective allusion—a condition foreclosed for classicism's forerunners, who obviously cannot remember and allude to what has not yet happened. Thus Egyptian art remains aesthetically inert. Not surprisingly, however, *Etruscan* art gives Winckelmann trouble: it is neither a forerunner nor an inheritor of fifth-century Greek art but rather a parallel development. Winckelmann's reader can be forgiven for failing to unravel all these tangles: the point is that the *History* manages the erotic—the wish for and memory of what is subjectively witnessed as beautiful and desirable in sexual, political, and ethical terms—almost entirely off stage, a transference, or "carrying over" *(Übertragung),* in the strict sense.[3]

But it is not enough to say that Winckelmann's division is a transposition of the subjective into the objective, of the erotic-ethical into the formal-historical, as I have so far described it, for this might imply that the one can be replaced by the other without any loss—the treatise on beautiful Greek statues perfectly translating its author's desiring of naked Italian boys. Because Winckelmann imagines an interminable oscillation between the two positions, his art history is not invented *through* division; it is invented *as* division and thus as an interminable mourning.

In a famous passage at the very end of the *History,* Winckelmann meditates on what he calls the "downfall" of Greek art in the late Roman Empire.[4] He describes the last work of art to be cited in his enormous work: an illuminated manuscript page from the reign of Justinian depicts "two female dancers with tucked-up dresses, who hold over their heads with both hands a floating drapery." The two dancers are "so beautiful," Winckelmann goes on to observe, "that we are compelled to believe they have been copied from an ancient picture"—that is, from a lost classical Greek painting. Thus, he says, to the end of art history—that is, to the end of Greek art—"may be applied the remark made by

3. Sigmund Freud, "The Dynamics of Transference," *Standard Edition,* 12:99–113. See also Chapter 11.

4. Quotations from Winckelmann's *History* are taken from the only complete English translation, by G. H. Lodge (4 vols., Boston, 1880), 4:364–65; a new rendition is long overdue. The French translation is worth consulting for its more nuanced representation of Winckelmann's prose (*Histoire de l'art chez les anciens, par Winckelmann, avec des notes historiques et critiques de différens auteurs* [Paris, 1802–3]).

Longinus of the *Odyssey,* that in it we see Homer as the setting sun; its greatness is there, but not its force." Examining these beautiful figures—the copy of a more "forceful" original, they are the trace of its loss—Winckelmann says, in the next-to-last paragraph of his history, that he feels "almost like the historian who, in narrating the history of his native land, is compelled to allude to its destruction, of which he was a witness" (4:364).

But Winckelmann does not actually indicate any specific work that the manuscript has "copied," although he has earlier given examples of prototype and copy. We are, he says, just "compelled to believe" the page is a "copy," and thus the trace of a loss, only because it is, itself, so "beautiful." Its apparent "beauty," for us, is what compels us to see a loss in it. But why should the beautiful dancers' being a "copy" imply that something has been lost or destroyed, when ordinarily Winckelmann recommends the imitation of classical art precisely as a *finding* or *restoration* of beauty? Of course, the late Roman copy might lose something because it *merely* copies rather than "imitates" in a more synthetic fashion; although Winckelmann does not say so, perhaps he thinks the dancers do not attain his recommended form of *Nachahmung.*[5] But then how could they be "beautiful," and how could he see them as the trace of a loss, when beauty is precisely the "imitation" and thus the finding—not the "copying" and thus the losing—of classical art?

Furthermore, in meditating on the loss that explains the beauty before him, in what sense can Winckelmann be a "witness" to the destruction of Greek art? Its "downfall" occurred between the age of Pericles and the age of Justinian—between the time of the unspecified lost prototype and the manuscript. By the same token, in what sense could Greek art—from the age of Pericles to the age of Justinian—be Winckelmann's "*native* land," the "destruction" of which he witnesses? Winckelmann was born in Prussia and came no closer to Greece than the Dresden collections of the King of Poland, the ruins of Herculaneum, and the Villa Albani (see Chapter 5). Indeed, in the terms of his own metaphor what Winckelmann witnesses does not obviously amount to a loss, a "downfall," at all. Although the sun may set, it always rises again. And although "Odysseus"—Greek art in the age of Justinian—may have wandered far from his native land, he *does* return home: it was other heroes of the *Iliad,* in all their "force," who left their native land of Greece to perish at Troy. It must be, then, that the late Roman manuscript is like a sun endlessly setting, without going down, or like Odysseus endlessly returning home without getting there. But what kind of a "downfall" is it that is always a downfalling without full presence or complete absence—as Longinus says, a "greatness" without "force"?

Now, it would be easy to say that Winckelmann witnesses the "downfall" of Greek art in writing his *History of Ancient Art.* As a historian, we could say, he witnesses the historical loss of the "force" of Greek art in the stylistic transformations that he chronicles—the setting of its sun from Pericles to Justinian. And it would be easy to conclude, in parallel, that it must be in his imagination and especially in his erotics that Winckelmann takes classical Greece as his "native land."[6] Thus we could say that Winckelmann, as historian,

5. J. J. Winckelmann, *Gedanken über die Nachahmung der griechischen Werke in der Mahlerey und Bildhauerkunst* (Dresden, 1755); an excellent English translation is *Reflections on the Imitation of Greek Works in Painting and Sculpture,* trans. Elfriede Heyer and Roger C. Norton (La Salle, Ill., 1987).

6. The most successful attempts to integrate Winckelmann's art historical writing and aesthetic theory with

witnesses the "downfall" of the object with which he identifies—"my native land"—by chronicling it, by producing a historical narrative of its transformation from Pericles to Justinian. If he were not the *historian* of Greek art, then he could not witness its destruction—seeing classical Greek art as something that art has historically lost. But the matter is not so simple. With typical nuance, Winckelmann says that as a historian he is "compelled to allude" to a destruction he has *already* witnessed—just as he has been "compelled to believe" that the beauty before his eyes is a copy of what has *already* been lost. Therefore it is not as a historian of art that he witnesses the destruction of Greek art; rather, it is as a historian that he writes about *a loss he has already witnessed*. Thus it may be his witnessing of the downfall of Greek art that constitutes him as its historian, rather than the other way around. The difference is between living through the loss to become its historian and becoming the historian of the loss to live through it. In the former case, the loss is already part of one's own history, a loss for oneself—although as a historian one writes about the loss as having taken place in history before oneself, a loss for art; the subjective loss of the object becomes the objective loss of the object. In the latter case, the loss is *not* part of one's own history, for it is only a loss for art, although as a historian one makes it so, a loss for oneself: objective loss becomes subjective. If Winckelmann acknowledges *two* losses, a loss within art history and a loss for oneself, as well as their complementary histories, the history one witnesses and the history within which one is witnessing history, his task will be to relate the two—to separate, conjoin, reduce, or transcend them.

Most modern art history can be seen as an "objective" account of the history of art using Winckelmann's instruments of periodization, stylistic criticism, iconography, historicism, and ethical valuation (now known as ideology critique, or political criticism) (see further Chapters 5 and 6). This practice is founded on radically polarizing the two fields I have identified (see further Chapter 11). Within the discipline, or, more accurately, *with* discipline, the loss—of the sexually, ethically, and politically beautiful or desirable—is always *outside* the art historian in the history of art as such; the art historian only "alludes" to what takes place in a "native land" in which he does not reside. Nonetheless, as Winckelmann's nuance implies, we must identify a necessary reflexive moment in which the loss must be *within* the art historian and *his* history in order for him to witness the history of art as any kind of loss—for if the loss were absolute, utterly unwitnessed by the art historian in his own history, then, for him, there would be no history of art he could "allude" to in the first place.

---

his sexuality and eroticism are Leopold D. Ettlinger, "Winckelmann: Or Marble Boys Are Better," in *Art the Ape of Nature: Studies in Honor of H. W. Janson*, ed. Moshe Barasch and Lucy Freeman Sandler (Englewood Cliffs, N.J., 1981), 505–11; Hans Mayer, "Winckelmann's Death and the Discovery of a Double Life," in *Outsiders: A Study in Life and Letters*, trans. Denis M. Sweet (Cambridge, 1982), 167–74; and Denis M. Sweet, "The Personal, the Political, and the Aesthetic: J. J. Winckelmann's German Enlightenment Life," in *The Pursuit of Sodomy: Male Homosexuality in Renaissance and Enlightenment Europe*, ed. Kent Gerard and Gert Hekma (San Francisco, 1988), 147–61; Kevin Parker, "Winckelmann and the Problem of the Boy," *Eighteenth-Century Studies* 25 (1992), 523–40. Alex Potts, *Flesh and the Ideal: Winckelmann and the Origins of Art History* (New Haven, 1994), is a superb substantive interpretation of Winckelmann's aesthetics; here, I merely treat Winckelmann's aesthetics and art history allegorically—as a figure for art historians' readings of art and their relation to it.

Again Winckelmann puts it carefully. In concluding his *History* with an example of the "downfall" of Greek art, he is "almost like" a historian writing about a destruction he has also witnessed. Yet in assuming this position, he has, as he says, "already overstepped the boundaries of the history of art." Strictly speaking, the history of art is the history of what has been lost in, and to, history. But one does not begin an art history unless what has been lost was once not unredeemably lost in an irreducibly past history one precisely did not witness. To begin an art history the loss must be in one's own history to be "witnessed" there. It is only there that it is *being seen to be being lost*. Something happens just outside the boundary of art history, at a horizon or place of sunsetting, where the object, the history of art, is witnessed as being lost—as being evacuated of its force despite its greatness, as departing or being destroyed; and the historian, writing his art history, alludes to his witnessing of this departing of the history of art.

Winckelmann depicts this condition in the final lines of the *History* in what I take to be the founding image of the discipline—or, more precisely, what founds the need for discipline. "Compelled to believe" that what is before his eyes, however beautiful, is just a "copy" of what has been lost, precisely because he takes it *as* beautiful, and "compelled to allude" to his "native land" being destroyed, finally he "cannot refrain," he writes, "from searching into the fate of works of art as far as my eye could reach," and he adds, "just as a maiden, standing on the shore of the ocean, follows with tearful eyes her departing lover with no hope of ever seeing him again, and fancies that in the distant sail she sees the image of her beloved." The metaphor is intricate, but Winckelmann glosses himself: "Like that loving maiden we too have nothing but a shadowy outline left of the object of our wishes, but that very indistinctness awakens only a more earnest longing for what we have lost" (4:364–65).

According to the logic I examined a moment ago, the "maiden" is not the art historian *as* art historian, the one who has just presented a history of Greek art and just ended it with this metaphor about the loss he has chronicled. Rather, she is that art historian *before* beginning his art history—witnessing the loss the history of which he will then chronicle. We should notice the shift here: before beginning the art history, witnessing the loss "she" is female; after writing the art history, "he" is a male "alluding" to the loss "she" witnessed.

Although it is not my topic here, one begins to see why androgyny, hermaphroditism, and other amalgamations or shifts of gender play a central role in Winckelmann's objective chronicle of the history of art: they animate the writer's *own* history—as a "she" witnessing the downfall of classical Greek art, the sailing of "her" lover, the departing to which "he" will allude. Indeed, the dynamic of subjective, feminized "witness" and objective, masculinized "allusion" is the very mode of Winckelmann's homosexuality or, if you like, homotextuality—to be specific, a *delayed* activation and *partial* transposition of loss from one register to the other, a fault line across which the observing, objective subject, male for the moment, never quite refinds the object that subjectively she never wholly lost.

If she is Penelope, then her "native land" will be destroyed because Odysseus has left it. She will be beset with false suitors like the modern arts Winckelmann deplored. But in weeping at the shore she cannot know this yet. She mourns not the destruction of her native land, which destruction she will only be able to see as the *historian* of the loss she also witnesses, but rather the departure of her lover, whom she has "no hope of ever seeing again." The art historian weeps not because he is a historian but because she is a lover; indeed, he becomes a historian because she was such a lover.

As a lover, she has lost her "object of desire." The loss occurred, however, not without having seen the beloved depart and not without the beloved's seeming to continue to appear to her, if only as an "image" in the "distant sail." That is to say, the loss preserves the possibility of writing its history as he "searches . . . as far as my eyes could reach," looking out to rediscover what she saw departing. But once become a historian, the maiden finds that the beloved has been destroyed. The image of the departing beloved—returned by the "distant sail" to the lover-historian standing on the shore of his native land—must be the image of the death of the beautiful beloved, the black sail of the ship's announcing the deaths of the Athenian boys and girls. Thus the "maiden" on the shore is not only a Penelope mourning her loss, being constituted as one who will write the history of her native land as it is destroyed. He is *also* the lover Theseus, who cannot accept the loss and sails off into story itself to *save* his native land from being destroyed. The historian begins his history in order to *prevent* the loss she has already witnessed: "he" is Theseus, sailing off from his native land in heroic rescue, because "she" is already Penelope, expecting never again to see Odysseus, who kept her native land alive. But if he sails off, Theseus becomes just like Odysseus mourned by Penelope—one who leaves his native land. Another maiden, of course, will guide Theseus out of his labyrinth and *back* to love: there is the barest hint that the widening circle of division might close, although even Ariadne must finally watch her Theseus depart.

In sum, the historian, to become a historian, remains partly behind himself, standing on the shore in his "native land," precisely in order to witness the departing that sets him off in the first place—at the same time as he goes partly ahead of himself, sailing away to rescue his "native land" from destruction, the loss she himself (if I can put it this way) will witness. What is the loss, then, but self-loss? She witnesses his departing and thus experiences the destruction of her native land; he alludes to her witnessing, and by chronicling the destruction thus partly prevents it. But although he sails off into the chronicle to prevent the destruction, he never actually returns to her except as image or copy, and the loss is never fully made up: her subjective "witness" always exceeds his objective "allusion" coming behind, too late and merely *as* allusion.

This might be the place to identify the "object of desire" that Winckelmann loses. Here we would need to consider Winckelmann's "beautiful young men"—the classical Greek athletes naked in the gymnasium—whose loss "she" witnesses while relaxing with Italian boys but to whom "he" can allude in the *History* of classical art, chronicling that which she has lost but which has been returning to her in the "image." The resulting divisions would require us to trace Winckelmann's inability fully to reconcile the time of the "beautiful" with the time of "freedom"; or to admit the place of "imitation" within the unfolding of classical art itself; or to conceive a Greece outside its afterimaging Rome or its forerunning Egypt and sidetracking Etruria; or to conceive classical art outside an imprint, copy, or fragment in the first place. In each context, the object of desire is the lost historical object toward which the historian moves in his allusions and the subjective object from which his very witness of loss proceeds—in this case, neither classical Greek art as such, merely a cold and lifeless fossil, nor beautiful Italian boys as such, merely available and nonethical embraces, but the image of their identity, an object in consciousness that neither real sculpture nor real boy can do anything but copy because they are always found only in the move away from or back to it.[7] (Of course, this object-in-consciousness, or subjective object, is, itself, a copy or repetition—the "transformational object" that creates a "holding environment," a "linking" object; however, I shall not pursue any particular model here [see Chapters 8 and 12], and merely recall that the constitution of this object is *defensive* and occurs in "defensive process" *[Abwehrvorgang]*.) Whatever kind of object we identify, and whatever its history might be, to excavate Winckelmann's object of desire would *also* be to recognize his *History* as a great and exemplary work, for it comes close, I think, to finding an objective subject that almost satisfies its subjective object—the bust of a faun gracing his apartment in Rome and noticed in his *History,* not merely, then, a token of his antiquarian scholarship but also a functioning relay of self-definition in the culture he inhabited. But this identification takes me in directions too particular and literal for the final observations I want to make in this chapter.[8]

We should look beyond the identification of a particular art historian's particular loss. Such losses require the discipline of art history because they are the objects for its subjectivity—not the artifacts in themselves, fossils with no intrinsic status, but rather the ways of their departing from art historians. Thus T. J. Clark, for example, mourns his loss—the "rendezvous between artistic practice and . . . alternative meanings to those of capital,"[9] here and there or once upon a time, he imagines, actually realized—like tradition, community, *jouissance,* truth, or equality: in any case, a subjective loss held by the historian as the objective nature of history. It is not the substance of the lost objects I want to notice; they are plainly the result, as Winckelmann engagingly put it, of an "interview with spirits" (4:365). But they all share a status as the motivating apparition of any art history that is, itself, interesting or *interested,* in the strict sense: troubled, "searching as far as the eyes can reach," the "tearful" witnessing of loss, what "compels" the historian's "allusion"—or, as Freud put it, what establishes the historian's "conviction" *(Überzeugung)* about his history-to-be-written, his "carrying-over" or "transference" *(Übertragung)* (see Chapter 11), or what I have been calling his subjective-objective "transposition," not the transformation of his practice but rather the placing of it "across" the division of positions. As Winckelmann's practice implies, the life of art history is the mourning of the loss of the history of art. Therefore the *death* of art history would be the loss of its life-in-mourning. But art history is not due to loss alone. Art history requires not only the loss of its objects but also its witnessing of that loss—that is, witnessing not of the loss itself, since that took place long ago, but of what has been lost *being lost for us*. The history of art is lost, but art history is still with us; and although art history often attempts to bring

7. Compare Michael Fried's insightful account of the temporality of the imitation of ancient art as recommended by Winckelmann, in "Antiquity Now: Reading Winckelmann on Imitation," *October* 37 (1986), 87–97.

8. See Whitney Davis, "Winckelmann's 'Homosexual' Teleologies," in *Sexuality in Ancient Art,* ed. Natalie Boymel Kampen (New York, 1996), 262–76.

9. T. J. Clark, *The Image of the People,* rev. ed. (Princeton, 1981), preface.

the object back to life, finally art history is our means of laying it to rest, of putting it in its history and taking it out of our own, where we have already witnessed its departure. To have the history of art as *history*—acknowledging the irreparable loss of the objects—we must give up art history as a bringing-to-life, as denial of departure. (In Chapter 4, I noted that the funereal interests and procedures of archaeology have not been fully realized in the discipline of archaeology.) If it is not to be pathological, art history must take leave of its objects, for they have already departed.

For many there is a dilemma here. To the extent that we acknowledge the loss of the objects, we can only have art history as a pathological not-letting-go; but to the extent that we admit our desire to mourn, we can only have the history of art as a pathological walking-of-the-dead. Do we want a pageant of corpses revivified by the historian, dead things reanimated with their supposed original ideas and passions, a ghastly puppet show—like that "social history of art" on such clairvoyant terms with the agencies and intentions, politics and subjectivities, of the departed? Or an echoing mausoleum of the vanished, crypts within crypts endlessly swept out by the historian forever coming across the bones—like that "deconstruction" so devoted to the vacated? (On the tensions between intentionalist and "deconstructive" archaeologies, see further Chapter 4.) But the supposed dilemma is a false one for art historical practice itself. Just as the departure is not an original, irreducible one—not a departure existing before our witnessing but always a departing *for us*—neither is the leave-taking completely outside the departure. It is always a *taking leave* of what we witness departing. Put another way, although the departing, the history of art, and the leave-taking, art history, take place at different times and in different places, they are not really two *different* histories—the histories of art and of the art historian—but inextricably *one* history. Art history is produced under "the shadow of the object," no matter how long ago or far away, by her who witnesses its retreat within him—an ongoing taking leave of a departing. It will not be pathological (it will not, for example, be truly fetishistic [Chapter 12]) precisely so long as it does *not* entirely divide into two different histories, subject and object, subjective and objective. We should remember that the "shadow of the object" is not only the field of death for and within the subject; the object "also offers the ego the inducement to live"—if I can put it paradoxically but accurately, to live *as* death.[10]

Winckelmann could have had two different histories utterly divided from one another—antiquarian and sodomite, let us say. But his division is reconciled—although not, of course, effaced—in the witness and allusion of his work, its ongoing mourning. Indeed he invents art history precisely because his two histories—she "witnessing" and he "alluding"—are conjoined in him without closure, without a full restoration, through "his" activity of alluding to what "she" witnesses being lost. If this mourning were to cease either through the absolute subjective departure of the object *or* its total objective restoration, then art history could not begin or would come to an end—but art history lived in Winckelmann because he and she mourn unceasingly, because as division *they* are a whole.

10. Sigmund Freud, "Mourning and Melancholia," *Standard Edition*, 14:245.

Chapter 10

Pleasure and Its Contents: Bersani and Dutoit's Assyrian Reliefs

To understand how subjective sexuality might be "in" a picture or other representation—where it might be "located" in the artifact itself and in the images or meanings that the artifact relays—requires us to recall that desire and representation are partly outside one another. What achieves representation is not—or, at least, not wholly—what is desired. And what is desired is not—or, at least, not wholly—what is represented. Moreover, the conventional concept of desire as wanting what one does not have must be supplemented. Psychoanalytic metapsychology, for instance, suggests that desire is *not* wanting what one does have. In recent years, one of the most suggestive and sophisticated views of this matter has been developed by Leo Bersani and Ulysse Dutoit. Here I focus on an extended example they have presented—a study of "sadistic" and "masochistic" formal and thematic rhythms, a system of presences and absences organized by pacing and pauses, in the historical narrative reliefs of Late Assyrian palaces at Nimrud and Nineveh.[1]

As much a reading of Freud as a contribution to the art history of Assyria, *The Forms of Violence* must be read with Freud (not just "on art") and with several post-Freudian works, specifically, Jean Laplanche's *Vie et mort en psychanalyse* of 1970 and Bersani's own *Freudian*

1. Leo Bersani and Ulysse Dutoit, *The Forms of Violence: Narrative in Assyrian Art and Modern Culture* (New York, 1986) (hereafter *FV*); Leo Bersani, *The Freudian Body: Psychoanalysis and Art* (New York, 1986) (hereafter

Body.[2] These brilliant books read "the Freudian text as if it were a work of art," "problematizing its own formalizing and structuralizing aspirations" (*FB,* 5). The "textual distress" of Freud's theoretical writing, "the only possible mode of adherence to its subject" (11), evokes the unconscious itself as essentially fractured and mobile. Similarly, representations—whether works of pictorial and cinematic art or literary texts—are "productively mistaken replications of sexual fantasy" elaborating the instability of desire (45–46), "formalizing" it or "rendering it visible" (122, compare 109–12). In criticism, it follows, "we map the moves of form" (90) (compare Chapter 8). Because desire destabilizes or shatters stable forms, we are always mapping "the erasures of form in art" (111).

I shall not bother with the objection that we can make no direct psychological observations of Late Assyrian artists from the ninth through the seventh centuries B.C. The objection applies to any interpretation imputing intentions or "meanings" to historical agents or artifacts; it is, in fact, the "archaeological" problem of interpretation as such (see further Chapters 1, 3, and 4). With Bersani and Dutoit, I assume that intentionality has its fossils or desire its signs. The question, for my purposes here, is what these fossils are—or how these signs can be deciphered.

Briefly, Bersani and Dutoit propose that although the Assyrian reliefs[3] involve a "mimetic fascination" with violence (*FV,* 39), they also "trace an escape from the very type of response which they appear so powerfully to solicit" (14). In this "sliding between narrative and non-narrative modes of organization" (14), "the very centers of anecdotal violence decenter themselves" (39). The Assyrians therefore "problematize" violence as "a subject easily identifiable and easily isolated" (47). Yet this turning away from climactic violence, or "sadistic" fulfillment (there is an ancient Egyptian parallel in the Narmer Palette and associated reliefs [Chapter 7]), is, in itself, supposedly a more fundamental violence, namely, the primal "masochistic" violence of sexuality itself, continually shattering any formation of desire—the "restlessness" of desire *being* the subject-in-sexuality, the subject of psychoanalysis. In sum, the Assyrian reliefs realize, or "render visible," desiring fantasy as such, or, in the more familiar terminology propagated by the *Standard Edition* of the works of Sigmund Freud, repeat the wish *(Wunsch)* of the drives *(Trieben)* in human experience.

NARRATIVE AND SADISM, SUBVERSION AND MASOCHISM

Bersani and Dutoit's analysis certainly fills a gap in our grasp of Assyrian art. Previous descriptions of the Late Assyrian relief cycles provided virtually no account of their coher-

FB), 67–78, is a condensed version of *FV.* See also Leo Bersani and Ulysse Dutoit, *The Culture of Redemption* (Cambridge, Mass., 1990), and idem, *Arts of Impoverishment: Beckett, Rothko, Resnais* (Cambridge, Mass., 1993). Although these more recent books are more complex developments of ideas presented in *FB* and *FV,* it is worth concentrating on the earlier books for both historical and expository purposes.

2. Jean Laplanche, *Life and Death in Psychoanalysis,* trans. Jeffrey Mehlman (Baltimore, 1976) (hereafter *LD*).

3. Accessible sources are R. D. Barnett, *Assyrian Sculpture in the British Museum* (Toronto, 1975), and Julian Reade, *Assyrian Sculpture* (Cambridge, Mass., 1983).

ence, beyond mere chronological sequence,[4] or accounted for it by implausibly assuming that a unitary Mesopotamian *Geist* underlay all production from the late fourth to the mid-first millennium B.C.[5] More recent accounts, such as the subtle reconstructions proposed by Irene Winter and John Malcolm Russell, recover the overt narrative systems of Late Assyrian relief and interpret them in terms of Assyrian political needs and interests.[6] But their accounts of the Assyrian political situation itself—of the geo-economic and sociocultural enterprises and aspirations of the Assyrian rulers, their subjects, and their enemies—generally fail to investigate what Bersani and Dutoit suggest must have been the important, if not determining, role of specifically sexualized *fantasy* in "political" affairs. Despite the great historical interest of their research, and the overall success of their archaeological reconstructions, there remains, then, a gap in their analysis. We cannot understand Late Assyrian politics without considering the scale and structure of its fantasies; but we can only identify these fantasies—in however broad an outline—by considering the formal structure of Late Assyrian relief and other cultural representations. Thus the "formal" and "stylistic" analysis that some art historians wish to replace with a sociopolitical one—typically through mechanical functionalist accounts of the role of art in "legitimating" existing or emerging sociopolitical authorities—cannot be avoided as readily as they seem to believe. The "formal" analysis (it must be tuned, of course, to the structures, rhythms, and signs of fantasy) suggests exactly what sociopolitical realities and possibilities might be at stake in the production of representations—and not the other way around. Historical criticism can always confirm or reject these suggestions; but if it proceeds from the belief that it already knows what the relevant sociopolitical interests and needs must have been, it will miss some of the most important histories. As Bersani and Dutoit imply, for example, an overt pictorial narrative of conquest or domination, which seems to be consistent with "royal rhetoric" or imperial policy, might actually repress or deny itself, at least in part. What is the "political" status of such a "counter-narrative" gesture, seemingly inconsistent with our simple—evidently simplistic—conception of what "domination" requires?

Bersani and Dutoit direct us to striking forms of order, or disorder, in Late Assyrian relief. They argue that the reliefs are characterized by a linear narrative "progression" from beginnings through "explanatory middles" to "climactic endings," usually violent (*FV,* 7, 51–52). From one discrete image of an event to the next, and within any single image, the narrative irresistibly exhibits a "calculated movement toward explosive climaxes" (40). The narrative is therefore "Sadean," in their loaded word: an "orgasmic climax"—humiliation, destruction, death—"closes an incidence of desire" (104, and compare *FB,* 51–67). Like the Freudian sexual sadist who must isolate and dominate his object and whose pleasure exists *at* or *in* the moment of violence (not the precondition but the climax of his pleasure), the Assyrian sculptors devise "immobilizations" and "stabilizations" within the

4. E.g., Hans Güterbock, "Narration in Anatolian, Syrian, and Assyrian Art," *American Journal of Archaeology* 61 (1957), 62–71.

5. E.g., Anton Moortgat, *The Art of Ancient Mesopotamia* (London, 1969), 125–57.

6. See Irene Winter, "Royal Rhetoric and the Development of Historical Narrative in Neo-Assyrian Reliefs," *Studies in Visual Communication* 7, no. 2 (1981), 2–38, and John Malcolm Russell, *Sennacherib's Palace Without Rival at Nineveh* (Chicago, 1991).

ongoing, potentially diffuse narrative. Although they are not always clear, I take Bersani and Dutoit to be referring here to several hierarchies in the reliefs—for example, the king is always distinguished from his enemy by pose, costume, and so forth—and to various formal devices, such as a dramatic distinction between foreground and background, compositional frames for foreground scenes of violence, and strong diagonals pointing to the climactic contacts within the violent scenes. "Violence is thus reduced to the level of a plot" (51). In turn, "the artist's privileging of the subject of violence encourages a mimetic excitation [in the viewer] focused on the very scene of violence" (51). The viewer feels a frisson of sexual excitement, a "secret attachment" to the spectacle of death (38).

In presenting a visual analysis of nonnarrative orders, Bersani and Dutoit in part invoke standard distinctions in the classical and more recent structural theories of narrative.[7] However, in identifying the rhythms, repetitions, and displacements of the narrative line with the history of desire—their real project—they go beyond familiar formulations. They argue that nonnarrative orders work a kind of violence against the manifest Sadean order. Almost by definition, these "counter"-narrative movements are a heterogeneous lot. Among such "forms of violence," Bersani and Dutoit focus on what they variously call "geometric," "abstract," or "formal" relations (*FV,* 9, 57, 58) "supplemental" to (56), if not directly "subversive" of, Sadean narrative coherence and visual rhetoric. It is important to notice here that Bersani and Dutoit, then, are not necessarily dealing with "style" or stylistic relations in the art historian's sense (see Chapter 6). Precisely because the "formal" relations do not wholly derive from Assyrian style—its institutionalized system for the regular production of standardized images—they can be used analytically, at least potentially, as indices of the eruption of desire in representation, or, in the broader terms explored in this book, of the eruption of materiality or literality in the rhetorical organization (see further Chapters 3 and 8). For "form" to betray the conflicts of the personal unconscious, it is required that it not be wholly stylistic or conventionalized but, instead,

7. This aspect of their book seems to be the least relevant to their project. Overall, Bersani and Dutoit associate *l'effet du réel* (or *ekphrasis* or both) with narrativity and take it to be the "dominant" representational strategy of Greco-Western culture (*FV,* 41). However, as Roland Barthes's gymnastics should have alerted us ("L'effet du réel," *Communications* 2 [1968], and "An Introduction to the Structural Study of Narrative," *New Literary History* 6 [1975], 237–72), the underlying distinction, as Bersani and Dutoit seem to suspect, is false. In visual media, *ekphrasis* and narrative are simply two different and incommensurable properties of representation, to be described in different, if sometimes crosscutting, ways (see further Chapter 7). Realistic description can be narrative or nonnarrative; narrative can be realistic or nonrealistic; *ekphrasis* is not, therefore, always straightforwardly antinarrative. In fact, if depiction necessarily attributes an indefinite number of possibly "real" spatial or other properties to its referents, then *ekphrasis* is one of the defining conditions or the very ground of the image itself (see Chapters 2 and 3); narration could be a function of only some of these depictions. Bersani and Dutoit's account of any particular realistic or nonrealistic technique in Assyrian pictorial narrative becomes convoluted. For example, they take the artists' "deliberate avoidance of the effects of perspective" (*FV,* 46)—or, put another way, the centrally placed figures in a "privileged" foreground (52)—to "reinstate" the full "presence" of objects for direct viewing, supposedly submerged or lost in the narrative line. *Geradvorstellig,* or "aspective," representation—this is what they are really describing (see Whitney Davis, *The Canonical Tradition in Ancient Egyptian Art* [New York, 1989], chap. 1, for references and discussion)—is counternarrative. However, the claim is hollow. Assyrian composition is thoroughly aspective and nevertheless exhibits that repetitive Sadean narrative the authors see in it. In fact, aspective composition enables a viewer to pick up the narrative of continuous temporal entities undergoing spatial relocations episodically plotted in the register frieze. "Avoidance of perspective" is not, therefore, antinarrative in and of itself.

at least partly unique, even though it is understood, in turn, that this "personal" morphology has been intersubjectively constructed (see further Chapters 6 and 11).

For example, visually dissimilar forms—man and animal, king and enemy—should be clearly distinguished by the Sadean narrative (see *FV,* 40–41), but, as Bersani and Dutoit observe, the Assyrian sculptor constantly fits them together, curve matching curve, like two bodies (the metaphor might be literal in the register of desire) gliding along one another or locking together in sexual love. Sometimes relations create stable visual units (for example, *FV,* figs. 38, 39) interrupting the linear narrative progress when victor and victim are framed (fig. 33) or even locked together (fig. 11). Sometimes they evade the climactic violence in the narrative, for example, when the huntsman's galloping horse leads our eyes away from his plunging spear (fig. 3). Or again, in handling visually similar forms the sculptors evince a preference for paired figures, but occasionally insert "radically heterogeneous differences" (89) or create "artful plays" and perceptual puzzles (89, 95).

Always leading us away from discrete sadistic moments of pleasure, the Assyrian sculptors express the primary "masochistic agitation" of sexuality (see *LD,* 102, 105; *FB,* 37–40)—mobile and nonclimactic, diversifying and shattering the self. Throughout, Bersani and Dutoit's discussion of this "shifting line of sensual [visual] experience" is clear and evocative (33–39, 66–68, 104–9, 115–22), argued as much in Dutoit's stunning photographs as in the text itself.

As a description of the material, however, the account has been obtained, in part, with some visual and historical sleight of hand. For example, the initial visual claim that the reliefs "are as close as any art we know to linear, nontransgressive story-telling" (52) is certainly exaggerated. It seems, rather, that the artists paid relatively little attention to so-called narrative beginnings and explanatory middles and instead depicted mostly climactic scenes of violence, perhaps drawing on an available stock of pictorial formulae.[8] By contrast, to take one example, Trajan's Column distributes its attention much more evenhandedly. Indeed, it might be said that the Roman sculptors' inclusion of lengthy "explanatory middles" containing many figures doing roughly the same thing creates a problem in marking important episodes or scenes (such as appearances of the figure of the emperor), leading, in turn, to the development of what we might call, in Bersani and Dutoit's terms, "Sadean" *counter*narrative devices—means of visually extracting the "climactic" moments from the narrative flow.[9]

Moreover, the horizontal order in Assyrian relief did not always observe "linear" spatio-temporal laws. For instance, in the Til-Tuba battle scene in Sennacherib Room XXIII, the enemy Teumman appears six times in the same composition. The scene therefore cannot depict a single "climactic" moment of the battle; in a fashion typical of much ancient art,

8. See Julian Reade, "Narrative Composition in Assyrian Sculpture," *Baghdader Mitteilungen (DAIK Baghdad)* 10 (1970), 25, 97. R. D. Barnett, *Assyrian Palace Reliefs* (London, 1960), 18, suggests that pattern books were used.

9. For Trajan's Column, see W. Gauer, *Untersuchungen zur Traianssäule,* vol. 1, *Darstellungsprogramm und künstlerische Entwurf* (Berlin, 1977). Richard Brilliant (*Visual Narratives: Storytelling in Etruscan and Roman Art* [Ithaca, N.Y., 1984], 97–101) persuasively suggests that vertical structures in the column stabilized the viewer's linear (roughly horizontal) experience of a complex narrative by emphasizing salient recurrent themata. See further Peter J. Holliday, ed., *Narrative and Event in Ancient Art* (New York, 1993), for recent studies of ancient pictorial narratives.

the image selects and combines separate moments. Even where linear logic was observed, it was offset by entirely nonlinear structures, such as the symbolic, as well as formal, echoes between event types positioned above or below one another in two-register blocks of relief.[10] Many of the "formal relations" described by Bersani and Dutoit could be, and usually are, regarded as the organic by-product of Assyrian representational technique as such, with its "aspective" construction, register composition, *horror vacui,* and decorative, heraldic, and apotropaic as well as narrative interests. In fact, strictly speaking, "linear" storytelling could not exist unsubverted in a visual medium anyway. Since depiction necessarily attributes particular properties to its object (color, shape, size, texture, etc.), and insofar as some of these could not possibly have a "narrative" significance or an intelligible place in its causal or spatiotemporal logics, images always already transgress narrativity.

Finally, Bersani and Dutoit tend to elide quite distinct works produced several generations apart. They say nothing about compositional differences between the reliefs of Ashurnasirpal II (883–859 B.C.) and Ashurbanipal (668–627 B.C.), or between reliefs produced for different palaces in the same reign and for different rooms in the same palace,[11] or between different parts of a single composition.[12] It might be thought, then, that Bersani and Dutoit can find "antinarrative," non- or counter-Sadean elements in the relief cycles because they have already accepted one kind of overall narrativity as the general condition of an artificially homogenized Assyrian style. In fact, Late Assyrian art exhibits several narrativities. The basic unit of composition—a single, one-register panel between two and four times as wide as it is high and containing a single stereotyped action formula or event type—was handled flexibly in different cycles. For instance, it could be indefinitely expanded by repetitively adding figures. This building-block method did not always admit narrative easily; it retains some of the hieratic qualities of earlier and contemporary glyptic. Most of the more striking antinarrative arrangements "subverting" the repetitive narratives in the art of Ashurnasirpal II are specifically to be found in Ashurbanipal's reliefs for his North Palace at Nineveh. Indeed, Assyrian narrative as such was itself a "subversion" of earlier Mesopotamian modes of representation. None of these historical distinctions necessarily contradict what Bersani and Dutoit say about tensions within a single relief cycle, such as Ashurbanipal's. Yet their elisions do reflect a fundamental silence in their text: *who is "subverted," and by whom?*

These warnings should not stop us dead in our tracks. They might, however, be used in some quarters to ward off the broader implications of an account like Bersani and Dutoit's. Suitably refined, their analysis could accommodate the visual and historical points I have just made—and others like them—and still make its basic case. What do these "formal relations" signify in the registers of perception, desire, and reflection, and for whom, for

10. See Reade, "Narrative Composition," 96–101, and William Stevenson Smith, *Interconnections in the Ancient Near East* (New Haven, Conn., 1965), 118–28.

11. See esp. Winter, "Royal Rhetoric," on the program of the throne room.

12. On different sculptors' "hands" in Assyrian relief, see Julian Reade, "Assyrian Architectural Decoration: Techniques and Subject-Matter," *Baghdader Mitteilungen (DAIK Baghdad)* 10 (1979), 24. Needless to say, we should not undertake authorial identification purely for its own sake—as if authorship were the most important cause of style—but clearly differences in authorship are at least potentially responsible for morphological differences in "formal relations" and in style, whether or not we go on to regard these differences as iconographically or iconologically significant (see further Chapter 6).

which system of the self or social group? In her analysis of "arrest and movement" in Late Assyrian art, cited but not much used by Bersani and Dutoit, Henrietta A. Groenewegen-Frankfort considered the distribution of repeating elements in the image field and pointed to nonnarrative (in her terms, "nonhierarchical") effects of "landscape" detail and of recession. She thought these procedures deliberately broke with older, religious Mesopotamian arts in order to depict the "secularized" space and time of the Assyrian elite, bent on glorifying the tale of Assyrian national triumph.[13] Bersani and Dutoit interpret differently but not incompatibly. Nonnarrative formal relations initiate the viewer's "perceptual mobility." They require us continually to compare one element of the image with another, verifying identities and locating differences (see Chapters 3 and 5). They push us away from any stable moment upon which to settle. They are formal signs of an Assyrian "ambivalence" about the "violence they have chosen to love" (131)—of the "restlessness of desire" and as such of the "primary masochism" of human unconscious sexuality.

The Nonsubject of Aggression in the Return to Freud

This is a provocative argument. Bersani and Dutoit give the appearance of deciphering some hitherto unknown *content* of Assyrian representation. Although presented without exaggerated theoretical fanfare, their argument is clearly linked to the classicizing "return to Freud" in postwar French psychoanalytic theory.[14] Like Jacques Lacan, Jean Laplanche, and others, Bersani and Dutoit privilege the metapsychological work of Freud in 1914–15 and his dynamic-economic model of libido over the later structural hypothesis (in *The Ego and the Id* [1923]) and assumption of a primal, nonlibidinal aggressive drive (in *Beyond the Pleasure Principle* [1920]). I argue that in so doing they fail to make specific sense of the aggressive content of Assyrian art. In an important sense, whatever its methodological virtues—I have touched on them already—they cannot really get beyond a descriptive formalism. Their problems are due, I think, to inconsistencies and gaps in Freud's own analysis of sexuality and aggression and to their avoidance (typical throughout the "return") of Freud's later, radical reformulations of the problem. Just as the Assyrians are said to have "subverted" aggression by binding it libidinally, so too the authors deflect the late Freud's disturbing views on aggression to return, indeed, to the restless embrace—but embrace nevertheless—of a mobile sexuality.

Let us begin by recalling Freud's tendentious maneuvers in sexualizing human aggression. In writing "Sexuality and the Aetiology of the Neuroses" (1898) and the *Three Essays on the Theory of Sexuality* (1905),[15] he was struck by how sadists simultaneously manifested

13. Henrietta A. Groenewegen-Frankfort, *Arrest and Movement: Space and Time in the Representational Art of the Ancient Near East* (London, 1951).

14. Pierre Fedida, "A propos du 'retour à Freud,'" *Regards sur la psychanalyse en France* (*Nouvelle revue de psychanalyse* 20), ed. J.-B. Pontalis (1979), 103–18, provides useful orientation.

15. *The Standard Edition of the Complete Psychological Works of Sigmund Freud,* 24 vols., ed. and trans. James Strachey et al. (London, 1953–74) (hereafter *SE*), 3:263–85 and 7:125–245. Hereafter references to Freud's writings are inserted parenthetically in the text following the first footnoted reference to *SE*.

what Richard von Krafft-Ebing had called "love and anger."[16] In the sadomasochistic perversion, "its active and passive forms are habitually found to occur together in the same individual. . . . A sadist is always at the same time a masochist" (*SE*, 7:159).[17] Freud's problem was to interpret a sexual behavior, or disorder, in which apparently *non*sexual activities, violence and the infliction of pain, had such an overwhelming place (see *LD*, 85–102; *FB*, 30–40).

From the beginning, Freud did not wholly resolve contradictions to be found between his own clinical sources. Krafft-Ebing had seen sadism as a pathology of power: a sadistic man does not court but violently subjugates his partner. Freud partly adopted this point of view. However, he recast Krafft-Ebing's terms somewhat: "[T]he sexuality of most male human beings," he writes, "*contains* an element of aggressiveness . . . which has become independent and exaggerated and, by displacement, has usurped the leading position" (*SE*, 7:157–58, emphasis added). To this Freud added a further characterization, adopted from the hypnotist and neurologist Albert Schrenck-Notzing, which has the sadist inflicting *pain* as his pleasure as such (what Schrenck-Notzing called "algolagnia"): for the sadist, the spectacle of pain *is* the pleasurable sexual act.[18] Freud's understanding has been colloquially successful to the extent that having pleasure-in-pain, in either active or passive variants, is now often casually conflated with sadomasochism. In general, sadism now tends to be seen as sexual desire that has been crosscut by an independent, and potentially extreme, hostility; this is closer to the view Freud ultimately elaborated. It is worth noting, however, that the field of "sadomasochism" has a complex topography that probably needs further differentiation. For example, consensual homosexual sadomasochism—"safe S & M"—seems close to the entity analyzed by Freud as thoroughly libidinized (self-)destructiveness, that is, mutually pleasurable pain-infliction, whereas violent sadistic assault, analyzed by con-

16. Richard von Krafft-Ebing's *Psychopathia Sexualis* (Vienna, 1886; 7th ed., Vienna, 1892) was the monumental source, although Freud does not directly cite it in the passages on masochism and sadism in the *Three Essays*. At this time, Freud apparently did not have substantial clinical experience with the sadomasochistic sexual "perversions." In addition to Krafft-Ebing, he may have depended on Havelock Ellis, *Studies in the Psychology of Sex*, vol. 3 (Philadelphia, 1903), and other sources. The several cases forming the basis for "A Child Is Being Beaten" [1919] (*SE*, 17:175–204) were apparently analyzed in the period 1910–14 to 1918.

17. Until at least 1924, Freud was never happy with this somewhat paradoxical formulation. In additions to the third (1915) edition of the *Three Essays*, he still said that "nothing has been done towards explaining [the] connection" between "cruelty and the sexual instinct" (*SE*, 17:159). See further Jacques Lacan, "Aggressivity in Psychoanalysis" [1948], in *Ecrits*, trans. Alan Sheridan (New York, 1977), 8–29, and Daniel Lagache, "Situation de l'agressivité" [1960], in *Agressivité, structure de la personnalité, et autres travaux: Oeuvres IV, 1952–62* (Paris, 1982), 145–75. Compare *FB*, 12–25, 56–67.

18. Albert Freiherr von Schrenck-Notzing, *Kriminalpsychologische und psychopathologische Studien* (Leipzig, 1902). Apart from the general acknowledgment at the opening of the *Three Essays*, Schrenck-Notzing appears nowhere else in Freud's publications and is not explicitly cited for his views on sadomasochism (we owe the reference to Strachey). In other important areas, Schrenck-Notzing's ideas prefigure Freud's (see Henri F. Ellenberger, *The Discovery of the Unconscious* [New York, 1970], 88, 164, 775), although in perhaps the most important area of all, Freud decisively rejected Schrenck-Notzing's claim to "cure" homosexuality as a wholly "acquired" pathology (see Whitney Davis, *Drawing the Dream of the Wolves: Homosexuality, Interpretation, and Freud's "Wolf Man"* [Bloomington, Ind., 1995], 113–29). With the exception of Freud, psychiatrists and even later psychoanalysts who clinically studied sadomasochism categorically rejected Schrenck-Notzing's formulations. For a telling instance, see the enormous treatise by Wilhelm Stekel, one of Freud's rejected disciples: *Sadism and Masochism: The Psychology of Hatred and Cruelty*, trans. L. Brink (New York, 1929), 1:57–58.

temporary sociologists as "rape," seems closer to the entity analyzed by Freud as one of the sexual diversions of pure outward-turned aggression. Although both safe S & M and rape probably manifest the fundamental "mobility" of desire, we want, of course, to be able to distinguish them in terms of a more nuanced topography. It is in part for this reason that I insist, below, on the importance of identifying the "content" of what might well be the morphologically or stylistically indiscernible "forms" of mobile desire.

Not without "textual distress," in "Instincts and Their Vicissitudes" (1915) Freud developed his contentions by strenuously applying the dynamic-economic model of libido theory.[19] Sadism and masochism can each be derived, one from the other, through chains of the two well-known transformations of drive—"reversal" (from active to passive) and "turning around" (subject to object, object to subject). "Where once the suffering of pain has been experienced as a masochistic aim, it can be carried back into the sadistic situation and result in a sadistic aim of *inflicting* pain, which will then be masochistically enjoyed by the subject while inflicting pain upon others, through his identification of himself with the suffering object" (*SE*, 14:128–29). As viewed here, masochism is derivative, for Freud takes it to be the "exercise of power or violence upon some other person" (14:127), "turned" upon the self. In *Life and Death in Psychoanalysis*, Jean Laplanche—closely followed by Bersani and Dutoit—makes much of this "reflexive moment" as the constitutive moment of sexuality itself. At this point, Freud says explicitly that "a primary masochism not derived from sadism [in the way just noted] does not appear to be met with" (14:128). It was only much later that Freud came to regard masochism as having the same fundamental character as sadism (aggression).

Despite its elegance, Freud's explication in "Instincts and Their Vicissitudes" is manifestly incomplete. First, he does not come to grips with one possible mode of "reversal" itself, so-called change of content, for he has let the pleasure-in-pain—the supposed "content" of sadomasochism—remain *un*changed in the active-to-passive and subject-to-object transformations.[20] Second, although the two more complex transformations of drive, repression and sublimation, are not explicitly incorporated in the model at all (or in Laplanche's famous diagrammatic restatement, *LD*, 89–95), covertly they must play a role. For example, the sadist must somehow be *repressing* his masochistic identification with his sexual object.[21] Finally, pain itself remains problematic. Freud seems unable to say where pain is felt—to specify the subject of pain—even though pleasure-in-*pain* is supposedly a distinctive "content" of sadomasochism throughout its reversals and turnings-round. Thus,

19. *SE*, 14:103–40.

20. In the second half of "Instincts," in some of its most striking passages (almost completely ignored by Laplanche), Freud worries about the "changing of love into hate" (*SE*, 14:133). He drops dynamic-economic language in part for biological and in part for tentatively "structural" speculation. He even seems to distance himself from the concept of libido as a single, unitary stream of energy: love and hate "did not originate," he says, "in a cleavage of any common primal element, but sprang from different sources and underwent each its own development *before* the influence of the pleasure-pain relation *constituted them antitheses to each other*" (*SE*, 14:138, emphasis added).

21. The vague arrows in Laplanche's diagrams (*LD*, 94) therefore document not only the genealogy or chronology of sadomasochism (for instance, "from" reflexive masochism "to" sexual sadism) but also its topography in the subject, for, of course, the whole perverse constellation exists for the subject all at once in the totality of his or her unconscious life ("a sadist is always at the same time a masochist").

for instance, masochism itself—underlying sexual sadism—is said to derive from an original nonsexual sadism, "the exercise of power or violence," turned inward. However, in the original nonsexual situation, although the subject exercises the violence, the *pain* is felt by someone else. Are we then to suppose that in the derivative masochism the subject's violence *and* the object's pain are both somehow simultaneously turned inward?

Without belaboring such puzzles, it is evident, I think, that we must break out of the closed circle inherent in conceiving "pleasure-in-pain" as a unitary content of a single subject's desire in turn conceived as sexual. Somewhere along the line, the sadomasochist's object (more properly, his representation of the object) must be the real source, in their intersubjective relationship, of an aggression-provoking pain. For example, the object might resist the "biological aggressiveness" of the male engaged in his "struggle . . . for self-preservation and self-maintenance" (*SE*, 14:138); indeed, he or she might be capable of an aggression in his or her turn. In either case, the primary pain—the real resistance of the object, the nonfulfillment of Oedipal desire, castration—is repressed. It is exchanged for what amount to the symbolic pains inflicted in the perverse practice (not pains at all but *pleasures*). However, Freud only wants to say that "it is not the pain itself which is enjoyed, but the accompanying sexual excitement" (14:128). This awkward distinction—"pain itself" and "accompanying" excitement—serves mostly to hold the dynamic-economic model of libido together in the first place by "separating out" sexual excitement from the "exercise of power or violence" as what must be analyzed. In sum, the interpretation definitionally guarantees "the autonomy of the field of human sexuality as the field of psychoanalysis" (*LD*, 122).[22]

If we conflate desire, the primal instinct(s), with sexuality, constituting it a priori "as the field of psychoanalysis," then aggression and pain "drop out" of the subject, or put another way, we have no good idea of what a subject's pain, as such, might be. "Certain fantasies about the possibilities of human power in the world" (*FV*, 31) therefore remain unintelligible. They have been emptied of substantial content—namely, that aggression or sadism which, if it is not specifically sexual, must be part of the "vital order" or, more likely, an intersubjective environment that has not been fully recognized by the psychoanalytic archaeology.

This gap is strikingly apparent in Freud's most important discussion of fantasy-representations of aggression, "A Child Is Being Beaten" (1919), the ultimate point of reference for an analysis like Bersani and Dutoit's (compare *LD*, 97–102).[23] In this paper, Freud discusses a sexually exciting fantasy of a child being beaten, reported to him by several female patients (and at least one male patient as well, possibly Serge Pankejeff, the "Wolf Man," whose case history had been published by Freud the previous year [see Chapter 11]). It is initially unclear who "the child" is (although it is not the patient herself), who is beating it, and "whether the pleasure attaching to the beating fantasy [should]

22. Compare *FB*, 101–2. *LD* emphasizes the "propping" of sexuality, in its "reflexive moment," on the nonsexual life of the organism, or its "vital order." Sexual excitement is "propped" on the organismic functioning of some bodily zone. But needless to say, in his effort to distinguish the "autonomy" of the sexual, Laplanche must recognize the founding reality of the "vital order" on which it is propped.

23. *SE*, 14:103–40.

be described as sadistic or masochistic" (*SE*, 17:181). Freud argues that the fantasy as consciously reported, carrying "strong and unambiguous sexual excitement attached to it" of an obviously sadistic nature (17:186), is actually the "latest phase" in a reversal and turning-round of an underlying *masochistic* fantasy of the female patient herself being beaten by her father (17:185), "never remembered" by her "in consequence of the intensity of the repression" of the wish (17:185, 189). Yet further, this masochistic phase of the beating fantasy is itself a transformation of a still more archaic fantasy, the "first phase," in which the father (now clearly represented as the one who beats) is (again) beating a child (not the girl herself) (17:185).[24]

Krafft-Ebing and others had understood masochism to have precisely the content of Freud's "masochistic" (second) phase of the beating fantasy, that is, to be *a fantasy of subjugation to another's power or aggression*. Freud strenuously libidinizes this view. In the fantasy nothing is said one way or another about *the father's* violence, and we must momentarily leave aside whether it actually ever occurred at all (*SE*, 17:185, 187). In the first phase of the fantasy, however, the fantasizer, the little girl, hates the child being beaten—and does so because the child is her rival for her father's love, or, more properly, impedes the fulfillment of her love for her father (17:185). Moreover, in the fantasy she appears to find confirmation of her father's love *for her*: "[H]e (my father) loves me, and not the other child, for he is beating it" (17:190). The first Freudian phase of the beating fantasy, then, arises in the Oedipus complex (17:188, 191–93). In part, therefore, the aggression represented in this phase is not merely the sexually affectless aggression—presumably a component of the "vital order"—Freud posited in "Instincts and Their Vicissitudes" as the ground of sadomasochism, using there the example of a child unthinkingly hurting another creature such as a pet or sibling. The participants in the first beating fantasy *wish* to inflict or witness pain, for they love or hate one another. In other words, sexual pleasure can be derived merely from the "reversals," or "turnings-round," of "the exercise of power or violence," by supposing "power or violence" always to have been sexualized.

Nonetheless, the thorough libidinization of sadomasochism does not wholly specify the impetus, aim, object, and source of the aggression *in and for the subject(s)*. It does not make explicit subjective and intersubjective sense for the aggressions depicted in the fantasy. For example, the content of the first phase of the beating fantasy is (1) "My father is beating the child whom I hate" (*SE*, 17:185). Freud proposes that the complete psychic translation or replication of this content, in the second phase of the fantasy, is (2) "My father loves only me, and not the other child, for he is beating it" (17:187). But in this "translation," the father's love manifested in and relayed by the aggressive act just materializes out of nowhere, for surely, despite Freud's effort, sentence 1 does not equal sentence 2. Even more striking, the fantasy has not said that the father beats "the child" *because* he loves the little girl—but only that he must love the little girl because he is not beating *her*. In Freud's

24. In a brilliant refinement, a tour de force of dynamic-economic principles, Freud can account for the fact that one *male* patient—perhaps the only one included in the series of beating fantasists—*did* consciously recall the masochistic fantasy of being beaten by his mother (*SE*, 17:189–90); supposedly because the male's transformation of an even more archaic fantasy already involves greater distortion, an additional "reversal," it escapes complete repression.

translation of the fantasy, then, the father's aggression itself just materializes out of nowhere. More precisely, as the subject matter but not the "content" of the little girl's fantasy-representation, his aggression (for Freud) has no place. Needless to say, the nameless "child" being beaten, whose own desire is not represented in the first fantasy at all, might provoke the father to beat it; and the fantasy as deciphered denies the possibility that the father beats the child because he loves *him or her*—that *beating the child* is the "content" of "love" in this situation, rather than *beating him or her so that the little girl may see her father's love for her*.

Whereas, then, the sexual component of the fantasy-representation in Freud's analysis subsists between two named subjects, father and little girl, who love one another, the aggressive component subsists only and separately between *each* of the two named subjects *and* an unnamed nonsubject, one whose desires are not represented, one who is not an Oedipal object, not named, this "child" beaten by the father and hated by the little girl. Aggression apparently has no vicissitudes, nor does it speak in fantasy or symptom. It does not occur between subjects, that is, beings constituted by one another's Oedipal desires, even though it is simultaneously the means by which libidinal subjects (not to be conflated with the subjects who might aggress) express their Oedipal desires. Despite the libidinal translations, aggression is always (though Freud hardly has terms for this in 1919) outside sexuality.

This gap certainly leads to some "distress" in the Freudian text (see *FB*, 11). In a famous passage, Freud is uneasy about the first and supposedly Oedipal beating fantasy, "not yet clearly sexual, not in itself sadistic, but the stuff from which both will later come" (*SE*, 17:185). Indeed, he is not certain whether to call the first phase a "fantasy" at all (17:185). Moreover, it becomes troublesome for him to show how the "not yet clearly" libidinal charge of the first is maintained in the second (masochistic) phase of the fantasy, "I am being beaten by my father." Freud is manifestly unhappy with his discussion of the second phase (17:185, 193). For example, the second phase cannot merely be a "turning round" of sadistic action upon the self, with the accompanying "reversal" from active to passive, for (1) in the first phase it is the father, not the self, who beats—or, at least, the aggression is already divided between father who beats and little girl who hates—and (2) the passivity of the one beaten, whether the unnamed child or the little girl, remains constant in relation to the father. In Freud's translation of the second fantasy, there are notable but unremarked cancellations:

FANTASY PHASE 1 (SADISTIC)	FANTASY PHASE 2 (MASOCHISTIC)
Father beats the child	Father beats me
I hate the child	(canceled)
Father loves me	(canceled) = Father "does not love" me
I love Father	(not spoken)

Although the beating continues, "the child" disappears completely in the second fantasy, and no one is said either to love or to hate. Pleasure, in the figure of "the child" being beaten, is eradicated, and libidinal subjectivity is canceled out, for no one is another's desire. In other words, sexuality itself disappears. Why, then, does Freud not regard this fantasy as a *non*libidinal masochistic representation of subjection to one who does not love the fantasizer? Why is the fantasy erotic?

By way of answer, Freud supposes that a "sense of guilt" having an "unknown origin" must appear at some point in the fantasizer's development (*SE*, 17:189, 194–95). Under its influence, the relevant terms of the first fantasy—love of the father, the pain of "the child"—are repressed and the residua condensed in the second fantasy:

1 (I love) Father (who loves me) beating (the child I hate) for me
2 . . . . Father . . . . beating . . . . me

Although the fantasy "content" surviving the repression is definitely truncated, the erotic charge of the repressed terms of the first fantasy cannot be lost. Since drive energy can merely be transformed, it must be compressed into the unrepressed terms of the second fantasy of "father beating me." But since it cannot be relocated in either "my father" or "myself" without precisely that eroticization about which "I" feel guilty, the only remaining term is, of course, *the beating* itself. "This being beaten is now a meeting-place between the sense of guilt and sexual love. It is not only the punishment for the forbidden genital relation, but also the regressive substitute for it, and from this latter source it derives the libidinal excitation. . . . Here for the first time we have the essence of masochism" (17:189).

We can agree with Laplanche and Bersani and Dutoit that Freudian sexuality—which I would define from the vantage point of the later Freud as the desiring self excited in one or both of its two instincts, aggressive and sexual, to an excess requiring "binding"—can be called primarily masochistic.[25] Since it can never be experienced as completely fulfilled pleasure, it is always in part unpleasurable—not so much pleasure-in-pain but pain-in-pleasure or, more simply, the inevitable partiality of pleasure. Sexuality is the self's discontent in pleasure. Although somewhat differently stated, Bersani and Dutoit interpret the "restlessness" of the anti-Sadean formal relations in Assyrian relief from this general perspective. Always leading us away from discrete sadistic moments of pleasure, the sculptors express the primary "masochistic agitation" of sexuality (see *LD*, 102, 105; *FB*, 37–40)—the product of the self-in-sexuality continually (re)constituting itself as the sub-

25. In Freud's later work, "diversion outwards" and "binding" or "taming" (*Bindung, Bändigung*) are the two processes of the "fusion" (*Mischung*) of the fundamental instinctual drives, aggression and libido. In "The Economic Problem of Masochism" [1924] (*SE*, 19:157–70), Freud no longer attempts to derive masochism from sadism but sees them as fundamental counterparts. Thus he wants to distinguish a "primary masochism"—on par with primary aggressiveness—from which what now becomes the "secondary masochism" is built, in the way suggested by "Instincts and Their Vicissitudes." But nonsexual aggression continues to occupy a secondary role, for in Freud's specific account of the sadomasochistic perversion itself (i.e., "secondary masochism") the "binding" of aggression by libido outweighs the "binding" of libido by aggression. The status of "primary masochism" is equally ambiguous. It is not identical with unbound, nonlibidinized "self-destructiveness," but how it is that the death instinct is, or becomes, so excited as to require libidinal binding (or taming by the life instinct)—thus becoming sexually pleasurable ("masochism")—remains unclear. There is no space here for further consideration of these matters.

ject (or object) of (another's) love. But because Bersani and Dutoit rely on Freud's earlier formulations on sexuality, as my reading of the relevant Freudian texts suggests, they cannot really find a place for aggressive subjectivity.

Ego, Aggression, and Representation

Following Lacan, let us say that desire narcissistically fantasizes illusory images of itself as stable and fulfilled—images with which it identifies.[26] But any subversion of the illusion, of course, will itself be subverted, for any subversion is another fantasy-representation inviting its negation. This is to say, I think, that desire can never see itself as it is—an endless and total subversive negativity—but only images of itself as *un*subverted or *before* negation. Subversion cannot be in the image as the subject matter of the image: if representation is desire's illusion, then desire can never represent its truth as subversion. Although it is the figure, representation is not the image of desire but rather of the death of desire, of desire stilled. In turn, if representation depicts, not what desire is, but rather what it has "masochistically" accepted for itself as its illusion of itself, then desire itself will appear sadistically in what is *not*-representation.[27]

Representation and not-representation may be morphologically indiscernible. One might even give the illusion, from an "outside" vantage point, of being the other (see Chapters 3 and 4). The first-order psychoanalytical problem must, then, be to distinguish representation from not-representation. It is supposedly in a technique of exchange between speakers, "psychoanalysis," that we discover whether formal morphology represents something for the one who produced it—whether it is, *for him,* if not for any other speaker, part of the structure of narcissistic illusion or the ground, negative, or subversion of that illusion, whether for him it is representation or not-representation. The question of *what* the morphology represents for the speakers—in the intersubjective exchanges of the psychoanalytic situation—is logically posterior to this question; here, not only is it possible that the morphology represents two different illusions for each speaker (see Chapter 11), it is also possible that for one speaker the morphology represents, while for the other it is pure not-representation (see Chapter 1).

Much current "psychoanalytically" oriented criticism effects only a mechanical "deconstruction" of morphology, so that its doubleness or equivocation is revealed (sometimes at the expense of making pure negativity *represent*). In principle, however, we would seek to expose the conflict of representation and not-representation occurring in and between the unconsciousness of ego *and* id respectively and for *all* drives—desires pitted against their death in or as the unconscious. Psychoanalysis becomes a critique of the possibility of all symbolism and its emergence from and devolution toward the natural, material, or "vital

26. Jacques Lacan, "Some Reflections on the Ego" [1951], *International Journal of Psycho-Analysis* 34 (1953), 11–17.

27. For a recent account of sadistic action against representation, see J. Chasseguet-Smirgel, *Creativity and Perversion* (New York, 1984), chap. 1.

order"—rather than merely a reconstruction of some "lost" symbolism of sexuality (see also *FB*, 110–11) (compare Chapter 11).

In this critical work, we must avoid mere formalistic delectation in the spectacle of subversion as a ratification of the success of subversive desire. In this respect we can, I think, be more precise than Bersani and Dutoit about the "masochistic subversion" performed by Assyrian reliefs. The "formal relations" Bersani and Dutoit have identified do not merely subsist as "formal relations" or not-representation subverting an overtly sadistic subject matter, figuring (but not depicting) the primary "restlessness of desire." They are not *merely* "erasures of form" (*FB*, 111). They also, I think, represent some specific alternative—the ego's inhibition of aggression (the pure not-representation of the drive) being the very condition of representation here.

We can look briefly to the ego psychologists' refinement of Freud's structural hypothesis for help with this. In a remarkable paper on the drives, Heinz Hartmann complains that "psychoanalytic psychology has frequently been considered a psychology of drives only."[28] The "return to Freud" has even been restrictive about the drives themselves; aggressive wishing is rarely conceived apart from its sexual "binding."[29] As Hartmann insists, however, "Freud's approach to the position of the drives . . . comprised from the outset the consideration of conflict (between the drives themselves, or between drives and other psychic tendencies)."[30] The study of conflict at the least requires the structural hypothesis—it posits the "other psychic tendencies" apart from the drives—and possibly the late Freudian concept of an autonomous aggression having the "same position" as sexuality as "part of the id."[31] Freud himself did not work out a psychoanalytic theory of aggression; even in his detailed studies of sadomasochism, aggression as such, or the pain it causes, has only a shadowy existence. Historically, a psychoanalytic theory of aggression—although in principle it might be independent—has evolved hand in hand with post-Freudian work on the ego.[32]

28. Heinz Hartmann, "Comments on the Psychoanalytic Theory of Instinctual Drives," *Psychoanalytic Quarterly* 17 (1948), 368–88 (quotation from 373). See further idem, "Comments on the Psychoanalytic Theory of the Ego," *Psychoanalytic Study of the Child* 5 (1950), 74–96; Heinz Hartmann, Ernst Kris, and Rudolph Loewenstein, "Comments on the Formation of Psychic Structure," *Psychoanalytic Study of the Child* 2 (1946), 11–38; and idem, "The Function of Theory in Psychoanalysis," in *Drives, Affects, Behavior*, ed. Rudolph Loewenstein (New York, 1953), 13–37.

29. *"It is sexuality,"* Laplanche asserts, *"which represents the model of every drive and probably constitutes the only drive in the strict sense of the term"* (*LD*, 8; emphasis in the original). See further Paul Stepansky, *A History of Aggression in Freud*, Psychological Issues Monograph 39 (New York, 1977). As Stepansky points out, Freud's concept of the "death instinct" was yet another way for him to avoid coming to terms with aggression (173). Bersani reminds us (*FB*, 56–67) that the "death instinct" is also a negation of sexuality—to the extent, that is, that it might succeed in wholly "binding" sexuality. Not surprisingly, then, it tends to be bracketed or rejected by many of those who call themselves psychoanalysts.

30. Hartmann, "Psychoanalytic Theory of the Ego," 373.

31. Hartmann, "Psychoanalytic Theory of the Ego," 385.

32. At this stage in our historical and critical understanding of the "return to Freud," especially in its Lacanian variant (see François Roustang, *Dire Mastery: Discipleship from Freud to Lacan*, trans. Ned Lukacher [Baltimore, Md., 1982]), it is probably unnecessary to recall that the Lacanian resistance to "American" ego psychology was as much personal and political as principled. The "return" partly constitutes itself in ritual dismissal of ego psychology. For instance, in a passage rhetorically different from the rest of his scrupulous text, Laplanche gives the title of "one of the texts inaugurating the [ego psychology] movement" but not its author's name (Hartmann) or any notes of reference and fires at it a barrage of quick questions left unanswered as if

Heinz Hartmann, Ernst Kris, and Rudolph Loewenstein take aggression, like libido, to be an independent and "primary" (innate) drive in the fullest sense, that is, one of the "general motor power(s)" of the self sited in the id. To be gratified at all, a drive in the psychoanalytic sense must be mediated in relation to the realities of the environment. In principle, this is the function of the system ego, whatever its origins, which modifies or inhibits the full, final discharge of the drive.[33] In Hartmann's account, this modification tends to be seen as "adaptive." For example, a deeply anxious young Viennese Jewish intellectual, analyzed by Kris in 1944, suffered from passive-homosexual fantasies of being overpowered by Gentile playmates of his childhood. In 1938, his fantasies were suddenly confirmed in reality. "One day he was confronted with a gang of young Nazis"; in the ensuing brawl, he fared surprisingly well. "Impressed by his courageous initiative, his violent and skillful defense, the gang did not try to prevent his retreat." The analysts presume, throughout their discussion of this case, that "passivity" in the face of objective danger, especially its "sexualization," would have been pathological; in situations such as the one described, "if aggressive reaction remains possible" within the bounds of reason, they insist, "it is normal,"[34] a wholly understandable opinion among the Jewish refugees in America in the late 1930s and early 1940s.

Modification or inhibition inevitably causes conflict. First, structural conflicts between aggression (id) and the ego and superego are genuinely intrapsychic. Second, conflict with reality itself ensues when an object resists the modified discharge of the drive. Finally, "aggression and libido may be involved in conflict when the cathexis of both drives is

---

unanswerable (*LD,* 51–52). Ironically, Laplanche's substantial conclusions (e.g., *LD,* 60, 62) are not far removed from some of the most familiar propositions of ego psychology. To take another example, in one Lacanian account the movement is "typically anglo-saxon" (or worse, "American"); this account conveniently ignores the fact that ego psychology was chiefly the work of Central European Freudians fleeing the Nazis (Roland Jaccard, "La psychanalyse aux Etats-Unis," in *Histoire de la psychanalyse,* ed. Roland Jaccard [Paris, 1982], 2:237–58; quotations from 252). Such gestures repeat the complaints voiced by Lacan, Laplanche's analyst, about the "American way" of analysis ("The Direction of the Treatment and the Principles of Its Power" [1958], in *Ecrits,* 230–31). It is worth recalling that in 1951 Lacan saw the ego as a narcissistic precipitate of the libido unconsciously defending, in its illusion of itself as unified and stable, against the "variations of desire" ("Reflections on the Ego," 15). This view was cited approvingly by Hartmann ("The Development of the Ego Concept in Freud's Work" [1956], in *Readings in Psychoanalytic Psychology,* ed. Morton Levitt [New York, 1959], 84–105)—for Hartmann himself, in work with Paul Schilder, had long emphasized the role of images of the body in psychic differentiation ("Körperinneres und Körperschema," *Zeitschrift für Neurologie und Psychiatrie* 109 [1927], 666–75), a point Lacan tried to make very much his own. The analyst in Lacan's famous "unfinished" analysis, Rudolph Loewenstein, was Hartmann's close associate in working out ego psychology; E. Roudinesco suggests Lacan's "classicism" led him to doubt Loewenstein's ideas, but we can suspect deeper conflicts (*La bataille de cent ans: Histoire de la psychanalyse en France, I, 1885–1939* [Paris, 1982], 355–56). It had been by supporting Lacan's election to the Paris Psychoanalytic Society that Loewenstein and others had secured Hartmann's simultaneous election; essentially Hartmann and Lacan were "trades" for each other in legitimation *as* analysts (see Celia Bertin, *Maria Bonaparte: A Life* [New York, 1982], 206).

33. Heinz Hartmann, Ernst Kris, and Rudolph Loewenstein, "Notes on the Theory of Aggression," *Psychoanalytic Study of the Child* 3/4 (1949), 9–36. The system ego might have its genesis in the id's narcissistic "imagination" of that very stabilized fulfillment of its drive impulsion (see *FB,* 94–97); analysis of structural conflict is not incompatible with the genetic story preferred by Lacan and elaborated by Hartmann, Kris, and Loewenstein later in their paper on aggression ("Theory of Aggression," 25–34).

34. Hartmann, Kris, and Loewenstein, "Theory of Aggression," 23–24.

vested in the same object."[35] Although all modifications may be regarded as a repression of the drive, it is worth distinguishing between them. Seeing them at work in Assyrian relief will be tentative. I shall merely suggest—as the necessary supplement to Bersani and Dutoit—some directions of interpreting the conflicted psychic content of "formal relations." I am, of course, moving back, for heuristic purposes, toward familiar psychoanalytic "theories of art."[36] Bersani and Dutoit's approach—to identify the formal rhythms of desire as it disturbs representation, the fossil of intrapsychic processes and object relations—cannot do without a psychoanalytic iconography of "content," whatever its theoretical and methodological difficulties, if only because "formal relations" as such could be the fossil of an indefinitely large number of actual intrapsychic processes and object relations, indiscernible from one another in a purely formal analysis. For example, many studies of supposedly "fetishistic" representations of female bodies in Euro-American painting have been unable adequately to distinguish genuine fetishisms from formally similar or identical formations—such as mourning—precisely because they do not sufficiently investigate the "content" of the form (see Chapter 12).

In the *displacement* of aggression, due to instinctual or structural prohibitions, discharge of the drive takes place against a substitute for the object. In classic theory, typical substitutes for aggression will be found among inanimate objects or in games and sports. Ashurbanipal's lions were caged in advance and released for the king's pleasure. However, contemporary texts assert that lions and other pests, like wild asses, ravaged the countryside; killing them was one of the king's civic achievements and became, as in ancient Egypt, a general symbol for human mastery over chaotic nature (see Chapter 7, especially Fig. 7.2). In other words, direct discharge of a "healthy" aggression may be embodied in some of the hunt reliefs—partly displaced onto the ritual, rather than real, act of extermination (on this point the form of Assyrian iconography may have somewhat misled Bersani and Dutoit).

In the *restriction* of aggressive aims, aggressive discharge against a protected object remains incomplete. The capture and display of prisoners, a stock formula in Assyrian war reliefs, might be interpreted as a restricted aggression. In Sennacherib's palace, the culmination of the narrative is the review of prisoners (rather than a Sadean episode of annihilation). In Ashurbanipal's reliefs of the wars with Teumman, strict distinctions are observed. The Elamites, who had sided with Teumman under duress, are liberated; not punished, they are depicted as welcoming the victors. Chaldeans, by contrast, are executed; they had been Teumman's allies. Finally, the Urartians, neutral in the Teumman wars, are shown as bystanders, as if the Assyrian king were merely issuing them a warning notice. At all times, rebels against Assyrian rule were generally depicted as more harshly treated than foreign enemies.[37]

Restriction of aggression for *external* reasons is not especially visible. It would neces-

35. Hartmann, Kris, and Loewenstein, "Theory of Aggression," 19.

36. The obvious point of reference is the writing of Ernst Kris on art: see esp. "Approaches to Art" [1938, 1946] and "On Preconscious Mental Processes" [1949], in *Psychoanalytic Explorations in Art* (New York, 1952), 26–29, 305–13. For a recent summary and extension of the general field, see Ellen Handler Spitz, *Art and Psyche* (New Haven, Conn., 1986).

37. Reade, *Assyrian Sculpture*, 22.

sarily imply that the object, or reality, is just as powerful—or more powerful—than the Assyrian king. Still, reality is admitted into official image making in subtle ways we can only begin to tease out. A striking example can be found in Ashurbanipal's lion-hunt reliefs. Although the lions are being "slain" by the king at close quarters, the sculptors generally show them as already pierced in the brain by an arrow safely delivered from afar. The poignancy of the lion's death partly derives from the viewer's knowledge that the beast is actually quite helpless against the missiles. Some episodes are ambiguous: perhaps the depicted king "holds up" a dying lion to deliver the coup de grâce rather than do battle with a very live and dangerous one.[38]

In the classic theory of sublimation, pure drive energy is neutralized. As such, it forms the reservoirs of psychic energy known as the structures or systems of ego and superego and may or may not result in pathological destabilizations.[39] In official Assyrian depiction, sublimation might take several directions. In certain works, notably the comparatively early Black Obelisk, the artist is almost single-mindedly occupied with the aftereffects of warfare—such as the bringing of tribute from subject states—without directly depicting strife itself. Is his motivation purely rhetorical (for example, to convince viewers to fight under the king), or does the representation manifest a turning away from aggression itself? Still, in the scenes of the battle of Til-Tuba, Ashurbanipal's sculptors depict the full chaos of battle, with corpse piled upon corpse; in the hunt reliefs, the death agony of the beast is unsparingly rendered. At least on the basis of our sketchy grasp of symbolic conventions and expressive nuance in its original contexts of beholding, Assyrian relief strikes most observers as vividly *un*sublimated.

Fusion (Mischung) may occur between the residua of otherwise unmodified aggressive and libidinal drives (compare *FB*, 85–90). The dynamics of fusion in representation will be complex. In principle, the modified discharge of aggression is more or less pleasurable for the self. In their few remarks on sadism, Hartmann, Kris, and Loewenstein do not worry about how *sexual* pleasures could be had in pain. Sadism is pleasure in pain *simpliciter:* when the pain of the object is observed, the pleasurable discharge of aggression takes place. However, this is not to say that there is nothing libidinal in sadomasochism. The fusion of drives Freud had struggled to express probably can be observed. If aggression is directed at unpleasurable objects, then we must ask in what way the sadist's object is, or was, unpleasurable for him. In part, we return to Krafft-Ebing's view of that object as resisting the self's sexual or aggressive advances. However, the adaptionalist perspective commonly found in the theory of the ego allows us to add that the sadist has represented the object *as aggressing him;* his counterposed aggression, as in the case of the student fighting off the Nazis, is perceived by him as necessary. Like sadism, masochism is also a way of avoiding the object's aggression, not as it were by the preemptive first strike of sadis-

38. Reade, *Assyrian Sculpture,* 58.

39. For Freud's early view of sublimation, see in detail "Leonardo da Vinci and a Memory of His Childhood" [1910], in *SE,* 11, 63–137; for the ego-psychological perspective, see Hartmann, "Psychoanalytic Theory of the Ego." In *FB,* 43–47, Bersani treats sublimation as an elaboration or "continuation," rather than a replacement, of sexual fantasy; this is surely correct. The problematic distinction between sublimation and repression can be expressed most economically by saying that repression handles a troubling wish by preventing it from being discharged into representation—this may leave its own traces, of course, such as gaps or slips—whereas sublimation handles it by discharging it in a revised form.

tic attack but rather by arms reduction. In masochism a lesser injury is accepted from the object in place of the greater injury fantasized or feared.[40] Presumably the anticipated injury is a fantasized denial of love. In fact, the self may have already formed a "masochistic character" (as Wilhelm Reich put it) in experiencing punishment for its own sexual advances on the object.[41] The self might even fantasize that the very guilt provoked in the object by a masochistic subjugation to it will reduce the object's aggressiveness or evoke a loving rapprochement. Only in its sadistic attack or masochistic subterfuge, then, can the self *have* its sexual relations. Therefore the practices of sadomasochism may stem from a primordial love fantasized as having been punished or denied.

Applied literally, these formulations raise several expectations about Assyrian narrative depiction. The king's aggression, for instance, is neither affectless nor his final, Sadean aim. It is a ritual action—signified less by the king's facial physiognomy, always expressionless, than by his costume—in which the Assyrians defend and extend the blessings of Ashur against forces seen as menacing the settled, farmed plains of the upper Tigris River. The sadism of the Assyrian king and army, then, is manifestly adaptive. But the very prominence of adaptive sadism suggests that objects resisting or aggressing Assyria were xenophobically fantasized *by* Assyria. After all, it was not the Elamites, Babylonians, or Urartians who increased their territory threefold in only two centuries. Furthermore, the plains had been successfully farmed for many millennia. If the poaching lion was seen as a "cruel enemy,"[42] it could only have been somewhat metaphorically. The lion hunt must have been a symbol for other competitions, the figure of the animal constituted in sublimation as a substitute for other hated objects. In other words, the possible sublimatory character of Assyrian reliefs directs us to investigate the *metaphorical* status of pictorial narratives otherwise seen, simplistically, as documentary (compare Chapter 7). If a "sadistic character" had already been formed closer to home, so to speak, then it required such an object to achieve any pleasurable discharge. When reality does not provide this object, it will be invented paranoiacally by the subject punished in his own past by others close to him. In sum, a pathology of power *internal* to Assyrian life may have resulted in its manifest outward and adaptive aggression.[43]

An official art will not directly depict familial, dynastic, or social conflicts over authority. Like all ancient despots, however, in reality the Assyrian king worked "directly, daily, and personally to maintain a trustworthy internal dominion."[44] Therefore the whole canon of depiction could be regarded as a substitute formation that nonetheless repeats the primary traumas. The depicted aggressor is not simply loved, as self, nor is the

40. Rudolph Loewenstein, "A Contribution to the Psychoanalytic Theory of Masochism," *Journal of the American Psychoanalytic Association* 5 (1957), 197–234.

41. Wilhelm Reich, *Character Analysis* (New York, 1949).

42. Reade, *Assyrian Sculpture*, 53.

43. In *Masking the Blow: The Scene of Representation in Late Prehistoric Egyptian Art* (Berkeley and Los Angeles, 1992), esp. chap. 9, I urge that the depiction of the king of Egypt striking his enemy is a metaphor for all situations of "rule" in Egypt—familial, professional, ethnic, and so on—and that the depicted characters, ruler and enemy, allegorize all psychic and social relations of dominance and submission, "sadism" and "masochism," and so on. It is on this basis, in fact, that the images were narratively intelligible in the first place, at least in part. For the Egyptian pictorial narratives of the ruler's "sadistic" mastery, see Chapter 7.

44. Pierre Bourdieu, *Outline of a Theory of Practice*, trans. R. Nice (Cambridge, 1977), 190.

aggressed simply hated; the aggressed are in part substitutes for objects who punished the aggressor and whom he in fact had loved. No doubt it is a vulgar Freudianism to see lion and lioness as parents—or king as artist and lion as authority. Nonetheless, in a very complex exchange of aggressive and libidinal charges the animals in Assyrian relief are rendered in their very destruction with extraordinary tenderness—the "fusion" we expect as one of the inhibitions of pure aggression.

In all of this, my point has been precisely not to produce cheap decipherments of some "lost" symbolism of sexuality or aggression as a "psychoanalytic" achievement. In fact, I have said nothing one way or another, in this chapter, about the iconographic, narratological, or other methods by which the psychic "content" of "formal relations" can be identified forensically in an archaeological analysis (see Chapters 3 and 7). We can recognize our interpretations, like the ones I have just been sketching, as necessarily crude, minimal, and banal—for *representation is just that banal illusion of "content" which desire essentially is not*. My point is rather to insist that we cannot merely delectate in the fact that desire always takes us beyond—in part because it always comes before—representation. The two cannot be understood at all except in interaction in a particular history of intrapsychic conflicts and object relations, whether we pursue this history at an individual level or, as I would prefer, at an intersubjective or social one (see Chapters 11 and 12). Discontented desire requires the banality of its illusions to find its subversive restless truth: and if not all illusions are alike, then neither can be all subversions. My point, then, is to recapture some specificity in the analysis of the conflict of image and desire, representation and not-representation. In order to produce a thorough map of that conflict for both drives and for all forms of repression and discharge, we would have to recognize—as neither Bersani and Dutoit nor I have done systematically—the differences as well as the identifications between sculptor, patron, tradition, depicted characters, and viewers, each and all of whom have, or are represented as having, a conflicted subjectivity.

In the end, I see no contradiction between what Bersani calls a "*confident and systematic interpretation* of desire," such as the ones I have been sketching in the last few pages, and a "*blocked but productive speculation* on pleasure," such as *The Forms of Violence* recommends to us (*FB*, 102). Thus I see no real contradiction between familiar forms of psychoanalytic iconography and the more recent development of topographies and tropologies of desire in (and outside) representation. The one cannot be had without the other. Desire necessarily blocks iconographic or symbolic decipherment, always and only, systematically and confidently, of precisely that which desire is not. The very production of particular representations—and consequently our confidence in the possibility of interpretation—is the condition, however, for restless desire having an individual history of specific subversions. The form of our desire—in its general mobility, it is ultimately "masochistic," but it devolves in innumerable constellations—must be the historical precipitate of the representations it fantasizes, fetishizes, and abandons. There is no such thing as pure desire we could, as it were, meditate upon abstractly as a play of "formal relations." We cannot somehow only map the "erasures of form," the appearances of negativity, and the "forms of violence." We are bound—and I use that term in its Freudian sense—to content.

Chapter 11

Sigmund Freud's Drawing of the Dream of the Wolves

Egocentric, demanding, intellectually and erotically voracious, Sigmund Freud and Serge Pankejeff, the "Wolf Man," saw and spoke with one another constantly for four years, from February 1910 until July 1914, and intermittently many times thereafter, including a second, brief psychoanalysis in 1919.[1] Freud described or otherwise represented the patient in ongoing session notes taken during the analysis;[2] in a brief publication of 1913 describing the patient's key dream; in the text of the great case history itself, "From the History of an Infantile Neurosis," written in winter 1914–15 after the close of the analysis and published, with additions, after the war, in 1918, a text that has become canonical in psychoanalytic training institutes around the world and a continual point of reference in the history of science and medicine, literary criticism, feminism and gay studies, and else-

1. The relevant data on the psychoanalysis is systematically collected and critically analyzed by Patrick Mahony, *Cries of the Wolf Man*, History of Psychoanalysis Monograph 1 (New York, 1984). Pertinent information can also be found in the sources noted below.

2. These notes do not survive, but they probably resembled those Freud kept for his analysis of the "Rat Man." For these, see *The Standard Edition of the Complete Psychological Works of Sigmund Freud*, 24 vols., ed. and trans. James Strachey et al. (London, 1953–74) (here-

where;[3] indirectly, in his polemical refutation of Alfred Adler and Carl G. Jung, "The History of the Psycho-Analytic Movement," written in 1914 as he was drafting the case history;[4] and elsewhere, including references in papers like "Remembering, Repeating, and Working Through" and the late, incompleted essay "Splitting of the Ego in Defensive Process" (for *Ichspaltung im Abwehrvorgang,* see also Chapter 9).[5] For his part, Serge presented an image of the "Professor," his analyst Freud, in eight curious essays published in the 1950s, now generally called his *Memoirs;*[6] in an intriguing series of interviews granted to a West German journalist in the 1970s before his death in 1979;[7] and in other ways.

In addition to this voluminous representation of each other's experience of the other, Sigmund and Serge literally exchanged several objects. Freud presented Serge with an autographed copy of Freud's publication of Serge's analysis; later, he helped Serge with cash for his flat in Vienna.[8] For his part, on the termination of the analysis Serge presented Freud with an Egyptian statuette to add to Freud's collection.[9] When Serge needed reanalysis in 1919, to make room for him Freud abruptly terminated another patient, his student Helene Deutsch, who fell into depression.[10] A dedicated amateur painter, Serge presented or sold more than forty paintings to psychoanalysts in Vienna and elsewhere; in his adolescence, he had studied formally with a Russian painter hired by his family, and submitted his work to a local exhibition.[11] Finally, he accepted and published under the name Freud gave to him, Wolf Man.[12]

The Wolf Man's most important gift exchange with Freud, of course, was the psychoanalysis itself. It afforded an intersubjective environment in which bisexual and homosexual conflicts could supposedly be resolved by interpretively deriving them from an archaic context, thus transposing subjective desires into an objective analysis of the very

after *SE,* followed by volume number and page), 10:251–317.

3. "The Occurrence in Dreams of Material from Fairy Tales," in *SE,* 12:279–87; the case history is translated in *SE,* 17:7–122. Hereafter, citations to it appear in the main body of the text in parentheses. For the German text followed here, see Sigmund Freud, *Gesammelte Schriften,* vol. 8, *Krankengeschichten* (Vienna, 1924), 439–567.

4. *SE,* 14:1–65.

5. *SE,* 12:145–56, 23:271–78. There are many other echoes of the case in Freud's writings; for a partial survey, see Mahony, *Cries of the Wolf Man,* 47.

6. [Serge Pankejeff], *The Wolf-Man by the Wolf-Man,* ed. and trans. Muriel Gardiner (New York, 1971), 3–152.

7. Karin Obholzer, *The Wolf Man Sixty Years Later: Conversations with Freud's Controversial Patient,* trans. M. Shaw (London, 1982) (a translation of *Gespräche mit dem Wolfsmann: Eine Psychoanalyse und die Folgen* [Hamburg, 1980]). There are important reviews of this publication by Mark Kanzer, *International Journal of Psycho-Analysis* 53 (1982), 419–22, and Jeffrey M. Masson, *International Review of Psychoanalysis* 9 (1982), 116–19; and see also Muriel Gardiner, "The Wolf Man's Last Years," *Journal of the American Psychoanalytic Association* 31 (1983), 867–97.

8. See Peter Gay, *Freud: A Life for Our Time* (New York, 1988), 285–92.

9. See Lynn Gamwell and Richard Wells, eds., *Sigmund Freud and Art: His Personal Collection of Antiquities* (New York, 1989); I have been unable to identify this particular object.

10. Paul Roazen, *Helene Deutsch: A Psychoanalyst's Life* (New York, 1985), 157–58.

11. *The Wolf-Man by the Wolf-Man,* 66–68. On the evidence, his teacher might have been the landscapist V. E. Borisoff-Mousatoff (1870–1905), whose work, as the Wolf Man tells us his teacher's had been, was exhibited in the Salon d'Automne in Paris, or perhaps a closely affiliated painter. As the Wolf Man's memoirs indicate, painting was one of his deepest interests throughout his life. More than forty of his paintings from the collections of Muriel Gardiner and K. R. Eissler are now in the Library of Congress.

12. Although he liked to think of himself as Freud's "most famous case" (*The Wolf Man Sixty Years Later,* 175), Serge's real name was not widely known until after his

origin *of* such desires (compare Chapter 9), in turn permitting the symbolic "overcoming" of their subjective reality. The objective ground from which another subject's sexuality is supposedly interpreted is, however, itself the site of subjective sexuality—of the observer's own sexuality. That the interpreter *remembers* such subjective sexuality in observing the other must be counted as a gift. Dependent on exactly what the other provides, such subjectivity is threatened by the demand that it be subtracted from the work of interpretation and replaced by that objectivity about the other which actually can only be its final, ideal effect. Without the energy provided by memory of the observer's own sexuality, the intersubjective interpretation of another's sexuality cannot get off the ground. At best, it can be an "objective" imitation of an interpretation of another's sexuality, precisely lacking the intersubjective construction of sexualized memories of others that *is* sexuality itself. Simply put, the objective interpretation of another's sexuality, such as one might undertake in a psychoanalytic inquiry, requires sexuality. A subjective object is required to interpret the objective subject of sexuality. This subjective object almost always involves actual artifacts or images existing in the tactile, visual, acoustic, and kinesthetic domains. In this chapter I look at this emergence of sexuality and the subjective object in Freud's interpretation of the Wolf Man, his objective subject of sexuality.

Freud's first comment on his new patient was made to his follower Sandor Ferenczi just days after the Wolf Man appeared for a consultation. "A rich young Russian"—Freud recounted—"admitted the following transferences to me after the first session: Jewish swindler, he would like to use me from behind and shit on my head."[13] At this point in February 1910, Freud was reasserting the fundamental status of infantile sexuality as he conceived it, resisting both Adler, who was developing his alternative theories of "organ inferiority" and psychic "protest," and Jung, who was beginning to object that Freud's interpretations of Freud's own infantile sexuality were manifestly incomplete.[14] In the first session, the Wolf Man informed Freud that he had previously consulted two of Freud's sci-

death, although several Freudians were in constant touch with him. Important psychoanalytic studies of the personal relationship between Freud and Pankejeff include William Offenkrantz and Arnold Tobin, "Problems of the Therapeutic Alliance: Freud and the Wolf Man," *International Journal of Psycho-Analysis* 54 (1973), 75–78, and Robert J. Langs, "The Misalliance Dimension on the Case of the Wolf Man," in *Freud and His Patients,* ed. Mark Kanzer and Jules Glenn (New York, 1980), 2:372–85, both with further references to the extensive clinical and theoretical literature on Freud's case history. In this chapter, I do not have space to consider certain challenging revisionary readings based in part on biographical and historical evidence (although see note 16 below). See esp. Jeffrey M. Masson, *The Assault on Truth: Freud's Suppression of the Seduction Theory* (New York, 1985), xxvii, who asserts (on the basis of documents unpublished at the time of his writing) that Freud did not know the Wolf Man had been anally raped in childhood, and Nicolas Abraham and Maria Torok, *The Wolf Man's Magic Word,* trans. Nicholas Rand (Minneapolis, 1986), who argue that Freud did not and could not interpret the "polyglot" speech of the Wolf Man's unconscious. I treat these and similar questions in a full-length study of the material presented here; see Whitney Davis, *Drawing the Dream of the Wolves: Homosexuality, Interpretation, and Freud's "Wolf Man"* (Bloomington, Ind., 1995).

13. Freud to Ferenczi, 13 February 1910, *The Correspondence of Sigmund Freud and Sandor Ferenczi,* vol. 1, *1908–1914,* trans. Peter T. Hoffer, ed. Eva Brabant, Ernst Falzeder, and Patrizia Giamperi-Deutsch (Cambridge, Mass., 1993), 138.

14. For Adler, Paul E. Stepansky, *In Freud's Shadow: Adler in Context* (Hillsdale, N.J., 1983), is detailed and reliable. Jung's complaints can be traced through his correspondence with Freud; see William McGuire, ed., *The Freud/Jung Letters,* trans. Ralph Manheim and R. F. C. Hull (Cambridge, Mass., 1988), e.g., 298–300, 392.

entific enemies, the psychiatrists Theodor Ziehen and Emil Kraepelin, both of whom had failed to help him; Serge required constant attendance, and could only move his bowels following enemas given by his manservant. I shall return to the specifically homosexual content of the first session, but broadly speaking, from the beginning the Wolf Man evidently appeared to Freud as a possible living confirmation of Freud's most closely defended intellectual commitment—his idea of the persistence of archaic, infantile sexualizations of the body in adult neurosis. The Wolf Man seems to have been quickly constituted, by Freud, as Freud's "case" both *of* and *for* psychoanalytic interpretation itself.

According to both Freud and the Wolf Man, "at a very early stage in the analysis" (33),[15] probably in the first weeks of the first year of analysis (April or May 1910), the Wolf Man recalled for Freud a dream he had had at the age of four years and, in Freud's words, "added a drawing which confirmed his description of the dream *[gibt dann noch eine Zeichnung . . . die seine Beschreibung bestätigt]*" (Fig. 11.1).

> I dreamt that it was night and that I was lying in my bed. (My bed stood with its foot towards the window; in front of the window there was a row of old walnut trees. I know it was winter time when I had the dream, and night-time.) Suddenly the window opened of its own accord, and I was terrified to see that some white wolves were sitting on the big walnut tree in front of the window. There were six or seven of them. The wolves were quite white, and looked more like foxes or sheep dogs, for they had big tails like foxes and they had their ears pricked like dogs when they are attending to something. In great terror, evidently of being eaten up by the wolves, I screamed and woke up. (29)

In the historical interpretation developed during the analysis and presented in the case history of 1914–15/1918, Freud deciphered the manifest elements of the wolf dream as a hallucinated repetition of what he called the dreamer's "primal scene." Specifically, he proposed that at the age of one and a half years the Wolf Man had witnessed three episodes of anal intercourse between his parents, disheveled in their white underclothes, at about five in the afternoon in their bedroom on his father's estate, while the very young Wolf Man lay transfixed in a crib nearby. As Freud realizes, his interpretation seems highly implausible. The question of the "reality" and "confirmation" of the primal scene preoccupies him.[16] Freud's account rests on the idea that no single event in any psychic history should be considered as fully the cause or fully the effect of any other single event. The historical status of events is conferred upon them by *Nachträglichkeit*, or "delayed action."

15. See also Pankejeff to Freud, 6 June 1926 ([B. D. Lewin, ed. and trans.], "Letters Pertaining to Freud's 'History of an Infantile Neurosis,'" *Psychoanalytic Quarterly* 26 [1957], 449). In 1926 Freud was impelled to query the Wolf Man on the date and other aspects of his report of the childhood dream because his disaffected follower Otto Rank had recently argued that the dream was partly fabricated by the patient to satisfy his analyst (see Phyllis Grosskurth, *The Secret Ring: Freud's Inner Circle and the Politics of Psychoanalysis* [Toronto, 1991], 179–81, although there are several small historical inaccuracies in her account).

16. In what follows I have benefited from the thorough scrutiny by Mahony, *Cries of the Wolf Man;* an elegant analysis by Ned Lukacher, *Primal Scenes: Literature, Philosophy, Psychoanalysis* (Ithaca, N.Y., 1986), chap. 4; and the general reflections of Peter Brooks, "Fictions of the Wolf Man: Freud and Narrative Understanding," in *Reading for the Plot: Design and Intention in Narrative* (New York, 1984), 264–85, and Stanley Fish, "Withholding the

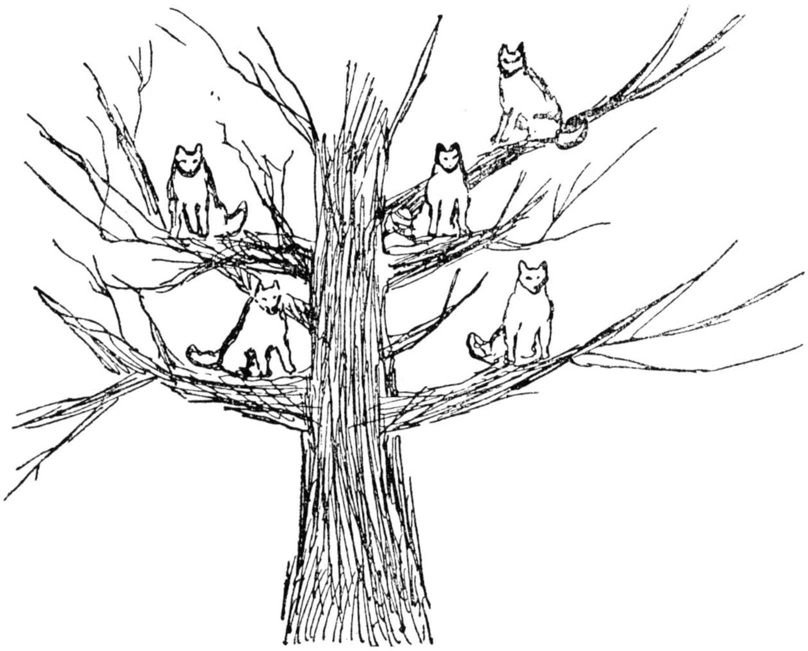

Fig. 11.1. Serge Pankejeff (the Wolf Man), drawing of his dream of the wolves, present whereabouts unknown.

Thus the Wolf Man's primal vision was relatively unimpressive to him. But in the historically forward direction of his life between one and a half and four years, the age of the dream, its sexual meaning was retrospectively created through the growing boy's maturing sexual knowledge. In particular, it was established in the sexualization of his body by others, for example, an attempted "seduction" by his sister at age three and a half and warnings about urination and display given by his beloved nursemaid, his foreign governess, and a maid in the household. By four years of age, the little Wolf Man *recollected* his "primal scene" as a very complex scene of "feminine identification" with his mother and desire for anal possession by his father, crosscut with a fear of castration and "masculine" protest against it. Very schematically, the fearful primality of the primal scene was only arrived at pro- and retrospectively in its repetitions and revisions. So much is familiar ground.

Now, the cycles of *Nachträglichkeit* that knot up the Wolf Man's psychic history *also* constitute the very interpretive activity in which Freud comprehends that subjectivity and writes out its history in the first place. The crucial wolf dream was related by the Wolf Man to Freud "at a very early stage in the analysis," sometime in 1910. But Freud remarks that "the interpretation was a task that dragged on over several years" (33). In fact, "it was only during the last months of analysis [that is, in the months before July 1914] that it became possible to understand it completely" (33). In the case history, immediately after describing the dream and its obvious connections with popular tales like "Little Red Rid-

Missing Portion: Psychoanalysis and Rhetoric," in *Doing What Comes Naturally: Change, Rhetoric, and the Practice of Theory in Literary and Legal Studies* (Durham, N.C., 1989), 525–54. My conclusions, however, diverge from theirs.

ing Hood," Freud outlines some of the patient's associations to the dream. "One day," for example, the patient interprets the opening of the window in the dream as meaning "my eyes suddenly open" (34). "On another occasion," he associates the tree in the dream with Christmas trees and suddenly remembers that he dreamed the dream on Christmas Eve, the night before his own birthday (34). Freud does not tell us when these "occasions" of association and recollection actually took place. But some of them almost certainly derive from the later period of the analysis, for Freud would have had no reason to pursue them had the patient not already produced the dream material itself. In sum, the meaning of the patient's report of the dream as the disguised primal scene was only progressively revealed through retrospective connections.

From the vantage point of 1914–15, when Freud was writing out the Wolf Man's case history, this *Nachträglichkeit* within the history of the analysis could be smoothed over or even somewhat obscured so that the *Nachträglichkeit* within the patient's life could be narrated. But from the vantage point of 1910, when the analysis was just beginning and the wolf dream had just been reported, there was no such hindsight to be had. There was no guarantee, for Freud, that the report of the dream had any special status for the hoped-for historical construction—for the "case" that the Wolf Man seemed, from the first consultation, to be offering.

Thus Freud's expressly stated response to the report of the wolf dream must interest us. Normally Freud recommends that an analyst maintain an uncommitted and unprejudiced attitude toward a patient's representations. However, with the wolf dream he immediately developed, he says, a "conviction that the causes of [the patient's] infantile neurosis lay concealed behind" it (33). In principle, Freud's "conviction" *(Überzeugung)* provided the expectation of and commitment to an interpretive construction using the materials of the wolf dream, the forward push animating the cycles of *Nachträglichkeit* within the analysis, by which the history of the patient's *Nachträglichkeit* was knotted up. From the vantage of 1914–15, when Freud was writing out the case history, the evidence for his "conviction" about the dream would have been the numerous associations and recollections the patient gradually offered in relation to it—the always troublesome "confirmations" *(Bestätigungen)* he found for the reconstructed primal scene. But from the vantage point of the day in 1910 when the dream was reported and Freud says his "conviction" was formed, this retrospective confirmation was not yet available. Whence, then, Freud's immediate "conviction"?

In 1910, when the wolf dream was reported, the patient *did* provide a "confirmation"—specifically, a confirmation of his report of the dream, namely, the *drawing* of the dream of the wolves (Fig. 11.1). At the same moment as the Wolf Man presented a "confirmation" of his report of the dream, Freud felt a "conviction" about the status of the dream for the hoped-for case, a foreknowledge that the dream could provide the forward energy animating the still-to-be-discovered connections of the patient's history. The Wolf Man's particular "confirmation," then, *was* Freud's "conviction." On these grounds, we can say that the drawing of the dream of the wolves was not fully distinguished from Freud's self, desire, and knowledge. As a real artifact, it was an objective manifestation of the Wolf Man's subjectivity, and deliberately used by Freud to reconstruct its history. But it was also Freud's own subjective object.

The "drawing of the tree with the wolves," of course, hardly "confirms" the reported dream. A very great deal has been left out. The dreamer dreamed that it was night; he was lying in his bed facing the window; the window opened of its own accord; the tree was in front of the window; wolves were sitting in the tree looking at him; he is frightened of being eaten up and—the dream ends—screams and wakes up. The drawing directly depicts neither the bed and room nor the opening of the window. At best, it depicts just one subordinate clause in the entire dream report—namely, "some white wolves were sitting on the big walnut tree." To be completely scrupulous, even here the drawing is vague. The wolves' *whiteness,* twice noted in the dream report, can only be implied in a black-and-white drawing; and that the tree is a large walnut is hardly obvious.

Some of this vagueness was resolved, but also reworked, in later paintings of his by-now-famous wolf dream the Wolf Man gave or sold to psychoanalysts, such as an example probably made in the early 1950s (Fig. 11.2). Here the wolves are definitely white. Moreover, a recollection about the circumstance in which the wolf dream was dreamed—the dreamer knows he had his dream during "winter time"—has been transferred, in the painting, into the dream story itself; here, it is winter outside the window. Probably this reworking partly reflects the Wolf Man's retrospective awareness of Freud's interest in aspects of the dream and drawing and his own desire to "confirm" Freud's published reconstruction in the text Freud had presented to him on its publication. But the painting of his wolf dream, although it was a special case, should not be totally detached from the Wolf Man's previous history, before and outside psychoanalysis. The Wolf Man's landscapes probably exhibit his educated-amateur understanding of pictorial tradition. Indeed, even the wolf-dream images themselves might have close pictorial associations with earlier works such as Caspar David Friedrich's 1822 *Solitary Tree,* with its imposing but damaged oak sheltering a shepherd—a conventional pastoral allegory for the artist, or perhaps a personification of nature—and sheep, iconographically transformable into wolves through a tissue of proverbs and folktales; or such as Friedrich's 1829 *Oak Tree in the Snow* (Fig. 11.3), an image that already situated the viewer's subjectivity without requiring the Wolf Man's greater literalization of nature as an other, an unsettling presence attentively "looking" at us.[17] Probably quite unknown to Freud, such iconographical possibilities remind us that the wolf drawing, from the vantage point of the Wolf Man, was originally a somewhat different object than that subjectively constructed by Freud. *Two* iconographies, two hermeneutic possibilities, had to meet and mutually inflect one another when the Wolf Man drew his dream *for* Freud, but using *his own* pictorial resources. But however we sort this out, the drawing was obviously a highly unstable object in the encounter between Freud and his patient.

There is one glaring discrepancy between the report and the drawing. The report says that there were "six or seven" wolves, but the drawing depicts only five. In writing out the case in 1914–15, Freud interpreted the numbers six and seven as the influence of the story "The Wolf and the Seven Little Goats" on the dreamer (31). But the significance of this

17. For the organization and iconography of these images, see Annabel Patterson, *Pastoral and Ideology* (Berkeley and Los Angeles, 1987), 56–57, and Joseph Leo Koerner, *Caspar David Friedrich and the Subject of Landscape* (New Haven, Conn., 1987).

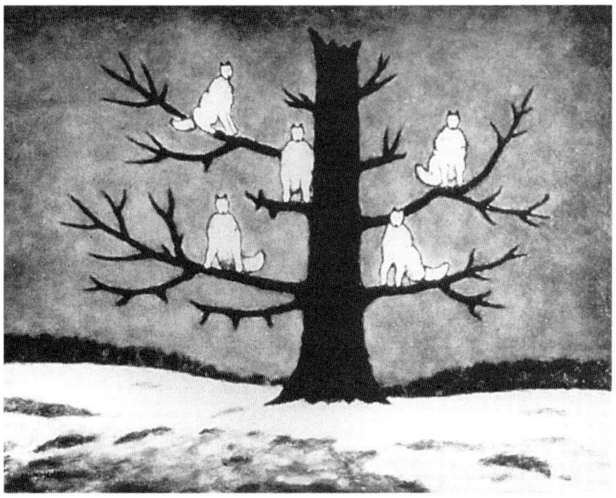

Fig. 11.2. Serge Pankejeff (the Wolf Man), untitled painting of his dream of the wolves, about 1950–60, from the collection of Muriel Gardiner.

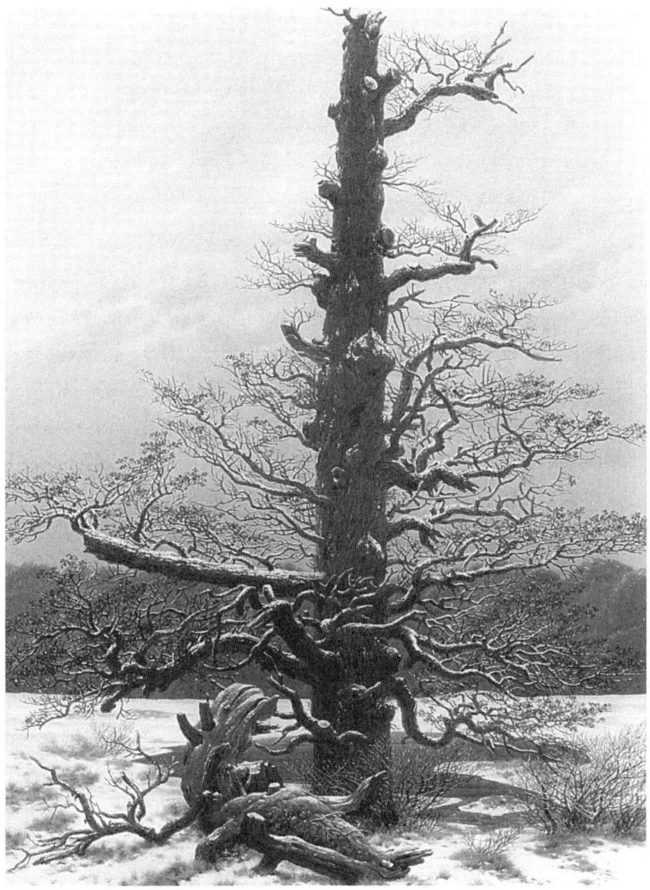

Fig. 11.3. Caspar David Friedrich, *Oak Tree in the Snow,* 1829. Collection of the National Gallery, Berlin, by permission.

folktale became evident only later in the analysis, after the dream report. At first "there seemed to be no answer to the question" why there were six or seven wolves (31). Furthermore, a few pages later, Freud does interpret the *five*foldness of the wolves in the drawing: he has discovered—again, after the dream report—that the little boy suffered from fevers that peaked at five o'clock in the afternoon (37). But if we go back to the dream report, we find that the dreamer dreamt that "it was night," not five in the afternoon (29). In order to tie the dream to the primal scene, in his final assessment Freud therefore takes the drawing illustrating five wolves as a "correction" of the dream's distortion of the "afternoon" of the primal scene into the "night" of the wolves (43): "In der zum Traum gefertigten Zeichnung hat der Träumer die 5 zum Ausdruck gebracht, die wahrscheinlich die Angabe: es war Nacht, korrigiert." In other words, the drawing is more accurate than the dream. Far from being a "confirmation" of the manifest dream thoughts, the drawing actually takes Freud well beyond them and supposedly closer to the disguised unconscious content that he finally reconstructs as the Wolf Man's primal scene. The drawing, then, becomes an interpretation not clearly distinguishable from Freud's own. Why?—and how? The drawing, I suggest, secured Freud's "conviction" about the dream precisely because it directly visualized—it pictorially realized—the very structure of the repression of infantile sexual drives of which the dream was supposedly the manifestation and, more broadly, of which the entire analysis was becoming Freud's "case," his example and proof. To anticipate, Freud had a picture of repression that was replicated in and as the drawing of the dream of the wolves.

In 1910, Freud depended on the models of the mind he had most fully expounded in the seventh chapter of *Die Traumdeutung* of 1899 (dated 1900). There he provided what he called "the most general schematic pictures of the psychical apparatus" (Fig. 11.4).[18] They depict the sequence and direction of nervous "excitation" passing through the mind from perception at one end (in the diagram, W = *Wahrnehmung*) to motor activities at the other. The passage of excitation leaves some traces in memory *(Erinnerungsspuren),* but since it is a basic axiom of psychophysics that nervous energy cannot be both transmitted and preserved by one and the same system, the memory system *(Er)* is said to be "unconscious" in relation to the conscious terminus. It is represented in Freud's diagram as lines branching off the main route of the arrow of excitation toward discharge.

As the explanations in *Die Traumdeutung* suggest, Freud conceived his pictures as schemas organizing the psyche as a branching network of mental contents and associations. For example, in the unpublished manuscript of autumn 1895 now known as the "Project for a Scientific Psychology," Freud considers the case of a patient, Emma, who sought therapy for an inability to shop for clothes by herself (Fig. 11.5).[19] He connects her present fear with two memories; one is a more recent memory of Emma, age twelve, being mocked on account of her clothing by two shop assistants, one of whom she feels attracted to; and the other is an earlier, more disturbing memory of Emma, age eight, being grabbed through her clothes by a shopkeeper. The set of relations is pictured as a set of intercon-

18. For *Die Traumdeutung,* see *SE,* 4 and 5; *SE,* 5:537–40, considers the schemas discussed here.

19. *SE,* 1:353–56.

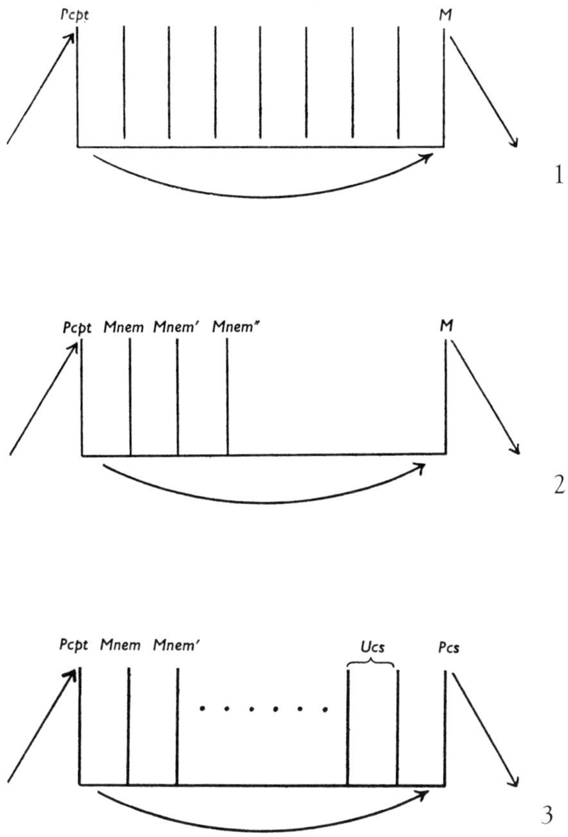

Fig. 11.4. Sigmund Freud, "Schematic pictures of the psychic apparatus."

nected nodes, with left and right in the picture indicating the beginning and end of a transmission of psychic energy and with up and down the relative antiquity of the memory traces. Freud's diagram of Emma's case assumes his own earlier "*Sexualschema*," or "basic schematic picture," for sexuality, formulated in January 1895 (Fig. 11.6).[20] Here he maps out the entire reflex arc from a sexually appealing perception to its ultimate discharge in erotic thought or action. Emma's problem is the dislocation and disturbance of the *Sexualschema;* in her illness, the arrow of discharge has supposedly been skewed by one branching-off too many. This "architecture of hysteria," as Freud put it, was schematically generalized in May 1897 in a letter to Wilhelm Fliess (Fig. 11.7).[21] In this beautiful dia-

20. Jeffrey M. Masson, ed. and trans., *The Complete Letters of Sigmund Freud to Wilhelm Fliess, 1887–1904* (Cambridge, Mass., 1985), 98–105 (hereafter *Freud-Fliess Letters*) (Masson's fig. 4 reproduces Freud's manuscript original); see also *SE,* 1:100–106.

21. *Freud-Fliess Letters,* 245–48; see also *SE,* 1:150–53. William J. McGrath, *Freud's Discovery of Psychoanalysis: The Politics of Hysteria* (Ithaca, N.Y., 1986), 191–94 and figs. 3 and 4, makes the suggestion that the diagram replicated the architecture of Nuremberg or other medieval German towns as Freud knew them or had seen them illustrated in early modern prints.

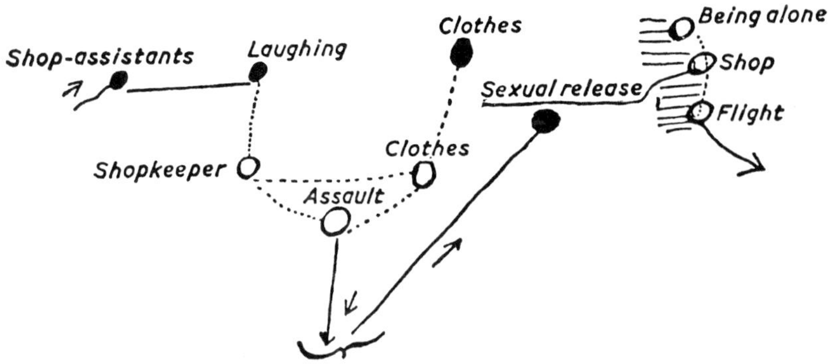

Fig. 11.5. Sigmund Freud, schema of the structure of Emma's hysterical repression.

gram, Freud depicts variously newer or older memory traces in the network attached to present-day symptoms, represented by little triangles like flowers or turrets. The analyst's work is represented by the broken lines as making "repeated loops through the background thoughts of the same symptoms" until analyst and patient manage to connect the deepest, oldest thoughts to the most recent symptom.

In such visualizations of the relations between mental contents, Freud's work of the late 1880s and early 1890s was decisive. In these years he completed detailed monographs on pathologies of perception, thought, and motor activity in cerebral palsy and aphasia; seldom read today, they made his scientific reputation. Two samples of his numerous intriguing schematizations must suffice for my purposes. Following Carl Wernicke, Freud pictured two "center aphasias" (Fig. 11.8), the sensory aphasia afflicting the perceptual nerve pathways and the motor aphasia afflicting the motor pathways, and the "conduction aphasias"—"confusion of words and uncertainty in their use"—afflicting an intermediate or interior area of the mind.[22] The similarity to the diagrams in *Die Traumdeutung* is obvious. Later in the monograph, Freud schematized the psychophysical analysis of words, underlying what he would later say about association generally (Fig. 11.9).[23] The word consists of two complexes of mental images—first, the sound image of the word with kinesthetic associations to the word spoken, scripted, and read; and second, the object associations of the word, with visual images of the object predominating. Whereas the sound image is relatively closed and stable, Freud depicts the largely visual object associations as branching out open-endedly as new perceptual impressions are added and associations forged.

As the very structure of these various schemas implies, Freud considered psychological relations to have a neurological basis and reality.[24] Ultimately the branching network of concepts should be explicable as the neuronal network itself. Nerve processes had been studied and drawn in detail by Freud himself all through his twenties, from 1876 to

22. Sigmund Freud, *Zur Auffassung der Aphasien* (Vienna, 1891), 5; cf. Carl Wernicke, "The Symptom Complex of Aphasia," trans. Norman Geschwind, *Boston Studies in the Philosophy of Science* 4 (1970), 40–42, fig. 2.

23. Freud, *Zur Auffassung der Aphasien*, 60.

24. A useful analysis is Peter Amacher, *Freud's Neurological Education and Its Influence on Psychoanalytic Theory*, Psychological Issues Monograph 16 (New York, 1965); for a wider-ranging treatment, see Frank Sulloway, *Freud, Biologist of the Mind: Beyond the Psychoanalytic Legend* (New York, 1979).

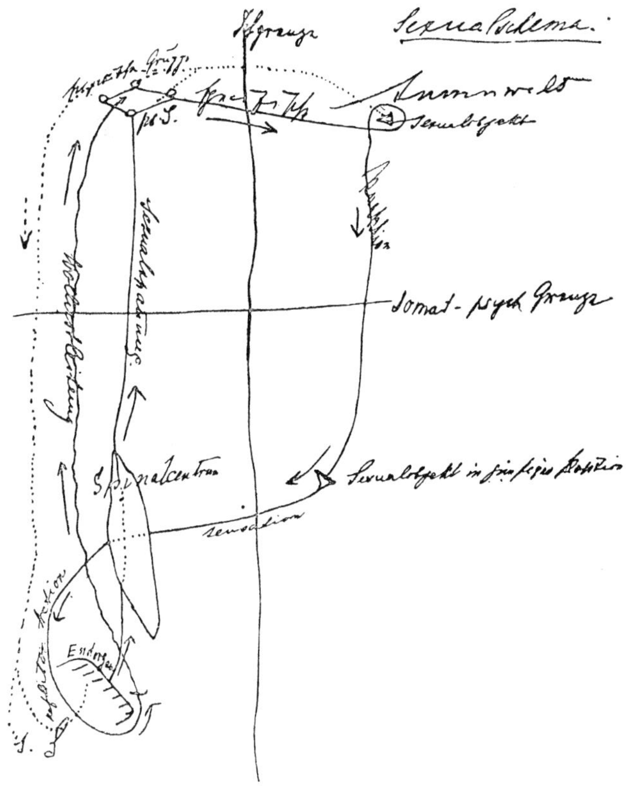

Fig. 11.6. Sigmund Freud, schematic picture of sexuality *(Sexualschema).*

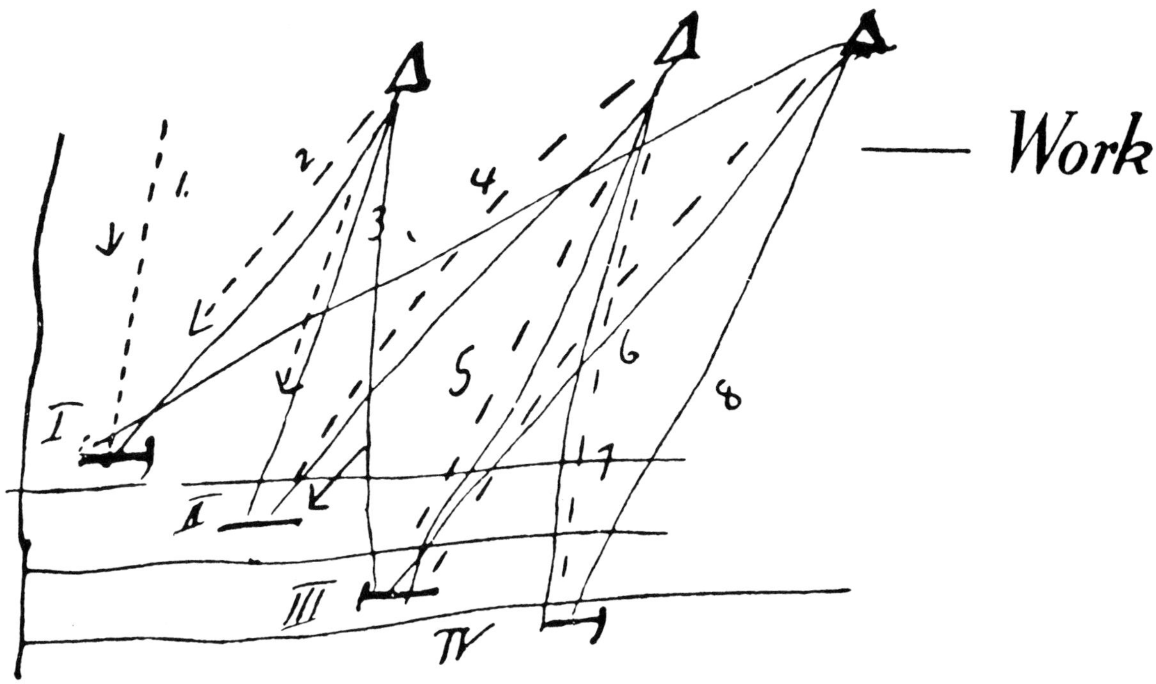

Fig. 11.7. Sigmund Freud, "The Architecture of Hysteria." In the original, the dotted lines, arrows, and numerals are in red ink, as well as the word "Work" and the line preceding it.

Fig. 1.

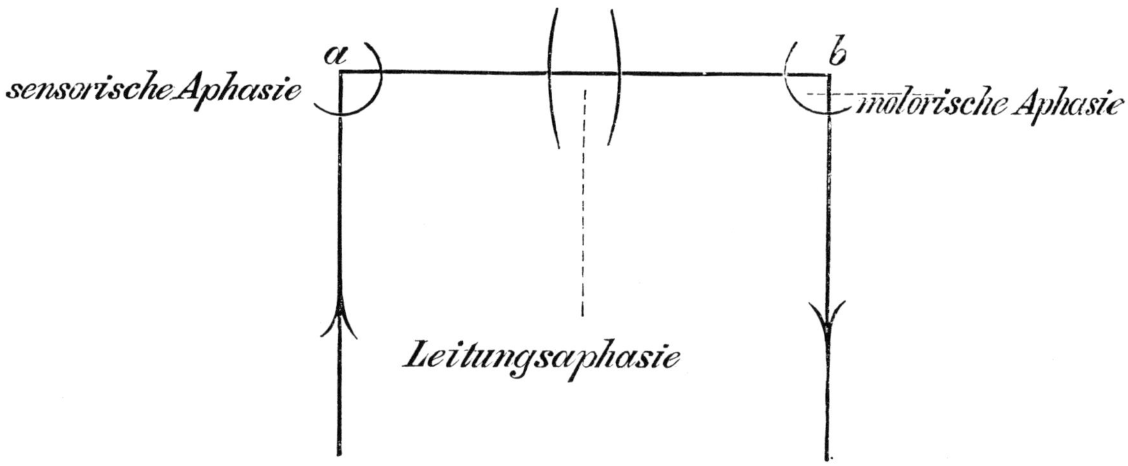

Fig. 11.8. Schema for sensory, motor, and conduction aphasias.

1886—so badly, in fact, that he was mercilessly mocked by his friends. (The subjective object considered here is connected, at various points, to Freud's professional anxieties and rivalries.) In one of his first scientific publications, of 1878, Freud surveyed the spinal ganglia of *Petromyzon* (Fig. 11.10), examining what he calls the "T-shaped branching of the fibers."[25] In one of the last histological publications (Fig. 11.11), written in Paris while working with Jean-Martin Charcot, Freud concerns himself—as his schema indicates—with the *Verbindung,* or "binding up," of the bodies and fibers of the lower brain stem.[26]

Although nerves are materially "bound up" with one another, "binding," as a *psychological* notion—later essential to Freud's psychoanalytic metapsychology—presented many logical difficulties.[27] As two important schematizations in the "Project" of 1895 attempt to show (Fig. 11.12), the quantity of energy passing through the mind supposedly varies with the strength of the stimulus. The mind is built to handle this variation, Freud supposes (Fig. 11.12*a*), in its differential construction of "thicker or thinner" pathways of discharge (*SE,* 1:314): a smaller quantity of energy (for example, "1Q") can be transmitted along one pathway (pathway I to neuron *alpha*), whereas larger quantities (for example, 2Q, 3Q) will be discharged along several pathways (pathways II and III to neurons *beta* and *gamma*). This schema, in fact, provides the minimal branching structure of repression—defined,

25. *SE,* 3:228–29, contains the abstract of Sigmund Freud, "Über Spinalganglien und Rückenmark des Petromyzon," *Sitzungsberichte der kaiserlichen Akademie der Wissenschaften* [Vienna], *Mathematisch-Naturwissenschaftliche Kl.* 78, no. 3 (1878), 81–167.

26. Sigmund Freud and L. O. von Darkschewitsch, "Über die Beziehung des Strickkörpers zum Hinterstrang und Hinterstrangskern nebst Bemerkungen über zwei Felder der Oblongata," *Neurologisches Centralblatt* 5 (1886), 121–29.

27. See esp. Robert R. Holt, "A Critical Examination of Freud's Concept of Bound Versus Free Cathexis," *Journal of the American Psychoanalytic Association* 10 (1962), 475–525; Sulloway, *Freud, Biologist of the Mind,* chap. 4; Jean Laplanche, *Life and Death in Psychoanalysis,* trans. Jeffrey Mehlman (Baltimore, Md., 1976), chap. 3. See also Chapter 10.

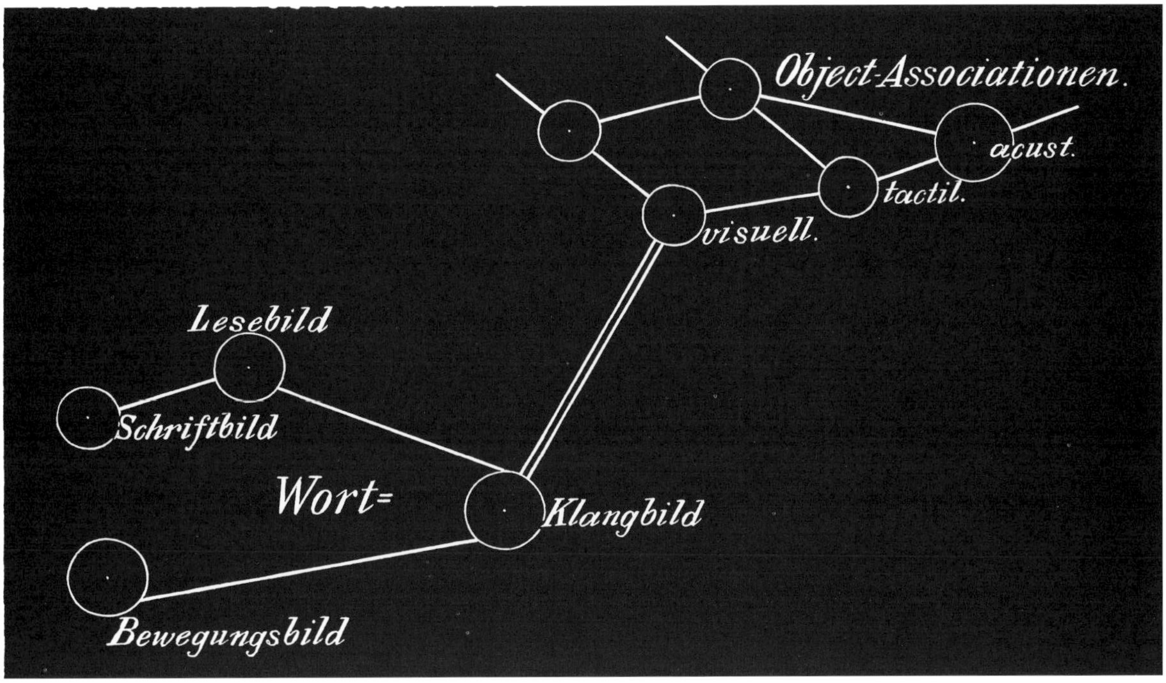

Fig. 11.9. Psychological schema for the word concept.

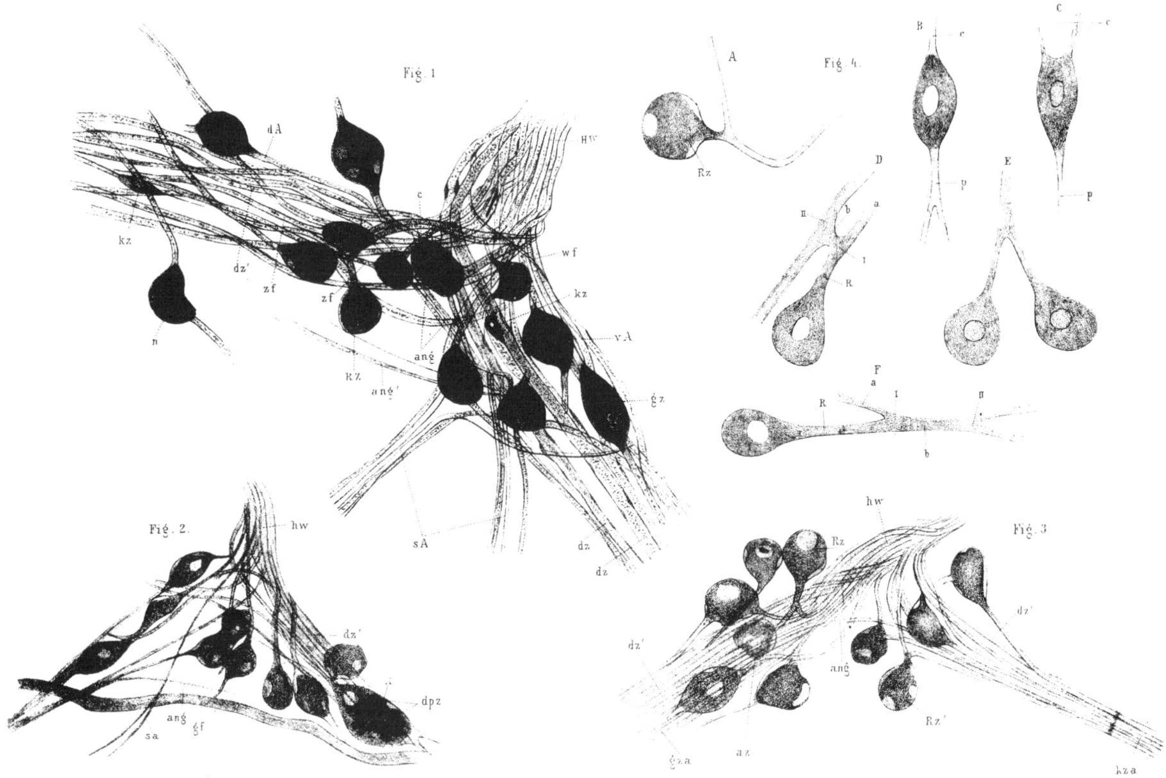

Fig. 11.10. Sigmund Freud, drawing of the nerve processes of the spinal ganglia of *Petromyzon*.

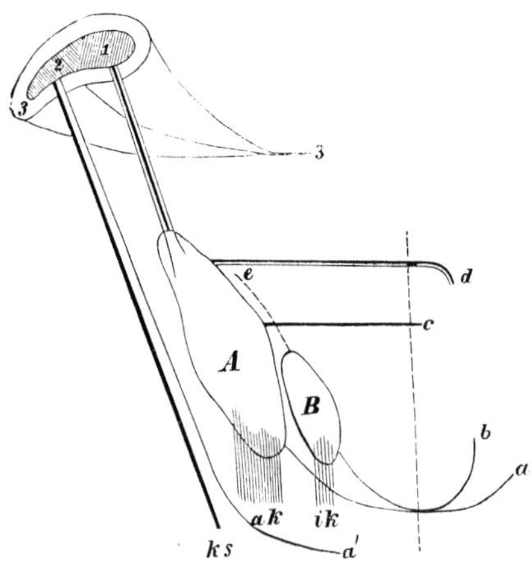

Schema des Hinterstrangskernes und seiner Verbindungen:
A Burdach'scher Kern.
B Goll'scher Kern.
1 Kopf des primären Strickkörpers.
2 Schweif desselben.
3 Secundärer Strickkörper (Olivensystem).
a } Faser aus unterem Bogenfasersystem
a' } zum Strickkörper der anderen Seite.
b unteres Bogenfasersystem (obere Pyramidenkreuzung) zur Olivenzwischenschichte.
c mittleres Bogenfasersystem.
d oberes Bogenfasersystem.
e Fasern aus Goll'schem Strang (Fibrae arcuatae externae).
Ks Kleinhirnseitenstrangfaser.
aK Aeusserer Keilstrang (Armfasern).
iK Innerer Keilstrang (Beinfasern).

Fig. 11.11. Schema for the binding of nerve fibers and bodies in the medulla oblongata.

that is, precisely as the dispersion of mental energy on its route toward discharge. But just as the quantity of incoming energy varies, so does its "quality" on a continuum from pleasurable to unpleasurable. A pleasurable sensation tends to discharge itself directly. But full discharge of an unpleasurable sensation would be damaging to the organism. Unpleasurable sensations, then, are diffused by being "defensively" siphoned off along alternative pathways—in the schema (Fig. 11.12*b*), the loop of neurons *"alpha-beta-gamma-delta"*—that Freud calls "*lateral* binding" (usually translated "cathexis"), that more specialized form of "repression" (or "defensive process" *[Abwehrvorgang]* of the "ego" *[Ich]*) which psychoanalysis later made its specific concern. The problem is that at the first "contact barrier" itself (in the schema, at neuron *a*/neuron *b* or neuron *a*/neuron *alpha*), the ego (defined in its most general Freudian sense as the self-preservative agency of the organism) must somehow know whether the incoming energy is pleasurable, thus leading to discharge, or unpleasurable, thus requiring lateral binding. Freud asserts that "it is easy to imagine how, with the help of a mechanism that draws the ego's *attention* to the imminent fresh cathexis of a hostile mnemic image, the ego can succeed in inhibiting the passage [of quantity] from a mnemic image to a release of unpleasure by a copious side-cathexis [lateral binding] which can be strengthened according to need" (*SE*, 1:324). Whence, though, this "attention," this observing homunculus that already knows what to do? In the last section of the "Project," Freud acknowledges the difficulty in giving "a mechanical (automatic) explanation of its origin," and supposes that it must be "biologically determined," "left over in the course of psychical evolution" (*SE*, 1:360). I shall return to the importance of this theory for his schematization of mental structure.

For the moment, I suggest that the first element in Freud's subjective object in or as the Wolf Man's drawing of his dream was simply the associative memory tree of repression as Freud himself had schematized it. This metaphorical visualization has haunted the conceptualizations of psychoanalysis right up to its most contemporary semiological and cognitive expressions.[28]

28. See, e.g., Jacques Lacan, *Ecrits,* trans. Alan Sheridan (London, 1977), 151, who reproduces Saussure's "classic" diagrammatic example of the meaning of the word "tree" to illustrate the concept of the "sliding"

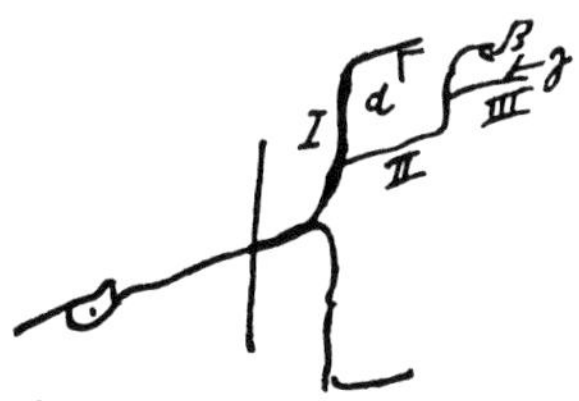

a

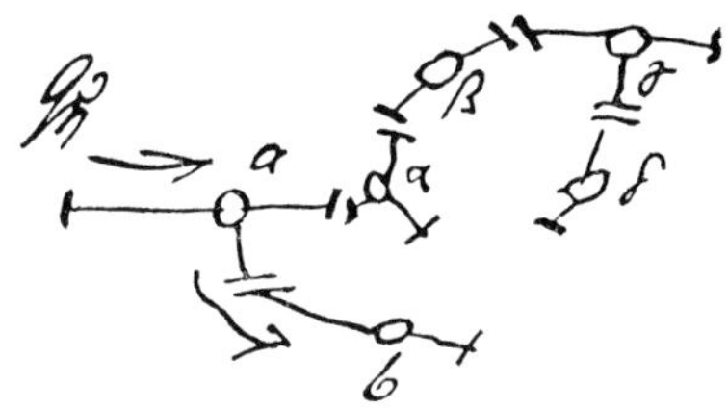

b

Fig. 11.12. *a.* Schema for the passage of quantity in the psychic system. *b.* Schema for the passage of quality in the psychic system.

From 1895 to 1900, Freud's research on the structure of repression was not confined to neurology, hysteria, or the general schema for the psychic apparatus. It also included his analysis of the structure of his own repressions. In the mid-1890s, Freud's public view was that repression siphons off unpleasurable memories of objectively traumatic events, such as Emma's memory of the abusive shopkeeper (Figs. 11.5, 11.6, 11.12*b*). But in his own self-analysis Freud could not always recall such origins. Rather, he uncovered an indefinitely ramifying network of memories of pleasant *and* unpleasant events *and* fantasies. He concluded that conflict between thoughts is *inherently* unpleasurable, independent of real-world correlates. On this view, repression cannot be tracked to a single point of origin; the root of repression is inherently divided.

The most important example of the dividedness of the origins of repression became the "specimen parapraxis" of psychoanalysis itself. In a letter to Fliess of 22 September 1898, Freud reported a slip that had taken place the previous week.[29] During a short train ride with a "lawyer from Berlin"—an obvious association to Fliess, who lived in Berlin—Freud "got to talking about pictures," as he and Fliess had done many times. "I could not find,"

(glissage) of the signifier; Stanley R. Palombo, "The Associative Memory Tree," *Psychoanalysis and Contemporary Science* 2 (1973), 205–19.

29. *Freud-Fliess Letters,* 326–27; less than a week later the slip had been written up as an essay ("The Psychical Mechanism of Forgetfulness," in *SE,* 2:287–97), reused in 1901 as the beginning of *The Psychopathology of Everyday Life* (*SE,* 3:2–7). For detailed considerations, see Jean Schimek, "The Specimen Parapraxis of Psychoanalysis," *Psychoanalysis and Contemporary Science* 3 (1974), 210–30, and Didier Anzieu, *Freud's Self-Analysis,* 2d ed., trans. Peter Graham (London, 1986), 359–62, although my reading differs from theirs.

he says, "the name of the renowned painter who did the *Last Judgment* in Orvieto, the greatest I have seen so far." There is no need to rehearse his well-known analysis of the repression of the name of Signorelli. As his diagram shows (Fig. 11.13), the repression was a fine instance of the lateral binding of thoughts, here concerning "death and sexuality." One thought was a joke he had heard about one's sexual activities' coming to an end as "death"; the other was the news of the suicide of a patient he was treating for a sexual disease. The repression, then, derived multiply from *two* memories connected with an inherently conflicted subject, "death-and-sexuality," that were themselves conflicting, one making light of it and the other deadly serious.

Indeed, the lateral binding that structured the forgetting of the name of Signorelli continues, I think, to structure Freud's own explication of his slip. Although he was unable to recall Signorelli's name, he could visualize the artist's self-portrait in the fresco; "with a serious face and folded hands," Signorelli's self-portrait was evidently the object of Freud's own identification. He also recalls, he says, that the artist's self-portrait was "put in a corner of one of the pictures, next to the portrait of his predecessor in the work, Fra Angelico da Fiesole." Despite the way the forgotten name of Signorelli was being disturbed by the name and image of Fra Angelico, however, this detail is *not* included in Freud's diagram of the structure of the repression (Fig. 11.13). It seems likely that the association with Fra Angelico was to Fliess himself. Initially repressed, it appears at the end of the essay, where Freud briefly describes a second slip. He forgets the address of someone he was supposed to visit in Berlin, because, he says, he would rather be "devoted entirely to his friend" in the city (that is, to Fliess). The duty to call on this unnamed person would "interfere with [Freud and Fliess] being together," like Signorelli and Fra Angelico, and therefore the address is forgotten.

Later on Freud was able to de-repress elements of the intense friendship with Fliess, which ended badly in 1904. Its erotic dynamics were repeated, he knew, with friends and rivals like Adler and Jung. In these relations, as he confessed to Ernest Jones in 1912, "there is some piece of unruly homosexual feeling at the root of the matter."[30] To be "homosexual," in Freud's lexicon at this time, is to be passive, receptive, or even seductive in relation to the desires of other men for oneself but also partly paranoid about these desires; it does not require overtly homosexual sexual attraction or activity.[31] His "unruly [homosexual] feeling" was complicated by public or professional competition that

30. Freud to Jones, 12 December 1912, quoted by Gay, *Freud*, 276. For penetrating treatments of Freud's bisexual conflicts, although debatable in points of detail, see Jim Swan, "Mater and Nannie: Freud's Two Mothers and the Discovery of the Oedipus Complex," *American Imago* 31 (1974), 1–64; Marianne Krüll, *Freud and His Father*, trans. Arnold J. Pomerans (New York, 1986); and McGrath, *Freud's Discovery of Psychoanalysis*, 278–88.

31. A useful introduction can be found in Kenneth Lewes, *The Psychoanalytic Theory of Male Homosexuality* (New York, 1988), 24–47. Freud's ideas are worked out not only in his studies of the memoirs of Judge Schreber (*SE*, 12:1–84) and of the life and art of Leonardo da Vinci (*SE*, 11:59–138) but also in the Wolf Man case itself. Whereas Schreber is a "repressed" homosexual and Leonardo an "ideal" homosexual, the Wolf Man is a "latent" homosexual. Freud means something quite specific and distinct by each of these terms. Although Schreber apparently never had a homosexual sexual experience—his only overt "perversion" consisted in cross-dressing—Freud's point is that "in the world of the unconscious" the judge's "homosexuality" determined his "paranoid" fantasy life (*SE*, 12:43). Whereas Schreber's homosexuality is merely "unconscious" (repressed), Leonardo's is "ideal" because he drained off or "sublimated" his sexual life, both unconscious and overt, in

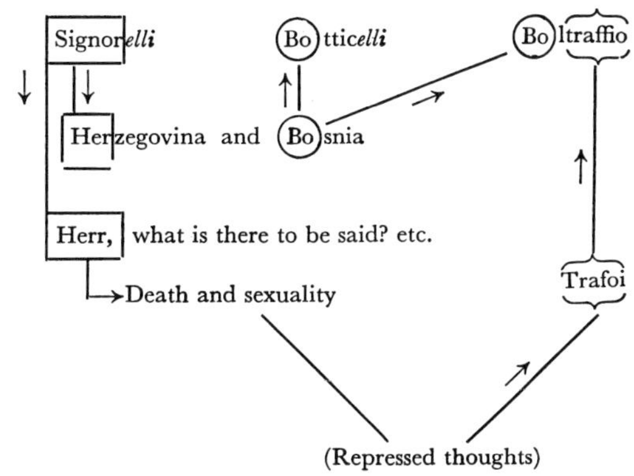

Fig. 11.13. Schema for the structure of the forgetting of the name of Signorelli.

grew up between the men. For instance, Freud grudgingly recognized Fliess as the predecessor of his own work, like Fra Angelico in Signorelli's fresco. Indeed, in 1901, despite growing trouble between the two men, Freud announced his adoption of one of Fliess's central ideas—namely, the theory of the "root" of repression as conflict deriving from the inherent possibility that any person can make both heterosexual and homosexual choices.[32]

The rooting of repression, of the branches of memory, is finally the intrinsic doubleness, or (in Fliess's term) "bisexuality," of the subject. In the simplest possible formula, bisexuality = repression. At some archaic point in the history of the subject, however, this network of lateral, deferred discharge, of repression, has not emerged, because no perceptual impression has yet activated bisexuality by laying down the first division, or branching, of the pathways to direct discharge. Such a perception might be called the "primal scene," a perception that first evokes the subject's double desire and that for the sake of the very preservation of the subject in turn requires the subject's division in repression.

The Wolf Man's primal scene is constructed by Freud from the material provided by the wolves. From their immobility, by the principle of distortion in the dreamwork, Freud

his creative work; that is, he partially discharged his repression (see esp. *SE,* 11:80–81). Finally, the Wolf Man supposedly does not benefit from Leonardo's (and Freud's) creative "overcoming" of homosexuality (here, of course, Freud ignores the Wolf Man's own creative activities); he is thus a "latent" homosexual, "shackled" by what Freud supposes is an "inherited" predisposition.

32. *Freud-Fliess Letters,* 447 (letter of 7 August 1901). In 1901 Freud publicly acknowledged his debt in *The Psychopathology of Everyday Life* (*SE,* 6:144), but by 1904, he clearly felt himself to be the actual inventor of the idea. If Fliess was his "predecessor in the work," in his own mind he was, without question, the real artist. It is significant, I think, that problems of originality and borrowing are at the heart of Vasari's biography of Signorelli, which evidently lies behind Freud's description of his slip of the tongue. The slip is not merely about Freud's dependence on Fliess in completing his scientific work (like Signorelli's completion of the frescoes begun by Fra Angelico); it is also about the great Michelangelo's (to say, Freud's) later "imitation"—Vasari describes it as "kind borrowing"—of Signorelli's (to say, Fliess's) "inventions" (Giorgio Vasari, *The Lives of the Artists,* trans. Julia Conway Bondanella and Peter Bondanella [Oxford, 1991], 271; Michelangelo was one of Freud's identificatory models throughout his life).

derives the "violent motion" of the primal scene (35). From the wolves' staring fixedly at the little boy, Freud derives the little boy staring fixedly at the scene. From their color, Freud derives characteristics of the setting—the parents' white underclothes, the bedding. From the "several" wolves, Freud derives the two parents; "as would be desirable," he asserts, "the dreamwork avoids showing the couple" (42). From the attitude of the wolves, sitting high in the tree, he derives the sexual act itself, a "climbing up" (43).

But, as Freud recognizes in two 1918 additions to the case history, from this material alone the primal scene as constructed—the Wolf Man's parents having anal sex—could be more plausibly interpreted as a distorted memory of animals copulating on his father's estate (see, for example, 58). In the dream report, the "wolves" *are* stated to look "more like foxes or sheep dogs" (29). Despite its plausibility, however, this version of the primal scene would, of course, disprove the "case" Freud had been trying to make with the Wolf Man from the beginning. In fact, it would tend to confirm Jung's skeptical opinion that neuroses, instead of reproducing (through repressing) an endogenous infantile sexuality as such, are actually retrospective formations in which the neurotic reorganizes postpubescent sexual fantasies as childhood memories. Because Freud's theoretical structure for repression requires an activation of the bisexual constitution in a primal scene, that scene must provide perceptual material giving pleasure to both the heterosexual and the homosexual currents in the subject. Freud's theory requires, then, that the little Wolf Man simultaneously saw the pleasured faces of both parents—for, of course, they are supposed to be making love *like animals*. In the retrospective interpretation produced in 1914–15 by historical construction and its writing out in the case history, the animals in the dream report become the parents in the primal scene. But in the forward thrust of Freud's "conviction" in 1910 about repression and its roots, it is the other way around: the *parents must become animals* to create the very possibility of the scene required by the theory of repression.[33]

The dream report itself, as recounted in spring 1910, gave no basis one way or another to

33. In his objective narrative of the Wolf Man's history, Freud constructs the parents' intercourse from behind as "especially favorable for observation" (36) or "for [making] certain observations" (55; see also 38). The little observer "was able to see his mother's genitals as well as his father's organ; and he [retroactively] understood the process [of their intercourse] as well as its significance" (37), namely, that in order to assume his mother's place in the scene he would have to possess genitals like hers rather than like his father's, a discovery terrifying him, for "he saw with his own eyes the wound of which his Nanya had spoken" (46). In other words, in the manifest text of the case history, the intercourse from behind is constructed to explain the boy's castration anxieties. However, as Serge Viderman says, "the position *a tergo* is the least favorable to observe the female genitals, unless the child enjoyed the optimal position neither behind nor before the couple but at their very juncture" (*Le céleste et le sublunaire* [Paris, 1977], 306, translated by the author). In fact, in this position—"which alone," Freud says, "offers the spectator a possibility of inspecting the genitals" (59)!—*both* parents' genitals would be invisible to the little observer if, as the account also has it, he was supposed to be seeing their facial expressions. Moreover, although in intercourse from behind both parents are "animals" (or make love the way animals do), they are, of course, different animals: the father, with whom the boy initially and strongly identifies but who later terrifies him, is the upright wolf, while the mother is just an (unidentified) animal, "bent down" (39) (see also Gilles Deleuze and Felix Guattari, "14 Mai 1914: Un seul ou plusieurs loups?" *Minuit* 5 [September 1973], 2–16). These and other turmoils in the text—I believe Freud was partially aware of them, for in the fourth edition of "Leonardo and a Memory of His Childhood," prepared in 1919, he added material on depictions of the position of intercourse (*SE*, 11:70–72)—simply reaffirm my argument here that behind the manifest interpretation of intercourse from behind as the objective historical root of the

take the wolves to be copulating animals or the little boy's parents. Assuming the principles of dreamwork, the violent motion, whiteness, two parents, and climbing up would be fully consistent with both versions. The evidence for the construction of Freud's *preferred* history was, I suggest, the *drawing* of the dream presented along with the dream report.

In addition to being the structure of laterally ramified thoughts requiring the "primal scene" of a repression of bisexuality, the tree with the wolves is, for Freud, also the structure of the evolution from animal to human sexuality—that is, of the individual inheritance of biologically acquired endowments, an idea that the theory of repression ultimately requires. The repression tree traces or retraces the phylogenetic tree. Although I shall not review them all here, phylogenetic arguments are crucial in the Wolf Man's case history. Three closely related images will have to make the immediate point. The phylogenetic tree was, of course, the subject of Darwin's famous 1859 diagram in *The Origin of Species,* known to Freud in the 1867 German translation by Victor Carus (Fig. 11.14). Darwin's diagram schematizes not only the growth and divergence of varieties and species. It also represents a history of competition and conflict between organisms—in Darwin's own words, "a constant tendency in the improved descendants of any one species to supplant and exterminate in each stage of descent their predecessors and original progenitor," somewhat, one might say, like Signorelli supplanting Fra Angelico.[34] In *Totem und Tabu,* written in 1912 while Freud was analyzing the Wolf Man, Freud rewrote Darwin's scenario to recount human psychogenesis as an Oedipal tale of the prehistoric sons' murder of the primal father; phylogeny is the historical site of the real lust, violence, and guilt that individual ontogeny inherits and repeats in the psychic register.

In turn, Freud's recapitulationist argument had its own well-known visualization: the comparative anatomist Ernst Haeckel's "systematic *Stammbaum* of mankind" (Fig. 11.15), well known to Freud by the early 1870s, placed species in relation to one another according to the law of recapitulation; in its individual development, every organism traverses the full phylogenetic emergence of its adult characteristics.[35] Haeckel's *Stammbaum,* then, represents *both* individual *and* species history. Haeckel concerned himself with the evolution of anatomy, and by the 1890s Freud had psychological characteristics in mind. In this regard, some portion of the psyche could certainly be conceived to derive from repressions; but to avoid a regress fatal to the whole Freudian theory of mind, some portion of the psyche has to emerge intrinsically; it has to be inherited.

A third source provided the schema—if not all the details—Freud required. Published in 1888, George Romanes's *Mental Evolution in Man* was carefully read by Freud in the

Wolf Man's subjectivity there lies a complex subjective object of Freud's own. Of course, the case had commenced with the Wolf Man's statement of his desire to "use [Freud] from behind."

34. Charles Darwin, *The Works of Charles Darwin,* vol. 16, *The Origin of Species,* ed. Paul H. Barrett and R. B. Freeman (1876; London, 1988), 97; see, generally, 94–103 for Darwin's fullest explanation of his diagram. For background material, see Lucille B. Ritvo, *Darwin's Influence on Freud: A Tale of Two Sciences* (New Haven, Conn., 1990).

35. Ernst Haeckel, *Anthropogenie oder Entwicklungsgeschichte des Menschen: Vorträge über die Grundzüge der menschlichen Keimes- und Stammesgeschichte* (Leipzig, 1874), pl. 15; I follow the explanation by Stephen Jay Gould, *Ontogeny and Phylogeny* (Cambridge, Mass., 1977), 170–73.

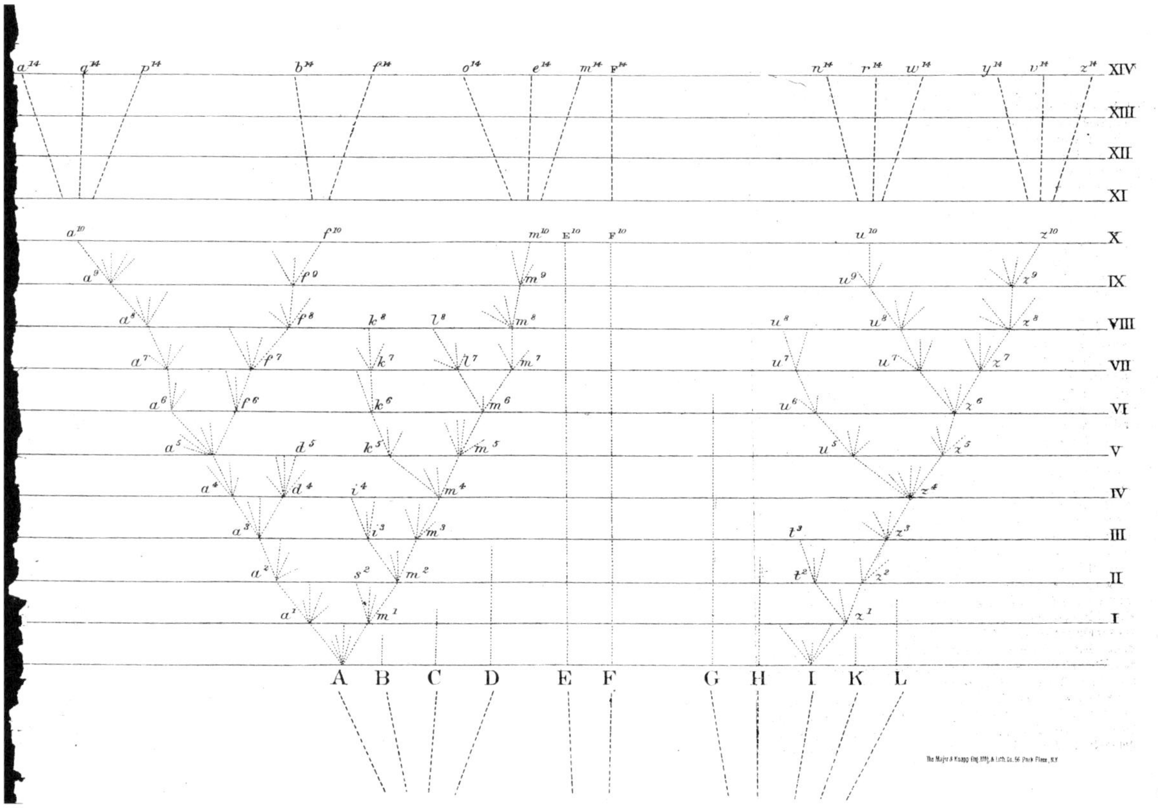

Fig. 11.14. "The probable effect of the action of natural selection through divergence of character and extinction, on the descendants of a common ancestor."

early 1890s.[36] In the foldout plate at the beginning of his book (Fig. 11.16), Romanes, a committed recapitulationist, visualized the psychogenesis of mankind: for example, at seven weeks, recapitulating through the insects and spiders, a human infant is "imagining" and "perceiving"; by the eighth month, the infant now recapitulating through the birds, "abstraction" appears; at fifteen months, abstraction sprouts a new branch, roughly equivalent to the associations, delayed discharges, and unconscious of Freudian metapsychology.

Introduced through his comprehension of the drawing, phylogenetic schemas enabled Freud to solve the pivotal historical problem of the Wolf Man's life story—namely, why the Wolf Man was neither a contented heterosexual nor an active homosexual but rather a "latent" or "shackled" homosexual whom analysis (according to Freud) actually "liberates" (71). As his life history suggested, the Wolf Man partially repressed but in various ways did partially discharge homosexually pleasurable thoughts, supposedly activated in the primal scene—for that scene, by definition, evokes both heterosexual and homosexual currents in primary bisexuality. But if this was so, then the Wolf Man was an anomaly. According not only to late-nineteenth-century stereotypes of sexuality but also to the prin-

36. George John Romanes, *Mental Evolution in Man* (London, 1888).

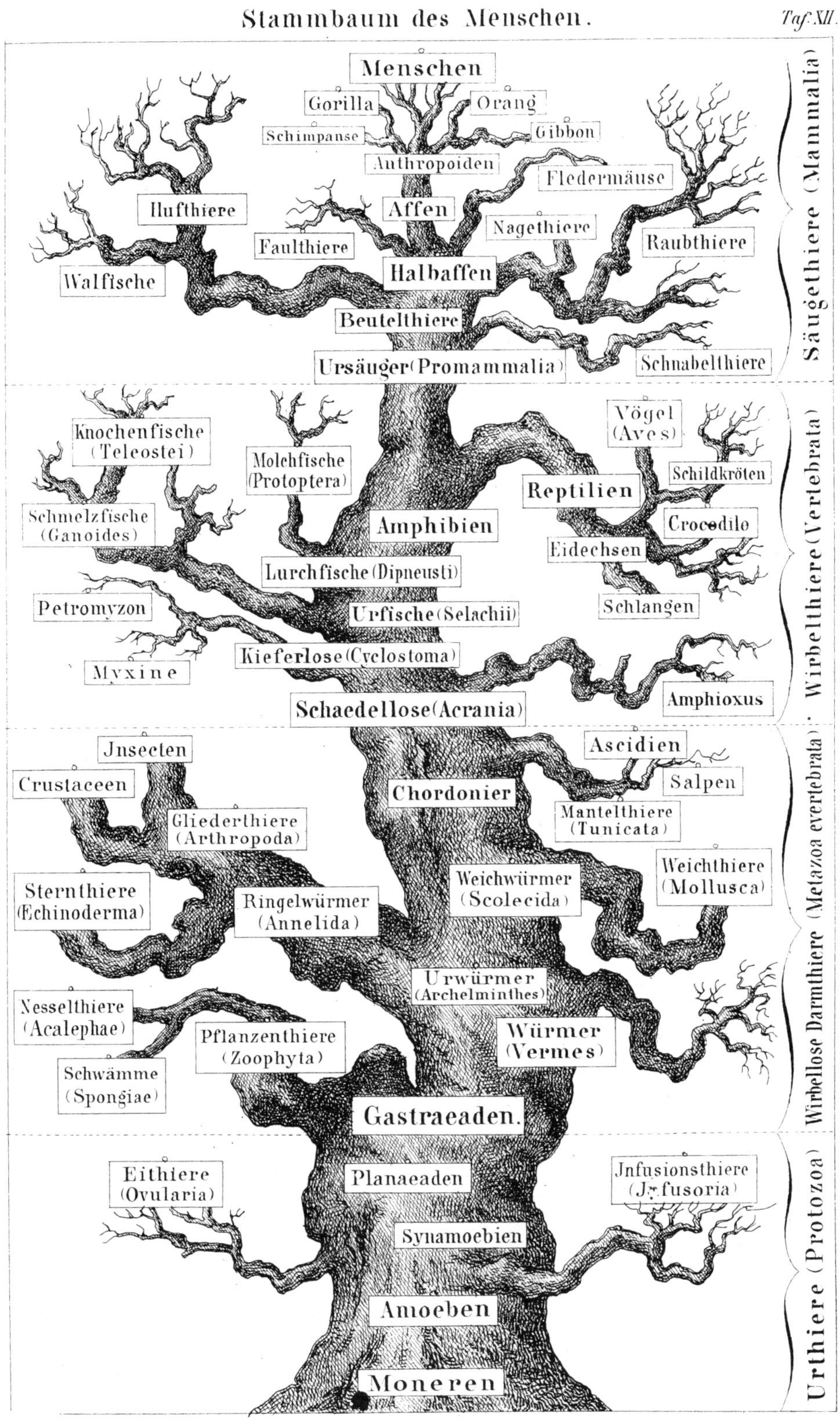

Fig. 11.15. "The lineage of mankind."

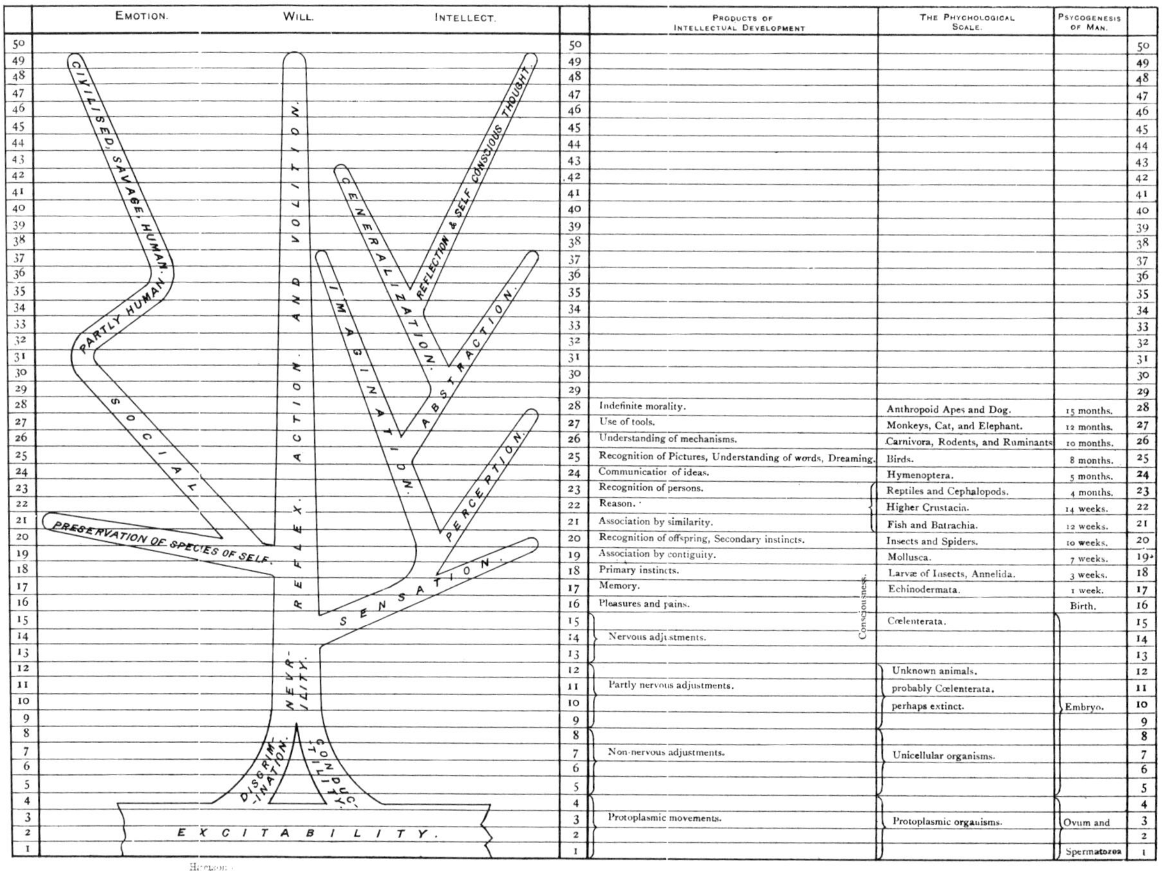

Fig. 11.16. Schema for the psychogenesis of mankind.

ciples of psychophysics, the two currents of primary bisexuality should be sorted out in repression by the time mature object choices are made; two different excitations toward discharge cannot be transmitted in the same system. Typically homosexual object choice is repressed by starving it of pleasure and overwhelming it with unpleasure (although rarer so-called inversions of this pattern might also be found).

But despite the splintered condition of his adult psyche, the Wolf Man somehow had the wherewithal to resist *either* such unilateral resolution of his bisexuality because his *inherited* predisposition supposedly contained two unusual psychic relays—namely, a disposition to take sexual pleasure from the male and a disposition to take pleasure in the anal region. Given their inherited strength, these relays continued to transmit toward discharge throughout the Wolf Man's life. In this respect, it was the homosexual content of the first consultation—apparently the Wolf Man wants to have anal sex with Freud and shit on his head and also complains of his homosexually relieved bowel disorders—that must have specified for Freud the "biologically determined" relays in the Wolf Man's endogenous sexuality, symbolized by the wolves, for they have no represented gender in either the dream report or the drawing but are somehow immediately taken by Freud as male or supporting masculine identifications. In fact, although the drawing is not a clear "confirmation" of the dream report, it does confirm the first consultation—confirming that Freud should seek an explanation of the Wolf Man's homosexuality in phylogenetically acquired endowments, such as the theory of repression broadly requires.

To generalize: according to Freud, the tree of phylogeny, the descent of human psychological characteristics, supports the tree of repression precisely by determining why, in the last instance, the subject's repression should have the *particular* form it does. The tree of descent produces a seed that grows up as the tree of repression. And thus there is yet another and final term to consider. The environment in which the tree of descent plants a seed that will grow up as the tree of repression is, of course, the *family tree*. Even if various graphic conventions for drawing kinship charts had not existed,[37] we can be fairly certain that the family tree completed Freud's subjective object, the Wolf Man's drawing as "confirmation" of the "case" of psychoanalysis concerning repression.

Freud probably knew at least one family tree of his own family (Fig. 11.17).[38] But if these images cannot do the historical work, another certainly can: a painting in Freud's immediate family's possession for many years (Fig. 11.18), at least since the late 1860s, presents a portrait of young Sigmund, at the far left, his younger brother Alexander, in the front, and their sisters, five little girls and "six or seven" children in all, depending on how we group them—five, counting all the girls; six, for all the girls and Freud's brother; seven, for all the girls plus the two boys.[39] As Freud would have argued, the history of congenital constitution and psychic repression—whether of Freud himself or of any other subject—intersect in the time and place represented in this image, by and large forgotten by all subjects and possibly by Freud himself, but remembered by him, I suggest, when in 1910 the Wolf Man presented its replication, with its five, six, or seven wolves, a drawing that because of its predecessors immediately realized itself, for Freud, as the psychic history of humankind—child, infant, and species.

Freud's past—specifically, his use of certain images, metaphors, and schemata—enables him to comprehend the Wolf Man's past. His approach to the case presented to him by the Wolf Man depends on the historical context of psychoanalytic polemic and, more to my point, on an art history, "within" Freud, that had set up and continued to provide an iconography for the history of minds and persons. Its history must take us from Darwin and Haeckel to histology and neurology to Freud's own personal artifacts and images—and I have only disentangled a few threads in the fabric. The meaningfulness of this iconography had been established, for Freud, well before the case commenced; it was activated during the case; and it provided the forward impetus by which the case resolved itself as the case history *for* that very iconography, that picture or schema of the mind.

37. For the use of these conventions, compare Sigmund Freud, *Totem und Tabu* (Vienna, 1916), 13, with Wilhelm Wundt, *Elemente der Völkerpsychologie: Grundlinien einer psychologischen Entwicklungsgeschichte der Menschheit*, 2d ed. (Leipzig, 1913), 160, 167.

38. Krüll, *Freud and His Father*, table 2, reproduces a family tree prepared from tombstones sometime after Freud's appointment to his professorship in 1902. I have been unable to determine whether Freud knew this drawing, although it seems very likely.

39. Published in Jonathan Miller, ed., *Freud: The Man, His World, His Influence* (Boston, 1972), 6 (top).

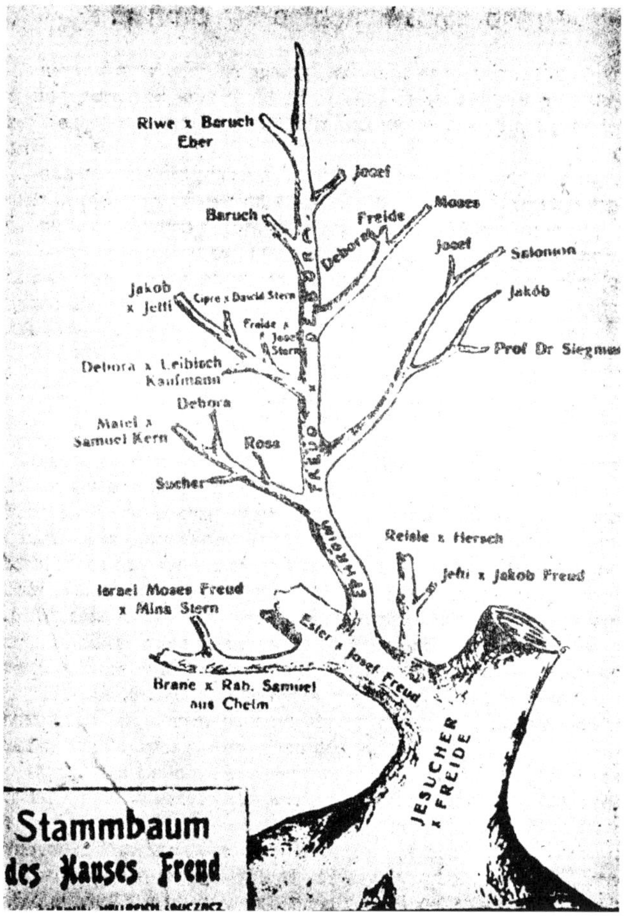

Fig. 11.17. Family tree of the Freud family, after 1902.

Rather than attack an art historical problem with psychoanalytic techniques, I have, as it were, attacked a psychoanalytic problem with art historical techniques.

Thus, I have not argued that Freud's use of the Wolf Man's drawing in his historical interpretation of the Wolf Man's subjectivity should be a general model for the authentic psychoanalytic interpretation of images, whatever that might be. Perhaps the case history could be taken as such a model; it is surprising to find that no treatment of the topic of "psychoanalysis and art" does anything with it.[40] In fact, Freud's essentially vulgar procedures in his 1910 essay "Leonardo da Vinci and a Memory of His Childhood" remain the usual illustration of psychoanalytic reasoning about images.[41] In the case history of the Wolf Man, an image could be interpreted through the artist's own associations, recollections, and transference in the specifically psychoanalytic situation, a context entirely lacking for Leonardo. In "Leonardo," Freud is constrained to construct Leonardo's subjectivity as a pure object for him. By contrast, in the Wolf Man case Freud's interpretation is constructed

40. There are possible exceptions; see Whitney Davis, "The Subject in the Scene of Representation," *Art Bulletin* 76 (1994), 570–75, for a discussion of the role of the case history in some contemporary art historical projects.

41. *SE*, 11:59–138.

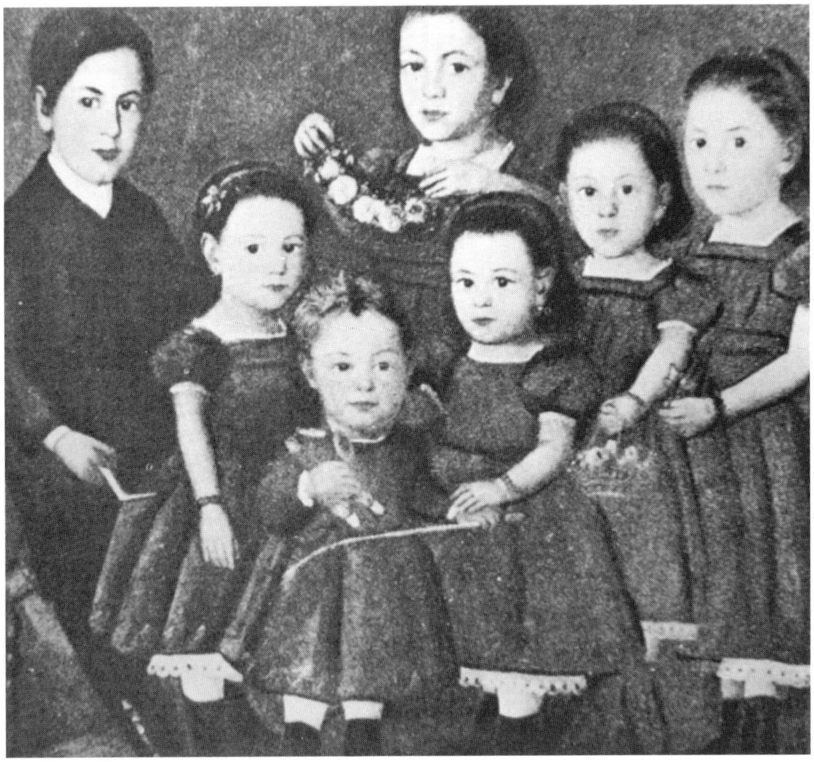

Fig. 11.18. Family portrait of Freud and his brother and sisters, about 1875.

intersubjectively: at least in principle, the subject could speak back to the ostensibly objective observer attempting to interpret him, and the observer could pursue this in direct exchange with the subject.

I have been interested in one aspect of this dynamic; in attempting objectively to interpret another's subjectivity, objects produced by that subject might function as what I have been calling subjective objects for the interpreter.[42] This phenomenon is partially inside the psychoanalytic situation to the extent that a psychoanalyst can witness it. But it is also partially *outside* the psychoanalysis, for it cannot be comprehended *psychoanalytically* without a complex fissuring of historical interpretation: the history by which an image becomes evidence for the objective history of a subject and the history by which an image becomes the subjective object of a historian are two different histories (see also

42. I have not attempted to relate this concept to its sources. I have learned, first, from the Lacanian concept of the *objet petit a:* Jacques Lacan, "Clivage du sujet et son identification," *Scilicet* 2/3 (1970), 103–36; see Antoine Vergote, "From Freud's 'Other Scene' to Lacan's 'Other,'" in *Interpreting Lacan,* ed. Joseph H. Smith and William Kerrigan (New Haven, Conn., 1983), 193–221—second, from object relations theory: see esp. D. W. Winnicott, "Transitional Objects and Transitional Phenomena: A Study of the First Not-Me Possession," *International Journal of Psycho-Analysis* 34 (1953), 86–97; idem, "The Subjective Object," in *Psycho-Analytic Explorations,* ed. Clare Winnicott, Ray Shepherd, and Madeleine Davis (Cambridge, Mass., 1989), 253–54; and Vamik D. Volkan, *Linking Objects and Linking Phenomena* (New York, 1981)—and, third, from studies of transference, countertransference, and the construction of objects in psychoanalysis: Heinrich Racker, *Transference and Countertransference* (London, 1968); Brian Bird, "Notes on Transference," *Journal of the American Psychoanalytic Association* 20 (1972), 267–301; and Irwin Z. Hoffman, "The Patient as Interpreter of the Analyst's Experience," *Contemporary Psychoanalysis* 19 (1983), 389–422.

Chapter 9). Moreover, subjective objects do not exist *only* within the psychoanalytic situation. *Any* interpretation of the ostensibly objective historical meaning of an image might proceed from the observer incorporating or projecting it as a subjective object (see Chapter 9). We could say that interpretation is vulgarly subjective when it proceeds, as it always partly does, merely from the interpreter's subjective objects—but can become *psychoanalytically* subjective when this history is, itself, recognized and interpreted. The opposite of subjectivity is not objectivity; the opposite of subjectivity is intersubjectivity.

Freud's past enables him to comprehend the Wolf Man's past; more accurately, an object produced by the Wolf Man is already part of Freud's past. Now this finding might tempt us to accept Stanley Fish's proposal that the "Wolf Man is, in short, a piece of language," a rhetorical construction by Freud to persuade a reader of the fitness of Freud's own interpretive conceptions: "At bottom the primal scene is the scene of persuasion."[43] But what I have described so far is not just more evidence for what we already know—that a historian's subjectivity is an inescapable touchstone for his or her construction of the subjectivities of others. Freud's construction of his patient was wide-ranging and penetrating, but the dynamic of the relation cannot be reduced to the construction of one subject "by" another.

The *Wolf Man's* share should not be forgotten. Freud made the "Wolf Man" who was the subject of his case history, for that "Wolf Man" is almost entirely a figure in Freud's narrative construction of him. Even the "Wolf Man's" most intimate manifestations, such as his report of his dream, come to us through Freud's transcription of them. But I say "almost entirely," for the Wolf Man, Serge Pankejeff himself, made something Freud needed to complete *himself* as a subject. Although that object necessarily becomes Freud's own subjective object, it is distinguished from Freud's representation, "the Wolf Man," as a representation *not* written "by" Freud but rather by the Wolf Man himself, written "into" Freud. More exactly, these very terms—representation "by" Freud or "by" the Wolf Man—break down. This effective intersubjectivity is what interests me.

Of course, we would need to investigate some other elements in the situation—such as the determinations of the Wolf Man's drawing of his dream of the wolves apart from *Freud's* drawing of the dream of the wolves. For example, as I have noted, the drawing probably replicates certain themes in the network of pastoral and landscape imagery that the Wolf Man, as an educated amateur painter, probably knew. Or again, the meaning of the Wolf Man's "wolves" should probably be partially situated for him, if not for Freud, in central European and Russian folk traditions of lycanthropy.[44] For the Wolf Man listening to Freud in 1914, the wolves in his dream could be legibly rendered as his parents, particularly his father, because in folk tradition the werewolf was already a punitive father transformed into a beast who will "eat you up" like the wolves in the dream. And other aspects of the cultural matrix of the Wolf Man's subjective object could also be identified, some of them as, or perhaps more, important than those briefly noted here.[45]

43. Fish, "Withholding the Missing Portion," 547.

44. This is the argument of Carlo Ginzburg's important essay "Freud, der Wolfsmann und die Werwölfe," *Poetik und Hermeneutik* 13 (1988), 217–27. However, Ginzburg, like Fish, does not come to terms with the intersubjective constructions in the case.

45. See Albert J. Lubin, "The Influence of the Russian Orthodox Church on Freud's Wolf-Man," *Psycho-*

More important for my immediate point, however, Freud subjectively *responded* to many aspects of this other history. Just as Freud projected his subjective object on the Wolf Man's drawing, so too did he incorporate the Wolf Man's subjective objects into his own representations. For example, in the text of the case history—immediately following his introduction of the drawing—Freud relates the Wolf Man's very first association to the dream. The patient connected the wolves with a wolf he had seen as a child in a picture book: the wolf was depicted "standing upright, striding out with one foot, with its claws stretched out and its ears pricked" (30)—like the wolves in the dream and drawing, with "their ears pricked like dogs when they are attending to something." Although he initially supposed that the picture illustrated the story of "Little Red Riding Hood," the Wolf Man searched the secondhand bookstores of Vienna until he found an old copy of the picture book; the story of "The Wolf and the Seven Little Goats" was illustrated with this image (31, 39). But predictably, we might now say, it was also *Freud* who had a treasured childhood picture book, which was awarded to him for his excellence in school and which he later passed to his own son Martin as an "heirloom," Friedrich Tschudi's *Animal Life in the Alpine World* (1865), which contains a striking illustration (Fig. 11.19) of an Alpine rescue dog, striding out with one foot forward and with its ears pricked, saving a little boy lost in the snowy mountains.[46] Toward the end of the case history, Freud explicitly discusses the issue of the delayed confirmation of material introduced, like the wolf dream, early in an analysis.

> It happens in many analyses that as one approaches their end new recollections emerge which have hitherto been kept carefully concealed. Or it may be that on one occasion some unpretentious remark is thrown out in an indifferent tone of voice as though it were superfluous; that then, on another occasion, something further is added, which begins to make the physician prick his ears; and that at last he comes to recognize this despised fragment of a memory as the key to the weightiest secrets that the patient's neurosis has veiled. (89)

The Wolf Man's *werewolf*, a terrifying gobbler, partially conflated by him with sheepdogs on his father's estate, is incorporated by Freud as a wolf-dog *doctor,* the attentive listener

analytic Forum 2 (1967), 160–81, and Florence J. Levy, "The Significance of Christmas for the 'Wolf Man,'" *Psychoanalytic Review* 55 (1968–69), 615–22. In *The Wolf Man's Magic Word,* Abraham and Torok argue that the Wolf Man's German speech to Freud was inflected by the connotations and homophonic associations of words both in Russian, his native tongue, and in English, the language of his first governess. Freud pursued German homophones (such as the important resemblance between the Wolf Man's initials, "S. P.," and the word for "wasp," *Wespe*), but he did not know Russian and never fully explains the relations between the Wolf Man's adult German-language representations and his childhood linguistic experiences. Abraham and Torok are surely correct that Freud was unable to work out this complex dimension of the Wolf Man's subjectivity. However, their dramatic thesis about the Wolf Man's "polyglot" (Russian/English) speech is not supported by the Wolf Man's independent, explicit testimony, whatever it is worth; the Wolf Man asserted he never learned English from his governess or anyone else (see Obholzer, *The Wolf Man Sixty Years Later,* 26, 73), and Abraham and Torok must suppose that his "English" comprehension was entirely unconscious.

46. See Lawrence M. Ginsburg and Sybil A. Ginsburg, "A Menagerie of Illustrations from Sigmund

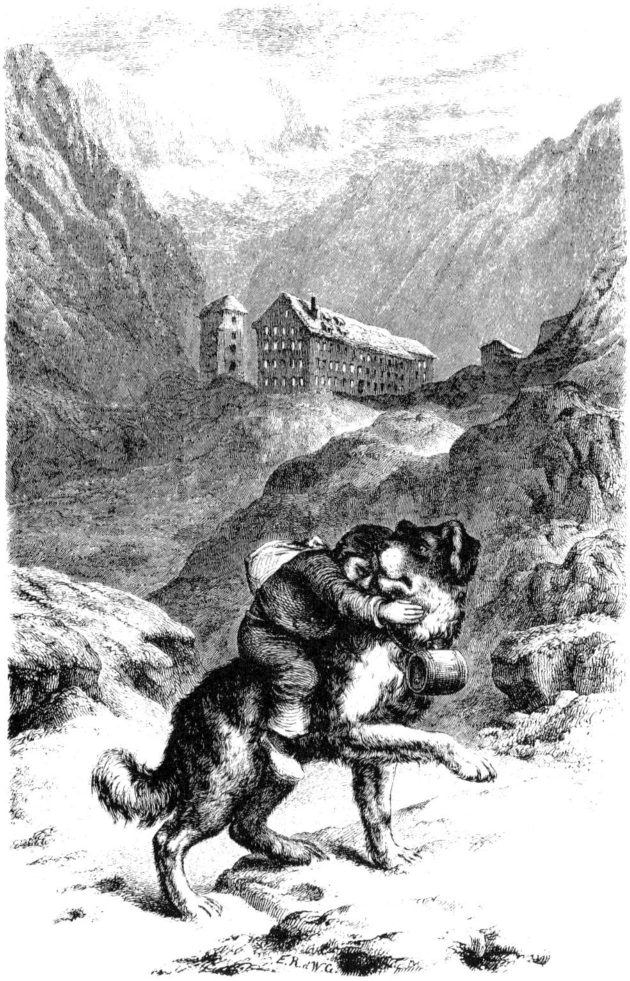

Fig. 11.19. Illustration from Freud's heirloom picture book.

who will rescue his patient from neurosis. The conversion is necessary because the Wolf Man's associations potentially cast Freud as a wolf-physician who connects up childhood imagery with the patient's history in the devouring activity of analysis.

Thus two objects, the Wolf Man's drawing and Freud's writing, become absorbed into one another in the lateral, deferred actions of psychoanalysis and writing. This intersubjective witness, transaction, and transformation should be distinguished from any merely unilateral subjective construction. Freud is not the same subject he was before the encounter takes place, for his own subjectivity—the discharging of partially unrealized desire that constitutes his own historical identity—is reorganized precisely by the incorporation and transformation of an object from the other, even as that object is the support screen for his own projections. Fish is right that the Wolf Man is a "piece of language." But that language is not *wholly* Freud's. It is forged between two subjects seeing and speak-

Freud's Boyhood," *Psychoanalytic Study of the Child* 42 (1987), 478–81.

ing with one another—jointly creating a new, intersubjective image out of their separate histories.

Of course, at the same time as the psychoanalytic situation includes this subjective incorporation and projection, this supposedly therapeutic intersubjectivity, it also claims objectively to identify and explain it, because the analyst, at least, has been previously analyzed. The analyst supposedly knows how he or she incorporates and projects subjective objects from or into the other, therefore qualifying as an objective historian of the other by knowing what to *subtract* from seeing and speaking with that other. The analyst's objectivity, however, is itself obtained by having another analyst subtract his or her subjectivity, in turn, from addressing that of the analyst-in-training; the analyst-in-training, to find objective subjectivity, awaits the training analyst's objective subjectivity; and so on. The moment of definitively interpreting the subjective objects in the history of the historian's intercourse with the other is, then, if not infinitely postponed, at least *laterally bound* in the deferred action of the historical emergence of psychoanalysis itself. It is referred to a place at the absolute horizon of historical interpretation, that is, to the "self-analysis" of Freud, in which the objective recognition of someone's subjective objects was supposedly secured *without* being addressed by another.[47] But this is a mythology of an objective subjectivity preceding intersubjectivity. Precisely because Freud's history of visualizing psychic history is replicated for him in the Wolf Man's drawing, to subtract these schemata would eliminate the basis on which the Wolf Man's drawing can be rendered intelligible to Freud in the first place: without the observer's subjective object in interpreting the other's representation, he would have not objectivity but illegibility. Despite the historian's cathexis to a horizon in which history was or becomes objective, there is no final subtraction or reservation of the subjective object—and this object is always mutually constructed.

This is not to say that the case history of the Wolf Man is based on *nothing but* the particular intersubjectivity of a psychoanalytic encounter an "authentic" psychoanalytic interpretation would seem to require. In the case history's conceptualization of homosexuality and masculinity, for example, Freud invoked concepts developed in earlier, "vulgar" interpretations—most notably his own reading of the memoirs of Judge Schreber, whom he never met, and his knowledge of patients analyzed by Alfred Adler, with whom he officially disagreed.[48] Indeed, a good case can be made that psychoanalytic "authenticity," whatever it might be, actually requires psychoanalytic vulgarity as well as unanalyzed subjective objects on the part of the supposedly analyzed or self-analyzed observer. But

47. The best detailed historical studies are Sulloway, *Freud, Biologist of the Mind,* and Anzieu, *Freud's Self-Analysis,* although they are quite different in their sources and conclusions; see also Alexander Grinstein, *Freud at the Crossroads* (New York, 1990). A suggestive contemporary interpretation is Mark Edmundson, *Towards Reading Freud: Self-Creation in Milton, Wordsworth, Emerson, and Sigmund Freud* (Princeton, 1990).

48. For the Schreber case, see *SE,* 12:1–84, and Zvi Lothane, "Schreber, Freud, Flechsig, and Weber Revisited: An Inquiry into Methods of Interpretation," *Psychoanalytic Review* 76 (1989), 203–61. Freud described his interest in Schreber's case to Jung as his "fighting off" Fliess (letter of 18 December 1910, *Freud/Jung Letters,* 380). In his interpretation of Schreber's psychosis, he explored the relation between homosexuality and paranoia; significantly, he had earlier described Fliess as developing a "paranoia" about Freud and psychoanalysis (letter of 17 February 1908, *Freud/Jung Letters,* 121). Throughout the Wolf Man case history, Freud is heavily but sometimes surreptitiously dependent on Adler's doctrine of the "masculine protest" (see Davis, *Drawing the Dream of the Wolves,* 219–20, 222–23).

the difference between this textual situation and psychoanalytical applications like "Leonardo" is that the vulgarity and subjectivity of "authentic" psychoanalytic interpretation exists in, and is motivated by, a real intersubjective exchange between observer and observed: and this is all the difference in the world.

I suggested earlier that the subjective object required to interpret the objective subject of sexuality is, itself, sexuality—more exactly, the interpreter's sexuality as it is brought to, evoked in, and reorganized by the intersubjective exchange in which a jointly, if differentially, meaningful history is being jointly, if differentially, constructed. In the very first session, the Wolf Man exclaimed his desire to "use [Freud] from behind and shit on his head." In developing his interpretation, Freud apparently carried this homosexual content forward into a theory of the "inherited" origin of the Wolf Man's homosexuality, a thesis derived in turn from Freud's schemata for the repression of bisexuality replicated in the Wolf Man's drawing. The conflicted, homosexualized origins of his own theory of repression itself were generally repressed by Freud—for instance in his explication of the Signorelli slip.

But in autumn 1910, six months after the case began, Freud told his friend Max Schur that he was "working through" his homosexual feelings toward Fliess,[49] although the two former friends had not spoken for eight years. He also told Ferenczi, to whom he had described the Wolf Man's first consultation a few months earlier, that "I feel myself to be a match for anything and approve of the overcoming of my homosexuality, with the result being greater independence"; in other words, he has overcome the dependent, paranoid desire for other men's desire for him.[50] Although the evidence is only circumstantial, we might say, then, that the Wolf Man's representations allowed the partial discharge of Freud's own sexuality to the extent that the case enabled him fully to appropriate Fliess's idea of inherited psychic bisexuality, combat his followers' doubts, and settle outstanding questions of originality and authority—that is, to "overcome the homosexuality" that the Wolf Man's first consultation elicited.

That the Wolf Man desires Freud is matched by the fact that Freud desires the Wolf Man. But over the course of their exchange, their two different homosexualities are intersubjectively reorganized for each subject as an overcoming of his homosexuality—mediated by the drawing that evokes those two pasts. Indeed, the drawing laterally binds or siphons off the subjective desire of each into the objective history of the other. For the Wolf Man, Freud's interpretation of his dream and drawing resituates his homosexuality, manifested in the real, "present-tense" intersubjective context of the first consultation, in an objective archaic past that once identified can be surmounted. And for Freud, the Wolf Man's dream and drawing allow *his* receptive, paranoid relation to the desires of other men, again evoked in the intersubjective context of the first consultation, to be resituated as an objective analysis of what other men really want. Freud's subjective object, the primal repression of bisexuality, is placed into the Wolf Man as the Wolf Man's objective history, now surmounted through therapy. And the Wolf Man's subjective object, a homo-

49. Max Schur, *Freud: Living and Dying* (New York, 1972), 256–57.

50. Freud to Ferenczi, 17 October 1910, *Correspondence of Sigmund Freud and Sandor Ferenczi,* 1:227. In his famous essay "Fetishism," of 1927 (*SE,* 21:146–58), Freud was later to interpret heterosexual male fetishism as an "overcoming," albeit "perverse," of the subject's primary homosexuality (see Chapter 12).

sexuality that threatens to gobble him up, is placed into Freud as Freud's objective history, now surmounted through theory—for he can now believe that the Wolf Man's desire for him wholly derives from the Wolf Man's history rather than from himself.

Thus a sexuality is constituted. Derived from originally separate histories, it is only realized mutually with another person who can represent and interpret it in the intersubjective exchange of subjective objects. No doubt it is a relation of misrepresentation and misinterpretation, of asymmetric (although not necessarily unequal) needs and powers. But there could never be a fully mutual absorption of subjective objects in the first place—a complete, objective recognition of the other as a subject. As I have stressed, intersubjectivity is not objectivity. The question, rather, is whether and how subjectivity can, or does, become intersubjective, and with what consequences for the balance of our lust, rage, guilt, and fear.

The lessons we could draw from the case might not be fully congenial to contemporary accounts of cultural objects. One lesson is compatible with a cliché of recent "cultural studies": broadly, a historian's "objective" analysis of another person's subjectivity is in part a subjective object of the historian's own making. But ironically, this lesson is *not* compatible with many supposed histories of others' subjectivity, for these do not display or establish any kind of intersubjective witness. Rather, histories of subjectivity often look "objectively" at what appears to be transpiring in another person: they take the other's subjectivity as a pure object. As the case history of the Wolf Man shows, the history of another's subjectivity is, in part, the history of the observer's own subjective object. And without a history of this latter object, a history of the other's subjectivity as an object is merely a fantasy of psychoanalytic interpretation.

It is sometimes assumed that we can surmount this problem merely by representing our own subjectivity, as interpreters, in our representation of another's history. But this supposed "positioning" is really no more than posturing. To represent one's own subjectivity is precisely to take it as an object. Whether we are claiming to add it to or subtract it from our objective interpretation of another, the subjective determination of that very representation remains unrecognized or uninterpreted as such.

Indeed, the lesson of the Wolf Man case must be that the historian writing the history of another person's subjectivity is not in a position to write the history of the subjective objects through which that history of the other is produced. The historian is not in the position to write the history of his or her own subjectivity as an object. This history could only be the work of another historian for whom the historian writing the history of an other is, in turn, an other—Whitney Davis writing the history of Freud writing the history of the Wolf Man; and so on, indefinitely. Thus I conclude that histories of the subjectivities of others, whatever they might be, remain only as a distant promise of an intersubjective practice of historians writing one another's histories. This practice would be one of great aesthetic, critical, and political interest, but it has yet to be realized.

Chapter 12

HomoVision: A Reading of Freud's "Fetishism"

The object is sought in its function as a signifier of transformation.

—Christopher Bollas, *The Shadow of the Object*

As with voyeurism and homosexuality, in his metapsychological writings Freud conceived fetishism as an instance of the vicissitudes of what he called psychic "interest," that is, of the directedness of the mind toward its objects of perception and reference in the world.[1] In this chapter, I explore Freud's two principal treatments of fetishism, a short section prepared for the third edition of *Three Essays on the Theory of Sexuality* and his well-known later essay "Fetishism," published in 1927.[2] Freud did explore the topic of fetishism in other places. In 1907, for example, he considered the "fetishistic" elements in the life story of the central character in Wilhelm Jensen's novel *Gradiva*, the fictional archaeologist Norbert

1. For psychic *Interesse* and the related problem of "attention," see Freud's "Project for a Scientific Psychology" [1895], in *The Standard Edition of the Complete Psychological Works of Sigmund Freud*, 24 vols., ed. and trans. James Strachey et al. (London, 1953–74) (hereafter *SE*, followed by volume number and page), 1:295–387, esp. pt. 1, sects. 1–18. In the simplest terms, we could say that "interest" is the subject's *attitude toward* an object of perception and reference in the world (as it is presented to the sensorium)—wanting it, hating it, fearing it, and so forth.

2. *Three Essays on the Theory of Sexuality* [1905], in *SE*, 7:125–248; "Fetishism" [1927], in *SE*, 21:146–58 (in German, "Fetischismus," in *Gesammelte Werke*, 18 vols. [Frankfurt am Main, 1940–68], 14:311–17). I usually quote the *Standard Edition*'s translation but sometimes provide my own rendering.

Hannold (modeled, to some extent, on the character of Winckelmann [see Chapter 9]).[3] More important, after publishing the first (1905) edition of the *Three Essays* he twice attempted, in oral communications, to conceptualize fetishism at a more general level.[4] These efforts lay behind his revisions to the third (1915) edition of the *Three Essays*, also partly beholden to the ongoing work of students.[5]

Unlike the classical sexologists' view of fetishism as a chance association of unrelated visual impressions, by 1909 Freud evidently conceived fetishism as a "question of the drive to look" and of its splitting into repressed and idealized components.[6] But it remained for the major essay of 1927 to coordinate Freud's specific theory of fetishism, and despite their historical interest, I shall not explore his earlier presentations here. Instead, my reading has been undertaken in the light of two essential later contributions built on Freud's major essay, Jacques Lacan and Wladimir Granoff's pithy discussion of the "symbolic," "imaginary," and "real" dimensions of fetishism[7] and Masud Khan's lengthy case study of the foreskin fetishism of a male homosexual patient.[8]

Through a close interpretive reading of Freud's text, I hope to draw out the structure and complexities of Freud's reasoning and language. Occasionally I attempt to extend or rewrite Freud's terms in order to suggest the continuing interest of Freud's thought and or to highlight its peculiarities.

Needless to say, the notion of a fetish or of a fetishist (a maker of fetishes or a user and viewer of them) has a central place in our thinking about images and objects not only in the psychoanalytic sense but also in many other senses. In this chapter, however, I do not consider "fetishism" as conceived within ethnology, economics, and anthropology or the "fetishisms" imagined by late-nineteenth-century psychiatry and sexology.[9] I do not pretend to offer a cultural history of modern discourses about fetishes and fetishism—a constellation of many overlapping representations. Instead, I focus on one particular, rather late, and quite individual contribution to this tradition, without attempting to

3. See "Delusions and Dreams in Jensen's 'Gradiva,'" in *SE*, 9:47, 50–51, and elsewhere.

4. See Louis Rose, "Freud and Fetishism: Previously Unpublished Minutes of the Vienna Psychoanalytic Society," *Psychoanalytic Quarterly* 57 (1988), 147–66, for Freud's views in February 1909; see Herman Nunberg and Ernst Federn, eds., *Minutes of the Vienna Psychoanalytic Society*, 4 vols. (New York, 1962–75), 4:243–46, for his views in March 1914. Elsewhere, Freud's remarks essentially repeat what he had written in 1905 (e.g., "Leonardo and a Memory of His Childhood," in *SE*, 11:96).

5. See esp. Karl Abraham, "Remarks on the Psycho-Analysis of a Case of Foot and Corset Fetishism" [1910], *Selected Papers of Karl Abraham*, trans. D. Bryan and A. Strachey (New York, 1989).

6. Rose, "Freud and Fetishism," 155.

7. Jacques Lacan and Wladimir Granoff, "Fetishism: The Symbolic, the Imaginary, and the Real," in *Perversions*, ed. Sandor Lorand (New York, 1956), 265–76.

8. M. Masud R. Khan, "Fetishism as Negation of the Self: Clinical Notes on Foreskin Fetishism in a Male Homosexual," in *Alienation in Perversions* (New York, 1963), 139–76. See also Octave Mannoni, "Je sais bien, mais quand même," in *Clefs pour l'imaginaire, où l'autre scène* (Paris, 1969), and Guy Rosolato, "Le fétichisme dont se dérobe l'objet," *Nouvelle Revue de Psychanalyse* 2 (1970), 31–39 (see also idem, "Etude des perversions sexuelles à partir du fétichisme," in *Le désir et la perversion* [Paris, 1967], 9–40). After this chapter had been written, a helpful, well-informed review came to my attention: see Marcia Ian, *Remembering the Phallic Mother: Psychoanalysis, Modernism, and the Fetish* (Ithaca, N.Y., 1993); Ian considers Binet's associationist analysis and Krafft-Ebing's medical analysis of fetishism (see note 33 below); the contributions of Freud, Melanie Klein, Jacques Lacan, and Julia Kristeva (see note 36 below); Marx's concept of "commodity fetishism"; and recent gender and critical theory.

9. The essential starting point is William Pietz, "The Problem of the Fetish," *Res* 9 (1985), 5–17; 13 (1987), 23–45; and 16 (1988), 105–23.

determine whether it should be regarded as a symptomatic expression of the tradition as a whole.

Any writing about gender and sexuality today finds itself in an ambiguous relationship with Freud's writing, for Freud seems simultaneously indispensable and inimical to many of our concerns. Although I take definite positions on particular issues and do not shrink from interpretation, my general approach is conservative in the strict sense. I try to secure an adequate reading of Freud's contribution as the sine qua non for further developments—theoretical, historical, and critical. What is adequate in this sense, then, is not what is true to Freud's text. Rather, it is what one post-Freudian reader—namely, *this* reader, with his own experiences and interests—takes to be worth saying about Freud's text today.

I do hope to provide a reading of Freud accurate enough to recall the subtlety of Freud's thought on fetishism. (Subtlety, of course, is not the same thing as truth, necessity, or relevance.) Thus I try to reconstruct the internal coherence of Freud's reasoning. The result, I think, speaks for itself. Freud's concept of fetishism is far more complex, and much richer, than it is usually represented to be. Although it must get low marks for its gender blindness and limited recognition of the social circuitry through which individual desire must circulate, it deserves high marks both for its depth—it offers a species of historical explanation—and for its specificity as a description of actual erotic practices not to be casually conflated with others. Post-Freudian revisionist concepts of fetishism tend to be just the opposite. Providing a more general analysis of fetishisms in gender and culture, they often lose sight of psychological process and differentiation as such.

A reading of "Fetishism" cannot ignore Freud's leaps of logic or rhetorical ruses. Freud was not able, for example, fully to integrate his claims about homosexuality into his account of fetishism, despite dealing with the matter at some length. But the relation between fetishism and homosexuality is also at the heart of Freud's analysis. Derivative or revisionist accounts of fetishism that ignore it overlook one of the essential meanings of fetishism. Here we have a good example of the ambiguous relationship between cultural criticism and psychoanalysis. Although the misogyny both exemplified and conceptualized in Freud's "Fetishism" is objectionable, Freud's recognition of the several roles of homosexual desire and homophobic flight in the constitution of normative male heterosexualities has relevance today: a certain kind of feminist and a certain kind of gay critic may find Freud's "Fetishism" salient in differing and not wholly compatible ways. I will be satisfied if this chapter suggests how Freud's text sustains—if it does not deliberately encourage—several complex possibilities of response.

The Difficulty of Identifying Fetishism

Contemporary psychology has long since assimilated and often rejected Freudian ideas. Recent cultural histories of sexuality—some of them investigating the social and cultural roots of psychoanalysis (see Chapter 11)—have been skeptical of Freudianism, seeing it as much the symptom as the explanation of modern sexual ideologies. But the fact remains that fetishism still tends to be characterized by many writers—from psychiatrists to cultural critics—in overly simple terms. Despite everything, Freud's writings provide a corrective to these crude, misleading, or damaging views.

For example, the 1987 edition of the *Diagnostic and Statistical Manual of Mental Disorders* of the American Psychiatric Association *(DSM-III-R)* defined the "essential feature" of fetishism as "recurrent, intense, sexual urges and sexually arousing fantasies, of at least six months' duration, involving the use of nonliving objects (fetishes)," usually "by themselves."[10] This characterization, reflecting the classical concept of fetishism developed by late-nineteenth-century sexologists, is clearly unsatisfying. What does *DSM-III-R* mean by the "fetishes" that must obviously define fetishism? Or, more exactly, how does it happen that certain "nonliving objects," the "fetishes," become the focus of sexual urges and fantasies, considering that other kinds of objects—such as the "transitional objects" of children, the mourning or "linking" objects of adults, and the like—do not qualify as fetishes although they can be understood to have sexual dimensions?[11]

Even confining ourselves to the descriptive, rather than the explanatory, level, as *DSM-III-R* itself does, there are certainly some oddities in the standard manual's treatment of the topic. For example, although "articles of female clothing used in cross-dressing" are designated as "fetishes" in the entry on fetishism, a diagnosis of "fetishism" is supposedly not to be made in the cross-dresser's case, because in "transvestic fetishism" the "recurrent, intense sexual urges and sexually arousing fantasies" involve the "cross-dressing" as such and not the "use of nonliving objects" as such. But it is not obvious how to distinguish the dressing, in which the dresser takes pleasure, from the dress articles providing such pleasure. And at any rate, it should be possible for an individual cross-dresser also to be a fetishist. Similarly, if a nonliving object is "genitally stimulating because it has been designed for that purpose," for *DSM-III-R* it cannot be a fetish. But again, there is no logical reason why for some people such a sex tool, irrespective of its design or intended function, could not be constituted as a fetish as well.[12]

Furthermore, *DSM-III-R*'s definition, if accepted, would eliminate the common practice of describing some men's or women's interests in one another's bodies as "fetishistic" interests—for they are, of course, directed at living things. Many statements about someone's supposed "fetishization" of "the female (or male) body," or parts of it, may not be informative, because the supposed "fetishization" has not really been distinguished from obsession, phobia, voyeurism, mourning, memorializing, and several other quite different mental

10. *Diagnostic and Statistical Manual of Mental Disorders*, 3d ed., rev. (Washington, D.C., 1987), 282–83 (sect. 302.81).

11. See esp. Vamik D. Volkan, *Linking Objects and Linking Phenomena* (New York, 1981), and Christopher Bollas, *The Shadow of the Object: Psychoanalysis of the Unthought Known* (New York, 1987); cf. Phyllis Greenacre, "The Transitional Object and the Fetish," *International Journal of Psycho-Analysis* 51 (1970), 447–56, and Robert Bak, "Distortions of the Concept of Fetishism," *Psychoanalytic Study of the Child* 29 (1974), 195–201.

12. E.g., see François Sirois, "Fétiche de femme," *Revue Français de Psychanalyse* 47 (1983), 409–11. In general, actual erotic practices outrun the clinicians' attempts to classify them.

interests. Nevertheless, on the face of it *DSM-III-R* does ignore hair, hand, or foot fetishisms—unless these parts of the human body are regarded as "nonliving" (presumably because they are "separated" from the whole body in the fetishist's psychic image of them as well as singled out in his or her erotic practice). To remedy this defect, more extended definitions of fetishism include fetishisms of "a body part of the [human] object not directly connected with the sexual act" and "ritualistic procedure[s] introducing or completing sexual intercourse."[13] Even here, however, not all erotic attentions to particular "body parts" or ritualized modes of intercourse are fetishistic.

As these attempts at definition suggest, we must look at the specific intrapsychic history, meaning, and use of the cross-dressing, sex tool, nonliving object, body part, or erotic act to determine whether it involves a fetishism. Unfortunately, this lesson often seems to be forgotten. All too frequently sociologists, historians, or cultural critics look at a person's activities, at a conventional representation, or at a cultural practice from the outside, pronouncing that it is "fetishistic" on the basis of its visual, semiotic, or other form and apparent content alone. "If it looks fetishistic," these accounts imply, "then it is"—a misleading elision of a colloquial concept of fetishism, an essentially formal description of ways in which people look at and refer to one another, and Freud's well-defined, limited concept of fetishism, an identification of the intrapsychic history and meaning of some such psychic "interests." On the one hand, practices that are clearly not fetishistic—for example, in painting, film, or daily life—have been labeled as such, leading to the introduction of vulgar psychoanalysis where none is warranted and to mistaken invocations of psychoanalytic theories and countertheories. And on the other hand, practices that are fetishistic or properly to be related to fetishism have gone unrecognized as such.

Needless to say, it is not enough merely to adopt a depth-psychological perspective. It is well known that for Freud fetishism is an intrapsychic phenomenon that "resumes within itself the structure of disavowal and multiple belief," as Christian Metz has put it in one formula.[14] But unfortunately "disavowal" seems to have been understood as the principal or even the sole mechanism of fetishism, whereas fetishism actually *avows* several beliefs by disavowing others. Even here, we need to say exactly how it does so—for there are many ways both of avowing and disavowing beliefs. Fetishism cannot just be "disavowal," at the same time as many disavowals are not fetishistic.

Because the multiple beliefs involved in a fetishism must vary among individuals, no fetishism or fetishist can be exactly like any other. We cannot generalize about what the specific *content* of a fetishist's practice must be: there are no specific limits on what fetishistic eroticism might be like. Putting the point the other way around, there are no particular practices that definitively identify a fetishist. Thus Freud offers a metapsychological analysis of the overall mental *structures and processes* of fetishisms. His framework leaves openings for an individual's particular beliefs, desires, and practices, to be filled in on the basis of detailed, nuanced clinical or historical study.

13. Henry E. Adams and Patricia B. Sutker, eds., *Comprehensive Handbook of Psychopathology* (New York, 1984), 785–86.

14. Christian Metz, *The Imaginary Signifier: Psychoanalysis and the Cinema*, trans. Celia Britton et al. (Bloomington, Ind., 1982), 71.

Diagnoses of Fetishism in Historical and Cultural Criticism

Unfortunately, commentators who label a person, a conventional representation, or a cultural practice as "fetishistic" often do not cite anything from life-historical evidence justifying the label of "fetishism" they have applied. (Calling something "fetishistic," then, may serve a function in repressive sexual ideology, whatever its ostensible moral vision or politics, that stereotypes the erotic practices of others without acknowledging their subjective realities.) Here again, fetishism can become confused with nonfetishistic obsessions (for example, interest in looking at certain things), phobias (for example, being afraid of certain things seen), longing (for example, hoping to see certain things never seen), mourning (for example, recalling certain important things that have been lost), and other entirely different psychological and cultural formations.[15]

The lack of specific historical evidence probably does not trouble writers who use the colloquial concept of fetishism. As a convenient description of ways in which people regard and refer to one another, the colloquial concept carries little explanatory weight. But when they diagnose "fetishism" in a person, representation, or practice, many cultural historians and critics obviously mean to invoke its psychoanalytic context—the scenarios of "castration" or "separation" anxiety, of Oedipal or pre-Oedipal struggle, of paternal rule or maternal fusion, of sexual hostility or dehumanization—in order to read from the apparent form and content of a person's actions, representations, or practices to psychological history and meaning. Once invoked, a psychoanalytic perspective imposes certain limits on a diagnosis of fetishism. Precise evidence is required to identify fetishism in an actual case and to distinguish it from (for instance) obsession, voyeurism, homosexual longing, mourning, or sadism.

15. On this point I wish to distinguish my account from those by other revisionist readers of Freud, such as Naomi Schor, "Female Fetishism: The Case of George Sand," *Poetics Today* 6 (1985), 301–10; idem, "Salammbô Bound," in *Breaking the Chain: Women, Theory, and French Realist Fiction* (New York, 1985), 111–16; and Emily Apter, *Feminizing the Fetish: Psychoanalysis and Narrative Obsession in Turn-of-the-Century France* (Ithaca, N.Y., 1991). At one level, Apter's book, for instance, is a rich cultural history of a late-nineteenth-century, largely French discourse on fetishism and a study of the "fetishisms" in nineteenth-century discourse more widely conceived. She considers fetishism "in its broadest applications" (43). However, in these studies' specific applications of psychoanalytic theory—they use it both to interpret and to criticize the systems of representation they consider—they do not fully succeed in distinguishing fetishism from other object relations or a subject's general, diffused interest in sexual difference and its supposed undecidability. Apter, for instance, wants to "associate fetishism with a blocking and fixating function *synonymous* with the repression of the scopic drive" (xiii, emphasis added)—despite the fact that Freud's "Fetishism" would recognize many unconscious vicissitudes of scopophilia that are not fetishistic or fetishism as such. Although Apter's ambition to "emphasize a broader, less gender-restricted conception of partial object substitutionisms in sexuality" (x; see 113–23) is understandable, it tends to assimilate fetishism to other psychic functions built on simultaneous recognition and denial, seeing and not-seeing, loss and remembrance, or eroticism and dread—some of them less commonly acknowledged than fetishism, no doubt, but often unrelated to fetishism's most essential meanings (such as its connection with homosexuality) and deserving separate conceptualization. What is needed in the study of sexuality is more differentiation, not less. In this chapter, I have, then, gone in the opposite direction. Rather than bring a host of psychic, erotic, and cultural phenomena under the umbrella of "fetishism," I have

As a typical example, Linda Williams has asserted, in her fascinating discussion of the "prehistory" of hard-core film pornography, that in Eadweard Muybridge's early photographic experiments "women's bodies are quite simply fetishized."[16] Between Freud's hypothetical scenario for the psychogenesis of fetishism and Muybridge's technical and aesthetic interests, Williams does recognize "enormous differences,"[17] not the least of which is the total absence of evidence that Muybridge and his viewers possessed the intrapsychic histories or the object relations of fetishists. Nonetheless, she goes on to invoke (if only in part to criticize) Freud's psychoanalytic concept and its metapsychological context, with its account of the female phallus, "castration anxiety," and the like. Now, it might well be true that "the obsessive gaze of Muybridge's [camera] apparatus on the naked female form attempts to reassure itself in the very sight of this [phallic] 'lack' by the fetish-substitutes that endow the woman with a surplus of erotic meaning."[18] Or it might be true that "the ejaculating penis of the money shot [in hard-core porn] could, in this [psychoanalytic] sense, be said to disavow castration by avoiding visual association with the women's genitalia."[19] Detailed textual or historical study might somehow manage to establish the point. But Williams's own examples do not inspire confidence in the possibility. Both the "obsession" with and the "avoidance" of the female body or genitals, which Williams sees in Muybridge's or the pornographers' images, must be distinguished from fetishism. They are non- or prefetishistic formations; with many other outlets in people's activities, in representation, or in cultural practice, they do not necessarily become a fetishism as such.

To take another example, Charles Bernheimer has argued that "in the male imaginary [of late-nineteenth-century aesthetic practice], the courtesan [depicted in nineteenth-century French painting] could be fantasized both voyeuristically, as the sexually desiring woman whose powerful independence provoked stimulating castration fears, and fetishistically, as an antidote to those fears embodying a modern aesthetic of artifice, illusion, duplicity."[20] Bernheimer regards "fetishism" as a general propensity of "the culture of late capitalism" as much as the "peculiar province" of fetishists as such.[21] If a "fetishistic" representation might not be Freudian fetishism as such, he can move in and out of psychoanalytic, anthropological, and other terminologies. But, like Williams, Bernheimer ultimately does rely upon the psychoanalytic concept of fetishism in using the colloquial term—for example, when he invokes men's "castration fears" to explain their "voyeuristic" fantasy of women.

focused on its specificity, at least in Freud's account of it. None of this detracts from the importance of Schor's and Apter's studies of cultural discourses on or about fetishism; it is only to interrogate the concepts of fetishism they use as instruments of cultural-historical interpretation.

16. Linda Williams, *Hard Core: Power, Pleasure, and the "Frenzy of the Visible"* (Berkeley and Los Angeles, 1989), 40.

17. Williams, *Hard Core,* 42.

18. Williams, *Hard Core,* 42.

19. Williams, *Hard Core,* 116.

20. Charles Bernheimer, "Degas' Brothels: Voyeurism and Ideology," *Representations* 20 (1987), 170. A more nuanced version of this article, modulating some of its claims, appears as chap. 6 of Bernheimer's *Figures of Ill Repute: Representing Prostitution in Nineteenth-Century France* (Cambridge, 1989).

21. Bernheimer, "Degas' Brothels," 171.

Some historians and critics who hope to apply psychoanalytic metapsychology to the interpretation of other subjects' representations have disavowed any interest in diagnosing the actual psychological states of the authors or artists in question. Supposedly the issue is not whether Muybridge was "really" a fetishist or Degas "really" the victim of separation or castration anxiety and masculine protest against it. The knowledge required to make such determinations is admittedly not available. Instead, following Lacanian directives, representation itself supposedly possesses the structure—the internal complexity, rhythm, and conflict—interpreted by metapsychological concepts like "fetishism" or "masochism" as organizations of the temporality and legibility of a language (see further Chapter 10). In addition, "fetishistic" or "masochistic" representations seem to solicit, or even to require, reading or viewing subjects of like constitution—if only in the act of reading or viewing itself, independent of their "real" subjective constitution as masochists or fetishists. In relation to certain representations, a reader or viewer is supposedly constructed or positioned as a masochist or fetishist. Because textual organizations can be fully conventional or stylized within a culture, they are not indices, in themselves, of any particular, individual subjectivity (see Chapter 6). Instead they exemplify social scripts for possible subjective positions with which individual real subjects might (or must) identify. Thus, to locate the masochistic or fetishistic structure of the textual organization is to discover the possibility of reading or viewing subjects socially constructed or positioned as masochists or fetishists.

This approach is preferable to the simpler form of authorial psychopathology. It does not, however, satisfy my objection. Some real process of "identification" in reading or viewing must be diagnosed—for it is supposedly what constructs or positions a reader or viewer "as" a masochist or fetishist in the reading or viewing of a particular representation. But evidence for the existence of the subject's requisite "identification" is as hard to obtain, and would need to be as differentiated and nuanced, as the evidence for the existence of masochism or fetishism as such. Whether metapsychological diagnosis is directed at actual historical persons or at the discursive organization and the possible identificatory positions it engenders, the historical and hermeneutic problem remains the same.

The Problem of Female and Homosexual Fetishisms

The description of particular fetishists or fetishisms, then, must be undertaken with an eye toward metapsychological precision and informed by actual evidence about subjective realities and identifications. But this stricture immediately raises a major problem for Freud's own, supposedly exemplary account. On the face of it, Freud's essay of 1927 sticks entirely to the cases of "heterosexual" male fetishists whose personal histories he had investigated psychoanalytically. (My exegesis, of course, necessarily mirrors this limitation, but I consider how it might be overcome.) And thus it would seem that the empirical and analytic precision of Freud's account ignores the fetishistic realities and identifications of anyone who is not a heterosexual male. Such people will not find that "Fetishism" acknowledges their histories.

It has often been said that psychoanalysis is unable to acknowledge female fetishism. In turn, this supposed blind spot is sometimes taken to be a fatal flaw in Freudian sexological metapsychology. Both textual and historical evidence, however, tells against this view. (As *DSM-III-R*'s definition shows, contemporary psychiatry does not make a gender distinction; the matter is mostly of doctrinal interest within orthodox psychoanalysis.) For one thing, the "fetishists" mentioned in the essay of 1927 indirectly refer to the people Freud had already discussed in an earlier paper, "A Child Is Being Beaten," of 1919 (see further Chapter 10).[22] The principal case in that paper was a woman reporting sexualized memories and neurotic fantasies of her childhood. Her adult erotic life apparently extended into a fetishism. Freud certainly knew other examples of female fetishisms or closely related practices and assumed the theoretical possibility of female fetishism in discussions with his followers. In his oral remarks of 1909, for example, he considered what he called a "passive" form of fetishism among women—namely, women desiring to be seen by men, "which is [in turn] repressed by clothes, and on account of which, clothes are raised to a fetish [for them]."[23] Although he draws the absurd (perhaps tongue-in-cheek) conclusion that such fetishists compose "half of humanity," because all women display clothes fetishism, there is no theoretical reason why certain clothes, for some women as for some men, could not be fetishes. There is plenty of room within psychoanalysis for an account of female (and male) sexuality and eroticism in which clothing and dressing manifest unconscious conflicts and defenses, including (but not, of course, limited to) fetishism.

Whatever Freud's own opinions, psychoanalysts in his circle wrote on the topic of female fetishism. As early as 1915, an example of female boot fetishism was published by one of the first female analysts, Hermine Hug-Hellmuth, in Freud's journal.[24] In fact, post-Freudian psychoanalytic literature does not lack considerations of female fetishists, although conservative Freudians have disputed them.[25] Homosexual male fetishists, likewise not directly represented in Freud's examples in the essay of 1927, have also been identified by later analysts and their histories recorded.[26]

Why Freud did not directly address female or homosexual male fetishisms in his major essay of 1927 is unclear. We could take his own usual explanation at face value: he had not himself personally psychoanalyzed such cases. More likely, he was aware that he would have to greatly elaborate his relatively brief essay in order to accommodate differences in the gender of subject and object between fetishists. Since he regarded masculinity and femininity (and heterosexuality and homosexuality) as continuous, it is also likely that he expected such accommodation could be made—even though his own strong bias inclined

22. *SE*, 17:175–204.

23. Rose, "Freud and Fetishism," 155–56.

24. See Arlene Kramer Richards, "Female Fetishes and Female Perversions: Hermine Hug-Hellmuth's 'A Case of Female Foot or More Properly Boot Fetishism' Reconsidered," *Psychoanalytic Review* 77 (1990), 11–23.

25. Both Bak, "Distortions of the Concept of Fetishism," and Georges Zavitzianos, "The Perversion of Fetishism in Women," *Psychoanalytic Quarterly* 51 (1982), 405–25, review earlier psychoanalytic literature on female fetishism, although they tend to reject the proposed examples. A search of psychological and medical databases turns up many more recent publications, stimulated, perhaps, by feminist criticisms of psychoanalysis.

26. See esp. Khan, "Fetishism as Negation of the Self."

him to adopt one supposedly normative position as the touchstone. Whatever we conclude, his reasoning about fetishism can be broadened to include women and homosexual men, whether or not Freud himself would have done so. As Emily Apter has put it, in Freudian theory "forms of female fetishisms unrecognized as such by psychoanalysis intersected with male fetishizations of femininity";[27] but there is no general reason for denying, as Naomi Schor has observed, that "the little girl's ego can be split along the very same fault lines as the little boy's."[28]

The Plot of "Fetishism"

To unravel the psychoanalytic concept of fetishism and read Freud's essay with anything like precision, we should distinguish between the *intrapsychic history* of a fetishism—what I call "prefetishism" followed by "fetishistic looking" leading finally to the "fetish-image"—and the *object relations* of a fetishism, what I call the fetishist's relation to the "fetish-effigy," as it is attached or belongs to the "fetishized object," in a "fetishistic practice." Figure 12.1 summarizes these distinctions using the terms of Freud's essay. A reading should also respect the two minimal criteria for any psychoanalytic account of human subjectivity—namely, that the vicissitudes of the drives (or egoistic, sexual, and aggressive desire) are organized, first, in repression and, second, in *Nachträglichkeit* (or "delayed activation") (for the former, see Chapter 10, and for the latter, Chapter 11). I observe these criteria in suggesting that (according to the logic of Freud's account) a fetishistic subjectivity is constituted in a doubled and reversed *Nachträglichkeit* of memory images as the embodiedness of vision itself.

The Grounds of Fetishism: Multiple Beliefs and Desires

In "Fetishism," Freud begins with a little boy endowed with at least one belief, namely, that his mother has a penis (Belief 1). For the purposes of an account of fetishism as such, his belief is taken for granted, an analytic primitive. But several well-known questions arise about its origin and status.

For one thing, we might ask: Why does the little boy believe his mother has a penis? Because he believes everyone has a penis. And why does he believe everyone has a penis? Because he believes everyone is just like him. One element in the bedrock of psychoanalytic metapsychology is always the claim that a very young child does not initially distinguish between itself, and its own properties, and the world and its properties. It is

27. Apter, *Feminizing the Fetish,* 244.

28. Schor, "Female Fetishism," 306, although see note 34 below.

Table 1. The Constitution of Fetishism According to Freud's "Fetishism" (1927)

1. Denegation (denial + repression, *Verleugnung* and *Verdrängung*	Prefetishism, phobic	Intrapsychic history
2. Compromise (*Kompromiss*) = *aversion* (*Entfremdung*)		
3. Reinforcement (*Steigerung*) (first *Nachtrag*)		
4. Denegation (denial + repression)	Fetishistic looking, obsessive	
5. Compromise = shock (*Schreck*) = *two incompatible propositions + double attitude*		
6. Reinforcement (second *Nachtrag*) = *monument* (*Denkmal*) = fetish image (*substitute, Ersatz*)	Classical fetishism, fixated	
7. Fetish-effigy (*Zeichen*) + fetishized object	Fetishistic practice	Object relations

Fig. 12.1. The constitution of fetishism according to Freud's "Fetishism" (1927).

upon this base, one says, that the subject/object relations of adulthood are gradually constructed. These two beliefs, at lesser and greater degrees of generality, form the background beliefs for the little boy's foreground belief that his mother has a penis.

Because of the twofold undergirding of the little boy's foreground belief, he might encounter two kinds of disturbance of this belief—depending on how the two background beliefs are challenged. First, he can discover that not everyone is just like him. For example, his father's penis is much larger, possesses hair, and is very differently shaped and colored than his own. Second, he can discover that not everyone has any kind of penis. For example, his mother does not have a penis.

For another thing, we can ask: Does the little boy believe his belief that his mother has a penis? Freud is not altogether clear on the point. Certainly the boy explores his parents' bodies—and those of siblings, friends, or other people—in order to investigate his belief. Although it is not logically entailed by the boy's belief as such, Freud endows the little boy with at least one desire along with his foreground belief—namely, in exploring his world he desires to confirm his belief, desires that his belief be true (Desire 1). But why does he desire to confirm his belief? Because he desires to confirm the background beliefs that undergird it. But why does he desire to confirm these beliefs? Because he desires to confirm all his beliefs. The other element in the bedrock of psychoanalytic metapsychology is its assumption that a very young child desires consistency and stability in the world and its properties. These two desires, at lesser and greater degrees of generality, are the background desires for the little boy's foreground desire to confirm his belief that his mother has a penis.

The little boy's foreground desire might encounter two kinds of disturbance—depending on how his two background desires are challenged. First, he can discover that his desire to confirm his initial belief cannot be sustained, for he may come to believe that not everyone has a penis just like his. Thus he may desire *not* to confirm his new belief in order to confirm his initial foreground belief (Belief 1)—because he desires to confirm the two background beliefs that undergird it. But second, he could desire to confirm his new belief that not everyone has a penis just like his: it is compatible with his most general background desire to confirm all his beliefs to admit as many of his (competing) beliefs with the most minimal cost to the whole set. Which price will he pay—the cost of maintaining the initial beliefs or the cost of admitting the new, incompatible beliefs? Are they equivalent costs, with desire thus evenly divided? In what way will beliefs and desires that initially imply one another become detached? It would be wrong to suppose that the little boy merely has to jettison, or "disavow," one set of beliefs and desires and replace them with another set. The initial set of beliefs and desires already contains multiple possibilities for partial discharge.

The Prefetishistic Elaborations: Denial, Repression, Compromise, Aversion

Looking up, down, or over his mother's body—or, like "Little Harry," crawling all over her[29]—the little boy's vision (we cannot assume a look) takes in a series of impressions: her hat, shoes, or gloves; face, eyes, and nose; hair; hands and feet; clothing and jewelry. In this setting, although not in every instance of it, the little boy's desire to confirm his initial foreground belief—his mother has a penis just like his—is activated precisely because he is already accumulating evidence against it. His mother is different from him, in size, in dress, or in odor. He is learning that she does not perfectly fulfill his needs, making an appearance at every demand, but can also be frustrating. Thus the little boy's vision—activated by belief and desire—gradually does become an "interest" *(Interesse)*, a look. And his interest is to look further up, or down, or around for his mother's penis. In Freud's considered phrase in the *Three Essays*, he is "peering up" at her *(aufgucken)*. Ultimately he makes the "unwished-for perception" *(unerwunschten Wahrnehmung)*—whether all at once or by collating many shadowy suggestions—that she does not have a penis just like his. Despite his desire to believe his belief, if the evidence of his eyes is any guide, then he must now believe that his mother does not have a penis (schematically, –Belief 1).

It is commonly asserted that fetishism is the "disavowal," or, more accurately, the "denegation" of this *new* belief (that is, –Belief 1): fetishism is supposedly the negation of the little boy's negated initial belief (schematically, –[–Belief 1]). However complete and convincing the evidence of his own eyes, the little boy can't believe that his mother does

29. Sandor Lorand, "Fetishism in Statu Nascendi," *International Journal of Psycho-Analysis* 11 (1930), 419–27.

not have a penis. As Freud puts it, the very "idea," the new perception, is "denied." In denial *(Verleugnung)* the little boy's initial foreground belief (Belief 1) is maintained, or restored, in the rejection of its negation (–Belief 1). It almost seems as if the "unwished-for perception" has fallen upon a blind spot in the retina and is thereby "scotomized": it occurs but does not register. Although built on a looking, it is a vision that does not result in a seeing. And indeed this denial is the first formation in the intrapsychic constitution of a fetishism (Fig. 12.1). Nonetheless, it is entirely prefetishistic.

The denegation of the "unwished-for perception," Freud takes care to indicate, is accompanied by emotional and intellectual disturbance. An unpleasant feeling, or "affect," has been introduced into the existing structure of the little boy's beliefs and desires. Like all unpleasant thoughts, then, it must be "repressed." (Repression *[Verdrängung]* is defined as the delay of the discharge of affect.) Therefore, although the "idea" formed as a result of the "unwished-for perception" can simply be ejected from thought, the psychic turbulence of having had this "idea" in the first place will linger on. For this reason the little boy is changed through having formed an idea, even though he later "denies" it. In the very moment of not believing his own eyes, the little boy must violate his background desire to confirm his beliefs—including, of course, any belief that his eyes do not deceive him. Simply put, it takes sustained effort for him not to believe his own eyes. Thus the prefetishist establishes a second formation in the forward temporality of his "interest" (Fig. 12.1), namely, what Freud aptly designates a "compromise" *(Kompromiss)*: the little boy maintains his initial belief (Belief 1) by denying its negative (–[–Belief 1]) and also represses the unpleasant sensation of having had to deny anything whatsoever (schematically, –[–Desire 1]).

What is the "quality" of the prefetishist's belief and desire, of his psychological "interest," after making his compromise?[30] Clearly the compromise must be a very rickety structure. In his ongoing interests, whatever they happen to be, the little boy would prefer not to have to tamper with an achieved compromise by ever having to deny the denial (schematically, –[–(–Belief 1)])—for example, by somehow confirming the evidence of the "unwished-for perception" and thereby discovering that he can't believe he can't believe his own eyes, negating his denegation.

Moving beyond the "compromise," then, in the forward temporality of his interest the prefetishist *loses interest* in the matter altogether. More exactly, the growing boy develops an interest in not being interested in female genitals (or anything else tending to confirm the initial "unwished-for perception"). Consistent with his most general background desire he now desires to confirm the "compromise" between his initial belief and the new,

30. For the "quality" of psychic "quantity," see *SE*, 1:295–307, pt. 1. The most perspicuous treatment of this most essential concept of Freudian thought is still Frank Sulloway, *Freud, Biologist of the Mind* (New York, 1979), 112–31; see also Jean Laplanche, *Life and Death in Psychoanalysis*, trans. J. Mehlman (Baltimore, 1975), chap. 1. Whereas quantity moves in a purely forward direction with a purely forward temporality, quality judges and distributes incoming quantities on the basis of established (repressed or even inherited) dispositions; as both backward- and forward-looking, it exemplifies *Nachträglichkeit* (see Chapter 11). This emphasis on the recursive temporal structure of intentionality (see Chapter 4) decisively distinguishes Freudian metapsychology from strictly mechanistic psychophysics.

"unwished-for" belief precisely by not desiring to confirm either one of these now former beliefs. He desires not to believe his own eyes but yet desires not to desire not to believe his own eyes. Henceforth he will continue to live in this condition of "vertigo," as Lacan and Granoff put it;[31] he will be defined by the normally neurotic, preperverse mode of masculinity that Freud labels "aversion to the female genitals" (the *Standard Edition* renders Freud's *die Entfremdung,* usually translated as "estrangement" or "alienation," as aversion).

Turning Toward Fetishism: Reinforcement

We can suppose, of course, that the prefetishist avoiding the female subject—and the subject of females—could somehow become the fetishist dehumanizing and dismembering her. But for all that we have seen so far, the latter does not necessarily follow from the former. Despite assertions in the secondary literature, neither denegation nor compromise, let alone aversion, constitute fetishism in themselves. They are among its necessary but are by no means its sufficient conditions.

In fact, where the prefetishist must lose interest in female sexuality through denegation and compromise, the fetishist continues to be interested. Because of his "aversion" the prefetishist—the normally neurotic, preperverse male—believes nothing one way or another about the female genitals, for he has lost interest in anything that would disturb his compromise. By contrast, the fetishist does, indeed, believe something about women; and despite his desire within the "compromise" not to confirm either the initial or the new beliefs one way or another, he tries to confirm this belief. Whereas the prefetishist accedes to having no interest in whether he can't believe his own eyes or can't believe he can't believe his own eyes, the fetishist can't believe that he has no interest in whether he can or can't believe his own eyes. In short, whereas the prefetishist has developed an "aversion," the fetishist becomes fascinated. But whence the different, added impulsion in the fetishist—interesting him where the prefetishist has completely lost interest?

The fetishist must have *additional* beliefs and desires that have not drawn notice so far. To be specific, the fetishist believes neither that his mother has a penis nor that his mother does not have a penis but instead believes that his mother had a penis but lost it before he looked for it (most exactly, before he sees that she does not have it). Freud specifically labels this belief in the mother's loss "an extraordinary heightening" (*Steigerung,* which the *Standard Edition* translates as "reinforcement") of the compromise as such. As a particular and presumably unusual interest, it is a special way of believing in the existing compromise of beliefs. (As I have noted, the question of psychic interest is not only about what the subject believes but also about whether and how the subject believes what is believed.) To this extent, the "heightening" is the third formation in the forward temporality of a fetishist's interest (Fig. 12.1).

31. Lacan and Granoff, "Fetishism," 273.

At this stage, it becomes quite obvious that the quality of a fetishist's repression must differ markedly from that of any prefetishist—despite the fact that they both count denegation, compromise, and aversion among their interests. A prefetishist "denies" the idea that his mother does not have a penis and "represses" the unpleasant affect of having to deny anything. But in relation to the idea, a fetishist must undo the denial. There is no longer any need for him to deny that his mother does not have a penis. In fact, he can believe that, as he sees, she does not have a penis—for what he now believes is that she lost it. And in terms of affect, the prefetishist's repression is, for a fetishist, now partially lifted, for what he has seen does not, now, require him to deny anything. His mother *did* have a penis, and he *did* see that she does not. The lifting of repression is the discharge of affect, and all discharge is, by definition, pleasurable. Thus a fetishist has an interest in believing in the compromise in his "heightened," or "reinforced," fashion—rather than acceding to the prefetishist's active lack of interest—because the third formation of his interest is pleasurable.

The Role of "Castration Anxiety"

But the "reinforcement" is not pleasurable indefinitely. In due time, the growing boy might ask what he believes about his mother's apparent loss. How did his mother, once like him, cease to be like him—as far as he can see, peering up at her? Here Freud's text becomes tangled.

In what I define as the fourth formation in the forward temporality of a fetishist's interest (Fig. 12.1), the belief that his mother has lost her penis is interpreted, in turn, by a belief that his father has removed it—that his mother has suffered "castration by the father." Although this conclusion creates horror—as the standard accounts recognize, the constitution of fetishism turns on it—it still functions as a "reinforcement" of the "compromise."

Like the previous formations, this formation must be maximally consistent with the immediately preexisting total structure of the little boy's beliefs and desires. Why, then, did his father castrate his mother? The fetishist supposes that his mother's penis, once just like his, was not as good as his father's—for in *another* scene of "peering up," not directly described by Freud, the little boy must be discovering that his *father's* penis is not just like his. Mother and father *both* lack the little boy's penis. Although I shall not follow out the process here, the boy's recognition of the father's lack must be constituted as an "unwished-for perception" that requires a resolution in its own compromise and reinforcement, running parallel to that of his interest in his mother. Given the preexisting structure of denegation, compromise, and reinforcement of beliefs about his mother's penis, his beliefs about his father's penis can only be assimilated into the *total* structure of his beliefs and desires by supposing that his father's penis must be better than his mother's because his father still has his—and, indeed, must be better than the boy's because mother's was just like his.

As with other formations of sexual subjectivity, then, fetishism cannot be conceptualized without referring to the father's difference from the child. Among other things, the inner connection between male fetishism and homosexuality—to be considered momentarily—depends on it. Freud himself, of course, explicitly focuses almost exclusively on the *mother's* difference as perceived by the little boy. In "Fetishism," he does not even mention the scene in which the little boy must recognize the father's difference, even though this scene runs parallel with the boy's recognition of the mother's difference and must combine with it in order to generate the "inexhaustible quadrature of the ego's verifications" in fetishism or any other formation.[32]

Freud's obvious biases—stressing the mother's at the expense of the father's difference from the boy—distorts the potential generality of psychoanalytic metapsychology into a tendentious history of specifically male (heterosexual) subjectivity. But in theory both male children and female children experience both mother's and father's "lack"—that is, the parents' difference from them and their corresponding "loss" in relation to the parents—from their own positions or perspectives as egos.

By this stage, the ongoing interest of the little boy peering up at his mother and peering up at his father is necessarily set into a fully imaginary history of other past and future looking. In fact, his "peering" occurs as an entry in an extended series that could only have begun with a looking, occurring between father and mother alone, that the boy cannot see—either to believe or to disbelieve—despite looking for it. According to the conclusion the boy has reached in his "reinforcement" of the "compromise," the father, looking down on the little boy peering up at him and lacking his father's penis, is also the one who looked down on his mother's penis, just like the boy's, and took it away. Thus in peering up at his mother, through *Nachträglichkeit*—the first true "delayed activation" in the forward temporality of the fetishist's interest—what the little boy sees becomes his evidence that someone else had also looked there. The measure of the difference between these two moments is, on the one hand, his mother's "castration" and, on the other hand, his father's "better" penis. In other words, it is the measure of the difference between him looking up at his father's big penis and his father imagined to be looking down at his nothing. But looking down at himself, the little boy believes that he still has a penis and even, indeed, that it is "better," because his mother lost hers and he still has his.

In sum, a second contradiction arises to replace the first contradiction (namely, his mother has a penis/his mother does not have a penis). Now he believes that it is he himself who does not have a penis and that it is he himself who does have a penis. As the fifth formation in the forward temporality of a fetishist's interest (Fig. 12.1), such "vertigo" is, in the language of psychoanalysis, the "shock of threatened castration" *(Kastrationsschreck)*. Because a second denegation—"I have a penis . . . I do not have a penis . . . I do not not have a penis"—has been mapped onto the first denegation, the quality of the boy's "shock" is not only aversion or horror at what he sees in others but also—a logically independent step—fear about what others see in him. Due to his preexisting and continued

32. Jacques Lacan, "The Mirror Stage As Formative of the Function of the I As Revealed in Psychoanalytic Experience," in *Ecrits*, trans. Alan Sheridan (New York, 1977), 4.

aversion, a prefetishist does not experience this fear; after peering up, he just looks away. A fetishist will also look away—but only after having peered down after peering up: and so his looking-away will be charged with an anxiety that the prefetishist does not share, namely, in the language of psychoanalysis, the "castration complex." Castration anxiety is precisely a peering up that necessitates a peering down.

Now, this second denegation ("castration anxiety"), like the first denegation, results in a compromise formation allowing the fetishist both to believe and not to believe. Since the second denegation is intercut with beliefs and desires organized in the first denegation, it contains four elements. They are usually described as the normally neurotic, preperverse male's "oscillation" *(Schwanken)* in castration anxiety. A fetishist entertains, as Freud puts it, "two incompatible propositions" (namely, that his mother has a penis and that his mother has been castrated by his father, the earliest and the latest beliefs that interested him in "peering up") and—a separate phenomenon—a "double attitude" toward the penis as such, namely, worshiping it or castrating it depending upon whether he identifies himself, in looking up and then looking down, with his father or with his mother.

Let us take stock. What I have been calling "prefetishism" is constituted in a normally neurotic, preperverse male as an "unwished-for perception" negating a previous foreground belief, followed by reversal of the negation itself (denegation), settling finally into a "compromise," namely, an "aversion" to the perception. In other words, the subject will do nothing to fill in, extend, or interpret the unpleasant perception: looking up ends in not looking at all. Prefetishism can be defined, then, as *active not-looking*.

In what I have been calling "fetishism," somewhat loosely so far, the process is carried further. The "reinforcement" provided by a new belief interpreting the first beliefs—namely, mother's loss of a penis = castration by the father—disturbs the equilibrium of the prefetishist's "compromise." Thus the fetishist has to begin all over again. For him, the negation of the unwished-for perception—mother does not have a penis because she has been castrated by the father—must be negated once more. Thus the second denegation settles into a second compromise, a rickety structure sustained as "two incompatible propositions" about and a "double attitude" toward the unwished-for perception. For a fetishist, looking up at mother ends, by way of imagining a whole history of other lookings, in looking down at himself. Fetishistic looking can be distinguished, then, from the prefetishist's *not-looking at the same thing* as a *looking at other things*.

At least in part. Fetishistic looking is the converse of prefetishistic looking and has been precipitated from it. However, the "oscillation" of castration anxiety—that is, obsession about the evidence of sexual sameness and difference—is the ordinary condition of *all* normally neurotic masculinity. The definition of fetishism as a specific erotics, even a "perversion," has not quite been achieved. One element remains to be filled in to complete the full doubling and reversal of prefetishistic looking in fetishism.

Whereas prefetishism is endless phobic not-looking at the same thing and fetishistic looking is endless obsessional looking at other things, fetishism is endless *looking at the same other thing*. It is, as it were, the accommodation between prefetishistic and fetishistic looking, between phobic and obsessive looking. More exactly, in terms of the schema I am developing (Fig. 12.1), it is an "extraordinary heightening" (or "reinforcement") of the otherwise stable, normally neurotic, preperverse compromise of ordinary male fetishistic looking in and as castration anxiety.

This reinforcement is what Freud calls the "permanent memorial" or "monument" *(Denkmal)* of the fetish-image or "substitute" *(Ersatz)*—the final, sixth formation in the forward temporality of a fetishist's interest. As the schema of the constitution of fetishism (Fig. 12.1) indicates, it is a full doubling and reversal of the subject's initial denegation. Like the first "reinforcement," then, the second "reinforcement" must require a return to, a revision of, the unwished-for perception as such, a second moment of *Nachträglichkeit* in the forward temporality of a fetishist's interest. Like the earlier "reinforcement," this *Nachtrag* allows him both to believe in his immediately preceding compromise and not to believe in it—for in the "monument" of the fetish-image, the fetishist now sees his mother pre-(not-)castrated by his father.

To be specific, by this point the unwished-for perception has become the evidence of his own eyes that his mother has been castrated by his father—an impression negating the belief with which he began peering up in the first place, namely, that she has a penis just like him. In the second *Nachtrag,* the little boy's look is "held up," as Freud puts it *(hier bleibt das Interesse wie unterwegs stehen),* at the "last impression" before the moment or sight of the "unwished-for" perception, now become not just unwished-for but also "uncanny, traumatic." His sight is now retroactively fixed on just those impressions experienced when the little boy had still wholly believed his mother had a penis: her hat, furs, or gloves; her clothes and jewelry; her mouth, eyes, nose, and lips; her hands and feet; her odor, shape, and size; the color or softness of the carpet, chair, or bed; the light in the room; the sound of music playing; the taste of a sweet in his mouth; and so on. Whereas the obsession of fetishistic looking requires him to continue to look up, triggering an endless history of imaginary lookings, the "monument" allows him to stop looking—neither the phobic not-looking of prefetishism nor the obsessive looking of fetishistic looking but rather a *fixated looking-away.*[33]

33. Within psychiatry, following an argument developed by Binet in 1887, Krafft-Ebing had stated the view that a fetishist "concentrates" on "partial impressions" based upon an "association" between the impressions and his or her "lust": see Alfred Binet, "Le fétichisme dans l'amour," *Revue Philosophique* 24 (1887), 143–52; Richard von Krafft-Ebing, *Psychopathia Sexualis,* 12th ed. [1934], trans. F. S. Klaf (New York, 1965), 144–47, 159. Roughly contemporary with Freud, the homosexualist sexologist Magnus Hirschfeld insisted upon fetishism as a "partial attraction," a "single-purposed train of thought" or "exclusive concentration" upon "parts" of the body of the desired object substituted for its "whole"; see *Sexual Pathology* [1932], trans. J. Gibbs (New York, 1945), 15, 22, 72. Despite superficial similarity between these associationist accounts and his own view, Freud rejected the sexological analysis, which tried to explain the apparently arbitrary connection, in a fetishism, between sexual pleasure and its special choices of object. Instead, Freud understands a fetishism as a continuous dynamic process in the recursively interrupted forward temporality of the psyche's interest (Fig. 12.1). For Freud, there is nothing arbitrary at all about the interconnection of a fetishist's ideas: they are interconnected from the beginning. The fetishist's problem is simply to maintain and interpret his or her ideas in the face of new experience. In this mental work, no mental "association" needs to be forged to link up previously separated impressions. The mind only requires the reinterconnections stitched up in *Nachträglichkeit.* A general description of fetishism as "substitutionism" or "synecdochic," sometimes encountered in secondary literature, is too vague to capture these connotations, for it does not differentiate associationist psychiatry and Freudian psychoanalysis on the essential role of *Nachträglichkeit,* arguably the most central component of the Freudian view of human intentionality.

The quality of this final relooking—directed at what is now the fetish-monument (an intrapsychic image, not a real object)—is quite different from the first, "unwished-for" look (mother does not have a penis) and the second, "traumatic" look (mother has been castrated by father). A natural reinforcement of the immediately preceding fetishistic looking, it would seem, would be to continue to look around. But a fetishist does not continue to look around at all. What, then, motivates him to break out of the obsessive looking-around of fetishistic looking—the looking of normally neurotic, preperverse males in the "castration complex"—to look determinedly away? Moreover, in looking away why does his look become altogether "held up" at what it now sees—the "last impression" before the unwished-for, traumatic perception—rather than continue to look *farther* away, folding back into the phobic not-looking and obsessive looking-around of earlier formations? Just as we had to ask what motivated the transformation of the prefetishist's ordinary phobia into the ordinary obsession of fetishistic looking, we must now ask what motivates the transformation of the looker's fetishistic looking into the "holding up" of his look in the "monument" of fetishism itself.

For the monument of fetishism is not an inevitable precipitate of fetishistic looking. To put the point the other way around, fetishistic looking cannot, in itself, be regarded as fetishism. As Freud notes, the "greater majority" of normally neurotic, preperverse males will "overcome" *(überwinden)* their castration complex, what I have defined as the obsessive looking-up, looking-around, and looking-down of fetishistic looking precipitated from phobic not-looking. They certainly do not become fetishists. Fetishistic looking at a woman does not, in itself, make the woman, or anything belonging to her, into a fetish or the looker into a fetishist. And a fetishism has not necessarily been constituted in male looking or male image making just because that look or image exemplifies denegation, compromise, aversion, reinforcement, and "castration anxiety." A real case of the full doubling and reversal of the little boy's initial belief (Fig. 12.1) must be rather special. Thus much or most of male looking or image making probably operates as essentially prefetishistic phobia and obsession rather than as fetishism—and only to the extent that the looking or the image making is ruled by quite particular initial beliefs and desires (namely, Belief 1 and Desire 1).[34]

34. This fact would have to be established in each case. If, for example, the little boy's initial belief is that he does not have a vagina (a possible Belief 2) and his desire is to confirm this belief (a Desire 2), his phobias, obsessions, and fetishisms in looking or image making might be quite different from those of the boy ruled by Belief 1 and Desire 1, even though, I believe, we can properly recognize such a little boy—or a little girl believing her father has a vagina (a possible Belief 3)—as potentially interested in a fetishism just to the extent that the belief could be doubled and reversed in the attempt to maintain and interpret it. Gerard Bonnet, "Fétichisme et exhibitionnisme chez un sujet féminin," *Psychanalyse à l'Université* 2 (1977), 231–57, suggests that a woman's belief and desire in a fetishism would be directed not at "having" but at "being" the maternal phallus. Bonnet is extremely conservative in his premises: the subject, here, must continue to believe in her mother's penis (because she wants to be just like the mother), and Bonnet simply attributes to the little girl the beliefs and desires with which the little boy is endowed. Zavitzianos, "Perversion of Fetishism in Women," makes a more radical revision by supposing that among women a fetish should symbolize the little girl's father's penis rather than her mother's; see also David L. Raphling, "Fetishism in a Woman," *Journal of the American Psychoanalytic Association* 37 (1989), 465–91. An entirely different line of thinking (recognized by both psychoanalysts and radical critics) drops the insistence of phallic anxiety altogether. Instead, it urges that a fetishism defends the subject, male or female, against sep-

In Lacan's terms, most males will supposedly "face" and "symbolize" the "imaginary," what I defined as the history of lookings imagined by the fetishistic looker and in which he determines and measures his own wholeness. By contrast, a fetishist will, as Lacan and Granoff put it, "give *reality* to the image."[35] He will set up a fetish-monument reinforcing, but also fixating, the obsession of fetishistic looking. Or, as Julia Kristeva has put it, "fetishism is a stasis that *acts* as a thesis."[36] What accounts for the difference between prefetishist and fetishist? In my terms, why does a fetishist desire to look only at the same other thing?

As he recognizes, Freud's notorious explication does not quite function as a full explanation. A fetishism, Freud claims (*SE,* 21:152), "also saves the fetishist from homosexuality *[erspart es dem Fetischisten auch, ein Homosexueller zu werden]*." The grammar of this striking statement implies that "homosexuality"—as much as fetishism itself or the alternative "overcoming" of the "castration complex"—can be one of the outcomes of phobic not-looking and obsessive looking-around: a phobic not-looker or an obsessive looker will become "homosexual" if he is not "saved" by a fetishism. But despite its apparently precise formulation and its pivotal role in his argument, Freud's meaning requires considerable elucidation.

According to Freud the construction of a fetishism is triggered by the little boy's not believing the evidence of his own eyes that his mother does not have a penis. In this context, both phobic not-looking and obsessive looking-around are successive ways for the little boy to believe "compromises" with his "unpleasant," "traumatic" knowledge. Now, if we follow the forward development of this interest (Fig. 12.1), it is noticeable that the penis has an increasingly prominent role as the subject's evolving beliefs and desires, challenged by the evidence of his own eyes, integrate and replace one another. For instance, in the first, phobic "compromise," the subject does not look at the evidence of his own eyes

aration from (and fears of fusion with) the mother. Here Freud's script for the constitution of a fetishism has been rewritten to replace the subject's initial belief in a maternal phallus with an initial belief in a symbiotic mother, whole, ever-present, and absolutely fulfilling. For my purposes, this revision does not introduce fundamental change. Whatever the subject's initial belief might be, an intrapsychic history of denegation, compromise, and reinforcement, doubled and reversed, must transpire in order to produce fetishism. In other words, the issue is not so much *what* form of sexual difference the subject initially believes and desires but *how* it is intrapsychically discharged.

35. Lacan and Granoff, "Fetishism," 273, emphasis added.

36. Julia Kristeva, "Substitutions in the Symbolic: Fetishism," in *Revolution in Poetic Language,* trans. M. Waller (New York, 1984), 64, emphasis added. In her brilliant (but exceedingly difficult) essay, Kristeva assumes Freud's crucial distinction (see below) between the fetish as substitute *(Ersatz)* and as sign *(Zeichen),* what I call image and effigy (Fig. 12.1). She conceives fetishism to straddle the fence between what she calls the "semiotic" and the "symbolic" domains. Because it is not just a sign (thus "symbolic") but also a substitute (thus "semiotic"), the fetish—as the "*ersatz* [replica] of the sign" (64), to follow Freud's phrasing—mimics but does not realize the essential function of symbolism, what Kristeva calls the "thetic": the fetish does not cross over the particular "threshold of language" in which a subject is constituted by his or her unconscious signifying process without being wholly reduced to it (43–45). In a fetishism, supposedly a subject is reduced to his or her fantasy and does not, as Lacan puts it, "face" and "symbolize" it in conventional, public, intersubjectively meaningful ("thetic") language. In turn, Kristeva's argument allows us to see that thetic representations of fetishes in paintings, novels, or films should not be confused with nonthetic fetishism as such—a point that often seems lost on cultural critics.

that his mother does not have a penis—precisely as a way of continuing to believe that she has a penis just like him. And in the second, obsessive "compromise," he looks all around rather than at the evidence of his own eyes that his mother has been "castrated" by his father because she did not have as good a penis as he—precisely as a way of continuing to believe that he himself has a penis as good as his father's. To be continually looking at, away from, and around the penis in this fashion—to be continually "interested" in the penis—is just to be "homosexual" until the phobia and obsession are "overcome." In Freud's sense, then, the fetishist is a homosexual until he becomes a fetishist, because to be "homosexual" is, finally, not to believe the evidence of his own eyes that everyone is not just like him. To be "homosexual" is, literally, to believe in one sex (one's own sex) only.[37]

On the view that underlies Freud's reasoning here, heterosexuality must be understood to have been gradually constructed on the basis of a primary homosexuality. The process includes not only the dynamics of fetishism as understood by Freud—fetishism "saves" the subject from his archaic, primary homosexuality—but many other dynamics as well. For example, an "aversion" to species of childhood or adult homosexuality might be the phobic/obsessive "compromise" of a heterosexual man unable to believe the evidence of his own eyes that he is homosexual. In fact, we should probably be able to identify many heterosexual male fetishizations of homosexual acts, images, or practices, as well as more pathological interests in them—for example, the unregenerate sadisms of some gay bashers. Freud's own depictions of homo- and heterosexualities in construction—for example, his studies of "latent homosexuality," in the Wolf Man case (see Chapter 11), "homosexuality and paranoia," in the Schreber case, or fetishism—do not build consistently from an explicit premise of primary homosexuality, even though he often requires and circles back to it. But in "Fetishism" Freud's bedrock is quite clearly exposed: Freud conceives a heterosexual fetishism as an interest evolving from and replacing primary homosexuality.[38]

Dehomosexualization and Blindness: The General Implications of Freud's Explication of Fetishism

Fetishism is the belief that ultimately substitutes—in an intrapsychic history having the form I have outlined—for the primary homosexual belief. It holds up the looker's looking at the "last impression" before the whole process tending toward and throughout requiring

37. On the principal Freudian texts dealing with male homosexuality, see Chapter 11, note 31; and see further Whitney Davis, *Drawing the Dream of the Wolves: Homosexuality, Interpretation, and Freud's "Wolf Man"* (Bloomington, Ind., 1995), 103–38.

38. Pre-Freudian psychiatrists as well as non-Freudian sexologists conceived a general connection between homosexuality and fetishism. For them, both formations displayed a man's fear and avoidance of women and an ostensibly nonreproductive eroticism. Moreover, a fetishist's supposed obsession with articles of female dress or adornment and his overly aestheticized attraction to ornamentation—a stereotype current in many late-nineteenth-century representations of the male fetishist—suggested his close proximity to "homosexuality" conceived as a feminized flight from appropriately masculine interests and comportment. (The hypermasculine imagery of male homosexual fetishism was barely acknowledged in the pre-Freudian literature, in part because the stereotype of the homosexual male could not

"homosexuality" is triggered. Fetishism, then, is the *dehomosexualization of fetishistic looking*. Whereas a "homosexual" prefetishist determinedly does not look at the female genitals, a "heterosexual" fetishist determinedly does not look at the male genitals. What is the difference between them? When the "homosexual" prefetishist looks away from the female genitals, he sees nothing of interest to him whatsoever. (Since he is not captured by an image of heterosexuality, he can enter its symbolic—that is, uninterested, purely linguistic—dimension; in the male symbolic, female sexuality is not interesting.) By contrast, when the "heterosexual" fetishist, further along in the forward temporality of a "perverse" interest (Fig. 12.1), looks away from the male genitals, he sees the *female* genitals, the "unwished-for perception" that had triggered the whole process to begin with and now animates it once again—and endlessly.

In short, homosexuality is the reality of fetishism, and fetishism is the imaginary of homosexuality.

On this account, fetishism stands midway between the gynophobia of normally neurotic male heterosexuality and the gynophobia of normally neurotic male homosexuality as a *gynophilic* fixation. It is "perverse" because nineteenth-century sexology was unable to imagine such a sexual interest as normal. But it is Freud's virtue that he does not quite accept this attitude. The fetishist, he says, is "saved," by "perversion," from what Freud himself was never willing to see *as* perversion but rather as an infantile or archaic form of sexuality, namely, homosexuality. Thus in "Fetishism" Freud finally offers a paradox in order to represent the vicissitudes of the subject's interest: the perversion of fetishism saves a "heterosexual" subject from his normal "homosexual" neurosis.

On Freud's analysis a "heterosexual" male seems to be placed in an impossible position. On the one hand, his gynophilia brings him perilously close to homosexuality: to the extent that it becomes fetishistic, it has been precipitated from homosexual interest. On the other hand, his gynophobia *also* brings him perilously close to homosexuality: to the extent that it becomes fetishistic, it too has been precipitated from homosexual interest. And to escape from this seemingly omnipresent homosexuality, the male subject has two alternatives. On the one hand, he can "overcome" aversion to the female genitals and obsession with them; he can escape gynophobia and gynophilia altogether by entering a domain in which female sexuality becomes, precisely, a blank attracting no real or imaginary interest but only its symbolic reversions. Freud imagines that most men must take

---

see him as other than effeminate.) Finally, to the extent that from the 1870s on fetishism was regarded, as Michel Foucault has put it, as the "model perversion" (*The History of Sexuality*, vol. 1, *An Introduction*, trans. Robert Hurley [New York: Vintage, 1980], 13), a fetishistic element tended to be seen in all nonstandard sexual practices, including homosexual ones. Quite apart from the crude stereotypes of both male homosexuality (as necessarily effeminate) and male fetishism (as necessarily heterosexual) to be found in these representations, they failed to explain how the two eroticisms became linked terms. Freud's reasoning was substantially discontinuous with this tradition. His emphasis on intrapsychic history required him to distinguish fetishism and homosexuality. The traditional stereotype only persisted in Freud's account to the extent that for him primary homosexuality was a more archaic formation than, and thus a precondition of, fetishism. Thus the fetishist, for the Freudian, is (or was) a homosexual, whereas the homosexual need not (but can) be a fetishist. Not to put too fine a point on the matter, if before Freud the "model perversion" is fetishism, with and after Freud it is homosexuality.

this route, in which the necessities of male heterosexuality construct female sexuality as uninteresting. On the other hand, however, the male subject could accede to the peculiar arrest of phobia and obsession in the endless dehomosexualizations of fetishism. But this is the route of heterosexual "perversion" because it violates the necessities of male heterosexuality even as it "saves" the subject from his homosexuality.

Both of these two alternatives—neurotic heterosexual male androcentrism or perverted heterosexual male gynocentrism—together constitute the field of a heterosexual's supposed "overcoming" of homosexuality, juxtaposed with homosexuality as its monument and substitute. In the forward temporality of the subject's interest, homosexuality is therefore the reality of heterosexuality and heterosexuality merely its symbol. In order for heterosexuality to become real itself in the forward temporality of the subject's interest, it must perform the imaginary "overcoming" of the homosexual real carried out in the symbolic of male neurosis, which erases women, or perversion, which erases men. But this full realization of heterosexuality is also impossible.

Presumably the opposite of a "monument" is an endless disremembering. As dehomosexualization, fetishism is the forgetting of men. The opposite of fetishism, then, can only be the forgetting of women—that is, the nonfetishism of "normal" male heterosexuality in which female sexuality attracts no interest. But how can the male forget what has been seen, the "unwished-for perception" that not everyone is just like himself, which triggers the process of phobic, obsessive, and fixated rememberings? How can the real of homosexuality be imaginarily overcome in the mere symbolic of heterosexuality? No matter what he does, in looking up, not looking, looking down, looking around, and looking away, the boy continues to be looking at something that will always remind him of what he has seen. Thus there can be no real or imaginary looking—if there might be some symbolic version of it—that does not sustain some degree of homosexuality and fetishism. Despite Freud's occasional faith in a normative teleology of heterosexuality, in order to "overcome" homosexuality and fetishism one could only go blind.

Does Freudian Fetishism Necessarily "Dehumanize" Its Object?

Freud's reasoning obliges us to conceive the essence of fetishism to be a dehomosexualization, the disremembering of men. The converse of fetishism, and that from which fetishism is precipitated, is the disremembering of women; the proper complement for fetishism—like exhibitionism for voyeurism—is sexual apathy. (In principle, in cases of female fetishism the genders would be symmetrically reversed in this structure.) Jointly, disremembering sexual difference from the ego results in the creation of the fetish-image.

Writers after Freud have gone much further in pursuing these ideas. They urge that what I am calling disremembering in the end amounts to an "objectification" in which the independent subjectivity of the fetishist's sexual partner is violated. On this view, fetishism can be regarded as sexually and ethically "perverted" because it supposedly inflicts moral and social damage on real subjects by disremembering, or "fetishizing," them.

Robert Stoller, for example, conceives fetishism as a fetishist's "dehumanization" of the fetishized object (in my terms [Fig. 12.1], discussed momentarily, this is the person to whom the fetish-effigy, the actual representation of the intrapsychic fetish-image, is attached in an erotic practice). According to Stoller, the human reality of the fetishized object is replaced by the fetish—a split-off, idealized substitute, triumphing over and revenging past traumas imagined to have been inflicted by the fetishized object or his or her psychic predecessors.[39] In what Stoller calls "benign" fetishism, the whole object might be partly *restored* through a fetishist's transient, nondamaging interest in it. In such cases fetishism is really a mode of loving interest in one's partner. But it is perverse, even pathological, when dehumanization and the current of "hostility" that animates it become unregenerate instruments in maintaining exploitative power. Along these lines many feminist and gay critics have taken the "fetishization" of objects as a dehumanizing symptom (and to some extent a cause) of male heterosexual hostility and anxiety in the face of female and homoerotic sexuality. In such cases, as Stoller puts it, supposedly the fetishist "cannot bear the totality of the object" that threatens him.[40]

Still, caution is necessary here. Although it may be accurate as a description of fetishistic practice, which is perhaps always crosscut by hostility (like any sexual relation) (see Chapter 10), Stoller's account leaves much unsaid as a theory of the intrapsychic constitution of fetishism. Needless to say, his description covers many formations of sexuality other than fetishism itself. According to one insidious modern stereotype, for example, homosexuality is the anxious, hostile response of some men who supposedly "cannot bear the totality" of women—or of their desire for women and women's desire for them. More specifically, how does the fetishist develop knowledge of the fetishized object such that it is felt to be unbearable as a "totality" in the first place? And how does the fetishist discover what is bearable, or safe, within the object—the aspect he will supposedly "fetishize"—if he cannot deal with its "totality" at least long enough to desire something about it *despite* its unbearability? To handle these questions Stoller points directly at the paradox he leaves unexplicated. "Only those who can perceive people as people," he writes, "are able to be perverse, for that perception, obviously, is needed in order to perform the act of dehumanization."[41] In other words, the object must somehow have been whole and "humanized" to be subsequently *de*humanized. But under what real conditions is the "totality" of an object ever known? In fact, of course, there are no such conditions: there is no state of "total" recognition of the other, a norm of full mutuality, from which acts

39. Robert J. Stoller, *Perversion: The Erotic Form of Hatred* (New York, 1975), 132–34. For a similar view, see Arnold Cooper, "The Unconscious Core of Perversion," in *Perversions and Near-Perversions in Clinical Practice: New Psychoanalytic Perspectives*, ed. G. I. Fogel and W. A. Myers (New Haven, Conn., 1991), 17–35.

40. Stoller, *Perversion*, 132. Stoller implicitly aligns Freudian fetishism with the Marxist conception of "commodity fetishism." This species of economic "perversion" supposedly alienates the worker from the product of his or her labor and dehumanizes both worker and artifact (now just a "commodity") in the process. (For a similar general synthesis, see Williams, *Hard Core*, chap. 4.) In sexual fetishism, we could say, the sexual laborer is alienated from the appropriate product of his or her work—namely, mutual recognition by and love of the other person, or "respect, intimacy, nonfetishizing, affection, friendship, love, [as] the opposite of dangerousness, of inflicting high, true trauma on others" (Robert J. Stoller, *Pain and Passion: A Psychoanalyst Explores the World of S & M* [New York, 1991], 54). Despite these suggestions, it remains unclear how the competing reductions of Freudian and Marxian determinism can really be reconciled. Stoller rightly does not attempt to do so.

41. Robert J. Stoller, *Sexual Excitement: Dynamics of Erotic Life* (New York, 1979), 7.

of "dehumanization" represent a deflection or deviance. Real subjectivity is only a continuum of states of "dehumanizing" the other. To put the point in less moralistic terms, a real subject always perceives the other according to his or her own unconscious beliefs and desires. Thus the internal object—like actual material images and artifacts (see Chapters 3, 4, and 8)—is *inherently* partial and fragmented. Only in this way could it appear to the subject as having both bearable and unbearable aspects.

In some contexts, fetishism might be crosscut by a profound hostility—the deep, seemingly independent force Stoller finds in all so-called sexual perversions—that results in a "dehumanizing" fetishistic practice in relation to the fetishized object. But fetishistic practice is not *inherently* dehumanizing. Experience suggests that fetishisms can play valuable roles within people's eroticisms; "constant, high attention to one's partner's experience is more caring and safer than the blundering, ignorant, noncommunicating obtuseness that governs so many 'normal' people's erotic motions."[42] Such humane fetishisms might be becoming more common than ever in the context of the revolutionary reconfiguration of erotic practice in recent "safe sex." For many gay men today, far from "dehumanizing" the sexual partner, fetishism develops as an interest in him precisely as a man with a past, a present, and a possible future—a local disremembering of aspects of genital sexuality in the service of a far greater, more important remembering.

Indeed, in strictly metapsychological terms we should find the so-called dehumanization of fetishism not within the *object relations* of a fetishist but rather within the *intrapsychic constitution* of his fetishism (Fig. 12.1). Fetishism does not necessarily involve the dehumanization of the fetishized object, but it does, in a sense, require the "dehumanization" of the fetishizing *subject*—for fetishism requires the subject's dehomosexualization, an avoiding of part of himself as real. (In "benign" fetishism or safe sex, such avoidance is both necessary and acceptable.) The dehumanization of fetishism thus seems somewhat like the dehumanization of heterosexuality itself, which also replaces or avoids primary homosexuality. Nonfetishistic heterosexuality, however, is not just an avoiding but a total "overcoming." Its dehumanization of the subject is more extensive—perhaps more irremediable and unregenerate—than his dehumanization within fetishism. Fetishism offers a persisting monument to what once was real. But nonfetishistic heterosexuality overcomes commemoration itself: in symbolic revision, the homosexual real is ejected from the past as much as from the present and the future.

Fetish-Image, Fetish-Effigy, Fetishistic Practice

What of fetishistic practice, the playing-out of the intrapsychic formation of a fetishism in a particular erotic activity, actual or desired? As I have shown, the fetish-image is constituted as a twofold *Nachträglichkeit* threading up the forward temporality of the fetishist's

42. Stoller, *Pain and Passion*, 21. Stoller is referring here to consensual sadomasochism.

interest. In "peering up," his interest gets "held up" at first impressions that progressively become his "last impressions" precisely because the last impression of which they are the first impressions has been retracted or, more exactly, "scotomized." It is as if the "unwished-for perception" falls on a blind spot that had been created *after* but retroactively *for* it. Put another way, first impressions become last impressions when the last impression of the first impression becomes traumatic.

Whereas an essentially non-Freudian account might place the "scotoma" of a fetishism at the very beginning of its intrapsychic constitution,[43] Freud's account places it at the very end. It is not a blind spot in perception but rather a blind spot in the *memory* of perceptions: "[I]t reminds one of the abrupt halt *(Haltmachen)* made by memory in traumatic amnesias" (*SE,* 21:154). The fetish-image is what is remembered as the last wished-for perception—although being last and being wished-for are only defined *retroactively* in terms of what was seen later but then not remembered (compare Chapter 8). As such, the fetish-image is, of course, a purely intrapsychic object, a constructed memory-fantasy. It is an internal object "collated" in what I have defined as the six successive intrapsychic formations in the constitution of a fetishism (Fig. 12.1).[44]

As a persisting intrapsychic object, the "permanent memorial" of the fetish-image should not be confused with the many transient external objects that could attract a fetishist's erotic interest—the gloves, furs, leathers, odors, or whatnot, in fetishistic practice. These transient objects—I call them the effigies of the fetish-image—are attached or belong to the fetishized object and must, in turn, be distinguished from him or her. In a male homosexual's "foreskin fetish," for example, the foreskin itself, the fetish-effigy, belongs to the fetishized objects, working-class boys picked up by the patient in his nocturnal rambles. In this case, personal relations between the fetishist and his fetishized objects go far beyond the relation between him and the fetish-effigy as such, although the former are determined, at least in part, by the latter.[45]

According to Freud and to psychoanalysts who have closely followed him, a fetish-effigy ultimately provides the fetishist with little or no "*imaginary* satisfaction."[46] No mere physical effigy can really replace the intrapsychic image (in turn, the replacement of a reality) but can only represent it. In Freud's terms in "Fetishism," the fetish-effigies are not *Ersätze* (substitutes) but *Zeichen* (signs). Moreover, the effigy can at best only partially represent the image: obviously it cannot represent what the fetishist does not remember, even though this forgotten material determined his memory-image.

On the one hand, because the fetish-effigy at least partially represents the fetish-image,

43. See René Laforgue, "Verdrängung und Skotomisation," *Internationale Zeitschrift für Psychoanalyse* 12 (1926), 54–61, to which Freud's essay is a polemical reply (see also Laforgue, "Überlegungen zum Begriff der Verdrängung," *Internationale Zeitschrift für Psychoanalyse* 14 [1928], 371–74). From their correspondence (see Sigmund Freud and René Laforgue, "Correspondance 1923–1937," *Nouvelle Revue de Psychanalyse* 15 [1977]: 262–67, 277), it is evident that Freud objected to Laforgue's thinking on fetishistic repression because it lacked a genuinely metapsychological (genetic and dynamic) perspective. Laforgue fell back on the prepsychoanalytic cliché that fetishism is the psychic equivalent of the obliteration of perception displayed in the actual scotomas.

44. M. Masud R. Khan, "The Role of the 'Collated Internal Object' in Perversions," in *Alienation in Perversions* (London, 1963), 134–48.

45. Khan, "Fetishism as Negation of the Self."

46. Lacan and Granoff, "Fetishism," 271, emphasis added.

in a fetishistic practice the fetishist can release himself from the image into a symbolic game. He can find workable "signs" in the real, outside world of objects and images for his desired "substitutes" in the psychic world of objects and images. Fetishists are well aware of the ritual or playful quality and limitations of their erotic practice. But on the other hand, because the fetish-effigy simultaneously cannot wholly represent the fetish-image, in a fetishistic practice the fetishist cannot escape his monumental interior image. Thus in a fetishistic practice the fetishist may experience a "hallucinatory imago" in, on, or as the fetish-effigy.[47] He is overwhelmed by an exhilarating, if horrifying, excitement. In sum, in fetishistic practice the fetishist is doomed to *Ichspaltung*—a division of his interest[48]—and to continual sexual disillusionment and repetition. He cannot decide whether a fetish-effigy satisfies him or does not satisfy him, because he cannot remember the whole of what the fetish-image, which the effigy is supposed to represent as its sign, itself represents as substitute.

In fetishistic practice, then, the fetishist peers at his own fetish-image but is held up at the fetish-effigy. Whereas the fetish-image is the last impression, which has become the first impression, the fetish-effigy is nothing but a first impression. In Freudian fetishism, one has seen it all before, yet finds it momentarily exciting because the fetish-effigy always works as the absolute first impression, with no past and no future.

The Real Body of Fetishism

In considering the vision and the body of fetishism according to Freud's "Fetishism," I have shown that fetishism (like many other psychic formations) requires looking and relooking. In fact, fetishism apparently begins as nothing but vision itself—pure, uncorrected vision, vision without memory. Indeed, it is scopic drive in its primal bodily condition, namely, *peering* as such. But how might Freud's metaphors for intrapsychic experience and history—a complex, evolving field of visible and invisible, written and erased perceptions, memories, traumas, substitutes, and signs—relate to the actual position and orientation of our eyes and bodies?

In our actual bodies, the eyes are in continual motion. They endlessly look up or look down. They look to one side and the other. They look away and look back. Even if we look at an object with head totally immobile and our two eyes fixed in their sockets, the eyes themselves move in very rapid saccades, which cease only when the eyes are turned in their sockets (with or without a turning of the head as well). The retina does, of course, contain a "blind spot" at the insertion of the vascular system into the interior structure of rods and cones. But one cannot see the blind spot as such—one does not experience seeing as containing a hole, blank, or gap—because socket or saccadic eye movements automatically compensate for it, building a "completed" retinal image in short-term optical memory (compare Chapters 2 and 3).

47. Khan, "Fetishism as Negation of the Self," 151.

48. Sigmund Freud, "Splitting of the Ego in Defensive Process" [1938], in *SE*, 23:271–78; for Freud, fetishism is one of its most important instances.

It is possible, however, completely to arrest socket and saccadic eye movements (for example, using a visual target fixed to a tight contact lens) to create a so-called stabilized retinal image. Under these conditions one does experience a "fading" of the target object being seen, because short-term optical memory rapidly degrades if eye movements are not feeding new information into it. Nevertheless, and in turn, the "faded" object is rapidly "filled in." Information from just outside the outermost boundary of the stabilized image will complete a new image "on top of" or "across" the place of the faded image. This filling-in contains no information derived from the faded image; instead, it transposes outside information across the central blank. Like the permanent blind spot, then, artificial fade spots are fully compensated. But as anyone who undertakes these experiments can attest, there is a just barely perceptible moment when the target dissolves into a visible haze or blank before disappearing into an apparently fully continuous visual world.[49]

In fetishism, "peering up" encounters an "unwished-for perception" that fades out and is then filled in from its immediate outside. In ordinary vision, of course, such a "stabilized image" can only be created artificially; otherwise the eyes naturally accommodate the faded spot and never stop moving or being moved. In fetishism, however, the "unwished-for perception" is fixed, as a "stabilized image," in memory—and it is memory that progressively constitutes it as unwelcome.[50]

So long as one is "peering" at the object of interest, he remains myopic or astigmatic: the image of the object forms too far in front of the retinal surface or literally forms without a point. In "peering," then, one does not quite know what the image is: one peers because one does not yet know what to believe. Not knowing what the image is becomes unwelcome when the evidence of the senses, what one seems to see, conflicts with beliefs and desires one already has. At that point, if peering wants to see but does not know what it sees, it is replaced by averting the eyes, which knows what it sees but does not want it. Beginning as pure scopic drive, then, seeing gets caught up by memory, belief, and desire, by looking; the body is caught up by the mind. But an actual human body is *always* caught up by the mind; it can have no other condition. Thus, it would seem, a real body has no alternatives to the vision of fetishism but the physical alternative of going blind or the psychic alternative of complete autism.[51] In its real embodiment, Freudian fetishism must

49. For a succinct account, see R. W. Ditchburn, "Retinal Images, Stabilization," in *The Oxford Companion to the Mind,* ed. R. L. Gregory (Oxford, 1989), 682–84, esp. fig. 5.

50. For the relation between geometrical and physiological optics in the nineteenth century, see Jonathan Crary, *Techniques of the Observer: On Vision and Modernity in the Nineteenth Century* (Cambridge, Mass., 1990). Although in this chapter I have not explored the scientific or social background of Freud's work (compare Chapter 11), I agree with Crary that "once vision became located in the empirical immediacy of the observer's body"—a construction of physiological optics—"it belonged to time, to flux, to death" (24): vision became a ripe field for Freudianization. Notice, however, that Freud's emphasis on the "quality" of psychic "quantity" (see note 30 above) and especially on the *nachträglich* vicissitudes of visual "interest" (see note 1 above), real or remembered, was a specifically psychoanalytic revision of the psychophysics discussed by Crary.

51. On the "inertia," "apathy," or "autism" of a fetishist outside the exhiliration of his or her fetishistic practice itself, see Khan, "Fetishism as Negation of the Self." This conceptual connection has deep roots in modern thought. For example, Roger Dadoun, "Fetishism in the Horror Film," *Enclitic* 1 (1977), 39–63 (esp. 59–60), rightly identifies the tension between Dracula's inertia or catatonia and his "paranoiac aggressivity" as the central story of the films (built, of course, on a wealth of earlier narratives).

be the necessary, unescapable consequence of the fact that the scopic drive is placed in a body that also contains a mind—a structure of memory, belief, and desire.

As the embodiedness of vision, then, Freudian fetishism—to extend and apply the logic of "Fetishism"—is the real historical and subjective condition of the abstract geometries of optics (compare Chapters 3, 8, and 9). Conversely, in modern discourse, we might say, optics is the symbolic overcoming of fetishistic realities. Along with voyeurism, homosexuality, and other vicissitudes of psychic interest, Freudian fetishism is the personal and social density of actual peering, seeing, and looking that really transpires in the pure, otherwise empty field of mere visibilities.

Index

aboriginal art, Australian, 67
Abri Blanchard, 69, 84
Abri Castanet, 69
Abri du Renne, 47, 69, 70, 84
Abri Labatut, 69, 70
Acheulean culture, 112, 157–64, 169. *See also* Berekhat Ram; Bilzingsleben; prehistory
Ackerman, James R., 171, 172, 185, 197
adaptation. *See* Binford, Lewis R.
Adler, Alfred, 287, 288, 302, 315
aesthetics. *See* art and aesthetics; art history
affect. *See* gender; meaning; sexuality
Albani, Alessandro, 145, 260
allegory, 18, 199, 237 n. 7, 248, 284 n. 43. *See also* tropology
Alpers, Svetlana, 181
Altamira, 71, 131, 133, 150–52, 153
anaclisis, 244, 246. See also *Nachträglichkeit*
anthropology. *See* replication(s), chains of: and culture or cultural analysis
Antinous, 258
Apollo XI Cave, 37
Apter, Emily, 323 n. 15, 327
Ara Pacis, 206
archaeological method. *See* archaeology; art history; *Nachträglichkeit*; psychoanalysis; replication(s), chains of; style
archaeology, 1–5, 6–11, 28–31, 36, 44–45, 72, 81–82, 94, 95–97, 99–100, 102–9, 142–48, 173, 188, 190, 194–97, 239, 244, 265, 267, 279–80, 282, 285. *See also* art history; prehistory; psychoanalysis; replication(s); style
Ariadne, 263
art and aesthetics, 3, 11–13, 15, 16, 20–21, 22, 24, 27, 47 n. 3, 51, 58, 64–65, 133–38, 142–48, 160–70, 178. *See also* art history; eighteenth century; nineteenth century; style
art history, 1–5, 11–20, 21, 28–31, 36, 46, 60 n. 31, 72, 75–76, 77, 81, 93–94, 103, 131–70, Chap. 6, 200–210, 233–36, 239–41, 244 n. 17, 248–50, 252, 257–65, 282, 310. *See also* archaeology; replication(s)
art, work of. *See* art and aesthetics; art history
Ashurbanipal, 271, 282, 283
Ashurnasirpal II, 271
Assyrian art, 22–23, 24, 266–85
Aurignacian culture, 47–48, 52, 54, 56, 58, 61, 62, 64, 67–70, 71 n. 19, 72, 73, 77, 82–85, 134 n. 8, 166. *See also* prehistory
Ayer, A. J., 75

Barrière, Claude, 39
Baudelaire, 234 n. 5
Beazley, John, 146 147, 184
Berekhat Ram, 157–60, 162, 164, 169. *See also* Acheulean culture
Berenson, Bernard, 146, 184
Bernheimer, Charles, 324
Bersani, Leo, 22, 24, 268–85
Bilzingsleben, 155, 164–68, 169. *See also* Acheulean culture
Binet, Alfred, 27, 335 n. 33
Binford, Lewis R., 8 n. 5, 96, 104–9, 113, 114, 116, 186
Black Obelisk, 283. *See also* Assyrian art
Blackburn, Simon, 36
Boucher de Perthes, Jacques, 150, 151
Breuil, Henri, 152–54
Burckhardt, Jakob, 146, 182
Buson, 194
Buto, 219

Carnac, 123
Carrier, David, 145
Carter, Howard, 133
Carthailac, Emile, 152–54, 162, 163, 165, 169, 184
Carus, Victor, 305
cave art. *See* Altamira; Aurignacian culture; Lascaux; prehistory
Chabot, 150
chain(s) of designation. *See* meaning
chains of replication(s). *See* replication(s), chains of
Charcot, Jean-Martin, 298
Christy, Henri, 150
Cicero, 144, 189
Clark, Grahame, 96
Clark, T. J., 76, 147 n. 28, 264
cognitive studies. *See* depiction; meaning; vision
color, 52, 58, 62, 63, 84, 155, 178
Combarelles, Les, 152

Courtauld Institute, 15
culture. *See* replication(s), chains of: and culture or cultural analysis
culturology. *See* replication(s), chains of: and culture or cultural analysis

Danto, Arthur, 73, 82
Darwin, Charles, 45, 151, 160, 305, 309
David, Jacques-Louis, 206
Davidson, Iain, 8, 127 n. 5, 155, 160–61, 167 n. 70
de Man, Paul, 5, 10, 18–20, 23, 58 n. 29, 232–53. *See also* deconstruction
deconstruction, 7, 10–11, 18, 97–100, 101, 102–4, 106, 109, 110 n. 36, 113, 114, 116, 117–18, 119, 123, 125, 147 n. 23, 207 n. 16, 234 n. 5, 236, 237, 238–39, 240–41, 242 n. 13, 244, 245, 246, 249 n. 26, 252–53, 265, 269, 279–80. *See also* de Man, Paul; Derrida, Jacques; disjunction; formalization; replication(s), chains of: and nonreplication
Deleuze, Gilles, 5
depiction, 6–7, 11, 13, 24, 36–45, 53, 58–59, 61–63, 72–80, 85–88, 92, 93, 127, 133, 157–60, 179, 181, 184, 193, 195, 206–8, 212, 214–15, 219, 231, 246, 248, 249, 251, 252–53, 269 n. 7, 271, 279, 284, 288, 289–90, 291–93, 294, 286–316, 325, 344. *See also* iconicity; vision
Derrida, Jacques, 96, 99, 107, 199, 126, 147 n. 28, 207 n. 16, 243 n. 15, 244 n. 17. *See also* deconstruction
designation. *See* meaning
Deutsch, Helene, 287
Dibble, Harold, 114–16
disavowal. *See* fetish(ism); replication(s), chains of: and nonreplication
disjunction, 125 n. 78, 126–27, 161, 187, 209–11, 216, 227, 235, 258, 316
Duchamp, Marcel, 172
Durkheim, Emile, 42, 44
Dutoit, Ulysse, 22, 24, 268–85

Eco, Umberto, 76
Egyptian art, ancient, 15, 16, 17, 73, 101, 105, 199–231, 233–34, 243 n. 15, 258, 259, 263, 267, 282, 284 n. 43, 287. *See also* Narmer Palette; pyramids
eighteenth century, aesthetics in, 13, 14, 29, 146, 192, 257–59
ekphrasis, 222–24, 227–28, 269 n. 7. *See also* narrative
"Emma" (Freud's patient), 294–95, 301
Estes, Richard, 135–37, 139
Etruscan art, 258, 259, 263
evolution. *See* Darwin, Charles; human evolution; morphology; paleoanthropology; replication(s), chains of
Eyzies, Les, 67, 151

fantasy. *See* sexuality; unconscious
femininity. *See* gender
Ferenczi, Sandor, 288, 316
Ferrassie, La, 69, 83, 84
fetish(ism), 3, 15 n. 11, 21, 23, 25, 248, 265, 282, 285, 318–46. *See also* homoeroticism; sexuality
Figuier, Louis, 155, 161
Fischl, Eric, 139, 153, 169
Fish, Stanley, 312, 314
Fliess, Wilhelm, 295, 301, 302–3
Fogg Art Museum, 15
Font-de-Gaume, 152
form and format, 173, 177–78, 184, 187, 190, 197, 209, 210. *See also* style
Formalism, 14, 15, 16, 182–88, 257, 267, 279–80. *See also* form and format; formalization; Riegl, Alois; style
formalization, 173, 178, 216, 241–47, 149–50, 251, 252–53, 267, 268–72, 282–85, 323–25. *See also* deconstruction; de Man, Paul; meaning; sublime; tropology
Foucault, Michel, 338 n. 38
Fra Angelico, 302, 303, 305
Freud, Martin, 313
Freud, Sigmund, 3, 17, 21, 22, 23, 25, 26, 27, 29, 30, 45, 81, 160, 248, 264, 267, 272, 273, 274, 275, 276, 277, 278, 279, 280, 283, 286–317, 318–46. *See also* fetish(ism); homosexuality; psychoanalysis; sexuality; unconscious
Fried, Michael, 147 n. 28, 207 n. 16, 264 n. 7
Friedrich, Caspar David, 292

Gargas, 6, 36–40, 85–90, 91 n. 54, 92
Gati, I., 177
gender, 262, 265, 280, 290, 308–9, 320, 325–27, 336 n. 34, 338 n. 38, 339–40, 341. *See also* sexuality
Gibbon, Guy R., 96
Gibson, J. J., 76
Giza, 233, 236, 238
Godelier, Maurice, 9
Gombrich, E. H., 57, 58, 66, 75, 133, 147, 167 n. 54, 172, 175, 189
Goodman, Nelson, 66, 71, 73 n. 20, 75, 82 n. 36, 160, 178, 181
Granoff, Wladimir, 319, 331, 337
Great Pyramid. *See* pyramids
Greek art, ancient, 20–21, 27, 124–25, 133, 134, 144, 145, 172, 196, 243 n. 15, 257
Grice, H. P., 77
Groenewegen-Frankfort, H. A., 271
Guattari, Felix, 5

habit. *See* style
Hadrian, 144

Haeckel, Ernst, 305, 309
Hartmann, Heinz, 280, 281, 283
Harvard University, 15, 147
Hathor, 205, 216
Hauser, Arnold, 15
Hegel, G. W. F., 18, 234 n. 5, 237 n. 7, 243 n. 15, 244 n. 17, 245
Heidegger, Martin, 18, 59 n. 30, 251 n. 29
Hennig, Willi, 180
Hesire, 147, 148, 166
Hierakonpolis, 201, 202
Hirschfeld, Magnus, 335 n. 33
historical materialism. *See* de Man, Paul; historicism; Marxism
historicism, 11–12, 17, 21, 22, 134–35, 257, 261, 268, 315
Hodder, Ian, 96, 117, 118–27, 240 n. 10
Hoffman, Michael, 207
Homer, 260
homin(o)id culture. *See* Acheulean culture; Neanderthal culture; Oldowan culture; prehistory; simian culture
homoeroticism, 20–21, 25, 26, 257–59, 262, 263, 265, 273, 281, 287–88, 289, 302–3, 304, 306–9, 316–17, 319, 320, 323, 325–27, 333, 338–40, 341, 342, 343, 346. *See also* sexuality; unconscious; Winckelmann, J. J.
homosexuality. *See* homoeroticism
Hornos de la Pena, Los, 48
Horus, 205, 218
Hug-Hellmuth, Hermine, 326
human evolution. *See* homin(o)id culture; paleoanthropology
Huxley, Thomas H., 151
hypoiconicity. *See* iconicity; Peirce, Charles Sanders

iconicity, 47, 50, 56–57, 64, 71, 72–77, 91, 215. *See also* depiction
iconography. *See* depiction; Panofsky, Erwin
idealism. *See* meaning
image. *See* depiction
intentionality. *See* formalization; meaning; nonintentional(ity)
Isaac, Glynn, 109–13, 114, 116

Janson, H. W., 131
Jensen, Wilhelm, 318
Jones, Ernest, 22, 302
Jung, Carl G., 287, 288, 302, 304
Justinian, 259, 260, 261

Kant, Immanuel, 18, 233, 234–35, 238 n. 9, 240, 242, 243 n. 15, 244, 248, 249, 250, 251
Kaschnitz-Weinberg, Guido von, 118
Kemp, Wolfgang, 147 n. 28
Khan, Masud R., 319
Kleist, Heinrich, 244 n. 17
Kraepelin, Emil, 288
Krafft-Ebing, Richard von, 273, 276, 283, 335 n. 33
Kripke, Saul, 5, 35, 77
Kris, Ernst, 281, 283
Kristeva, Julia, 337
Kroeber, Alfred R., 183
Kubler, George, 42, 58 n. 29, 78 n. 33, 182 n. 31, 184 n. 35, 187, 210

La Grèze, 70
Lacan, Jacques, 272, 279, 280 n. 32, 281 n. 33, 300 n. 28, 319, 325, 331, 337
Laforgue, Rene, 27, 343
Lamarckianism, 23
Laplanche, Jean, 22–23, 246 n. 19, 226, 272, 274, 275 n. 22, 278, 280 n. 29, 280 n. 32, 298 n. 27
Lartet, Edouard, 150
Lascaux, 51, 71, 131, 132–35
Leonardo da Vinci, 38, 57, 133, 134, 164, 168, 302 n. 31, 310–11, 315
Lepenski Vir, 123, 125
Lermolieff, Ivan. *See* Morelli, Giovanni
Leroi-Gourhan, André, 54, 154
Levalloisian method. *See* reduction sequence
Lévi-Strauss, Claude, 117, 120, 121
Levinson, Jerrold, 132
Lewis-Williams, J. D., 117, 126, 127 n. 85
literary criticism. *See* deconstruction; de Man, Paul; formalization; narrative; semiotics
"Little Harry" (patient), 329
Livy, 144
Loewenstein, R., 280 n. 32, 281, 283
logocentrism. *See* deconstruction
Longinus, 260
Lotman, Juri, 215
Lubbock, Sir John, 150
Lumley, Henry de, 162–64

Magdalenian culture. *See* cave art
making. *See* replication(s); style
Malraux, André, 29
Manet, Eduard, 67, 76
marking, 6–7, 36–40, 46–65, 66–93, 106–9; *See also* depiction
Marshack, Alexander, 54, 61, 92, 153
Marxism, 9, 14, 15, 25, 104, 144, 247 n. 21, 253 n. 33, 341 n. 40
masculinity. *See* gender
masochism, 22, 24, 267–79, 325. *See also* gender; homoeroticism; sexuality; unconscious
materialism. *See* historical materialism; replication(s), chains of
Matz, Friedrich, 118

meaning, 3–4, 5, 7, 8, 9, 10, 13, 17, 37, 40, 45, 52 n. 19, 57, 58, 63–64, 65, 77–78, 92, 95–97, 99–102, 104, 105, 106–9, 110, 112–14, 117–27, 141, 142, 144, 155–60, 167–70, 173, 178, 179, 191–93, 199–200, 208–209, 210, 212, 215–16, 231, 232–36, 238–39, 240, 242, 243, 244–47, 249–51, 267, 271, 272, 274, 275, 279, 282–85, 289–90, 309–17, 318, 322, 323, 327, 330–31, 335 n. 33, 345 n. 50. *See also* formalization; *Nachträglichkeit*; narrative; nonintentional(ity); replication(s), chains of; semiotics; tropology
Mellaart, James, 123
memory. See *Nachträglichkeit*
Memphis, 219
Mesopotamian art. *See* Assyrian art
metaphor. *See* tropology
method of residuals. *See* Isaac, Glynn; reduction sequence
metonymy. *See* tropology
Metz, Christian, 322
Michelangelo, 67, 106 n. 26, 134, 155
Millet, N. B., 206
Moore, Henry, 187
morphology. *See* form and format; formalization; replication(s), chains of: and nonreplication; style
Morelli, Giovanni, 14, 16, 146, 184. *See also* style
Morris, Desmond, 157
Morris, Robert, 94, 195, 236
Mortillet, Gabriel de, 15, 155
Mousterian culture. *See* Neanderthal culture
Mouthe, La, 150, 151–52, 153, 155
Muybridge, Eadweard, 324, 325

Nachträglichkeit, 17–18, 19, 21, 22, 24, 160, 169, 250–51, 262, 289–90, 291, 295–96, 303–4, 327–28, 330 n. 30, 333, 335, 342–43, 345 n. 50. *See also* anaclisis; meaning; psychoanalysis; tropology
Nagada, 201
Narmer Palette, 17, 18, 147, 148, 181, 199–231, 264. *See also* Egyptian art; narrative; prehistoric art
narrative, 133–34, 137, 199–231, 232, 236, 246–51, 266, 267–72, 278–79, 284, 325. *See also* ekphrasis; tropology; semiotics
Neanderthal culture, 37, 46, 52, 54, 61, 68, 83, 133, 155–57, 172, 196, 197. *See also* prehistory
neolithic, 118–27
New Archaeology. *See* Binford, Lewis R.; Isaac, Glynn
New Historicism, 9
Nimrud, 166
nineteenth century, aesthetics in, 5, 13, 25, 29, 145–46
Nineveh, 266, 271
Noble, William, 8, 127 n. 5, 155, 160–61, 167 n. 70
nonintentional(ity). *See* deconstruction; morphology; replication(s), chains of: and nonreplication; unconscious

Oakley, K. P., 51
Odysseus, 260, 262, 263
Oldowan culture, 10, 111–13

paleoanthropology. *See* Binford, Lewis R.; Isaac, Glynn; prehistory
paleolithic art, 46–94. *See also* Aurignacian culture; cave art; prehistory
Palermo Stone, 206
Pankejeff, Serge, 275, 286, 312. *See also* "Wolf Man"
Panofsky, Erwin, 125 n. 78, 187, 210. *See also* disjunction
Pech-Merle, 52, 71
Peirce, Charles Sanders, 91, 160. *See also* iconicity; semiotics
Penelope, 262, 263
Pergamon, 144
Petrie, W. M. F., 234
phenomenology. *See* deconstruction; formalization; psychoanalysis; tropology
Picasso, Pablo, 175
picturing. *See* depiction
Piette, Edouard, 151
Pissarro, Camille, 135–37, 139
Plato, 98, 124
Pliny, 144
Pollock, Jackson, 67, 197
postmodernism, 15 n. 11, 96, 103–4, 188–19
post-processual archaeology. *See* archaeology; deconstruction; Hodder, Ian
Potts, Alex, 257–58
Potts, Richard, 111
predynastic art. *See* Egyptian art, ancient; Narmer Palette
prehistoric art. *See* Aurignacian culture; cave art; Narmer Palette; prehistory
prehistory, 2, 4–5, 6, 44, 63, 104–14, 120, 131–69, 191, 193, 199, 200, 239–40, 241, 242 n. 14, 243 n. 15, 248, 249, 253. *See also* Acheulean culture; Aurignacian culture; Narmer Palette; Neanderthal culture; neolithic culture; Oldowan culture; reduction sequence; simian culture
Preziosi, Donald, 162–64
primal scene. *See* psychoanalysis
Proust, Marcel, 238, 244 n. 17
psychoanalytic archaeology. *See* psychoanalysis
psychoanalysis, 1–5, 7, 14, 19, 20–28, 29–31, 45, 100 n. 36, 123, 124, 180, 193, 197, 275, 279, 282, 286–317, 318–46. *See also* affect; anaclisis; Freud; meaning; *Nachträglichkeit*; unconscious; sexuality
pyramids, 234, 235, 239, 242, 243, 245–46, 248, 250–51, 276. *See also* Giza; Kant, Immanuel; Savary, Claude Etienne

Quintilian, 144, 189

Rank, Otto, 289 n. 15
Raphael, 145, 155, 178, 187
reduction sequence, 114–16. *See also* prehistory
reference. *See* depiction; meaning
Reich, Wilhelm, 284
Renaissance, 13, 40, 44, 133, 187
Riegl, Alois, 14, 15, 182, 185. *See also* Formalism; style
replication(s), chains of, 1–2, 3–4, 5, 7, 17, 38–44, 61–63, 71 n. 19, 78–81, 82, 84, 85, 88, 91–94, 119, 134–35, 136, 138, 141, 142–70, 155, 158, 164–68, 174–76, 178–81, 182–84, 193–97, 201–2, 209–11, 231, 234, 241, 247, 260, 274, 276, 277–78, 289–90, 292, 301, 303–4, 309, 310–12, 316–17, 320–335, 339–40
  and aesthetics. *See* art and aesthetics; art history
  and culture or cultural analysis, 4–5, 6, 9, 17, 22, 23–24, 27–28, 38, 42–44, 45, 60 n. 31, 62 n. 33, 64, 66–67, 76, 77, 79–81, 94, 97, 98, 103, 105, 107–9, 110, 112, 114, 120, 121–23, 177, 185–86, 190, 193, 194, 201, 208–9, 239, 260, 317–19, 320, 322–35
  and evolution. *See* adaptation; archaeology
  and intentionality. *See* formalization; meaning; tropology
  and making. *See* style
  and meaning. *See* depiction; meaning; tropology
  and morphology. *See* form and format; formalization; style
  nature of, 1–5, 6–7, 11–12, 13, 17, 20, 21–22, 24, 28, 30–31, 38–45, 56, 60 n. 31, 61–65, 78 n. 31, 91 n. 54, 114–16, 176–81
  and nonintentional. *See* deconstruction; prehistory; psychoanalysis
  and nonreplication, 2, 7, 11, 12, 15–17, 18, 19, 21, 22, 25, 40, 52, 74, 80, 83, 175–80, 181, 184, 196, 214, 233–36, 244, 269, 276, 279–80, 285, 329–32
  and seeing. *See* depiction; vision
  study of. *See* archaeology; art history; deconstruction; disjunction; formalization; *Nachträglichkeit*; psychoanalysis; style; tropology
  and vision. *See* depiction; vision
repression. *See* unconscious
resemblance. *See* depiction; iconicity; replication(s), chains of
Rilke, Rainer Maria, 244 n. 17
Rivière, Emile, 150, 152
Roman art, ancient, 144–45, 151, 187, 258, 259, 260, 263, 270
Romanes, George John, 305–6
Romantic poetics. *See* de Man, Paul; formalization; sublime
Russell, John Malcolm, 168

Sackett, James R., 114, 189–91
sadism. *See* masochism
sadomasochism. *See* masochism
Saint Peter's Basilica (Rome), 234, 235, 239
Sais, 219
San rock art, 126
Sauerländer, W., 76, 179, 182, 192
Sautuola, Marcelino Sanz de, 150–52
Savary, Claude Etienne, 233–39
Schäfer, Heinrich, 228
Schapiro, Meyer, 14, 171, 184 n. 35
schema. *See* depiction; Gombrich, E. H.
Schiffer, Michael B., 106
Schiller, Paul, 157
Schliemann, Heinrich, 133
Schor, Naomi, 323 n. 15, 327
Schott, Siegfried, 206
Schreber, Daniel Paul, 302 n. 31, 315, 338
Schrenck-Notzing, Albert von, 273
Schur, Max, 316
scotoma. *See* fetish(ism); vision
seeing-as. *See* depiction; iconicity
semiotics, 12, 15 n. 11, 41, 49, 52–54, 71 n. 18, 73–77, 78, 132, 160–64, 168, 179, 181, 187–94, 196, 209, 232, 237 n. 7, 239, 246 n. 19, 248, 250, 251–52, 258, 259, 262, 264, 266, 267, 300. *See also* deconstruction; iconicity; narrative; tropology
Sennacherib, 270, 282
sense. *See* depiction; meaning
Seurat, Georges, 73
sexuality, 246, 252 n. 32, 257–65, 266, 267–79, 287–89, 295–96, 304, 306–9, 316–17, 320. *See also* fetishism; gender; homoeroticism; masochism; voyeurism
Shelley, Percy B., 249
sign(s). *See* semiotics
Signorelli, Luca, 302, 303, 305, 316
simian culture, 38, 41, 53–54, 111, 157, 172. *See also* homin(o)id culture; paleoanthropology
similarity. *See* iconicity; replication(s), chains of
Smith, William Stevenson, 15, 147
Stieglitz, Alfred, 184
Stoller, Robert, 340–41
Stosch, Philipp von, 145
structuralism. *See* Lévi-Strauss, Claude; semiotics
style, 4, 5, 11, 12, 13–17, 20, 22, 24, 25, 27, 37, 41, 42, 57, 60 n. 31, 70, 74, 84 n. 40, 96–97, 116, 137 n. 12, 138, 144, 146, 147, 149, 154, 160, 165, Chap. 6, 201, 209–10, 249 n. 17, 261, 268, 269, 271 n. 12, 274, 325. *See also* replication(s), chains of
sublimation. *See* unconscious
sublime, 234 n. 4, 235–36, 238 n. 9, 239, 241, 249–51. *See also* de Man; formalization; Kant, Immanuel
substitutability. *See* replication(s), chains of
symbolism. *See* depiction; meaning; narrative; semiotics; tropology

Terra Amata, 161–64, 169
Teumann, 270, 282

Theseus, 263
tool making. *See* homin(o)id culture; prehistory
Trajan's Column, 270
transference. *See* psychoanalysis
tropology, 232–54, 269, 285. *See also* disjunction; meaning; *Nachträglichkeit*; narrative
Tschudi, Friedrich von, 313
Tutankhamen, 133
Tversky, Amos, 177

unconscious, 28, 269, 275–79, 282–85, 294–300, 302–3, 327, 332, 339, 341. *See also* Freud, Sigmund; *Nachträglichkeit*; psychoanalysis; sexuality

Vandier, Jacques, 206
Vasari, Giorgio, 145, 146
Velazquez, Diego, 174
Vermeer, Jan, 139, 153, 169, 172, 175, 187, 195, 196
Villa Albani, 145, 260
da Vinci, Leonardo. *See* Leonardo da Vinci
vision, 28, 45, 47, 49–50, 61–62, 127, 233, 234 n. 3, 235–36, 237–38, 239, 240–43, 245–51, 258, 294, 318–19, 323, 327, 329–46. *See also* depiction
voyeurism, 321, 323, 324, 340, 346

Walton, Kendall, 296
Warburg Institute, 15
Warhol, Andy, 139, 169
Wernicke, Carl, 296
Williams, Linda R., 324
Wilson, George R., 100–101
Winckelmann, J. J., 20–21, 26, 27, 145, 257–65, 319
Winter, Irene J., 168
Wittgenstein, Ludwig, 5, 6, 35, 59 n. 30
"Wolf Man" (Freud's patient), 25–26, 275, 286–317, 338. *See also* Pankejeff, Serge
Wölfflin, Heinrich, 146, 182
Wollheim, Richard, 66, 77, 139, 167, 171, 180, 185, 195

Yeats, W. B., 244 n. 17

Ziehen, Theodor, 288